Nuclear Battlefields

Nuclear Battlefields

GLOBAL LINKS IN THE ARMS RACE

William M. Arkin
and
Richard W. Fieldhouse

An Institute for Policy Studies Book

BALLINGER PUBLISHING COMPANY
Cambridge, Massachusetts
A Subsidiary of Harper & Row, Publishers, Inc.

International Standard Book Number: 0-88730-021-9 (CL)
0-88730-002-2 (PB)

Library of Congress Catalog Card Number: 84-24236

Printed in the United States of America

Library of Congress Cataloging in Publication Data

Arkin, William M.
Nuclear battlefields.

"An Institute for Policy Studies book."
Bibliography: p.
Includes index.
1. Nuclear weapons. 2. Strategic forces.
I. Fieldhouse, Richard W. II. Title.
U264.A75 1985 355.8'25119 84-24236
ISBN 0-88730-021-9
ISBN 0-88730-002-2 (pbk.)

Map artwork by John Michael Yanson
Design by Virginia J. Mason

Some of our men were overheard talking about nuclear weapons at the EM club. This is strictly forbidden by law. The words "nuclear weapons" should not even be mentioned ashore. If questioned about nuclear weapons there is only one reply: "It is the policy of the Department of the Navy to neither confirm nor deny the presence of nuclear weapons onboard naval ships or shore stations . . ." To illustrate the sensitivity of the subject of nuclear weapons overseas, be advised that ships have been refused entrance to Japan and required to get underway from Japan because of rumors that nuclear weapons were on board and because someone mentioned nuclear weapons on liberty one time. There is only one way to avoid trouble in this area and that is by not talking about our cargo at all when you are ashore.

"Plan of the day for Saturday 16 October 1976,"
Subic Bay, Philippines, *USS Kiska* (AE-35)

It is U.S. policy that we will resist attacks on the United States and its allies and interests by whatever means are necessary, and that accordingly, the Soviets, in contemplating aggression could not assume that merely because they attacked in some particular geographic area, the United States would for that reason alone consider itself barred from using nuclear weapons. There is no reason to believe that the USSR regards any part of the world as out of bounds for use of nuclear weapons when it would be in Soviet interests to do so. Thus, any direct U.S.-Soviet confrontation carries with it the risk of intensification and geographical spread of that conflict.

Carter administration response to question at Hearing on Nuclear War Strategy before the Senate Foreign Relations Committee, Sept. 16, 1980

Contents

List of Figures

List of Tables

Acknowledgments

THIS BOOK BEGAN ten years ago with research on the U.S. base structure. Our understanding of the way the military works has grown since then, spurred on by the work of a small group of diligent scholars who are on the leading edge of knowledge about military affairs. They deserve our main debt. This book would not have been possible, however, without the many hours of direct spade work, map reading, discovery, and editing by Andrew Burrows, David Chappell, Robert S. Norris, and Jeffrey Sands.

We are also indebted to many other people who lent us their assistance in the preparation of this book. Many were generous with information, advice, and support, and others were inspirations by virtue of their own work: Ruth Adams, Scott Armstrong, Duncan Campbell, Roberto Cicciomessere, Paul Claesson, Thomas Cochran, Nils Peter Gleditsch, Steve Goose, Mark Lynch, Andrew Mack, Andreas Orth, Giovanni Pace, Chris Paine, John Pike, Peter Pringle, Jeffrey Richelson, Jorge Rodriguez Beruff, Paul Rogers, Wilke Schram, Robert Scott, Malcolm Spaven, Paul Stares, Owen Wilkes, Fumi Yamashita, John Michael Yanson, Uwe Zimmer.

In the course of our research, we corresponded with well over 200 bases, laboratories, and commands of the U.S. military, collecting information on the nuclear infrastructure. We would like to thank the conscientious officers who helped us.

We would also like to thank W.H. Ferry, Carol Guyer, Stewart Mott, the Youth Project, the Field Foundation, the Cudahy Fund, and the Myrdal Foundation for helping to fund this project. Robert Borosage, director of the Institute for Policy Studies, consistently supported our work. Finally, we would like to thank Carol Franco, president of Ballinger, and her colleagues for fully committing themselves to this book.

Introduction

LOCAL PEACE GROUPS are disappointed and sometimes even hostile when they are informed that the military facility in their backyard is not a nuclear weapons storage site or high priority target. People in upstate New York, Iceland, West Germany, Italy, Japan, Palau, Greece, Puerto Rico, and hundreds of other places want to believe they are at the center of military planning and are a "strategic" region. A morbid desire to have secret bases and nuclear-related facilities, to be a disaster waiting to happen, to be a target, animates public concern.

The nuclear status symbol is often required to mobilize even minimal public interest in national security and military issues. Nuclear weapons and everything connected with them have been hidden from view for so long that virtually no one—not peace groups, not professors, not journalists, not even the Pentagon specialists—has a full picture of the nuclear weapons infrastructure. The public sees every military base as a nuclear weapons storage site because governments have never divulged basic facts the enemy already knows. Citizens see every city or factory as a nuclear target, and governments let the hysteria boil. Governments have never cared to explain military basing, nuclear plans, or targeting strategies. Public ignorance in these complex matters is then used as the evidence for their need to surrender total control and decision-making to the government.

Nothing makes the military have more contempt for the public than to have to respond to these concerns or to hear the simple-minded yardsticks used to fathom the nuclear arms race—that the nuclear arsenals contain the equivalent of X-tons of explosive power for each person on earth, and each could be killed X-times over. Yet the military's rhetoric sets the hyperbolic tone of such discussions with its references to the "biggest build-up in history", the "finest fighter jet," the "fastest tank," the "most accurate" missile. The government created bomber and missile "gaps," not the public. Pick up any promotional brochure written by the Navy about its Trident submarine and it's sure to make a comparison in size to the Washington monument. This stems partly from our public relations culture. But the system is so huge and pervasive that even the "experts" need help to comprehend or explain it.

A close examination of the nuclear system (which we refer to as the nuclear infrastructure) reveals that superpower military activity is constant and senseless; it has no real, long-term objective. The infrastructure itself perpetuates constant tension and threatens to cause war. Whether it be the height of "detente" or the height of East-West hostility, at any given moment the collection of "intelligence" continues, the airwaves stay filled with messages, forces maneuver, weapons get developed and tested, and the missiles, submarines, and bombers stand ready for instant action, oblivious to the world around them. These activities guarantee that the other side will do at least the same; each side uses them as evidence that the other side is planning and preparing for the worst.

Millions of people and dozens of countries are directly vulnerable to this system. Whether countries provide direct assistance to the nuclear powers or are merely in proximity to the endless potential targets and theaters of war, their security is threatened. The purpose of this book is to explain how.

The nuclear powers have spread their nuclear infrastructures around the world. They have carved up the globe among competing military commands, placed nuclear warheads in foreign countries, and integrated nuclear arms into every level of their military forces. They have created huge "theater" nuclear forces and put thousands of nuclear weapons at sea. The nuclear support structure for these weapons extends the reach and influence of the nuclear powers far beyond national borders and far beyond where combat forces are deployed. Military research on the earth's features takes place on seven continents, from the bottom of the seas into outer space. Testing of nuclear missiles extends into four oceans. Military transmitters and electronic stations wire together the entire globe.

Our inquiry focuses on the factors that would determine what a nuclear war would look like, how it would progress, and what its targets would be. The field we have tried to enter is largely unmapped. Much of what we have pieced together deserves further study and revision. While the nuclear infrastructure is the object of constant scrutiny by opposing militaries and governments, it is largely invisible to the public. Occasionally, when U.S. and Soviet ships collide, or planes get shot down, we are reminded that something is going on out there that seems to have a life of its own. Some in the military call it the "pre-attack phase;" most of us refer to it as peace.

William M. Arkin and Richard W. Fieldhouse
Washington, November 1984

Nuclear Battlefields

1

State of War

EVERY MINUTE OF every day, at thousands of locations around the world—from the plains of North Dakota and Montana, from the Ukraine and Siberia, from southern France and central China, to beneath the Arctic icepack, to the Sea of Okhotsk, to the Yellow Sea—nuclear missiles sit ready to be launched. In Western Europe nuclear aircraft sit cocked on alert. On and under the high seas, nuclear-armed ships and submarines patrol, waiting for their day to go into battle. The weapons could reach their targets thousands of miles away quicker than it takes most people to get to work in the morning.

At scores of military command centers around the world, nuclear war plans are continuously tested, revised, and updated. Planners record the latest personnel and equipment strengths and enemy dispositions, consult weather forecasts, and sift through and assimilate mountains of constantly arriving data giving the details of the next war.

In the air, endless streams of dispatches fly back and forth between bureaucracies, naval vessels, and military forces dispersed around the globe. Spy satellites, ships, and airplanes keep a close watch, covertly intercepting, recording, and photographing. The five nuclear powers and many military alliances work in rhythm, feeding off each other's actions. It is "a world that's only nominally at peace," says Admiral James Watkins, U.S. Chief of Naval Operations.[1] "Peace, crisis, conflict: often in today's world there are no clear demarcations," he told Congress in early 1984.[2]

To support the huge nuclear arsenals and war plans, a global infrastructure has been created. It comprises much more than the 50,000 warheads the five nuclear nations have stockpiled. The infrastructure includes hundreds of laboratories, testing sites, and electronic support facilities. It encompasses the factories, military bases, transportation networks, command centers, computers, and satellites that feed the system. It is the lifeblood of the war plans. The infrastructure knows no boundaries and observes no borders; the battlefields are virtually everywhere. Scores of nations are linked, wittingly and unwittingly; all of them are on the front lines. Just as the distinction between peace and war is blurred, so is the distinction between military and civilian. The nuclear infrastructure has a priority claim on all resources. To recognize the full scope of this infrastructure is to fathom the true extent of the arms race. Simply tallying up the number of nuclear weapons in a nation's arsenal does not indicate how ready or able it is to use nuclear weapons in a war.

Most of us go about our daily lives unaware of how close to war we constantly are. Every day, all over the globe, endless military activity insures that war planners never let down their guard. On a normal day, U.S. military radars and command centers must catalog and distinguish between 1,700 flights that enter and leave U.S. airspace. They must determine whether each flight is a valid civilian aircraft or a covert military one. A difference of five minutes or twenty-five miles between flight plans and radar contacts will cause interceptor jets to "scramble" and investigate. In a typical year, there are also over 500 "major" rocket launches around the world, at least one every day. Last year, about 400 were Soviet launches, and for each one, the U.S. early-warning system clicked into operation. Within five minutes, officers in command posts had to determine whether a satellite was being propelled into orbit, whether a routine missile test was taking place, or whether World War III had just begun.

The level of peacetime military preparedness has reached wartime dimensions. This is most clearly seen with naval forces, the focus of superpower signaling and posturing. U.S. and Soviet naval operations routinely include provocative maneuvers such as shadowing and mock attacks. The superpowers continually use geographic advantages such as "choke points" for peacetime positioning. Recently, for instance, the United States resumed aircraft-carrier operations in the Sea of Japan after a thirteen-year absence, and U.S. attack submarines have conducted patrols in such protected Soviet waters as the Sea of Okhotsk. The Soviets have responded by using naval bombers for simulated strikes against U.S. ships and by increasing the tempo and range of their own naval operations.

The two sides carry out these cat-and-mouse antics in a cavalier fashion. In September 1982 the U.S. Navy conducted an unprecedented exercise in the north Pacific with two aircraft-

Air Force and Navy fighter aircraft "scramble" to intercept all Soviet military aircraft that come near U.S. airspace. Here, a U.S. Navy F-14 "escorts" a Soviet "Bear" reconnaissance plane. Regular flights by U.S. and Soviet reconnaissance and maritime patrol planes skirt each other's national borders and patrol the world's oceans.

carrier battle groups. Admiral Watkins, Chief of Naval Operations, stated that the exercise was "to show the Soviet Union we were back in the vicinity of our western reaches of the Aleutian Islands within 500 miles of Petropavlovsk."[3] The exercise was enough, according to Admiral S.R. Foley, Jr., Commander of the Pacific Fleet, for the Soviets to have "Backfires conduct flights against our carrier battle force in the North Pacific . . . the first such use of Backfires anywhere." The United States then followed with another exercise in April 1983, this time with three carrier battle groups off the Aleutian Islands, "to deliberately simulate the conditions of the Falklands conflict," Admiral Foley stated. "I believe the Soviets were surprised to see us conduct such a large-scale exercise, nearly back to back with the annual 'Team Spirit' exercise in Korea." In his words, the exercise "gave the Soviets a few more things to ponder."[4]

Even in the absence of these provocative maneuvers, conflicts rage on among more than forty-five nations in forty wars around the globe. That the nuclear powers are among those involved in these conflicts is often ignored. In the past few years, all of the five nuclear powers have been (or continue to be) at war: the Soviet Union in Afghanistan, China against Vietnam,

France against Libya and in Lebanon, Britain against Argentina, the United States in Grenada, Central America, and Lebanon.

The links between the nuclear powers in these conflicts are significant. The United States and China provide covert assistance to Afghani guerilla fighters. The Soviet Union provides military support to Cuba, Nicaragua, Vietnam, Syria, and Libya. The United States, committed by treaty to both Britain's and Argentina's defense, provided intelligence and communications assistance to Britain during the Falklands War. The United States also provided satellite reconnaissance information to France for its operations in Chad. Meanwhile, French aircraft and missiles were the most potent weapons used by the Argentines against the British.

The five nuclear powers have spread the arms race beyond their own soil by placing nuclear-related facilities in sixty-five countries and territories. Some 11,800 nuclear weapons are stored or deployed outside the homelands of these five powers. About 70 percent of U.S. tactical nuclear weapons are stored in foreign countries or on ships at sea. The Soviet Union has 15 percent of its Navy at sea (presumed to be nuclear-armed) and stores nuclear weapons in four Eastern European countries. Britain has nuclear weapons in West Germany. The infrastructure extends underground and into the oceans, across the land, and into the atmosphere and space. No continent is immune; no border, river, mountain range, or political frontier divides one battlefield from another. A new geography has been created.

WORLD CONFLICT

The nuclear powers have divided the continents, oceans, and seas into military theaters; each has special command structures and represents special interests. Nuclear weapons are divided not only by strategic, theater, and tactical categories, but are allocated to military services and regional commands. The current and potential conflicts most likely to escalate to nuclear warfare are highlighted along with the naval choke points which would become the focus of naval operations.

Nuclear Geography

Geography is the military's domain. The land, water, and ice surface of the globe are potential battlefields. The

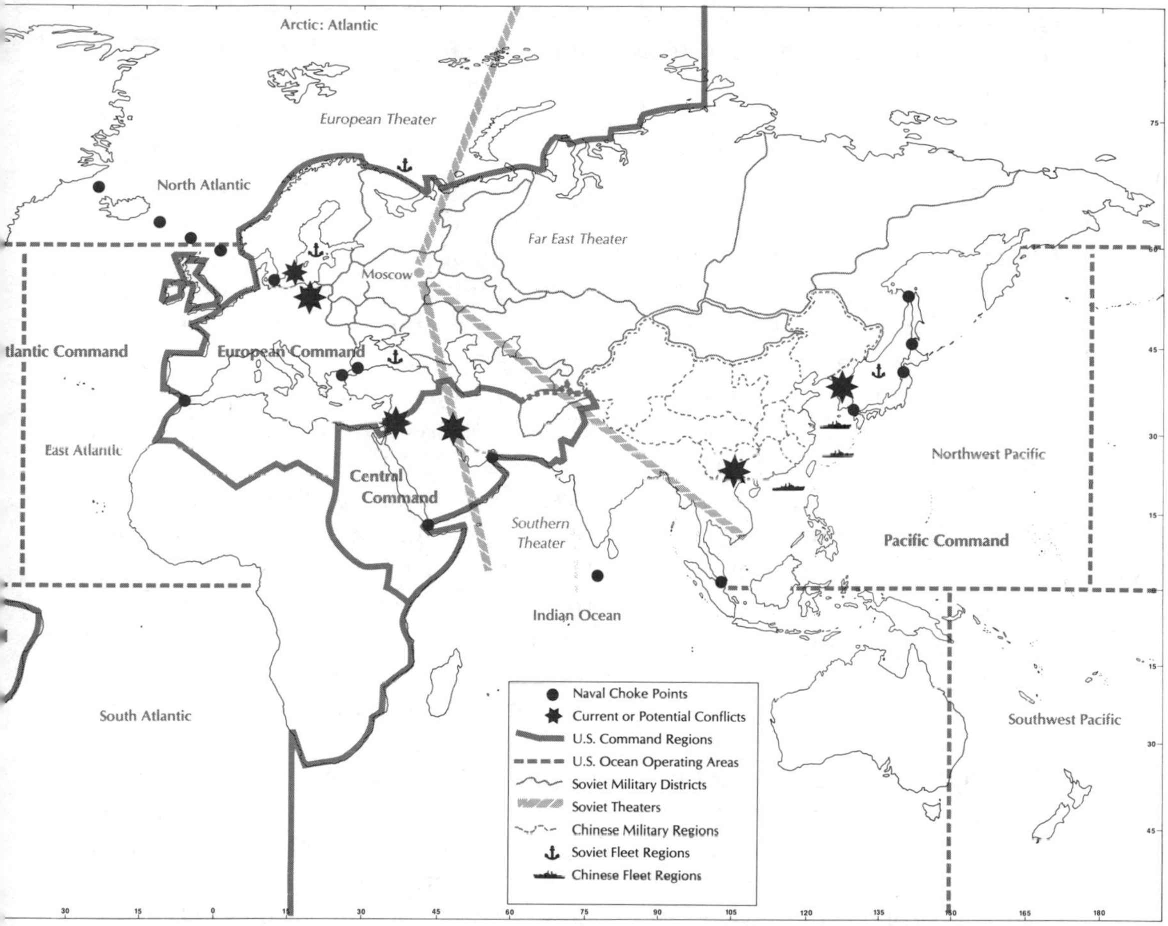

military studies the political and topographic divisions, the climate, natural resources, inhabitants, and economies as gauges of power and as determinants for strategy. The standard view is that "geographic considerations, in their broadest sense, are the cause of most wars."[5] The military considers "realistic" its "preparedness" to fight all possible forms of war in all areas of the globe, based on its scientific understanding of each.

Yet given the global striking power of nuclear weapons, the creation of peacetime military alliances, and the apparent lack of interest of any nuclear powers for actual conquest, the nuclear infrastructure is anachronistic. Overseas access is perhaps the most important case in point. There is little evidence to support the position many analysts propound that overseas bases have direct military importance. In their view these facilities not only cement relations but provide important tactical advantages.

A fuller analysis tells a different story. Many countries hosting superpower military facilities have begun to insist on a more explicit and fair quid pro quo, particularly as they have concluded that the bases may not correspond with their own interests. During the past few years military facilities have increasingly become the subject of contention and crisis rather than a means of international security: the use of the Azores in arms resupply of Israel in 1973, the closing of U.S. bases in Turkey following the Cyprus invasion, the loss of bases in Iran to verify SALT, the establishment of new bases in China, and Turkey's denial of U.S use of Turkish airspace for spy overflights along the Soviet border.

Increasingly, bases that support nuclear weapons and preparations for nuclear warfare are becoming the center of attention. Many countries have long-standing non-nuclear policies and have established policies barring nuclear weapons from their soil and waters. Yet at the same time a new type of military facility—for research, testing, intelligence, communications, and ocean and space surveillance—has emerged, in many ways more important than a base harboring nuclear weapons. The importance of these facilities can be fully appreciated only in the context of the entire network (e.g., ocean surveillance and global anti-submarine warfare). Each individual base seems almost trivial by itself. More than 3,000 foreign military bases circle the globe. Many of their functions are shrouded in secrecy. It is often impossible for the host country to determine what advantages accrue to it from hosting these technical or electronic facilities. The globe is so fully wired that it is difficult to comprehend the entire infrastructure. The countries that house facilities and serve as hosts for the nuclear powers (U.S. naval vessels, for instance, made 2,331 port visits in 110 countries in 1982), end up accepting the entire war-making machinery.[6] This is a reality of today's geography.

What special features characterize this new nuclear geography? First and foremost is the heightened awareness by the military of needing to know the exact position, area, and physical characteristics of land and water areas, and the air and space above them. The short flight times of highly accurate missiles, coupled with the global deployment of forces, demands the most exacting knowledge about every feature of the earth, oceans, atmosphere, and space. Second, the global nature of the arms race has meant that conflict could break out anywhere. This has led to defining the most prominent as well as the most obscure sites around the world as having vital "strategic" importance. Third, the new demands of the infrastructure require that all resources of a society be available to support war plans. Thus the demarcation between what is civilian and what is military is blurred. The nuclear infrastructure is both omnivorous and voracious. The globe is its battlefield; no one and nothing escapes.

Since World War II, territorial disputes have greatly diminished in importance to the nuclear powers. Conflicts have arisen over the control of territory, but geographic conquest has been a minor feature of the nuclear era. The United States and Great Britain are no longer "secure" because of their locations. Some analysts insist that the United States enjoys a great geographic advantage over the Soviet Union because the U.S. is not "surrounded" by hostile neighbors. Even though the Soviet Union is "surrounded," it is not threatened by land forces. Likewise, the "grand strategy" justification for the Soviet Union's 191 divisions because it is, in contrast to the United States, a land power, is as anachronistic as the "forward base" strategy of the United States. Differences in basic land geography have influenced the development and the collective psyches of the United States and the Soviet Union, but those differences can also distort the significance of geography for today's military operations. The importance of being an island nation, of lacking natural borders, or of having "depth" in resources for a prolonged mobilization disappears in the nuclear era.

Today's military operations concentrate more on day-to-day problems of "access" and position. Both the United States and the Soviet Union claim the right of access to any region of the earth where they have interests, self-defined as everywhere. Freedom of access, freedom of the seas, and freedom of space have become the military's goals. Disputes occur not over ambiguous interpretations of where national territory ends and international space begins, but from demonstrations of access to these areas. Jockeying for geographic position in peacetime, together with demonstrations of access, thus become major threats to peace.

This is not to say that traditional geographic axioms do not continue to dominate some military realities. Locations close to the enemy are better suited for intelligence collection or anti-submarine warfare. Peacetime positioning allows for the creation of a ready infrastructure and superior tactical positions on "day one" of the next war. But while the United States and its allies clearly have the geographic advantages, military planners concoct the opposite interpretations. For example, the Commander of the U.S. Pacific Fleet told a Naval War College Forum in June 1983 that "As the British established the capability to control world trade from Singapore, Gibraltar, South Africa, Suez, and Hong Kong, the Soviets have created regional political nodes in their intervention system, capable of power projection and disruption of free world sea routes."[7]

The relation between traditional geography and current military planning partially explains the obsession with nuclear targeting. Nuclear weapons are in many ways products of World War II thinking and strategy. After the war, it was thought that the massive bombing of Germany and Japan was the decisive factor in destroying the fabric of the enemy's society and their ability and will to continue. Nuclear weapons were seen as better weapons to carry out the newly created function of strategic bombing. As the number of nuclear warheads grew, the plans also grew. Yet fundamental thinking is still the same: The enemy can be brought to its knees through massive bombing.

Targeters and planners ply their trade by claiming links between military power and traditional geography. Nonetheless, geography does not always correspond with the reality of nuclear weapons. To arbitrarily categorize weapons by ranges, and then produce war plans for them is an example of poor geographic thinking. War scenarios for Europe ignore the thousands of additional warheads on submarines and in U.S. strategic forces that could attack any target that weapons in Europe could attack. The vulnerability of fixed U.S. missiles has disappeared as a justification for the MX missile, but at the same time this type of piecemeal geographic analysis is applied to the bomber forces. The Air Force spent millions of dollars moving B-52s from coastal bases because of their supposed vulnerability to Soviet submarines patrolling off the U.S. coast. Yet it continues to use several other coastal bases for the deployment of B-52s and air-launched cruise missiles.[8] Why? It is simply more convenient for a whole host of political and economic reasons, to have bomber bases in Maine, Washington, and Guam. The geographic analysis only bolsters the public impression that there must be good reasons for military decisions.

Large size may be a determinant of raw power in traditional geography, but it is overemphasized in the nuclear era. This is particularly true of the Soviet Union, where an area larger than the United States is almost constantly frozen and undeveloped. Soviet nuclear targets are actually more concentrated and vulnerable than those in the U.S. Traditional geography also overemphasizes the depth of the United States and the Soviet Union as a source of protection. "Unfortunately, the United States has large concentrations of industry along her vulnerable coastlines," one simplistic military geography textbook states.[9] Yet in the nuclear era this is not a vulnerability.

A close examination of the demography and distribution of industry in the United States and the Soviet Union gives a new picture for nuclear war planning. It is often asserted that the Soviet Union has an "advantage" over the United States in terms of distribution of its population and thus an advantage in "damage limitation" and civil defense. A secret U.S. government study on Soviet civil defense paints a different picture, however. In fact, a majority of the Soviet population is located close to industrial concentrations, the study states. The proportion of the Soviet population five miles or more from industrial targets is 65 percent compared to about 50 percent of the U.S. population. The proportion of the Soviet population within 1.5 miles of industrial installations is nearly twice that of the United States.

The density of urban populations is another criterion in the new nuclear geography. While the number of concentrations of at least 25,000 population is similar in both the United States and Soviet Union, 50 percent of the Soviet population that lives in such concentrations is in a single area of approximately 1,000 square miles. One hundred percent lives in a total land area of about 5,000 square miles. By comparison the total U.S. urban population lives in an area of about 13,000 square miles.

A comparison of rural populations is even more revealing. Although the land mass of the Soviet Union is about 2.5 times that of the United States, with a rural population about 40 percent larger, both rural populations occupy approximately the same land area (about one million square miles). The density of the Soviet rural population is much higher. Some six million square miles of the Soviet Union is uninhabited.

Intelligence analysts estimate that the Soviet population will have grown by about 40 million between 1970 and 1985 and that the number of persons living in cities of 10,000 or more will increase by almost 70 million. The Soviet population is shifting from a predominantly rural society to one in which almost two-thirds of the population is urban. To a military planner, this means the population is more and more vulnerable to the effects of nuclear war.

Oceans and Space

Geography shapes the naval policies and strategies of the United States and the Soviet Union. The United States has more than fifteen protected ports on two ice-free coasts with direct access to open oceans. No other nation has the freedom and flexibility of the U.S. position. Though the Soviet Union has the world's longest coastline (primarily along the Arctic Ocean), it is restrained by remote ports that lack access to the open seas. Ice impedes almost every Soviet port in winter, except for bases in the Black, Baltic, and Barents Seas. Even when weather is favorable, Soviet naval forces must funnel through nine natural "choke points" to reach open waters. Only Petropavlovsk on the Bering Sea has open access to the oceans.

Space has many features similar to the oceans. Beyond the short distance that is regulated as national "territory," it is an ocean-like zone of international free passage. "The atmosphere trails off to almost nothing within a hundred miles of the ground," writes one space analyst, "meaning that space is closer to most people than they are to their national capitals."[10] The military's exploitation of space has developed quickly. It is an environment favorable to military systems. Satellites can orbit the earth almost indefinitely without maneuvering. From a high orbit they can view almost half the planet at once or, in a low orbit, periodically approach every point on earth to within 100 kilometers. It is an ideal vantage point for communicating, navigating, and observing and is one of the key arenas of the nuclear infrastructure. Control of space may have a more significant global influence than control of either sea or land.

The militaries have used space increasingly over the past twenty-five years, and its limits are not known. The development of weapons for space has given birth to yet another battlefield, in which planners seek to outmaneuver the enemy in orbit. Space contains minor peacetime obstacles that, like naval choke points, would become a main focus of military operations during a war. The difference is that vantage points in space are mobile. Consequently, just as the navies focus on choke points in peacetime, military forces must direct their attention to space orbits to attempt to close them to the enemy in wartime.

Just as the omnipresence of naval forces in peacetime will ensure the rapid transition to war, the scope of naval activity will ensure that the war is global. The globalization of military power first began in the oceans, with their huge, borderless expanses. U.S. Secretary of the Navy John Lehman stated before the Senate in February 1982 that "Unlike land warfare, should deterrence break down and conflict begin between the navies of the U.S. and the Soviet Union, it will be instantaneously a global naval conflict."[11]

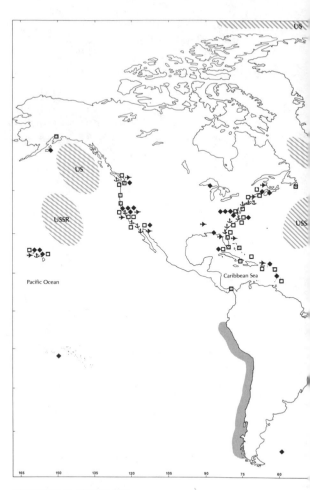

NUCLEAR OCEANS

The world's oceans have become the most active and dangerous theater for nuclear operations. U.S. and Soviet nuclear ships "rub up" against each other every day, seeking tactical advantages that could determine the course of naval confrontations. Submarine operating areas, known and presumed, are shown. Increasingly, submarine and anti-submarine activity is moving into the Arctic. A huge ocean surveillance and anti-submarine network tracks global naval activity.

Nuclear weapons are included in all scenarios for this conflict. They also provide a link between naval warfare and global nuclear warfare. The secret Defense Guidance for 1984–1988 stated that "It will be U.S. policy that a nuclear war beginning with Soviet nuclear attacks at sea will not necessarily remain limited to the sea . . . . The prospect of losing their fleet to U.S. naval theater forces may not be sufficient to deter the Soviets from initiating a nuclear campaign at sea."

While the oceans are the peacetime battlefield of the superpowers, the military importance of ocean geography can be overstated. "Throughout our history, the surrounding oceans have afforded us physical protection, critical trade routes, valuable resources, an important strategic arena, and other tangible benefits," a U.S. Navy officer recently wrote. "Perhaps more importantly, the oceans have granted us a sense of distance, a chance for reflection, and a psychological buffer zone between us and the world."[12] The distances afforded by the oceans may be useful for conventional warfare but have little relevance in the nuclear era. The nuclearization of the oceans (and the ocean nuclear infrastructure, see Figure) is so complete that a conflict involving superpower navies could not long remain conventional.

One naval expert cites eight natural elements that affect or govern naval tactics: presence of land nearby, depth of water, force and direction of the wind, "sea state," visibility from the surface, visibility from aloft, electronic conditions, and sonic (water conditions for sonar) conditions.[13] The presence and potential use of nuclear weapons can render each of these immaterial.

Any nuclear navy fearing its own imminent destruction would feel com-

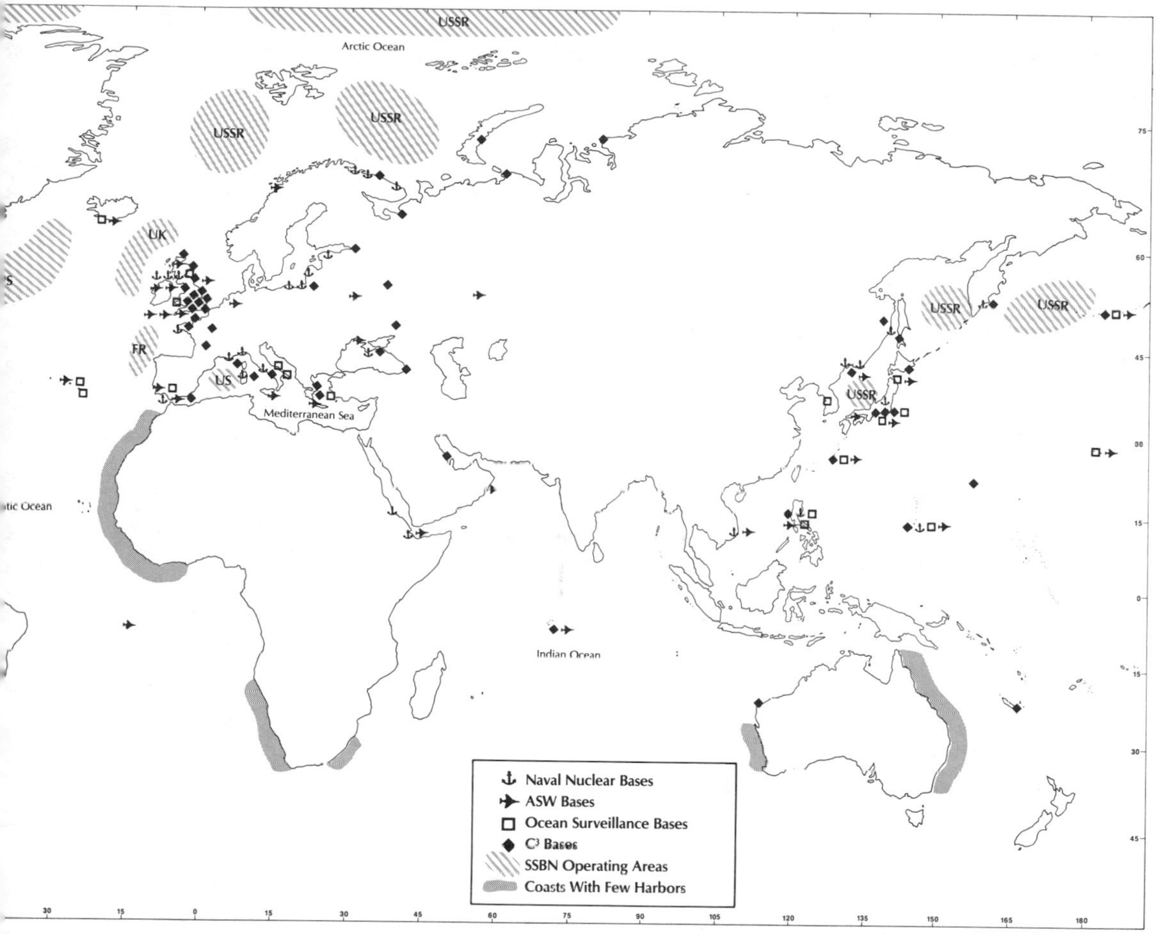

pelled to use the only weapons capable of obliterating enemy forces—nuclear weapons. The ensuing battle would produce effects no navy has yet encountered. Underwater shock waves, surface tidal waves, and the immobilizing effects of electromagnetic pulse (EMP) on electronic equipment would overwhelm carefully drawn plans. Nuclear explosions would cause serious failures of electronics and sound signals (known as "blue out"). Since naval ships are floating sensor platforms, the loss of computers, radars, and sonars would be devastating.

The influence of environmental conditions on naval warfare, particularly submarine and anti-submarine warfare, can create a false impression of the importance of those conditions in wartime. Much of the military interest in exploring the oceans has gone into acoustic research. Unlocking the secrets of ocean surveillance and anti-submarine warfare (ASW) has become an obsession with naval planners. The oceans are studded with "arrays" of hydrophones that collect acoustic information on ships and submarines. Nonacoustic detectors—such as lasers designed to penetrate sea water, sensitive magnetic detectors, infrared and heat detectors—are also part of the infrastructure. It is difficult to determine how effective the global ASW network is. But it is clear that a few well-placed nuclear weapons aimed at a dozen ocean surveillance processing facilities could destroy the empire.

Because the seas are not transparent it remains difficult to locate enemy submarines with precision. Accordingly, ASW forces have large numbers of nuclear warheads assigned to them (see Chapter 3). Yet there also does not seem to be much truth in the common liberal concern about "the importance of opaque oceans to the stability of the balance of power."[14] If the seas were transparent, a major and provocative superpower activity—peacetime ocean surveillance and anti-submarine warfare—would most likely decrease. The supposed "stabilizing" feature of strategic missile-carrying submarines, their covertness and survivability, would not be affected. There are two reasons for this. First, the deployment of highly accurate, submarine-launched counterforce missiles in the late 1980s will end the era in which submarines were seen as less destabilizing than land-based missiles. Second, while there may be some reason to think that survivable submarines were not destabilizing, it is wrong to think that they have "stabilized" the arms race.

Strategic submarines, and the oceans, cannot just be plucked out of the rest of the nuclear infrastructure and analyzed in isolation. Nuclear warfare at sea is closely linked to nuclear warfare on land and in space. Oceans and seas, and therefore theaters of war, are linked together at their choke points, where much of the fighting is likely to take place. The nuclear arsenal at sea, no matter how "stabilizing" some analysts would like to believe it is, is part of the same world at war.

Nuclear Links

Two kinds of links exist in the global nuclear infrastructure. The first kind is the relatively open and obvious set of military alliances, base agreements, joint exercises and planning, and programs of nuclear cooperation. The second kind is more subtle, indirect, and obscure. It includes the mobilization of science and technology, and the use of civilian resources for military purposes that relate to nuclear weapons. But the role of civilian assets is always indirect. Much is still unknown here, but it is clear that as nuclear strategy shifts toward warfighting and long-term "endurance," the importance of civilian facilities grows. It is critical to make explicit all of the links in the nuclear infrastructure. Many of those links are "known" to the experts but many more are not. It is time to show how all-encompassing the nuclear infrastructure actually is.

Many of the first type of nuclear links involve the deployment of nuclear weapons. In the past, virtually all nuclear deployments were highly secret. Few people know, for instance, that at one time the United States deployed nuclear weapons in Spain, Morocco, Greenland, Puerto Rico, Bermuda, Taiwan, Thailand, and Okinawa. Today that secrecy continues. It has never been publicly acknowledged that the United States has nuclear weapons in eight foreign countries. No agreements exist between the nuclear powers and foreign countries concerning port calls of nuclear-armed ships and submarines or the overflight of "neutral" countries with nuclear cargo.

The links between the United States and Britain on nuclear matters are well known. But the U.S. link with France, which continues in the era of the French "independent" nuclear force, is much less obvious. French submarines have relied on U.S. Transit navigation satellites since they have been in orbit, long before other countries were using the signals. U.S. navigation technology played a key role in France's development of its own strategic submarine force. French bombers also depend on the U.S.-supplied aerial refueling planes purchased in the 1960s. In 1981 France and the United States signed an agreement to put new engines in the French tanker aircraft.[15] France (together with West Germany and Britain) also has close links with the United States in research on the simulation of the effects of nuclear weapons.[16]

While the links with Britain and France deal directly with nuclear weapons, some seemingly non-nuclear links exist with many other countries that deal with the less obvious parts of the nuclear infrastructure. Many non-nuclear countries (for example, Japan, the Scandinavian countries, and the countries in the Latin American Nuclear Free Zone) do not have nuclear weapons on their soil but provide technical facilities that play direct roles in the nuclear infrastructure. One of the most dramatic examples is Japan, where a civilian satellite, purportedly for scientific research, is used by the U.S. military. A report of Air Force Global Weather Central described the link between this satellite and the nuclear infrastructure:

> Another large data loss was due to the switching off of the Engineering Test Satellite (ETS-2), a Japanese owned satellite used by WSE [a branch of the Air Force Global Weather Central] to collect total electron content (TEC) data for Shemya, Alaska and Osan, Korea [two U.S. bases]. The satellite was shut off on 21 February 1983 to preserve its batteries because it was entering the eclipse period. Data flow was not restored until 9 April 1983. This data loss severly degraded support to the Cobra Dane Phased Array Radar [an intelligence radar that monitors Soviet missile testing] at Shemya.[17]

As described in Chapter 2, the military collects explicit data about the physical features of the earth to assist in missile accuracy, timing, navigation, and research on nuclear effects. Buried in a 1984 U.S. Naval Observatory document is one of the most bizarre links in the nuclear infrastructure. To justify a new means to observe distant radio sources with radio interferometers, the Observatory stated that more accurate data was important as it would "remove reliance on foreign observatories":

> For a wide range of applications including geodesy, satellite navigation, and weapons delivery, it is necessary to know the the rotational attitude and spin-axis orientation of the Earth with respect to a stellar reference system. This can be accomplished by observing the rotation of the Earth and motion of its pole by a photographic zenith tube (PZT). Observations

from such instruments at the Naval Observatory have routinely been sent, and are still being sent, to the Bureau International de l'Heure (BIH) for averaging with similar data from 75 other observatories, 40 of which are located in communist countries.[18]

Even enemies are linked and help each other to make their missiles more accurate.

The military usefulness of scientific research is similar to the military usefulness of civilian resources. In one area, "civilian" communications, there is a close and growing link with the nuclear infrastructure. About 95 percent of the communications that support U.S. nuclear weapons release orders and the command and control of nuclear forces are provided by commercial carriers in the United States. The Primary Alerting System (PAS), or "Red Phones," that link all SAC bases uses commercial carriers to communicate with missile silos and bomber bases. For routine military communications, military bases lease telephone networks connected to commercial satellites.

The shift to a nuclear warfighting strategy has meant that these assets, long used by the military, now have to be "hardened" to survive nuclear attack. According to *Business Week*, for instance, "The Pentagon is 'hardening' all 21 major switching stations through which its messages are now carried by American Telephone & Telegraph Co and is installing electromagnetic pulse surge 'arrestors' at these stations."[19] At the same time, Presidential Directive 37 (PD-37), issued by the Carter administration, established procedures allowing the U.S. military full access to civil and commercial satellites if U.S. systems were destroyed in a nuclear war.

"Reconstituting" communications after a nuclear war has become an obsession among war planners, and they have not overlooked civilian assets to serve this purpose. One program called GWEN (Ground Wave Emergency Network) will set up a "post-attack" and "reconstitutable" communications network of some 300 to 500 radio towers in the United States to survive an attack and serve as the backbone of "post-strike" communications (see Chapter 2 for a description of the system). According to *Air Force Magazine*, "Wherever possible, GWEN will use existing AM and FM radio towers."[20] The Defense Advanced Research Projects Agency (DARPA) has also eyed radio stations for an "AM internetting" scheme that would survive a nuclear war, "a program to form the AM radio broadcast stations into a network capable of surviving an electro-magnetic pulse attack." According to DARPA, "a small area network of broadcast stations will be linked together to demonstrate the AM internetting concept."[21]

A new U.S. Army program in Europe links such "strategic locations" as hotels into a network to serve the military when it disperses into the field during a nuclear war. The program, called the U.S. Communications Grid Network (USCGNET), will "supplement . . . limited theater wartime communications at potential war headquarters sites. HQ USAREUR [U.S. Army, Europe] and major subordinate command elements must be able to set up and communicate quickly in towns, cities, and villages from designated locations such as civil government buildings, office buildings, inns, etc. The USCGNET will consist of leased . . . telephone circuits which are terminated in locked junction boxes at several hundred predetermined locations."[22]

The military seems determined to leave no stone unturned in trying to "reconstitute" after a nuclear attack. A 1983 National Academy of Sciences study, *National Joint Planning for Reliable Emergency Communications*, stated that "The cable television industry has not yet participated in national security and emergency preparedness joint planning activities." Cable stations use satellites to send and receive signals and operate in remote areas. Most important, according to an article about the study in *Defense Week*, "The nation's full network of cable communications has not yet been spun. This means there is plenty of time for the government to demand that cable networks meet its national-security specifications."[23]

The very size and complexity of the nuclear infrastructure is its largest limitation. Not everything can be monitored, collected, or known. The so-called transparency revolution does not exist. It is a creation of military propaganda to justify the deployment of weapons like the MX, cruise missiles, and new submarines. Twenty years ago B-47 bombers and other forward-based nuclear weapons were removed from forward bases because they were considered vulnerable to preemptive Soviet attacks. Today Pershing II and cruise missiles are placed in the same "vulnerable" positions. Land forces in West Germany and South Korea continue to shrink while the size of enemy forces grows.

The global infrastructure will determine the course of the next war; it will, in fact, contribute to the outbreak of the next war. We live in a "hair trigger" society. Permanent readiness for war is embodied in the nuclear infrastructure. In the United States, the behavior of ordinary civilians suggests that they do not believe nuclear weapons will ever be used. The military, on the other hand, keeps thousands of nuclear weapons in a high state of alert. The global struggle has moved from being a definable line or "front" around Eurasia to a much more dispersed battlefield. Operational tactics now cover a global screen. Contested terrain now encompasses the globe.

2

The Earth

THE EARTH IS not round. The surface stretches, rises, and falls. Modern military operations, from amphibious assaults to shooting missiles thousands of miles away, require a precise and detailed understanding of the earth. Geophysical phenomena such as magnetospheric storms, seismic activity, clouds, winds, atmospheric disturbances, and auroras, adversely affect the performance of virtually all military systems. The sun constantly bombards the earth with electrons and protons. Radiation and other naturally occurring disturbances can disrupt communications, satellite electronics and sensors, and surveillance and tracking systems.

The military controls massive scientific programs to determine the size, shape, gravity field, motions, and conditions of the earth. These relate directly to the nuclear infrastructure. Since World War II, enormous scientific resources have been committed to understanding the fundamental forces of nature and to harnessing them for military purposes. Technological advances have created a new understanding of the planet. These findings are used to solve military problems relating to missile operations, navigation, communications, and guidance. Military research in the physical sciences—in oceanography, geology, seismology, geophysics, aeronomy (the study of the physical and chemical properties of the earth's upper atmosphere), and astrophysics—seeks to mitigate the negative effects of the natural environment while taking advantage of those effects that can be enlisted for military advantage.

As discussed in Chapter 1, the importance of standard geography has not diminished. It has changed. The earth has not changed, but the military significance of its natural features has evolved with shifts in technology. Climate is critical in military operations. Earthquakes are key to detecting underground nuclear tests. The military strives for better geodetic and geophysical understanding of the planet in order to improve missile accuracy. Better weather forecasting can improve reconnaissance, communications, and low-level aircraft operations. Mastery of the environment is important for research on nuclear effects. Today, no one knows the earth better than the military.

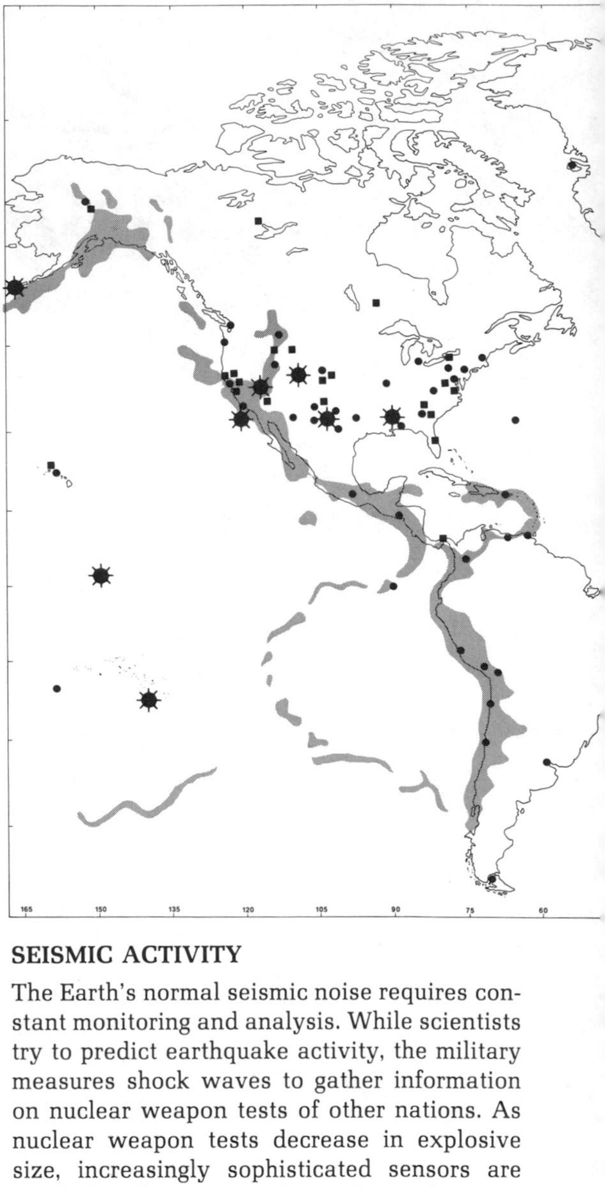

SEISMIC ACTIVITY

The Earth's normal seismic noise requires constant monitoring and analysis. While scientists try to predict earthquake activity, the military measures shock waves to gather information on nuclear weapon tests of other nations. As nuclear weapon tests decrease in explosive size, increasingly sophisticated sensors are needed to detect more data. The nuclear test detection networks are already shrouded in secrecy, to protect the identity of countries that cooperate in the monitoring effort.

Seismology and Nuclear Test Detection

Seismology is one scientific field that has become dominated by nuclear concerns. Scientists have probed the mass of the earth because of nuclear testing. Since 1945 there have been more than 1,250 nuclear test detonations: over 750 by the United States, 335 by the Soviet Union, 37 by Britain, over 100 by France, 27 by China, and one by India.[1] During the late 1950s, seismologists could barely distinguish between large nuclear explosions and natural earthquakes. Since then seismologists have learned how pressure waves travel through the earth's crust, how to determine the depth of seismic activity (which can distinguish an explosion from an earthquake), and how

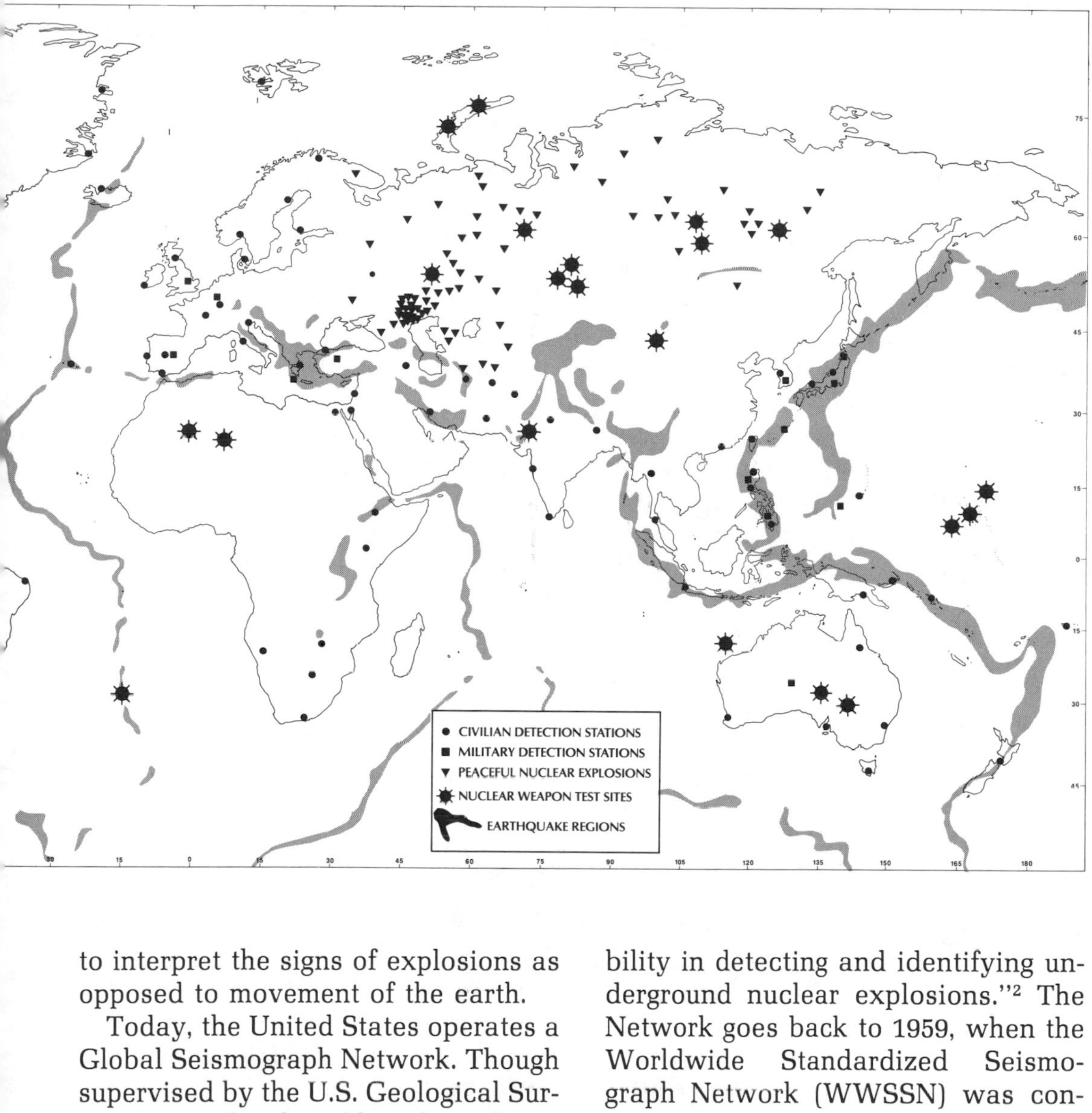

to interpret the signs of explosions as opposed to movement of the earth.

Today, the United States operates a Global Seismograph Network. Though supervised by the U.S. Geological Survey, it was developed largely with Department of Defense funds. This worldwide network consists of seismic listening stations in over sixty countries, ostensibly to study earthquakes but also to monitor underground nuclear tests (see Figure). According to the National Research Council, "The history of global seismographic networks is closely tied to the U.S. national need for improved capability in detecting and identifying underground nuclear explosions."[2] The Network goes back to 1959, when the Worldwide Standardized Seismograph Network (WWSSN) was conceived.[3] Because WWSSN was able to detect only large explosions, it has gradually been supplemented by an accurate military detection network. The Air Force Technical Applications Center (AFTAC) operates this separate and secret network, which includes "more than 50 equipment locations around the globe" in "more than thirty-five countries."[4] The ground sites have been carefully selected for low background noise and have been tied together for precise synchronization. The ground stations are but one part of the U.S. Atomic Energy Detection System, which also includes sea-bottom detectors, aircraft, submarines, and satellites that collect data on nuclear detonations.[5]

The nuclear detection system has also expanded into space, where it has become the most far-flung component of the nuclear infrastructure. Orbiting the earth at more than 70,000 miles—a third of the way to the moon—are two Vela nuclear detection spacecraft, the oldest satellites in continuous operation. The current Vela generation (launched in 1970) is supplemented by nuclear detection sensors placed on early-warning satellites and will soon be replaced by the Nuclear Detonation Detection System (NDDS) (previously known as the Integrated Operational Nuclear Detection System) aboard NAVSTAR navigation satellites.

New generations of sensors have improved Vela from its original ability to detect only large clandestine nuclear explosions in space to the collection of a full range of infrared, particle, X-ray, gamma-ray, and electromagnetic pulse (EMP) signals. The new NDDS system will move nuclear detonation detection into the warfighting age. NDDS sensors will be able not only to detect explosions but to determine the type of warhead, size, and location (within 100 meters) anywhere in the world.[6] Secretary of Defense Harold Brown wrote in his 1981 Report to Congress that IONDS (NDDS) would "provide nuclear trans– and post-attack damage assessment information to the NCA [National Command Authorities]."[7] The data from NDDS will aid war planners in "force management," that is, the determination of the effectiveness of U.S. strikes, the targeting of follow-on nuclear strikes, and the "reconstitution" of military forces and communications facilities during and after a nuclear war. According to the Defense Department, NDDS provides "a war-fighting capability."[8] As noted in Chapter 4, NDDS is only one of many electronic programs devoted to improving the ability to fight a nuclear war.

Even though nuclear detection has progressed to the warfighting phase, the original problem—discriminating between the earth's natural seismic activity and nuclear explosions—still remains. Just as the means of submarine detection improve while submarines are getting quieter, so too is nuclear detection advancing while nuclear detonations are becoming smaller.

Mapping and Navigation

More accurate geodetic and geophysical data is central to supporting the development of more sophisticated nuclear weapons. It is the "necessary positional, gravitational and navigational data required to ensure the effectiveness of ICBM and SLBM systems," according to the Defense Mapping Agency (DMA).[9] DMA produces traditional aeronautical, hydrographic, and topographic maps and charts, but it is increasingly turning to electronic data on the size, shape, and features of the earth for advanced nuclear weapon systems. About one-third of the earth's 39 million square-mile surface has been "digitized" by

DMA. In fiscal year 1983, it collected a billion and a half elevation readings from the earth's surface and mapped, in digital form, 4.4 million square miles of the earth's surface (one-tenth).[10]

Cruise missiles provide the best examples of the importance of digital data.[11] The newest models fly at varied altitudes on a preplanned flight path, often just above treetop level, to evade enemy defenses, for hundreds of miles. The missile's internal guidance computer provides steering information by correlating digital data to the terrain contours, elevation, and vertical obstructions. Terrain contour data is the most important. It is used in the missile's guidance system (called TERCOM, for terrain contour matching) to correct navigation errors after the missile's launch. At predetermined points along its flight path, the missile compares radar altimeter readings to its known height above sea level, computes the profile of the terrain below, and corrects errors to keep the inertial-guidance system up to date.

Digital mapping data is also used for the Pershing II missile and will be used in the future for maneuvering reentry vehicles (MaRVs). According to the DMA director, "The Pershing II's operating area will approach one-and-a-half million square miles. To provide the missile a 'target-of-opportunity' capability we will need digital terrain and radar data over the entire area. That means a data base with elevations on roughly a 100 meter (or about 300 foot) grid, plus hundreds of thousands of future data 'digits.'"[12]

The increasing use of flight training simulators, which have grown in importance since the price of oil shot up in the early 1970s, also creates demand for digital data from DMA. It is essential to produce realistic radar and visual scene simulations for B-52 and KC-135 crews to practice their bombing of the Soviet Union. In fact, the demand for digital data is so large that DMA has begun to exploit civilian LANDSAT satellite data for "landscape feature extraction."[13]

Directly related to mapping are gravity and positioning measurements used to increase missile accuracy. The gravitational field of the earth is not uniform because large sections of the earth's crust have different densities. Finding the exact variations in gravity can reduce the "bias" factor caused by variations in the earth's shape, atmosphere and magnetic fields. The director of DMA testified in 1984 that "The perturbations due to gravity combined with the precise target position makes up over 25 percent of the total accuracy error" of a missile.[14] The MX, for instance, requires specific geodetic and gravity surveys, gravity models of the earth and the launch region, launch and target positions, and "gravity intensity profiles" that might affect the missile's trajectory.

"Accurate geodetic information," according to the Air Force Geophysics Laboratory, "is necessary for the accurate determination of positions, distances and directions for launch sites, tracking sensors and targets. The geodetic and gravimetric parameters for the earth and geodetic information for positioning not only form the structural framework for mapping, charting and navigational aids, but are also direct data inputs for missile inertial guidance systems."[15] Studying the earth's size, shape, mass, and its orientation in inertial space is no longer pure scientific inquiry; it serves the military's effort (and its illusion) to control a nuclear war.

Within the past ten years, major breakthroughs have occurred in geodesy (the study of the size, shape, and mass of the earth) that have significantly improved weapons accuracy. The old transit and steel tape method of surveying has been replaced by highly accurate lasers, infrared-beam devices, and satellites. Since 1960, when the military took over NASA's Project Anna, the first geodetic satellite, the accuracy of locating a point in the Soviet Union relative to a point in the United States has improved from 100 to less than 5 meters. In the coming years, the full deployment of NAVSTAR (see below) may totally solve the problem of geodesy because it will provide positioning and gravity accuracies in the ½- to 1-foot range.

Today, geodetic data is gathered from ground sites around the world and by satellites from millions of spots on earth. A DOD radar altimeter satellite, GEOSAT, launched in 1981, collects accurate geodetic measurements. In addition to GEOSAT, ground-based laser ranging systems and radio interferometers routinely measure the moon and satellites and record phase signals from quasars and satellites to study earth rotation and polar motion.

Very long baseline interferometry (VLBI) is a new technique that uses signals from quasars "for precisely determining the time difference by the cross correlation of the signals recorded" at two observatories on earth. "As the earth rotates, the time difference changes, and the VLBI data can be used to determine earth rotation and polar motion, source directions, and the relative positions of the observatories."[16] By using observatories in the United States, West Germany, and Sweden, the U.S. Air Force has been able to measure the distances between two points widely separated on earth to within 34 millimeters.

In the future, mobile missiles and counterforce submarines will require even more accurate geodetic data. One of the major tasks of military geodesy is precise measurement of the gravity field over the entire earth. A 1983 report of the Defense Intelligence Agency stated that "Of particular importance in mobile applications are the errors arising from the nonuniform nature of the gravitational field. These errors are variable from one location to another. Therefore, the gravitational model must be tailored to the area of its intended use and cannot be used outside the area without incurring accuracy losses."[17] Increasingly accurate gravity measurements are obtained from research satellites that are ostensibly civilian. The GEOS-3 satellite launched in 1976 and SEASAT launched in 1978 have played a major role in improvements in the military's knowledge of the ocean's gravity field.

Probably no satellite will have a greater impact on the military's understanding of the earth and military operations than the NAVSTAR (Navigation System Time And Ranging) Global Positioning System (GPS).[18] When the eighteen NAVSTAR satellites become operational in the late 1980s, users will be able to obtain their precise locations and time, as well as data on how fast they are moving, anytime, in any weather, anywhere on or above the earth. It is "the star that always shines" according to the military. NAVSTAR will supplement and eventually replace a host of ground-based navigational systems. These systems—LORAN-C, VLF transmitters, and Omega—are subject to errors as large as two miles, or 100 times less accurate than NAVSTAR.[19] Systems like LORAN-C help to develop and test submarine-launched missiles and synchronize radar systems.

Satellite navigation goes back to the original Sputnik flight in 1957, when scientists noted that the "bleeps" from the satellite formed a curve that could be plotted as the satellite approached or receded from a tracking station. Changes in the signal were consistent so that an accurate measure of the change and of the orbit yielded the exact location of the ground tracker. A bomber or submarine could thus use a set of satellites to find their positions accurately anywhere in the world. The Navy started two satellite-navigation programs in the late 1950s—Transit and Timation—as an integral part of Polaris ballistic-missile submarine development. The Soviet Union developed its first navigation satellite starting in 1967, and currently has third- and fourth-generation satellites in orbit.

Unlike earlier systems, NAVSTAR will be more accurate and "three dimensional" (important in the guidance of aircraft or missiles in flight), and its signal will be continuously available. The NAVSTAR satellites are being "hardened" against nuclear effects and will be able to operate two weeks at a time without ground updates so that mobile emergency control stations on the ground can be "reconstituted" if ground stations are destroyed. NAVSTAR satellites will also carry Nuclear Detonation Detection System (NDDS) sensors (previously called the Integrated Operational Nuclear Detection System) (discussed above). The Soviet Union is deploying its own new NAVSTAR system, called GLONASS (Global Navigation Satellite System), first launched in October 1982.

The primary military interest in NAVSTAR is not to find one's way in the dark but to increase the accuracy of weapons. As receivers become smaller, weapons such as cruise missiles will use NAVSTAR as a reliable internal guidance and updating system.[20] NAVSTAR will directly enable submarine-fired missiles to be as accurate as those fired from land, by providing "the precision data available during test launches."[21] NAVSTAR will also contribute to better geodetic measurements, surveillance systems, computer and communications networks, and astronomical measurements. NAVSTAR is already being "fully exploited" by the DMA, which claims that it "dramatically improves our strategic target mapping capability, the probability of target acquisition, low-level ingress/egress, flexible routing, and the accuracy of delivered weapons."[22]

Timing

The key to most sophisticated systems in the nuclear infrastructure is timing. The military's ability to synchronize its watches is central to every aspect of research, testing, communications, and, if need be, battle. Each NAV-

ARCTIC OPERATIONS

On an increasing scale the Arctic is becoming a nuclear theater of operations for the superpowers. The Arctic is unique because of the "extreme climate and the unusual geophysical phenomena associated with its polar location."[1] Arctic ice expands each year from roughly 5.2 million to 11.7 million square kilometers (See Figure "Early Warning" in Chapter 4). Ships require icebreakers to clear passages through most of the "ice-locked" Arctic Ocean. Submarines navigating below the ice must be specially equipped with ice sensors, special navigation aids, and strengthened hulls. The uneven formations of the Arctic ice pose tremendous challenges for submarine and anti-submarine operations. Pressure ridges and glacial ice can extend as deep as 170 feet and 1,500 feet, respectively, and can trap submarines. A submarine captain with Arctic experience stated that "Maneuvering a submarine under the ice is the most challenging and unforgiving operation a submarine can do."[2]

The chief of U.S. Naval Intelligence, Admiral John C. Butts, believes that "the Soviets intend to make maximum use of the natural obstacle presented by acoustic conditions in the Arctic to enhance the survivability of their SSBN [strategic missile submarine] force." Accordingly, the Navy's strategy for destroying Soviet submarines states: "The majority of Soviet forces must be contained as far north as possible. This can be accomplished by offensive actions that keep the Soviet Navy focused on the threats to their forces in the Norwegian and Barents Seas. If [Soviet] offensive operations are allowed to break out into the broad Atlantic, many more [U.S.] forces may be required to defeat the threat."

Both the U.S. and the Soviet Union are making greater use of the Arctic for their naval operations. Submarine operations have been focusing more on the Arctic in recent years. "Much of the high Arctic," Admiral Butts told the Senate in April 1983, "is relatively, I say relatively smooth, with no more than about two meters of ice over much of it, even in the dead of winter, and so surfacing through the ice is a practical thing to consider. We have done it and the Soviets have done it." In addition to surfacing through the ice, submarines can also surface in open water areas called polynyas, where pockets of warm water melt away the surface ice.

Advances in submarine design and communications have made operation of U.S. and Soviet missile submarines under the Arctic ice cap possible. The Typhoon class submarines of the Soviet Navy have distinctive features which, many speculate, give it the ability to operate under the ice cap's protection and "punch through" the ice to fire missiles. Soviet Delta and Typhoon submarine deployments in the Arctic have already begun. The FY 1984 Navy budget refers to "urgent requirements in Arctic ASW" as a result of these operations.[3] New U.S. Trident submarines have also patrolled under the ice cap and Los Angeles class attack submarines are being upgraded with an "Arctic warfare capability."[4] Research is underway to develop sonobuoys that can drill their way through the ice. Submarine patrols under the ice are largely possible as a result of the activation of the extremely low frequency (ELF) system which allows communications with submarines on covert missions. The USS Ohio, lead ship of the Trident-class strategic missile submarines, and five attack submarines are already equipped with experimental ELF receivers. One DOD official reported that with ELF "the Navy has had excellent reception under the ice."[5]

There has been a surge in research to understand the dynamic interaction of Arctic weather, ocean, and ice phenomena. Experiments like the Arctic Ice Dynamics Joint Experiment and the Marginal Ice Zone Experiment, sponsored by the U.S. Navy, aim to improve the Navy's ability to fight in the Arctic. Each year the edge of the polar icefield moves as much as 375 miles north to south; according to the Navy this "affects the weather patterns of the entire northern hemisphere and has a significant effect on naval operations." Current experiments include acoustics, biology, ice meteorology, oceanography, remote sensing, and will examine ice properties, the atmospheric boundary layer, and upper ocean characteristics. Another program, the Arctic Submarine Lab Project (SUBICEX), involves "testing special [i.e. nuclear] weapons in the Arctic area." The Navy stated that "the number of SUBICEX exercises and participants is doubling in FY 1985."[6]

NOTES

1. For a good discussion of Arctic phenomena see Central Intelligence Agency, *Polar Regions Atlas* (Washington, D.C.: U.S. GPO, 1978).
2. Norman Polmar, "Sailing Under the Ice," *Proceedings* (June 1984), p. 121.
3. U.S. Navy, FY 1984 RDT&E Descriptive Summary, pt. 1, p.184.
4. HASC, FY 1984 DOD, pt. 4, p. 206.
5. HAC, FY 1984 DOD, pt. 8, p. 325.
6. HAC, FY 1985 DOD, pt. 3, p. 602.

STAR satellite, for instance, carries four atomic clocks. These clocks are accurate to within fifty nanoseconds (billionths of one second); they will lose or gain only one second every 65,000 years. In operation, an airplane or ship will receive signals from NAVSTAR satellites, measure the range by calculating time delays, and then use simple triangulation to locate precise positions at the intersection of separate satellite signals. Since the receivers' and the satellites' clocks can be off by up to ten milliseconds, four satellites' signals are used. The NAVSTAR satellite clocks still have to be synchronized to within three nanoseconds; this is accomplished by resetting their clocks via ground commands.

The "master clock" of the U.S. military (the most accurate and reliable time standard in the world) is at the Naval Observatory in Washington, D.C. currently providing an accuracy of five to twenty nanoseconds. But the Observatory says, "Requirements of a number of DOD platforms and systems over the next decade will demand an absolute accuracy of 1 nanosecond."[23]

These measurements of time (precise time and time intervals) are used to synchronize satellite operations, which contribute to the improvement of nuclear weapons and plans. The Air Force Global Weather Central, in a 1983 report, demonstrated the importance of this data. AFGWC discovered a "serious error" of twenty seconds "in the orbital element sets of all weather satellites," in the scheduling of satellite orbits. According to the report, "The ephemeris files provide satellite locations and altitudes to data mapping programs, and the 20 second error would have produced mapping errors of over 60 nautical miles. Mapping errors that large would have been disastrous."[24] Not every timing error is that spectacular, but considering that NAVSTAR signals are based on light-travel time, the accuracy of ten nanoseconds can correspond to three meters on the ground. The electronic satellite transmission from one point to another itself introduces a delay of about 250 milliseconds.

The Observatory attains its precision from continuous observation of the stars, planets, moon, sun, and other natural and artificial celestial bodies to determine their position, motions, and physical characteristics. Accurate stellar position and timing data, according to the Observatory, "is needed for the calibration of inertial and satellite navigation systems, satellite orbit calculations and predictions, precise guidance in space, precise positioning of launch sites and tracking stations, geodesy, and observational input to the improvement of planetary theories and ephemerides."[25]

Weather

Weather has become more and more important as modern weapons have evolved. Its effects on the electronic systems of the nuclear infrastructure have been especially important. The increasing use of sensors that operate between the visible electromagnetic spectrum and radar frequencies—infrared devices, lasers, and electro-optics—and the pursuit of greater weapons accuracy have meant that an accurate knowledge of the weather is essential for the employment of nuclear forces. Military history is full of apocryphal stories about campaigns lost because of the weather. A recent reminder came in the spring of 1980 when the hostage rescue attempt in Iran failed because of a sandstorm during total darkness.

Local weather conditions, such as temperature inversions or fronts, can cause "ducting," which distorts the performance and propagation of radars and can significantly change the quality of communications. In the eastern Mediterranean, for instance, warm desert air from the south produces significant radar ducting. In the Arabian Sea, ships often encounter sandstorms hundreds of miles from shore. Collecting precise weather data in remote parts of the world has thus become important for a global war strategy.

The weather requirements of the nuclear era go far beyond conventional forecasts. Weather data directly aids the planning of bomber flights by selecting the optimum routes and altitudes from sophisticated computer models of aircraft performance in different atmospheric conditions. Winds can severely hamper the attacks of bombers or cruise missiles.[26] Accurate wind data is also critical in the military's predictions of nuclear fallout patterns. Measurement of cloud properties is used in "specifying cloud particle characteristics along reentry vehicle trajectories for nosecone erosion testing applications."[27]

The military has its own infrastructure to collect weather forecasts: ground observations and radar, upper-air sensors (aircraft, balloons, and rockets), specialized weather-reconnaissance aircraft (to collect weather in "data sparse areas"), and satellites.[28] Since missiles will be shot and bombers will fly primarily over the North Pole, a nuclear war will depend heavily on support from satellites in polar orbits. Weather satellites provide the degree of accuracy and global coverage the nuclear infrastructure demands. The U.S. military's own weather satellite—the Defense Meteorological Satellite Program (DMSP), which reports directly

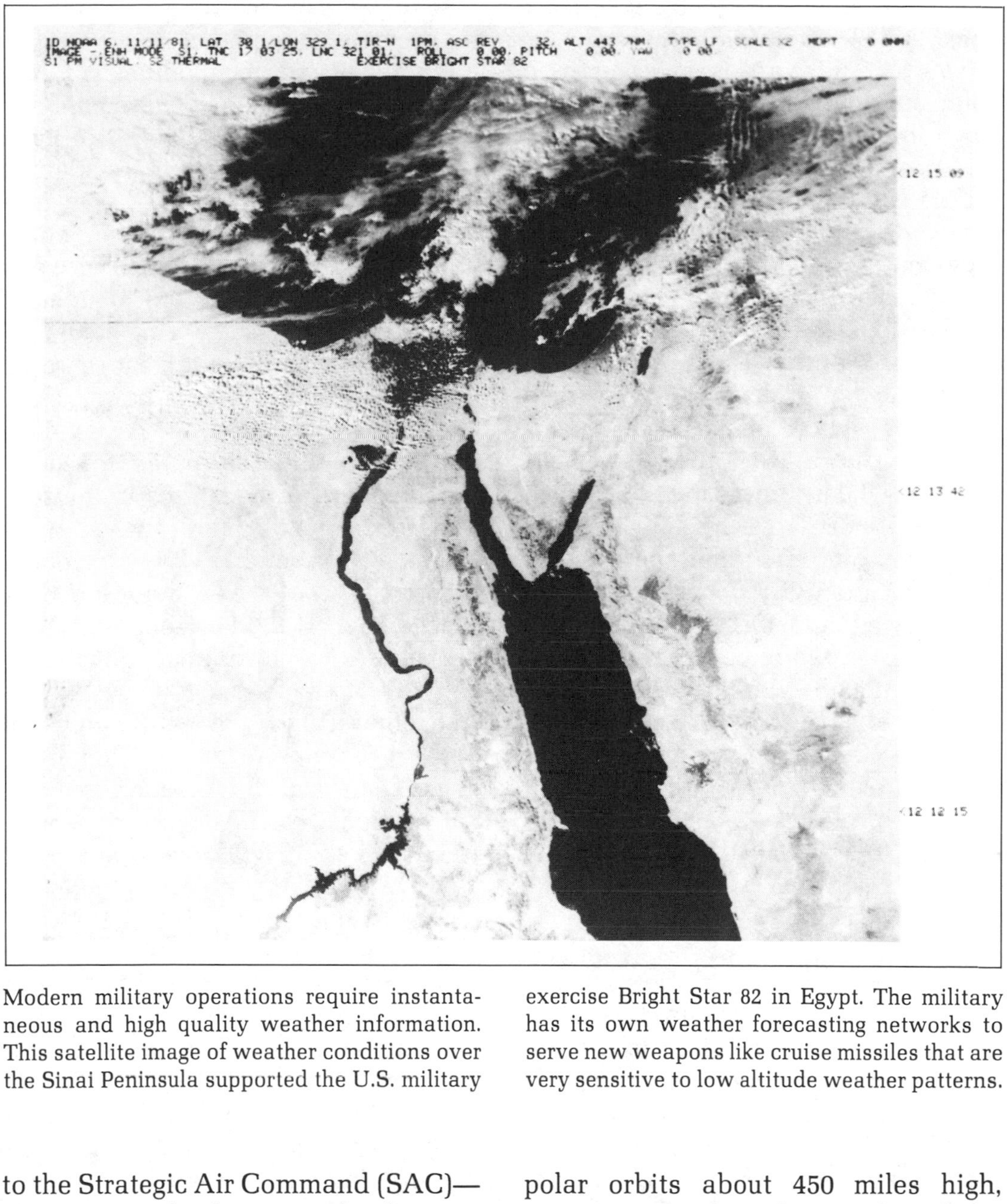

Modern military operations require instantaneous and high quality weather information. This satellite image of weather conditions over the Sinai Peninsula supported the U.S. military exercise Bright Star 82 in Egypt. The military has its own weather forecasting networks to serve new weapons like cruise missiles that are very sensitive to low altitude weather patterns.

to the Strategic Air Command (SAC)—can accurately forecast cloud cover (which is crucial for aiming reconnaissance satellites) or predict the behavior of low-altitude weather systems on the other side of the earth (to aid low-level bomber and cruise missile penetrations).[29]

The DMSP satellites, from near-polar orbits about 450 miles high, cover 1,600-mile-wide swaths of the earth during each orbit, or the entire earth in about twelve hours. DMSP sensors provide local forecasts directly to military bases and ships. Bulk data is also stored on tapes and sent via commercial communications satellite links (AMSAT/WESTAR) to one of three readout stations in Hawaii, Washington, and Maine.[30]

The U.S. military operates its own solar observation network: the Space Environmental Support System, for observing solar flares and activity, and for detection and forecasting of auroral activity. Outbursts of solar energy, equivalent to billions of nuclear explosions, constantly strike the earth's upper atmosphere and affect a variety of military systems. When these energy particles become trapped in the ionosphere, they can result in a visible Aurora Borealis ("northern lights"), which affects high-frequency (HF) and short-wave communications, satellite orbits, and radar operations.[31] Solar flare activity occurs in eleven-year cycles, and the early 1980s is a high point of activity. From six locations around the world, Air Force solar telescopes observe the sun around-the-clock. By measuring light intensity and wavelength (to one-ten-billionth of one meter), these sites can alert the military to adverse conditions.

Communications and Electronics

The condition of the atmosphere and its physical and chemical properties affect many aspects of the nuclear infrastructure. Military aeronomy research investigates the effects of energy sources such as ultraviolet radiation from the sun on "missile surveillance and tracking, spacecraft horizon sensing, atmospheric/ionospheric sensing for communication and detection purposes, and technical intelligence."[32] Communications are probably affected more than any other activity.

In the field of electronic communications, each medium and frequency has advantages and disadvantages. Radio signals propagate in electromagnetic waves, traveling at the speed of light. Each wave has a different wavelength (the distance between one point in a wave and the next corresponding point) and cycle (one complete wave motion). Frequency is the number of times a cycle passes during each second (known as a hertz). Since radio waves travel in different patterns according to frequency, they provide a number of different paths for communications. Radio waves in the four lowest frequency bands travel what are called "groundwaves" and follow the curvature of the earth for long distances beyond the horizon. Thus they are useful for communications with ships far from land.[33] Extremely-low-frequency (ELF) waves (below 300 hertz) can penetrate water to hundreds of feet (perfect for submarine communications), while extremely-high-frequencies (EHF) (above 30 gigahertz) have difficulty penetrating even a heavy rainstorm.

Several conditions determine the best frequency to choose. The size of the transmitting antennas is a significant military consideration. For frequencies below the HF band, antennas are too large for ships or aircraft. A very-low-frequency (VLF) or ELF transmitting antenna must be several miles long. A second consideration is "data rate,"—the amount of information the frequency can transmit in a given time. The higher the frequency, the greater the data rate. Since each cycle can be modified to carry a fragment of information (a letter of the alphabet, for example), a frequency of 30

Before going on operational patrol U.S. submarines have their magnetic "signatures" reduced so that they will be undetectable to enemy antisubmarine warfare forces. This magnetic silencing facility, located in Puget Sound, Washington, serves strategic missile and attack submarines.

megahertz, for instance, would have a data rate of 30 million cycles (letters) per second. Thus even though the ELF frequency may be the best means to penetrate water, it has an extremely low data rate and would require a long time to send just a few characters. The amount of power required or the interference a signal receives also determines frequency and data rate. A third consideration is reliability—how much a frequency is subject to interference, fading, or jamming.

The military uses high-frequency (HF) radio communications (3 to 30 megahertz) widely. HF is long-range, cheap, low-power, small, and highly portable but requires constant adjustments in specific frequencies to deal with atmospheric conditions.[34] Because of shifting in the ionospheric layers, the radio propagation varies. Long-distance HF radio transmissions depend on refraction of radio waves by layers of the ionosphere, a region in the upper atmosphere where free electrons are produced by the ionizing effects of radiation from the sun. The height and ion density of layers within the ionosphere vary significantly with the time of day, season of the year, location, and the eleven-year cycle of sunspot activity.[35] With HF, the frequency must be selected to achieve the best possible "signal fidelity" given atmospheric conditions. This is based on propagation predictions, essentially charts based on past observations, that on this day, at this hour, this frequency would be the best over certain paths. The solar observatories (discussed above) collect the relevant solar-activity data.

Natural events, such as atmospheric disturbances or solar flares (which can cause magnetic storms), interfere with transmissions. The Air Force Global Weather Central history for the first half of 1983 gives some idea of the military implications of solar and geophysical activity:

> The first half of 1983 began on quiet note. Both solar and geophysical activity were at relatively quiet levels throughout January picking up slightly during February. However, a very large flare occurred in February. Intense optical, radio, particle, and X-ray emissions accompanied this flare and resulted in severe degradation in high frequency (HF) communications in the sunlit hemisphere for nearly an hour. This flare also ejected a large number of protons which caused a polar cap absorbtion (PCA) event. The PCA caused a disruption of HF radio communications in and through the polar regions. In addition, solar material ejected by the flare produced a major geomagnetic storm starting on the 4th and lasting two days. This major geomagnetic storm severely degraded HF communications between 40 and 75 degrees latitude. It may have resulted in spacecraft charging on geostationary satellites and increased atmospheric drag on lower earth orbiting satellites.[36]

These effects have given high frequencies a reputation for unreliability, especially because of their tendency to fade in response to the sun's position relative to the propagation path between points on the earth. The low reliability of HF communications, together with "crowding" of the frequency spectrum (interference) and the advent of computers and satellites (which operate at higher frequencies and data rates), led to a shift away from HF for military purposes in the 1960s and 1970s. Satellites were hailed as the means to satisfy all communication needs because they were largely immune to ionospheric disturbances. To the military planner, however, satellites could fail or be attacked. This led to the rebirth of military interest in HF.

New technology and techniques can now be used to increase the reliability of HF communications. "Sounders" (devices that automatically sense the environment) can alert an entire HF network to change frequencies instantly to get more reliable and clear transmissions. More reliable than ordinary HF radios are solid-state transmitters and microprocessors that can form a finer beam, adapt a signal to ionospheric conditions, and protect the signal from jamming or detection.

The renewed interest in HF is linked to nuclear war planning. Military planners want to build "endurance" into the command, control, and communications (C3) system for a "protracted" nuclear war. As one military officer has written, "From a military viewpoint, the principal advantage [of HF radio] is that the transmission relay system—the ionosphere of the Earth's surface —is very difficult to permanently interrupt." It is "the satellite which doesn't fall down."[37]

The ionosphere can also be used to

reflect radio signals from long-range radar and thus provide "over-the-horizon" (OTH) detection.[38] Because radar does not follow the curvature of the earth past the visible horizon, in order to detect low-flying aircraft and cruise missiles, the military has had to develop OTH radars. The United States is testing an OTH "backscatter" radar in Maine that sends high-powered radar signals 500 to 1,800 miles away and reflects back to a receiver where large computers extract target data. Since the operation of a northern-looking OTH radar would be affected by auroral and ionospheric disturbance, the radar in Maine and a future site on the Oregon/ California border will probe east and west. The Soviet Union also operates three OTH radars, but they are primarily for the detection of ballistic missiles, not low-level cruise missiles or aircraft.

A special satellite, the high latitude research satellite (or HILAT), funded by the Defense Nuclear Agency (DNA), is investigating the Aurora Borealis.[39] Given the huge amount of electrical power in the auroral zone of the atmosphere (it carries currents of 1 to 100 million amperes), HILAT can use this region to simulate nuclear bursts and their effects in the atmosphere. This will help the study of the atmospheric effects of high-altitude nuclear explosions. Data from HILAT will be collected at ground stations in Canada, Greenland, the United States, and Norway.

The military endlessly studies the effects of nuclear blasts on communications (nuclear "blackout") and has spawned numerous programs to provide the new "endurance" requirements of a long-term nuclear war. "Following a nuclear exchange," one military consultant has stated, "mobile (or proliferated) HF may well be the only long-haul communication resource that will survive intact."[40] But HF is not the only frequency being examined. Groundwave communications are only moderately affected by nuclear explosions in the atmosphere. The military is examining VLF and LF frequencies because they are reliable, can penetrate sea water, and have relatively good performance in a nuclear-disturbed environment.

The key "enduring" system is the Ground Wave Emergency Network (or GWEN). GWEN will be a grid of 300-foot unmanned relay stations, with EMP hardened LF transmitters and receivers. By transmitting "groundwaves," the radio signals will follow the earth's surface and will continue to function in spite of the nuclear disruption of the ionosphere. By using "automatic diverse routing," the GWEN network of some 300 to 500 relay stations will ensure that there is a "communications backbone even after a nuclear laydown."[41] The network will be constructed in three stages in the United States (and eventually into Canada): "initial connectivity" (9 stations), "thin-line connectivity" (57 stations), and "fully proliferated" (300 to 500 stations) (see Figure).[42]

The theory behind GWEN holds that, with hundreds of relays eventually installed in the United States, the network could never be fully destroyed in any but an all-out nuclear attack. Thus the system would "deter" an attack on communications (instead of on weapons) meant to disarm the United States. "The fact that this system will maintain communications

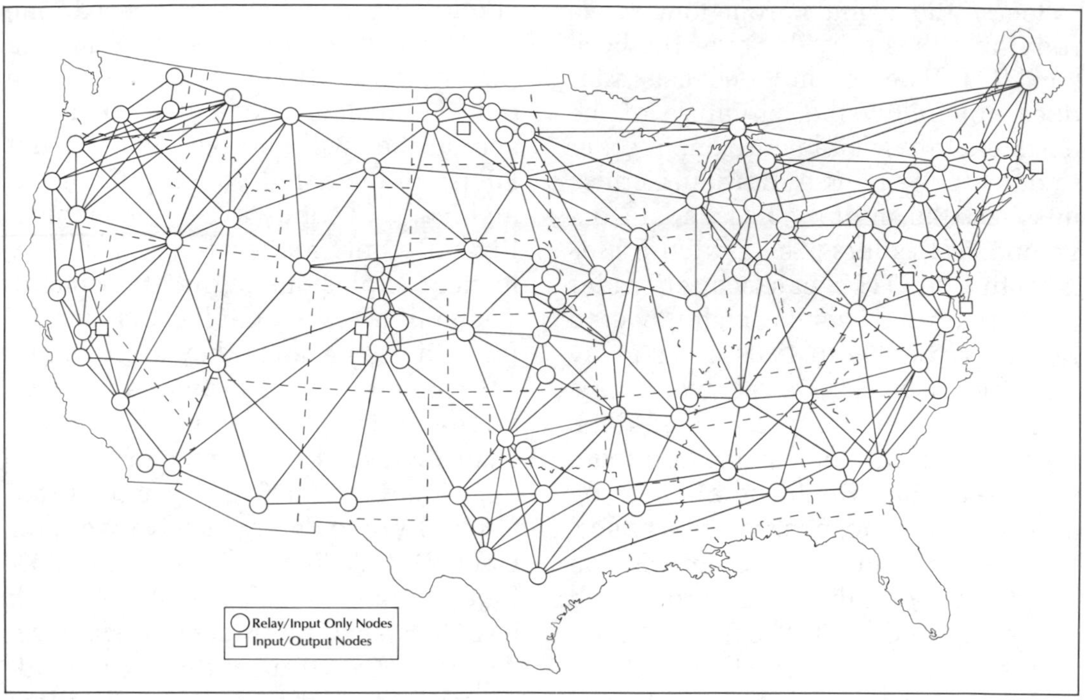

SURVIVABILITY

Worries about being "decapitated" by a nuclear attack aimed at communications links has led war planners to dream up schemes like the Ground Wave Emergency Network (GWEN). It is intended to create too many targets to destroy in less than a massive attack, thus allowing the military to communicate through even concerted targeting of communications assets, or after the first salvos of a nuclear war. Each relay node will be in a location that the military feels is not yet a target and will connect with all nearby sites, allowing it to seek out other surviving sites after nuclear attack. This map shows only a small portion of the eventual planned network.

connectivity even after a nuclear attack will discourage attacks on terrestrial communications links," a top DOD official told Congress in early 1983.[43]

The GWEN theory will work only if there is a limitation on the number of attacking warheads or if there are at least as many essential communications targets as weapons targets. But GWEN will have only about ten critical "input/output" stations (not hundreds), while there are more than 100 hardened missile launch control centers. It will be easy to knock GWEN out in comparison to the missile force. Nevertheless, GWEN is being built because it is a challenge. According to the Air Force "To the maximum extent possible, GWEN relay nodes will be installed at effective ground wave radio ranges in low risk target areas."[44] One result will be to put targets into towns across America. The initial network of nine test stations uses three commercial radio towers, in

Manhattan and Colby, Kansas; and Canton, Oklahoma.[45]

Another communications medium for use in nuclear war is "meteor burst communications" (MBC). According to one MBC engineer, "When a meteor the size of a grain of sand enters the earth's atmosphere and ionizes, it generates a trail of (typically) one meter in diameter at the nose and 25 kilometers long."[46] Billions of ionized meteor trails, constantly present in the atmosphere, can be used to reflect very-high-frequency (VHF) radio signals. Due to the enormous amount of debris, and the wonders of modern technology, communications at the rate of 100 words per minute over distances of 1,200 miles can be reflected off the meteor trails.[47] Since the average duration of a meteor trail is between 200 and 400 milliseconds, MBC stations depend on precise synchronization and "bursts" of data. The Alaskan Air Command has already successfully tested MBC technology to backup satellite communications. The Federal Emergency Management Agency (FEMA) also operates two portable stations and five remote terminals for testing a post-nuclear war communications system. Since ionization would increase in a nuclear war, and thus enhance MBC communications, MBC plays a prominent role in the official fantasies of post-attack communications.[48]

Nuclear Effects Research

Pursuit of the perfect infrastructure to survive and fight a nuclear war infuses a great deal of research. A Defense Nuclear Agency research program, for instance, uses "natural and artificial phenomena such as aurora and metal releases in the atmosphere . . . to simulate important aspects of atmospheric conditions following nuclear detonations."[49] "In the absence of atmospheric nuclear testing," DNA budget documents state, information on the effects of nuclear weapons is collected using solar-induced disturbances, which are probed by satellites, rockets, the space shuttle, and ground-based instruments that "discern the IR chemistry processes [for infrared space-based target acquisition] and the effects on propagation of radio signals." To test the effects of "emissions from weapon debris," the military plans to release barium and uranium in near space. Similarly, test detonations of conventional explosives "lend insight into the propagation of radar signals through dust clouds lofted by surface or near surface nuclear detonations."[50]

DNA's research also extends into the propagation disturbances that would result from high-altitude nuclear detonations. DNA investigations of natural ionospheric disturbances (which use the HILAT satellite and research radars) and of nuclear simulation (which use high-altitude barium and uranium releases) seek to predict nuclear disturbances and their impact, and counter with new systems like "adaptive HF" and groundwave LF radios.

The Air Force Geophysics Laboratory (AFGL) also has research programs relating to "upper atmosphere impact on Air Force systems." It is using rockets and satellites to "provide knowledge concerning winds, density, turbulence, and temperature"

This is the world's largest glue-laminated wood structure, located at Kirtland Air Force Base in New Mexico. The Air Force uses it to pump huge electric shocks through aircraft, like this B-52 bomber, to test their vulnerability to the electromagnetic pulses that nuclear explosions cause. Scores of military laboritories and test facilities conduct such "nuclear effects" research on military equipment.

of the atmosphere above 35 kilometers. "These models," an AFGL report states, "include undisturbed and naturally-disturbed conditions, and disturbances due to the detonation of a nuclear weapon. The design and operation of various Air Force satellites and missiles operating in this environment can be simulated over a wide range of conditions."[51] The "Earth Motion Effects" program "is to measure and characterize the effects of motions, both natural and those due to nuclear detonations, on various Air Force systems, e.g., the MX."[52]

The military's interest in the earth, of course, does not translate into an interest in protecting the enviornment. Its main worries about radiation or nuclear weapons effects concern disruption of military equipment and operations. The history of nuclear production includes numerous incidents that released radioactivity into the environment.[53] At least twelve of the numerous "serious" nuclear weapons accidents have spread radiation. In at least six accidents, nuclear weapons have been "lost."

Radiation from the more than 1,250 nuclear tests conducted since 1945 have affected much of the globe.[54] Six nations have tested nuclear weapons at thirty-five sites around the world, in the Atlantic and Pacific oceans, on four continents, and in the Arctic circle. China may still test nuclear weapons in the atmosphere and France tests beneath an atoll in the South Pacific. Manmade nuclear materials and waste created in the nuclear fuel cycle will have to be perpetually stored, as there is still no permanent method for disposal of nuclear waste.

The military's urge to understand and control the enormous nuclear infrastructure drives science to serve the needs of managing (and fighting) a nuclear war. Military planners and scientists perpetuate the illusion that they can understand and control the nuclear links with scientific accuracy instead of throwing up their hands and admitting that they don't have a clue what will happen in a nuclear war.

3

Nuclear Arsenals

NOTHING IN HUMAN experience can adequately describe the enormity of the nuclear weapons arsenals. More than 50,000 warheads, most smaller than suitcases, can each obliterate cities. Just a few can kill millions of people and destroy the environment for decades hence. The smallest nuclear warheads are ten times more powerful than the largest conventional weapons. The largest have the power of forty billion pounds of conventional explosives.

Why does the military stock such a huge arsenal of weapons? Warheads are bureaucratically and regionally categorized for seemingly specific and separate tasks. Half of the arsenals are "strategic" or long-range weapons for attacking enemy homelands: land-based missiles, submarine-launched missiles, and strategic bombers—all widely dispersed to increase their chances of surviving a surprise attack. Thousands of warheads from each category always sit at high readiness levels to meet the hair-trigger requirements of the nuclear infrastructure.

The remainder of the arsenals are nonstrategic forces. Their various labels indicate confusion or internal competition over roles: battlefield nuclear weapons, tactical nuclear weapons, theater nuclear weapons, intermediate-range nuclear weapons, and sea-control nuclear weapons. Unlike strategic weap-

World Nuclear Stockpiles

United States	24,898
Soviet Union	22,709–32,823
Britain	686
France	514
China	251–331
Total	49,058–59,252

ons, most nonstrategic weapons are "dual capable," that is, their delivery systems or missiles can carry either nuclear or conventional (or chemical) warheads. Each military service and each geographic command—Europe, the Pacific, Middle East, or "reserve" —has its own nuclear weapons. Within the commands, the weapons are further divided and dispersed for different missions, flexibility, and survivability.

The 26,000 warheads of the United States form the most widespread arsenal in the world.[1] It was the first country to send nuclear weapons abroad (in 1952). Within the United States, nuclear warheads are permanently stored in twenty-eight states (see Table). Overseas, they are in Guam and eight foreign countries: Belgium, Greece, Italy, the Netherlands, Turkey, South Korea, the United Kingdom, and West Germany. The armed forces of these foreign countries (except South Korea) also use U.S. warheads for their own nuclear delivery systems. The United States maintains about 5,800 warheads in Europe, another 580 in Asia (South Korea and Guam), and some 1,400 at sea. They are routinely present in the Atlantic, Pacific, and Indian Oceans and the Mediterranean Sea. About 13,000 warheads could strike targets in the Soviet Union, some 9,000 are intended for battlefield roles, and 1,900 are for nuclear warfare at sea.

The Soviet nuclear arsenal is thought to consist of some 22,000 to 33,000 warheads. Although the exact composition of the Soviet stockpile is unclear, particularly the nonstrategic warheads, roughly half of the Soviet arsenal is estimated to be long-range strategic weapons (just as in the U.S. arsenal).[2] Another 10,000 are available for theater attacks in Europe or Asia (and beyond), and 3,000 for naval warfare. Soviet nuclear weapons span the full range of delivery means and missions, from a single warhead 20-megaton SS-18 missile to nuclear artillery. Like the United States, the Soviet Union has a "triad" of strategic weapons, and a full complement of "theater," "battlefield," and naval nuclear weapons.

Until recently, it was unclear whether the Soviet Union deployed nuclear warheads on foreign soil. It now appears that Czechoslovakia, East Germany, Hungary, and Poland host Soviet nuclear warheads. Unlike the United States, the Soviet Union does not share warheads with its Warsaw Pact allies. Nonetheless, the Soviet nuclear infrastructure is quite similar to the U.S. infrastructure in its balance between tactical dispersal and centralization. Strategic missiles are deployed at about twenty main bases, submarines operate from four bases, and long-range nuclear bombers fly from twenty airfields backed up by five Arctic "staging bases" where bombers can land en route to targets in North America. There are probably about thirty Soviet nuclear storage sites in Eastern Europe.

The only nuclear weapons aimed at America belong to the Soviet Union, but the Soviet Union faces the weapons not only of the United States but of Britain, France, and China who have a combined total of roughly 1,500 nuclear warheads, 900 of which could strike targets in the Soviet Union or other Warsaw Pact countries (and are called "strategic"). While Britain and France are often lumped together as the "other" western nuclear forces, their positions are quite different. Although each country has between 500 and 700 warheads, France has maintained its nuclear independence while Britain has chosen to integrate its weapons into U.S./NATO war plans, which makes them an adjunct of U.S. nuclear forces. Britain has a combination of British-made and U.S.-supplied warheads (controlled by the U.S.), thus requiring a smaller infrastructure for development and support than France.

Technological cooperation between Britain and the United States in nuclear matters is unique. Britain has access to a wide variety of technologies for the development or manufacture of warheads, missiles, and submarines. Britain relies on the United States for training assistance and testing. It tests its warheads in Nevada and fires its missiles on the U.S. Eastern Test Range. It also relies on the United States for a large portion of its targeting data. In the future, Britiain's new Trident-equipped submarines will be serviced at the U.S. submarine base at Kings Bay, Georgia. In return, Britain incorporates its nuclear weapons into U.S. nuclear plans and provides the United States with support for its nuclear weapons, including a submarine base at Holy Loch in Scotland, major nuclear air bases, the Ballistic Missile Early Warning System (BMEWS) radar at Fylingdales, and key strategic communications and intelligence facilities.

Like America, Britain has a tradition of basing portions of its nuclear forces abroad. For twenty-two years, between 1954 and 1975, British nuclear aircraft and bombs were stationed in two overseas territories: Cyprus and Singapore. Today, Britain continues to base aircraft and nuclear bombs in West Germany, at Brüggen, and Laarbruch air bases. Britain also has the capacity, as demonstrated in the Falklands War, to bring nuclear weapons into the Third World.[3]

French nuclear forces exist for the same ostensible reason as Britain's (to have nuclear weapons independent of the U.S. and NATO) but have been independent since 1966, when France withdrew from NATO's military structure. The French forces consist of missile-carrying submarines, land-based long-range and short-range missiles, and nuclear-capable aircraft (see Table). All French weapons are stationed in France; they are widely dispersed to ensure that only a massive preemptive attack could be successful. Of the 514 French warheads, about 270 can be delivered against targets in the Soviet Union, 204 are for battlefield purposes, and 40 are available for use in the Third World. The "survivable" French deterrent consists of three submarines (with 48 missiles) that are always at sea.

China is the newest and most mysterious nuclear power. It developed nuclear weapons for two reasons: to offset Soviet nuclear weapons and to

The U.S. Nuclear Infrastructure

State	*Warhead Deployments* Number (a)	*Warhead Deployments* Rank	*All Military Facilities* Number	*All Military Facilities* Rank	*Nuclear Facilities* Number (b)	*Nuclear Facilities* Rank
Alabama	0	—	70	22	6	36
Alaska	70	25	210	5	42	2
Arizona	10	28	52	27	14	15
Arkansas	430	10	44	32	7	32
California	1,437	4	299	2	79	1
Colorado	138	23	82	16	17	11
Connecticut	20	26	33	41	2	45
Delaware	0	—	12	49	1	48
Dist. Columbia	0	—	15	48	—	—
Florida	230	20	135	8	33	4
Georgia	406	12	55	24	14	16
Hawaii	345	14	76	17	29	6
Idaho	0	—	27	44	10	23
Illinois	0	—	73	19	8	28
Indiana	0	—	35	37	5	38
Iowa	0	—	29	43	4	40
Kansas	20	26	48	28	9	26
Kentucky	0	—	18	47	4	40
Louisiana	530	9	45	30	8	28
Maine	320	15	43	33	16	14
Maryland	0	—	83	15	35	3
Massachusetts	0	—	71	21	17	11
Michigan	630	6	53	25	13	19
Minnesota	0	—	36	36	4	40
Mississippi	0	—	38	35	6	36
Missouri	155	22	218	4	7	32
Montana	315	16	254	3	14	16
Nebraska	255	18	118	11	10	23
Nevada	260	17	32	42	15	15
New Hampshire	190	21	12	49	2	45
New Jersey	100	24	53	25	12	20
New Mexico	410	11	25	45	17	11
New York	1,900	2	132	9	26	7
North Carolina	0	—	70	22	11	21
North Dakota	1,510	3	361	1	18	10
Ohio	0	—	74	18	11	21
Oklahoma	0	—	46	29	6	35
Oregon	0	—	34	39	7	32
Pennsylvania	0	—	124	10	10	23
Rhode Island	0	—	35	37	3	43
South Carolina	1,962	1	45	30	9	26
South Dakota	365	13	180	6	7	32
Tennessee	0	—	34	39	5	38
Texas	630	6	140	7	21	9
Utah	0	—	72	20	8	28
Vermont	0	—	9	50	2	45
Virginia	542	8	109	12	30	5

The U.S. Nuclear Infrastructure *(Continued)*

State	Warhead Deployments Number (a)	Rank	All Military Facilities Number	Rank	Nuclear Facilities Number (b)	Rank
Washington	1,172	5	106	13	24	8
West Virginia	0	—	23	46	1	48
Wisconsin	0	—	41	34	3	43
Wyoming	247	19	85	14	8	28
TOTAL	14,599	—	4115	—	670	—

(a) peacetime deployments *(b)* Nuclear facilities do not include individual missile silos and launch control centers

attain thc political advantages of a nuclear power. The Chinese, stressing the political status achieved by the nuclear nations, sought to "break the monopoly of the Superpowers." Little is known about the size or types of Chinese nuclear weapons. Like France, it possesses both land-based and submarine-launched missiles, in addition to several models of nuclear bombers (see Tablc). Its deployment schemes (totally within China) include a high degree of mobility and dispersal to complicate the enemy's targeting. While a handful of full-range ICBMs could strike the United States and Europe, the weapons are thought to be aimed exclusively at targets in the Soviet Union.

Soviet technical, scientific, and military assistance in the 1950s helped China attain its nuclear status. Russia shared its aircraft, missile, and submarine designs with China and jointly developed "civilian" nuclear power resources. In return, the Soviets extracted Chinese uranium for their own nuclear weapons programs. The Soviets, however, never shared nuclear warhead tcchnology with China, as they had initially promised.

Strategic Nuclear Forces

Strategic nuclear weapons are generally of intercontinental range, deliverable by land-based and sea-based missiles and bombers. These three categories of weapons form the so-called triad of U.S. and Soviet (and to a lesser extent French and Chinese) arsenals. The justification for the three types lies in differences of range, yield, accuracy, level of reliability, survivability, and readiness. Nearly all U.S. land-based missiles (over 95 percent), one-third of the bombers and half of the submarines—totaling some 5,000 warheads—are constantly ready to go to war. On the Soviet side, the readiness level is much lower. No bombers are kept on alert, and only about 15 percent of the submarine force is away from home waters on a regular basis. Nonetheless, some 5,000 Soviet warheads could be launched at any moment. Britain and France maintain one and three submarines, respectively, at sea at all times, and about 80 percent of France's eighteen land-based missiles could probably be launched immediately.

The United States maintains slightly over 1,000 intercontinental ballistic

French Nuclear Forces

Delivery Mode	Weapon System Number	Weapon System Type	Year Deployed	Range (km)	Warheads / Yield	Warhead Type	Number in Stockpile
Strategic							
Land-based IRBMs	18	S3	1980	3,500	1 × 1 Mt	TN-61	18
Submarines (SLBMs)	80	M-20	1977	3,000	1 × 1 Mt	TN-61	80
	16	M-4	1985	4,000	6 × 150 kt	TN-70	96
Bombers *(a)*	34	Mirage IVA	1964	1,500	2 × 70 kt	AN-22	75
Aerial refuelers	11	C-135F	1965	—	—	—	—
Nonstrategic							
Aircraft *(a)*	45	Jaguar A	1973	720	1 × 6–8/30 kt	*(b)*	50
	30	Mirage IIIE	1964	800	1 × 6–8/30 kt	*(b)*	35
SRBMs	42	Pluton	1974	120	1 × 15–25 kt	ANT-51	120
Naval							
Carrier aircraft	36	Super Etendard	1978	650	1 × 6–8/30 kt	*(b)*	40

(a) The AN-51 warhead is also possibly a secondary bomb for tactical aircraft and the AN-52 is also possibly a secondary bomb for the Mirage IVA.

(b) Warheads include ANT-51, ANT-52, and possibly a third type.

Sources: Robin F. Laird, "French Nuclear Forces in the 1980s and the 1990s," *Comparative Strategy,* 4(4) (1984), pp. 387–412; Pierre Langereux, "Missiles Tactiques et Engins: Cibles Francais en Service, en Developpment ou en etude," *Air et Cosmos* (May 28, 1983), p. 180; Defense Intelligence Agency, "A Guide to Foreign Tactical Nucear Weapon Systems Under the Control of Ground Force Commanders," DST-1040S-541-83-CHG 1 (Secret, partially declassified) (Aug. 17, 1984); International Institute for Strategic Studies, *The Military Balance 1983–84* (London: IISS, annual).

missiles (ICBMs), which carry a total of 2,100 nuclear warheads (see Table). The ICBMs—550 Minuteman III, 450 Minuteman II, and about 30 Titan II missiles (now being retired)—are housed in hardened underground launchers (called silos) in ten states, covering an area of 80,000 square miles (roughly the size of the state of Minnesota) (see Figure).

The Soviet Union has 1,398 ICBMs—550 SS-11s, 60 SS-13s, 150 SS-17s, 308 SS-18s, and 330 SS-19s—capable of carrying over 6,000 warheads (see Table). There are at least three modifications (or variations) of the three newest ICBMs, and the number of warheads varies accordingly. Soviet ICBMs are deployed in hardened un-

NUCLEAR FORCES OF THE SOVIET UNION [*following page*]

Most major Soviet strategic nuclear forces and facilities lie along the Trans-Siberian railroad, the only major transcontinental transportation network, or in the Western Soviet Union. The Soviet military has a much larger number of separate missile and submarine bases, command centers, and communications sites than the U.S. military. Arctic "staging" bases for aircraft would launch bombers on their way over the North Pole.

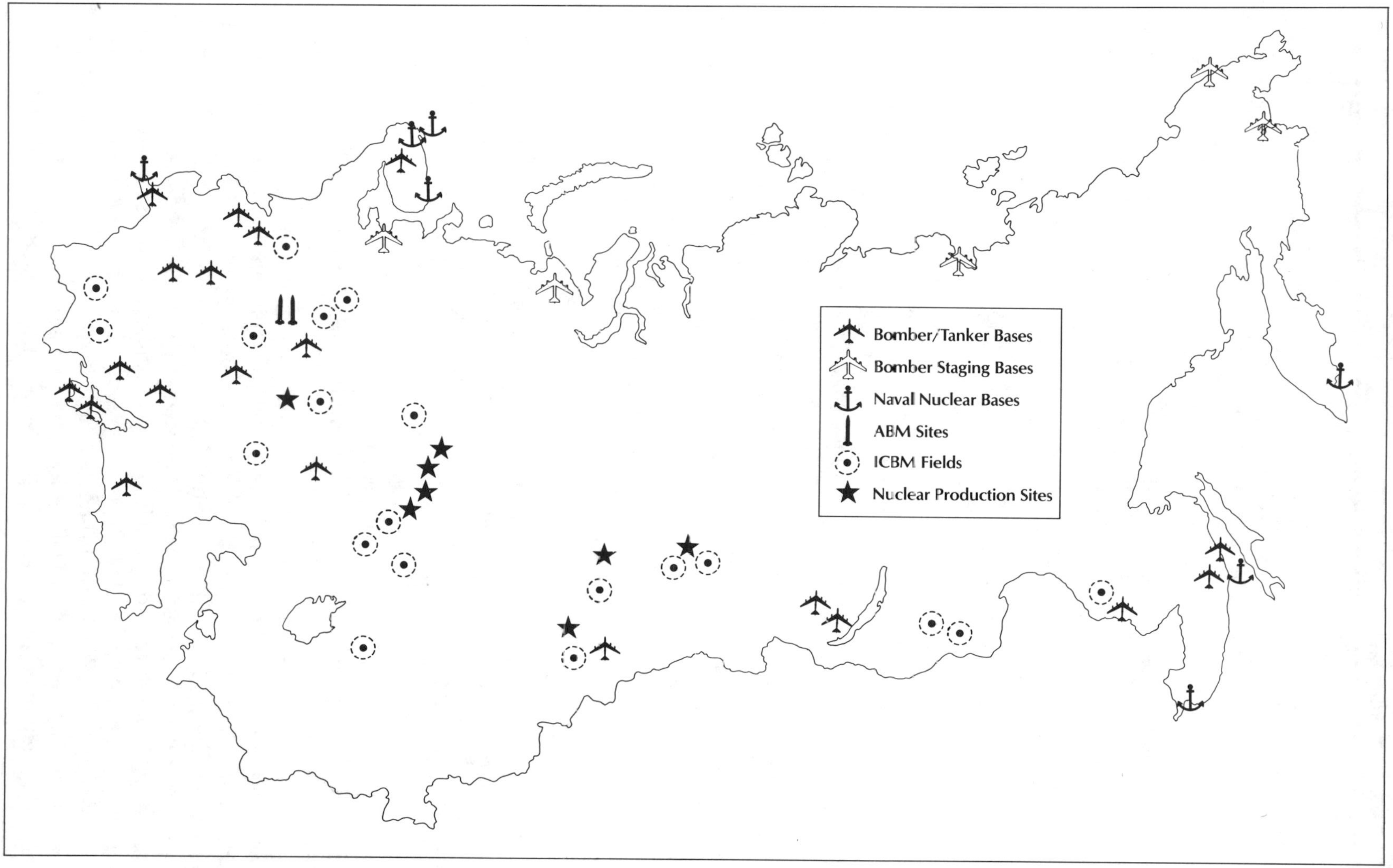

NUCLEAR FORCES OF THE SOVIET UNION

Chinese Nuclear Forces

Delivery Mode	*Weapon System Number*	*Type*	*Year Deployed*	*Range (km)*	*Warheads / Yield*	*Number in Stockpile*
Strategic						
Land-based missiles	40–60	CSS-1 (DF-2)	1966	1,100	1 × 20 kt	40–60
	85–125	CSS-2 (DF-3)	1972	2,600	1 × 2–3 Mt	85–125
	~5	CSS-3 (DF-4)	1978	7,000	1 × 1 Mt	10
	~5	CSS-4 (DF-5)	1980	12,000	1 × 5–10 Mt	10
Submarines (SLBMs)	26	CSS-N-3	1983	3,300	1 × 200 kt–1 Mt	26
Bombers *(a)*	30	B-4 (Bull)	1966	6,100	1–4 × bombs	30
	10	B-5 (Beagle)	1974	1,850	1 × 1 Mt	10
	100	B-6 (Badger)	1966	5,900	1–3 × 1 Mt	30
Nonstrategic						
SRBMs *(b)*	10–30	DF-1	1966	650	1 × 2–10 kt	10–30

(a) All figures for bombers refer to nuclear-capable versions only. Hundreds of these aircraft are also deployed in non-nuclear versions.

(b) A number of SRBMs (DF-1) have been deployed in "theater support" roles, although they may no longer be active. Some of the MRBM and IRBM missiles are assigned to "regional nuclear roles." China has tested a number of warheads with yields from 2–20 kt.

Sources: Joint Chiefs of Staff, *Military Posture* (annual report) FY 1978, 1980, 1982, 1983; Department of Defense, *Annual Report for 1982;* Defense Intelligence Agency, *Handbook on the Chinese Armed Forces,* (April 1976); Defense Intelligence Agency, "A Guide to Foreign Tactical Nuclear Weapon Systems Under the Control of Ground Force Commanders," DST-1040S-541-83-CHG 1 (Secret, partially declassified) (Aug. 17, 1984); Paul H. Godwin, *The Chinese Tactical Airforces and Strategic Weapons Program: Development, Doctrine, and Strategy,* (Maxwell AFB, Ala.: Air University, 1978); Captain Thomas D. Washburn, "The People's Republic of China and Nuclear Weapons: Effects of China's Evolving Arsenal," (Washington, D.C.: NTIS (ADA 067350), 1979); U.S. Congress, Joint Economic Committee, *Allocation of Resources in the Soviet Union and China 1976,* pt. 2, pp. 94–96; Jack Anderson, "China Shows Confidence in Its Missiles," *Washington Post,* (Dec. 19, 1984), p. F11; International Institute for Strategic Studies, *The Military Balance 1983–84* (London: IISS, annual).

derground silos at bases roughly following the route of the Trans-Siberian Railroad across the Soviet Union.

The United States and the Soviet Union are developing two and three new ICBM types, respectively. In the United States, the ten-warhead MX missile will first be deployed in late 1986, and a single-warhead small ICBM (SICBM or "Midgetman") is planned for the early 1990s. In the Soviet Union, the SS-X-24, SS-X-25, and SS-X-26 are under development.

China has also developed an ICBM capability, with a handful of CSS-3 (limited-range) and CSS-4 (full-range) missiles (perhaps ten and five each respectively) deployed in hardened underground silos. The full-range CSS-4 could strike targets throughout the Soviet Union, Europe, and North America.

Submarine Forces

All five nuclear powers deploy a major part of their missile forces on submarines because of advantages in mobility and survivability, and soon, missile accuracy equal to the best land-based missiles. At any time, seventeen to twenty U.S., ten Soviet, one to two British, and three French missile submarines are at sea, "on station," with some 3,100 nuclear warheads com-

U. S. Strategic Nuclear Forces

Delivery Mode	Weapon System Number	Weapon System Type	Year Deployed	Range (km)	Warheads / Yield	Warhead Type	Number in Stockpile
Land-based missiles	450	Minuteman II	1966	11,300	1 × 1.2 Mt	W56	480
	550	Minuteman III	1970	13,000	3 × 170 kt/	W62	825
					3 × 335 kt	W78	1,000
	30	Titan II	1963	15,000	1 × 9 Mt	W53	50
Submarines (SLBMs)	304	Poseidon	1971	4,600	10 × 40 kt	W68	3,300
	288	Trident I	1979	7,400	8 × 100 kt	W76	3,000
Bombers	264	B-52G/H	1955	16,000	8–24 *(a)*	*(a)*	4,733
	60	FB-111	1969	4,700	6 *(a)*	*(a)*	360
Aerial Refuelers	615	KC-135	1957	—	—	—	—

(a) Bomber weapons include five different nuclear bomb designs with yields from 70 kt–9 Mt, air-launched cruise missiles (ALCMs) with yield of 200 kt and short-range attack missile (SRAM) with yield of 200 kt. FB-111s do not carry ALCMs or the 9 Mt bomb.

Sources: Thomas B. Cochran, William M. Arkin, Milton H. Hoenig, *Nuclear Weapons Databook, Volume 1: U.S. Forces and Capabilities* (Cambridge, Mass.: Ballinger, 1984); updated in *Bulletin of the Atomic Scientists* (Aug.–Sept. 1984).

bined. Soviet long-range SLBMs and U.S. Trident I missiles can hit targets in each other's country from home waters.[4] China is the only nuclear power that does not yet regularly deploy submarines at sea, although it has two SSBNs that could probably go to sea during a crisis.

The U.S. submarine force consists of 36 missile-carrying submarines (SSBNs) with a total of 640 launch tubes containing over 5,500 nuclear warheads. Nineteen SSBNs carry the Poseidon C3 missile, and twelve carry the newer Trident I C4. The new Trident SSBNs (Ohio class) are also being armed with Trident I, which has a longer range and more than twice the yield of the Poseidon.

U.S. SSBNs are stationed at four bases, three in the Atlantic Ocean (at Kings Bay, Georgia; Charleston, South Carolina; and Holy Loch, Scotland) and one in the Pacific (at Bangor, Washington). Little is known about where U.S. submarines patrol, but they are thought to transit to "stations" well away from shipping lanes. They regularly operate in the Arctic, North Atlantic, and North Pacific Oceans and in the Mediterranean Sea. While about 30 percent of the total submarine force is "on station" on day-to-day alert, another 25 to 30 percent is at sea in transit or on training missions. U.S. submarines go to sea for about seventy days at a time, and because they are each assigned two crews they operate almost constantly.

In the Soviet fleet, 66 SSBNs and 14 SSBs (nuclear and non-nuclear powered missile-carrying submarines respectively) serve a combination of strategic and nonstrategic roles. There are ten classes of submarines armed with six different missiles, comprising 981 SLBMs with as many as 2,400 nuclear warheads. Soviet submarines

Soviet Strategic Nuclear Forces

Delivery Mode	Weapon System Number	Weapon System Type	Year Deployed	Range (km)	Warheads / Yield	Number in Stockpile *(a)*
Land-based missiles	520	SS-11 Mod 1 *(b)*	1966	11,000	1 × 1 Mt	640–1280
		Mod 2/3	1973		3 × 250–350 kt (MRV)	
	60	SS-13 Mod 2	1972	9,400	1 × 600–750 kt	60–120
	150	SS-17 Mod 3 *(c)*	1979	10,000	4 × 750 kt	600–1,200
	308	SS-18 Mod 4	1979	11,000	10 × 550 kt	3,080–6,160
	360	SS-19 Mod 3 *(d)*	1979	10,000	6 × 550 kt	2,160–4,320
Submarines (SLBMs)	42	SS-N-5	1963	1,400	1 × 1 Mt	42–60
	368	SS-N-6 Mod 1/2	1967	2,400	1 × 1 Mt	368–736
		Mod 3	1973	3,000	2 × 200–350 kt (MRV)	
	292	SS-N-8	1973	7,800	1 × 800 kt–1 Mt	292–584
	12	SS-N-17	1977	3,900	1 × 1 Mt	12–24
	224	SS-N-18 Mod 1/3	1978	6,500	3–7 × 200–500 kt	672–2,510
		Mod 2	1978	8,000	1 × 450 kt–1 Mt	
	40	SS-N-20	1983	8,300	6–9 × 350–500 kt	240–288
Bombers	45	Mya-4 Bison	1956	8,000	2 × bombs	90–180
	125	Tu-95 Bear	1956	8,300	2 × bombs and ASMs	386–872
	130	Tu-22M Backfire	1974	5,500	2 × bombs and ASMs	390–780
	125	Tankers *(e)*	—	—	—	—
ABMs	32	Galosh	1964	750	1 × 3–5 Mt	32–64

(a) Warheads represent low and high estimates of possible force loadings (including reloads).
(b) Approximately 100 Mod 1 with 1 warhead, 360 Mod 2, and 60 Mod 3 are deployed.
(c) Some SS-17 Mod 2 missiles with one warhead may also be deployed.
(d) Some SS-19 Mod 2 missiles with one warhead may also be deployed.
(e) Includes Badger and Bison A bomber converted for aerial refueling

Sources: Authors estimates derived from: William M. Arkin and Jeffrey I. Sands, "The Soviet Nuclear Stockpile," *Arms Control Today* (June 1984), pp. 1–7; Department of Defense, *Soviet Military Power,* 1st, 2d, 3d eds.; NATO, "NATO-Warsaw Pact Force Comparisons, 1st, 2d eds.; Robert P. Berman and John C. Baker, *Soviet Strategic Forces; Requirements and Responses* (Washington, D.C.: Brookings, 1982); Defense Intelligence Agency, *Unclassified Communist Naval Orders of Battle,* DDB-1200-124-84, (May 1984).

tend to have much lower at-sea deployment rates than U.S. submarines. At any time some fifteen to twenty Soviet submarines are away from their home bases and about ten to twelve (15 percent) are on station within range of targets.[5] Soviet submarines, unlike their U.S. counterparts, have only one crew.

Since the mid-1970s the overall number of Soviet SSBNs has not increased, as new Delta III and Typhoon commissionings have been offset by Yankee and older submarine retirements. Soviet SSBNs spend most of their time in port, primarily assigned to four main bases in the Northern and Pacific Fleets: Petropavlovsk and Vladivostok in the Pacific and Polyarnyy and Severomorsk in the North. "Submarine tunnels" have reportedly been built for them.[6] While Delta-class submarines can strike U.S. targets from Soviet home waters, older submarines must go through "choke points" to Atlantic and Pacific stations to be within range.[7] Delta-class submarines patrol primarily east of Greenland, in the Norwegian and Barents Seas, and in the northern Pacific Ocean. Beginning in January 1984, some long-range Delta submarines have also been stationed "forward" in the Atlantic Ocean as a Soviet reponse to deployment of U.S. Pershing II and ground-launched cruise missiles in Europe.

Some submarines with shorter-range missiles have European strike roles. Six Golf II-class submarines have been stationed in the Baltic since 1976, and four are assigned to the Northern Fleet. The United States, rather than using different submarine classes for European war plans, has allocated 400 Poseidon warheads for NATO targeting, carried on submarines operating out of Holy Loch, Scotland.

Britain has four Resolution-class SSBNs, each carrying sixteen Polaris A3 missiles with two or three MRVs (multiple reentry vehicles, not independently targeted).[8] These submarines are routinely under the control of NATO and targeted in accordance with NATO plans, although British targeting plans are also thought to exist for possible unilateral use. The British submarines are based at Faslane on the Clyde Estuary in Scotland (near the U.S. base at Holy Loch) (see Figure). One or two are on patrol at any time (one of the four boats is usually out of service undergoing maintenance at the Rosyth shipyard). Each SSBN has two crews, which rotate on twelve-week cycles: four weeks of trials and maintenance and eight weeks on patrol. Submarines transit north between Scotland and Ireland into the Atlantic Ocean to a specified "block" of water to the southwest of Ireland where they patrol.

The French Force Océanique Stratégique (FOST) consists of five Redoutable-class SSBNs, each armed with sixteen M20 missiles, and the first Inflexible-class SSBN carrying 16 MIRVed SLBMs, each of which carries 6 warheads—thus doubling the number of FOST warheads in one step. The submarines, based at Île Longue in Brest (on the Atlantic Ocean), go on two-month patrols in the eastern Atlantic off the coast of France and Portugal. Three French submarines are at sea at any time, and French policy is to have a fourth submarine available at all times for patrol.

NUCLEAR AMERICA *[following page]*

U.S. nuclear weapons and forces are spread across the entire country. Only nine states do not have some major nuclear force component —bomber bases, missile silos, submarine bases, command centers—within their borders. The inset of F.E. Warren Air Force Base in Wyoming shows how underground missile silos are spread out over thousands of square miles, in this case across three states.

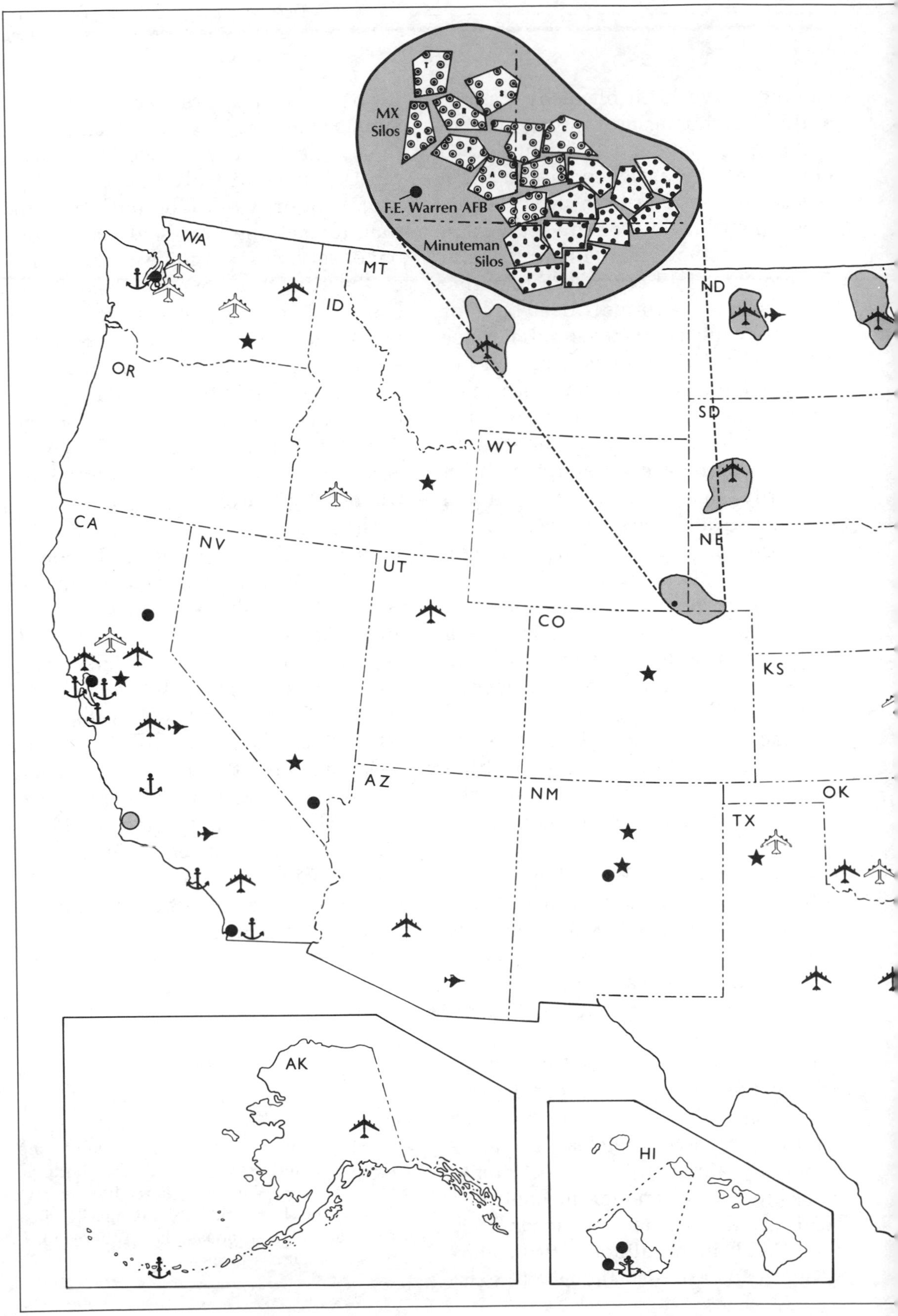
MX Silos
F.E. Warren AFB
Minuteman Silos
WA
MT
ID
OR
ND
SD
WY
NE
CA
NV
UT
CO
KS
AZ
NM
OK
TX
AK
HI

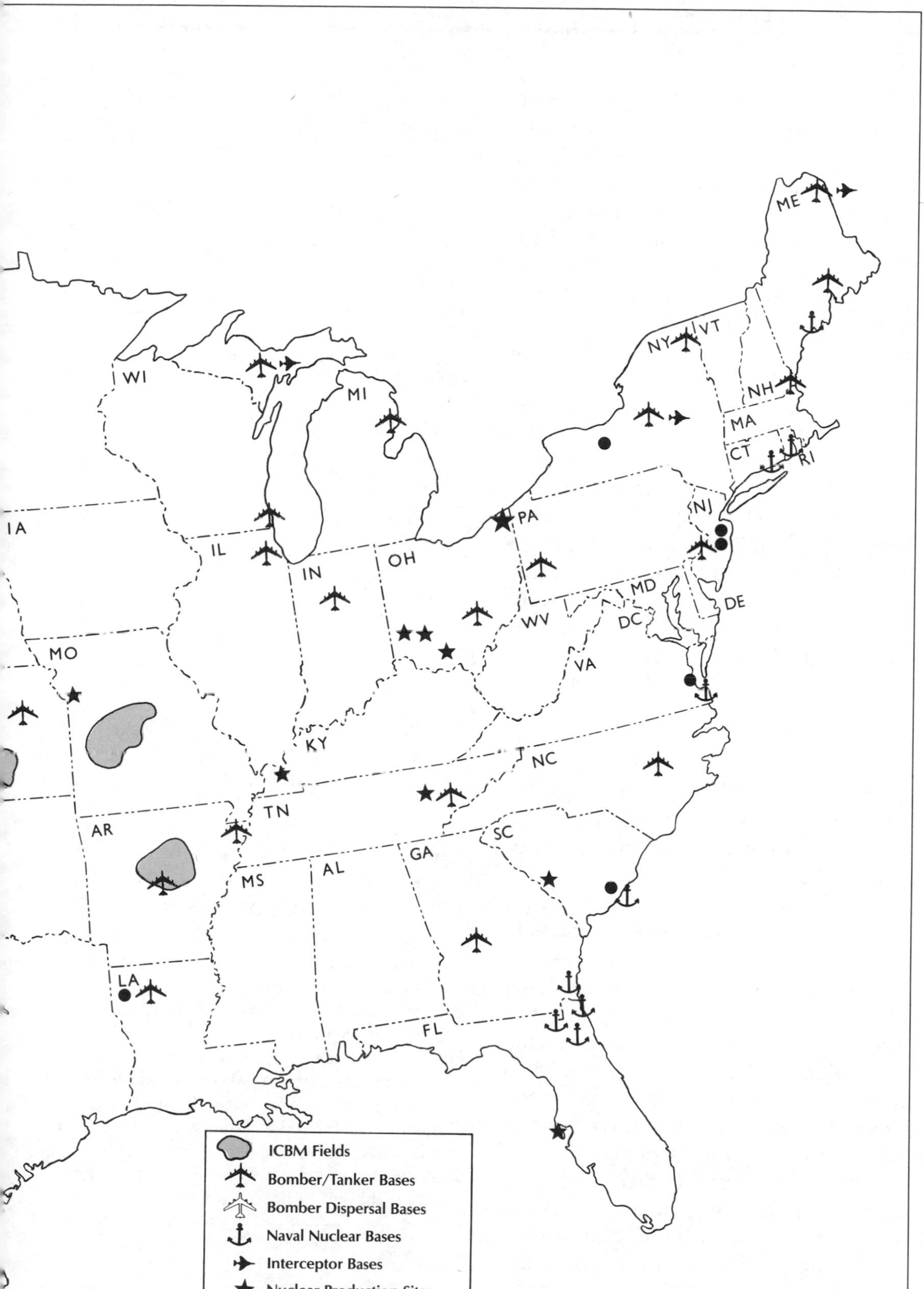
ME
NY
VT
NH
MA
CT
RI
NJ
PA
DE
MD
DC
WV
VA
WI
MI
IA
IL
IN
OH
MO
KY
NC
TN
AR
SC
GA
AL
MS
LA
FL
ICBM Fields
Bomber/Tanker Bases
Bomber Dispersal Bases
Naval Nuclear Bases
Interceptor Bases
Nuclear Production Sites
Other Nuclear Weapon Sites

China has one Golf-class SSB, which it built from Soviet parts. This submarine has two or three missile tubes in the conning tower, thought to be used only for testing and not normally loaded with operational missiles. China launched the first Chinese-designed SSBN, of the Xia-class, in April 1981 and a second in October 1982. Each has twelve launch tubes and carries the CSS-N-3 missile.[9] The Chinese have been working on national SLBM development since the late 1950s, but only recently developed a reliable solid fuel missile for the Xia. In October 1982 China announced a successful test flight of the CSS-N-3 SLBM from a submerged submarine.[10] Latest estimates of Chinese plans foresee a total of eight Xia class submarines with CSS-N-3 missiles. These submarines could begin patrol in 1985.[11]

The submarine forces of the nuclear powers are all undergoing major programs of modification and upgrade. The new U.S. Trident II missile will be loaded into the ninth Ohio-class submarine in 1989. Trident II will be as accurate as the most accurate land-based missiles and expand the missile range (and thereby the patrol area) of U.S. submarines to 4,000 miles. Each Trident II will probably carry eight 475 kiloton warheads so that each missile could destroy the "complete spectrum of targets in the Soviet Union."[12] Between twenty and twenty-five submarines will carry the Trident II.

The Soviet Union is also deploying new submarine and missile classes. Two large Typhoon submarines are already deployed with twenty solid fuel SS-N-20 missiles. The long-range SS-N-20 carries six to nine warheads and

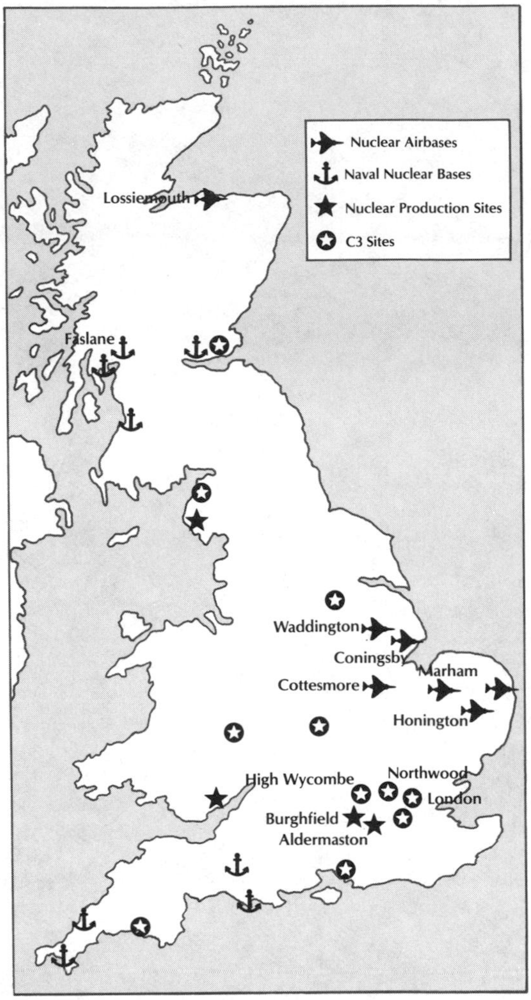

NUCLEAR FORCES OF BRITAIN

An adjunct of the U.S. nuclear force, Britain has the capacity with its Tornado fighters and Polaris submarines to strike targets in the Soviet Union and Eastern Europe. The British submarine force will expand tenfold with deployment of the Trident II missile in the mid-1990s. British national nuclear weapons include Polaris, bombs for fighter aircraft, and nuclear depth bombs for naval helicopters. This map shows only British nuclear forces. The U.S. military stores more nuclear weapons in Britain than the entire British arsenal.

is the most accurate Soviet submarine missile in the water. There has also been speculation that the submarine's design is geared toward patrols under the Arctic ice cap.[13] Another new Soviet SLBM, the SS-NX-23, is also being tested for deployment aboard Delta submarines in 1985 or 1986.[14] The DOD has called it "a Trident II-equivalent" weapon.

In the mid-1990s, Britain will begin to deploy new submarines to replace its Polaris force and arm them with the U.S. Trident II missile (but with British nuclear warheads). A force of four or five new British submarines will carry some 512 to 640 multiple independently targetable reentry vehicles (MIRVs) (compared to 64 warheads today). Besides the huge increase in warheads, the Trident II's ability to destroy any targets (including "hardened" ones) will radically transform the British submarine force.

The French are upgrading too. In 1985 a sixth French submarine became operational with a new missile, the M4, which will carry six 150-kiloton warheads. By 1992 the French will load the M4 into four of the five existing Redoubtable-class SSBNs (one is too old and will be retired in 1995). The M4 program will expand the French submarine force from today's 80 warheads to 496 warheads. France will begin development of a fully MIRVed M5 missile in the late 1980s, and plans to build a seventh submarine, of a new design, to join the fleet in the mid-1990s.

Bomber Forces

Strategic bomber forces constitute a large and flexible element of the nuclear arsenals. Although bombers fly slowly, and are thus normally excluded from first-strike scenarios and computer-simulated war games, they are in many ways the "warfighting" arm of strategic forces. War planners endlessly construct complex bomber loading, routing, refueling, penetrating, targeting, and recovery plans. Bombers carry a variety of bombs and air-launched missiles and can fit into virtually any war plan. While missiles cannot be recalled or redirected once launched (and are thus "inflexible"), bombers can attack hardened, mobile, or previously unlocated targets and can be called back before reaching them. If they overcome air defenses and complete their mission, bombers can return to a "recovery" base and reload for more bombing missions.

The United States maintains a fleet of 264 B-52 and 61 FB-111 bombers, all assigned to the Strategic Air Command (SAC), with 615 KC-135 aerial-refueling tankers to support them. According to the JCS, "The primary role of this tanker force, which includes 125 aircraft operated by the Air National Guard and Air Force Reserve, is to support plans for nuclear retaliation."[15] The bombers are stationed at nineteen air bases in thirteen states and at Andersen AFB in Guam. The United States also maintains "dispersal" and "recovery" bases for the bombers. Overall, the force comprises some 5,000 nuclear warheads, including a variety of nuclear bombs, short-range attack missiles (SRAMs), and air-launched cruise missiles (ALCMs).

The Soviet bomber force includes 100 Bear and 45 Bison intercontinental bombers and 230 shorter range Backfire, Badger, and Blinder bomb-

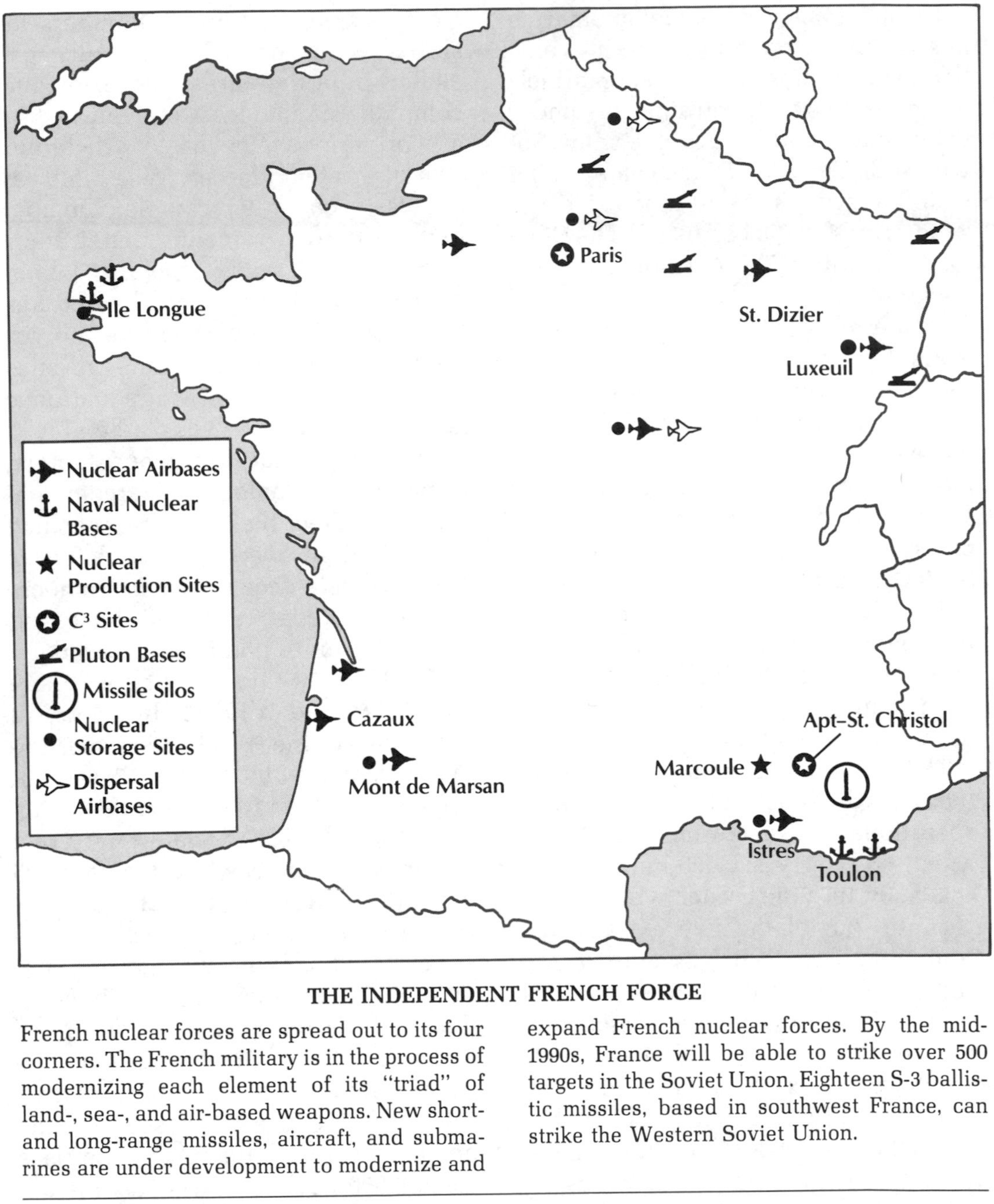

THE INDEPENDENT FRENCH FORCE

French nuclear forces are spread out to its four corners. The French military is in the process of modernizing each element of its "triad" of land-, sea-, and air-based weapons. New short- and long-range missiles, aircraft, and submarines are under development to modernize and expand French nuclear forces. By the mid-1990s, France will be able to strike over 500 targets in the Soviet Union. Eighteen S-3 ballistic missiles, based in southwest France, can strike the Western Soviet Union.

---

ers. The 36th Air Army, the Soviet counterpart to SAC, controls long-range bombers. Some Backfires in the western Soviet Union and in the Far East are also assigned to long-range aviation. An Arctic Control Group maintains five northern staging and dispersal bases from which bombers can begin their attacks closer to U.S. targets.

Soviet bombers carry two types of gravity bombs and a variety of air-to-surface cruise missiles, including the AS-4 and AS-6 nuclear-capable missiles. As with U.S. bombers, in-flight refueling extends the range of properly equipped aircraft, particularly important in the case of the newest Backfire, which otherwise lacks the range for round-trip missions into the interior of the United States.

Britain, France, and China all have bombers that can strike the Soviet Union. Britain has retired the last of its Vulcan bombers but is reinforcing its nuclear air arm with Tornado strike aircraft, which are suitable for long-range bombing. By the end of the decade, Britain will have 220 nuclear-capable attack versions of the Tornado. France has four squadrons of about thirty-four Mirage IVA bombers in its Strategic Air Force (FAS), armed with 70-kiloton nuclear bombs. The squadrons are located at four bases in France supported by five additional dispersal bases (see Figure). They will be replaced by Mirage IVP aircraft with a new nuclear air-to-surface missile starting in 1986. Eleven C-135F tankers (purchased from the United States in the mid-1960s) can provide aerial refueling to allow the bombers to reach deep into Soviet territory.

China has one type of nuclear bomber, the B-6, modeled after the Soviet Badger design. Latest estimates put roughly ninety B-6 bombers into three regiments. Two older aircraft, the B-4 and B-5 (modeled after Soviet Tu-4 and Il-28 bombers respectively), are also believed nuclear-capable. China is estimated to have about 100 airfields that can accomodate these bombers, which are reportedly rotated randomly among them to complicate Soviet targeting.[16]

Both the U.S. and Soviet bomber forces are in the midst of significant change. The armaments of both forces will soon include long-range air-launched cruise missiles (ALCMs). The United States introduced its ALCMs in 1981, and the Soviet Union is expected to field its 2,000 mile range AS-X-15 in the near future. The U.S. is also developing a new air-to-surface missile for its bomber force and has introduced a new, more accurate bomb. Both countries are about to field new generations of bombers: the B-1B (U.S.) and the Blackjack A (Soviet). Currently, two Soviet bomber models are in production, the new Backfire, at the rate of some thirty per year (about half are for naval aviation), and the Bear-H, the latest configuration of the 1956 plane, which will carry the AS-X-15. The United States is developing an Advanced Technology Bomber (Stealth), which it could deploy in the mid-1990s.

The Soviet Union has an active, nuclear-armed anti-ballistic missile (ABM) system, based around Moscow and made up of thirty-two Galosh missiles armed with 3.5-megaton warheads. Two launch complexes each contain two launcher sites with eight missiles at each site. Work continues on designing and building new missile silos and installing new ABM radars and tracking equipment. The United States does not have an active ABM system, although two nuclear missile systems deployed in the mid-1970s—Sprint and Spartan—are still in storage and available for reactivation.

Nonstrategic Forces

Although they receive far less scrutiny, nonstrategic nuclear weapons are far more likely to be used before strategic nuclear weapons. Nonstrategic nuclear forces include numerous types of weapons for battlefield missions: nuclear bombs, atomic land mines, and weapons that resulted from nuclearizing an array of delivery systems since the 1950s: surface-to-surface, surface-to-air, and air-to-surface missiles as well as artillery shells. Developed before long-range weapons, these forces now augment strategic weapons.

Nonstrategic forces fall into many categories, representing geographic interests and dispersal of military forces, and competing military services and roles. Nonetheless, an increasing number of nonstrategic weapons are "crossover systems" (sometimes called "gray area" weapons), highly mobile and long-range, and usable in more than one "theater" of war or even for "strategic" strikes. Such systems include many types of naval nuclear weapons, as well as long-range cruise missiles and land-based aircraft.

The so-called long-range intermediate forces have received the most attention, particularly the highly mobile U.S. Pershing II ballistic missile and the ground-launched cruise missile (GLCM). Both weapons fall into the "gray area" category. The Pershing II is the first long-range terminally guided missile deployed anywhere; the GLCM is the first reliable long-range cruise missile deployed on land. Both weapons, with nuclear warheads of 80 and 150 kilotons maximum yield, respectively, are highly accurate and can destroy hardened military targets. By 1988 the United States will have deployed 108 Pershing II launchers and 464 GLCMs in five European countries. The entire force will be spread among thirteen bases in peacetime. In a crisis or during wartime the force would disperse in platoons of three launchers (for Pershings) or "flights" of four launchers (for GLCMs), for a total of thirty-six Pershing dispersal sites and twenty-nine GLCM dispersal sites.

Pershing and cruise have been touted as counters to Soviet intermediate-range missiles, particularly the triple-warhead SS-20, first deployed in 1977. From its bases in the Soviet Union, the SS-20 can hit targets throughout Asia, the Middle East, North Africa, and Europe. Two-thirds of the launchers are deployed in the western Soviet Union, and one-third are in the Far East. The 150-kiloton yield and moderate accuracy of the SS-20 make it suitable for striking virtually any target within range. In addition to the SS-20, the Soviets still deploy some older medium-range SS-4s, which were first deployed in 1958. About 224 SS-4s are in the western Soviet Union; all those in the Far East have been retired.

Another new class of weapon, as important as the Pershing II and SS-20, is the long-range sea-launched cruise missile (SLCM), entering service in the U.S. and Soviet navies. The U.S. Tomahawk SLCM is the same as the GLCM but configured for naval use. It was first deployed in June 1984 aboard attack submarines, battleships, and two destroyers. Out of 3,994 planned SLCMs, 758 will be the nuclear land-

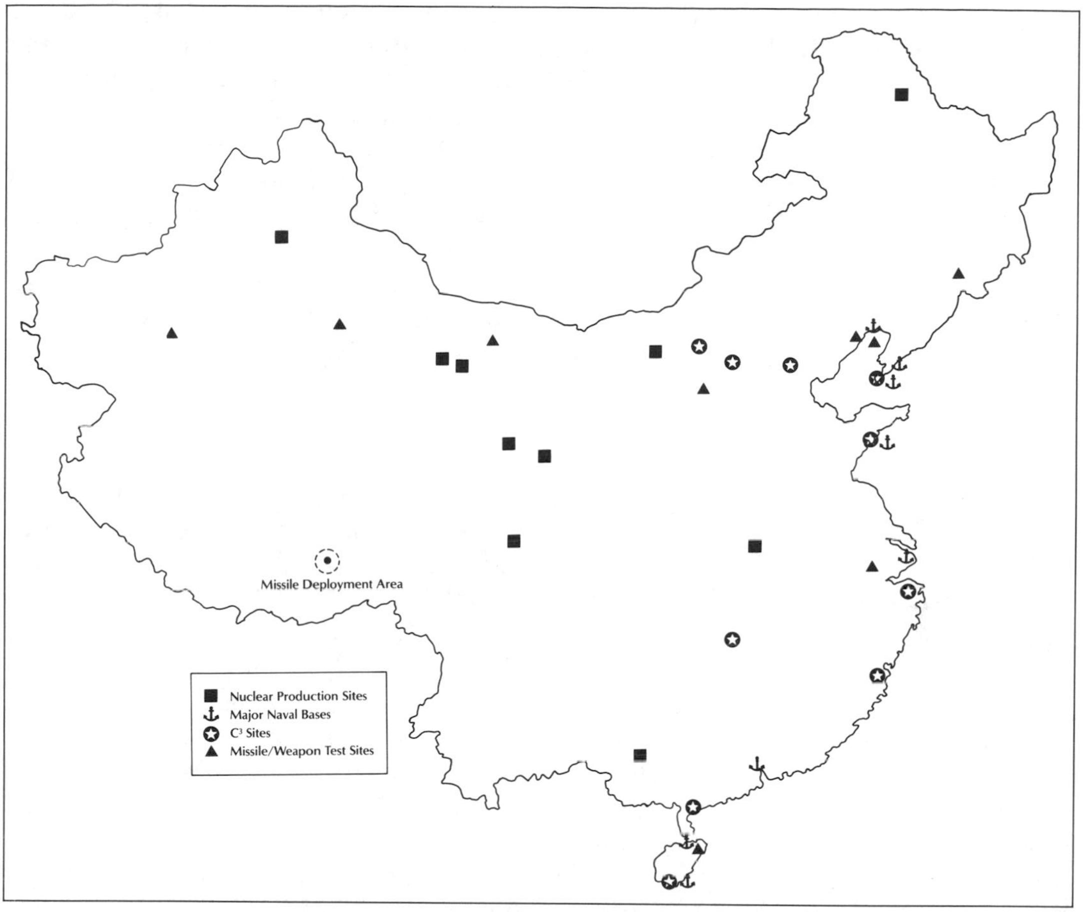

CHINA'S NUCLEAR ARSENAL

Most mysterious of all the nuclear powers is China. Although it has taken great pains to demonstrate its nuclear status and capabilities, China protects its nuclear forces from a surprise attack by moving them often and hiding them well. Thus its deployments defy simple mapping. Nonetheless, China does have a well established nuclear support infrastructure, depicted in the map.

attack version (called the TLAM(N) for Tomahawk Land-Attack Missile - Nuclear). This nuclear missile will have three separate roles: "strategic reserve," theater strike, and tactical naval strike. It will be the first "strategic" platform not reserved specifically for that role (see Chapter 7 for a full discussion of the SLCM). By 1992, sixty-five ships and eighty-three submarines will be able to carry the nuclear SLCM, and by the end of deployment, 204 ships and submarines will have this capability.[17] In addition to the new Tomahawk, the secret Defense Guidance for 1984-1988 instructed the Navy to prepare an "advanced concepts study" for a new land-attack missile with a longer range and better targeting features.

The Soviet counterpart to the Tomahawk is the SS-NX-21 SLCM, which became operational in late 1984. This missile not only improves Soviet accuracy but extends the striking range of Soviet naval forces to 3,000 kilometers, giving them their first long-range nuclear capability at sea.[18] The SS-NX-21 is launched from standard 21-inch (533mm) torpedo tubes (which are on almost all the Soviet Navy's ships and submarines). A second long-range strategic land-attack SLCM is under development, as is a long-range GLCM, designated the SS-CX-4, which could be deployed in the next few years.[19]

Both France and China deploy land-based intermediate-range missiles (IRBMs). France has eighteen silo-based S-3 IRBMs on the Plateau d'Albion in southeastern France. With their 3,500-kilometer range, S-3s can reach targets throughout Eastern Europe and the western Soviet Union. A new mobile land-based missile, the S-X (designated "Danone"), is under development for deployment in the mid-1990s. As many as 100 S-X missiles and warheads could be deployed.[20]

Since 1972 China has deployed 85 to 125 CSS-2 IRBMs, with a range of 1,500 to 2,000 miles and a warhead of one to three megatons. The CSS-2s are mobile and are reported to be deployed in underground silos as well as in man-made caves.

Battlefield Nuclear Forces

Tactical aircraft (of less than intercontinental range) are the most versatile arm of nuclear forces.[21] Nuclear-capable fighters and bombers afford greater control than missiles, are by far the most accurate means of delivering nuclear weapons, are capable of delivering a variety of nuclear weapons, and pilots can use their judgment to find and strike mobile or imprecisely located targets. All five nuclear powers maintain tactical aircraft. The Soviet Union has both a medium (capacity) bomber force and tactical nuclear aircraft. The United States has a wide variety of nuclear-certified fighters (see Table). Britain and France both have nuclear fighters. It is unclear how many nuclear bombs are allocated to the nuclear-capable planes of other countries, but in the United States, where the numbers are known, the percentage of warheads allocated for aircraft delivery is significant. For instance, of 5,800 forward-deployed U.S. warheads in Europe, about 1,700 (almost one-third) are bombs for aircraft delivery.

The Soviet medium-range bomber force is very large, consisting of 350 Badger, Blinder, and Backfire aircraft. These can carry nuclear bombs or air-to-surface missiles, but the precise number of warheads in the Soviet arsenal is unknown.[22] All of the bombers are assigned to bases within the Soviet Union, except for one Badger unit in Vietnam. The typical base has about forty-five aircraft, compared with a comparable U.S. tactical fighter unit of seventy-two planes. The Soviet Union also has six different tactical fighters thought to have nuclear weapons roles (see Table). The Fencer is the primary strike plane and has been deployed with nuclear weapons since 1981 in Czechoslovakia, East Germany, Hungary, and Poland.

U. S. Nonstrategic Nuclear Forces

Delivery Mode	*Weapon System* *Number*	*Type*	*Year Deployed*	*Range (km)*	*Warheads / Yield*	*Warhead Type*	*Number in Stockpile*
Nonstrategic							
Aircraft	2,000	*(a)*	—	1,060–2,400	1–3 × bombs	*(a)*	2,800
IRBMs/MRBMs	54	Pershing II	1983	1,790	1 × .3–80 kt	W85	63
	64	GLCM	1983	2,500	1 × .2–150 kt	W84	100
SRBMs	126	Pershing 1a	1962	740	1 × 60–400 kt	W50	280
	100	Lance	1972	125	1 × 1–100 kt	W70	1,282
	24	Honest John	1954	38	1 × 1–20 kt	W31	200
Land-based SAM	200	Nike Hercules	1958	160	1 × 1–20 kt	W31	500
Artillery (b)	4,300	*(b)*	1956	30	1 × .1–12 kt	*(b)*	2,422
ADMs	610	Medium/Special	1964	—	1 × .01–15 kt	W45/54	610
Naval							
Carrier aircraft	900	*(c)*	—	550–1,800	1–2 × bombs	*(c)*	1,000
Land attack cruise missile	50	Tomahawk	1984	2,500	1 × 5–150 kt	W80	50
ASW							
Ship-based	n.a.	ASROC	1961	10	1 × 5–10 kt	W44	574
Submarine based	n.a.	SUBROC	1965	60	1 × 5–10 kt	W55	285
Air-delivered	630	P-3/S-3/SH-3	1964	Max 2,500	1 × sub–20 kt	B57	897
Ship-based SAM	n.a.	Terrier	1956	35	1 × 1 kt	W45	100

(a) Aircraft include Air Force F-4, F-16, and F-111 and NATO F-16, F-100, F-104, and Tornado. Bombs include four types with yields from sub kt–1.45 Mt.

(b) There are two types of nuclear artillery—155mm and 203mm—with three different warheads, a 0.1 kt W48 155 mm shell, a 1–12 kt W33 203mm shell, and a 1 kt W79 enhanced radiation 203mm shell.

(c) Aircraft include Navy A-6, A-7, F/A-18, and Marine Corps A-4, A-6, and AV-8B. Bombs include three types with yields from 20 kt–1 Mt.

Sources: Thomas B. Cochran, William M. Arkin, and Milton H. Hoenig, *Nuclear Weapons Databook, Volume 1: U.S. Forces and Capabilities* (Cambridge, Mass.: Ballinger, 1984); updated in *Bulletin of the Atomic Scientists* (Aug./Sept. 1984).

The United States has a wide variety of tactical nuclear aircraft and nuclear bombs. Some 3,800 bombs arm these tactical aircraft: 1,700 in Europe, 130 in the Pacific, 720 aboard aircraft carriers at sea (on the average), and 1,250 in reserve. Although the United States does not have medium-range bombers, the F-111 is essentially equivalent to Soviet planes of that category. The United States has about 250 F-111s, with about 150 stationed at two forward bases in Britain, and the other 100 in the United States. About 600 nuclear bombs are allocated to the forward force. Most U.S. aircraft intended for interdiction or close air-support missions, whether Air Force, Marine Corps, or Navy, have been nuclear-certified, including the AV-8B Harrier, F-16, and F/A-18s currently in production.

The U.S. Air Force's nuclear planes are stationed overseas in Britain, Italy, South Korea, Turkey, and West Germany. The U.S. Air Force keeps nuclear bombs at a dozen NATO air bases for the planes of the Belgian, Greek, Italian, Dutch, Turkish, and West German Air Force. At seventeen bases in Europe, U.S. and NATO planes stand on nuclear alert at all times. Five or six aircraft carriers at sea also carry various land-attack nu-

Soviet Nonstrategic Nuclear Forces

Delivery Mode	Weapon System Number	Weapon System Type	Year Deployed	Range (km)	Warheads / Yield	Number in Stockpile (a)
Nonstrategic						
Bombers	316	Tu-16 Badger	1955	4,800	2 × bombs and ASMs	632
	139	Tu-22 Blinder	1962	2,200	1 × bombs or ASMs	139
Tactical aircraft	2,545	*(b)*	—	700–1,800	1–2 × bombs	2,545
IRBMs/MRBMs	378	SS-20	1977	5,000	3 × 150 kt	2,268
	224	SS-4	1959	2,000	1 × 1 Mt	224
SRBMs	120	SS-12	1969	800	1 × 200 kt–1 Mt	120
	100	SS-22	1979	900	1 × 1 Mt	100
	570	SCUD-b	1965	280	1 × 100–500 kt	1,140
	48	SS-23	1982	350	1 × 100 kt	48
	620	FROG	1965	70	1 × 10–200 kt	2,480
	120	SS-21	1978	120	1 × 20–100 kt	480
Artillery	900	*(c)*	1974	10–30	1 × low kt	900
ADMs	n.a.	n.a.	n.a.	—	n.a.	n.a.
Land-based anti-ship	100	SS-C-1b	1962	450	1 × 50–200 kt	100
Land-based SAMs	n.a.	*(d)*	1956	40–300	1 × low kt	n.a.
Naval						
Aircraft	105	Tu-22M Backfire	1974	5,500	2 × bombs or ASMs	210
	240	Tu-16 Badger	1961	4,800	1–2 × bombs or ASMs	480
	35	Tu-22 Blinder	1962	2,200	1 × bombs	35
	200	ASW aircraft *(e)*			1 × depth bombs	200
Anti-ship cruise missiles	336	SS-N-3	1962	450	1 × 350 kt	336
	96	SS-N-7	1968	56	1 × 200 kt	96
	200	SS-N-9	1968	280	1 × 200 kt	200
	136	SS-N-12	1976	500	1 × 350 kt	136
	88	SS-N-19	1980	460	1 × 500 kt	88
	28	SS-N-22	1981	110	1 × unk kt	28
ASW missiles and torpedoes	310	SS-N-14	1968	50	1 × low kt	310
	76	SS-N-15	1972	40	1 × 10 kt	76
	10	SUW-N-1	1967	30	1 × 5 kt	10
	n.a.	torpedoes	1957	16	1 × low kt	n.a.
Ship-based SAMs	264	SA-N-6	1977	55	1 × low kt	264

(a) Estimates of total warheads are based upon minimal loadings of delivery systems.

(b) Nuclear-capable tactical aircraft models include Su-24 Fencer, Su-17 Fitter, Mig-27 Flogger, Mig-21 Fishbed, Yak-28 Brewer, Mig-25 Foxbat, and Su-25 Frogfoot.

(c) Artillery includes 152mm towed and self-propelled guns, and 180mm, 203mm, and 240mm calibers.

(d) Nuclear-capable SAMs probably include SA-1, SA-2, SA-5, and SA-10.

(e) Includes Bear, Mail, and May aircraft.

Sources: William M. Arkin and Jeffrey I. Sands, "The Soviet Nuclear Stockpile," *Arms Control Today* (June 1984), pp. 1–7; Norman Polmar, *Guide to the Soviet Navy,* 3d ed. (Annapolis, Md.: U.S. Naval Institute, 1983); Department of Defense, *Soviet Military Power,* 1st, 2d, 3d eds.; NATO, "NATO-Warsaw Pact Force Comparisons," 1st and 2d eds.; DIA, "A Guide to Foreign Tactical Nuclear Weapon Systems Under the Control of Ground Force Commanders," DST-1040S-541-83 (Secret, partially declassified) (Sept. 9, 1983).

British Nuclear Forces

Delivery Mode	Weapon System Number	Type	Year Deployed	Range (km)	Warheads / Yield	Number in Stockpile
Strategic						
Submarines (SLBMs)	32	Polaris A3	1968	4,600	3 × 200 kt	96
	32	Polaris A3TK	1982	4,700	2 × 40 kt	64
Nonstrategic						
Aircraft	30	Buccaneer S2 *(a)*	1962	1,700	2 × bombs	60
	36	Jaguar A *(a)*	1973	1,400	1 × bombs	36
	140	Tornado GR1 *(b)*	1982	1,300	2 × bombs	280
Naval						
Carrier aircraft	30	Sea Harrier	1980	450	1 × bombs	30
ASW helicopters	69	Sea King	1976	—	1 × depth bombs	69
	16	Wasp	1963	—	1 × depth bombs	16
	35	Lynx	1976	—	1 × depth bombs	35

(a) Some 6 Buccaneer and 36 Jaguar aircraft withdrawn from bases in West Germany may be assigned nuclear roles in the U.K.

(b) 220 Tornado attack aircraft (GR1) are on order for the Royal Air Force, and continue to replace Jaguar aircraft.

Note: 34 Nimrod ASW aircraft, 12 Lance launchers, and artillery guns are also certified to use U.S. nuclear weapons.

Sources: John Moore, ed., *Jane's Fighting Ships 1982–83, 1983–84* (London: Jane's, annual); John W.R. Taylor, *Jane's All the World's Aircraft, 1982–83, 1983–84* (London: Jane's, annual); Paul Beaver, *The Encyclopedia of the Modern Royal Navy* (London, 1982); U.K. Ministry of Defence, *Statement on the Defence Estimates,* 1980, 1981, 1982, 1983, and 1984 (London: H.M. Stationer's Office, annual); Paul Rogers, *Guide to Nuclear Weapons 1984–85* (Bradford: University of Bradford, 1984); U.K., House of Commons, "Defence Committee Report, Session 79/80," (July 23, 1980).

clear planes. Aboard these six forward-deployed aircraft carriers are over 700 nuclear bombs.

Some 300 British-made nuclear warheads are carried on about 200 nuclear-capable tactical aircraft of three types: Jaguar, Buccaneer, and Tornado (see Table). These aircraft are stationed at four air bases in Britain and two in West Germany, Britain's only permanent overseas nuclear weapons bases. The new Tornado fighter bombers will replace the current Buccaneers and Jaguars. Eleven squadrons will be equipped with Tornado by 1987, three in Britain and eight in West Germany. Nuclear-armed Sea Harrier aircraft are stationed on three aircraft carriers.

An important element of the French military force is nuclear-capable aircraft. Nuclear-armed air units include two squadrons of thirty Mirage IIIEs and three squadrons of forty-five Jaguar aircraft. According to the Defense Intelligence Agency, these aircraft can deliver "a 6-to 8- or 30- kt tactical nuclear weapon."[23] The aircraft are stationed at three airbases in France, and will eventually be replaced by a new nuclear-strike aircraft, the Mirage 2000N, beginning in 1988. The French Navy's only tactical nuclear weapons equip thirty-six Super Étendard nuclear aircraft aboard two aircraft carriers based at Toulon in the Mediterranean. At any moment, one French carrier is in the Mediterranean Sea, and one periodically deploys to the Atlantic or Indian Oceans.[24] France is also developing a 150-kiloton medium-range air-to-surface nuclear missile, the ASMP (Air-Sol Moyenne Portée), for the Mirage IVA, Mirage 2000N, and the naval Super Étendard.

The Soviet Union's large array of battlefield missiles includes short-range "division support missiles," Army support missiles, and longer range "Front support missiles." All three are being modernized. The FROG-7 (Free-Rocket-Over-Ground) (a division support missile with a range of forty miles) is being replaced by the longer range SS-21. Virtually all of the FROG-7 missiles in Soviet divisions in East Germany and Czechoslovakia (four launchers per division is the standard allocation) have been upgraded. The SCUD missile, allocated to the Army formations, is about to be replaced by the SS-23 (whose range is 300 miles, compared to the SCUD's 110). The SS-12 Scaleboard, currently assigned to the Front formations, is being replaced by the SS-22.

Most Soviet battlefield missiles have conventional and nuclear capabilities; only the SS-12 and SS-22 missiles are thought to lack conventional warheads. There is, in addition, evidence that the new SS-21 and SS-23 have primarily non-nuclear roles.[25] The SS-12 was never deployed outside of the Soviet Union, although FROG and SCUD missiles (and SS-21s) have been routinely based with Soviet forces in Czechoslovakia, East Germany, Hungary and Poland. The SS-22 has been reportedly been deployed in East Germany, a significant departure from previous Soviet nuclear-basing practices.[26]

The medium-range Pershing 1a missile, deployed in West Germany, is assigned to the U.S. and West German militaries. The U.S. missiles and launchers are being replaced by the Pershing II, but the future status of the seventy-two West German launchers is still uncertain.[27] The mobile, dual-capable Lance missile, which has a maximum range of 125 kilometers, provides artillery support to numerous NATO armies. Some 692 Lance nuclear warheads are deployed in Europe (608 in West Germany), for Belgian, British, Italian, Dutch, U.S., and West German launchers. About 380 enhanced radiation warheads ("neutron bombs") for the Lance missiles were built in the United States between 1981 and 1983, but are stored in the United States pending European approval to station them in Europe. A successor to the Lance, with a longer range and greater accuracy, is under development. Only the the armies of Greece and Turkey continue to use the U.S. Honest John missile, first deployed in 1954.

The Chinese have one MRBM deployed, the CSS-1, its first missile fielded in 1966. The CSS-1 has a range of 600 to 700 miles. About forty to sixty missiles are deployed, each with one 20-kiloton warhead. From their bases in Shanxi province, these missile can strike Far Eastern Soviet targets.[28]

The United States and the Soviet Union both deploy nuclear artillery shells. In the U.S. military there are two sizes—155mm (6-inch) and 203mm (8-inch)—assigned to the Army and the Marines. About 920 155mm shells and 1,500 203mm shells are in the stockpile. The 155mm shell was introduced in 1967 and is slated to be replaced by a more versatile, higher yield, longer range shell in the next few years. The more numerous 203mm shell (the W-33) is one of the oldest nuclear warheads in the U.S. stockpile, but a replacement, the W-79, is in production (to be stockpiled in the United States while awaiting approval for storage in Europe). U.S. nuclear artillery shells are stored in five countries in Europe, in South Korea, and in Guam. Some 570 warheads are allocated for NATO use, by Belgium, Britain, Greece, Italy, the Netherlands, Turkey, and West Germany.

Soviet nuclear artillery has been in the field since the mid-1970s, but it is still unclear how important a role it will play in comparison to short-range missiles. For some time, there were U.S. government mentions of the existence of 180mm and 240mm Soviet nuclear guns, but it was not until 1981 that the Soviets' widespread adoption of nuclear artillery was confirmed. Now, DOD has concluded that the 152mm, 180mm, 203mm, and 240mm calibers are nuclear-capable, but large-scale production of four different nuclear warheads seems unlikely. A more important development in the Soviet Army is the conversion from towed to self-propelled artillery since the mid-1970s. (Self-propelled artillery is far more mobile and logistically sustainable than towed artillery.) Nuclear-capable self-propelled 152mm artillery guns are now assigned to Soviet divisions.[29]

The French Army maintains forty-two Pluton short-range ballistic missile launchers with reload missiles. The Pluton force is made up of five regiments, deployed in northeastern France. A new longer range missile, called Hadés, will be deployed beginning in 1992. France may decide to use an enhanced radiation warhead for the 350-kilometer range Hadés.

The two remaining battlefield nuclear weapons, comprising about 5 percent of the U.S. nuclear arsenal, are probably present in the Soviet arsenal as well: surface-to-air missiles (SAMs) and atomic demolition munitions (ADMs). Nuclear Nike Hercules SAMs are deployed in Europe, arming the United States, Belgium, Italy, Greece, West Germany, and the Netherlands. The U.S. and Belgian nuclear missiles are in the process of retirement (the U.S. missiles will be completely withdrawn by mid-1985), to be replaced by the conventionally armed Patriot. There are numerous reports of the existence of nuclear warheads for Soviet SAMs, particularly the SA-2 Mod 4 and SA-5 systems.[30]

Two types of ADMs are deployed in the U.S. military: Medium ADMs and Special ADMs. ADMs are intended for the destruction of physical features such as bridges, mountain passes, dams, and forests. The U.S. arsenal contains 608 ADMs, assigned to regular Army engineers, Marines, and "unconventional warfare forces." Some 372 are stored in Europe (351 in West Germany and 21 in Italy). Units of the British, Dutch, and West German armies also train with ADMs. ADMs are stored in South Korea and Guam, for Pacific nuclear "contingencies." There are reports of the existence of Soviet ADMs, but nothing is known about them.[31] The Defense Intelligence

Agency has stated that ADMs "may also be used" by the Chinese.[32]

Naval Nuclear Weapons

The nuclear arsenals at sea include anti-submarine, anti-air and anti-ship weapons.[33] The nuclear-armed ships and submarines of the U.S. Navy comprise (as of early 1984): all of its 13 large aircraft carriers, all 5 helicopter and Marine Corps carriers, two recommissioned battleships, all 112 cruisers and destroyers, 64 nuclear attack submarines, and 61 of 86 frigates. Approximately 30 percent of these ships and submarines are at sea at any time. Soviet nuclear-capable ships consist of 69 of 281 surface ships (cruisers, destroyers, and frigates), and 119 of 268 attack and cruise-missile submarines. About 15 percent of Soviet ocean-going vessels are out of home waters at any time.

The West counters the large Soviet submarine force with a combined British and U.S. nuclear anti-submarine warfare (ASW) arsenal of 1,900 warheads (20 times the number of Soviet submarines). U.S. naval forces have 1,750 nuclear ASW warheads, stockpiled at sixteen bases in peacetime. Attack submarines carry nuclear-armed submarine rocket (SUBROC) missiles. A nuclear-capable weapon similar to SUBROC, the ASROC, is also deployed aboard 150 surface ships.[34]

The U.S. Navy has 412 land-based P-3 Orion ASW patrol aircraft, which can carry B-57 nuclear depth bombs. They are organized into 37 squadrons of 9 aircraft, 24 active and 13 reserve. The planes rotate to numerous bases around the world: Bermuda, the Azores, Puerto Rico, Ascension Island, Spain, Italy, Iceland, Oman, Diego Garcia, the Philippines, Japan, Alaska, and Guam. The 187 carrier-based S-3A Viking aircraft and 104 SH-3 ASW helicopters can also deliver the nuclear depth bomb. Dutch P-3 Orion, Italian Atlantique, and British Nimrod ASW aircraft are all certified to carry U.S. B-57s, which are stored for their use on British and Italian soil. The British Navy also has three nuclear-capable aircraft carriers and fifty-nine ASW surface ships (which carry ASW helicopters). The carriers can operate with nuclear-capable Sea Harrier attack aircraft and Sea King helicopters. About 120 Lynx, Wasp, and Sea King nuclear-capable ASW helicopters operate from ships (Sea Kings also operate from shore). These helicopters can reportedly carry a British-made nuclear depth bomb, about which nothing is known. Britain's nuclear-capable naval aviation force is comprised of thirty Buccaneer and thirty Sea Harrier strike aircraft.

The Soviet Navy has approximately 1,200 ASW nuclear warheads, including rockets, torpedoes, and depth bombs. The Soviets deploy a nuclear-capable ASW rocket similar to SUBROC, the SS-N-15, which is estimated to be aboard about sixty-five submarines. A wide variety of ASW ships in the Soviet Navy carry either the SS-N-14 (a nuclear weapon similar to ASROC) or the SUW-N-1 nuclear depth charge. Both ships and submarines are thought capable of carrying nuclear-tipped 21-inch torpedoes. Two types of Soviet ASW aircraft, about fifty-one TU-142 Bear Fs and ninety-four BE-12 Mails, are nuclear-capable.

The U.S. Navy deploys the nuclear-armed Terrier surface-to-air missile (SAM), now in the process of being withdrawn and retired, on cruisers and destroyers. With the development of Soviet Backfire bombers and the increasing cruise missile threat to ships, nuclear-armed surface-to-air missiles have gained in importance to Naval planners who see them as last-ditch weapons to shoot down aircraft and nuclear missiles. Two warheads are now being developed for missiles that will replace the Terrier, one for the longer range Standard-2 SAM and one for the Phoenix air-to-air missile.

An important nuclear weapon in the Soviet naval arsenal is the sea-launched anti-ship cruise missile (ASCM) (the United States does not deploy anti-ship nuclear weapons). Seventy of 354 Soviet submarines are cruise missile launchers, all of them thought to be nuclear-capable. Most of the recently deployed cruise missile submarines (SSGNs) have short-range SS-N-7, SS-N-9, or supersonic SS-N-12 cruise missiles. In 1982 the Soviets deployed a new medium-range SS-N-19 cruise missile aboard the large, fast new Oscar-class submarines. The supersonic SS-N-19 has a range of around 460 km and can be launched from underwater. It is thus the most versatile Soviet ASCM to date.

An important component of the Soviet anti-ship nuclear force is its Naval aircraft force (called Soviet Naval Aviation or SNA), which is based on land since the Soviets have no aircraft carriers capable of carrying such nuclear-capable aircraft. Current Soviet "carriers" are equipped with helicopters and a few non-nuclear vertical take-off planes. SNA includes 423 land-based nuclear bombers: 105 Backfires, 279 Badgers, and 39 Blinders. All SNA bombers can carry nuclear bombs, and the Backfires and Badgers can carry AS-4 and AS-6 air-to-surface missiles (ASMs) as well.

Over the past decade, technological improvements have greatly reduced the number of weapons needed to destroy a given target. One logical consequence would be a reduction in the size of the nuclear arsenals. But as the nuclear powers build ever more effective weapons, they rarely reduce the number of weapons. And they never reduce their nuclear capabilities.

Forty years into the atomic age, there has not yet been a nuclear war: some therefore accept the vast nuclear arsenals; some even credit them with preventing nuclear war. But whatever the number of weapons, whatever the intentions of planners, the danger is ever greater. Technological advances and improvements in planning, command, and communications have seemingly shaved away uncertainties. Nuclear weapons have become more accurate, more reliable, more enduring —more usable.

4

The Arsenal's Tentacles

NUCLEAR FORCES ARE only one part of the nuclear infrastructure, a complex made up of hundreds of obscure research, testing, electronic, and command facilities. Virtually every laboratory, test range, military base, or communications transmitter contributes to preparations for nuclear warfare. Military exercises and maneuvers, communications, surveillance, and testing keep the system alive.

The activities of the nuclear infrastructure are not passive. Most operations that the military justifies on the basis of "preparedness" are seen by the other side as aggressive. Scientific research, information gathering, and early warning surveillance are part of a qualitative arms race. The superior ability to detect and target the enemy's forces, to hide and communicate with one's own, and to control military operations has become more important than the weapons themselves. The means to chart the realms important for military operations—observatories, electronic and technical facilities, oceanographic labs, and satellites—are integral to the military forces of the nuclear era.

There are eight categories of activities in the nuclear infrastructure (see Table):

1. the arsenals (the missiles, ships, aircraft, guns, and warheads) and the bases involved in training, maintenance,

The Nuclear Weapons Infrastructure

				Category					
	Arsenals	*Warhead Production*	*Research & Testing*	*Early Warning*	*Surveil-lance*	*Communi-cations*	*Planning & Control*	*Civil Defense*	*TOTAL*
United States									
Domestic	245	36	192	127	52	121	35	20	830
Foreign	348	1	93	71	48	120	68	—	749
Soviet Union									
Domestic	251	16	26	18	14	23	37	n.a.	385
Foreign	85	—	5	—	1	7	7	n.a.	105
United Kingdom									
Domestic	40	6	32	19	4	23	14	27	165
Foreign	15	1	1	1	—	3	4	—	25
France									
Domestic	47	20	24	18	3	9	11	n.a.	132
Foreign	4	5	3	—	—	4	—	—	16
China									
Domestic	17	16	16	n.a.	17	8	1	1	76
TOTALS	1,053	101	392	254	139	318	178	48	2,483

storage, and supply of nuclear forces that were described in Chapter 3;

2. the production complex, which manufactures and designs nuclear warheads and radioactive materials;
3. the research, development, and testing complex comprised of scores of laboratories and test facilities;
4. the surveillance system whose facilities collect information related to nuclear weapons, particularly as a part of ocean surveillance and monitoring foreign nuclear tests (a growing complex of satellite tracking and control stations also supports the nuclear arsenals);
5. the early-warning and "attack-assessment" complex of radars and processing stations that detect and describe attacks;
6. the communications system that links all of these;
7. the planning and command structure that controls the nuclear battlefields (this category is described in Chapter 5); and
8. civil defense.

The surveillance, early-warning, communications, and command facilities are collectively called the C^3I (pronounced "see-cubed-eye") system, for command, control, communications, and intelligence. C^3I is the nervous system of the nuclear arsenal. Nuclear commanders have fixed, mobile, and airborne command centers connected by specialized communications networks. Everything from simple telephones to protected underground cables to satellites are used to control nuclear forces. "If deterrence fails," the Air Force says, "the C^3 system must then provide the necessary information, command facilities, and communications to prosecute a nuclear war effectively."[1]

The Production Complex

The governments of the nuclear powers design, manufacture, and test nuclear warheads. Special government agencies are responsible for building and dismantling nuclear warheads and their component parts. The nuclear materials—predominantly plutonium, highly enriched uranium, and tritium—must be manufactured (in the case of plutonium or tritium) or enriched (uranium) from raw materials and then fabricated in special facilities. An extraordinarily complex and costly process must be followed to produce the materials in the concentrations and quantities required to manufacture nuclear warheads.

The U.S. production complex is operated by the Department of Energy (DOE). Roughly 45,000 people work in thirty-six laboratories and production centers in thirteen states that in total take up over 2,000 square miles of land (about the size of Delaware).[2] Very little is known about the production complexes of other nuclear powers. The Soviet complex is under the control of the Medium Machine Building Ministry. Its size and level of technology is thought to be equivalent to the U.S. complex. The British nuclear complex is managed by the Controller Research and Development Establishments, Research and Nuclear Programmes (CERN) in the Ministry of Defence. It consists of three primary facilities and employs some 8,000 personnel. The French complex is controlled by the Commissariat à l'Énergie Atomique (CEA). Ten French locations have been identified as nuclear weapons production sites, but little is known about the specific facilities for warhead fabrication. The Chinese ministry in charge of nuclear weapons is unknown; some forty Chinese locations have been identified as uranium mining and enrichment facilities, but little is known about nuclear weapons technology or production.

Worldwide, nuclear weapons research is concentrated at less than ten major laboratories. In the United States, three laboratories are responsible for warhead research, design and testing: the Lawrence Livermore National Laboratory in California; the Los Alamos National Laboratory in New Mexico; and the Sandia National Laboratory in Albuquerque, New Mexico. The Arzamas Laboratory, south of Gorky, and facilities at Kyshtym, Moscow, Leningrad, and Semipalatinsk are reportedly responsible for Soviet nuclear weapons design. One laboratory in Britain, the Atomic Weapons Research Establishment at Aldermaston, works on nuclear warheads. French laboratories include the Saclay and Grenoble Centers for Nuclear Studies and the laboratories under CEA's military applications branch.

The uranium, plutonium, and tritium for warheads are produced or processed in nuclear reactors and enrichment plants. Seven U.S. facilities produce materials.[3] In the Soviet Union uranium and plutonium are produced at more than ten major facilities, both military and civilian. British nuclear materials are produced mainly at Calder Hall, Chapelcross, and Windscale. French materials are produced at Marcoule, Miramas, and Pierrelatte. Chinese nuclear materials are produced at Lanzhou, Yumen, Baotou, Hong Yuan, Jiuquan, and Urumqui.

Nuclear warheads are assembled and mated with their nuclear materials at government-owned production facilities that build one-of-a-kind components and assemble entire warheads. There are seven U.S. production facilities that produce the thousands of subcomponents needed for the twenty-eight different warheads in the U.S. arsenal.[4] Final assembly occurs at the Pantex Plant in Amarillo, Texas. In the Soviet Union the main production plants are in Sverdlovsk and Novosibirsk; final assembly takes place at Chelyabinsk. British production facilities are at Aldermaston, Cardiff, and Burghfield, where final warheads are assembled. In France the CEA is responsible for all warhead fabrication, although the functions of specific CEA facilities are not known. Nuclear weapons production and assembly plants have been identified at Lanzhou, Baotou, and Haiyen in China.

Nuclear warheads are currently tested at five sites worldwide. All U.S. and British warheads are detonated at the Nevada Test Site. Testing has ceased at sixteen earlier sites.[5] The U.S. maintains a "readiness to test" facility at Johnston Island, Hawaii in case it ever again wants to test nuclear warheads in the atmosphere. The Soviets have tested nuclear warheads at twenty sites, including East and West Kazakh, five sites in Siberia, Semipalatinsk, and two on the island of Novaya Zemlya. The Novaya Zemlya and Semipalatinsk sites are still active. France tests nuclear weapons at Mururoa Atoll in French Polynesia.[6] Chinese tests are conducted at Lop Nor. Although China's last atmospheric test was in 1980, the U.S. Atomic Energy Detection System registered seismic signals coming from Lop Nor on October 6, 1983, and October 3, 1984. Underground nuclear tests almost surely caused the signals.[7]

Research, Development, and Testing

The complex that develops and tests nuclear weapon systems (minus the warheads) is almost ten times larger than the warhead complex. Military laboratories conduct research from basic scientific and technical experiments to engineering and prototype manufacture of weapon systems. Inquiries by these laboratories in such fields as oceanography and meteorology contribute to the development of virtually every weapon. Large research and development centers specialize in classes of weapons—such as aircraft, missiles, artillery, and ships—and generally manage a weapon program from conception to procurement. Nuclear weapon systems require extensive testing before and after deployment. Nuclear delivery vehicles—ballistic and cruise missiles, bombers, and submarines—have a testing infrastructure that spans the globe (see Figure). The test ranges contain instruments to record every possible facet of a weapon's operation: They photograph the launch, track the missile by radar, and measure its range and accurary (the accurate timing and positional data necessary for the test program was discussed in Chapter 2). During test flights a missile sends diagnostic data on its internal workings (called telemetry) to observers on land, on tracking ships, and on special aircraft. After collecting and analyzing the test data the military adjusts the weapon to refine accuracy and reliability.

Tests are followed by "operational training." Submarines are taken out to sea to fire their missiles with special telemetry packages in the place of warheads. Missiles are fired from inland and coastal test ranges and, by the Soviets, from operational silos. Bombers and tankers fly along low-level routes and drop bombs on practice ranges. The United States operates more than a dozen Strategic Training Range complexes where it conducts over 100,000 simulated bombing missions a year. Bombardiers on unarmed planes are tested by overflying "radar bomb scoring" sites that "electronically score the accuracy of SAC aircrews."[8]

The major missile launch complexes are among the world's most sophisticated facilities. Because testing ranges require extensive space, small countries like Britain and France do much of their testing on foreign soil. Britain tests its nuclear warheads and missiles in the United States. France conducts its missile tests in the Atlantic and its nuclear warhead tests in the South Pacific.

The United States, though it has abundant land, also conducts much of its research, development, and testing (RD&T) on foreign soil. These RD&T facilities constitute one of the major elements of the U.S. nuclear infrastructure overseas. Missiles shot from Vandenberg AFB, California, and Cape Canaveral, Florida, into the Pacific and Atlantic oceans are tracked by radars and telescopes in fifteen foreign countries. The ocean floor is studded with sensors to gauge the accuracy of warheads that land in the water.

Overseas testing and training are often justified on climatic conditions. Air-launched cruise missiles (ALCMs), for instance, are tested from the Canadian Arctic to the Primrose range near Cold Lake where Soviet Arctic terrain can be simulated. Climatic testing of aircraft, missiles, and nuclear artillery also takes place in Canada, Panama, and the Philippines.

Much of the nuclear weapons training overseas is primarily related to the deployment of forces. U.S. training in tactical nuclear bombing with mock weapons that duplicate the weight and shape of real nuclear bombs takes place in Canada, Italy, Spain, Turkey, West Germany, the Netherlands, France, Britain, the Philippines, Japan, and South Korea.[9] At a major nuclear bombing range at Crow Valley in the Philippines, targets include mock railyards and military bases.[10] Simulated nuclear weapons training by the Soviet Union is no less common. In East Germany, for instance, Soviet aircraft and missiles are known to conduct simulated nuclear missions at ranges in Belgern, Retzow, Rossow, Sperenberg, and Letzlinger Heide. Soviet training facilities also have models of U.S. weapons systems and bases.[11]

Surveillance

Production, research, testing, and training all provide information about the nuclear powers to their adversaries. Enemy missile tests are tracked, and the telemetry is intercepted. Com-

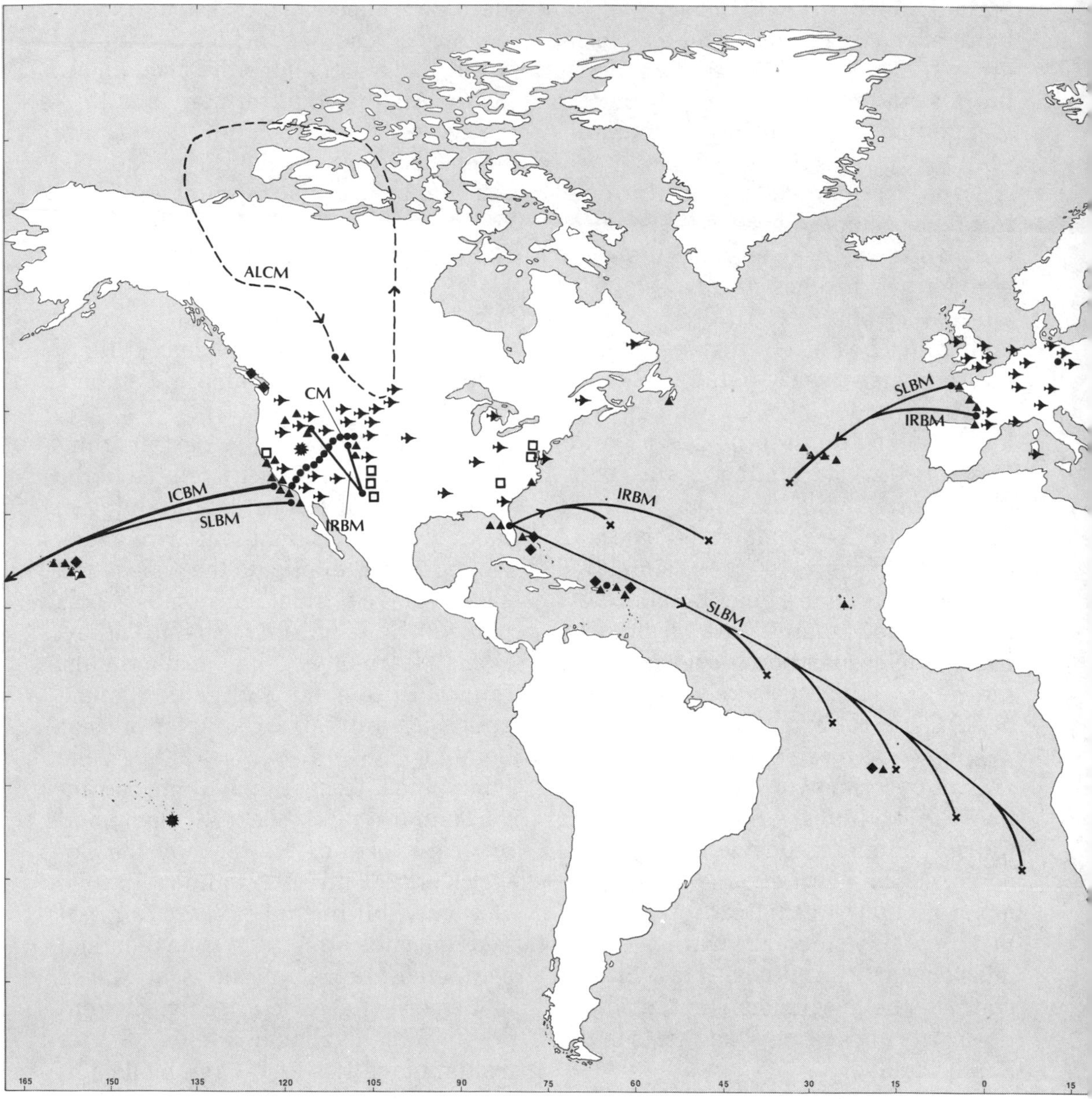

TESTING AND TRAINING

The nuclear powers use the land, sea, air, and space extensively for missile and aircraft testing and training. Tracking and support sites for weapons testing number in the hundreds and are spread over seven continents. All play a role in the development of nuclear weapons and delivery systems. Each dot in the U.S. from California to Utah represents a separate support site (radar, telemetry or communications) to monitor missile tests in the western U.S.

munications between pilots or ships during mock nuclear missions are intercepted and analyzed. Photographs of maneuvers are "fused" with communications intercepts and background data to obtain a picture of the enemy's doctrine and capabilities. Ocean surveillance networks above

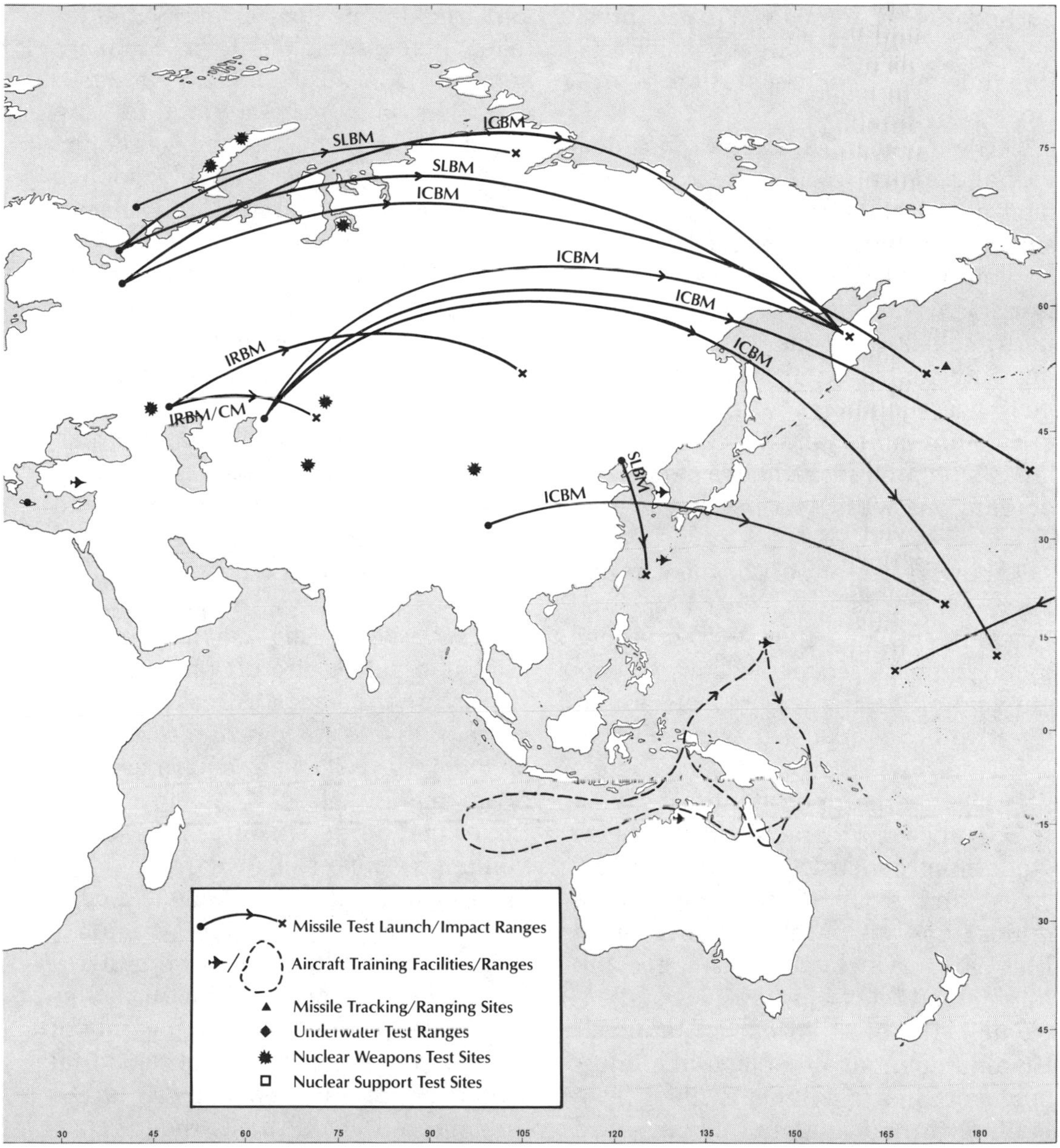

and below the surface track the movement of ships and submarines. Planes and ships collect "intelligence" while they conduct anti-submarine warfare, early-warning and space-surveillance operations.

Since the interception of signals and satellite monitoring—the so-called National Technical Means of verification—are technical processes, the information they produce is heavily slanted toward hardware. This makes the intelligence establishment a part of the nuclear infrastructure, either by collecting and analyzing information about enemy nuclear forces or supporting nuclear forces and plans. Intelligence collection directly supports targeting and the preparation of nuclear war plans.[12]

The nuclear infrastructure includes virtually every intelligence collection facility around the world. This discussion concerns only those facilities that are known to collect "strategic" (that is, nuclear) intelligence, or clearly support nuclear weapons: satellite tracking and control facilities, ocean surveillance stations, and nuclear explosion and missile-test surveillance sites (the surveillance of nuclear detonations was described in Chapter 2).

The most secret part of the surveillance system is in space where four types of satellites collect information: photographic reconnaissance, communications interceptors, electronic interceptors, and ocean surveillance. U.S. and Soviet reconnaissance satellites fly over the globe at altitudes of 75 to 200 miles photographing military installations, construction activity, exercises, and troop dispositions. Using optical and electronic sensors, satellites can survey large areas or specific targets and relay film capsules or electronic data back to earth stations.[13] Communications and electronic intercept satellites monitor everything from civilian broadcasts to military and government messages to radar and telemetry signals. Flying in a variety of orbits, both in stationary positions at 22,300 miles or at low altitudes, they can cover huge areas in search of specific radio frequencies and "targets." Low-flying ocean-surveillance satellites use either active radar (Soviet) or passive infrared sensors and antennas (U.S.) to monitor ship traffic. Control and tracking of the various satellites takes place from eighteen countries and territories. The U.S. tracking network has some forty-six facilities, including radars whose primary function is early warning, and highly sophisticated optical cameras and electo-optical observatories.

One of the largest components of the surveillance system is the ocean surveillance network, which provides instant anti-ship and anti-submarine targeting data. Ocean surveillance is therefore not just a neutral information gathering enterprise. Nor are oceanography and bathymetry, or the pursuit of understanding the oceans.[14]

Ocean surveillance data come from hundreds of sources. Ships carry sonars and electronic collection gear. Maritime patrol aircraft operate from scores of land bases. Aircraft carriers serve as bases for patrol aircraft and helicopters. Attack submarines covertly operate close to enemy naval forces and borders. Many of these surveillance sources also carry nuclear arms, which further links the ocean surveillance system to the arsenals.

Ocean surveillance can be either a local or global activity. Small navies and lesser powers are capable only of detecting naval activities in territorial waters or geographic choke points. Detection on a global basis requires access to land facilities around the world to service naval forces and to serve as staging bases for aircraft, or as processing stations for acoustic and electronic data. Moored to the ocean floor around the world are U.S. (and allied) hydrophone listening arrays, part of the SOSUS (Sound Surveillance System) network, also known as Caesar. Caesar, which began operation in

1954, "is a network of ocean bottom hydrophone arrays which feed back oceanographic and acoustic data to a shore processing site."[15]

Operating with less access to military bases around the world, the Soviet Union's ocean-surveillance network depends almost exclusively on mobile assets: ships, aircraft, and satellites. The Soviet Union has nothing equivalent to the SOSUS system but has about fifty intelligence-collection ships (called AGIs). They keep watch on U.S. naval activities and maintain a constant presence near important bases such as Holy Loch, Scotland; Charleston, South Carolina; Kings Bay, Georgia; Norfolk, Virginia; Mayport, Florida; and Bangor, Washington.[16] Soviet Bear-D, Bear-F, and May maritime patrol aircraft fly regular routes over the oceans, as do U.S. P-3 Orion planes. Soviet planes regularly operate from airfields in Cuba, Angola, Vietnam, South Yemen, and Ethiopia. U.S. P-3s operate from some fifteen countries. All of the data gathered from ocean-surveillance systems are correlated at a few large processing stations where a complete picture of naval activity can be drawn. In the United States the main processing center is in Suitland, Maryland, supported by five regional centers.[17]

Many of the surveillance stations monitor strategic missile tests. Satellites are a major source of data on tests, augmented by ground-based radars and signals-intelligence stations. The U.S. systems include the Cobra Dane radar on Shemya Island in the Aleutians, detection and tracking radars at Pirinclik, Turkey, radars at Kwajalein Atoll in the Marshall Islands, and covert interception facilities in Norway and China. Reconnaissance aircraft allow the United States to get closer to missile tests. Planes include high-altitude U-2s and SR-71s and special aircraft configured for telemetry interception. These include RC-135 Cobra Ball planes, which fly from Shemya to cover Soviet Pacific tests, and EC-135N Advanced Range Instrumentation Aircraft (ARIA) based at Wright-Patterson AFB, Ohio, which fly out of forty airfields throughout the world to monitor tests.

Since much of the missile testing is over water, ships are also used for surveillance, particularly to get close to the impact points of reentry vehicles. The U.S. ship Observation Island, stationed in Hawaii, carries the Cobra Judy radar to monitor Soviet testing. Soviet monitoring of U.S. and foreign testing relies on its fleet of ships, which are usually around the Florida and California coasts during launches. The only ocean-going ships in the Chinese Navy are its fleet of missile-tracking, telemetry, and recovery ships, which are used to support Chinese missile testing but also could monitor U.S. and Soviet testing in the Pacific.

Early Warning and Attack Assessment

The surveillance system is backed up by an early warning system that directly supports nuclear warmaking. While the primary goal of the surveillance system is to assess the likelihood of conflict, the early warning and attack assessment system lies dormant until an attack. It will then operate for perhaps a day to detect and characterize the nature of the attack and provide information to decision-makers to set nuclear war plans in motion. When the early warning system swings into operation, military and political planners will have less than thirty minutes to choose nuclear options. In peacetime the early warning sensors spend their time monitoring missile testing and space activity.

The first warning of missile attack would come from early warning satellites. When a missile launch occurs, the satellites sense the heat from the rocket and burning motor within a minute of liftoff.[18] U.S. ground stations at Nurrungar, Australia; Aurora, Colorado; and Kapaun, West Germany, all scrutinize some 400 major foreign rocket launches a year to determine whether they are tests, satellite liftoffs, or nuclear attacks.

As soon as rockets rise above the horizon, five to ten minutes into their thirty-minute intercontinental flights, information from land-based radars can confirm an attack and precisely assess its nature. Both the United States and the Soviet Union operate a handful of early warning and attack assessment radars (see Figure). There are three primary sets of missile warning radars in the U.S. system. The largest are the three radars of the Ballistic Missile Early Warning System (BMEWS), at Clear, Alaska; Thule, Greenland; and Fylingdales Moor, England (the Fylingdales radar is a joint U.S.-British radar that also provides warning for Britain and Europe). Two Pave Paws submarine missile radars supplement BMEWS on the Atlantic and Pacific coasts, on Cape Cod, Massachusetts, and at Beale AFB, California. Two more Pave Paws are to be built in Georgia and Texas to detect attacks from the southeast and southwest, replacing two older radars in Florida. The Perimeter Acquisition Radar Characterization System (PARCS) is operated in North Dakota to provide detailed attack assessment data on the number and targets of incoming reentry vehicles.

The Soviet Union operates numerous large types of radar for early warning. There are three over-the-horizon radars, two directed at the United States and one at China. There are about a dozen Hen House, Hen Roost, and Hen Egg phased-array radars around the periphery of Soviet Union.[19] The anti-ballistic missile system around Moscow also has specialized detection and tracking radars—at Chekhov, Naro-Fominsk, Pushkino, and Skrunda—to provide early warning and attack assessment. China has one major phased-array radar in Xinjiang province.

Immediately after detection of an attack by early-warning satellites,

---

EARLY WARNING *[facing page]*

Poised for imminent war, the two superpowers ceaselessly watch for missile launches or aircraft intrusions that could signal an attack. Here are the main missile and bomber early warning radars and their respective tracking ranges. (Note that the actual arc of each radar's coverage extends farther than the map symbols indicate. The radar at Fylingdales, for example, can "see" farther than Lyaki.) American and Soviet early warning satellites, not shown here, give the first indication of missile launches. Several minutes later land-based radars confirm the launches. National leaders then have 10-25 minutes between confirmation and impact. One of the many bomber early warning systems, the DEW Line, is shown on the map of Canada.

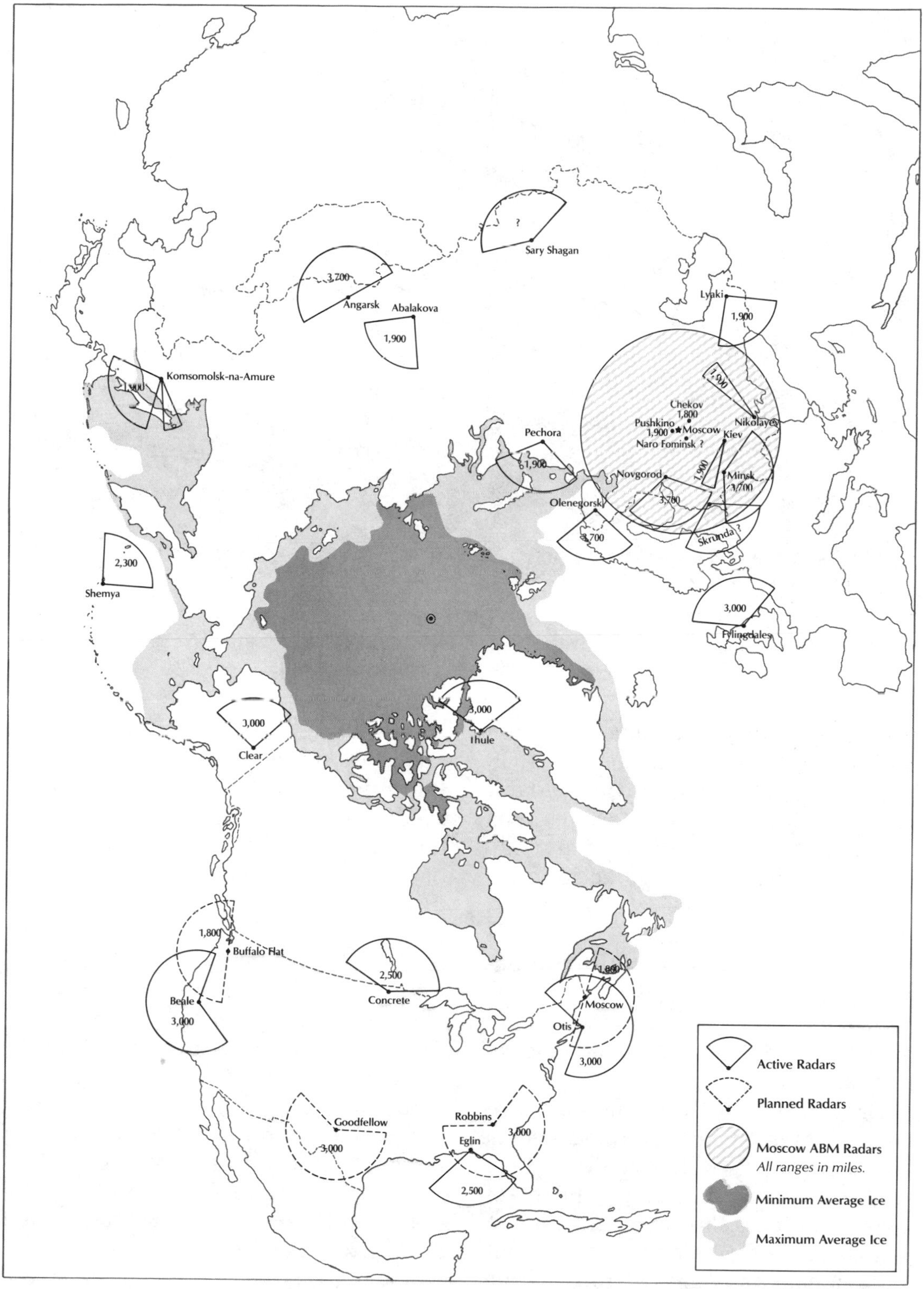
Sary Shagan
Angarsk
3,700
Abalakova
1,900
Komsomolsk-na-Amure
Lyaki
1,900
Chekov
1,800
Pushkino
1,900
Moscow
Naro Fominsk ?
Nikolayev
Kiev
Minsk
Novgorod
Pechora
Olenegorsk
3,700
Skrunda ?
3,000
Fylingdales
2,300
Shemya
3,000
Clear
3,000
Thule
1,800
Buffalo Flat
Beale
3,000
2,500
Concrete
Moscow
Otis
3,000
Goodfellow
3,000
Robbins
3,000
Eglin
2,500
Active Radars
Planned Radars
Moscow ABM Radars
All ranges in miles.
Minimum Average Ice
Maximum Average Ice

"Fat Albert," one of two blimps the U.S. uses to carry "early warning" radar, sits 12,000 feet over Florida watching over the Keys and the straits of Florida. These "aerostats" (and AWACS flying radar planes) can plug low altitude "gaps" in radar coverage.

"missile impact computers" from the BMEWS, Pave Paws, and PARCS (and the equivalent Soviet radars) begin sorting out hundreds, perhaps thousands, of warheads and provide command centers with precise information about the nature of an attack. The PARCS radar in North Dakota would detect warheads in the terminal phase of their flight and contribute the most detailed information, which would then go into planning responses.

Backing up the large missile-warning radars is an early-warning system to detect aircraft. The United States and Canada operate three "lines" of over 100 radars that are constantly on watch for bombers and other aircraft intrusions. The lines stretch from Alaska through Canada and Greenland into Iceland and Europe. The thirty-three radars of the northern DEW Line (the Distant Early Warning Line) are augmented by thirteen radars in Alaska, twenty-four radars in the Canadian-operated CADIN-Pinetree line, and other more specialized regional radars such as Seek Skyhook (two balloons tethered 12,000 feet above Florida), or an over-the-horizon radar in Maine.[20] The Joint Surveillance System in the United States incorporates civil and military radars that feed data into five Region Operations Control Centers (ROCCs). To cope with the large U.S. bomber force, the Soviets have some 7,000 radars at some 1,200 sites, comprised of border-detection, and aircraft-control and fire-control radars for surface-to-air missiles.

The aircraft early-warning system is reproduced in miniature in the rest of the world, where it is closely linked to the nuclear powers. NATO's integrated warning is provided by a conglomeration of forty-two radars extending from the tip of Norway to southern Turkey. Even France, which left NATO's military structure in 1966, ties its early-warning system into the NATO NADGE network. Other systems are tied into U.S. networks, such as Combat Grande in Spain, BADGE in Japan, and similar systems in the Philippines. Eastern European air-defense radars are tied into the Soviet system.

Communications

Tying all the weapons, test ranges, surveillance, and early warning systems together is a vast communications network of wires, submarine cables, radio stations, and satellites. Satellites, now only two decades old, link the entire globe with instantaneous communication. According to Admiral Gordon Nagler, chief of Naval communications, "we can talk to any ship any place on the surface of the Earth, 365 days a year, 24 hours a day."[21]

The largest communications system in the world is that of the United States. The Defense Communications System, a peacetime and crisis operations network, serves 3,161 locations in seventy-five countries and islands.[22] Nearly two-thirds of it is overseas. It combines many lesser networks comprising 35 million miles of circuits, operated by 15,000 people. Every command center, headquarters, submarine, missile silo, or bomber constantly receives messages over it.

The day-to-day networks are supplemented by a bewildering array of special networks that support nuclear weapons. The most important is the Minimum Essential Emergency Communications Network (MEECN), set up in 1970. The MEECN, according to the Department of Defense, "is intended to survive and to provide those links essential [to] . . . exercise deliberate and precise control of strategic nuclear options for the SIOP execution and termination."[23] It is made up of airborne command posts, satellite systems, ground transmitters, and more exotic relays, all able to operate during and after a nuclear war.

The most important ground system of the MEECN is the Survivable Low Frequency Communications System (SLFCS), a teletype network composed of eight Air Force and Navy transmitters, connected to over 200 receivers at command centers, missile launch centers, submarines, and radio sites (for further relay to bombers). The most exotic system is the Emergency Rocket Communications System (ERCS), deployed aboard ten Minuteman II missiles based near Whiteman AFB in Missouri.[24] In place of the 1.2 megaton nuclear warheads are radio transmitters providing "alternate communications with the nuclear force under surprise attack conditions."[25]

MEECN space systems include the Air Force Satellite Communications System (AFSATCOM), a network dedicated to nuclear weapons. Put into operation in 1979, there are AFSATCOM repeaters on military and commercial "host" satellites. There are 900 terminals installed in nuclear com-

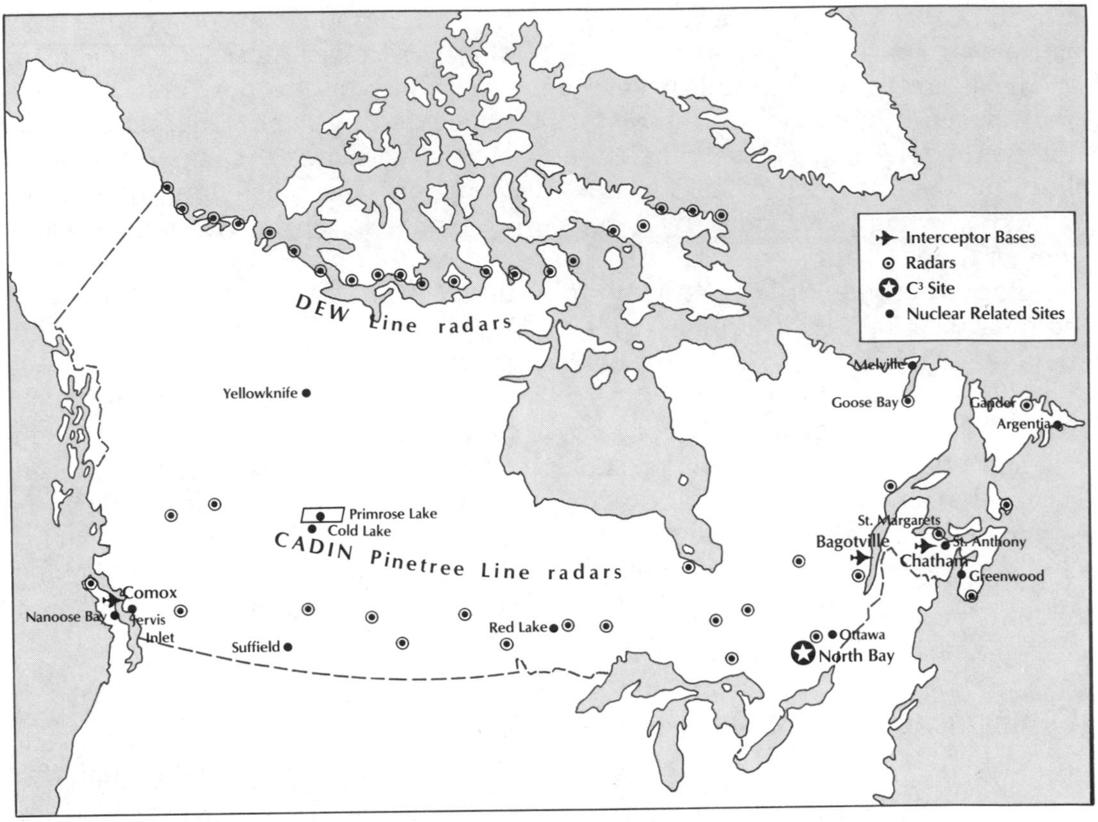

CANADA AND THE NUCLEAR INFRASTRUCTURE

Canada is unique in the thoroughness of its support of the U.S. nuclear infrastructure. It provides links in six of the eight categories and is second only to West Germany in hosting nuclear-related facilities, with nearly eighty separate installations. As a member of the North American Aerospace Defense Command (NORAD), Canada has become closely linked to U.S. early warning and nuclear war planning. NORAD was the first peacetime organization the U.S. set up for joint contingency planning with another country. As a member of NATO, Canada fits closely into nuclear-related anti-submarine warfare plans. With huge expanses of uninhabited land above the Arctic circle, Canada is well-suited for testing weapons, electronic equipment, and communications systems in northern latitudes. Some of Canada's more important support roles are outlined below.

- The Strategic Air Command plans to use Canadian airfields for dispersal of the U.S. bomber force. Nuclear-loaded B-52s would fly to Cold Lake and other Canadian bases during an alert. KC-135 aerial refueling planes would also use Canadian airfields such as Goose Bay, Labrador, and Namao for dispersal and refueling operations.
- The NORAD treaty with Canada allows U.S. bombers and refueling planes to fly without restrictions over Canadian airspace on their way to the Soviet Union. Upon warning of impending action, "safe passage of SAC aircraft must be guaranteed."
- Canada participates in several nuclear

war planning programs, including the North American Air Defense Master Plan, and the Strategic Defense Architecture 2000 Plan, both linked to the Nuclear Weapons Employment and Acquisition Master Plan. One goal of this long-term plan is to achieve "enduring air defense—something that you could actually have in place that would actually last through a nuclear strike."[1]

• Canada hosts several radar systems important for early warning of attacking aircraft: 21 DEW Line radars across northern Canada and 24 CADIN (Continental Air Defense Integration North) Pinetree radars closer to the U.S.-Canada border. The DEW Line system is being upgraded to detect low-flying aircraft and cruise missiles. The new "North Warning System" will expand the number of sites to 52 (excluding Alaska). The radars report to a NORAD Region Operations Control Center at North Bay, Ontario. From this hardened command center, U.S. and Canadian operators could run the entire NORAD aircraft early warning system, directing U.S. and Canadian aircraft to intercept attacking bombers. Canadian technicians are being trained to operate the E-3A AWACs planes for NORAD.

• Canada permits the U.S. Air Force to test its air-launched cruise missiles (ALCMs) from over the Canadian Arctic to the Primrose Weapons Evaluation Range near Cold Lake, Alberta. According to the Air Force Secretary, the ALCM's terrain guidance system will see Canadian Arctic terrain, "like that we might encounter in enemy territory," so that it won't be "snowblind" when fired at northern Soviet targets. He stated that these tests "will give us the most realistic training we could have."[2] The U.S. Army also uses Canada for cold weather tests of its nuclear artillery shells.[3]

• Numerous nuclear-related communications programs are researched, developed, tested, or operated in Canada. SAC's Northern Area Communication System, called Green Pine, for communicating with bombers and tankers in northern latitudes, has stations at Argentia, Newfoundland, and Melville Air Station, Labrador. The nuclear-war surviving Ground-wave Emergency Network (GWEN) is planned to extend into Canada to connect with Canadian Air Defense Forces.[4] Canada participates in research on propagation of satellite communications in northern latitudes, including research on extremely-high-frequency (EHF) communications between the Canadian Forces Station (CFS) Alert on Ellesmere Island and two U.S. satellites of the Minimum Essential Emergency Communications Network (MEECN). CFS Alert is the northernmost active military installation in the world. A joint U.S.-Canadian development program is also developing navigation systems for the NAVSTAR Global Positioning System (GPS) and measuring "high latitude effects on GPS signal propagation."[5]

• Canada helps the U.S. in its anti-submarine warfare tasks by hosting the Naval Facility at Argentia, Newfoundland, one of the main data processing stations for the SOSUS submarine detection system in the northern Atlantic. Canada also operates its own ASW monitoring bases for the U.S. The United States uses the Advanced Underwater Acoustic Measurement System at Jervis Inlet, and the Canadian Forces Maritime Experimental and Test Range at Nanoose Bay, both in British Colubia, as deepwater testing and training areas for submarines and ASW weapons system evaluation, including nuclear-capable ASROC and SUBROC weapons. Canadian CP-140 Aurora maritime patrol aircraft are also "compatible with [U.S.] ASW opertations centers throughout the world" and supply targeting data on Soviet submarines to the U.S. Navy and intelligence community.[6]

• Two sites in Canada (Yellowknife, Northwest Territories, and Red Lake, Ontario) host seismic detection stations of the U.S. Department of Energy's Regional Seismic Test Network. Along with three other such stations in the U.S., these RSTN stations are used in researching the seismic signal characteristics of nuclear tests for future use in collecting information on Soviet nuclear weapons tests.

NOTES

1. HAC, FY 1984 DOD, pt. 8, p. 319.

2. HAC, FY 1984 DOD, pt. 2, p. 167.

3. U.S. Army Armament, Munitions and Chemical Command, "AMCCOM Laboratory Posture Report FY 83," No. RCS-DRCLD-101 (Rock Island, Ill.: AMCCOM, n.d.), p. 1-26.

4. HAC, FY 1984 DOD, pt. 8, p. 341.

5. U.S. Department of State, Memorandum of Understanding Between the United States of America and Canada, "Satellite Based Global Positioning and Navigation System," *Treaties and Other International Acts* Series No. 9689 (Washington, D.C.: U.S. Government Printing Office, 1978).

6. Lieutenant Maurice S. Joyce, "Dawn of the Aurora," *Proceedings* (March 1980), p. 129.

mand centers, storage sites, and units. The next generation of nuclear weapons communications satellite will be MILSTAR, which will replace AFSATCOM. MILSTAR is "more capable of effectively operating in a nuclear environment,"[26], "so we can better manage our forces in a protracted war."[27]

Newer systems such as the Groundwave Emergency Network (GWEN) (discussed earlier) will further extend communications during a nuclear war. Other specialized systems, not direct elements of the MEECN, such as the presidential Mystic Star network, also play a role in the "release" of nuclear weapons. Each component of the nuclear force has its own network to ensure receipt of nuclear orders. Land-based ICBMs have redundant and protected underground cables and a wide variety of radios. Bombers have their own radio nets to transmit "execution instructions," including the Green Pine/Northern Area Communications System (NACS) in the Arctic, and Giant Talk/Scope Signal III, a system of fourteen stations with coverage in all areas of the world other than the Arctic.[28]

Submarines have the greatest number of special communications networks. The primary components are twenty-seven U.S. Navy low- and very-low-frequency transmitters (code-named Verdin), a fleet of eighteen TACAMO ("Take-charge-and-move-out") radio-relay aircraft, and the new extremely-low-frequency (ELF) system in Michigan and Wisconsin. MEECN elements, ship-based radio systems, "various acoustic signalling methods" and satellites, are also used for submarine communications.[29] One unique system is Clarinet Pilgrim, deployed in the North Pacific (and possibly in the Atlantic), a shore-to-submarine network that works by superimposing data on the wave transmitted by LORAN-C radio-navigation stations.[30]

The covert use of civilian or seemingly non-nuclear systems (such as the Clarinet Pilgrim network) is most common in the field of communications. The GWEN system will use commercial radio towers as antennas. Another noteworthy program is the Military Affiliate Radio System (MARS), a network of amateur ham-radio stations on military bases throughout the world. The MARS system of shortwave radios is most often used to transmit birthday messages home, but according to an Air Force regulation, "In the event normal base communications fail, Pacific area MARS stations are authorized entry into the Commando Escort network to activate emergency communications nets."[31]

The communication systems of the other nuclear powers are not as complex but are similar in design to the U.S. system. The Soviets have made extensive use of buried cables and special networks. Some airborne command posts and radio relays are also deployed, but mobile systems do not appear to be as important as they are to the United States. The Soviet Union, like the United States, is shifting much of its communications infrastructure into space. Additionally, it is building systems like ELF antennas (on the Kola Peninsula) and experimenting with laser and acoustic communications.

France is developing four planes like the U.S. TACAMO to communicate with its submarines and other nuclear forces.[32] All five nuclear powers are making greater use of satellite systems for the full spectrum of nuclear services. One common goal of these initiatives is to increase the "nuclear" survivability of communications assets by reducing their susceptibility to jamming, electromagnetic pulse, or other nuclear effects. The communications revolution brought on by satellites and other advanced technologies has falsely promoted the notion that nuclear war can be controlled.

Civil Defense

Continual improvements in the flexibility (or usability) and control of nuclear weapons, and demonstrations of national preparedness to fight and win a nuclear war, bring us to the final component of the nuclear infrastructure: civil defense. The civil defense complex has three missions: protection of the population, continuity of government, and improvement of the prospects for postwar recovery. The United States, Britain, and the Soviet Union have massive programs to carry out some or all of these goals (the programs of France and China are not publicly known). They are driven by the prospects of preparing for the effects of a war that would harm the homeland (as opposed to a war in some "forward area"), for which the only possibility is nuclear war.

In order to make civil defense seem plausible, highest priority is placed on the easiest and most unobtrusive task: "continuity of government," (assuring that a skeletal central government survives a nuclear war). The other tasks are attended to with differing degrees of detailed study and action. "Low-" and "high-" "risk areas" are designated, and population relocation plans are formulated for cities. Plans are prepared for protection of factories, provisions for post-nuclear war postal service, and shelters to safeguard government documents. Scare campaigns are periodically mounted to raise the specter of the dangerous intent of enemy civil defense programs. The most interesting observation to make in a brief treatment of civil defense is that the actual program is so immense.

In the United States some 1,480 of 3,135 localities that are identified to evacuate in the event of nuclear war have complete "crisis relocation plans." Current plans call for 3,063 local "emergency operations centers" and 5,828 state and local centers throughout the country. Three hundred fifty of the 3,063 centers are "fully capable of post nuclear attack operations" and can provide "radioactive fallout protection; an emergency generator; a 14-day fuel supply; and adequate ventilation, sanitation, and water."[33] There are 607 "protected commercial broadcast stations" and plans to have 2,771 by 1989.[34] Twice each day, the National Weather Service feeds wind data into civil defense computers to update fallout prediction forecasts should nuclear war occur that day. The Federal Aviation Administration is prepared at a moment's notice to implement SCATANA (Security Control of Air Traffic and Air Navigation Aids), a plan that would ground all commercial aircraft within the United States and Canada.

The U.S. civil defense infrastructure is thus massive and pervasive. Whatever its effectiveness, its sheer size is in stark contrast to the image of almost totally lacking U.S. civil defense measures portrayed when U.S. officials discuss Soviet civil defense. The Soviet Union and Great Britain have huge infrastructures as well. Preparations exist at all levels of government, particularly in cities, for evacuation and survival.

Conclusion

The obscure installations of the nuclear infrastructure deserve the closest scrutiny for their role in the nuclear arms race. Since many of the keys to victory in warfare today are electronic—radars, communications, satellites, computers—it is important to question whether those systems merely support decisionmakers and weapons or dominate them. The military sponsored the majority of the early work on computers, and today's thumbnail-size chips have more power than the first room-size computers. In the next ten years very-high-speed integrated circuits will be a hundred times faster and more compact than today's systems.

As systems become smaller and faster, the ability of humans to manage the whole nuclear apparatus at a central location diminishes. The process places herculean demands on its human creators, who are unable to assimilate and comprehend such oceans of information. Ultimately, this will lead to changes in the way nuclear weapons are controlled because it decentralizes and automates greater amounts of analysis and decisionmaking. While electronic technology is a significant "force multiplier," it is also more vulnerable and perishable than weapons, which ultimately will lead to a loss of control. In the end, the destruction of electronic systems will have a more profound effect than the destruction of weapons during a nuclear war.

The existence of thousands of analysts, planners, and technicians is very sanguine, evoking images of skilled air-traffic controllers and well-informed managers who advise decisionmakers on the enemy's nuclear forays, and suggest optimum reactions. This is based on the mistaken belief that nuclear war is like other wars. The electronically dominated infrastructure produces mountains of technical data but no real answers. It is the war planners, and not the policymakers, who will be served, kept apprised of minute developments to establish and reorder targeting priorities and select options in a nuclear war.

5

Going to War

THE MOST DEVASTATING nuclear war scenario for the United States is the "bolt-out-of-the-blue" attack. Soviet missiles and bombers would be fired at U.S. nuclear forces caught in their normal "day-to-day alert." Without a "launch on warning" or "launch under attack," 90 percent of land-based ICBMs, 70 percent of strategic bombers, and 45 percent of submarines would be destroyed.

If an attack occurred during a "fully generated alert," as much as 90 percent of the bombers and 85 percent of the submarines could survive an initial attack. Unless the United States launched its land-based missiles while the Soviet missiles were on their way, 90 percent of them would still be destroyed.

Using hundreds of computer inputs, calculations, and qualifications, the Pentagon's worst-case scenario assumes that a bolt-out-of-the-blue attack would reduce the U.S. retaliatory force to 3,800 surviving nuclear warheads with some 500 megatons of explosive force. In their "fully generated" alert state, U.S. strategic forces could muster 7,000 warheads of 1,200 megatons. Incredibly, to some these are the calculations that prove "ICBM vulnerability" and evoke dire pessimism about the state of deterrence. Those who want to expand U.S. forces use the most pessimistic assumptions. Their opponents use the most optimistic.

The arcane art of nuclear war planning is based on untested and untestable assumptions that masquerade as scientifically rigorous precepts. Complex planning creates the illusion that all variables about what might happen in an endless set of possible circumstances have been thought out. In this way, preparing to respond to any type of attack theoretically aids deterrence of that attack. The lack of any real experience with nuclear war means that assumptions form the basis of all justification, structuring, and criticism of nuclear forces. The assumptions are far removed from the roots or the ultimate effects of the war that would occur if the scenarios were to become reality.

This kind of planning promotes nuclear self-esteem. The military believes that the "credibility" behind its policy is what ultimately deters. The planners have grown so used to destroying the enemy in their computers that the actual war has become secondary to the game. When the "balloon goes up," civilian decisionmakers will have to weigh the political circumstances, moral dimensions, and motives of an attack and determine the appropriate response. Military planners do not waste their time pondering ultimate national goals or the purpose of nuclear war; they concentrate on the details of executing it.

Nuclear Decisionmaking

All nuclear nations have granted nuclear weapons a special status by placing their control firmly under political leaders who have the sole authority to order their use. In the United States this authority rests with the so-called National Command Authority (NCA), a civilian body consisting of the President and the Secretary of Defense, "or their duly deputized alternates and successors."[1] Ultimate and exclusive authority to make nuclear decisions resides in the Soviet Union with the Politburo; in Britain, the Prime Minister; in France, the President; and in China, the Communist Party Central Committee.

The NCAs enforce their control through devices that inhibit the unauthorized or inadvertent use of nuclear weapons and procedures that govern their security. In each country, specially constructed command facilities and communications links connect the NCA to the nuclear forces. In the United States (and presumably in other countries) release of nuclear weapons requires both voice and written commands (over teletype) that are validated by codes and "authenticators."

The United States maintains four primary command centers to support nuclear operations. They collect and process all the required information on forces, planning, intelligence, and early warning to allow "informed" decisions on the use of nuclear weapons. If the NCA and the civilian successors were destroyed in a nuclear attack, the chain of command would not fail. The United States maintains a network of airborne and other alternate command centers. At least one airborne command center is always in the air (and has been since 1962) as part of the day-to-day alert posture. Secret plans set forth policies for delegating authority of the NCA to the succeeding military officers when

In an effort to build communication systems that could survive and operate through a nuclear war, the nuclear powers are making "hardened" equipment like this microwave antenna on the side of Cheyenne Mountain in Colorado, which houses the NORAD underground command center. The command center is connected by hardened underground communcation cables and microwave radio relays to civilian communication stations as far as 165 miles away.

all means of communication to civilians fail.

The Strategic Air Command maintains the largest fleet of airborne command centers (the Looking Glass command planes and Coverall airborne relays), which are always manned by General officers prepared to take over the reins of the nuclear forces. Each head of the nuclear-armed commands (Europe, Pacific, Atlantic, Central (Middle East) and North American Aerospace Defense [NORAD]) have primary and alternate command posts ready to lead the entire military. The three major nuclear commands fly their own airborne command planes: Silk Purse, based in Britain for Europe, Blue Eagle, based in Hawaii for the Pacific, and Scope Light, based in Virginia for the Atlantic.

The authority over nuclear weapons in the Soviet Union resides in the General Secretary of the CPSU, who is also head of the Politburo, Defense Council, and Supreme Commander-in-Chief of the Armed Forces. The use of nuclear weapons would probably be approved by the Politburo, which is advised in wartime by a Defense Committee that would take over from the peacetime Defense Council. Nuclear orders would be controlled by the Supreme High Command (VGK or Stavka) and passed by the General Staff to the nuclear commands: Strategic Rocket Forces (SRF), Air Force, Navy, and the five Theaters of Military Operations (TVD).[2]

The Soviets command their nuclear forces from underground, mobile, and airborne command centers. The Air Defense Forces (PVO) headquarters near Moscow makes the early warning and attack assessment and would pass it on to some thirty military NCA support bunkers. The Defense Council, General Staff, Politburo, and other higher commands "have multiple hardened facilities and mobile command vehicles and aircraft available for their use."[3] There are fewer airborne command centers in the Soviet Union, and they are not as important as their U.S. counterparts. Command ships and submarines augment the airborne centers. Nine intermediate SRF "Army" headquarters and approximately 300 SRF launch centers control the land-based ICBM force. The alert rates (the percentage of nuclear forces kept ready for instant use) are lower in the Soviet Union than in the United States, reflecting tight control of nuclear forces, as well as Soviet fear of losing control during a nuclear alert.

Authority over British nuclear weapons rests with the Prime Minister.[4] Commands emanate from the Defence Ministry in London to two main nuclear centers: Northwood (for Polaris submarines) and High Wycombe (for aircraft). These command centers serve both British and NATO functions. Six secondary nuclear command centers augment the central bunkers.

In France, the President would order the use of nuclear weapons.[5] He would send his commands through the Centre de l'Opération des Forces Aériennes Stratégiques (COFAS) in a hardened command center at Taverny, near Paris, to the nuclear forces. The ALFOST (Admiral in charge of the submarines), headquartered at Houilles, northwest of Paris, exercises command of the submarine force. Two launch control centers command the land-based missiles. Eight other primary military control centers and two secondary control centers back up the main centers. Command of tactical nuclear aircraft and Pluton missiles would flow directly to military commands. According to the DIA, "Once the French President decides to use nuclear weapons, the authority for Pluton employment is delegated directly to Army and Corps."[6]

In China, the Chairman of the Central Committee of the Communist Party, advised by the Standing Committee of the Politburo, would decide whether to use nuclear weapons.[7] The Chinese nuclear forces have consolidated training and operations under a special command (formerly called the Second Artillery). That it lies outside the normal chain of command assures its unique mission and control.

Strategic Nuclear War Plans

The central strategic war plan of the United States is called the Single Integrated Operational Plan (SIOP), currently SIOP-6, which went into effect on October 1, 1983. It reportedly includes instructions for everything "from a show of force to a trans/post SIOP environment."[8] The Joint Strategic Target Planning Staff (JSTPS) at Offutt AFB in Omaha, Nebraska, develops the plan. The JSTPS coordinates the nuclear forces to strike targets under preplanned "options" available to the NCA.

Plans to use nuclear weapons have changed since the early days after World War II when bombers were aimed at industry, transportation links, and other bombers. In the early 1960s, options for "limited" nuclear war were created. These options distinguished attacks on military or "counterforce" targets from those on cities or "countervalue" targets. "Damage-limiting counterforce" strikes would presumably destroy the enemy's nuclear forces with the "countervalue attack" retained for revenge. Beginning in 1974, "more-selective options, relatively small scale, were added to the existing large-scale options."[9]

When President Carter took office, he ordered a review of nuclear targeting policy (PD-18) that eventually resulted in the "countervailing" doctrine, a strategy that stressed "that no plausible outcome [of a Soviet nuclear attack] would represent a success—or any rational definition of success."[10] The recapitulation of the long evolving trend towards a wider range of nuclear options came in Presidential Directive 59 (PD-59), Nuclear Weapons Employment Policy, dated July 25, 1980. According to then-Secretary of Defense Harold Brown, "Our planning must provide a continuum of options, ranging from use of small numbers of strategic and/or theater nuclear weapons aimed at narrowly defined targets, to employment of large portions of our nuclear forces against a broad spectrum of targets."[11] PD-59 instructed the military to integrate strategic and nonstrategic nuclear forces into the SIOP and develop options for attacks against the Soviet command structure (the military, party, and internal security control apparatus within the Soviet Union), "power projection forces" (that is, the combat troops the Soviet Union could "project" into foreign countries), and the Soviet industrial and "economic recovery base." It called for a secure "strategic reserve" force to carry out countervalue strikes after the initial salvos of a nuclear war.[12] It extended the possible timespan of a nuclear war to sixty days and called for better C^3 support.

The Reagan administration reaffirmed the guidelines of PD-59 in National Security Decision Directive 13 (NSDD-13), issued in October 1981. NSDD-13 accepted the arbitrary assumptions set forth in PD-59 about the duration, extent, and character of a nuclear war. It stressed making improvements in the command and control system to bolster "post-attack" control over nuclear forces as the first priority and called for greater coordination of theater and strategic plans.

Ever since limited war became the main feature of U.S. nuclear plans, the interaction between U.S. and Soviet nuclear strategy has grown. The PD-18 targeting review grew out of a new U.S. intelligence analysis that concluded Soviet planners believed a prolonged nuclear war was possible. The sense of the United States having options for precise targeting or "escalation control" depends largely on the Soviet Union having a strategy other than the massive use of nuclear weapons. According to the 1984 edition of *Soviet Military Power*, "Priority targets of all Soviet forces would be the enemy's nuclear delivery systems and weapons, nuclear C^3, air defenses and politico-administrative centers."[13] The Joint Chiefs of Staff stated:

> They have sized their strategic missile warhead inventory to their worldwide targeting requirements, plus a substantial reserve to support military operations after the initial exchange and to dominate the post-war world. They plan to use their inventory to ensure high confidence in achieving the required degree of damage to selected targets by striking the same target two or three times.[14]

Although virtually nothing is known about actual Soviet nuclear war plans, U.S. interpretations of the Soviet proclivities for selective targeting justify U.S. weapons and nuclear plans.

U.S. planners derive what they view as operational principles for the use of Soviet nuclear forces from broad tenets of doctrine and strategy. Soviet military writings stress certain basic rules that may apply to its nuclear war plans:

- "preemption consistently has been the preferred Soviet strategic option";[15]
- "second strike has been the residual option if the Soviets do not succeed in preempting";[16]
- "launch on warning was adopted as the second option (after preempting)" in 1966-67;[17]
- nuclear forces are the first targets in a nuclear exchange, to be destroyed in their entirety, through such possible measures as barrage attacks with land-based missiles against suspected submarine patrol areas;[18]
- neutralization of non-nuclear military forces is a secondary objective to be carried out by whatever means possible; Soviet forces would simultaneously have to engage enemy front line forces and rear area targets;
- destruction of the enemy political control system and preservation of Soviet state power and control are high priorities;
- industrial and other economic targets important for sustaining warfare would be a high priority in a world war;
- defense of the Soviet homeland is the overall objective of any military operation;
- a prolonged nuclear war is possible;
- victory is a theoretical possibility, although it is rarely defined in the context of nuclear war.

The Soviet Union appears to recognize the futility of a disarming attack on U.S. nuclear forces (although its planning vis-a-vis Europe seems quite different, as seen below), since large numbers of weapons would survive even in their best case scenario. Nonetheless, Soviet nuclear war options call for massive attacks if they feared that the United States or its allies were about to strike with nuclear forces.

All of Britain's nuclear forces are integrated into U.S. and NATO plans, though Britain retains the right to use its nuclear weapons independently when it is in its "supreme national interest" to do so. Given its close ties to U.S. planning, the main justification today for continuing to have national nuclear weapons is to maintain a "second center of decisionmaking." "Even if in some future situation Soviet leaders imagined that the United States might not be prepared to use nuclear weapons," Britain's *Statement on the Defence Estimates* for 1981 stated, "having to take account of enormous destructive power in European hands would compel them to regard the risks of aggression in Europe as still very grave."[19]

France also justifies its independent nuclear arsenal on the basis of a second center of decisionmaking. Unlike the pseudo-independent British force, it is a direct challenge to U.S. credibility in risking nuclear war to defend Europe. The central theme of French nuclear plans is that the use of its weapons is credibile only if the survival of the nation is at stake. What there is of French strategic writing tends to belittle counterforce concepts, stating that anti-city attacks are the only true deterrent.

Little information is available on the specific targeting of either French or British nuclear weapons. One British government document has referred to "key aspects of Soviet state power."[20] It states that "Selective air attacks with nuclear weapons against specific targets might be necessary to demonstrate political will and to induce an opponent to stop aggression."[21] Most British and French strategic forces are believed to be targeted on cities and "command" targets. The expansion of British and French submarine forces each to about 500 warheads will have a significant impact on targeting. Aircraft like the Mirage IVA and Tornado, as well as the versatile submarines and ship-based aircraft, could be used anywhere in the world, as demonstrated during the Falklands War in 1983.

Chinese nuclear weapons, according to the judgment of most observers, "appear to be targeted almost exclusively on the Soviet Union."[22] The Defense Intelligence Agency stated that the CSS-2 missile "is probably intended for relatively large population centers in central and eastern Russia."[23]

U.S. Targeting

The growth in nuclear arsenals has led to the identification and categorization of a vast number of targets, called the target "complex." The complex has grown from a few Soviet cities and bomber bases to some 40,000 military bases, economic and industrial facilities, natural features, and centers of government in the Soviet Union and Eastern Europe.[24] Nuclear war planners spend most of their time selecting, examining, and ranking the potential targets, then matching individual weapons to each. The planners calculate their assumptions about the capabilities of weapon systems (reliability, range, explosive yield, speed) and the characteristics of the targets (hardness, time sensitivity, importance) to match the arsenal with specific tactical and political objectives (destruction requirements, damage levels, avoidance of "collateral damage").

Since readiness for nuclear war is a 24-hour-a-day, 365-day-a-year reality, the war plan is under constant revision. A change in the readiness of a

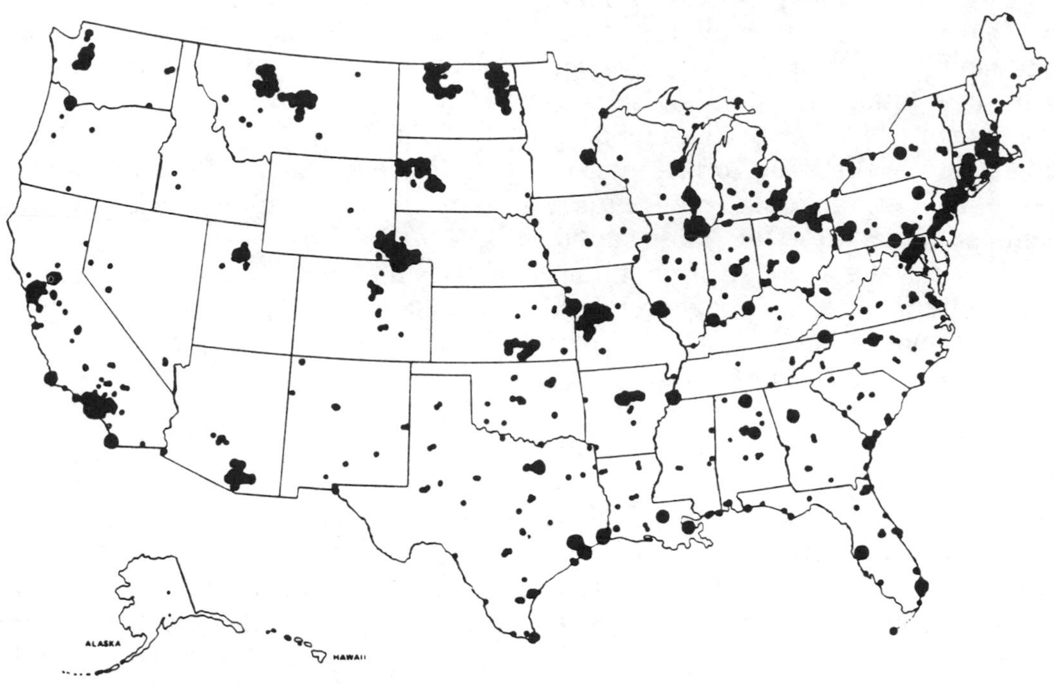

NUCLEAR TARGETING

According to the Federal Emergency Management Agency, responsible for U.S. civil defense, the "high risk areas" which would be targets in a large scale nuclear attack include 63 "counterforce" areas that contain strategic offensive forces (ICBMs, bomber bases, and submarine ports), 250 metropolitan areas with over 50,000 population, and 100 additional areas of "important military and economic installations" (map above). In a counterforce nuclear exchange, however, the following types of targets would be the highest priority to the Soviets: strategic nuclear forces, naval nuclear forces, essential nuclear communications sites, command and control sites, nuclear weapons production sites, and early warning facilities (map right). Cities would not be targeted per se, but Seattle, San Francisco, San Diego, Washington, D.C. and Oahu, Hawaii, with high concentrations of nuclear-related facilities virtually disappear even in the "limited" counterforce scenario. This more realistic targeting complex, which does not assume any industrial, economic, or population targets, is as extensive as the FEMA targeting scheme which assumes cities as targets.

portion of the nuclear force leaves certain targets uncovered. A new calculation of the ability of Soviet defenses to shoot down bombers requires compensating changes in their loading and routing. The deployment of a new Trident submarine with 192 individual warheads or a planeload of twelve new air-launched cruise missiles requires not only new targets but changes in the distribution of targets allocated to other forces. Target assignments and instructions change almost daily.

The war plan is based on assumptions about weapons reliability, "penetration" (for bombers), type of target, and timing of attacks. In the

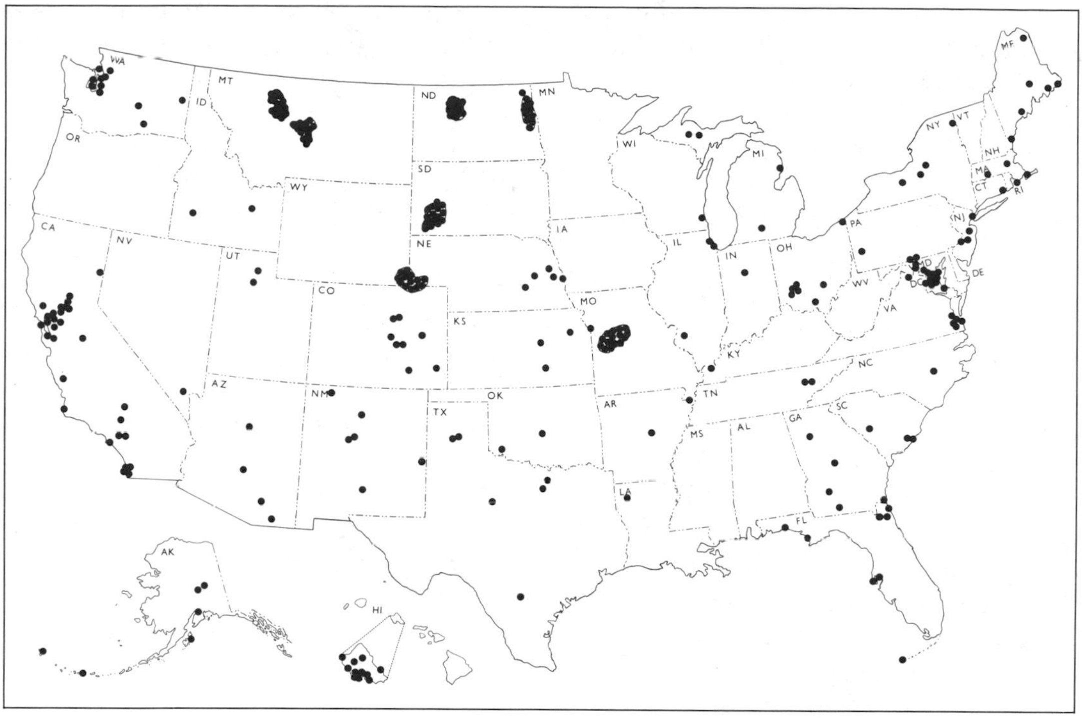

current SIOP, some of the assumptions are:

- The "probability of arrival" to enemy targets for weapons carried on bombers (a calculation of bomber penetration and weapons reliability) is about 77 percent for ALCMs, 72 percent for SRAMs, and 60 percent for bombs;
- Submarine-launched missile warheads would be used in a "defense suppression" attack against Soviet interceptor and air defenses and thus aid bomber penetration;
- The "probability of arrival" for submarine missiles is equal to the 80 percent reliability of the overall system;
- The bombers attack targets no farther than 2,500 kilometers from Soviet borders;
- The first warhead allocated to each "aimpoint" will be detonated reliably at an optimum height of burst, destroying surface structures and killing all people at the target;
- If a second warhead is required to physically destroy hardened targets (no targets currently receive more than two warheads), it will be detonated on the surface;
- ICBM and SLBM targets include ICBM silos and command centers in a combination of air and surface bursts;
- ICBM and bomber weapons are targeted on "other military targets" almost exclusively in airbursts; and
- SLBM and bomber weapons are aimed at economic and industrial targets.

The process of choosing targets starts with the collection of "intelligence." Support for nuclear war planning has become one of the primary responsibilities of the intelligence community. Once a facility of military interest (that is, factory, military barracks, bridge) is identified, intelligence analysts enter it in the Basic Encyclopedia (BE), a massive list compiled by the Defense Intelligence Agency (DIA). From the BE, a more detailed Target Data Inventory (TDI) is compiled, a list produced by the DIA that contains the "identification, location, relative importance and physical vulnerability of installations and complexes that have been evaluated as possessing current or potential target significance."[25] The TDI is further refined into the National Target Base (NTB) compiled by the Joint Strategic Target Planning Staff. The NTB forms the data base to compile the National Strategic Target List (NSTL) from which SIOP targets are drawn. The process of identifying and updating the target lists never ends. Monthly, for instance, DIA produces the Accepted Change List, a new computer tape of updates to the TDI, and the process of refinements to the plans follows.[26]

The war planning process goes far beyond the identification of targets. Targets are put into groups that form the so-called "packages" that would be destroyed under different "options." Planners then analyze targets to see how "hard" they are: how many pounds per square inch (PSI) overpressure they can withstand. There are four primary categories of target hardness: soft (10 psi), semi-hard (100 psi), hard (600 psi), very hard (2,500 psi). A typical brick or concrete structure can withstand only 3 to 5 psi overpressure. Modern ICBM silos are hardened to at least 2,000 psi. The hardness analysis is constantly revised to determine the appropriate "mix" of weapons. According to the Defense Department, "The number of targets which the U.S. must threaten to deny Soviet war aims that are hardened to 200 psi or more is roughly triple the number of similar targets that the USSR must be prepared to destroy or neutralize in order to achieve Soviet war aims against the U.S., NATO Europe and the PRC."[27] Target hardness is one of the major motives to develop new weapons with greater accuracy, better fuzing, and higher explosive yield.

After the planners identify the targets and determine their hardness and proximity, they group the targets into what they call "aimpoints" (or "desired ground zeros"). This accounts for the pairing of targets that could be destroyed by one nuclear explosion with a blast radius of thousands of feet. For instance, in the current plan 1,400 of the most important industrial facilities in the Soviet Union form 900 aimpoints. For the bomber force, planners collect additional data such as the radiation signatures of electric power facilities or other "radar significant" points to determine "Offset Aiming Points" to aid aiming of bomber weapons.

SIOP planners do not consider just fixed targets. As assumptions have changed about how long a nuclear war could last, nuclear targeting plans have changed to take into account the movement of forces, which is a "difficult challenge for the targeteers." As the DOD sees it, "Peacetime installations lose their value, and dispersal locations gain value as the Soviets mobilize and relocate their forces in the crisis period . . . . New targets are created. Target values rise and fall as

Targets in the United States and the Soviet Union

Target Class	*United States*	*Soviet Union*
Strategic Nuclear Forces		
ICBM silos and launch control centers	1,134	1,500
Strategic submarine bases and support facilities	36	130
Bomber airfields (operating and staging bases)	68	80
Medium-range missile bases	16	140
Nuclear weapon storage sites	44	94
Communications and Strategic Defense		
Command Posts	36	50
Key Communications facilities	850	2,240
Ballistic Missile Defense	—	20
Interceptor Aircraft bases	32	67
Fixed strategic SAM sites	—	900
Early warning radars	127	1,200
Conventional Military Forces		
Major complexes	250	250
Airfields	233	420

Sources: William Beecher, "U.S. Drafts New N-War Strategy vs. Soviets," *Boston Globe* (July 27, 1980), p. 1; Defense Communications Agency, National Security Telecommunications Conference Papers, March 16, 1982; HAC, FY 1984 DOD, pt. 8, p. 256; DOD, *Soviet Military Power,* 1982, 1983, 1984; U.S. Air Force, *Soviet Military Power Briefing,* (Feb. 22, 1982); SASC, FY 1981 DOD, pt. 5, p. 2721; General Accounting Office, "Potential Joint Civil and Military Use of Military Airfields," RCED-83-98 (March 1, 1983); JCS, FY 1985, p. 32; U.S. Arms Control and Disarmament Agency, "Effectiveness of Soviet Civil Defense in Limiting Damage to Population," ACDA Civil Defense Study Report No. 1, (declassified) (Nov. 16, 1977).

leadership organizations and military units disperse, mobilize, train, move forward, [or] suffer attrition during conventional operations."[28]

Targeting at the regional level follows the same SIOP process. The Critical Installation List of the Allied Command, Europe, identifies "priority targets" in Eastern Europe and Western Soviet Union: missile bases, nuclear-armed airfields, nuclear storage sites, and command and control installations. Other potential targets include a large number of supporting installations that would be important in combat: munitions and petroleum storage and shipping facilities, "choke points" in the terrain, troop concentrations, staging and assembly areas, rail yards, bridges, and logistic lines of communication such as roads, railroads, and ports.

The Supreme Allied Commander, Europe (SACEUR) annually produces a Nuclear Weapons Requirement Study that contains the 18,000 to 25,000 Eastern European and Soviet targets in the European TDI. Many of the targets are economic and industrial installations that in previous plans were exclusively the targets of strategic forces. As a result of PD-59's instruction to integrate forces, these are now also targets of European nuclear forces.

NATO planners have reportedly identified about 10 percent of the European TDI as "high-priority military targets." Two-thirds of these targets are in Eastern Europe, and one-third are in the Soviet Union. This includes roughly 10 percent of Soviet strategic forces and all SS-4s and SS-20s in the western Soviet Union. Over 70 percent of all targets identified in the western Soviet Union are within range of European-based missiles.

The Table above identifies and categorizes the targets in the United States and Soviet Union that are thought to correspond to actual military installations. According to the DOD, "we see a target structure that is about twice as large as the one the Soviet Union looks at when they look at us."[29] The targets are assigned to the four main types of options identified in the SIOP: Major Attack Options (MAOs), Selected Attack Options (SAOs), Limited Nuclear Options (LNOs), and Regional Nuclear Options (RNOs). The targets are divided into four principal classes: counterforce (nuclear forces), other military targets (OMT), leadership, and economic.

Whereas targeting of counterforce, other military, and leadership targets is fairly straightforward, economic targeting is more complicated. Two methods are used to target economic and industrial activity. The first is to identify individual plants or factories of high enough value to warrant destruction. There are about 2,300 of these industrial "war support" installations, which translate into 1,472 aimpoints (DGZs) in the SIOP.[30] About 200 to 400 of these targets are "key factories."[31] The second method is to identify areas of concentrated economic activity within which individual installations may not be high priority. This second method results in the creation of "E-95 circles" where 95 percent of the industrial war supporting activity in that area lies within a circle of at least 0.5 and no more than 4 miles radius. According to one report there are about 6,700 E-95 circles in the Soviet Union (2,100 aimpoints), excluding the 2,300 individually listed installations.[32]

The DOD has outlined three objectives for economic targeting: to deny the enemy access to war-supporting industry, to destroy a fraction of economic activity, and to impede Soviet economic recovery after a nuclear war. Since industry is highly concentrated in the Soviet Union ("the destruction of twenty blast furnace shops would eliminate 95 percent of pig iron production," for instance) targeting has concentrated on economic "bottlenecks." The underlying assumption is that surgical economic strikes can achieve military objectives that the destruction of military targets did not already achieve. The large size of the Soviet or U.S. economic base, though, makes that assumption absurd. In spite of all the precise identification of targets, today's targeting plans would destroy the same population centers as the "massive retaliation" plans of the 1950s.

U.S. policy since the early 1970s is not to target "population per se." Likewise, according to the JCS, "The Soviets do not target the general population but may target selected elite groups."[33] Like the United States, the Soviets select "those economic targets they consider essential to the U.S./NATO ability to support a war."[34] Population concentrations also have "P-95 circles" where within each circle of at least 0.5 and no more than 4 miles radius there are at least 25,000 people. P-95 circles in the Soviet Union represent about 50 percent

Industrial and Economic Target Classes

Direct War Supporting Industry
  "Key factories"
  Ammunition Factories
  Tank and Armored Personnel Carrier Factories
Production/Manufacturing/Processing Installations
  Energy Production
    Electric Power Generation
      Specialized Equipment for Power Plants
    Petroleum Products Refining
  Metallurgy
    Primary Metals
      Specialized Machinery and Equipment
    Basic Aluminum
    Basic Steel
  Chemicals
  Food Chain
    Food Processing
    Agricultural Machinery
    Fertilizers
  Construction and Other
    Earth Moving and Heavy Construction Equipment
    Cement
    Locomotive and Railroad Cars
    Metal Cutting and Forming Tools
    Ball and Roller Bearings
    Turbines (other than Marine)
    Stationary High Pressure Steam Boilers
    Communications and Electronics Equipment
    Rubber
    Tires and Tubes
    Shipyards
Support Installations
  Energy
    Electric Power Substations
    Pump Stations, Petroleum Product Pipelines
    Storage Areas Petroleum Products
    Compressor Stations for Natural Gas
  Research and Development
  Repair
    Locomotive and Railroad Cars
    Commercial Ships
  Computing and Data Processing Centers
Selected Transportation Facilities
  Railroads
    Classification Yards
    Transloading Facilities
  Other
    Waterborne Trade (ports)
    Locks (Inland Waterways)
Communications Facilities

of the population. Soviet (and U.S.) cities are targeted because the specific targets (counterforce, other military, leadership, and economic) are located in population centers. In fact, in each of the 200 largest Soviet cities, an average of 19.1 warheads with 6.33 equivalent megatons (EMT) would be exploded. A 1978 ACDA report on civil defense stated: "Keep in mind that cities per se were not targeted; these cities were attacked because they contained the military and industrial facilities that were targeted."[35]

Regional Nuclear Plans

The SIOP is reproduced in miniature in four U.S. commands that have responsibility for "theater" nuclear war planning: European, Atlantic, Pacific, and Central (for the Persian Gulf region). Each of the commands considers the capabilities of nuclear forces, targets, and options just as the authors of the SIOP consider them. The only difference is that the four field commands prepare for two types of nuclear war: an orchestrated "preplanned" war directed against specific targets and a fluid battlefield war (on land or at sea) where the use of nuclear weapons would be "adaptively planned."

The most information available about regional nuclear war planning concerns Europe, for which planning is an integrated activity of the fourteen nations that belong to the NATO Nuclear Planning Group. European nuclear planning is shared between the U.S. European Command, headquartered at Stuttgart-Vaihingen, and the NATO International Military Staff, and in turn by three NATO nuclear commands: Allied Command Europe (ACE), in Casteau-Mons, Belgium, Allied Command Atlantic (ACLANT), in Norfolk, Virginia, and Allied Command Channel (ACCHAN), in Northwood, England.[36] Together they produce NATO's equivalent of the SIOP: the Nuclear Operations Plan (NOP), officially known as SACEUR SUPPLAN 10001A (Supreme Allied Commander Europe Supplementary Plan).

The NOP derives from a NATO Military Committee statement of January 16, 1968, entitled "Overall Strategic Concept for the Defense of the NATO Area" and known as MC (Military Committee) 14/3.[37] This document established the "flexible response" doctrine, designed to "respond appropriately to any level of potential attack and . . . pose the risk of escalation to higher levels of conflict."[38] If deterrence "fails," MC 14/3 calls for three successive responses open to the Alliance.

The first is "direct defense": defeating the enemy "on the level at which he chooses to fight," including the use of nuclear weapons "as may be authorized either on a pre-planned or case-by-case basis."[39] Since Soviet doctrine for war in Europe prominently includes the use of nuclear weapons, even the basic "direct defense" plan anticipates nuclear warfare. "We do not rule out the use of nuclear weapons by the United States and its allies if that should prove necessary to contain or repel a major conventional attack by the Warsaw Pact," Secretary of Defense Schlesinger stated in 1975.[40] NATO plans include "first use," according to a 1976 DOD report, "in response to attacks by nuclear powers or states assisted by them in the face of a major failure of the conventional defense due to enemy use of conventional forces more effective than expected."[41]

If "direct defense" fails, the next response is "deliberate escalation," a process of intentionally raising "but where possible controlling" the intensity and scope of combat to make the threat of nuclear response "progressively more imminent."[42] According to the Joint Chiefs of Staff statement for 1975, "the doctrine of flexible response provides for a carefully controlled, deliberate raising of the scope and intensity of combat to a level where the costs and risks of continuation become disproportionate to the aggressor's objectives."[43] The targeting objectives of such escalation would be "to induce the enemy to limit the scope of his aggression, to yield allied territory, to act to avoid an extended war of attrition, or to make the political decision to restore peace short of all-out destruction."[44]

Should deliberate escalation fail to stop the war, the third alternative, all-out destruction, is called "general nuclear response." General nuclear response is defined in a U.S. Senate report as "massive nuclear strikes against the total nuclear threat, other military targets and urban industrial targets."[45] Initiation of the general nuclear response in Europe would occur in conjunction with implementation of the SIOP. NATO and JSTPS planners have "deconflicted" targets within range of nuclear weapons in Europe to ensure that these attacks would complement one another and that two weapons will not be aimed at the same targets.

This "strategic" role of nuclear forces in Europe continues to grow with changes in strategic policy. The U.S. Defense Department's Defense Guidance for 1985–89 calls for greater integration of plans for theater and strategic weapons, to eliminate "any arbitrary division between categories of nuclear weapons systems."[46] Weapons "capable of executing non-strategic nuclear options may be tasked for strategic missions" the Guidance states. The Guidance also directs the Air Force to investigate new ways for its strategic bombers to augment nuclear forces in Europe.

Allied Command Europe, responsible for the majority of the nuclear weapons in Europe, has implemented MC 14/3 with another document entitled "Concepts for the Role of Theater Nuclear Strike Forces in ACE." This guidance document identifies two distinct goals: "selective use" and "general nuclear response." Selective use covers every scenario from the first use of nuclear weapons, including a single "demonstration" attack, to a widespread European "theater nuclear campaign" involving hundreds of weapons. A variety of nuclear weapons in Europe are kept on alert like strategic forces, under the "priority strike program," to destroy the most important Warsaw Pact installations at a moment's notice.

NATO war planners believe that any Soviet attack will include the use of nuclear weapons. "Current doctrine and training indicate a readiness . . . for conducting a war in Europe with theater-wide, large scale nuclear strikes," according to one secret DOD report. The high alert posture of NATO forces provides a threat of nuclear escalation that NATO planners believe could convince Soviet planners to restrain their use of nuclear weapons. The same posture, however, and the existence of plans to use nuclear weapons at lower levels, probably have convinced Soviet war planners that it is not worth the risk of letting NATO use nuclear weapons. A Soviet attack in Europe would therefore have to include nuclear strikes.

The nuclear infrastructure in central Europe (discussed in Chapter 6) is so huge that only massive strikes against it could be effective. A Brookings Institution study of Soviet nuclear forces interprets Soviet intentions differently: "The USSR's plans for the wartime occupation of Europe suggest that its nuclear strikes would be discriminate in their targeting."[47] But the density of nuclear units in West Germany means that even discriminate attacks would have to be massive.[48] The JCS have stated that "Operational-tactical [forces] (missiles and aircraft) target enemy military forces in the forward areas. Yields are matched to targets in order to ensure the required damage to the target proper."[49]

In U.S. war plans, "battlefield" nuclear weapons are distinct from "theater" nuclear systems. Although DOD documents state that battlefield operations could include "selective employment of nuclear weapons against armored thrusts,"[50] precise plans do not exist for such use. The escalation to nuclear warfare, however, would probably begin at the battlefield level, as nuclear artillery, short-range missiles, mines, and close support aircraft destroyed mobile military formations, their supporting command centers, and support bases. Since the circumstances that would determine use of battlefield nuclear weapons depend on a certain type of attack and the state of defenses, those who write the plans for using battlefield nuclear weapons spend most of their time speculating about and quantifying the effects of small nuclear explosions on different kinds of targets: a Soviet tank division in a breakthrough formation, a FROG rocket battalion at a typical launch site, a division command post. From these guidelines, commanders in an actual war will create target "packages" at the division level to achieve tactical goals with a specific number of weapons in a specific time frame.[51] When officers on the battlefield felt the tactical situation required the use of nuclear weapons, they would send requests for release up the chain of command to the NCA.

As contingent and undefined as nuclear planning is in Europe, it is even more vague in other theaters. Even though Pacific, Central (Middle East), and Atlantic Command planners identify targets suitable for nuclear attack, their "contingencies" are so sketchy that nuclear planning entails little more than target selection. The Pacific Command is responsible for planning nuclear strikes against North Korea, China, and the Soviet Far East. The Atlantic Command is responsible for Cuba, the Caribbean, and West Africa. Each command has aircraft carriers and land-based aircraft that would become the primary platforms for launching nuclear strikes. Strategic bombers would also contribute to theater war: a special Contingency Command Operational Priority Requirements List (COPRL) identifies non-SIOP bomber targets (see Chapters 7 and 8 for further discussion of nuclear contingencies in these theaters).

Conclusions

Nuclear planning has become so immersed in the process of worst-case analysis and targeting that it has lost touch with the reality of the effects of nuclear war or the objectives it is supposed to achieve. As the appendices show, large numbers of targets are intermingled with urban areas and overlap so much in function that limited nuclear warfare is at best an exercise in self-deception. Demands for new weapons derive from the target system in terms of levels of hardness or requirements to minimize "collateral damage." The war plans, which require ever greater flexibility and endurance, create a demand for new weapons with better retargeting capacities and survivability. The "fire control" computers of each strategic submarine contain the targets of every other submarine. According to the Navy, "For ad-hoc coverage, the data required can be as little as latitude, longitude, and altitude of the individual installations, if they are not already in the computer memory."[52]

Nuclear Wargames

AEM—Arsenal Exchange Model: "four types of scenarios: one-strike against military and value target; a two-strike game, and two types of three-strike games with suboptimization problems of selecting a weapons reserve or selecting a value target reserve for the initiator's third strike."

AMM—Strat Missiler: "analysis of total strategic ballistic missile attacks . . . model limitations . . . 5,000 mobile base aimpoints . . . 10,000 mobile launch locations, 15,000 population circles, 50,000 installations, 6,000 rural cells."

CIVIC III: "estimates civilian fatalities and casualties resulting from the prompt and fallout environments of a nuclear weapons laydown."

DACOMP—Damage Assessment Computer Program: "damage assessment exercise involving an attack of 1,261 nuclear weapons against 3,615 population resource points in the United States."

Force Mix Model: "to calculate an optimum mix of U.S. strategic forces . . . collateral damage to population when targeting military targets, is not accounted for."

HARLOT: "Height of Burst; Altitude of Targets; Resources; Location; Objectives; and Time"

MEM—Multiple Engagement Module: "general war model"

OASIS: Operation Analysis Strategic Interaction Simulator: "computer program for simulating the effects of strategic nuclear and non-nuclear engagements"

Source: Organization of the Joint Chiefs of Staff, Studies, Analysis, and Gaming Agency, *Catalog of Wargaming and Military Simulation Models,* 9th ed. SAGA Manual 120-82 (May 1982)

All of this added flexibility and targeting can hardly be shown to have enhanced deterrence, which depends on defensive responses. The plans themselves do not stand up to close scrutiny of their own objectives. "[E]mphasizing flexibility in strategic targeting is costly and complex," one study by a military targeting specialist noted. "Smaller and more numerous attack options degrade the synergism of the triad, weaken the integrity of the remaining force structure, and lower the confidence associated with the large number of sorties involved in major attack options."[53]

One of the reasons that the process continues, as the data get more refined and the assumptions come to look more like facts, is the use of computer simulations in the planning process. The system long ago became too complex to be handled by human beings. The SIOP is constantly evaluated in computer war games, where it is pitted against the JCS's best interpretation of the Soviet war plan, which it calls the RISOP or Red Integrated Strategic Operational Plan. The Table above discusses some of the simulations the DOD uses to measure nuclear force effectiveness.

Modifications of U.S. war plans are always justified on the basis of new interpretations of the proclivities of the Soviet war planner. Two methods are used. One is to analyze statements and intelligence about Soviet doctrine and strategy. The other is to examine the nuclear force structure. A balanced view of the two might provide some insight when mixed with political and historical understanding of Soviet intentions. The reason that political leaders have reserved exclusive authority over nuclear weapons is that they alone have the breadth of information to consider the questions and implications that nuclear weapons raise. Nuclear war planning, however, is so isolated and self-contained that it cannot serve that broad purpose. Worst-case scenarios, "windows of vulnerability," and endless "contingencies" determine nuclear decisions: It is all hypothetical. The absurdity of staking the survival of the world on a game so removed from reality becomes even more clear in the following statement of General John Vessey, Chairman of the Joint Chiefs of Staff, submitted for the record of a 1983 Senate hearing. He revealed not only that the particulars but the fundamental premise of U.S. war planning is unreal:

> A war between the USSR/Pact and the U.S./NATO would be the third and decisive conflict between Soviet "socialism" and Western "imperialism" to determine which social system will inherit the Earth. Such a war will be an intercontinental, coalition war involving all of the "basic" states. Such a war would be "just" war for the USSR but "unjust" for the West. Like previous wars, a nuclear war would be the continuation of politics by violent means. The use of nuclear weapons by the USSR would be "just," but because a world nuclear war would be so destructive the USSR could not logically rationalize initiating one. The Soviets, therefore, reject any unprovoked surprise attack ("out-of-the-blue") on the "imperialists."[54]

6

Europe

"BY VIRTUALLY EVERY yardstick you care to use," a U.S. Army official told Congress in 1983, "Germany probably has the greatest imposed defense burden of any nation."[1] With 62 million people, it is equal in population to the United States west of the Mississippi. Yet it is no larger than the state of Oregon. Stationed on West German soil are more than 725,000 foreign soldiers (including their family members) and 495,000 West German military personnel. If the United States had the same proportion, it would have a standing military of about 3.4 million, or five times what it currently has stationed in the fifty states.

There are over 4,000 individual military facilities in West Germany (Oregon, by comparison, has thirty-four) and the U.S. military maintains well over 1,000 of these. In this densely populated and highly developed country, NATO military forces have free rights to maneuver on both public and private land. The United States conducts about 5,000 military exercises a year at 226 training areas. Eighty of these are considered "major" maneuvers.

Germany's highways, railroads, airports, utilities, and communications are built to maximize their wartime usefulness. Highways are designed to serve as alternate landing strips for military aircraft.[2] About ninety civilian and military airports are earmarked for

U.S. Nuclear Weapons in Europe

Nuclear Weapon (Warhead)	*Number of Warheads* *U.S. use*	*non-U.S. use*	*Total*	*Allied Users*
Bombs (B-61, B-57, B-43, B-28)	1,416	324	1,740	Belgium, Greece, Italy, Netherlands, Turkey, West Germany
Depth Bombs (B-57)	129	63	192	Italy, Netherlands, United Kingdom
Long-range Missiles				
Pershing II (W-85)	54	—	54	
GLCM (W-84)	100	—	100	
Short-range Missiles				
Pershing 1a (W-50)	120	100	220	West Germany
Lance (W-70)	324	368	690	Belgium, Greece, Italy, Netherlands, West Germany, United Kingdom
Honest John (W-31)	—	198	198	Greece, Turkey
Artillery				
8-inch (W-33)	506	432	938	Belgium, Greece, Italy, Netherlands, Turkey, West Germany, United Kingdom
155mm (W-48)	594	138	732	Belgium, Greece, Italy, Netherlands, Turkey, West Germany, United Kingdom
Nike Hercules (W-31)	296	390	686	Belgium, Greece, Italy, Netherlands, West Germany
ADMs (W-45, W-54)	372	unk	372	Belgium, Netherlands, West Germany, United Kingdom
TOTALS	3,911	2,013	5,922	

military cargo and troops.[3] Bridges, highways, and rail tunnels are built with demolition chambers, ready for destruction in the face of advancing enemy forces. Even the rivers and canals, which are primary commercial thoroughfares, are periodically closed for military exercises.

West Germany is the military center of Europe, the most heavily armed and densely nuclearized region in the world. The most discussed war scenario is for war in Europe. Over 2,700 NATO and 3,500 Soviet nuclear delivery vehicles and 9,000 warheads are deployed in Europe or facing Europe. Additional weapons in the Soviet Union and the United States are ready to "reinforce" the theater. In the surrounding seas, naval forces have still more warheads, bringing the region's total to about 17,000 or one-third of the world's arsenals.

Hundreds of military units and locations make up the peacetime nuclear infrastructure. Nuclear warheads are stationed in eleven European countries and span the full range of types: long-range "strategic" missiles and bombers for European contingencies, tactical aircraft and bombs, short- and medium-range ballistic missiles, artillery, surface-to-air missiles, and land mines (The Table above provides a breakdown of U.S. nuclear weapons in Europe). Almost all of the weapons are "dual capable"; that is, they can deliver either nuclear or conventional (and in some cases chemical) warheads.

Preparations for warfare by the two superpower military alliances are more extensive in Europe than anywhere else, although conventional wisdom holds that war is least likely to erupt there. Europe's geography is an important reason why the Soviets would want to avoid war. Small, densely populated, and heavily industrialized, it is a valuable prize intact, and any war would destroy it. The nuclear infrastructure in Europe is so extensive that even the most limited nuclear exchanges would involve hundreds of targets. As many as 1,000 of these potential targets are located in West Germany and East Germany alone.[4]

Nuclear weapons are so highly integrated into each bloc's structures that any conflict would turn into a nuclear war. With the density of military forces and the level of conventional firepower this high, it is difficult to imagine any type of invasion or defense that would not resort to nuclear weapons. The farther west the Warsaw Pact penetrates, the worse transportation, logistics, and communications systems become; this alone makes the theory of sustained conventional attack untenable. Inevitable breakdowns in communications and command systems would unleash uncontrolled and uncontrollable fighting. Nuclear weapons would have to be used to accomplish either offensive or defensive objectives. Many bases have air defenses and hardened shelters to protect equipment from conventional attack; only nuclear weapons can assure their destruction. Nuclear systems are designed to evade destruction by moving out into "the field" where they are harder to detect and destroy with conventional weapons.

Since most military planners do not believe that the Soviet Union desires to invade and take over all of Europe, they promote scenarios of limited Soviet attacks to disrupt NATO before its nuclear weapons could be dispersed or before authority to use them could be obtained through political channels. The current theory is that a Soviet attack against NATO would begin without use of nuclear weapons in the pursuit of these limited tactical objectives. Europe's nuclear infrastructure, however, lends meager credibility to these canned scenarios.

Nuclear Infrastructure in Europe

The deadly seriousness with which military analysts dissect NATO and Warsaw Pact capabilities creates the illusion, as with geography, of scientific certainty about "deterrence" and "defense." As Paul Bracken has written, "The . . . problem in examining NATO defense is that it involves so many bizarre issues, especially when tactical nuclear weapons are brought into the picture, that any analysis of the problem in peacetime takes on an aura of either sterility or surrealism."[5]

The majority of U.S. nuclear weapons in Europe are short-range and in-

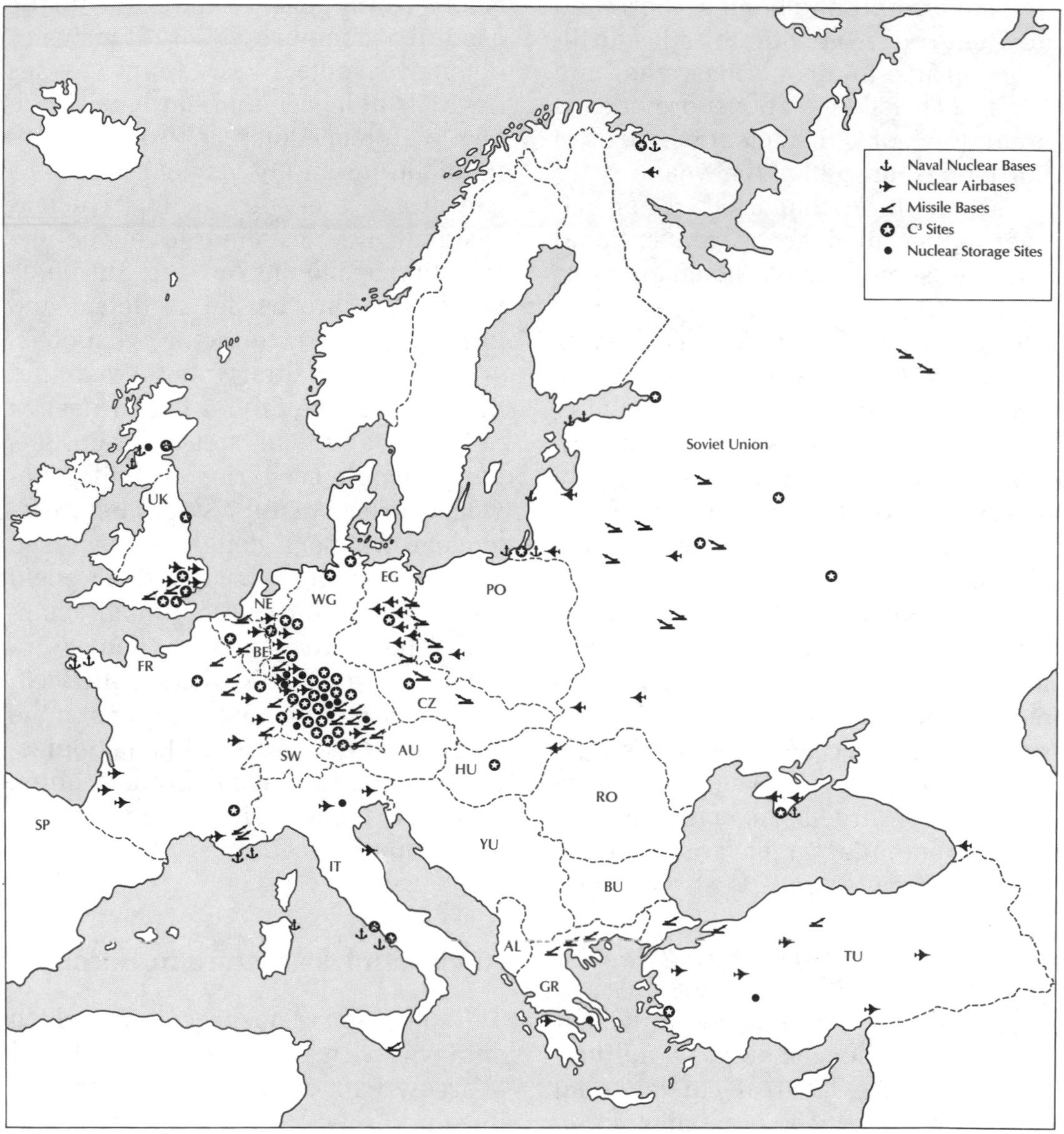

NUCLEAR EUROPE

The largest concentration of nuclear weapons in the world is in central Europe. Long-range missiles and aircraft around the periphery of the continent supplement the shorter range weapons in the central region. Since 1980 new long-range nuclear weapons have been introduced into seven European countries and Soviet nuclear warheads have been "forward deployed" in four Eastern European nations. Only "theater" forces are depicted here, not "strategic" or battlefield weapons.

tended for battlefield roles. They are concentrated in Central Europe and particularly in West Germany. The rest of the nuclear warheads are long-range, for preplanned strikes against fixed targets. Many of these are on Combat Alert Status (also known as "quick reaction alert"), able to fire within fifteen minutes. These include ground-launched cruise missiles, Pershing II, F-111, F-4, and Tornado aircraft, and shorter range aircraft in Turkey, all of which have the range to reach targets within the Soviet Union.

The largest concentration of NATO nuclear weapons is in West Germany (see Figure). Six foreign nations have military forces there with about 3,400 nuclear warheads. Dozens of nuclear storage sites, from the Danish to the Swiss border, serve military units throughout the country.

There are more short-range nuclear artillery weapons in West Germany than any other nuclear weapon (over 100 nuclear-capable artillery units and 1,500 warheads). Second in number are surface-to-surface missiles such as Lance and Pershing. There are 78 NATO Lance launchers and 600 warheads in Germany, 126 Pershing 1a launchers (72 West German and 54 U.S.), and 54 U.S. Pershing IIs. The Pershing II will replace all the U.S. Pershing 1as by about early 1986. Five types of aircraft at eight air bases in West Germany also have nuclear missions. These include U.S. and West German units (with U.S. nuclear warheads) and British units. There are approximately 500 nuclear bombs for these aircraft. Other nuclear systems include Nike-Hercules surface-to-air missiles, with some 300 nuclear warheads, and about 250 atomic demolition munitions (ADMs) (nuclear land mines).

Soviet nuclear forces in Eastern Europe are now essentially equivalent in size and strength to those of NATO. They are reported to have some 4,000 nuclear warheads, with delivery systems from artillery to long-range missiles and aircraft. The recent deployment of the 560 mile-range SS-22 missile and long-range Fencer aircraft (both with nuclear warheads) in East Germany represents a significant departure from previous Soviet practice: Never before had the Soviet Union permanently put nuclear weapons outside its borders. Fencers and nuclear bombs have also been deployed in Poland, Hungary, and Czechoslovakia. New SS-21 missiles have been delivered to Soviet units in East Germany and Czechoslovakia, and 152mm nuclear artillery guns have been sent to Soviet forces in East Germany. Some thirty nuclear storage facilities are now reported in Eastern Europe.[6]

The nuclear forces of NATO and the Warsaw Pact are not structured to serve their stated military purpose. The nuclear infrastructures can be explained only in terms of internal bureaucratic or security concerns. U.S., Soviet, and NATO military forces still occupy the facilities they took over from the Nazis. They continue to follow the structures of conventional, World War II models. The occupying powers deploy nuclear weapons in response to political concerns or internal bargaining processes that have little regard for military functions or necessity. None of this is to suggest that either side has structural advantages or that there is a need to tinker with the nuclear forces to improve deterrence.

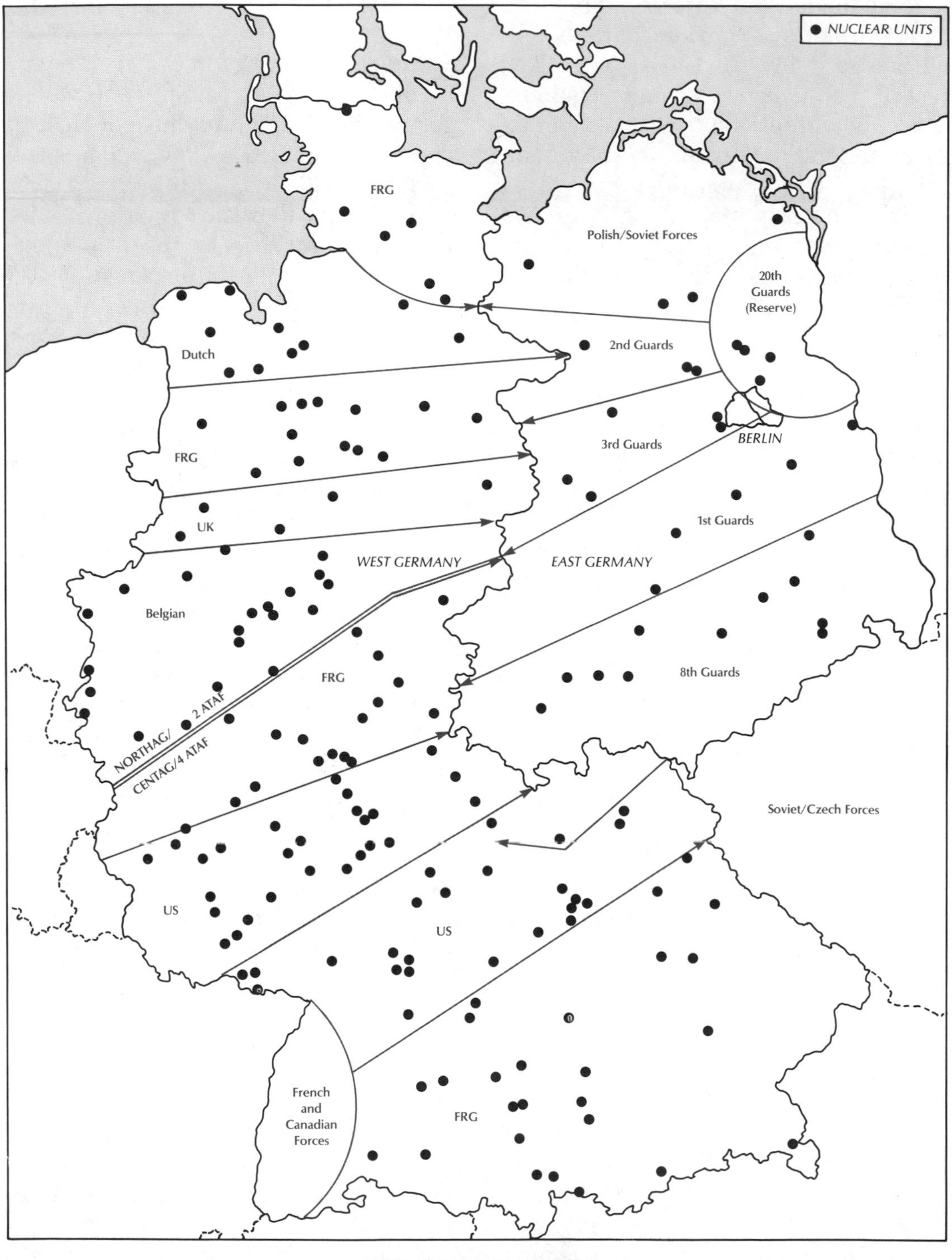

THE CENTRAL FRONT

Nowhere on earth are nuclear weapons so numerous and so densely deployed as in East and West Germany. Nearly 150 primary NATO nuclear units and more than 30 primary Warsaw Pact nuclear units have over 4,000 warheads allocated to them for missiles, aircraft bombs, artillery shells, and atomic land mines. Any war here could quickly become a nuclear war.

The nuclear infrastructure is a combination of bureaucratic inertia, national selfishness, and confusion.

The Soviets concentrate their military forces in as few installations as possible. While the Warsaw Pact has many training areas and radar and communications sites, it has far fewer bases for its major combat units. In the Soviet Army, one division will quite often be housed in a single installation. NATO, on the other hand, disperses its military units, technical sites, and logistic facilities. One NATO division often spreads over a dozen facilities many miles apart.

The Soviets have nuclear warheads concentrated at a small number of specially guarded, central storage sites and airbases. NATO, again, disperses nuclear weapons widely. The reason for the difference lies, partly, in the unique NATO practice of sharing U.S. nuclear weapons with allies and maintaining some nuclear weapons on permanent alert. The Soviets concentrate their deployments because of their ability to call on nuclear forces stationed in the Soviet Union for a war in Europe, their extreme security and secrecy requirements, their lack of nuclear units on day-to-day alert, and their consequent lack of formal allocation of nuclear weapons to Soviet combat units.

These basing practices influence the way war will be fought in Europe. Most Soviet nuclear forces targeted at Europe are in the Soviet Union. This partially determines the type of retaliatory strikes open to NATO and the prospect for escalation. Both alliances will try to disperse their nuclear systems during a crisis. Three Pershing battalions (108 launchers), for instance, will move to thirty-six separate firing sites. According to Colonel William Fiorentino, then Pershing program manager, the missiles would be "hidden in forests and various other locations—villages for example."[7] Anywhere there is "six feet of clear sky," the Army says, it can hide and fire a Pershing missile.[8]

Nuclear weapons in Europe are under the strict control of the United States, the Soviet Union, France, or Britain. They support national forces at the expense of their allies. In West Germany, for instance, the United States deploys approximately 2,250 nuclear warheads for its own use in the U.S. sector of responsibility (see Figure) and deploys only 1,500 warheads in the much larger Belgian, British, Dutch, and West German sectors. Soviet forces in eastern Europe are uniformly deployed throughout each country of occupation. Unlike the United States, however, the Soviet Union does not share nuclear responsibilities with any of its allies.

Almost one-third of NATO's nuclear warheads are artillery projectiles. But of the 1,600 artillery shells, 1,100 are for U.S. use and 500 are for non-U.S. use. The 1,100 U.S. shells are for 570 "certified" guns. The 500 NATO shells are for 700 "certified" guns. Virtually all U.S. artillery units in Europe (about thirty-five battalions and six independent batteries) are nuclear-certified. By contrast, only a few of the units of the other NATO countries are nuclear-certified. These non-U.S. units cover a much larger area of territory than the U.S. sector in central West Germany and include NATO forces in Italy, Greece, and Turkey.

In light of these features of the nu-

Photo courtesy of IKV, reprinted by permission.

U.S. nuclear warheads are stored at over 150 special facilities scattered around the world. Protected "igloos," partially underground like this one in Europe, each store from 10 to 25 warheads. Nuclear storage sites are surrounded by double fences, and have special lighting, security sensors, and guard towers.

clear infrastructure, the justification for nuclear modernization seems confused. The Army claims, for instance, that "because the number of 8-inch howitzers that NATO Allies possess is so small, the targeting problems for the Soviets are much simplified in [the non-U.S.] sectors of the battlefield."[9] Therefore, the Army argues, NATO should procure new 155mm artillery shells and distribute them to allies. But since a 155mm shell can be fired as far as an 8-inch shell, and there are more 155mm guns than 8-inch guns, the question should be why hasn't NATO already distributed more of its existing 155mm nuclear shells to allied sectors? And what type of Soviet targeting is the Army talking about? In a small area of northern Germany and the Netherlands, there are 112 non-U.S. 8-inch nuclear-certified guns, supported by a dozen nuclear storage sites. But these are not the only nuclear systems in these allied sectors. They are supplemented by nuclear air bases, nuclear-armed 155mm artillery, and Lance and Pershing missiles.

Soviet targeting of 8-inch artillery would be relevant only as part of a total attack on NATO's nuclear infrastructure. This includes well over 200 locations in central Europe alone. The Soviet Union, of course, has a sufficient number of nuclear warheads to strike every one of these 200 targets. That very fact raises serious questions about any of the limited strike scenarios that posit attacks against only one category of weapons bases.

The U.S. military claims it will increase its military capability if it deploys new 155mm nuclear shells in Europe. Unlike some new nuclear weapons with a smaller explosive yield, these nuclear shells have three times the yield of the shells they would replace. This increased yield seems to contradict the concern to limit "collateral damage." The huge number of weapons already in West Germany raises serious doubts whether NATO nuclear planners consider collateral damage at all.

These issues—unexplainable locations, piecemeal analysis, and inconsistent justifications—plague the rest of the European nuclear system as well. Consider nuclear bombs. The United States stores over 1,700 nuclear bombs in Europe, of which 1,400 are allocated to U.S. aircraft, and only 300 to NATO aircraft. Although most NATO nuclear aircraft could be nuclear-certified, it appears that planners find it both more convenient and prudent to keep nuclear weapons on U.S. bases and under U.S. control. If NATO approval to use nuclear weapons became politically difficult or impossible to obtain, U.S. planes and bombs could be released unilaterally. U.S. control is also crucial in some scenarios that go beyond the scope of NATO's treaty limits and plans: a strategic attack on the Soviet Union or in the Middle East or Africa.

Nuclear politics in NATO frequently lead to deployments that make neither military nor political sense. The Honest John rocket, for instance, has been withdrawn and replaced by Lance missiles in every NATO army except those of Greece and Turkey. These countries were unable to afford the Lance missile, and it is now no longer in production. Thus Greece and Turkey are saddled with a weapon that one DOD official calls "essentially unusable."[10] Why haven't the 200 nuclear warheads for the Honest Johns been withdrawn? According to one military official, "to further reduce their number without compensating modernization would diminish the valuable . . . political commitment they represent for those nations."[11] In other words it has less to do with "deterrence" and more to do with managing the alliance.

Reload missiles for the Pershing system exemplify disingenuous government behavior. Prior to deployment of the Pershing II in December 1983, 180 Pershing 1a launchers were deployed in U.S. and West German units with some 300 nuclear warheads. Plans called for reloading the Pershing launcher after initial firing. This reload capability, however, was never publicly announced or officially acknowledged. The number of Pershing II replacements, therefore, was widely assumed to be exactly 108 until it was revealed in October 1982 that Army plans included reloads. This revelation caused a furor in West Germany that forced the United States to pledge to change its reload plans.[12] Nonetheless, Army training of Pershing II crews continues to include practice reloading.[13]

The U.S./NATO analysis of Soviet nuclear weapons improvements in Eastern Europe typified official incoherence. In late 1981 it became clear that the Soviets were deploying nuclear weapons in Eastern Europe.[14] This began with deployment of Fencer aircraft to Poland and East Germany (with nuclear bombs) and the replacement of old Soviet short-range missiles (with SS-21s, SS-22s, and SS-23s). The debate in Europe about deployment of cruise and Pershing II missiles caused the Pentagon to downplay these Soviet nuclear force improvements. Secretary of Defense Caspar Weinberger, visiting Europe in May 1983, stated that Soviet deployment of nuclear warheads in Eastern Europe was "common knowledge in the United States" and gave the impression it was no big deal. In fact, it was an unprecedented breach of Soviet practice. For years the Soviets benefitted in the propaganda war in Europe by stating they had no permanent deployments of nuclear weapons—"targets"—on their allies' soil. The Pentagon could not admit that its deployment caused a Soviet counterdeployment, a development that makes confrontation and escalation more likely.

One noteworthy case of poor logic is the argument for increasing conventional capabilities so as to raise the nuclear "threshold" in Europe. If NATO's theoretical nuclear threshold were to rise because of additional conventional strength, the Warsaw Pact's nuclear threshold would be lowered because its conventional options would become less viable. This point about lowering the Warsaw Pact nuclear threshold is often dismissed by the claim that increased NATO conventional strength would help to deter a Soviet attack, and thus make use of nuclear weapons moot. Why should this point be accepted? The probability that the Soviets would attack NATO with or without provocation depends on such intangibles as Soviet "interests," "intentions," will, and the like. The question of whether they would risk all-out nuclear war for whatever gains might accrue from an invasion of Western Europe raises fundamental issues that the Pentagon never tackles.

Instead, the debate is limited to technical and tactical points. Like strategic war planning, the game has become more important than the war. Lost in all the "balances" and scenarios are not only the questions about whether the Soviets would ever attack but a host of other considerations for the Kremlin: NATO's superior economic mobilization base, NATO's larger population, the dubious reliability of Warsaw Pact allies, and the role of the Chinese. All of these factors would influence a Soviet decision to attack NATO and, if war broke out, compel the Soviets to use nuclear weapons to win the war quickly.

Less prominent than West Germany and the central front but very important are Europe's so-called flanks, southern and northern; the former providing a link to the Middle East and the

Third World, the latter a link in the continuum from peace to strategic nuclear war. The U.S. Defense Guidance for 1984-1988 states that "In recognition of the weaker in-place defense on the northern and southern regions . . . [the U.S. military should] place more emphasis and provide more visibility to NATO offensive exercises in the northern and southern regions." It states that "emphasis will be given to offensive moves against Warsaw Pact flanks" and that "this role should include both nuclear and conventional weapons." This strategy has come to be known as "horizontal escalation." The offensive strategy on the flanks, in the words of Admiral James Watkins, Chief of Naval Operations, is "to diffuse enemy strength and shift the battlefield from allied to enemy territory . . . . NATO faces the Soviet homeland across a single border on the flanks and can carry the war directly to the Soviets."[15]

Southern Europe

The southern "flank" of Europe provides NATO's nuclear link to the Middle East and the Third World. The new military strategy of horizontal escalation is increasing the importance of this link. NATO war plans are focusing more and more on areas to the south—North Africa, the Middle East, and beyond—moving farther and farther away from NATO's traditional battlefields.

Italy, far from the NATO central region, and not bordering Warsaw Pact territory, is the hub of NATO southern operations. Most of the nuclear weapons in Italy are, ironically, concentrated in Italy's northeast where their presence is unnecessary and their usefulness is highly questionable (see Figure). But as the center of NATO's southern flank, Italy's importance as a naval base and headquarters for coordinating NATO military operations in Greece, Turkey, and the Mediterranean is tremendous.

The Soviet naval presence in the Mediterranean consists of about forty-five ships: ten to twelve surface warships, seven to eight attack submarines, and two cruise missile submarines. According to a U.S. briefing, "The numbers of Soviet ships have not increased [as] dramatically in the Medditerranean as they have worldwide."[16] In addition, the Soviet Union has no permanent naval bases in Mediterranean countries; its ships spend most of their time at sea anchorages: near the Spanish island of Alboran; near the Greek island of Kithira; in the Gulf of Sollum; and in the Gulf of Hamamet between Tunisia and Sicily. The Strait of Gibraltar at the entrance to the Mediterranean severely restricts Soviet access to the sea. Turkey controls the straits from the Black Sea into the Mediterranean under the terms of the Montreux Convention. Consequently, the Soviets do not operate strategic missile submarines in either the Mediterranean or Black Seas.[17] The majority of Soviet naval forces are concentrated in the eastern Mediterranean helping focus NATO's attention toward long-range southward operations.

As the Mediterranean naval hub, Italy provides the best location from which to dominate ASW and other naval operations. The U.S. Sixth Fleet consists of at least one and sometimes

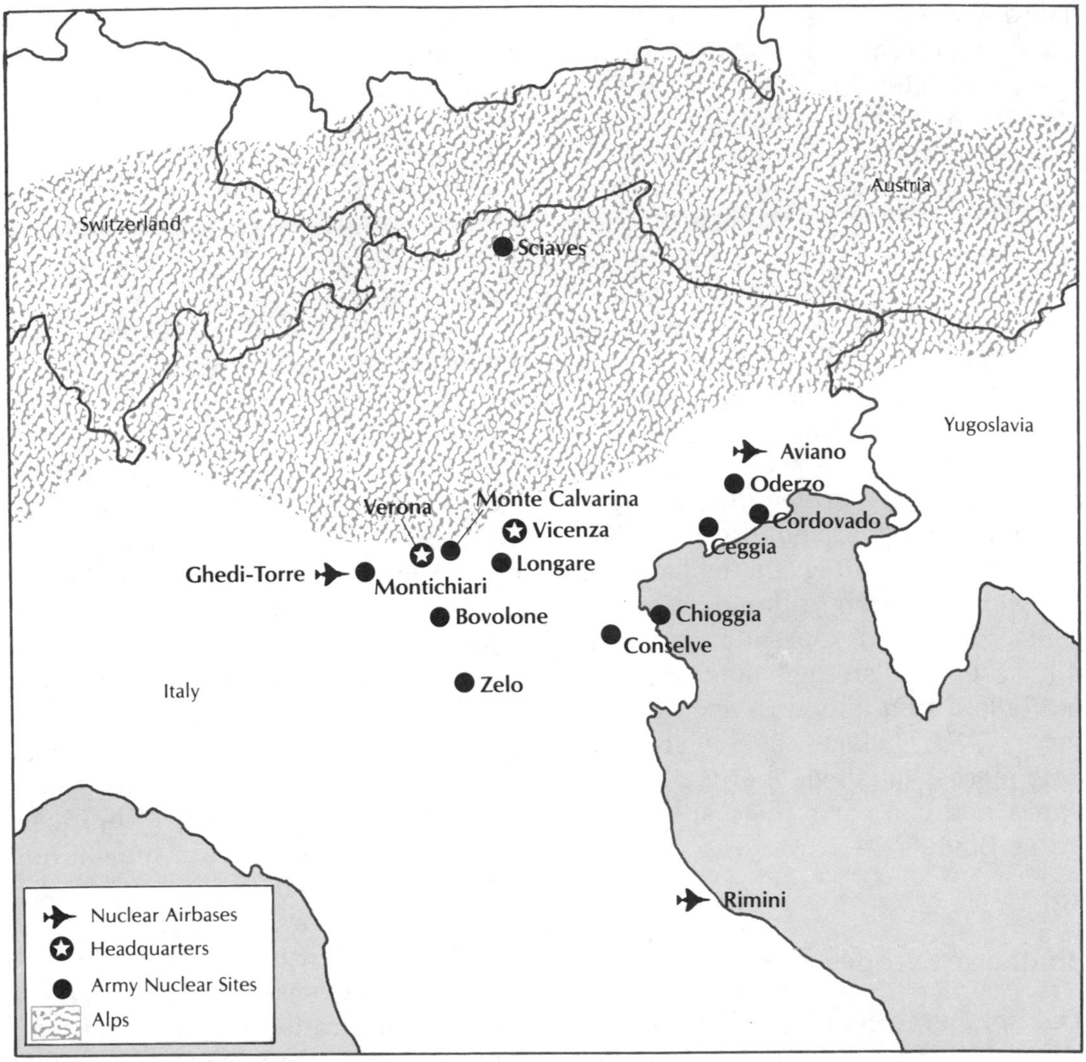

NORTHERN ITALY'S NUCLEAR WEAPONS

Thirty-five miles from the Yugoslav border is Aviano, a U.S. airbase and nuclear storage site. This southern flank base, which contains some 200 nuclear bombs, serves as the "staging base" for part of NATO's nuclear strike force, nuclear-certified F-16s on "quick reaction alert" (QRA). Aviano is also the center of the U.S. Air Force's nuclear operations in the Mediterranean (partly because the Spanish government does not allow the deployment of nuclear weapons on its soil). Two Italian Air Force bases, Ghedi-Torre and Rimini, each house about 25 U.S. nuclear bombs and, to carry them, NATO's Tornado and F-104 strike aircraft with the range to strike into the Soviet Union.

NATO planners believe that the ground threat to Italy lies primarily along the Yugoslavian border. There, in an area of about 50 kilometers between the edge of the Alps and the Adriatic Sea is the "Gorizia Gap," the only suitable invasion route for Warsaw Pact forces. Non-aligned Yugoslavia and neutral Austria act as buffer states. According to one NATO commander, they "offer a guarantee of strategic warning time which will most probably allow the timely deployment of [western] forces along the frontier."[1]

Virtually every analysis of the defense of northern Italy points to the difficulties a Warsaw Pact invasion would face. According to the Chief of Staff of the Italian Army, Lieutenant General Umberto Cappuzzo, "The Alps as a whole are basically a complex 'obstacle' area in which movement and manoeuvres are restricted to the few easily identifiable valleys and this is particularly true for mechanized and armoured forces."[2] Admiral W. J. Crowe, former Commander of Allied Forces, Southern Europe, has written that "the narrow width of the [Gorizia] Gap will cause constriction of forces and inhibit attempts to mass across a wide front."[3] The mountainous terrain of northern Italy greatly benefits the defender. There is a limited road network and a large number of bridges, viaducts, and dams which, if destroyed, could easily bring an invasion to a halt.

This sector of NATO's pseudo front lines is the home of thirteen sites for short-range and medium-range nuclear weapons. These are unnecessary to defend against or deter an attack no one expects to come across Austria and Yugoslavia. Even if there were an attack through the "Gap," NATO could defend the area easily with its special mountain troops and other conventional forces. Since it is militarily gratuitous, the nuclear infrastructure's political purpose here is it's only purpose: it brings Italy into NATO's joint nuclear operations and planning, and assures the U.S. access to Italian soil. The deployment of nuclear weapons in Italy also perpetuates U.S. domination of defense planning: as long as NATO members are "unable" to defend themselves with conventional forces the U.S. must be the senior partner in the alliance.

NOTES

1. General Giorgio Donati, "The Defence of North-East Italy," *NATO's Sixteen Nations* (June/July 1983), pp. 28-30.

2. Leiutenant General Umberto Cappuzzo, "Mountain Warfare in the North-East Frontier," *NATO's Sixteen Nations* (Special 1/83), pp. 52-57.

3. Admiral W. J. Crowe, Jr., "Allied Defence of the Southern Region—A Commander's Perspective," *NATO's Sixteen Nations* (June/July 1983), pp. 18-25.

two carrier battle groups (over ninety aircraft each), about fourteen warships, about four attack submarines, one Marine amphibious group, and twelve auxiliaries augmented by land-based surveillance and ASW forces. Poseidon strategic submarines also patrol the Mediterranean Sea from time to time, committed to NATO nuclear war plans.[18] Sixth Fleet ships carry approximately 300 nuclear warheads for land attack, anti-air, and ASW operations.

Even without the U.S. Navy, NATO and French naval forces outnumber Soviet forces in the Mediterranean. One or two French aircraft carriers (with Super Étendard nuclear strike planes) homeported in Toulon patrol regularly in the Mediterranean. The British also assign one or two frigates or destroyers with Lynx or Wasp nuclear-capable ASW helicopters to the Gibraltar "guardship." U.S. naval forces are thus free to venture throughout the Mediterranean, to provide everything from political "presence" to nuclear attacks on Soviet targets. U.S. naval forces in the Mediterranean are crucial not only for naval warfare but for attacking the Soviet southern flank, the Middle East and Africa.[19]

Anti-submarine warfare is one of the major naval nuclear activities in the Mediterranean. Over twenty principal ASW bases are located in five countries. The top priority of NATO ASW is to keep a close watch on Soviet naval deployments and ship traffic. Besides naval activity, the Soviet Union ships some 50 percent of its imports and 60 percent of its exports through the Mediterranean. Nuclear-capable U.S. P-3C Orion and Italian Atlantique patrol aircraft operate out of Sigonella and Catania respectively on Sicily. Major ocean surveillance centers at Sigonella, San Vito dei Normani, and Naples, Italy, and at Rota, Spain, collect information about deployments of Soviet ships. Attack submarines from La Maddalena, off the northern coast of Sardinia, cruise around the Mediterranean, assisted by aircraft, ASW ships, and aircraft carriers, in search of Soviet targets.

The only U.S. Army combat unit in the southern region is an airborne battalion (the only U.S. parachute unit stationed in all of Europe) from the 82d Airborne Division. Although ostensibly earmarked for rapid intervention to reinforce NATO's weak points in Greece or Turkey, it is also a lead element of U.S. forces that would quickly move to North Africa or the Middle East.

The Air Force link to the Middle East and Africa is its storage of nuclear bombs in northern Italy and south central Turkey (see Chapter 8) and the recent deployment of ground-launched cruise missiles (GLCM) to Comiso in Sicily. The GLCMs, with a range of 2,500 kilometers, give the United States new targeting flexibility north and south. The claim that the purpose of the GLCMs is to attack the Middle East and threaten Libya, seems farfetched. But, just as other forces on the flanks are increasingly focusing on "out-of-area" missions, so could the cruise missiles become the primary nuclear weapons link in a U.S.-Soviet war south of Europe. The nuclear weapons in Italy and the Mediterranean have much wider missions than those in West Germany or Britain.

Northern Europe

War plans in the northern flank play a crucial role in global war strategy. They are the most important link between Europe and strategic nuclear war. The goal of the new strategy to shift warfare to the far north—into the Norwegian Sea and the Arctic—is, according to the Defense Guidance for 1984–1988, "to force diversion of Pact resources from the Central Front." The implementation of this guidance will depend on the interception of Soviet forces before they can attack U.S. and NATO forces and on offensive attacks against Soviet homeland bases. "We must be able to prevent the Soviets from achieving the initiative," says Secretary of the Navy John Lehman. The Defense Guidance stated that "Naval forces, with the assistance of Air Forces, will give first priority to establishing control of LOCs [lines of communication] in the North Atlantic by attacking and destroying naval and air forces and defending . . . key island bases."

This strategy would do more than just prevent Soviet initiation of a blitzkrieg in central Europe. Attacks against homeland bases threaten principal centers of Soviet strategic power. Within the past ten years the Soviet Union has added long-range submarine-launched ballistic missiles (SLBMs), which can hit the United States from Soviet home waters, to its Northern Fleet short-range SLBMs, which had to move to forward positions to hit U.S. targets. Soviet Naval Aviation has received the long-range Backfire bomber which can threaten U.S. and NATO forces from northern Soviet bases. Based around the Kola peninsula (to the east of northern Norway), the Soviet Fleet is relatively protected.

The new U.S. strategy, however, includes offensives to protect U.S. and Western European operations and SLOCs (sea lines of communication). This is a significant departure from a strategy to control "choke points," to prevent Soviet ships and submarines from threatening U.S. targets or disrupt reinforcement of Europe. The Navy now describes its goal as "Military superiority . . . over, on, and under the sea in areas such as the Norwegian Sea, the Greenland-Iceland-Norway gap, the North and Atlantic sea lines of communication and in the mid-Atlantic."[20] Admiral Lee Baggett, Director of Naval Warfare, testified before the House Armed Services Committee in April 1983 that "Our answer to . . . [the Soviet] threat cannot be simply to throw a passive barrier across the Greenland-Iceland-U.K. gap."[21] The preferred approach is to destroy enemy bombers before they can reach missile launch range. This threat against Soviet homeland bases will force the Soviets to escalate conflict. No other aspect of military planning is as shortsighted and dangerous as this.

Plans for the northern European battlefield and their scenarios for strikes against strategic weapons and homeland bases do not take into account that the region is full of non-nuclear countries. Iceland and Norway, though they adhere to non-nuclear principles, are both members of NATO and are in fact the key launching pads for the new strategy. "We would perceive," says Admiral Wesley L. McDonald, Commander of the Atlantic Command, "that Norwegian air defense, U.S. Air Force squadrons based in Norway, would be the first line of intercept."[22] The Navy has proposed to upgrade its base at Keflavik, in Iceland, with a "semi-hardened" operations center, for seven days of self-contained "full wartime operations under applicable war plans."[23] The new plans provide forty-five days' worth of fuel storage in Iceland "for aircraft not assigned to NATO, such as strategic bombers."[24]

Neutralization of Soviet submarines and naval forces would depend on the U.S. Navy's nuclear attacks. Up to four aircraft carrier battle groups with nuclear-armed anti-submarine aircraft and attack submarines would operate in the area. Attack submarines will carry the battle to the enemy's home waters and adjacent sea areas as necessary to engage the Soviet submarine fleet before it can disperse. Assignment of a naval "surface action group" to New York will, according to the Navy, improve its responsiveness in the Northern Atlantic area. British, Dutch, and U.S. nuclear-armed ASW aircraft would operate together in the region. They would fly from Iceland, Greenland, the Netherlands, and Scotland. Britain could also contribute up to two nuclear-capable ASW carriers to war in the North Atlantic.

The strategy in Northern Europe is the logical extension of strategy in Europe. Moreover, "there is a striking symmetry," Admiral Baggett stated in 1983, "between the Atlantic and Pacific in terms of elements of strategy. Fundamental importance is placed on a forward strategy . . . [to] keep the Soviet threat away from CONUS [the continental U.S.] and SLOCs by early forward defense and attrition."[25] This link between the Atlantic and Pacific is only one of many the military recognizes. The military recognizes that global warfare is the most likely outcome of conflict. In Europe, as in other regions, it prepares for this battle by positioning forces to outfox the enemy and strike quickly at enemy vulnerabilities. The more the military prepares for conflict, the less it makes a distinction between peacetime and wartime. Since the military's decisions are all that separate the world from war, this is a foreboding trend.

In spite of all the "peacetime" maneuvers, the outbreak of war in Europe still appears unlikely. But it cannot be said that there is no crisis in sight that would lead the military to risk war in Europe. The European nuclear battlefield is tied to the Pacific and the Third World and will erupt in due course when nuclear war breaks out in some less stable area.

7

The Pacific

THE EXPANSE AND geographic extremes of Asia influence its role in the nuclear infrastructure. The superpowers consistently and extensively exploit Asia to support their nuclear plans and programs. Although the region has rarely been at the top of the strategic agenda, it is presently the focus of a growing and irrational nuclear arms race.

Poor weather conditions, transportation problems, and huge distances seriously constrain Soviet forces in the Pacific, which are largely concentrated around coastal cities, particularly Vladivostok (thirty-five miles from the Chinese border) and Petropavlovsk, and along the Sino-Soviet border. China is the primary Asian concern of Soviet military planners. According to a U.S. Pacific Command (PACOM) briefing, 90 percent of Soviet ground forces in the Far East are directed against China and are preoccupied with the "growing Chinese nuclear capability."[1] "Moscow's military posture and Beijing's response to it," the Deputy Undersecretary of Defense for Pacific Affairs stated in May 1984, "have resulted in the largest single concentration of forces along any bi-national border."[2]

More than half of the combatants in the Soviet Pacific Fleet are stationed at just two naval bases. Most Soviet naval forces are cut off from the open ocean by narrow straits, which have thus become the focus of

U.S. military plans. The Sea of Okhotsk and ports in the Bering Sea are further restricted by heavy winter icing. The Korea Strait (or Tsushima Strait) is the widest (at 110 miles) of four passages that connect the Sea of Japan with the Pacific Ocean. Japan's Tsushima Island, in the center of the strait, would become the focal point of anti-submarine warfare (ASW) and other naval warfare, waged in unison by South Korean, U.S., and Japanese forces supported by U.S. nuclear firepower.

The Soviet Pacific coast is more accessible than its other coasts, and its proximity to Alaska gives it a special status. The area between the northeastern tip of the Soviet Union and Alaska is the only place where the U.S. and Soviet territories meet. Defending Alaska is a high priority; U.S. war plans call for the deployment of large forces to the Aleutians. Joint Chiefs of Staff Chairman General John Vessey testified in February 1983 that "The Chiefs are in the process right now of examining the alternatives for improving the defenses of the Western Aleutians and Alaska."[3]

Petropavlovsk, on the tip of the tip of the Kamchatka peninsula, is where Soviet naval forces, including strategic submarines, are closest to U.S. ASW and interdiction operations. Although the only major Soviet base in the Pacific that is not hemmed in by "choke points," Petropavlovsk is the weakest major Soviet base: It depends on supply lines, airlift, and sealift that are highly vulnerable and inefficient.

Soviet forces in the region face larger and more capable Chinese, Japanese, U.S., and allied forces. The Soviet build-up, while portrayed by the U.S. military as designed to put pressure on Japan and the United States, is more realistically a response to tense relations with the Chinese, prospects of Japanese remilitarization, and shifts in U.S. strategy. The United States pressure on Japan to "rearm," is due more to increased attention to the Middle East, where the U.S. would like to focus its forces, than to changes in the Soviet Pacific threat.

Military interest in Asia has not declined, as predicted, since the U.S. withdrew from Southeast Asia and normalized relations with China. The United States continues to base half of its Navy in the Pacific and to put new Trident SSBNs there. Soviet naval and military forces in the Far East have grown steadily, including new operations and bases in the Indian Ocean and Vietnam. U.S. and Soviet forces are renewing their plans for a multitude of military "contingencies" for war in the Sea of Japan, on the Korean peninsula, and in the Persian Gulf.

Since the Soviet invasion of Afghanistan and the subsequent U.S. declaration of America's global military strategy, the Pacific has become prominent in U.S. war planning, even though its rank fell on the U.S. priority list. Pacific war planners have devised an offensively oriented and increasingly aggressive surveillance, exercise, and training schedule, creating an environment that invites naval collisions or acts of quasi-war (such as the downing of KAL flight 007). The change in the U.S. Navy's operational doctrine in 1982 to promote greater flexibility, variety, and offensiveness (this new doctrine is called "Flex-ops") is part of the preparation for global war. After 1979, U.S. naval forces had too many roles,

For the first time since World War II the U.S. brought together three aircraft carrier battle groups for exercises off Alaska's Aleutian Islands in 1983, just 500 miles from the Soviet Union. The force, carrying over 300 nuclear weapons, would operate in wartime to destroy the Soviet Pacific Fleet and Far East bases and to isolate the Soviet Asian region.

and neglected their traditional "presence" operations—to touch base with friends, clients, and adversaries. Since the introduction of flex-ops, the Navy has varied the predictability and tempo of its operations to assure that deployments and training conform to overall political objectives.

New nuclear weapons figure prominently in the new strategy and in the increased tempo of operations since 1979, when units of the Pacific Fleet rushed to the Indian Ocean and Southwest Asia rose from third to second priority in U.S. military planning. This diverted the attention of the PACOM (which has jurisdiction over the naval forces in the Indian Ocean) from East Asia to the Middle East. In 1983 a radical change in U.S. planning led to the creation of a new unified command to take over responsibilities for Southwest Asia (see Chapter 8). This swung the Pacific Command's attention back to East Asia.

PACOM had to reexamine its status and future "needs."[4] Studies done by the rival European Command to justify deployment of U.S. cruise and Pershing II missiles on the basis of Soviet nuclear modernization led PACOM to assert similar "needs." By 1980 these studies induced the Navy to increase its nuclear capabilities, especially through the introduction of land-attack sea-launched cruise missiles (SLCMs), which are becoming the main nuclear weapons for the Pacific theater.

Bureaucratic bickering and reorganization also influenced the structure of military forces in the region. U.S. military planners are partially absorbed in such issues as the growth of Japanese forces and South Korean and Philippine internal political conflicts over the presence of U.S. forces. South Korea faces large and militant North Korean forces in an intractable standoff. U.S. Army divisions, Air Force units, Marines, and a huge logistics infrastructure in Japan remain committed to contingency plans (formulated at the end of the Korean War) that assume a long, conventional war in Korea. U.S. planners put Korea on the back burner in their zeal to justify new operations in the Persian Gulf, but South Korea is the only place in the world where U.S. forces maintain a permanent DEFCON 4 (Defense Readiness Condition Four, one level of readiness above the normal DEFCON 5).[5] Planning in the Pacific is not limited to Korea. In terms of winning resources in competition with other commands, Pacific Command planners have found it more challenging and fruitful to focus their attention on the Soviet Union; they are thus assured an important place in the latest global strategy.

Nuclear Forces in the Pacific

The United States, China, and the Soviet Union have some 3,000 nuclear warheads committed to warfare in the Pacific. The Soviets and Chinese probably aim their missile warheads at predetermined targets for mini-strategic scenarios. But the remainder of their tactical and naval warheads, as well as most U.S. Pacific nuclear weapons, are intended for battlefield use. The U.S. and Soviet navies routinely carry nuclear weapons in the region, but the U.S. is the only country that deploys warheads on foreign territory. About 150 U.S. nuclear warheads are in South Korea for use

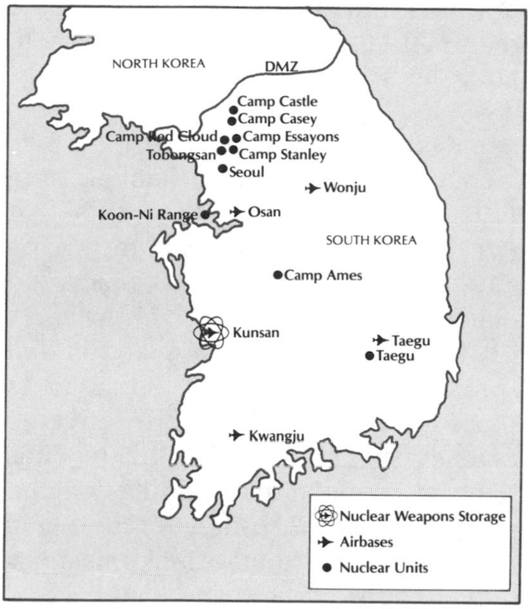

SOUTH KOREA

The only place in the world where nuclear weapons face a non-nuclear foe is South Korea. Nuclear bombs, artillery, and atomic demolition munitions are stored at Kunsan airbase and would be dispersed to a number of military units at the outbreak of hostilities. Korea is the only country where U.S. military forces are kept permanently at DEFCON 4, one level above normal alert.

against North Korea (see Figure). Since returning Okinawa to Japan in the early 1970s, the United States has deployed no nuclear weapons on Japanese soil, and there is no evidence that the United States permanently stations warheads in the Philippines either. Guam (legally a U.S. territory) is the main stockpile for U.S. nuclear weapons in the western Pacific.

Since the late 1970s the nuclear dimension has increased in the Pacific. In early 1980, just after the NATO decision to deploy cruise and Pershing II missiles was announced, Defense Nuclear Agency (DNA) officials testified before Congress that "the JCS [Joint Chiefs of Staff] has requested DNA to assist in an assessment of the theater nuclear balance in the Pacific Command area."[6] DNA stated that "many of the tools and methodologies that were developed for the European theater will have direct transferability to PACOM" and that DNA's assessment of the Pacific Command's nuclear modernization needs comes from "successful assessments and support programs in the European theater over the past five years."[7] In FY 1982 the DNA announced plans "for improving the nuclear force effectiveness of those assets under CINCPAC" and "enhancing Pacific theater nuclear targeting capability and assisting PACOM staffs to determine specific TNF weapon systems requirements."[8] The next year the DNA budget reported to Congress that the agency was investigating "PACOM's needs for enhanced nuclear forces based on a detailed assessment of the command's forces vis-a-vis the Soviet Union's for a broad spectrum of situations." The results would "prescribe the nuclear forces and weapons needed by the Pacific area commanders."[9] In testimony before Congress in February 1984, Admiral William J. Crowe, commander of PACOM, stated, "In my view, all of our military efforts in the PACOM area must rest on the foundation of a viable and credible nuclear deterrent. I cannot hypothesize a situation where it is in our interest to be dealing [from a position of] nuclear inferiority. Upgrading our theater nuclear posture combined with the supporting survivable and enduring C^3 system is also important."[10]

The need for upgraded nuclear weapons derives from a distorted view of Soviet forces. One need not be a military expert to understand the centrality of China to Soviet planners. Western military analysts have traditionally viewed large Soviet forces in the Far East as a boon because they depleted forces that would otherwise be committed to Europe. With more than a quarter of its forces "tied down" by Chinese forces in the Far East, the Soviet Union's Asian ground deployments and inferior Navy were relegated to a secondary threat status. Yet as the Soviets followed their European nuclear "modernization" with new SS-20s and Backfire bombers in its Pacific forces, the threat was reinterpreted by the Pentagon. Secretary of Defense Weinberger stated in 1982 that "the nuclear balance in the region has. . . shifted in favor of the Soviet Union."[11]

Soviet military deployments in the Far East now number some 52 Army divisions, 120 major ships, and 130 submarines. The Soviet Pacific Fleet has become the largest and most active of its four Fleets, with permanent naval deployments also in the South China Sea and Indian Ocean. In 1979, as part of a major shift in its peacetime readiness, the Soviets created a headquarters of the Far Eastern "Theater of Military Operations" (TVD) at Chita to command forces in the Far East, Transbaikal, Siberian, and Central Asian military districts (and forces in Mongolia) and to facilitate the transition to war. A secret briefing by the Defense Intelligence Agency in 1982 stated "In the Far Eastern TMO, the Soviets have the capability to seize Manchuria and fix Chinese forces in the western region of China, but such an incursion would require massive additional forces to hold the areas."[12]

Soviet theater nuclear forces in the Far East include more than 135 SS-20 launchers and about 80 Backfire and 120 Badger bombers of the Irkutsk Air Army (50 additional Bear and Bison strategic bombers are discussed below). According to a DIA briefing, "The SS-20s have taken over some of the missions previously allocated to those ICBMs which were targeted against China."[13] The Pacific Fleet has nuclear-armed cruise missile submarines that are intended for anti-ship and short-range land-attack missions. Other naval vessels and tactical aircraft also carry nuclear arms.

To counter Soviet Far East forces the United States has deployed new naval forces, tactical air, and ground units to the Pacific region. A direct comparison, division-for-division, is meaningless because the U.S. and Soviet forces focus on very different threats. The majority of Soviet forces (including 90 percent of their ground forces) are tied down by the prospect of Sino-Soviet conflict, and only a few Soviet combat divisions or aircraft could be deployed outside the Soviet Union. Some Soviet naval forces and bombers assigned to long-range and naval aviation could form part of a mobile strike force. The primary missions of the Soviet Pacific Fleet, according to the DIA, "are to protect the Pacific flank of the Soviet Union, to help secure the Delta SSBN launch areas and provide limited interdiction."[14]

U.S. forces, on the other hand, have an offensive structure to counter deployable Soviet forces and to "project" U.S. power ashore, primarily to attack

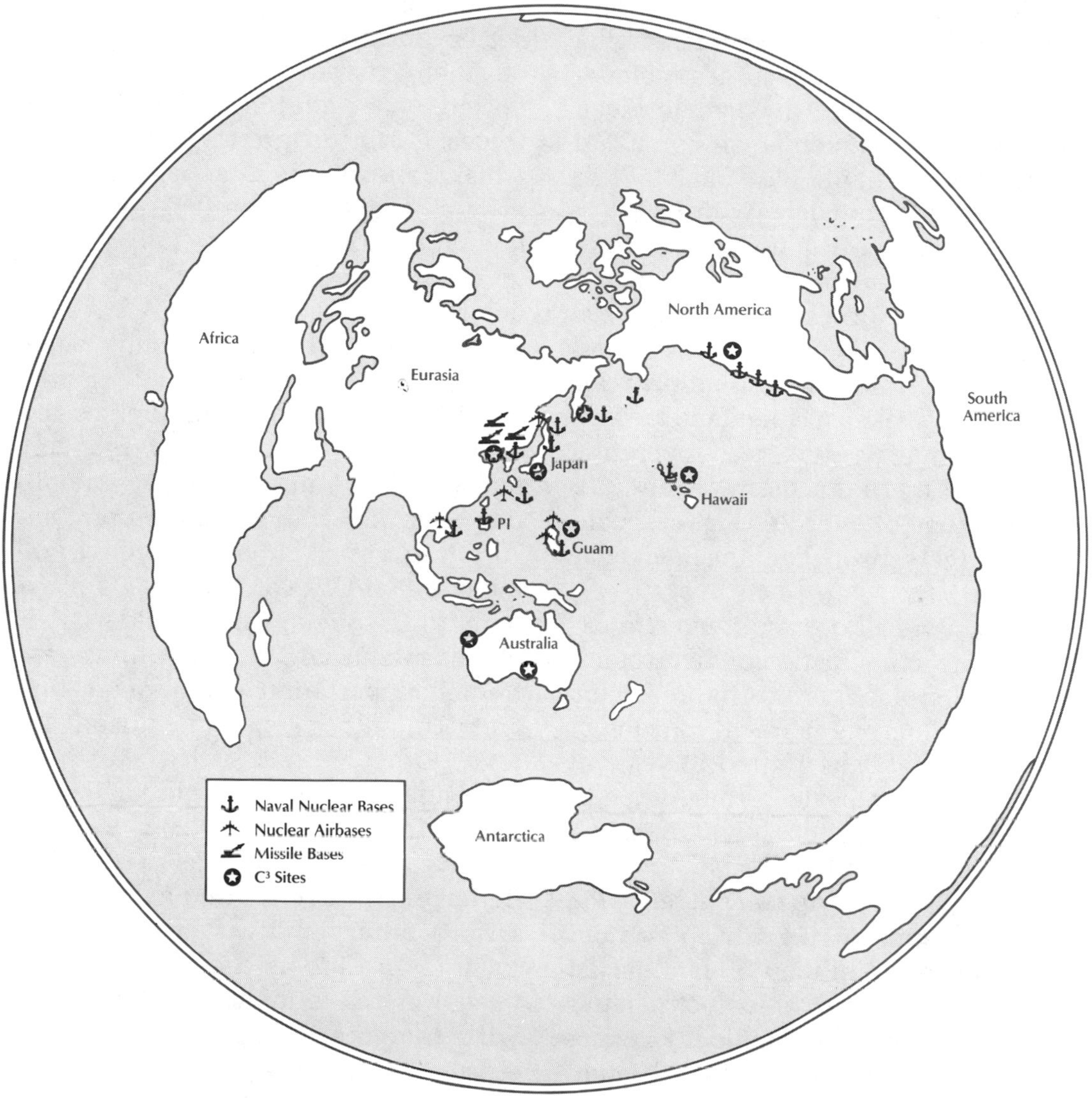

PACIFIC NUCLEAR FORCES

Nuclear activities in the Pacific take on a new dimension when seen from the perspective of the huge distances involved in this military theater. Soviet naval forces, concentrated at two base complexes in the Far East, are the foci of U.S. surveillance operations and military planning. U.S. forward basing clusters around the Soviet Pacific coast. On land the primary Soviet concern is China, which stations about one million troops along its northern border. This distorted view of the world centers on Guam, which is the center of U.S. nuclear planning and storage in the western Pacific.

Soviet bases, troop concentrations, and nuclear weapons facilities on the Soviet homeland. The largest component of PACOM is the Pacific Fleet, backed by large, mobile Air Force and Marine components. The Pacific Fleet has six aircraft carriers (with 1,800 aircraft), about ninety major surface combatants, and forty-four attack submarines. These forces carry some 700 nuclear warheads, about 300 for naval nuclear warfare and about 400 for long-range strikes against land targets. Flying from aircraft carriers operating in the northern Pacific, A-6 aircraft, with a range of over 1,900 miles, could reach targets throughout the Soviet Far East.

The U.S. Air Force continues to examine the idea of deploying ground-launched cruise missiles in the Pacific but, for numerous political reasons, it is unlikely that the United States will be able to deploy long-range theater nuclear weapons on land in Asia.[15] The sea-launched cruise missile (SLCM), which accomplishes the offensive aims of the GLCM without the political liabilities of land-based nuclear weapons, is much better suited to the geographically widespread and naval-dominated command. The SLCM is becoming the centerpiece of U.S. nuclear force in PACOM (see shaded box).

The greatest contrast between Soviet and U.S. forces, of course, is their locations. U.S. forces are "forward deployed" in Japan, the Philippines, Hawaii, and Guam. From these bases, they can better prevent the Soviet Union from taking the offensive against any point in the Pacific. A U.S. naval exercise in April 1983 demonstrated the offensive advantage of forward operations. The United States set up an attack submarine "barrier" off the coast of Petropavlovsk supported by five additional lines of ASW forces: P-3 Orion aircraft staging out of Alaska and Japan, attack submarines in support of carrier battle groups, two layers of sonar arrays, and a final layer of aircraft carriers and ASW helicopters.

U.S. forward deployment also means that military forces in Japan, South Korea, and the Philippines are closely linked to U.S. military plans and strategy. Joint air defense and anti-submarine warfare structures ensure that any U.S.-Soviet conflict will include non-U.S. forces. Japan's proximity to the Soviet Union makes its air defense and ASW operations extremely important to exploiting the Soviet Union's geographic disadvantages. Other nations, such as Australia and New Zealand, also figure in Pacific war plans.

The Soviet Union has a growing military presence in Vietnam where it has established two major naval facilities, intelligence collection bases, and rotational airfields (those with temporarily assigned aircraft). Admiral Crowe stated that, "On any given day, up to 20 Soviet surface ships and four or more submarines" are at Cam Ranh Bay.[16] In November 1983 the Soviets deployed nine Badger H light bombers to Cam Ranh Bay, the first such planes deployed in Asia outside the Soviet Union. There are no nuclear weapons in Vietnam, but deployment there of nuclear-capable forces like the Badgers and Tu-142 Bear F anti-submarine warfare (ASW) aircraft represents a significant increase in capabilities.

SEA-LAUNCHED CRUISE MISSILES

The Tomahawk sea-launched cruise missile (SLCM) is emerging as the most important nuclear strike system in the Pacific Command and other naval forces worldwide. According to the Navy, the 1,350 mile range, land-attack version of the SLCM "will significantly increase the Pacific Fleet's theater nuclear arsenal and provide the capability to strike land targets from survivable sea-based platforms."[1] The nuclear-armed SLCM is the most versatile weapon in the U.S. nuclear arsenal. It will serve strategic, "theater," and tactical roles.

Though SLCMs will serve primarily as "theater nuclear strike" weapons in regional plans "for selective release in non-SIOP options," they will also remain available as part of the post-nuclear war "strategic reserve force." Admiral Kelso, Director of the Navy's Strategic Submarine Division, explained to Congress in 1981 that SLCMs "will not be automatically launched in a general war scenario." The Navy may hold them back so that "the United States would, in any post-nuclear exchange environment, retain a measure of coercive power."[2]

The primary nonstrategic role of SLCM will be "conveying to the Soviet Union that its territory is not a sanctuary."[3] The presence of SLCMs in naval forces, according to the Navy, will enhance "the capability to execute a variety of options within both sea control and power projection functions." Nonstrategic roles for the SLCM named by the Navy include the capability to:

- "strike selected naval targets ashore to enhance sea control operations;
- strike selected fixed targets in support of the land war;
- strike quasi-fixed targets to disrupt enemy second and third echelon movement; and
- strike or hold at risk selected targets after a major theater nuclear exchange."[4]

By the early 1990s, over 140 ships and submarines, armed with over 2,500 launchers, will carry Tomahawk. Of the 3,994 missiles planned, 758 will be for nuclear land attack missions, 593 will be for conventional anti-ship missions, and 2,643 will be for conventional land attack missions; 2,739 will be for surface ships and 1,255 will be for submarines. Four Battleships, virtually all cruisers and all Spruance class destroyers, and SSN 637 and Los Angeles class attack submarines will be converted to carry the SLCM. These "platforms" will be able to launch the SLCM from standard 21-inch torpedo tubes, from deck mounted "armored box launchers" or new vertical launchers. New Los Angeles class submarines, the first of which will be deployed in 1985, will have 12 vertical launch tubes in the forward section of the bow. When all SLCMs are deployed, DOD officials said, they will increase the Navy's land-attack "platforms" from the presently planned 14 aircraft carriers to over 200 ships and submarines.

SLCMs will supplement rather than replace nuclear-armed aircraft on carriers. SLCM targets that are not assigned to carrier-based aircraft include "targets deep inside enemy territory, currently outside the combat radius of tactical aircraft, point targets of extreme hardness, previously unable to be attacked with a high kill probability, and targets close to the FEBA [forward edge of the battle area] that are so heavily defended as to cause excessively high levels of aircraft attrition."[5] "The increased strike range [that SLCM will provide from] . . . a larger number of surface platforms operating under carrier air cover and independent, covert, forward-deployed submarines presents the Soviets a formidable threat" the chief nuclear planner told Congress in March. This will mean that "Soviet firepower cannot concentrate on the carrier alone. . . (and result in) an increase in the range of escalation control options available to the nation without resort to central strategic systems."[6]

NOTES

1. SASC, FY 1983 DOD, pt. 5, p. 3083.

2. SASC, Strategic Force Modernization Programs, FY 1982, 97th Cong., 1st Sess. (Oct./Nov. 1981), p. 203.

3. ACDA, FY 1984 ACIS, p. 142.

4. HAC, FY 1980 DOD, pt. 3, pp. 754-755.

5. HAC, FY 1980 DOD, pt. 3, p. 755.

6. Statement of Commodore Roger F. Bacon, Director, Strategic and Theater Nuclear Warfare Division in the Office of the Chief of Naval Operations before the Strategic and Theater Nuclear Forces Subcommittee of the Senate Armed Services Committee on Sea-based Deterrent, 13 March 1984.

Strategic Operations in the Pacific

Along with the increasing nuclear commitment to regional warfare plans, the Pacific is gaining strategic importance. The interests, territories, supply lines, and testing facilities of four nuclear powers converge in the Pacific and include strategic submarines, bombers, and cruise missiles. As elsewhere, a warfighting infrastructure of intelligence collection, ASW, and command and control facilities, spread across six countries and one territory in the Pacific, accompanies the deployment of strategic nuclear weapons.

The strategic importance of the Pacific Ocean has increased substantially in the last decade as the Soviet Union has deployed Delta III-class submarines and the United States has deployed Trident submarines. Since 1966 the number of ballistic missile submarines in the Soviet Pacific Fleet has tripled. Soviet submarines are about evenly split between its Northern and Pacific Fleets, with nearly 40 percent of total submarine warheads in the Pacific. U.S. Pacific-based Trident submarines replaced a squadron of ten Polaris submarines (based in Guam), decommissioned in 1981.

Soviet submarines operate out of Vladivostok and Petropavlovsk. Petropavlovsk offers immediate access to the open waters of the Pacific Ocean; Vladivostok lies behind several choke points. Most of the submarines based at Petropavlovsk and Vladivostok, however, do not generally stray far from the Soviet mainland. Within the past ten years the Sea of Okhotsk, sheltered by the Kamchatka Peninsula and the Kurile Islands, has become the main area for deployment of Soviet submarines. As many as a quarter of Soviet submarines could launch their missiles from the Sea of Okhotsk. The DIA believes the build-up of military forces on Sakhalin Island and the Kuriles probably relates "to the Soviet requirement to maintain the Sea of Okhotsk as a relatively secure wartime patrol and launch area for their Delta-class ballistic missile submarines."[17]

The Soviets have fifty long-range Bear and Bison strategic bombers based in the Far East as part of the Irkutsk Air Army. These bombers (along with Backfires discussed above) "can strike targets in Japan, China and the northern Pacific, and could operate as far as the South China Sea."[18] The Soviets maintain two staging bases in the extreme northeast of the Soviet mainland, only 570 miles from Prudhoe Bay in Alaska, for forward operations. Soviet strategic missile forces have regional roles too. The DIA reported that "some ICBMs. . . now have a peripheral role in targeting China and other targets in the region. . .[and] Soviet Yankee SSBNs also provide flexibility for Soviet nuclear strikes against China and Japan."[19]

The United States has a squadron of B-52G bombers based in Guam. These bombers are committed to the SIOP (Single Integrated Operational Plan) and take part in regional bombing, mining, and sea surveillance exercises. KC-135 aerial refueling planes are based at Kadena Air Base, Okinawa, to refuel B-52Gs flying to bomb the Soviet Union from Guam. In addition to the B-52s, the United States has now deployed its first nuclear-armed sea-launched cruise missiles (SLCMs) in the Pacific. From U.S. attack submarines and surface ships, SLCMs will be able to strike targets deep in the Soviet Union. U.S. and Soviet deployment of SLCMs will change the focus of Pacific nuclear planning as the search begins for suitable targets and justifications grow on both sides to counter the new weapon.

Pacific Nuclear Infrastructure

Anti-submarine warfare (ASW) is the primary role for nuclear weapons in the Pacific. The United States could immediately deliver some 400 ASW nuclear warheads from aircraft carriers, attack submarines, and ASW patrol planes. The main U.S. ASW base is at Adak in the middle of the Aleutian Islands. In peacetime about sixty B-57 nuclear depth bombs are stored at Adak. P-3 maritime patrol aircraft fly regularly from the island; they collect information from the ocean surveillance network (described in Chapter 4) and follow the movements of Soviet submarines and surface ships. In wartime the number of ASW aircraft based at Adak would increase. Elsewhere in the Pacific nuclear-certified P-3 planes would "stage" out of Canada, Hawaii, Midway Island, Misawa and Kadena in Japan, Cubi Point in the Philippines, and Guam. They would coordinate with U.S. nuclear attack submarines to locate and destroy Soviet submarines.

Since submarines are protected when submerged, ASW forces could more efficiently destroy their communication facilities. Four of the U.S. Navy's six facilities to contact submerged submarines via very-low-frequency (VLF) transmissions are in the Pacific: at Northwest Cape, Australia; at Yosami, Japan; at Jim Creek, Washington; and at Wahiawa, Hawaii. TACAMO communications aircraft, which serve as airborne VLF radio relays, supplement the VLF ground stations. These aircraft operate from Barbers Point, Hawaii and Alameda, California (they moved from Guam when the Polaris submarines left, though Guam remains an "alternate field" to serve TACAMO planes). The Soviets have numerous VLF stations to transmit to the region.

Communication with submarines is not limited to the land-based VLF and TACAMO systems. One system unique to the northern Pacific for communications with U.S. Trident submarines is the Clarinet Pilgrim network, a series of five specially converted LORAN-C navigation beacons (four in Japan and one on Yap Island) that can produce a signal for broadcast to strategic submarines.

The single most important strategic base in the Pacific is the processing station of the U.S. Defense Support Program's (DSP) early-warning satellites, one of three such stations in the world, at Nurrungar, in central Australia. Nurrungar would receive the first information of Soviet missile launches from infrared detection satellites and transmit it to U.S. command centers for instant analysis and action. Plans to purchase six "mobile ground terminals," to supplement the three fixed and vulnerable ground stations, point up the importance of Nurrungar as a prime nuclear target.

Other weapons-related long-range communications networks operate in the region. High-frequency (HF) radio stations, which serve as ground links for bombers and airborne command planes, operate from ten main locations. These stations are part of the PACOM- and SAC-operated Giant Talk/Scope Signal III, Commando Escort, Global Command and Control, and Mystic Star networks (described in Chapter 4). The U.S. Pacific Command's airborne command post, Blue Eagle, operates out of Hickam AFB, Hawaii as a mobile and survivable center to make decisions and direct strategic or theater warfare. It can communicate (primarily through the Commando Escort stations) with bases and forces throughout the region or with any other U.S. nuclear forces worldwide.

Four of the nuclear powers use the Pacific region for testing and development of nuclear weapons. France, with no conveniently located uninhabited domestic site, uses Mururoa Atoll in French Polynesia to test its warheads. The United States, Soviet Union, and China operate numerous strategic development and testing facilities (see Figure in Chapter 4) and all launch their missiles into the Pacific.

The United States launches strategic missiles from submarines off the California coast and from Vandenberg AFB, California, into the Kwajalein Atoll and the ocean area north and east of Midway Island. The Soviets launch SLBMs and ICBMs from submarines and from three land bases to three impact areas: on the Kamchatka peninsula, in the Sea of Okhotsk, and in the open ocean north of Midway. China tests its missiles from Shuangchengzi in Kansu province, the Wuzhai rangehead in Shanxi province, and Jinxi on the Bohai Gulf in Liaoning province. Impact ares include the East China Sea and the Pacific Ocean, as far south as the Gilbert Islands.

Conclusions

The nuclear arms race in the Pacific is becoming particularly dangerous. None of the conventional forces of the nuclear powers in the region threaten the others. As the DIA concluded about the Soviets, "much of the Soviet strength in the Far East is represented by the nuclear forces, with the SS-20 as a major addition for operations in the region."[20] One has to wonder what all those Yankee- and Golf-class submarines, SS-20s, Backfire, Badger, and Bear bombers and SS-11s north of

China have their sights set on. The Soviets have built up a force of more than 500 regionally targeted nuclear warheads, far exceeding any calculation of nuclear targets within their range. According to one informed source, "Intelligence officials are unwilling to talk about details, but there are disturbing indications that the USSR has reacted to U.S. superiority in the Pacific (and the problems inherent in any conventional conflict with China) by adopting a strategy that relies heavily on the initial or early use of nuclear weapons in anything other than a limited border war."[21] A purely military analysis of the Soviet force structure could come only to that conclusion.

But the context of the Soviet nuclear build-up in the Pacific must be expanded from a general appreciation of the superiority of anti-Soviet forces to the specific provocations that ensue from PACOM's new forward offensive strategy. PACOM calls its new "General Warplan Concept of Operations" the "Full Forward Pressure Maritime Strategy." Its "basic premises" were laid out before Congress in a secret session last year:

> Objective of warfighting is war termination on terms favorable to United States: War termination requires sufficient pressure on Soviets to convince them of no gain in continuing aggression.
>
> Favorable terms to United States means: Soviets see no advantage in further escalating conflict; requires secure strategic nuclear reserve; and requires sustained capabilities of conventional forces.
>
> Carry fight to enemy to: Gain/regain territory [deleted]; and strike vulnerabilities [deleted].[22]

Soviet SS-20s and Backfire bombers are a response to the new offensive posture of the United States; U.S. SLCMs redress some "balance" lost with the new Soviet deployments. But the question must be asked, Threat against what, and for what purpose? Neither side has an answer.

Counterbalancing is the mode of the arms race. And these developments make confrontation, even war, more likely. Increasing and improving combined U.S.-Japanese ASW operations, in conjunction with actions to "bottle up" the Soviet Pacific Fleet during a crisis, will elicit nuclear retaliation, not the cleanly choreographed naval battle the military envisions. Any attempt to restrict the operations of the Soviet Navy, particularly during a crisis, will result in swift escalation to nuclear war. Yet the forward strategy puts a premium on rapid, decisive, offensive action.

Most military analysts see the Pacific nuclear problem as isolated and peripheral. This was clear when Western officials discussed the merits of reducing the SS-20 threat to Europe by simply having the Soviets move SS-20s east of the Urals. The Soviets, in a subsequent maneuver to curry Western favor, declared a "moratorium" on SS-20 deployments. Later, after it became clear this "moratorium" only applied to SS-20s west of the Urals, well-meaning Western arms controllers in their zeal to achieve a "balance," any balance at all, clung to the "moratorium" and defended its attributes. They "balanced" and "stabilized" the arms race into yet another region.

8

Nuclear Weapons and the Third World

SINCE THE MID-1960s, military analysts have set their sights on the Third World. Following the independence of scores of former colonies, the Arab-Israeli wars, and the oil embargo, U.S. military priorities have evolved into a complex strategy to enforce international "stability." The new focus has led to a greater concentration on overseas bases, naval forces, and improved "power projection" into distant regions. As the superpowers adjusted to the perceived Third World military "realities," they increased the level of forces committed to those regions and changed their war planning.

Attention to the Third World has not diminished interest in other battlefields—in strategic nuclear weapons, or in the European and Asian theaters. Although events in the Third World are credited with the shift to global engagement, superpower military planning there focuses on the nuclear arms race and superpower rivalry in the Third World, not on local security concerns. Wherever war planners shift their attention, the assumed military challenge is the Soviet threat.

Virtually every commentator on the military status quo—from hard-nosed geopolitical experts to peace movement activists—recognizes the increasing likelihood of superpower conflict in the Third World. This danger is due not to the epidemic warfare there but to the designation of the region as a U.S.-Soviet battlefield. The Defense Department's principal policy expert on unconventional warfare stated before the Congress in April 1984: "Today, 21 countries are threatened by insurgencies and, counting the 'small wars' in progress around the world, one out of every four countries is in conflict. In part, this level of violence reflects the endemic instability of the Third World but, more to the point, it reflects the success of Soviet efforts to undermine the west."[1] "Whether inspired by historical, economic, political or social factors," the Army Posture Statement said in early 1984, "Third World conflicts provide prime opportunities for Soviet inroads."[2] In 1978 Ronald Reagan stated: "In every one of the far-flung trouble spots, dig deep enough and you'll find the Soviet Union stirring a witch's brew."[3]

The belief that the Third World is a superpower battlefield elevates every region to "strategic" status. Military planners make the Third World part of the nuclear infrastructure, forcing European land warfare doctrines, numerical balances and counterbalances, and nuclear theories to fit new military terrain. "Much of the world," Secretary of the Navy John Lehman wrote in 1980, "wherein lies the vital interests of the United States and its allies, is now for the first time outside of the nuclear umbrella."[4]

As war planners carve out new battlefields and dust off war plans or draft new ones, nuclear weapons become an important part of planning. After the fall of the Shah, for instance, the Pentagon prepared a secret report titled "Capabilities in the Persian Gulf" that examined various scenarios for future conflict there.[5] One of the conclusions of the report was that "To prevail in an Iranian scenario, we might have to threaten or make use of tactical nuclear weapons." "Contingency plans" to use nuclear weapons preceded President Carter's statement that any outside attempt to gain control of the Persian Gulf would be "repelled by use of any means necessary, including military force."[6] Secretary of Defense Caspar Weinberger confirmed this policy in his nomination hearing: "Any time you get into a war the possibility that you will use every weapon available has to be left open."[7]

Nuclear Weapons for the Third World

Four of the five nuclear powers have earmarked nuclear weapons—as many as 3,000 warheads—for use outside of Europe and north Asia. Naval weapons are the most numerous, and include land- and carrier-based aircraft, and a vast array of anti-air, anti-ship, and anti-submarine weapons. The aircraft carrier is the preeminent means of nuclear attack available to western powers, with its long-range capability to strike virtually any targets. A 1982 U.S. Congressional Budget Office (CBO) study found that the presence of such a potent delivery platform in a conflict could itself lead the Soviets to use nuclear weapons: "Certainly the temptation would be great, given the difficulty of defeating a battle group with conventional weapons."[8]

The long-range, sea-launched cruise missile (SLCM) is emerging as an important new weapon for nuclear warfare in the Third World. Both the United States and the Soviet Union are deploying new SLCM generations on hundreds of ships and submarines. The SLCM "will allow virtually all Navy combatants, not just the carrier battle groups, to go on the offensive whenever necessary and from any corner of the globe," the director of the U.S. cruise missile program told Congress in early 1983.[9] The advantage of the SLCM will be to "bring nuclear forces to bear in areas where they are not forward deployed ashore,"[10] and "strike selected targets in contingencies such as third world crises involving Soviet intervention or introduction of nuclear weapons."[11] One chief naval nuclear planner posited the advantage of SLCM in the Third World: "providing a new threat spectrum to the Soviets through a worldwide strike capability, achieved with minimum risks and costs."[12]

Naval forces that operate around Third World countries routinely carry nuclear arms. On a typical day, some 2,000 non-strategic warheads are aboard ships and submarines at sea; this includes regular nuclear patrols in the northwestern Indian Ocean, eastern Mediterranean, Caribbean, South China Sea, and the Gulf of Guinea. Britain and France also deploy their nuclear-capable carriers and other ships in the Third World. It is likely that Britain carried nuclear weapons into the South Atlantic during the Falklands War.

Ground forces are also nuclear equipped. Hundreds of warheads are estimated to be stockpiled in the United States and Soviet Union for use by intervention troops in conflicts outside of Europe or Asia. If U.S. and Soviet units were deployed overseas, nuclear-capable and nuclear-certified units would accompany them. The Soviet Union routinely included nuclear-capable FROG missile units in the army divisions it sent to Afghanistan. The structure of each side's forces keeps the nuclear option open at all times.

The role of battlefield nuclear weapons in Third World war plans is not as clear as that of naval or air weapons. The U.S. Army is converting to a "light division" system for the express purpose of creating a force to respond to crises in the Third World. The new light divisions, which will form the core of U.S. intervention forces, will be armed with 155mm nuclear-capable guns, although it was originally proposed that they have only non-nuclear 105mm guns. Soviet airborne divisions, the bulk of Soviet intervention forces, have no nuclear capacity. Preserving the option to use battlefield nuclear weapons influences both training and planning. The U.S. Army is developing a number of new nuclear systems and reexamining old systems for use in the Third World. In 1983 the Joint Chiefs of Staff requested funds to study "the potential role of future special nuclear weapon designs in support of U.S. intervention forces."[13] In anticipation of "the Central Command's early need for Lance fire support," a missile unit stationed at Fort Sill, Oklahoma, has been developing a "rapid deployment" plan which will use smaller, more transportable Lance launchers.[14]

The U.S. Marine Corps is also increasing its nuclear capacity: It has about 400 nuclear warheads of seven types. Two types of specialized nu-

Marine Corps Nuclear Weapons

Nuclear Bombs	225
Artillery Projectiles	115
Atomic Demolitions	60
Total	400

clear units—Nuclear Ordnance Platoons (NOP) for ground weapons and Marine Wing Weapons Units (MWWU) for air-delivered bombs—belong to each of the three active Marine Divisions and Marine Air Wings, respectively. Each NOP has sixty nuclear weapons technicians who are reponsible for 155mm and 8-inch nuclear artillery and medium and special atomic demolition munitions. The MWWUs have forty-nine technicians each, who provide technical support to Marine aircraft units that use nuclear bombs.[15]

The Marine Corps' nuclear-capable aircraft include the A-4 and A-6, which have had nuclear roles for over two decades. The F/A-18 fighter/light attack aircraft is beginning to replace the Marine's F-4N, which is not nuclear certified, and "will more than double" the number of nuclear-capable Marine Corps aircraft.[16] In 1985 the nuclear capable AV-8B Harrier II aircraft will start to replace the A-4 and the non-nuclear AV-8A. Under current plans the marines will buy twelve squadrons of F/A-18s and eight squadrons of Harrier IIs.

In 1981 the new nuclear-capable M-198 155mm howitzer began to replace non-nuclear 105mm howitzers in all three Marine divisions. Introduction of the M-198 "will increase the number and range of Marine dual-capable artillery weapons by more than 300 percent and 60 percent, respectively."[17] The Marines also use Medium and Special Atomic Demolition Munitions (ADMs).

The Marine Corps would bring nuclear weapons to the Third World on the Navy's amphibious ships. Aboard the ship, the Amphibious Task Force commander would determine target priorities and detailed plans to hit each target. Helicopters, landing craft, or armored personnel carriers would then transport nuclear weapons to land. The preferred method is by helicopter. According to a Marine Corps regulation, "Movement of nuclear weapons ashore must be made to appear ordinary. A helicopter or landing craft escorted by numerous helicopter gunships will attract the attention of enemy observers and could result in the very thing they are intended to prevent: attack by the enemy."[18]

Southwest Asia and the Indian Ocean

No area of the globe has received more high-level military attention than the Persian Gulf ("Southwest Asia" to the Pentagon). Political instability in the Middle East has led the military to increase preparations for war between the superpowers in the region. Despite the regional roots of the war between Iran and Iraq, U.S. war planners are primarily concerned with the Soviets' role. "The Soviets are using Afghanistan to extend their own zone of security, and as a potential staging area for power projection to the south," General Robert C. Kingston, commander of U.S. forces in the region, told the Senate in February 1984. "Operating from southern Russia and Afghanistan," he said, "Soviet forces could conduct a ground assault on Iran; to either seize the oil fields or secure their long standing goal of a warm water port. Clearly, the most dangerous potential threat to the area is the Soviet Union."[19]

The U.S. response includes strengthening the infrastructure of U.S. bases in the Middle East, increasing the number of exercises there, and keeping a large naval presence in the Indian Ocean. The Indian Ocean, which only five years ago the United States deemed of such low "strategic" value to consider letting it become a nuclear-free zone, has turned into the fastest-growing area of military competition between the United States and the Soviet Union.[20] The United States and Soviet Union now maintain permanent naval forces in the region, and France keeps about 20 ships based in Djibouti and Reunion. The U.S. "Middle East Force," first established at Bahrain in 1949, has grown since 1980 from three to five ships and now has nuclear roles.[21] U.S. naval forces in the Indian Ocean consist of about twenty-five ships, centered around a nuclear-armed aircraft carrier (with over 100 nuclear bombs), and a Marine Amphibious Unit. Nuclear-capable P-3 Orion ASW aircraft now regularly patrol the area in search of Soviet targets. The United States gets support from bases and other facilities at Diego Garcia (a British island in the Indian Ocean), Oman, Egypt, Somalia, and Kenya.

Since early 1983 Soviet naval forces in the Indian Ocean have numbered about thirty ships at a time (they have fewer combatant ships than the United States, however): one submarine; four to five surface combatants (including one amphibous ship); and about fifteen support ships (all from their Pacific fleet). Nuclear-capable IL-38 May and TU-142 Bear ASW planes regularly fly over the area, primarily from bases in South Yemen and Ethiopia.

Partly because of political crises in the areas and partly because of insecurity about oil supplies, the United States elevated "Southwest Asia" in 1981 to the second ranked theater of war (after Europe and before the Pacific). In response to the change, the DOD established a new Middle East command, the U.S. Central Command (CENTCOM). CENTCOM, formed on January 1, 1983, at MacDill AFB, Florida, replaced the short-lived Rapid Deployment Joint Task Force. It serves as the planning headquarters for war in the Persian Gulf and has a variety of forces from the four military services loosely committed to it for use in contingency planning.

Activation of CENTCOM has been the largest post-war change in the Joint Chiefs of Staff's "Unified Command Plan," which partitioned the world into U.S. military commands. "When the Unified Command Plan was created at the end of World War II," a CENTCOM pamphlet states, "it was not possible to foresee the significant security and economic issues that would focus on the Central region in the eighties."[22] In the words of the CENTCOM commander, "in 1980, had the President of the United States directed the military to send a sizable force to the Middle East, to protect Iran and block the Russians, nobody, at that time, could have told you where the force would come from, what the force would consist of, how long it

Scenario for War in Southwest Asia

Time (Days)	*Activity*	*Responses*
−50	"Rising tensions"	"national, Naval, and Air Force broad area surveillance systems and combat forces surged to wartime rates"
−23	"Soviet mobilize forces north of Iran"	
−14	"USSR Activity reaches critical level"	"U.S. forward-deployed carrier, amphibious forces . . . U.S. begins precautionary actions"
−7		"President exercises limited reserve component call-up . . . RDF units alerted"
"C-Day"		"U.S. declares partial mobilization . . . orders its forces worldwide to DEFCON-2 . . . deployment of RDF to Southwest Asia"
+2	"Warsaw Pact mobilizes" [in Europe]	"U.S. declares full mobilization"
+7	"Soviets enter Iran"	"U.S. begins to deploy forces into Iran . . . forces begin to deploy to Europe"
+17	"North Korea attacks South Korea . . . Warsaw Pact attacks" [Europe]	"first convoy sails to Europe . . . tacair deploys to ROK [Republic of Korea]"

Source: U.S. Secretary of Defense secret Defense Guidance for FY 1984–1988

would take them to get there, how they would get there, the sequence, how they would be sustained, and who would be in command."[23]

The Soviets recently established a command for Southwest Asia, the Southwestern Theater of Military Operations (TVD), based at Tashkent. The Southwestern TVD controls Soviet forces in the Turkestan, North Caucasus, and Transcaucasus military districts, and the war in Afghanistan. The Southwestern TVD's peacetime responsibilities include military planning and operations in the Middle East.

The Defense Intelligence Agency estimates there are no strategic nuclear forces in the Southwestern TVD, and "there are no projections for the future basing of SS-20 IRBMs in the TVD."[24] "All ground forces, within the TVD," DIA says, however, "including Afghanistan, have nuclear and chemical delivery capabilities."[25] The Soviets have about twenty-five divisions in the region, most of which are "cadre" divisions with small numbers of men. There are 105,000 additional Soviet troops in Afghanistan.

Despite greater superpower interest in the region, there is no evidence of any Soviet preparations for an invasion of countries around the Persian Gulf. According to the DIA, "generally, forces in the [Southwestern] TVD, less the 40th Army in Afghanistan, are being modernized and restructured at a much slower pace than Soviet forces opposite NATO and the PRC."[26] A Soviet invasion of the Gulf region would encounter significant geographic problems. "The rough, rugged and widely varying Iranian geography poses the most immediate military problems for a nation like the Soviet Union, which is inordinately dependent upon tank and mechanized divisions with little organic logistical support," according to an Army analyst.[27] An overland attack through northern Iran would be difficult, even in the absence of local opposition given mountain ranges that run from east to west with narrow passes and deep gorges. Soviet tactical aircraft from Afghanistan or the Caucasus do not have the range to provide continuous tactical support for forces moving south. The Soviets would have to establish and hold staging bases in Iran. Even though this type of invasion is highly implausible, U.S. planning is based on the the assumption that it will happen.

The Atlantic and Caribbean

As links to other theaters of war, the Atlantic and Caribbean are at the center of the U.S. Navy's global plans, again focusing on the Soviets. Shipment of fuel and other goods through the region in peacetime and the planned transit of U.S. forces to Europe in wartime influence its military importance. The Atlantic Ocean is the military planner's deepest naval concern because it links the United States with its forces in Europe (the headquarters of the NATO Atlantic Command, for instance, is at Norfolk, Virginia). More strategic missile carrying submarines (SSBNs) operate in the Atlantic than anywhere else. All British and French, and virtually all U.S. SSBNs patrol in the Atlantic. At any given moment, two or three Soviet SSBNs are in the open waters of the central Atlantic, off the U.S. coast near Bermuda.

The Atlantic splits into two major regions. North of the "gap" between Greenland, Iceland, the Faeroes, the United Kingdom, and Norway (called the GIUK or GIN gap), NATO and Soviet forces vie for control. South of the GIUK gap, Western forces dominate and if war broke out could quickly close the region to Soviet naval forces. Despite this advantage, U.S. war planners are far more concerned with the prospects for global war caused by Soviet (or Cuban) military forces in the region than they are with such politically tumultuous areas as Central or South America. Admiral Wesley L. McDonald, Commander of the U.S. Atlantic Command, told Congress in February 1984 that the current focus of his planning was "if, and when required, [to] counter the Cuban air and naval offensive capability, to ensure the unimpeded flow of seaborne traffic through the straits of Florida, the Gulf of Mexico and the Panama Canal."[28] Thus the sea lines of communication (SLOCs) from the United States to Europe and the Middle East figure prominently in U.S. plans. These focus to a surprising degree on Cuba. "We have continued to revise and improve our operations plans for dealing with the Caribbean situation," Admiral McDonald continued. "How to best deal with the increasing Cuban threat will be a major political decision that must be made very early in any crisis."[29]

Cuba is important to U.S. military planners because the Caribbean is an integral element of the U.S. defense of both Europe and North America. The existence of a Latin American Nuclear-Free Zone Treaty (the Treaty of Tlatelolco; see Chapter 9) and a Soviet pledge (emerging from the Cuban missile crisis) not to place offensive weapons in Cuba, have not denuclearized the Caribbean. U.S. and Soviet naval forces routinely carry nuclear weapons through the region. The U.S. has nuclear anti-submarine warfare (ASW) plans for the region and has prepared bases at Key West, Florida, and Roosevelt Roads, Puerto Rico for nuclear ASW. The United States has numerous nuclear weapons-related training, C^3, and research and development facilities in the "nuclear-free" zone. While the Tlatelolco Treaty has apparently prevented permanent storage of nuclear weapons in Latin America and the Caribbean, it has not prevented preparations for nuclear warfare there.

Twice since taking office, President Reagan has questioned Soviet compliance with U.S.-Soviet agreements on offensive weapons in Cuba. He stated in September 1983 that the "agreement has been abrogated many times by the Soviet Union and Cuba in the bringing of what can only be considered offensive weapons, not defensive, there."[30] Regular Soviet port visits to Cuba began in 1969. Bear reconnaissance planes regularly use Cuban airfields. In 1983 the Soviets deployed nuclear-capable Bear-F anti-submarine warfare planes to Cuba for the first time. During 1982, after the United States increased its naval deployments off the coast of Central America, the Soviets dispatched a cruiser-destroyer-submarine task force to Cuba.[31] One well-informed military expert has referred to Soviet nuclear weapons deployments in the Caribbean.[32] Although little is known about Soviet nuclear plans or operations in the region, they are minimal compared to the powerful U.S. presence there.

Protection of the sea lines in the Caribbean is a great challenge to the U.S. military because its forces are either deployed overseas or committed to warfare in theaters far away. Forces stationed in the southern part of the United States might as well be in Europe, since their location does not enable them to defend America's backyard. U.S. military planners seldom consider the ground and naval forces stationed in the United States for an active role from their home bases: They are a pool of resources to reinforce overseas commands.

Just as in Southwest Asia, increased military interest in the Caribbean entails new war plans and additional forces for deployment there. The Navy recently announced plans to station a seven-ship "Surface Action Group," including the battleship Wisconsin, in the Gulf of Mexico, the first such homeporting of naval forces in the Caribbean in many years. Within the past year military activity in Central America has led to the creation of a permanent Army planning cell for the area. Designated Army Forces, Southern Command (SOUTHCOM), and located with the headquarters for all U.S. forces in Central America, it is "a headquarters designed to plan for the worst, the contingency that will happen out there."[33]

Africa

Since 1970, when Soviet ships began calling at West African ports and reconnaissance aircraft began using airfields in Guinea and Angola, U.S. military strategy for the Atlantic has extended to Africa. "Although other areas of the world may be more critical to the vital interests of the United States than Africa," the Army reported in 1984, "continued growth of the Soviet presence and influence in this mineral-rich continent must be considered potentially dangerous to the security of the United States and its allies."[34] The CENTCOM commander, General Robert C. Kingston, stated in 1984 that "We must also seek to deny the Soviet Union or its surrogates, domination or hegemony in Africa."[35] There is confusion over what the military threats are.

Admiral Harry Train, former Commander of the Atlantic Fleet, told Congress in March 1982 that he was "seriously concerned about the number of countries which currently provide port facilities to the Soviet Union along the vital South Atlantic shipping routes."[36] According to other military testimony, "there is a 50,000 ton oil tanker every 40 nautical miles" in the waters off the west coast of Africa.[37] Naval analysts point to the year-round presence of the Soviet navy in the Gulf of Guinea and speak of the inadequacy of potential U.S. "offensive operations against Soviet support installations fronting the South Atlantic."[38]

Protection of the sea lines is only one military formula applied to Africa. Admiral Train has voiced additional concern about the Soviet Union establishing a strategic presence in Africa: "It is entirely possible that over the course of the next 10 years, we will see the establishment in the South Atlantic of a fifth Soviet Fleet." The Soviets, according to the Admiral, are "running out of sea room in which they can deploy and employ their ballistic missile submarines," and the south Atlantic may prove a suitable place.[39]

The military's abuse of geographical arguments becomes particularly apparent in its plans for Africa. The Director of Naval Intelligence, Admiral John L. Butts, stated in early 1984 that Soviet "naval related activity in the Southwest Indian Ocean may presage an attempt to establish a naval support facility in that critical area astride the SLOCs to the South Atlantic."[40] One has to wonder why the U.S. military would worry about Soviet interdiction of oil routes around southern Africa when interdiction would be much easier and more effective in or near the Persian Gulf itself.

One explanation of this concoction is that in creating a global warfighting structure a U.S. military alliance with South Africa cannot be ruled out. As long as military planners think they might someday need such an alliance, they will need to posit a concrete (or concrete sounding) military necessity to override or overwhelm congressional and public qualms about maintaining relations with such a state. One military study states that "our ability to deny the Soviets a submarine resupply sanctuary near the Cape of Good Hope will depend on cooperation from South Africa"[41] (as if this were a credible concern). There are also reports of U.S.-South African cooperation in intelligence collection: covert links that could seem justifiable to policymakers on the basis of the "strategic" importance of South Africa.[42]

The U.S. military presence in Africa is minimal, and while the Atlantic Fleet organizes an annual West African training cruise to develop working relations with African navies, part of its purpose is to indoctrinate African militaries on global war. When it comes to the South Atlantic, military planners foresee the involvement not only of African nations: "It is most important that we continue to encourage the improvement of the forces of our Central and South American allies," Admiral Wesley McDonald stated in early 1984, "and continue to conduct periodic training with them so they will be capable of contributing to the defense of . . . sea lines of communications."[43]

Global War

As crises in each region of the Third World grab the attention of war planners, the relative importance of each theater fluctuates accordingly. The commands compete for high man on the totem pole and first dibs on the common pool of military forces. The military planners can maneuver and withdraw forces very quickly to and from whichever region is hottest. During 1983, for instance, the second aircraft carrier in the Indian Ocean, rushed there in 1979 to deal with Iran, was withdrawn as crises in Central America and Lebanon preempted even the number-one hotspot.

The U.S. military's global warfighting strategy links all of these potential battlefields, but common forces, facilities, and plans link region to adjacent region to create a global strategy. SLOCs link the Caribbean and West Africa to war in Europe and the Middle East. Southern Africa links Europe and the Atlantic to the Middle East. The Pacific and Indian Ocean are linked by the forces one ocean supplies to another.

The Defense Nuclear Agency is studying "the use of Third World assets in an extended conflict."[44] Some assets are already linked, such as the three high-frequency radio stations in the Philippines, Turkey, and Britain, that connect to U.S. military forces in the Middle East.[45] Preparations for global war are resulting in the growth of intelligence collection, communications, and technical facilities in the Third World.

The superpowers' plans also link their allies into global war. France, Britain, and the Netherlands, for instance, are linked to U.S. war planning outside of the NATO framework because of their possessions in the Caribbean.[46]

A significant shift in war planning for the Third World is NATO's increasing links to "out-of-area" military contingencies outside Europe. The traditional boundaries of NATO military planning are Europe, North America, and the Tropic of Cancer. The Soviet invasion of Afghanistan, however, forced NATO planners to reconsider those boundaries. The Commander of the U.S. Sixth Fleet in the Mediterranean wrote in 1983 that "An inventory of the instability and potential crisis points around the littoral of the Mediterranean leads to the conclusion that a serious threat to peace of the Southern Region [of NATO], and perhaps to all of NATO, is not necesarily restricted to Europe, but also lies south and east of the traditional NATO area of interest and responsibility."[47] NATO's Southern European commander wrote in 1983 that the Sixth Fleet was "continually looking over their

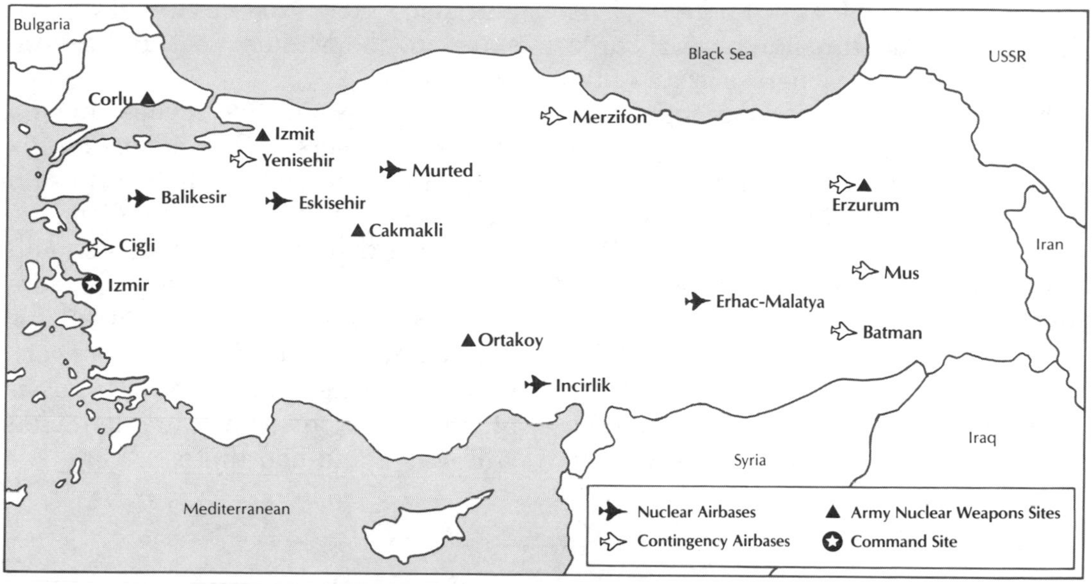

GATEWAY TO THE THIRD WORLD

Turkey is perhaps the most overlooked NATO member with U.S. nuclear weapons deployed on its soil. Not only is it adjacent to the Soviet Union, but it is also the military link to the Middle East. From Incirlik on the south coast, U.S. F-16 aircraft armed with nuclear weapons can cover the entire region. Dispersal bases in eastern Turkey are crucial for attacks on the Soviet Union, just 150 miles away, or for military intervention in the Persian Gulf region.

shoulders at events and possible dangers from the South and East—outside the formal boundaries of NATO."[48] The Deputy Commander of NATO's Iberian Atlantic Command wrote about "increasing our capabilities to counter potential Soviet threats in developing Africa."[49]

NATO planners have closely examined the impact on Europe of a war in Southwest Asia, especially if U.S. forces earmarked for Europe were rushed to the Persian Gulf. A "Southwest Asia Impact Study" concluded that "civil and military compensatory measures . . . could—if implemented—considerably offset the most serious effects of such deployments."[50] There is an even more direct European link to global strategy. The direct link between the NATO southern region and new areas (discussed in Chapter 6) is nowhere clearer than in Turkey, the NATO country with the longest border adjacent to the Soviet Union. The United States stores almost 500 nuclear warheads in Turkey (see Figure).

In addition to the nuclear infrastructure already in Turkey, the United States is building two new air bases in the eastern part of the country—at Mus and Batman—to handle U.S. reinforcements in wartime. Because NATO pays for part of these air bases, Assistant Secretary of Defense Richard Perle has stated that "these bases will be used in a strictly NATO context and not for forces of the Rapid

Deployment Joint Task Force."[51] This is untrue. The director of Air Force construction told Congress in 1983 that "the strategic value of bases in eastern Turkey became very evident to protect not only the southern flank of NATO but other contingencies."[52] The Joint Chiefs of Staff responded to a written question in Congress in 1984 by stating that "Mus is essential as the base will provide significant NATO capability within 120 miles of the Soviet border. Additionally, because of the strategic location of Southeastern Turkey, Mus will also deter possible Soviet expansion into the Middle East and Southwest Asia."[53]

One of the main criticisms leveled on war planners and policymakers is that they do not establish priorities. In light of the abundant links between the numerous theaters of war this should not be surprising. The superpowers cannot hope to contend with all (or even some) of their military contingencies around the globe. Nor is it possible that superpower war in one region will stay contained there.

9

Denuclearizing

THE NUCLEAR-FREE PACIFIC movement has a slogan: If it's safe, test it in Paris, dump it in Tokyo, but keep our Pacific nuclear-free. Around the world, citizen campaigns are challenging the nuclear system, linking local concerns to the issues of international conflict and the arms race.

Nuclear relations have claimed the attention of citizens and officials alike, prompting a spate of proposals for "nuclear-free zones" for the Nordic region, Central Europe, the Mediterranean, the Balkans, the Middle East, South Asia, the Indian Ocean, Africa, and the Pacific. The government of Greece pledged to remove American bases and, by 1989, all nuclear weapons. In 1984 the Canadian government removed the last American nuclear warheads from its soil. The Parliaments of Norway and Denmark voted to cut national funding for U.S. nuclear missile bases in Europe. Eight of sixteen NATO members prohibit deployment of U.S. nuclear warheads on their soil (Norway, Denmark, Canada, Portugal, Luxembourg, Spain, Iceland, and France). The Netherlands is already in the process of reducing its NATO nuclear "tasks," and popular pressure has prevented the Dutch goverment from deciding whether to accept U.S. ground-launched cruise missiles. Egypt, Sri Lanka, India, and other countries restrict nuclear ships from their territorial waters. Australia, New Zealand, and Fiji have sued France in the International Court of Justice to force cessation of atmospheric nuclear testing. The New Zealand government declared its country a nuclear-free zone and banned U.S. nuclear weapons and nuclear-powered ships.

Even Soviet allies have managed to make some gestures against Soviet nuclear prerogatives, including the deployment of new Soviet missiles on their soil. Romania stated in 1981 that it would not accept Soviet missiles. In fact, Romania regards all foreign bases and foreign stationing of troops as a violation of its sovereignty. Bulgaria also denies any peacetime basing of Soviet nuclear weapons.

In the United States, local campaigns are challenging the course of the arms race. Residents of the Pacific Northwest and New York City protested the stationing of nuclear-capable ships and submarines near their homes. Environmentalists in Michigan and Wisconsin have halted construction of a new extremely-low-frequency antenna for submarine communications. "Ranchers and Mormons" successfully fought deployment of the MX missile in their backyards.

Many anti-nuclear actions take the form of non-violent civil disobedience. At the General Dynamics Shipyard in Groton, Connecticut, activists hammered the hulls of Trident missile-carrying submarines. In King of Prussia, Pennsylvania, protesters removed missile re-entry vehicles from a General Electric plant. Activists in California hiked miles across restricted areas of Vandenberg Air Force Base to obstruct MX missile testing. Fishermen from Vieques Island, Puerto Rico, staged a "fish-in" to interfere with the Navy's bombing practice. Hawaiians launched a boat blockade to stop naval shelling of their sacred island of Kahoolawe.

What common thread ties these extraordinary public and governmental actions together? It is the refusal to host a link in the nuclear infrastructure. The fear of being a nuclear target stands out in peace movement literature, in anti-nuclear government statements, and in campaigns around the world to designate towns, cities, counties, nations, and regions "nuclear-free zones."[1] Beneath the fear lies a much more powerful conviction: the growing belief of citizens, parliaments, and governments that they are being deceived, that they are being used to perpetuate a system that does not serve their interests and indeed increasingly threatens war. Anti-nuclear activists are asserting their rights: They seek to control their own future.

Secrecy and the Nuclear Infrastructure

The most serious impediment to citizen participation has been secrecy. Although much technical data on nuclear weapons has been made public through the arms control process, there remains a dearth of information on the infrastructure, war plans, and the peacetime practices of the nuclear system. Officials have kept quiet for an obvious reason: It's going on in everyone's backyard. Secrecy obscures the link between a local inconvenience or eyesore and world events. It is the prime weapon in a calculated effort to discourage public inquiry.

As a result, the military establishment can dismiss public concern as uninformed and hysterical. Local campaigns, for want of a more tangible role in national security policy, concentrate on nuclear accidents, safety, environmental impact, and health hazards. The government instinctively responds by glossing over any problems with assurances that the system is safe. In 1981, for example, when the U.S. Department of Defense released a new "official" list of nuclear weapons accidents, it included five earlier accidents that had never been disclosed.[2] What was so signficant about these five new accidents to have warranted decades of cover-up? Nothing. The military was not hiding a specific catastrophe, inefficiency, or negligence. But to admit that accidents happen is to admit that things are not as foolproof as they are promoted to be. Concealing the five accidents averted an embarrassing public discussion of safety. Why then did they disclose them in 1981? That in itself was an accident, an inadvertent disclosure.

Increasing activism and public interest have forced changes in secrecy practices. Military officials have breached the long-standing U.S. and British policies to "neither confirm nor deny" the presence of nuclear weapons. In 1980 the British Ministry of Defence, as part of its attempt to refute claims that deployment of ground-launched cruise missiles would increase the likelihood of nuclear accidents, stated in a public brochure that "Nuclear weapons have been stored in this country for many years."[3] In Seal Beach, California, concerns about the safety of a naval weapons depot led to a General Accounting Office investigation that stated in its audit report:

> In response to our inquiries, the Navy provided the following written statements concerning Seal Beach's nuclear capabilities:
>
> 'The Naval Weapons Station, Seal Beach, currently has no nuclear weapons capability. No assigned 'EMERGENCY CAPABILITY' exists at Seal Beach; however, ordnance storage facilities exist there and would be utilized with proper authorization, during emergency situations.
>
> The Naval Weapons Station, Seal Beach, capability for storage of nuclear weapons no longer exists. This action was executed at the direction of the Chief of Naval Operations. At present, there are no plans to resume this capability.'[4]

Governments have attempted to use such revelations to pacify activists, but have kept the public uninformed about the state of nuclear affairs. Increased public interest in nuclear issues has reinforced the military's secrecy fetish. But because the technology is often arcane, and its military role inscrutable, secrecy is often unnecessary to preclude public involvement. Links between ordinary military and nuclear operations, between civilian and military assets, and between scientific research and nuclear weapons are diffuse, protean, and hidden from view. There is a pervasive lack of understanding—even within the military—of the pervasiveness of the arms race.

Of the 115 nations that have signed the Nuclear Non-Proliferation Treaty (NPT), fourteen play important roles in the nuclear arms race: they host nuclear weapons under foreign control; some can even use those weapons when released by the controlling nation. The NPT does not proscribe nuclear alliances or nuclear delivery systems, only the warheads. An NPT signatory can be intimately involved in nuclear weapons planning and preparations, even to the point of having its delivery systems "certified" to fire nuclear warheads. Ten signatories have such a status: Belgium, Czechoslovakia, East Germany, Greece, Hungary, Italy, the Netherlands, Poland, Turkey, and West Germany.

The tentacles of the nuclear infrastructure are so obscure that most countries do not understand their own contribution to the arms race. Members of nuclear alliances often do not know the worldwide strategic role of facilities on their soil. "Non-nuclear" countries frequently house nuclear-related facilities; indeed virtually every "non-nuclear" country allied with the United States houses such facilities, almost always without public knowledge, and often without the government's knowledge.

Secrecy does not necessarily have the purpose of concealing information from a potential enemy. According to a 1975 Congressional report,

> The U.S. Government security policy regarding nuclear weapons locations is that it will neither confirm nor deny the existence or location of U.S. nuclear weapons located anywhere. In part, this is at the request of the nations where the weapons are deployed, since in most nations the existence of U.S. nuclear weapons within their borders is a difficult internal political issue. Thus they generally have requested that the United States not declassify the fact that U.S. nuclear weapons are located in their specific nation—even though the evidence that they are there is obvious and generally known by their population.[5]

The United States permanently stores nuclear warheads in eight foreign countries, the Soviet Union in four, and Britain in one (see Table). Though the United States, which at one time also stored nuclear weapons in Canada, France, Greenland, Libya, Morocco, Okinawa, the Philippines, Spain, Taiwan, and Thailand, has reduced the number of its peacetime nuclear storage sites overseas, it has established top secret plans to base nuclear warheads overseas during a crisis or war. According to Pentagon documents, the President has given "conditional deployment authorization" for wartime storage of nuclear warheads in the Azores, Bermuda, Canada, Diego Garcia, Iceland, the Philippines, Puerto Rico, and Spain.

None of these governments were informed of the U.S. President's authorization to send nuclear anti-submarine depth-bombs there in wartime. Since five of these nations do not permit nuclear weapons on their soil, it is easy to see why such plans would be kept top secret. The political sensitivity of such plans is heightened by the non-nuclear status of numerous other countries (Denmark, Finland, Norway, Sweden, New Zealand) which, in addition to prohibiting peacetime deployment of nuclear warheads on their soil, are all actively pursuing nuclear-free zones.

Puerto Rico, where the United States also plans to deploy nuclear depth bombs in wartime, presents a different problem. Although Puerto Rico is U.S. territory, the United States has ratified the Latin American Nuclear-Free Zone Treaty (the "Treaty of Tlatelolco") which prohibits "the testing, use, manufacture, pro-

The U.S. Nuclear Infrastructure Overseas

Country / Territory	*Warhead Deployments Number (a)*	*Rank*	*Military Facilities Number*	*Rank*	*Nuclear Infrastructure Number*	*Rank*
Australia	0	—	4	17	10	12
Bahamas	0	—	23	10	15	9
Belgium	25	9	14	14	7	15
Canada	0	—	25	8	78	2
Greece	164	6	27	7	20	8
Greenland	0	—	7	16	9	13
Guam	428	5	20	13	8	14
Iceland	0	—	1	19	5	17
Italy	549	3	54	6	39	3
Japan	0	—	82	4	28	5
Netherlands	81	8	8	15	11	11
Norway	0	—	2	18	9	13
Panama	0	—	21	12	6	16
Philippines	0	—	22	11	20	8
Portugal	0	—	21	12	8	14
Puerto Rico	0	—	25	8	13	10
South Korea	151	7	136	2	21	7
Spain	0	—	24	9	11	11
Turkey	489	4	66	5	22	6
United Kingdom	1,268	2	121	3	34	4
West Germany	3,396	1	892	1	241	1
TOTALS	6,551		1,595		615	

(a) peacetime deployments

Countries with fewer than five facilities or no nuclear weapons on their soil have been excluded from this table (see Appendix A): Antigua, Ascension Island, Argentina, Barbados, Bermuda, Cape Verde Islands, Denmark, Diego Garcia, Djibouti, Enewetok, Gibralter, Johnston Atoll, Kwajalein, Liberia, Midway Island, New Zealand, Oman, Saipan, Seychelles, Turks and Caicos, and Yap Island.

duction or acquisition by any means whatsoever of any nuclear weapons, . . . and the receipt, storage, installation, deployment, and any form of possession of any nuclear weapons, directly or indirectly" in the Zone (which includes Puerto Rico).[6] Though the United States does not now store nuclear warheads in Puerto Rico (it withdrew them between 1976 and 1978 before ratifying the Protocol of the Treaty dealing with Puerto Rico), it maintains a specially certified "advanced underwater weapons (AUW) shop" at the Roosevelt Roads Naval Station to receive nuclear depth bombs in wartime.[7] The Bar Association of Puerto Rico has declared that these preparations, along with other parts of the nuclear infrastructure on the island, violate the Treaty.[8]

Thirteen facilities in Puerto Rico are part of the infrastructure (see Figure and Appendix A). The intimate involvement of these facilities in U.S. preparations for nuclear warfare, and training, testing, command, and communications, undermines the Treaty's

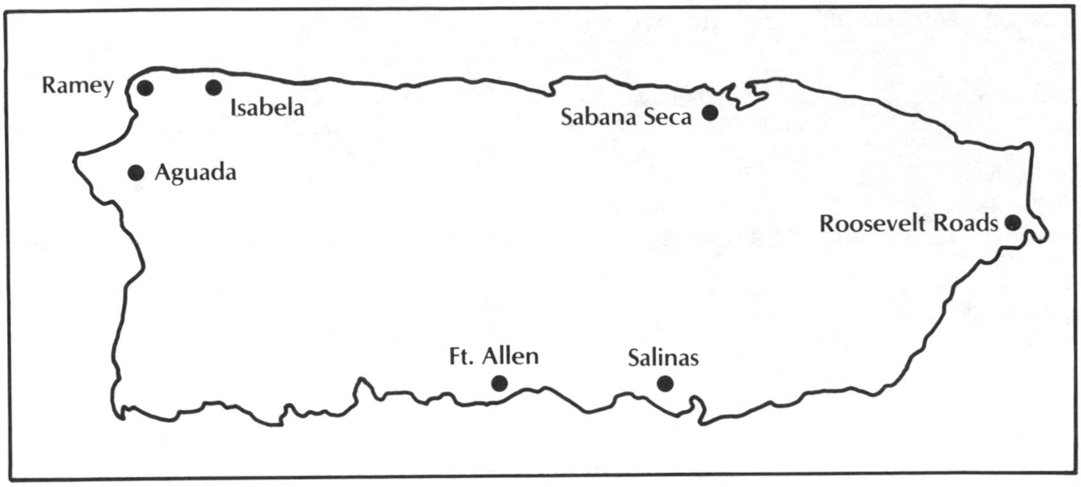

PUERTO RICO

Though it lies in the Latin American Nuclear Free Zone, Puerto Rico houses a number of nuclear-related installations and would house U.S. nuclear depth bombs in wartime. Nuclear-armed anti-submarine aircraft would fly out of Roosevelt Roads naval station.

stated goal: abolition of the nuclear arms race in Latin America. Beyond the facilities in Puerto Rico, activity in other parts of the Latin American Nuclear-Free Zone make a mockery of the Treaty. The United States uses four ranges that extend into the Zone for nuclear weapons certification and training.[9] A chain of tracking sites in the Bahamas and Antigua support U.S. and British strategic missile testing from Florida. The Atlantic Undersea Test and Evaluation Center on Andros Island in the Bahamas plays a key role in certification of Trident submarines.

In Japan, another "non-nuclear" country, the system of U.S. bases serves preparations for nuclear war. Though the United States does not station nuclear warheads there in peacetime, its infrastructure in Japan, comprising twenty-eight facilities, is the most extensive in the Pacific (see Figure). At Kadena Air Base on Okinawa, Strategic Air Command KC-135 aerial refueling planes stand on constant alert; their mission is to refuel B-52 bombers, stationed in Guam and the United States, en route to targets in the Soviet Union. Communications sites in Japan such as the Pacific Command's "Commando Escort" system and Strategic Air Command's "Giant Talk/-Scope Signal III" high frequency radio networks at Kadena, Iruma, Owada, and Tokorozawa, as well as the Navy's fleet and submarine transmitters at Totsuka and Yosami, all serve direct nuclear missions. Airborne command planes also depend on a ground link at Kadena Air Base and a "mobile ground entry point" at Yokota Air Base (it would move out of Yokota to the Japanese countryside during a crisis). Five LORAN-C navigation stations in Japan double as "Clarinet Pilgrim" stations for emergency submarine communications.

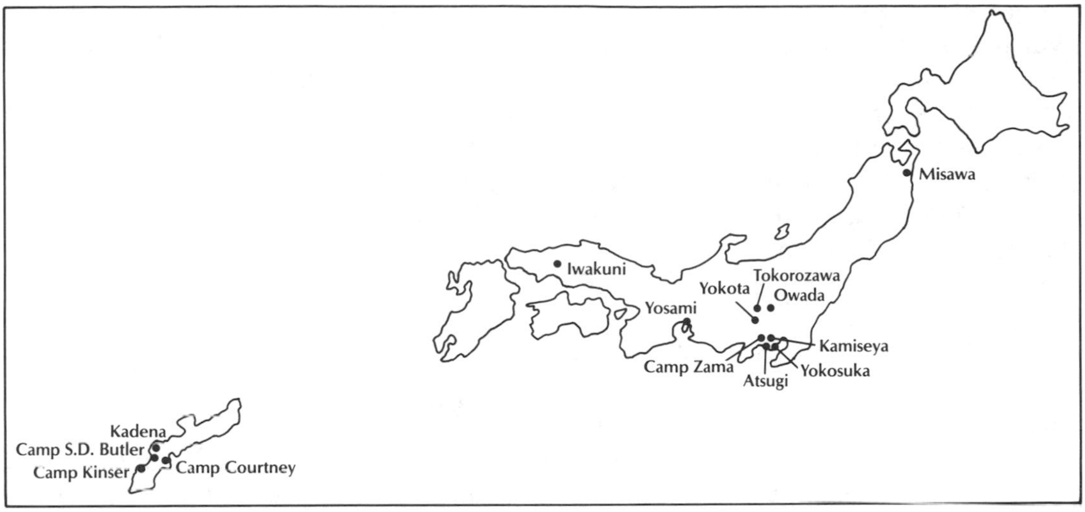

JAPAN

Japan, in spite of its "non-nuclear" policy, houses the most extensive forward nuclear infrastructure in the Pacific. Even though there are no nuclear warheads in the country, there are numerous anti-submarine, surveillance, communications, and command bases important to U.S. nuclear war plans. The bulk of the U.S. Naval and Marine strength in Asia is also in Japan.

Japan is also the headquarters of the U.S. Navy's Seventh Fleet, which has nuclear war plans for the entire western and northern Pacific. From its command base at Yokosuka, the Seventh Fleet would direct aircraft carrier, surface ship, amphibious, and submarine attacks on the Soviet navy and its bases in the Soviet Union. The Seventh Fleet's command center at Kamiseya would direct anti-submarine and surveillance operations in the northern Pacific. Nuclear-capable P-3 Orion planes, flying from Iwakuni, Misawa, and Kadena would track down and destroy Soviet submarines. Army, Marine, and Air Force bases in Japan would also support nuclear operations (see Appendix A).

U.S. military commands in Japan cannot be isolated from the overall U.S. posture in the Pacific. The United States need not violate Japan's non-nuclear policy by putting warheads there: The communications, planning, targeting, and refueling infrastructure firmly links Japan into its nuclear war plans. Moreover, there is evidence that the United States plans to move nuclear warheads into Japan in wartime. At Misawa, an "advanced undersea weapons shop" exists, ready to be activated for storage and preparation of nuclear anti-submarine depth bombs. Naval ships and submarines carrying nuclear weapons will also use Japanese bases during wartime to receive supplies and fuel.

The extension of the nuclear infrastructure into "nuclear-free" areas demonstrates how secrecy hides nuclear war preparations from the citizenry. It also shows that arms control—if it is to be effective—must restrict more than the presence of nuclear warheads. The flaw in the "nuclear-free" policies of Japan and Iceland, in the Treaty of Tlatelolco, and in most proposals for new "nuclear-free zones," is that they set up a system whereby "non-nuclear" means nothing but the absence of nuclear warheads; the infrastructure is ignored. This may have made sense in the 1950s and 1960s when nuclear weapons were large and difficult to transport and assemble. But today warheads are small, lightweight, and require minimal preparation and upkeep. Virtually every ship and airplane available to the nuclear powers can carry them anywhere on earth—as long as the intelligence, targeting, basing, training, and communications infrastructure is in place around the world. The Defense Department itself made this point in 1981 when it began to build neutron bombs even though European governments had refused their deployment in Europe. The DOD's justification was that during a crisis it would only take a few hours to fly the warheads to Europe from their storage depot in upstate New York.

The nuclear-related facilities in Iceland, Puerto Rico, Japan, and other "non-nuclear" countries are as important as warheads to U.S. plans to fight a nuclear war. Indeed, as far as these countries are concerned, they are more important. The once passive-sounding "reconnaissance" and "surveillance" planes, and "defensive" anti-submarine forces, are active instruments to prepare and implement nuclear attacks. The technical facilities of the nuclear infrastructure do not at first appear to be provocative, but they are as deadly as the nuclear arsenal. They tie these countries into nuclear plans in such a way that they not only become nuclear targets, but nuclear catapults on the front lines of the next war.

The Failures of Traditional Arms Control

The United States and the Soviet Union are embarking on programs to expand their strategic nuclear forces, programs that all presently planned "arms control" will do nothing to prevent. Neither side shows the inclination to accept limits on qualitative or quantitative improvements. But arms control was not designed to denuclearize the world or restrain nuclear war-making capacities. It has been dominated by the desire to institutionalize nuclear operating rules created by the superpowers to assure their freedom of movement, to secure advantages gained over the other side, and to appease public opinion.

Even the modest limits achieved in existing arms control agreements are dissolving. The Anti-Ballistic Missile (ABM) Treaty stands on the verge of collapse. Both the United States and Soviet Union have publicly questioned each other's compliance with the terms of previous treaties, including SALT (Strategic Arms Limitation Talks) I and SALT II, which the United States has not ratified. Negotiations for a Comprehensive Test Ban Treaty ceased in 1981. Two older nuclear treaties, the Threshold Test Ban Treaty and the Peaceful Nuclear Ex-

Future Nuclear Weapons Programs

United States	MX ICBM Small ICBM B-1B bomber Advanced Technology Bomber ("Stealth") Advanced Cruise Missile Advanced Air-to-surface Missile Trident II (D5) SLBM Intercontinental cruise missile Joint Tactical Missile System 155mm AFAP (W-82) Standard-2 Nuclear ASWSOW Nuclear Phoenix MARV
Soviet	SS-X-24 (MX class) solid fuel ICBM Improved Liquid Propellant ICBMs SS-X-25 small solid fuel ICBM SS-X-26 large ICBM SS-NX-23 (Trident II class) SLBM Blackjack (B-1 class) heavy bomber AS-X-15 air-launched cruise missile Bear H ALCM carrier SS-NX-21 (Tomahawk class) SLCM Yankee class cruise missile submarine Modified Galosh ABM interceptor High acceleration ABM interceptor SS-CX-4 GLCM SS-X-23 SRBM SS-X-28 (SS-20 replacement)
British	Trident II (D5) SLBM Harrier II GR5
French	ASMP air-to-surface missile SX mobile IRBM ASLP long-range attack missile M-5 MIRVed SLBM Hades SRBM Mirage 2000N
Chinese	CSS-NX-3 SLBM CSS-NX-4 SLBM CSS-5 ICBM

plosions Treaty, have not been ratified by the United States.

Regional arms control has also failed. A growing number of SS-20s face a growing number of Pershing IIs, ground-launched cruise missiles, and British and French missiles. The United States and the Soviet Union are upgrading their theater and battlefield nuclear forces. Britain and France are about to deploy new submarine missiles with improved, multiple warheads. Negotiators from NATO and the Warsaw Pact are entering their second decade of talks on "Mutual Reduction of Forces and Armaments and Associated Measures in Central Europe" without any result. Huge numbers of nuclear weapons—those designed for "tactical" fighting, naval warfare, and non-European contingencies—remain outside any negotiations.

Official attitudes toward the control of naval operations illustrate why traditional "arms-control" fails to restrain warmaking capacity. Much of the formal debate about the Latin American Nuclear-Free Zone centered on naval operations, particularly the "transit" of nuclear weapons. France, the Soviet Union, and the United States all asserted a right to unrestricted operations on the high seas, including those waters within an internationally mandated Nuclear-Free Zone. The Treaty, therefore, was made to fit the lowest common denominator. The superpowers valued the political symbolism of the Treaty (and its restraint on nuclear proliferation within Latin America) but rejected any contraints on their military operations and future options. Thus, without violating the letter of the Treaty, Britain reportedly brought ships armed with nuclear depth charges into the Nuclear-Free Zone during the Falklands War[10]; the United States can continue preparations for nuclear anti-submarine warfare in the Caribbean; and the Soviet Union can now regularly operate nuclear-capable naval vessels and Bear anti-submarine planes in the Zone.

Although strategic nuclear weapons and long-range theater missiles have been included in arms control negotiations, the military has successfully insisted on excluding non-strategic naval nuclear weapons. A Naval expert explained the basis of this position in 1980: "In land warfare, the main reasons for distinguishing between nuclear and conventional battlefield ordnance stem from the scale of devastation and the dangers of escalation. Both reasons lose much of their significance in maritime warfare."[11] Another expert, who later became Assistant Director of the U.S. Arms Control and Disarmament Agency, opposed the control of naval nuclear weapons because "there does not seem to be any compelling argument that limitations on nuclear weapons at sea provide more than ambiguous military, economic, or political benefits."[12] He argued that

> the risk of a gradual escalation to strategic nuclear war from conventional conflict is a far more serious problem for ground forces than for the Navies of the United States and the Soviet Union. In fact, if there had to be a tactical nuclear war between the superpowers, it would be better to fight it at sea . . ..[13]

These arguments do not hold water. First, the most numerous naval nuclear weapons are land-attack weapons—aircraft carrier bombs and cruise missiles. Nuclear weapons that would affect only other naval forces are far less numerous. Second, naval nuclear forces operate from U.S. and Soviet land bases (Backfire bombers, for example, and maritime patrol planes); any naval battle with those forces would involve attacks on them, and assure swift escalation to other "strategic" targets. Third, it is U.S. policy not to allow a nuclear war at sea to remain limited to the sea[14]: Any use of Soviet naval nuclear weapons would provoke U.S. retaliation against land targets, thus guaranteeing total escalation. Fourth, since a "tactical" nuclear exchange at sea would not initially endanger any population, cities, or territory, the temptation to cross the nuclear threshold at sea may actually be much greater than on land. Finally, the policy aim of the recent deployment of long-range sea-launched cruise missiles is to increase the "scale of devastation and the dangers of escalation" from the use of naval nuclear weapons.

The military employs a rhetoric of piecemeal analysis and spurious geographic analogy to avoid controls of its nuclear weapons, plans, operations, and infrastructure. Defense officials issue expert statements about the feasibility or infeasibility of whatever they do or do not want to do, sprinkling in vague concepts like "strategic" to lend authority to their language. One of the most common arguments against relinquishing any option is its irreplaceability. The military insists it cannot sacrifice control of Micronesia because it needs those islands just in case it loses bases in the Philippines. Yet at the same time it argues that Philippine bases are "irreplaceable" and completely secure. It argues that tropical testing grounds in Micronesia are extremely valuable, yet at the same time states it cannot give up identical facilities in Panama because there is no other location (including Micronesia) that could replace them. When the U.S. military wanted to expand its bases in Australia in the 1970s it argued such expansion was necessary because of the possibility of losing Philippine bases.[15] Later, when the Indian Ocean became an area of military competition, Australian bases became "necessary" because of their proximity to the Indian Ocean. Secrecy prevents the public—and the Congress—from scrutinizing such arguments, from finding the incoherence beneath phrases like "strategically vital area." The military's compartmentalization of geographic jurisdictions, and competition among the armed services, prevent the military itself from having an overall view.

The military issues grave warnings about every Soviet move and every new Soviet weapon. When the public questions whether Western counter-deployments might escalate the arms race, rather than impel the Soviets to negotiate, the U.S. military dismisses Soviet actions as unimportant or unrelated to U.S. actions. In May 1983 Secretary of Defense Weinberger downplayed new Soviet deployments of nuclear warheads to Eastern Europe.[16] In February 1984 Secretary of the Navy John Lehman made light of new Soviet deployments of Delta-class submarines in the western Atlantic: "We would invite them to deploy all their Deltas there," he said, because they would be easier to detect and destroy by anti-submarine forces. Joint Chiefs of Staff Chairman General John Vessey added, "The primary purpose of these deployments is political."[17] In October the Pentagon labeled the deployment of Soviet long-range cruise missiles "routine," not an escalation in the arms race.[18]

There is always some reason why

the public is wrong. When the "nuclear winter" effects of nuclear war were introduced into the public debate in 1983, military experts quickly took exception to the scientific and targeting assumptions. But the nuclear winter issue had an impact. Interviews with Pentagon officials revealed that they

> are plainly worried about the nuclear-winter problem, and plainly at a loss over what to do about it. In conversations with officials at the nuts-and-bolts level one picks up interesting nuances of reaction: a wistful hope that "more study" will make the nuclear-winter problem go away, embarrassment at having overlooked it for nearly forty years, resentment that the peacenik doom-mongers might have been right all these years, even if they didn't know why they were.[19]

The nuclear winter dispute offers yet another reminder that forty years into the nuclear era, much about nuclear weapons is still unquantified, unexplained, unknown. Nuclear winter studies suggest that the arms race affects everyone, and that nuclear war could be as bad as people's worst fears.

The arms race and nuclear plans proceed unchecked while nuclear governments issue assurances about controlling the system and reducing its risks. How ironic that the best argument the British Ministry of Defence could offer against denuclearization of Britain was that it would be a target anyway: "Whether we like the fact or not, and whether nuclear weapons are based here or not, our country's size and location make it militarily crucial to NATO and so an inevitable target in war."[20] Military experts scoff at the loose talk that everything is a target. In the next war it will be.

Restraining the Nuclear Infrastructure

From declarations of "nuclear-free" zones, to prohibitions on weapon deployments, to protests against military facilities, the nuclear system is under attack. Governments and citizens have launched campaigns to rein the nuclear powers. Yet none of these actions have meant much militarily. None have restrained the ability of the superpowers to wage war. Bans on warheads, for instance, do not impinge on superpower military prerogatives. The warheads are not needed in peacetime, and in war all bets are off: The nuclear militaries flout any treaty that limits their options. Whether launched by international organizations, national governments, or local citizen groups, "nuclear-free" proposals fail to heed the infrastructure, the crux of the nuclear system. Cast in official secrecy, the nuclear infrastructure has survived, vast and recondite; it has subverted efforts to control it.

The nuclear militaries nonetheless view the "nuclear-free" trend as a threat. Apprehensive that calls for control could someday lead to limits on military options, the superpowers counter "nuclear-free" proposals with ominous incantations: vital interests are at stake, threats in the region are growing, and non-nuclear status would make it impossible to defend in a war. But nothing has changed. U.S. allies in "nuclear-free" zones are still under the "nuclear umbrella," still tied in to military plans. "Nuclear-free" countries must recognize that, given the infrastructural requirements of U.S. war plans, nuclear protection entails nuclear provocation.

Preparing for the next war means preparing to fight it any second and every second, anywhere and everywhere. Behind every move lurks the threat of hair-trigger annihilation. Computer simulations, training maneuvers, and wargames act out every war that planners can imagine. To let down their guard, even for an instant, is to cede an advantage. Both sides are already fighting the next war—with everything but the warheads. Plotting targets, chasing submarines, testing missiles, collecting intelligence, and positioning forces, all could be the figment or fact of superiority. And superiority, even illusory, could provoke attack. The infrastructure is a moving target, ever changing, never safe. It is not only the means to fight the next war, it is likely to be the cause of it.

Everyone opposes nuclear war. Preventing it would require dismantling the nuclear infrastructure, and thereby restrict the worldwide war-making capabilities, nuclear and conventional, of the superpowers. Denuclearization would entail restraints not just on weapons, but on war. The long-term goals should be to redefine security, reshape superpower relations, and reduce interbloc tensions. A move toward a truly nuclear-free world would challenge superpower control. Denuclearization can only begin with widespread knowledge of the infrastructure that makes the world a nuclear battlefield. It can only be achieved by worldwide action to check the nuclear system, a system that threatens the peace.

Notes

ABBREVIATIONS

ACDA.	Arms Control and Disarmament Agency.
AFGL.	Air Force Geophysics Laboratory.
CBO.	Congressional Budget Office.
CRS.	Congressional Research Service.
DARPA.	Defense Advanced Research Projects Agency.
DIA.	Defense Intelligence Agency.
DOD.	Department of Defense.
DOE.	Department of Energy.
DMA.	Defense Mapping Agency.
DNA.	Defense Nuclear Agency.
GAO.	General Accounting Office.
GPO.	Government Printing Office.
HAC.	House Appropriations Committee.
HASC.	House Armed Services Committee.
JCS.	Joint Chiefs of Staff.
SAC.	Senate Appropriations Committee.
SASC.	Senate Armed Services Committee.
SIPRI.	Stockholm International Peace Research Institute.

Annual Congressional hearings on the Department of Defense and Department of Energy budgets are referred to in the notes as, Congressional Committee (HAC, HASC, SAC, SASC), Fiscal Year, Hearing (DOD, Energy and Water Development Appropriations, Military Construction), part number, page number (e.g.: HAC, FY 1984 DOD, pt. 1, p. 562.)

Chapter One: State of War

1. HASC, FY 1985 DOD, pt. 1, p. 563.
2. Ibid., p. 567.
3. HAC, FY 1984 DOD, pt. 2, p. 454.
4. Admiral S.R. Foley, Jr., Commander-in-Chief, U.S. Pacific Fleet, *Current Strategy Forum,* (Newport, R.I.: Naval War College, June 23, 1983).
5. William W. Jeffries, *Geography and National Power,* 4th ed. (Annapolis, Md.: U.S. Naval Institute, 1967), p. 1.
6. SASC, Report on Omnibus Defense Authorization Act, 1984, Report No. 98–174 (July 5, 1983), p. 14.
7. Foley, *Current Strategy Forum,* p. 8.
8. HAC, FY 1982 Military Construction, pt. 4, pp. 106–09.
9. Jeffries, *Geography and National Power,* p. 5.
10. Daniel Deudney, *Whole Earth Security: A Geopolitics of Peace,* Worldwatch Paper 55 (Washington, D.C.: Worldwatch Institute, July 1983), p. 15.
11. SASC, FY 1983 DOD, pt. 2, p. 1059.
12. Lieutenant Commander James Stavridis, "Naval Strategy and National Ocean Policy," U.S. Naval Institute *Proceedings* (July 1984), p. 43.
13. Frank Uhlig, "Naval Tactics: Examples and Analogies," *Naval War College Review* (March-April 1981), pp. 92–104.
14. Daniel Deudney, *Whole Earth Security*, p. 26.
15. *Air Force Magazine* (June 1981), p. 26.
16. U.S. Army Armament R&D Center, "Laboratory Posture Report FY 1983," No. RCS-DRCLD-101 (Dover, N.J., 1984), p. 1–15: "BRL [Ballistic Research Laboratory] has provided simulation technology pertaining to thermal and blast signatures of nuclear weapons to France, Germany, U.K., and the DNA. The above mentioned countries are developing facilities for nuclear weapons effects research and verifying equipment nuclear hardness."
17. U.S. Air Force, Air Weather Service, "History of Air Force Global Weather Central (AFGWC), Offutt Air Force Base, Neb., 1 January 1983—30 June 1983," No. RCS: HAF-CHO (AR) 7101 (Offutt AFB, Neb.: AWS, Sept. 30, 1983), p. 32. Total electron content (TEC) is the total number of electrons in a vertical meter squared from the earth's surface to the top of the world.
18. U.S. Naval Observatory, "Astronomy and Astrophysics," rev. ed., No. PE 62759, Subproject No. XF 59–554, FY 1984 (Washington, D.C.: U.S. Naval Observatory, n.d.), p. 7.
19. "Keeping the Lines Open during a Nuclear War," *Business Week* (Feb. 7, 1983), pp. 116–17.
20. Edgar Ulsamer, "C^3: Technolgical Edge for the '80s," *Air Force Magazine* (July 1982), p. 55.
21. DARPA, FY 1984 Budget Justification, pp. 134–35.
22. HASC, FY 1985 DOD, pt. 3, p. 157.
23. "After the Holocaust, Cable Television Is the Tie to Rebind," *Defense Week* (April 24, 1983), p. 14.

Chapter Two: The Earth

1. These figures are taken from DOE, "Summary of Foreign Nuclear Detonations Through December 31, 1983" (annual) (Las Vegas, Nev.: DOE, n.d.); DOE, "Announced U.S. Nuclear Tests, July 1945 through December 1983," No. NVO-209, 4th rev. (Las Vegas, Nev.: DOE, Jan. 1983). Outside of the nuclear nations themselves, U.S. tests have taken place at Bikini, Johnston, and Eniwetok Atolls in the western Pacific; British tests have taken place in the Monte Bello Islands, at Emu Field and Maralinga, Australia, and in the Christmas Islands in the central Pacific; French tests have taken place in Reggan and the southern Sahara desert in Algeria, as well as at Mururoa, Fangataufa, and Reao Island in French Polynesia.
2. National Research Council, *Seismographic Networks: Problems and Outlook for the 1980s* (Washington, D.C.: National Academy Press, 1983), p. 7.
3. Jack Oliver and Leonard Murphy, "WWNSS: Seismology's Global Network of Observing Stations" *Science* (Oct. 15, 1971), p. 255.
4. "Air Force Technical Applications Center," *Air Force Magazine* (May 1982), p. 143; (May 1984), p. 152.

5. The Glomar Challenger was used in 1981 to emplace marine seismic sensors in "boreholes several hundred meters deep that are drilled into firm bedrock . . . in the mid-Atlantic." Defense Advanced Research Projects Agency, FY 1983 R&D Program (Washington, D.C.: DARPA, March 30, 1982), p. III-5.
6. HASC, FY 1984 DOD, pt. 3, pp. 826, 1306.
7. DOD Annual Report, FY 1981, p. 143.
8. SASC, FY 1983 DOD, pt. 7, p. 4625.
9. DMA, FY 1984 Budget Justification, p. 9.
10. HAC, FY 1985 DOD, pt. 3, pp. 425, 431.
11. "DMA: The Cruise Missile's Silent Partner," *Air Force Magazine* (April 1980), pp. 60–62.
12. Major General W.L. Nicholson III, Director, Defense Mapping Agency, "Progress with a Purpose." (Keynote address presented to the American Congress on Surveying and Mapping at the annual convention of the American Society of Photogrammetry, St. Louis, Missouri, March 10, 1980).
13. Ibid.
14. HASC, FY 1985 DOD, pt. 3, p. 431.
15. Air Force Geophysics Laboratory, "Report on Research for the Period January 1979—December 1980," No. AFGL-TR-82–0132 (Hanscom AFB, Mass.: AFGL, April 1982), pp. 161–62.
16. Ibid., pp. 162–63.
17. DIA, "Ballistic Missile Guidance and Control—USSR and China," No. DST-1000S-294–83 (Washington, D.C.: DIA, April 15, 1983), pp. 110–11. Uncertainties cited by DIA for mobile land basing included "launch position uncertainty, the uncertainty in the deflection of the gravity vector from the normal to the reference ellipsoid, and the uncertainty in the magnitude of the gravity vector."
18. See K.D. McDonald, "Navigation Satellite Systems: Their Characteristics, Potential and Military Applications," in Bhupendra Jasani, ed., *Outer Space: A New Dimension of the Arms Race* (London: Taylor & Francis, 1982); James A. Austin, "GPS: Global Positioning System, An 18-Star Navigation Constellation," *Military Communications/Electronics* (June 1980), pp. 63–70; Robert P. Denaro, "Navstar: The All-Purpose Satellite," *IEEE Spectrum* (May 1981), pp. 35–40.
19. There are eight stations in the Omega network, located in Norway, Liberia, Hawaii, North Dakota, La Reunion, Argentina, Australia, and Japan. Nine VLF transmitters (also used for communications) are part of the coordinated navigation network: Yosami, Japan; North West Cape, Australia; Rugby and Anthorn, United Kingdom; Cutler, Maine, Annapolis, Maryland, Jim Creek, Washington, and Wahiawa, Hawaii. The land-based LORAN-C system could provide accuracy on the order of 150 meters but LORAN-C covers only 14 percent of the earth's surface.
20. The Air Force Armament Laboratory is developing a NAVSTAR receiver that could provide mid-course guidance to Tomahawk sea-launched cruise missiles.
21. HAC, FY 1984 DOD, pt. 8, p. 394.
22. DMA, FY 1984 Budget Justification, p. 12; Air Force, FY 1984 RDT&E Descriptive Summary, p. 747.
23. U.S. Naval Observatory, "Astronomy and Astrophysics: Accuracte Improvement of NAVOBSY Data, in support of NAVOBSY Operational Mission," No. PE 62759, Subproject No. XF 59–554, FY 1984 (Washington, D.C.: NAVOBSY, n.d.), p. 5.
24. U.S. Air Force, Air Weather Service, "History of Air Force Global Weather Central (AFGWC), Offutt AFB, Neb., 1 January 1983 — 30 June 1983," No. RCS: HAF-CHO(AR)7101 (Offutt AFB, Neb.: AWS, Sept. 30, 1983), p. 68.
25. Naval Observatory, "Astronomy and Astrophysics," p. 10.
26. Commander Linton Wells II, "Weather and Darkness in Contemporary Naval Operations," *Proceedings* (May 1982), pp. 151–67; U.S. Air Force, "Atmospheric Effects on Detecting/Tracking Radars," NORAD/SPACECOM Pamphlet 105–3 (May 20, 1983).
27. Air Force Geophysics Laboratory, "AFGL, Fiscal Year 1984 Air Force Technical Objectives Document," Special Report No. 232, AFGL-TR-82–0293 (Nov. 1982), p. 11.
28. HAC, FY 1984 DOD, pt. 3, p. 350.
29. Low-level route forecasts including altimeter settings, winds, temperatures, and D-values (a measurement of altitude correction) are actually provided by the National Oceanographic and Atmospheric Administration (NOAA), the central government

weather agency. DOD pays for NOAA mapping and weather services.

30. Use of civilian satellites like AMSTAR further extends the nuclear infrastructure into civilian areas, as is the case with AMSTAR facilities, including the control center in Glenwood, New Jersey, and the tracking, telemetry, and control centers in Dallas, Texas, and Atlanta, Georgia.
31. The NAVSTAR satellite navigation signal, for instance, must be corrected to take into consideration ionospheric disturbances or delays which occur during transmission. See Bruce Brown, "The Shining: The Mysterious Power of the Northern Lights," *New York Times Magazine* (December 12, 1982).
32. Air Force Geophysics Laboratory, "AFGL Fiscal Year 1984", p. 7.
33. Groundwaves are propagated within the troposphere (first 7–10 miles above the Earth's surface).
34. HF communications networks currently include the SAC Giant Talk/Scope Signal III network, the air/ground/air Global Command and Control System network, the Mystic Star Presidential/VIP network, and the Defense Communications System (DCS) "entry sites."
35. A good discussion of HF communications is "High Frequncy Transmissions Enjoy a Renewed Life," *Defense Systems Review* (June 1983), pp. 59–66.
36. U.S. Air Force, Air Weather Service, "History of Air Force Global Weather Central" p. 29. PCA is a total loss of HF radio communications in polar areas due to a large increase in ionospheric absorption; the Navy is conducting a program in northern Norway to monitor PCAs. Ibid., p. 30.
37. Commander Harley Higgins, "The Rediscovery of HF for Command and Control," *Signal* (March 1981), p. 57.
38. Bernard Blake, "Beyond the Horizon: A New Concept in Detection," *Jane's Defence Weekly* (March 17, 1984), pp. 414–16.
39. See "The HILAT Satellite" articles, *Johns Hopkins APL Technical Digest* 5(2) (April-June 1984).
40. G. Wetmore, "HF Radio: A Major Asset for 'Enduring C³'," *Journal of Defense Electronics* (May/June 1981), p. 57.
41. SASC, FY 1984 DOD, pt. 5, p. 2471.
42. HAC, FY 1984 DOD, pt. 8, p. 341.
43. SASC, FY 1984 DOD, pt. 5, p. 2471.
44. Edgar Ulsamer, "C³: Technological Edge for the '80s," *Air Force Magazine* (July 1982), p. 55.
45. "Systems Command Probes C³ Potential," *Aviation Week & Space Technology* (March 28, 1983), p. 65.
46. Willis E. Day, "Meteor Burst Communications Offer a Vital Alternative," *Defense Systems Review* (January 1984), pp. 49–51.
47. Robert L. Richmond, "Meteor Burst Communications, Part I: MBC Advances Assist C³ Objectives," *Military Communications/Electronics* (August 1982), pp. 68–72; Kenneth G. Gray, "Meteor Burst Communications," *Signal* (May/June 1982), pp. 125–34.
48. Philip J. Klass, "Meteor Trails May Aid Communications," *Aviation Week & Space Technology* (Aug. 15, 1983), pp. 166–69.
49. DNA, FY 1984 RDT&E Descriptive Summary, p. 330.
50. Ibid.
51. AFGL, "AFGL, Fiscal Year 1984," p. 10.
52. Ibid., p. 11.
53. See, for instance, Fred Pearce, "Secrets of the Windscale Fire Revealed," *New Scientist* (Sept. 29, 1983), p. 911; "Search Begins for Bomb-Test Victims," *New Scientist* (Oct. 6, 1983), p. 3. The Windscale fire in 1957 released polonium-210 into the atmosphere. Britain also conducted tests at Maralinga, South Australia, mostly in the late 1950s and early 1960s, in which "some radioactive materials were dispersed into the environment." Thousands of servicemen were also present at U.S. nuclear tests. Other examples include the impact of Soviet satellite Cosmos 954, which rained radioactive debris on Canada in 1978, and the plans to dispose of nuclear-powered submarines at sea.
54. Almost one-third (233) of the nuclear tests announced by the U.S. Department of Energy have resulted in releases of detectable radiation, either on-site or off-site.

Chapter Three: Nuclear Arsenals

1. Most of the information in this chapter on U.S. nuclear weapons comes from Thomas B. Cochran, William M. Arkin, and Milton

H. Hoenig, *Nuclear Weapons Databook: Vol. 1: U.S. Nuclear Forces and Capabilities* (Cambridge, Mass.: Ballinger, 1984); updated in *Bulletin of the Atomic Scientists* (August-September 1984).
2. Most of the information in this chapter on Soviet nuclear weapons comes from William M. Arkin and Jeffrey I. Sands, "The Soviet Nuclear Stockpile," *Arms Control Today* (June 1984), and Thomas B. Cochran, William M. Arkin, and Jeffrey I. Sands, *Nuclear Weapons Databook, Vol. 3: Soviet Nuclear Weapons* (Cambridge, Mass.: Ballinger, forthcoming).
3. The presence of British nuclear weapons in the Falklands is discussed in two unpublished papers: William M. Arkin and Andrew Burrows, "British Nuclear Weapons in the Falklands" (Washington, D.C.: Institute for Policy Studies, 1984), and George H. Quester, "Nuclear Implications of the South Atlantic War" (College Park, Md.: University of Maryland, 1984).
4. JCS, FY 1985, p. 25.
5. JCS, FY 1979, p. 28.
6. SAC, "S. Con. Res. 26, A Resolution to Approve Funding for the MX Missile," *S. Hearing* 98–444, 98th Cong. 1st Sess. (1983), p. 260.
7. Five to six older Yankee I-class submarines with shorter range missiles patrol in the Atlantic and Pacific and "conduct lengthy transits in order to be within range of targets in North America." DOD, *Soviet Military Power, 3d ed.* (Washington, D.C.: U.S. Government Printing Office, 1983), p. 23. (hereinafter DOD *Soviet Military Power*).
8. Two of the submarines have been upgraded to carry the new Chevaline "front end" which includes new and more accurate warheads and penetration aids. The other two submarines will be converted in the late 1980s.
9. "China Launches First Nuclear-Missile Sub," *Baltimore Sun,* (Nov. 29, 1981), p. 19; Antony Preston, "The PLA Navy's Underwater Deterrent," *Jane's Defence Weekly* (April 28, 1984), pp. 659–60.
10. Lieutenant Commander David G. Muller, Jr., "China's SSBN in Perspective," *Proceedings* (March 1982), pp. 125–27.
11. Bradley Hahn, "China in the SLBM Club," *Pacific Defence Reporter* (Feb. 1984), p. 18.
12. DOD, FY 1984 RDA, p. V-7.
13. J.M. McConnell, "Possible Counterforce Role for the Typhoon," *Professional Papers 347* (Washington, D.C.: Center for Naval Analysis, March 1982).
14. Rear Admiral John L. Butts, Director of Naval Intelligence, Statement on "The Naval Threat" before the Seapower and Strategic and Critical Materials Subcommittee of the House Armed Services Committee, 98th Cong., 2d Sess. (Feb. 28, 1984), p. 5.
15. JCS, FY 1984, p. 17.
16. Captain Thomas D. Washburn, "The People's Republic of China and Nuclear Weapons: Effects of China's Evolving Arsenal" (M.A. thesis, University of South Carolina, March 15, 1979).
17. HAC, FY 1985 DOD, pt. 1, pp. 511–12.
18. DOD, *Soviet Military Power* (1983), p. 23.
19. Butts, "The Naval Threat," pp. 2, 6.
20. Charles Hernu, "France's Defense: Choices and Means," *Le Figaro,* Jan. 30–31, 1982 (reprinted by the Press and Information Service of the French Embassy, New York).
21. William M. Arkin, "Flying in the Face of Arms Control," *Bulletin of the Atomic Scientists* (Feb. 1984), pp. 5–6.
22. "Normally the majority of INF aircraft carry only one warhead but some types of aircraft, particularly those with longer ranges, can carry a second or third warhead." NATO, "NATO and the Warsaw Pact: Force Comparisons, 1st ed. (Brussels: NATO Information Service, 1982), p. 31.
23. Defense Intelligence Agency, *A Guide to the Foreign Tactical Nuclear Weapon Systems Under the Control of Ground Force Commanders,* No. DST-1040S-541–83-CHG 1 (Aug.17, 1984) (Secret, partially declassified), p. xviii.
24. French plans call for the replacement of the Clemenceau carrier with a nuclear-powered Bretagne class carrier in the mid-1990s.
25. U.S. Air Force Tactical Air Command, "Soviet Short Range Ballistic Missiles: New Generation," Slide 1, TAC Intelligence Briefing 79–10 (1979) (partially declassified).
26. *Jane's Defence Weekly* (June 2, 1984), p. 867.
27. William M. Arkin and Richard W. Fieldhouse, "Pershing and Cruise: No Room for Compromise," *ADIU Report* (March/April 1983), pp. 4–7.
28. S.K. Ghosh and Sreedhar, eds., *China's Nu-*

clear and Political Strategy (New Dehli: Young Asia Publications, 1975).

29. Defense Intelligence Agency, "Soviet Self-Propelled Artillery," No. DDI-1130–6-76 (May 1976) (Confidential, partially declassified).
30. DIA, *A Guide,* p. xii.
31. Ibid., pp. x, xii.
32. Defense Intelligence Agency, "Handbook on the Chinese Armed Forces," No. DDI-2682–32-76 (July 1976), p. 3–15.
33. See William M. Arkin, Andrew Burrows, Richard Fieldhouse, Jeffrey I. Sands, "Nuclearization of the Oceans," Background paper presented at the Symposium on the Denuclearization of the Oceans, Norrtalje, Sweden, May 11–14, 1984.
34. A replacement missile for ASROC and SUBROC, called the ASW Stand-off Weapon (ASWSOW), has been in development for some time.

Chapter Four: The Arsenal's Tentacles

1. SASC, FY 1984 DOD, pt.2, p. 886.
2. HAC, FY 1985 EWDA, pt. 6, p. 35.
3. These facilities are the Gaseous Diffusion Plant in Paducah, Kentucky; the Portsmouth Gaseous Diffusion Plant in Piketon, Ohio; the Feed Materials Production Center in Fernald, Ohio; the Ashtabula Extrusion Plant in Ashtabula, Ohio; the Hanford Reservation in Richland, Washington; the Savannah River Plant in Aiken, South Carolina; and the Idaho National Engineering Laboratory in Idaho Falls, Idaho.
4. These facilities are the Rocky Flats Plant in Golden, Colorado; the Kansas City Plant in Kansas City, Missouri; the Mound Laboratory in Miamisburg, Ohio; the Pinellas Plant in Clearwater, Florida; and the Y-12 Plant in Oak Ridge, Tennessee.
5. In the United States, tests have been held at Amchitka, in the Aleutian Islands; Alamogordo, Carlsbad, and Farmington, New Mexico; Hattiesburg, Mississippi; Grand Valley and Rifle, Colorado; Eniwetok and Bikini Atolls and the Johnston Island area; and in the east Pacific and South Atlantic Ocean areas. Before starting to use NTS in 1962, Britain also tested weapons near the Monte Bello Islands off the north coast of Australia; at Christmas Island in the Pacific; and at Woomera and Maralinga in central Australia.
6. Previous French detonations have occurred at Fangataufa and Reao Islands in French Polynesia and in Algeria.
7. See U.S. Department of Energy, Nevada Operations Office, "Summary of Foreign Nuclear Detonations through December 31, 1983" (annual) (Las Vegas, Nev.: DOE, 1984). China, which is not a signatory to the Limited Test Ban Treaty of 1963 (nor is France) has tested nuclear warheads in the atmosphere on twenty-two of its known twenty-seven tests.
8. "DOD Memo for Correspondents," April 22, 1983.
9. HASC, FY 1982 DOD, pt. 2, p. 177.
10. U.S. Air Force, "Operations: Airspace Management in the Philippines," Thirteenth Air Force Regulation 55–2 (March 1, 1982), pp. 4–5–4–7.
11. DOD, *Soviet Military Power,* 3d ed.(1984), p. 70.
12. See Peter Pringle and William Arkin, *S.I.O.P.: The Secret U.S. Plan for Nuclear War* (New York: W.W. Norton, 1983).
13. See Jeffrey T. Richelson, "United States Strategic Reconnaissance: Photographic/Imaging Satellites," *ACIS Working Paper No. 38* (Los Angeles: Center for International and Strategic Affairs, UCLA, 1983).
14. See, for instance, Lieutenant Commander Edwin W. Shaar, Jr., "ASW and the Naval Officer Oceanographer," *Proceedings* (Feb. 1978), pp. 43–49.
15. SAC, FY 1981 DOD, pt. 4, p. 356.
16. SASC, FY 1983 DOD, pt. 6, p. 3578.
17. These are at Dam Neck, Virginia; Makalapa, Hawaii; London, England; Rota, Spain; and Kamiseya, Japan. See Vice Admiral Samuel L. Gravely, Jr., "OSIS Extends Intelligence Coverage Beyond Radar Horizon," *Defense Electronics* (April 1982), pp. 69–76.
18. See William Arkin and Richard Fieldhouse, "Nuclear Weapon Command, Control and Communications," in *World Armaments and Disarmament: SIPRI Yearbook 1984* (London: Taylor & Francis, 1984), p. 470, (hereinafter referred to as "SIPRI C^3"); Senator Gary Hart and Senator Barry Goldwa-

ter, "Recent False Alerts from the Nation's Missile Attack Warning System," *Report to the Senate Committee on Armed Services,* 96th Cong., 2d Sess. (Oct. 9, 1980), p. 3.
19. SIPRI C^3, p. 495.
20. SIPRI C^3, p. 475.
21. HASC, FY 1983 DOD, pt. 3, p. 865.
22. DOD, Defense Communications Agency, "Meeting the Challenge of the 80's: The Defense Communications System in Transition" (Washington, D.C.: DCA, n.d.); and "DCA," (Washington, D.C.: DCA, n.d.), p. 12.
23. HASC, FY 1983 DOD, pt. 3, p. 152.
24. SIPRI C^3, p. 479.
25. JCS, FY 1984, p. 15.
26. SASC, FY 1984 DOD, pt. 5, p. 2470.
27. DOD, Annual Report, FY 1983, p. I-40.
28. SIPRI C^3, p. 483.
29. SAC, FY 1980 DOD, pt. 3, p. 1362.
30. R.J. Carlin, "Communicating with the Silent Service," *Proceedings* (Dec. 1981), pp. 75–78; see also "Promulgation of Commander in Chief, Atlantic Organization and Regulations Manual," CINCLANT/CINCLANTFLT/CINCWESTLANT/COMOCEANLANT Staff Instruction 5200.1N (July 29, 1981), p. 2-4-13.
31. U.S. Pacific Command, "PACAF Command Control HF/SSB Radio Network (Commando Escort)," Pacific Air Forces Regulation 100–2, (June 3, 1981), p. 2–8.
32. Four C-160 Transalls will be hardened and equipped as VLF transmitters by 1988. See Jeffrey M. Lenrovitz, "French Budget Sets $8 Billion for Equipment," *Aviation Week & Space Technology* (Nov. 1983), pp. 31–32.
33. General Accounting Office, "The Federal Emergency Management Agency's Plan For Revitalizing U.S. Civil Defense: A Review of Three Major Plan Components," Report No. NSIAD-84–11 (April 16, 1984), p. 37.
34. Ibid.

Chapter Five: Going to War

1. DOD, "World-wide Military Command and Control System (WWMCCS)," DOD Directive 5100.30 (December 2, 1971).
2. A complete discussion of Soviet C^3 is contained in William M. Arkin and Richard W. Fieldhouse, "Nuclear Weapon Command, Control and Communications," in *World Armaments and Disarmament: SIPRI Yearbook 1984* (London: Taylor and Francis, 1984).
3. DOD, *Soviet Military Power,* 2d ed.(1983), p. 17.
4. Congressional Research Service, "Authority to Order the Use of Nuclear Weapons (United States, United Kingdom, France, Soviet Union, People's Republic of China)," Committee Print prepared for the Subcommittee on International Security and Scientific Affairs of the House Committee on International Relations, 94th Cong., 1st Sess. (Dec. 1, 1975), pp. 10–14.
5. Ibid., pp. 15–17.
6. DIA, *A Guide to Foreign Tactical Nuclear Weapon Systems Under the Control of Ground Force Commanders,* No. DST-1040S-541–83, (Sept. 9, 1983) (partially declassified).
7. CRS, "Authority to Order the Use," pp. 23–29.
8. Strategic Air Command, "Units, Organizations, and Functions of Strategic Air Command Units," SAC Regulation 23–9 (July 31, 1981), p. 7–101.
9. Richard Lee Walker, *Strategic Target Planning: Bridging the Gap between Theory and Practice* (Washington, D.C.: U.S. Government Printing Office, National Defense University, 1983), p. 6.
10. DOD Annual Report, FY 1981, p. 55.
11. DOD Annual Report, FY 1982, p. 40.
12. 200 SLBM warheads are allocated to the Strategic Reserve force in day-to-day alerts. Under generated alerts, the number would be increased to 400 warheads.
13. DOD, *Soviet Military Power,* 3rd ed.(1984), p. 11.
14. SAC, "S. Con. Res. 26, A Resolution to Approve Funding for the MX Missile," S. Hearing 444, 98th Cong., 1st Sess.(1983), p. 245.
15. Ibid., p. 245.
16. Ibid., p. 245.
17. Ibid., p. 249.
18. Robert P. Berman and John C. Baker, *Soviet Strategic Forces: Requirements and Responses* (Washington, D.C.: Brookings Institution, 1982). This contains a good over-

view discussion of what is known about Soviet doctrine.
19. U.K., Ministry of Defence, *Statement on Defence Estimates for 1981,* vol. 1 (London: H.M. Stationery Office, 1982), p. 11.
20. Ibid., p. 12.
21. Ibid., p. 23.
22. Harlan W. Jencks, *From Muskets to Missiles: Politics and Professionalism in the Chinese Army, 1945–1981* (Boulder, Colo.: Westview, 1982), p. 159.
23. DIA, *Handbook on the Chinese Armed Forces,* No. DDI-2682-32-76 (July 1976), p. 142.
24. In 1974, the number of installations in the target system was more than 25,000. Senate Foreign Relations Committee, "US-USSR Strategic Policies Hearing," 93rd Cong., 2d Sess. (March 4, 1974), p. 38. In 1979, the Air Force reported an "annual average increase in the target list of approximately 10 percent over the past several years." SASC, FY 1980 DOD, pt. 1, p. 397.
25. Strategic Air Command, "The SAC Air Target Materials Program," SAC Regulation 96–1 (Sept. 12, 1980), p. 2–2
26. Ibid.
27. S. Con. Res. 26, p. 259.
28. Ibid.
29. HAC, FY 1984 DOD, pt. 8, p. 257.
30. Arms Control and Disarmament Agency, "Effectivėness of Soviet Civil Defense in Limiting Damage to Population," *ACDA Civil Defense Study Report No. 1* (Nov. 16, 1977) (declassified).
31. William Beecher, "U.S. Drafts New N-War Strategy vs. Soviets," *Boston Globe* (July 27, 1980), p. 1.
32. ACDA, "Effectiveness of Soviet Civil Defense."
33. S. Con. Res. 26, p. 249.
34. Ibid, p. 245.
35. Arms Control and Disarmament Agency, "An Analysis of Civil Defense in Nuclear War" (Washington, D.C.: ACDA, December 1978).
36. HAC, FY 1985 DOD, pt. 1, p. 511.
37. Senate Foreign Relations Committee, *U.S. Security Issues in Europe: Burden Sharing and Offset, MBFR and Nuclear Weapons,* Staff Report (Comm. Print, Dec. 2, 1973) 93rd Cong., 1st Sess.
38. DOD, Annual Report, FY 1982, p. 64.
39. Senate Foreign Relations Committee, *U.S. Security Issues in Europe,* p. 19.
40. DOD, Annual Report, FY 1976, p. III-2.
41. DOD, FY 1977 RDA, p. IV-103.
42. Senate Foreign Relations Committee, *U.S. Security Issues in Europe,* p. 19.
43. JCS, FY 1976, p. 107.
44. JCS, FY 1977, p. 69.
45. Senate Foreign Relations Committee, *U.S. Security Issues in Europe,* p. 19.
46. Richard Halloran, "New Weinberger Directive Refines Military Policy," *New York Times,* March 22, 1983, p. 1.
47. Berman and Baker, *Soviet Strategic Forces,* p. 29.
48. See William Arkin, Frank Von Hippel, and Barbara G. Levi, "The Consequences of a 'Limited' Nuclear War in East and West Germany," in Jeannie Peterson, ed., *The Aftermath: The Human and Ecological Consequences of Nuclear War* (New York: Pantheon, 1983); also in *AMBIO,* 11(2–3) (Spring, 1982), pp. 163–73.
49. S. Con. Res. 26, p. 249.
50. JCS, FY 1978, p. 85.
51. Department of the Army, *Operations, Field Manual* 100–5 (Baltimore, Md.: Army AG Publications Center, July 1, 1976), p. 10–6.
52. SAC, FY 1984 DOD, pt. 1, p. 419.
53. Walker, *Strategic Target Planning,* p. 35.
54. S. Con. Res. 26, pp. 247–48.

Chapter Six: Europe

1. HASC, FY 1984 Military Construction, pp. 332–341.
2. The highway outside Ramstein Air Base, for instance, is already prepared with taxiways.
3. SAC, FY 1981 Military Construction, p. 250.
4. See William Arkin, Frank von Hippel, and Barbara G. Levi, "The Consequences of a 'Limited' Nuclear War in East and West Germany," in Jeannie Peterson, ed., *The Aftermath: The Human and Ecological Consequences of Nuclear War* (New York: Pantheon, 1983); also in *AMBIO,* 11(2–3) (Spring, 1982), pp. 163–73.
5. Paul Bracken, "The NATO Defense Problem," *ORBIS* (Spring 1983), p. 83.
6. *Soviet Aerospace* (June 13, 1983), p. 46.

7. HAC, FY 1983 DOD, pt. 4, p. 402.
8. HASC, FY 1984 DOD, pt. 3, p. 1046.
9. SAC, FY 1984 Energy and Water Development Appropriations, pt. 2, p. 1175.
10. Ibid., p. 1215.
11. Ibid., p. 1155.
12. See William M. Arkin, "Pershing II and U.S. Nuclear Strategy," *Bulletin of the Atomic Scientists* (June/July 1983), pp. 12–13.
13. Captain Robert Sankner and Captain Peter H. Norris, "One Up on 1a," *Field Artillery Journal* (July-August 1984), pp. 16–19.
14. See William M. Arkin and David Chappell, "The Impact of Soviet Theater Nuclear Force Improvements," *ADIU Report* (July/August 1983), pp. 11–13.
15. HASC, FY 1985 DOD, pt. 1, pp. 562, 578.
16. U.S. Sixth Fleet Threat Briefing (1983) (mimeo).
17. A single Golf V-class SSB is used in the Black Sea for missile research and development. Defense Intelligence Agency, "Unclassified Communist Naval Order of Battle" (June 1983), p. 1.
18. NAVCAMS MED in Naples, for instance, is "Broadcast Control Authority (BCA) terminal facility for command and control of U.S. and NATO ballistic and Fleet submarine forces in the Mediterranean." Naval Telecommunications Command Instruction 5450.22C, "Mission and Functions Assigned to U.S. Naval Communications Area Master Station, Mediterranean, Naples, Italy" (Sept. 26, 1979).
19. This is seen in the recent reorganization of U.S. naval forces in Europe, transferring the position of Commander-in-Chief, U.S. Naval Forces in Europe (CINCUSNAVEUR) from headquarters in London to Naples. The command responsibilities for all U.S. naval forces in Europe and NATO forces in the southern region have been consolidated with the Commander-in-Chief of Allied Forces Southern Europe (CINCSOUTH). Previously CINCUSNAVEUR was purely a U.S. command with no NATO forces. CINCSOUTH was a NATO command with no U.S. responsibilities. Consolidating U.S. and NATO commanders in the Mediterranean and stressing the improved "command relationships" of a U.S. Admiral commanding all naval forces in the southern region and Europe is indicative of growing NATO interest in regions outside of its traditional focus.
20. HASC, FY 1984 DOD, pt. 1, p. 1336.
21. HASC, FY 1984 DOD, pt. 3, p. 1388.
22. HASC, FY 1984 DOD, pt. 1, p. 1351.
23. HAC, FY 1984 Military Construction, pt. 4, p. 183.
24. HASC, FY 1984 Military Construction, p. 293.
25. HASC, FY 1984 DOD, pt. 3, pp. 1375–1376.

Chapter Seven: The Pacific

1. Pacific Command, "Pacific Area Update," No. P4080.1P1–4 (Feb. 17, 1984).
2. James A. Kelly, Deputy Undersecretary of Defense for East Asian and Pacific Affairs, *Statement before the House Foreign Affairs Committee,* May 6, 1984.
3. HAC, FY 1983 DOD, pt. 1, p. 596.
4. See William M. Arkin, "The Nuclear Balancing Act in the Pacific," *Bulletin of the Atomic Scientists* (Dec. 1983), pp. 9–10.
5. A discussion of DEFCON levels is contained in Peter Pringle and William Arkin, *S.I.O.P.: The Secret U.S. Plan for Nuclear War* (New York: W.W. Norton, 1983).
6. SAC, FY 1981 DOD, pt. 3, p. 729.
7. Ibid.
8. Defense Nuclear Agency Budget Justification, in Office of the Secretary of Defense, "Justification of Estimates for Fiscal Year 1982," (Jan. 1981), p. 422 (hereinafter DNA Justification).
9. DNA Justification, FY 1983, p. 437.
10. Admiral William J. Crowe, Jr., Commander-in-Chief, Pacific, *Statement on the Pacific Area before the Senate Armed Services Committee,* 23 February 1984, p. 14.
11. DOD, Annual Report, FY 1983, p. II-21.
12. Intelligence briefing of the DIA (undated, circa 1982) (partially declassified).
13. Dr. Wallace G. Magathan, Jr., Defense Intelligence Officer/General Purpose Forces and MBFR, Defense Intelligence Agency, *Statement on the Soviet Role in Asia before the Foreign Affairs Committee of the House of Representatives, Subcommittee on Europe and the Middle East and Subcommittee on Asian and Pacific Affairs,* July 1982 (partially declassified).

14. Ibid.
15. According to Pacific Air Forces, "Organization and Mission of PACAF Air Combat Operations Staff," PACAFR 20–6, (Dec. 20, 1981), a staff member is assigned duties as "operational point of contact for development of GLCM beddown in PACOM." According to information obtained by the authors from the Air Force, future deployment of the GLCM in the Pacific was still under active consideration in December 1982.
16. Crowe, *Statement on the Pacific Area,* p. 8.
17. Magathan, *Statement on the Soviet Role in Asia.*
18. Ibid.
19. Ibid.
20. Ibid.
21. Anthony H. Cordesman, "The Military Balance in Northeast Asia: The Challenge to Japan and Korea," *Armed Forces Journal International* (November 1983), p. 101.
22. HASC, FY 1984 DOD, pt. 3, pp. 1374–1375.

Chapter Eight: Nuclear Weapons and the Third World

1. HAC, FY 1985 DOD, pt. 8, p. 791.
2. HASC, FY 1985 DOD, pt. 1, p. 396.
3. Cited in *The New Republic* (April 15, 1980).
4. John F. Lehman, "The Soviet Strategic Nuclear Advantage and How to Eliminate It," *International Security Review,* (Fall 1980), pp. 271–86.
5. Richard Burt, "Study Says Soviet Thrust in Iran Might Require U.S. Atom Arms," *New York Times,* (Feb. 2 1980), p. 1.
6. President Jimmy Carter, *State of the Union Address before the Congress,* Jan. 23, 1980.
7. Senate Armed Services Committee, *Nomination of Caspar W. Weinberger to be Secretary of Defense, Hearing,* 97th Cong., 1st Sess. (Jan 6, 1981), p. 45.
8. U.S. Congressional Budget Office, *Building a 600-ship Navy: Costs, Timing, and Alternative Approaches* (Washington, D.C.: CBO, March 1982), p. 17.
9. SASC, FY 1984 DOD, pt. 6, p. 3211.
10. ACDA, FY 1984 ACIS, p. 142.
11. HAC, FY 1980 DOD, pt. 3, p. 755.
12. Commodore Roger F. Bacon, Director, Strategic and Theater Nuclear Warfare Division in the Chief of Naval Operations, *Statement on the Sea-based Deterrent before the Stategic and Theater Nuclear Forces Subcommittee of the Senate Armed Services Committee,* 98th Cong., 2d Sess. (March 13, 1984).
13. JCS, Budget Justification, FY 1984, p. 28.
14. "Minuteman Concept," Field Artillery Journal (March-April 1984), p. 44.
15. SASC, FY 1981 DOD, pt. 3, p. 1282.
16. JCS, FY 1982, p. 79.
17. JCS, FY 1981, p. 49.
18. Commander Amphibious Group Eastern Pacific, "Movement and Storage of Nuclear Weapons during Amphibious Operations," CPGEPINST 3401.1 (June 24, 1980), p. 7.
19. Lieutenant General Robert C. Kingston, Commander in Chief, U.S. Central Command, *Statement on the Status of the United States Central Command before the Senate Armed Service Committee,* 98th Cong., 2d Sess. (Feb. 23, 1984).
20. Bargaining during the 1970s laid the foundation for bilateral agreements to restrict forces in the Indian Ocean and establish a "zone of peace." In March 1977 President Carter proposed complete demilitarization of the Indian Ocean. That spring Soviet President Podgorny pledged the Soviet Union's willingness to participate in a zone of peace. However, discussions between the superpowers on limitation of their naval operations ceased when the Soviet Union lost access to Somalian bases and after the fall of the Shah of Iran in 1979.
21. Middle East Force, "Organization Manual," COMIDEASTFORINST 5400.1C, 15 March 1983.
22. U.S. Central Command, "United States Central Command," (n.d. (1983)).
23. "An exclusive AFJ interview with Lt. Gen. Robert C. Kingston, Commander-in-Chief, U.S. Central Command," *Armed Forces Journal International* (July 1984), pp. 67–73.
24. Dr. Wallace G. Magathan, Jr., Defense Intelligence Officer/General Purpose Forces and MBFR, Defense Intelligence Agency, *Statement on the Soviet Role in Asia before the Subcommittee on Europe and the Middle East and the Subcommittee on Asian and Pacific Affairs of the House Committee on Foreign Affairs* (July 1982) (partially declassified).

25. Ibid.
26. Ibid.
27. Keith A. Dunn, "Constraints on the USSR in Southwest Asia: A Military Analysis," *Orbis,* 25(3) (Fall 1981), pp. 607–29.
28. Admiral Wesley L. McDonald, Commander-in-Chief, U.S. Atlantic Command, "Status of the Atlantic Command," *Statement before the Senate Armed Services Committee,* 98th Cong., 2d Sess. (Feb. 23, 1984).
29. Ibid.
30. Quoted in "Questions About the Kennedy-Krushchev Agreement," *Air Force Magazine* (Dec. 1983), pp. 17–18.
31. SASC, FY 1984 DOD, pt. 2, p. 1008.
32. John Collins, *U.S.-Soviet Military Balance: Concepts and Capabilities,* 1960–1980 (New York: McGraw-Hill, 1980), p. 20.
33. HAC, FY 1984 DOD, pt. 3, p. 128.
34. HASC, FY 1985 DOD, pt. 1, p. 397.
35. Kingston, *Statement.*
36. SASC, FY 1983 DOD, pt. 5, pp. 3060–79.
37. HAC, FY 1985 DOD, pt. 1, p. 826.
38. Rear Admiral John L. Butts, Director of Naval Intelligence, *Statement on the Naval Threat before the Seapower and Strategic and Critical Materials Subcommittee of the House Armed Services Committee,* 98th Cong., 2d Sess. (Feb. 28, 1984); SASC, FY 1983 DOD, pt. 5, pp. 3060–79.
39. SASC, FY 1983 DOD, pt. 5, pp. 3060–79.
40. Butts, *Statement.*
41. Burt, "Study Says Soviet Thrust in Iran," p. 1.
42. Thomas O'Toole, "South African's Spying Seen as Painful Blow to West," *The Washington Post,* June 11, 1984, p. A10.
43. McDonald, "Status of the Atlantic Command."
44. DNA, FY 1984 RDT&E, p. 362.
45. SAC, FY 1984 DOD, pt. 2, p. 841.
46. U.S. Atlantic Command, "Promulgation of Commander in Chief, Atlantic Organization and Regulations Manual," CINCLANT/CINCLANTFLT/ CINCWESTLANT/COMOCEANLANT Staff Instruction 5200.1N, (29 July 1981); p. 2-4-4 refers to an Atlantic Command "bilateral agreement for Netherlands/U.S. surveillance in the Caribbean."
47. Vice Admiral William H. Rowden, "New Challenges on an Ancient Sea: The U.S. Sixth Fleet and NATO," *NATO's Sixteen Nations* (June/July, 1983), pp. 47–49.
48. Admiral W.J. Crowe, Jr., "Allied Defence of the Southern Region," *NATO's Sixteen Nations* (June/July 1983), pp. 18–25.
49. Rear Admiral Louis A. Williams, "The Atlantic Connection: IBERLANT," *NATO's Sixteen Nations,* 28(6) (Special 2/1983), pp. 30–38.
50. Caspar W. Weinberger, "Report on Allied Contributions to the Common Defense, A Report to United States Congress," (March 1983), p. 58.
51. HAC, FY 1984 Military Construction, pt. 5, p. 298. See also Sam Cohen, "Turkey Allows U.S. Marines to Use Air Base as Transit Point," *Christian Science Monitor,* December 12, 1983.
52. SASC, FY 1984 Military Construction, p. 212.
53. HAC, FY 1985 DOD, pt. 1, p. 614.

Chapter Nine: Denuclearizing

1. For a discussion of the impact of local nuclear-free zones, see Andrew Ryerson, "Small-Town Freeze," *The New Republic* (Oct. 15, 1984), pp. 14–16.
2. Stephen Talbot, "The H-Bombs Next Door," The Nation (Feb. 7, 1981), pp. 143–148; Center for Defense Information, "U.S. Nuclear Weapons Accidents: Danger in Our Midst," *Defense Monitor,* 10(5) (1981).
3. Duncan Campbell, *The Unsinkable Aircraft Carrier: American Military Power in Britain* (London: Michael Joseph, 1984), p. 51. The statement by the British government was, in fact, a lie, given that there was a serious U.S. nuclear weapons accident at RAF Lakenheath in 1956, an accident which has never been officially acknowledged.
4. U.S. General Accounting Office, "Safety at the Navy's Seal Beach, California, Weapons Station Has Improved," Report No. PLRD-83-87 (June 10, 1983), p. 12.
5. U.S. Congress, Joint Committee on Atomic Energy, Development, Use, and Control of Nuclear Energy for the Common Defense and Security and for Peaceful Purposes, *First Annual Report to the U.S. Congress,* 94th Cong., 2d Sess. (June 30, 1975).

6. U.S. Arms Control and Disarmament Agency, *Arms Control and Disarmament Agreements: Texts and Histories of Negotiations* (1982 Edition) (Washington, D.C.: U.S. Government Printing Office, 1982), pp. 59–82.
7. U.S. Navy, "Naval Station Roosevelt Roads Nuclear Weapons Security Plan," NAVSTAROOSRDSINST C5510.16A (Sept. 17, 1979) (Confidential-Formerly Restricted Data, partially declassified).
8. Colegio de Abogados de Puerto Rico, *Report of the Special Commission on Nuclear Weapons and the Treaty for the Prohibition of Nuclear Weapons in Latin America* (San Juan, Puerto Rico: CAPR, Aug. 17, 1984).
9. Department of Defense, "Major Range and Test Facility Base," DOD Directive 3200.11D (June 1983).
10. Duncan Campbell and John Rentoul, "All Out War," *New Statesman* (Aug. 24, 1984), p. 8.
11. Michael MccGwire, "Soviet-American Arms Control," in George H. Quester, ed., *Navies and Arms Control* (New York: Praeger, 1980).
12. Barry M. Blechman, *The Control of Naval Armaments: Prospects and Possibilities* (Washington, D.C.: Brookings Institution, 1975).
13. DOD, FY 1984 Annual Report, p. 139.
14. George C. Wilson, "Pentagon Guidance Document Seeks Tougher Sea Defenses," *Washington Post,* (May 25, 1982), p. 1.
15. Robert E. Harkavy, *Great Power Competition for Overseas Bases: The Geopolitics of Access Diplomacy* (New York: Pergamon, 1982), p. 210.
16. "U.S.: Nuclear Warheads in Eastern Europe," *Washington Post* (June 4, 1984), p. A1; "Soviet A-Arms in Europe No Surprise, U.S. Says," *New York Times* (Oct. 19, 1983), p. A5.
17. *Boston Globe,* (Feb. 15, 1984).
18. See for instance, Gerald F. Seib, "New Soviet Submarine Moves Close to U.S. In a Move Seen as Politically Motivated," *Wall Street Journal* (Jan. 27, 1984), p. 6; "The U.S. Response on Cruise Missiles," *New York Times* (Aug. 28, 1984), p. 12.
19. Thomas Powers, "Nuclear Winter and Nuclear Strategy," *The Atlantic,* (Nov. 1984), pp. 53–64.
20. U.K. Ministry of Defence, *Statement on Defence Estimates for 1981, vol. 1* (London: H.M. Stationery Office, 1982), p. 14.

Appendices

The five appendices that follow list all the locations that have been identified as part of the nuclear infrastructure: nuclear forces; decisionmaking centers; research and development facilities; nuclear testing and training sites; surveillance facilities; command, control and communications facilities; and scientific or electronic installations that provide peacetime or wartime support for the nuclear forces (weather, navigation, radar and optical tracking, and civil defense). The largest category of locations covers "nuclear-certified" and "nuclear-capable" combat units, and their controlling headquarters and command centers. More obscure facilities and forces, such as those for anti-submarine warfare, are also identified when they have a direct link to nuclear forces or plans. (Because anti-submarine warfare operations depend on nuclear weapons, all facilities that contribute to ocean surveillance also support nuclear capabilities.) Similar standards have been applied in other fields to determine which facilities appear in these lists. In each appendix, those bases where nuclear warheads are stored in peacetime are highlighted with an asterisk (*). Descriptions of different facilities at the same location are separated by a bullet (•).

The appendices are divided by state and overseas country (including territories such as Guam and Puerto Rico). In the U.S. Appendix, an overview of locations in most states and overseas country summarizes key facilities and assesses the overall role the state or country plays in the nuclear arms race. Each state is ranked in terms of the number of nuclear warheads deployed and the number of separate facilities in the nuclear infrastructure. Locations in the Soviet Appendix are identified by Military District. This should serve as an aid in locating the bases. British and French locations are identified by county and department, respectively.

The greatest amount of detail, of course, is in the U.S. Appendix. Many new facilities are revealed whose nuclear role was previously unknown. Footnotes identify specific documents that refer to the nuclear connections. The British and French Appendices are second in terms of detail and reliability. Through multiple sources, virtually every location in the U.S., British, and French appendices has been confirmed. This has not been possible for the Soviet and Chinese appendices, however, and they should be used with care: There is no way to confirm the locations or unit names of most facilities. Our intention was to lay out what is known for these two countries to demonstrate that the numbers and types of facilities in their nuclear infrastructures are similar to those of the West, and that their deployments are at least as pervasive. The main sources for all five appendices are listed after the Chinese appendix.

Appendix A

United States Nuclear Weapons Infrastructure

INSIDE THE UNITED STATES

Location	*Organization and Activity*

ALABAMA

The Army dominates the state of Alabama, where the most important nuclear facilities are in Huntsville. Missile Command at Redstone Arsenal and the Army's Ballistic Missile Defense Systems Command coordinate all Army nuclear missile development and training, including work on Pershing II and the "Star Wars" strategic defense initiative. No nuclear warheads are deployed in the state.

Anniston	Anniston Army Depot: fuels, seals and performs final check and packaging of Lance missiles
Fort McClellan, Anniston	Army Military Police School/Training Center: nuclear weapons guard and security training, newly built prototype nuclear weapons storage site operated by the Defense Nuclear Agency for nuclear security training • LORAN-D transmitter
Grand Bay	JSS radar
Huntsville	Milton K. Cummings Research Park: Army Ballistic Missile Defense Systems Command/Advanced Technology Center, coordinates all ballistic missile defense R&D, operates the Kwajalein Missile Range
Jordan Lake	Naval Space Surveillance System transmitter
Redstone Arsenal, Huntsville	Army Missile Munitions Center and School: Army missile training and doctrinal development • Army Missile Command: R&D and management of Lance, Pershing and other Army nuclear missiles, including future battlefield nuclear weapons • 515th Ordnance Det: mobile nuclear weapons support training for Army reserve units
Montgomery	187th Tactical Fighter Group (ALANG): nuclear-capable F-4D

ALASKA

Even though Alaska ranks 25th in number of nuclear warheads deployed, it ranks 2d with 42 facilities in the nuclear infrastructure. Its location makes it a significant strategic command and control headquarters. Military forces will be deployed to and operate from Alaska in wartime, in many ways equivalent to an overseas base. Less than 3 miles separate U.S. and Soviet territory at Little Diomede and Big Diomede Islands. Shemya and Adak Islands at the tip of the Aleutians are critical for monitoring Soviet missile testing and for nuclear anti-submarine warfare.

***Adak Island**	Naval Station • Patrol Wings Pacific Det Adak/Adak Air Patrol and Reconnaissance Group: rotational deployment base for nuclear-capable P-3s from Moffett Field, CA, center of ASW operations in the northern Pacific, command facilities include ASW Operations Center • Advanced Underwater Weapons Det: storage of 70 nuclear depth bombs, guarded by Marines • Naval Facility: processing station for SOSUS • Naval Radio Transmitting Facility (Mt. Moffett): HF network control station for naval communications, LF transmissions to the Pacific area • Coast Guard LORAN-C Monitor Station: serving north Pacific chain • Green Pine communications station[1]
Attu Island	Attu Research Site: nuclear test detection station • Coast Guard LORAN-C Station: serving north Pacific chain
Barter Island	DEW line radar (BAR) and Bar Main Site
Burnt Mountain	Burnt Mountain Research Site: AFTAC seismic detection station consisting of 5 remote detection sites, containing radio isotope thermoelectric generators, 10.3 miles of specialized data transmission cables
Campion AFS	743d Aerospace Defense Squadron: surveillance station and GCI site reporting to Murphy Dome RCC
Cape Lisburne AFS, Kapalowa	711th Aerospace Defense Squadron: surveillance station reporting to Murphy Dome RCC, AN/FPS 117 Seek Igloo radar site
Cape Newenham AFS, Platinum	794th Aerospace Defense Squadron: surveillance station reporting to King Salmon RCC, Seek Igloo radar site

Cape Prince of Wales	Arctic ASW research field station of Naval Ocean Systems Center, San Diego, CA: monitors sea and Arctic ice conditions
Cape Romanzoff AFS, Igiak	795th Aerospace Defense Squadron: surveillance station reporting to King Salmon RCC, seek Igloo radar site
Chatanika	AF Geophysics Laboratory radar supporting Poker Flat rocket launches and atmospheric research
Chena River	Chena River Research Site: Det 460, AFTAC: nuclear test detection station
Clear AFS, Anderson	13th Missile Warning Squadron: BMEWS Site II, one of three Ballistic Missile Early Warning System stations providing early warning and initial confirmation of missile launches after detection by DSP satellites, secondary satellite tracking mission, radars include 3 FPS-50 detection radars (400 feet wide by 165 feet high) and 1 tracking radar
Cold Bay AFS	714th Aerospace Defense Squadron: surveillance station reporting to King Salmon RCC, Seek Igloo radar site
Eielson AFB	6th Strategic Wing (SAC): forward aerial refueling and reconnaissance base supporting KC-135s (Alaska Tanker Task Force) and RC-135 reconnaissance aircraft, provides bomber refueling in wartime • Giant Talk transmitter moved to Elmendorf AFB as part of Scope Signal III upgrade • Det 406, AFTAC: operates and maintains several unmanned seismic arrays throughout Alaska, also processes air samples from WC-135 aircraft
Elmendorf AFB, Anchorage	HQ, Alaskan Air Command/Joint Task Force Alaska: major AF command and JCS designated joint command for wartime control of Alaskan theater, coordinates nuclear weapons custody and planning in Alaska • Alaskan NORAD Region: operation of ROCC for radar sites and interceptors in Alaska • 11th Tactical Control Group (formerly 531st ACW Group): mans the ROCC and operates 13 radar sites and two intermediate regional control centers • 21st Tactical Fighter Wing: F-15 air defense unit, converted from F-4 in 1982 • dispersal base for B-52 bombers from Castle AFB, CA • 5021st Tactical Operations Squadron: T-33 aircraft flying "unknown targets" to test Alaskan radar sites by simulating Soviet bombers • Global Command and Control station, Giant Talk/Scope Signal III station • DSCS communication terminal linked to Sunnyvale, CA, Offutt, NE, and Ft. Detrick, MD • NAVSTAR monitor station • Det 471, AFTAC: nuclear detection station[2]
Flaxsman Island	DEW line radar
Fort Greely, Fairbanks	Army Cold Regions Test Center: cold climate testing of military equipment
Fort Richardson, Anchorage	172d Infantry Brigade: senior Army command in Alaska, includes nuclear-capable 155mm artillery
Fort Yukon AFS	709th Aerospace Defense Squadron: surveillance station and GCI site reporting to Murphy Dome RCC, Seek Igloo radar site
Galena Airport	forward F-15 air defense operations from Elmendorf AFB • Seek Igloo radar surveillance station
Indian Mountain AFS	708th Aerospace Defense Squadron: surveillance station and GCI site reporting to Murphy Dome RCC, Seek Igloo radar site
Juneau	Coast Guard LORAN-C Monitor Station: serving Gulf of Alaska chain
Kenai	FAA radar reporting to the ROCC at Elmendorf AFB
King Salmon Airport Naknek	forward F-15 air defense operations from Elmendorf AFB • 705th Aerospace Defense Squadron: Southern Alaskan Regional Control Center (RCC) and first AN/FPS-117 Seek Igloo radar surveillance station
Kodiak	Coast Guard LORAN-C Monitor Station and Control Site: serving Gulf of Alaska and north Pacific chains • VLF radio transmitter, operating worldwide, LF to Pacific and Arctic Oceans
Kotzebue AFS	748th Aerospace Defense Squadron: surveillance station reporting to Murphy Dome RCC, Seek Igloo radar site
Lonely	DEW line radar (POW 1)
Murphy Dome AFS	744th Aerospace Defense Squadron: Northern Alaska Regional Control Center (RCC), Seek Igloo radar site

Narrow Cape	Coast Guard LORAN-C Station: serving north Pacific and Gulf of Alaska chains
Oliktok	DEW line radar (POW 2)
Point Barrow	DEW line radar (POW) and POW Main Site
Point Lay	DEW line radar (LIZ 2)
Poker Flat	Poker Flat Research Range: AF Geophysics Laboratory range for study of the disturbed lower ionosphere, also used for possible nuclear detection station
Port Clarence	Coast Guard LORAN-C Station: serving north Pacific chain
St. Paul Island	Coast Guard LORAN-C Station and Monitor Station: serving north Pacific chain
Shemya AFB, Shemya Island	16th Surveillance Squadron: operates "Cobra Dane" AN/FPS-108 phased array radar, "collect technical intelligence data on Soviet ballistic missile (ICBM/SLBM) test launches to the Kamchatka peninsula and the Pacific Broad Ocean area. Provides tactical warning and attack assessment (TW/AA) of ICBM/SLBM attack on the continental United States and southern Canada," satellite tracking is secondary peacetime mission • Det 1, 6th Strategic Wing: 2 RC-135S "Cobra Ball" aircraft forward based from Eielson AFB for immediate launch to collect intelligence on Soviet missile testing • Det 461, AFTAC: nuclear test detection station • DSCS satellite communications terminal[3]
Shoal Cove	Coast Guard LORAN-C Station: serving Gulf of Alaska and Canadian west coast chains
Sparrevohn AFS, Iliamna	719th Aerospace Defense Squadron: surveillance station and GCI site reporting to King Salmon RCC, Seek Igloo radar site
Tatalina AFS, McGrath	717th Aerospace Defense Squadron: surveillance station and GCI site reporting to King Salmon RCC, Seek Igloo radar site
Tin City AFS, Wales	710th Aerospace Defense Squadron: surveillance station reporting to Murphy Dome RCC, Seek Igloo radar site, closest active military base to the Soviet Union (50 miles)
Tok	Coast Guard LORAN-C Station: serving Gulf of Alaska chain
Wainwright	DEW line radar (LIZ 3)

ARIZONA

The open land of southern Arizona houses extensive military training and testing areas, and until 1984 18 Titan II missile silos around Tuscon. Training is the biggest activity, with Davis-Monthan AFB being used for ground-launched cruise missiles, Luke AFB for F-16s, Fort Huachuca for communications and electronic equipment, and MCAS Yuma for Marine Corps aviation.

Benson	Site Sibyl, Electronic Proving Ground, Ft. Huachuca: communications test facility
Cave Creek	JSS radar
***Davis-Monthan AFB, Tucson**	former locaton of 390th Strategic Missile Wing with 18 Titan II missiles, deactivated in early 1984 with retirement of Titan II • 868th Tactical Missile Training Squadron: primary training base for ground-launched cruise missiles • Det 1, 5th Fighter Interceptor Squadron: 2 F-106 on alert with Genie nuclear missiles, some 10 warheads probably stored • Military Aircraft Storage and Distribution Center/"The Boneyard:" location of retired aircraft and bombers awaiting canabalization or reactivation
Flagstaff	Naval Observatory Flagstaff Station: astronometric and astrophysical observations • NEACP ground entry point • GWEN relay site to be activated in 1985[4]
Fort Huachuca, Sierra Vista	HQ, Army Communications Command: worldwide Army non-tactical communications, including nuclear weapons command and control • Army Electronic Proving Ground: T&E of electronic equipment, including radioactive detection equipment

Gila River	Naval Space Surveillance System transmitter
Holbrook	Holbrook RBS Site: 15th AF SAC radar bomb scoring site for nuclear bomb delivery practice, to be upgraded to Strategic Training Range
Luke AFB, Litchfield	58th Tactical Training Wing: F-16 conversion training • former SAGE RCC and 26th NORAD Region headquarters, deactivated and moved to March AFB, CA
Mount Lemon	Electronic Proving Ground communications test facility and tracking radar
Mule Mountain	Electronic Proving Ground communications test facility
Oatman Mountain	Electronic Proving Ground communications and radar test facility
Sky Harbor IAP, Phoenix	161st Aerial Refueling Group (AZANG): KC-135 tankers
Tucson IAP	162d Tactical Fighter Group (AZANG): nuclear capable A-7D training
MCAS Yuma	Marine Aviation Weapons and Tactics Squadron One (MAWTS-1): Marine Corps advanced aviation training, including nuclear weapons delivery and AV-8B Harrier testing • Marine Wing Weapons Unit 3 (MWWU 3), 3d Marine Air Wing: nuclear bomb technical support to west coast Marine Corps aviation units, including operation of an "instrumented special weapons delivery range" (called Panel Stager)
Yuma	Yuma Proving Ground: development and testing range for artillery and air delivered weapons, including Lance missile, one of the largest uninhabited areas in the U.S. increasingly important in Army equipment testing in the desert environment, range is 1,400 sqare miles, used for test firing of nuclear artillery projectiles • NAVSTAR system test site

ARKANSAS

Arkansas ranks 10th in nuclear weapons with 430 warheads deployed at two SAC bases, Blytheville and Little Rock. The number of warheads will increase to more than 600 with deployment of air-launched cruise missiles to Blytheville in early 1985.

Blackwell	SACDIN terminal supporting Little Rock AFB
***Blytheville AFB**	HQ, 42d Air Division, SAC: intermediate SAC headquarters • 97th Bombardment Wing: B-52G and KC-135, nuclear warheads include 150 bombs and 60 SRAMs, to receive 244 ALCMs at full deployment • GWEN receive-only station
Fayetteville	GWEN relay node to Barksdale AFB, Little Rock AFB and Blytheville AFB
Ft. Smith MAP	188th Tactical Fighter Group (ARANG): nuclear-capable F-4C
Judsonia	SACDIN terminal supporting Little Rock AFB
***Little Rock AFB**	309th Strategic Missile Wing: 17 Titan II missiles, to be retired by 1986 • 189th Aerial Refueling Group (ARANG): KC-135 tankers • Primary Nuclear Airlift Support Base for AF nuclear weapons transportation • GWEN receive-only station[5]
Red River	Naval Space Surveillance System receiver

CALIFORNIA

California ranks first in the nuclear infrastructure with 80 locations and fourth in nuclear warheads with 1,437. It has the largest number of military installations of any state (not counting individual missile silos). Every category of the nuclear infrastructure is in the state. The variety of bases include naval complexes around San Diego, Long Beach and San Francisco, SAC bomber bases, Castle and Mather, and one of two main Army nuclear storage sites in the U.S., Sierra Army Depot (the other is in New York). Radar and electronic sites abound in the state supporting four major research, development, and testing centers: China Lake, Edwards AFB, Point Mugu, and Vandenberg AFB. Twelve communications and ten early warning radars directly support strategic forces.

NAS Alameda, San Francisco	Carrier Group 3: homeport for two aircraft carriers • intermittent nuclear weapons storage aboard ships and on land (long-term storage at Concord) • HQ, Carrier Air Wing 30: naval reserve air wing for Pacific units, including 2 nuclear-capable attack squadrons and 1 ASW helicopter squadron • Marine

	Corps Reserve nuclear-capable A-4 squadron • Naval Air Rework Facility: depot rework of A-6, P-3 and S-3 aircraft, 4,600 civilian employees[6]
Almaden AFS, New Almaden	682d Radar Squadron: JSS radar, also provides surveillance information to WSMC for missile testing safety checks
Anderson Peak, Big Sur	large-aperture optical tracking site supporting missile launches from Vandenberg AFB, B-1 and cruise missile testing, located in "one of the few remaining clear sky areas in the continental U.S."[7]
Bakersfield	GWEN relay site to be activated in 1985
Beale AFB, Marysville	HQ, 14th Air Division, SAC: intermediate SAC headquarters • 9th Strategic Reconnaissance Wing: operates SR-71, U-2 and TR-1 reconnaissance aircraft, U-2 is used for Operation "Bugle Rag" which supports SAC training in the U.S., the preparation of bomber targeting folders, and nuclear test monitoring • 100th Aerial Refueling Wing: 2 KC-135 tanker squadrons supporting bombers and reconnaissance planes • "ready dispersal base" for B-52s from Mather AFB • 7th Missile Warning Squadron: west coast Pave Paws AN/FPS-115 early warning radar, "provides tactical warning and supports attack assessment of an SLBM attack against the continental U.S and southern Canada. Another mission is to provide warning and support attack assessment of an ICBM attack against these areas," peacetime secondary mission is satellite tracking[8]
Boron AFS	Kramer Radar Annex: 750th Radar Squadron: JSS radar
Cambria AFS	775th Radar Squadron: JSS radar, also provides surveillance information to WSMC for missile testing safety checks
MCB Camp Pendleton	HQ, I Marine Amphibious Force/1st Marine Division/Landing Force, Third Fleet (CTF 39): west coast Marine Corps HQ, including one division and support troops • 11th Marine Regt (Artillery) of the 1st Marine Division, comprised of 3 155mm nuclear-capable artillery battalions • 1st Combat Engineer Bn has possible ADM mission • 5th Marine Amphibious Brigade: HQ for deployments to Middle East
Camp Roberts, Paso Robles	major satellite communications station operated by the Army, serves as west coast entry point, net control station for the Pacific DSCS satellite, linked to Japan, Hawaii, Kwajalein, Philippines, and between the DSP station at Nurrungar, Australia and NORAD (linked to San Luis Obispo AUTOVON switch) • JSS radar (possibly located at Santa Margarita)
***Castle AFB, Atwater**	93d Bombardment Wing: B-52G/H and KC-135 training (2 KC-135 squadrons), full combat readiness with 150 nuclear bombs and 70 SRAM missiles • 84th Fighter Interceptor Squadron: F-106 interceptors with Genie nuclear missiles, 10 warheads deployed on base
Centerville Beach, Ferndale	Naval Facility: processing station for SOSUS
Chico MAP	AF Geophysics Laboratory site activated to support balloon flights from Holloman AFB, NM
China Lake, Ridgecrest	Naval Weapons Center: "principal Navy RDT&E center for air warfare systems (except ASW) and missile weapon systems," including work on cruise missiles, antisubmarine stand-off weapon (ASWSOW), and vertical-launch ASROC (VLA), 4,000 civilian employees, nuclear bombing practice range in Coso target area • Operational Test and Evaluation Squadron 5 (VX-5): test of airborne attack weapon systems[9]
Chollas Heights, San Diego	Naval Radio Transmitter Facility: LF and HF transmitter for fleet communications to the Pacific Ocean, inactive VLF transmitter for worldwide communications
***Concord**	Naval Weapons Station: major nuclear weapons storage depot supporting 7 homeported ammunition ships of the Pacific Fleet, NAS Alameda, and NAS Moffett Field, weapons stored include 175 nuclear bombs for Navy and Marine Corps aircraft, 45 artillery warheads and 30 ADMs for the Marines, and 55 nuclear depth bombs for NAS Moffett Field P-3s, 1,100 civilian employees, nuclear weapons guarded by large Marine Barracks[10]
NAB Coronado, San Diego	HQ, Naval Surface Forces Pacific: type command of the Pacific Fleet •

	Naval Special Warfare Group One: Pacific Fleet "SEALs" commando unit with probable ADM mission
Davis	HF transmitter of McClellan AFB supporting Giant Talk/Scope Signal III and Global Command and Control systems
Dixon (Sacramento)	Naval Radio Transmitter Facility: LF transmitter to Pacific Ocean
Edwards AFB	AF Rocket Propulsion Laboratory: R&D of future missiles and spacecraft • AF Flight Test Center: DT&E of all aircraft and bombers, 65 sqare miles of landing area • B-1 Test Force: 3 prototype B-1As built for initial B-1 program • Special Weapons Maintenance Facility: DOE support for drop testing of nuclear bombs and parachute flight testing of nuclear missiles and reentry vehicles • 4200th Test & Evaluation Squadron, SAC: bomber and missile operational testing, including B-1B, B-52, and ALCM[11]
El Paso	microwave relay station supporting the AFFTC and overland cruise missile testing from PMTC to Utah
MCAS El Toro, Santa Ana	HQ, 3d Marine Aircraft Wing: west coast Marine Corps aviation HQ, including A-4, A-6 and F/A-18 nuclear-capable squadrons • Air Weapons Training Unit 3: training in nuclear weapons loading, transportation and handling
Fort Ord, Seaside	7th Infantry Division: in the process of converting to 6th Infantry Division (Light), nuclear units currently include 4 artillery battalions[12]
Fresno	Fresno Air Terminal: 144th Fighter Interceptor Wing (CAANG): F-4D interceptors
George AFB	35th Tactical Fighter Wing: nuclear-capable F-4E • Det 1, 84th Fighter Interceptor Squadron: 2 F-106 interceptors on alert, possible Genie nuclear missile storage on base
Hawes AFS, Hinkley	AF operated VLF/LF transmitter/receiver, one of two sites in the Survivable Low-frequency Communications System, 1,260 foot tower, receiver antennas are buried and protected
Honda Ridge	FAA Air Route Surveillance Radar (ARSR-1D) provides sea and air traffic status supporting missile launches from WSMC
Imperial Beach	Naval Radio Receiver Facility: HF radio receiver
Klamath AFS, Crescent City	FAA owned and operated long-range radar, part of JSS, provides surveillance data to WSMC for missile testing safety checks
Laguna Peak, Point Mugu	command and control site for missile launches from Vandenburg AFB • tracking and injection station for Transit navigation satellites (from Point Mugu)
NAS Lemoore	HQ, Light Attack Wing Pacific: operation of 12 nuclear capable A-7 squadrons, small Marine Barracks indicates possible nuclear weapons storage
Lincoln	Lincoln Communications Annex: HF receiver of McClellan AFB supporting Giant Talk/Scope Signal III and Global Command and Control systems
Livermore	Lawrence Livermore Laboratory: DOE laboratory conducting RD&T on nuclear warheads, technical verification and seismology, Defense Nuclear Agency and Sandia Laboratories have dets at the Laboratory • Regional Seismic Test Network (RSTN) monitoring station • DOE Satellite Earth Station (WESTAR) for communications
Long Beach	Naval Station: homeport for the battleship New Jersey and other nuclear-capable surface ships
Los Angeles AFS	HQ, Space Division: development, production and testing of DOD space and missile systems • NAVSTAR Joint Program Office
Los Banos	Over-the-horizon radar built for OTH technology program, used by DOE for nuclear weapons test detection research[13]
March AFB, Riverside	HQ, 15th Air Force, SAC: alternate SAC command post • 22d Aerial Refueling Wing: converted from bomber wing when B-52Ds were retired in 1983, KC-135 and KC-10A tankers • Southwest ROCC: NORAD air defense warning and control center, 26th NORAD Region, 26th Air Division • Giant

	Talk/Scope Signal III receiver (transmitter at Mira Loma) • NEACP ground entry point • 452d Aerial Refueling Wing (AFRES): 1 KC-135 squadron, crews for KC-10 tankers • 163d Tactical Fighter Group (CAANG): nuclear-capable F-4D[14]
Mare Island, Vallejo	Naval Shipyard: maintenance and overhaul of attack and ballistic missile submarines and surface ships • Navy Nuclear Power School • DOE Naval Reactors Office
***Mather AFB, Sacramento**	320th Bombardment Wing: B-52G and KC-135, nuclear weapons include 150 nuclear bombs and 60 SRAM missiles • 323d Fighter Training Wing: navigator-bombardier training, uses B-52s and KC-135s of 320th BW • 940th Aerial Refueling Group (AFRES): KC-135 tankers
McClellan AFB,	Sacramento Air Logistics Center: logistics management for F-111, FB-111, early warning surveillance and Sacramento radar systems, strategic communications including SLFCS/VLF and Green Pine, some 12,000 civilian employees • 1155th TOS, AFTAC: logistics support of Atomic Energy Detection System, AFTAC processing laboratory and equipment storage for nuclear air sampling operations and equipent, R&D and analysis of nuclear test detection techniques • Global Command and Control station, Giant Talk/Scope Signal III station (sites at Davis and Lincoln) • AUTODIN switching center • DMSP repair facility • "standby dispersal base" for B-52s from Mather AFB
Middletown	Coast Guard LORAN-C Station and Control Site: serving U.S. west coast chain
Mill Valley AFS	Det 3, 14th Missile Warning Squadron: inactive FSS-7 SLBM detection radar, could be returned to active service • JSS radar, also provides surveillance data to WSMC for missile testing safety checks
Mira Loma	SAC Radio Transmitter Facility: HF transmitter of March AFB supporting Giant Talk/Scope Signal III
NAS Miramar, San Diego	shore base for carrier air wings when in port in San Diego
NAS Moffett Field	Patrol Wings Pacific/Patrol and Reconnaissance Force, Third Fleet (CTF 32)/Moffett Air Patrol and Reconnaissance Group: 8 nuclear-capable P-3 squadrons, forward operations in the Pacific and Indian Ocean • Reserve Patrol Wings Pacific: coordinates naval reserve P-3 operations in the Pacific • TACAMO deployment station for rotations from Barbers Point, HI • "contingency support" nuclear depth bomb storage site supported by Concord[15]
Monterey	Fleet Numerical Oceanography Center: furnishes nuclear weapons radiological fallout predictions to naval forces, provides DMSP and weather broadcasts for naval forces
Morris Dam, Azusa	Naval Ocean Systems Center, San Diego Test Range: testing of underwater ordnance
Mt. Laguna AFS	Det 4, 14th Missile Warning Squadron: inactive FSS-7 SLBM detection radar, could be returned to active service • JSS radar
Mt. Pinos	microwave relay station operated to support the AFFTC and cruise missile testing from PMTC to Utah
***NAS North Island, Coronado**	Nuclear Weapons Training Group Pacific: nuclear weapons training for the Pacific Fleet • nuclear weapons storage for ships in the San Diego area, including 100 nuclear bombs, 32 Terrier warheads, 60 nuclear depth bombs, guarded by large Marine Barracks • HQ, Naval Air Forces, Pacific, including ASW Wing Pacific: 6 nuclear-capable S-3 and 6 SH-3H squadrons • San Diego Air Patrol and Reconnaissance Group: wartime ASW operations • Carrier Group One: support of San Diego homeported carriers • Naval Air Rework Facility: 6,000 civilian employees[16]
Norton AFB, San Bernadino	Ballistic Missile Office, AF Systems Command: plans, implements and manages ballistic missile programs, including MX missile development, basing, and reentry systems • Small Missile Program Office
Oakland	Naval Supply Center, Nuclear Weapons Supply Department: "supply support for inert nuclear ordnance materials [limited life components, neutron

	generators, non-nuclear components of nuclear weapons] and services is provided western continental U.S. Navy and Marine Corps units and the Pacific Fleet"[17]
Owens Valley	AF Geophysics Laboratory very-long baseline interferometry observatory
Pillar Point AFS, Half Moon Bay	tracking radar, telemetry and command and control site for missile launches from Vandenberg AFB, provides a "side view" of ICBM launches to minimize "flame attenuation" of radar and telemetry signals
Pinion Peak	microwave relay station operated to support the AFFTC and cruise missile testing from PMTC to Utah
Point Arena AFS	JSS radar
Point Arguello	Navy offshore gunnery range used by SAC bombers[18]
Point Cabrillo	Coast Guard LORAN-C Monitor Station: serving U.S. west coast chain
***Point Loma (San Diego)**	Naval Weapons Station, Laplaya Annex: nuclear weapons storage supporting submarines and ships in San Diego, including 25 SUBROC, 55 ASROC, and about 25 SLCM warheads
Point Mugu, Oxnard	Pacific Missile Test Center: DT&E of naval and DOD weapons, including Trident, MX, cruise missiles, B-1B, advanced intercept air-to-air missile (AIAAM), and Minuteman, highly instrumented sea test range off the coast includes radars, telemetry, and command and control sites supporting Tomahawk operational T&E as well as missile firings from WSMC, 35,000 sqare mile open ocean test area extends 180 miles seaward, more than 1,900 missile launches annually, 2 P-3 aircraft are modified with Sonobuoy Missile Impact Locator System (SMILS) which provides MX and Trident II accuracy test support in "broad ocean areas" of the Pacific, 60 miles north of Kwajalein Atoll • Navy Astronautics Group: satellite monitoring and control center for Transit, the Navy navigation satellite, station at Laguna Peak • Operational Test & Evaluation Squadron 4 (VX-4): evaluation of fighter weapon systems • President Reagan uses the Point Mugu airfield when in California • Patrol Squadron 65 (VP-65): reserve nuclear-capable P-3s
Point Pinos	Coast Guard LORAN-C Monitor Station: serving U.S. west coast chain
Point Sur, Big Sur	Naval Facility: processing station for SOSUS
Port Hueneme	Naval Ships Weapons System Engineering Station: Tomahawk sea launched cruise missile ship installation, T&E, and logistics support, 1,600 civilian employees • homeport for Norton Sound and Point Loma: Trident program launch area support ships
Rimrock Lake, Alturas	future receiver site for west coast Over-the-horizon-backscatter early warning radar
San Clemente	launch point for Tomahawk cruise missile overland testing from Pacific Ocean to Utah • Naval Ocean Systems Center test range: underwater launch facility supporting Harpoon and Tomahawk • Capistrano Test Site: high energy laser test programs • tracking radar supporting missile tests from Point Mugu • Sea Echo HF radar research facility operated by the Naval Research Laboratory
San Diego	Naval Station: homeport for majority of Pacific Fleet surface ships assigned to 3 cruiser-destroyer groups • Amhibious Group 3: homeport for amphibious lift ships • Submarine Base: Submarine Group 5: homeport for 2 attack submarine squadrons • Submarine Development Group One • Submarine Training Facility • Fleet ASW Training Center: training in the technical aspects of ASW weapons and systems • Naval Ocean Systems Center: RDT&E for naval C3, ocean surveillance, surface ASW, submarine arctic warfare, ASW nuclear weapons, and acoustics, 2,500 civilian employees • Naval Space Surveillance System receiver • (nuclear weapons for San Diego naval units are stored at North Island and Point Loma)
San Francisco	HQ, FEMA Region IX: command center operated at Santa Rosa
San Nicolas Island	Naval Facility: processing station for SOSUS • principal instrumentation site supporting missile launches from Point Mugu and WSMC, facilities include tracking radar and telemetry collection, the area between the island and

	Point Mugu (known as the Inner Sea Test Range) is one of the most heavily instrumented areas of the world
San Pedro Hill	JSS radar
Santa Cruz Island	instrumentation site and relay station supporting missile launches from Point Mugu and WSMC
Santa Rosa	FEMA Region IX "Federal Regional Center": underground civil defense command center
Santa Ynez Peak	large aperture optical tracking system supporting westerly and southerly missile launches from WSMC
Seal Beach	Naval Weapons Station: ordnance support for Long Beach and San Diego, "classified ordnance facility," no nuclear warheads are stored at Seal Beach in peacetime, coordinates the worldwide "Navy-Marine Corps Nuclear Weapons Stockpile Evaluation and Reliability Program"[19]
***Sierra Army Depot, Herlong**	major west coast Army nuclear weapons storage depot, including 110 retired ABM warheads, 125 artillery shells, 100 Lance warheads, and 60 ADMs, nuclear mission transferred from Savanna Army Depot, IL when it ceased operation in 1975, receives nuclear weapons and components for shipment throughout the Pacific and South Korea, the depot is served by railways and has its own airfield (Amedee Army Airfield)[20]
Stockton	Naval Communications Station: HF fleet communications and FLTSATCOM net control station
Styx	GWEN relay station to be activated in 1985
Sunnyvale AFS, San Jose	Air Force Satellite Control Facility: control and tracking of reconnaissance satellites from 7 worldwide stations • DSCS III Operations Center: network control center for DSCS Pacific satellites, communications link to Guam, Australia, Shemya, Alaska and Hawaii • Operating Location AX (OL-AX), AFTAC: processing of satellite nuclear test detection data
Travis AFB	HQ, 22d Air Force, MAC: coordinates airlift and nuclear weapons transportation in the Pacific region and west coast, "Primary Nuclear Airlift Support Base" • 307th Aerial Refueling Group: KC-135 tankers, one squadron with 19 KC-135 deactivated in 1983[21]
MCAS Tustin, Santa Ana	Marine Aircraft Group 16: CH-46 and CH-53E heavy helicopters responsible for nuclear weapons transportation, used by AWTU-3 at El Toro for nuclear weapons training[22]
Twenty-Nine Palms	Marine Air Ground Combat Training Center: Force Troops Pacific: combat support units for Pacific Marine Divisions, including Nuclear Ordnance Platoon • 1st Field Artillery Group: 155mm and 8" nuclear artillery supporting I MAF • 4th Battalion, 11th Marines: 2 nuclear-certified 8" and 2 155mm batteries • HQ, 7th Marine Amphibious Brigade: nucleus of an armored force for Marine Corps rapid deployment planning
Vandenberg AFB, Lompoc	Western Space and Missile Center (AFSC): manages the Western Test Range (WTR), including launch, tracking, telemetry and command and control of development and operational ICBMs (MX, Titan II, Minuteman) and cruise missile tests, base covers 98,400 acres, including 35 miles of Pacific coastline, 16 missile silos at the north side of the base are used for testing but also maintain a "latent EWO [Emergency War Order] capability" and could be converted to operational missile silos in crisis, approximately 65 missile launches take place from Vandenberg each year • 1st Strategic Air Division: SAC missile crew training, preparation of ICBM performance data for war planning purposes • AF Satellite Control Facility satellite tracking station • NAVSTAR Master Control and Monitor Station[23]

COLORADO

Colorado is the center of U.S. early warning with NORAD headquarters and the Cheyenne Mountain command center as well as the DSP satellite early warning ground station at Buckley ANGB in Aurora. Seven strategic communications bases serve these installations. Important nuclear weapons installations include the Rocky Flats plant in Golden which manufactures the plutonium cores of nuclear warheads and

46 Minuteman silos (138 warheads) of F.E. Warren AFB, WY spread out in the northeast corner of the state.

Aurora	GWEN relay node linked to Buckley ANGB
Boulder	AF Global Weather Central Operating Location: collocated with the National Space Environmental Services Center of NOAA, collection and analysis of upper atmosphere and solar activity information
Buckley ANGB, Aurora	"Aerospace Data Facility": 2d Communications Squadron, SPACECOM: one of two main DSP satellite early warning system ground stations (the other is at Nurrungar, Australia), the station is connected to Camp Roberts, CA and Australia via cable and satellite • Operating Location BN (OL-BN), AFTAC: processing of nuclear test detection data from sensors aboard the DSP satellites • GWEN input/output station • 140th Tactical Fighter Wing (COANG): nuclear-capable A-7D
Cedarwood	terminal node of hardened microwave link providing communications to Cheyenne Mountain, 67 miles south
Cheyenne Mountain Complex, Colorado Springs	NORAD Combat Operations Center: hardened NCA command center, 300 operational personnel, to expand to 1,000 in wartime, 30 days of supplies, 4.5 acre grid of excavated chambers, 15 steel buildings, terminal point for worldwide surveillance, early warning and attack warning networks, provides data on detection of nuclear events, WWMCCS terminal includes access to the Nuclear Capabilities Plan and Single Integrated Damage Analysis Capabilities system • Air Defense Operations Center: command of interceptor forces • National Warning Center, FEMA: initiates all civil defense warning throughout Canada and the U.S. • 4 communication spokes emanate from Cheyenne Mountain, 2 microwave and 2 hardened cable, connected to terminals at least 50 miles away at Westcreek, Hugo, Lamar, and Cedarwood • GWEN input/output station
Denver	HQ, FEMA Region VIII
Falcon AFS, Colorado Springs	Consolidated Space Operations Center: command and control of military space shuttle and satellite missions, to become operational in 1986–1990, facilities will include Satellite Operations Center and Shuttle Operations Planning Complex • NAVSTAR Passive Monitoring Station, to become Master Control Station by late 1980s
Fort Carson, Colorado Springs	HQ, 4th Infantry Division: units include 4 nuclear capable 155mm and 8" artillery battalions, "special weapons shop" providing "direct and general support maintenance, calibration and load testing services on special weapons under controlled secure conditions, . . . store and maintain special weapon trainers and associated classified training materials for use by certain 4th Infantry Division units stationed at Ft. Carson, and selected National Guard units from an eight state area."[24]
Golden	Rocky Flats Plant, DOE: GOCO facility operated by Rockwell International, fabrication, assembly and testing of plutonium/uranium cores and tampers of pits of nuclear warheads, 3,745 civilian employees
Hugo	terminal node of hardened microwave link providing communications to Cheyenne Mountain 79 miles away
La Junta	8th AF SAC radar bomb scoring nuclear bombing practice site, to be upgraded to Strategic Training Range
Lamar AFS	NEACP/SAC airborne command post ground entry point • terminal node of buried blast-resistant coaxial cable providing communications to Cheyenne Mountain, 165 miles away, linked to AT&T hardened central office and and transcontinental hardened cable[25]
Lowry AFB, Denver	Lowry Technical Training Center: AF nuclear warhead and bomb training, primary center for space systems training for all AF satellites • Det 057, AFTAC: space systems training related to nuclear test detection
Menafee Peak	telemetry site supporting missile testing from White Sands, NM
Peterson AFB, Colorado Springs	HQ, North American Aerospace Defense Command (NORAD): administrative offices including Cheyenne Mountain back-up facility (BUF) • Rapid Emergency Reconstitution Team (RAPIER): mobile NORAD command

	center activated in 1983 • Aerospace Defense Center, SPACECOM: satellite surveillance and space operations • HQ, Space Command (SPACECOM): control of AF satellite and space activities • Space Communications Division, AFCC: support for SPACECOM and NORAD
Pueblo	GWEN relay node • Pueblo Army Depot Activity: Pershing missile logistics and technical support
Westcreek	terminal node of buried, blast-resistant coaxial cable providing communications to Cheyenne Mountain, 50 miles away

CONNECTICUT

No nuclear weapons are stored on land in Connecticut, but the Naval Submarine Base at New London/Groton is home to over 20 nuclear-capable attack submarines. Warheads are not stored on land when those submarines are present. The crews for ballistic missile submarines are also stationed at Groton, but the submarines operate from Holy Loch, Scotland.

Groton	Naval Submarine Base, New London: Submarine Group 2/Submarine Squadron 10/Submarine Development Squadron 12: homeport for ballistic missile and attack submarines, ballistic missile submarines are not actually at the base, crews fly to meet them at Holy Loch • Naval Submarine School • Naval Reactors Office: monitors construction of nuclear powered submarines at the General Dynamics Electric Boat shipbuilding complex • Naval Underwater Systems Center, Newport, RI, Laboratory: 1,200 civilian employees • Marine Barracks: nuclear weapons and submarine security
Windsor	Nuclear Power Training Unit: submarine reactor training • DOE Naval Reactors Office

DELAWARE

The Naval Facility at Lewes, a processing station for SOSUS has been deactivated, leaving the state with no installations in the nuclear infrastructure.

DISTRICT OF COLUMBIA

The District of Columbia houses a number of military headquarters and commands (the Pentagon is located in Arlington, VA) as well as the White House.

Anacostia	Naval Station: houses offices of the White House Communications Agency, the Defense Communications Operations Unit, and the Defense Communications Support Unit, all providing military communications support to the President, operating the White House telephone switchboard and emergency links with top officials • Naval Research Laboratory: basic scientific research, advanced technology research, computer science, directed energy, early warning, environmental effects, surveillance and sensors, anti-submarine warfare, space systems and ocean surveillance research • Marine Executive Flight Det (HMX-1): alert helicopters providing Presidential transportation and evacuation, squadron HQ is at Quantico, VA
Bolling AFB	Air Force Office of Scientific Research: coordinates basic scientific research in the Air Force, including electronics, radar, communications, computers, surveillance, material technology • HQ, Defense Intelligence Agency: new analysis center of DIA opened in 1984 • DOE Regional Seismic Test Network receiving station
Forrestal Building	HQ, Department of Energy: control of all aspects of the development and production of nuclear warheads, research, nuclear materials production, components production, testing and assembly
Naval Observatory	HQ, Defense Mapping Agency: mapping support to military forces, electronic mapping support for cruise missile and Pershing II, development of a geodetic research and data base • Naval Observatory: operates the "Atomic Clock," the U.S. military time standard, also conducts research in navigation and timing • Oceanographer of the Navy

Washington Navy Yard	National Photographic Interpretation Center: joint CIA/DIA photographic imagery interpretation center
White House	White House Situation Room/White House Communications Agency/Office of Military Support: support to the President and National Security Council in crisis management, continuity of presidential operations, communications, and release of nuclear weapons
4401 Massachusetts Avenue, NW	HQ, Naval Telecommunications Command: operation of the non-tactical Navy communications systems as well as development of communications systems for nuclear weapons command and control

FLORIDA

Florida ranks 4th with 34 installations in the nuclear infrastructure, with a large naval presence around Mayport and Jacksonville, Eglin and MacDill Air Force bases, and numerous facilities supporting missile testing from Cape Canaveral. Major headquarters include Readiness and Central Commands at MacDill AFB and U.S. Forces, Caribbean in Key West. 230 nuclear warheads support naval units in the Jacksonville/Mayport area.

Cape Canaveral AFS	Eastern Space and Missile Center: launch sites and missile assembly facilities for military flight tests into the Atlantic Ocean, includes numerous technical facilities, optics, command and control, navigation, timing, meteorological, and radar for monitoring missile tests, which average 50 major launches per year, missiles supported include Pershing 1&II, Trident I&II, Poseidon, British Polaris and Chevaline, SRAM and Small ICBM • Seek Skyhook: aerostat borne radar, one of two air defense balloons in Florida, tethered at 12,000 feet • Acoustic Trials Det, DTNSRDC: operates MONOB (YAG-61) noise monitoring platform used in submarine noise reduction research and testing, operates mostly in Exuma Sound, Bahamas • Naval Ordnance Test Unit: maintains the Trident basin and Navy testing facilities at Cape Canaveral • Fleet Ballistic Missile Operational Test Support Unit 2: operates the USNS Range Sentinel, Trident launch support ship • AF Satellite Control Facility Remote Vehicle Checkout Facility: supports satellite launches from Cape Canaveral
***NAS Cecil Field, Jacksonville**	Light Attack Wing 1: 12 nuclear-capable A-7/F-18 squadrons, conversion to F-18 began in early 1984 • Anti-submarine Wing 1: 6 nuclear-capable S-3 squadrons • Carrier Air Wings 3, 17, 20: land base when not at sea aboard aircraft carriers • nuclear weapons storage at "Yellow Water," adjacent to the NAS, 13 miles from Jacksonville, guarded by about 200 Marines, warheads include about 140 nuclear depth bombs[26]
Cocoa Beach	optical tracking station supporting missile launches from ESMC
Cross City AFS	FAA owned and operated long-range radar, part of JSS and reporting data to the military
Cudjoe Key AFS	671st Radar Squadron: Seek Skyhook aerostat borne radar, one of two air defense balloons in Florida, tethered at 12,000 feet
Destin	Coast Guard LORAN-C Monitor Station: serving southeast U.S. and Great Lakes chains
Eglin AFB, Fort Walton Beach	AF Armament Division: mostly involved in conventional air armament DT&E, also contains a "Base Installation Security System" (BISS) test and training site, 752 acres used for evaluation of nuclear security systems • electronic warfare range used in testing of tail warning system for B-52s • AF Armament Laboratory: responsible for the preparation of all ballistic tables for nuclear warheads in the Air Force • 20th Missile Warning Squadron: FPS-85 SLBM and satellite tracking radar, to be deactivated when new Pave Paws radars are built in Georgia and Texas[27]
Flagler Beach	timing transponder supporting missile launches from ESMC
Ft. Lauderdale	homeport of acoustic research vessel Deer Island (YAG-62), part of the DTNSRDC • Naval Surface Weapons Center Ft. Lauderdale facility: field trials of air, surface and underwater ordnance
Ft. Lonesome	JSS radar

Homestead AFB	31st Tactical Fighter Wing: F-15 with full time air defense role • 482d Tactical Fighter Wing (AFRES): nuclear-capable F-4C • 644th Radar Squadron: JSS radar
Jacksonville AFS, Orange Park	JSS radar
Jacksonville IAP	125th Fighter Interceptor Group (FLANG): nuclear-capable F-106, to be replaced by 18 F-4D in air defense role
NAS Jacksonville	Sea-based ASW Wings, Atlantic: command of all ship-based Atlantic Fleet nuclear-capable S-3 and SH-3 squadrons • Patrol Wing 11: 7 nuclear-capable P-3 squadrons, aircraft rotate to overseas bases in the Atlantic and Caribbean, facilities include ASW Operations Center and Advanced Underwater Weapons Detachment for storing nuclear depth bombs at the airfield in war, they are stored in peacetime at "Yellow Water" (see Cecil Field) • Helicopter ASW Wing 1: 7 nuclear-capable SH-3 squadrons • Patrol Squadron 62: reserve nuclear-capable P-3 • LF transmitter operating to the Western Atlantic Ocean[28]
Jonathan Dickenson	new ESMC tracking and telemetry station which replaced the closed Turks and Caicos Islands site, facilities will include command and control and timing transponders
Jupiter Inlet	Coast Guard LORAN-C Station: serving U.S. east coast chain and providing remote ranging for missile tests from ESMC, including navigational and timing fixes
NAS Key West, Boca Chica	HQ, U.S. Forces, Caribbean/Joint Task Force 140: contingency planning for the Caribbean area • Advanced Underwater Weapons Det: stand-by storage site for nuclear depth bombs, to be activated in wartime • JSS radar[29]
Leesburg	Naval Research Laboratory Underwater Sound Reference Det: acoustics measurements range at Bugg Spring
Macdill AFB, Tampa	HQ, Readiness Command (REDCOM): worldwide Joint Task Force HQ for support of military operations in areas of the world unassigned to other U.S. commands, also responsible for the land defense of North America and joint military planning with Canada, WWMCCS facilities include access to Single Integrated Damage Analysis Capabilities System and Nuclear Capabilities Plan • HQ, Central Command (CENTCOM): newly established (1983) joint command responsible for contingency planning for Southwest Asia, replaced the Rapid Deployment Joint Task Force • Det 1, 20th Missile Warning Squadron: FSS-7 SLBM warning radar, only one of six still active, to be deactivated when new Pave Paws radars in Georgia and Texas are activated • Global Command and Control Station • 660th Radar Squadron: JSS radar • 56th Tactical Training Wing: F-16 training
Malabar	optical tracking station supporting missile launches from ESMC
Malone	Coast Guard LORAN-C station and control site, serving southeast U.S. and Great Lakes chains
***Mayport**	Naval Station: Carrier Group 6/Cruiser-Destroyer Group 12: homeport for 2 carriers and 40 surface ships, nuclear weapons storage includes 50 Navy bombs and 40 ASROC warheads • Coast Guard LORAN-C Monitor Station: serving southeast U.S. chain
McCoy AFB, Orlando	former SAC base, remains a bomber and tanker dispersal base
Melbourne Beach	optical tracking station supporting missile launches from ESMC
Merritt Island	tracking radar and telemetry site supporting missile launches ESMC, includes optics and weather facilities
New Smyrna Beach	timing transponder supporting missile launches from ESMC
Orlando	Naval Training Center: operates Nuclear Power School • Naval Research Laboratory Underwater Sound Reference Det: underwater acoustic R&D at two clear quiet lakes near Orlando
Patrick AFB	HQ, AF Technical Applications Center (AFTAC)/1035th TOG: operation of the Atomic Energy Detection System (AEDS) for monitoring nuclear weapons explosions by collecting and analyzing data from satellites, ships,

	submarines, aircraft, ground and underwater stations, data received includes EMP, hydroacoustic and seismic signals, more than 50 locations worldwide in 35 countries • HQ, Eastern Space and Missile Center: administrative, technical and logistics center for Eastern Test Range, facilities at Patrick include tracking radars and cameras (see also Cape Canaveral)
Pinellas Plant, Clearwater	Pinellas Plant, DOE: GOCO operated by GE Company, production of neutron generators, electrical and electronic components of nuclear warheads (lightning arrestor connectors, capacitors, switches, batteries), 1,550 civilian employees
Ponce de Leon	instrumentation site supporting missile launches from ESMC
Richmond AFS	Naval Observatory Richmond Substation: astronomical observations • JSS radar jointly operated with FAA
Saddle Bunch Keys	Navy LF and HF communications station transmitting to the Caribbean and south Atlantic areas
Tyndall AFB, Panama City	Air Defense Weapons Center: AF air defense training and doctrinal development • Southeast ROCC/23d NORAD Region/23d Air Division: first of 8 Region Operations Control Centers, opened in March 1983 • 678th Radar Squadron: JSS radar
Whitehouse	JSS radar

GEORGIA

Nuclear warheads at the King's Bay missile submarine base currently rank Georgia 12th with 406 warheads deployed and will result in a significant increase starting in the late 1980s as the first squadron of Trident II submarines is stationed there.

Albany	AUTODIN switching center
Atlanta	HQ, FEMA Region IV: command center operated at Thomasville
Dobbins AFB	116th Tactical Fighter Wing (GAANG): nuclear-capable F-4D
Fort McPherson, Atlanta	HQ, Army Forces Command (FORSCOM)/Army Forces, Atlantic Command (ARLANT): training and maintaining the U.S. Army combat base, WWMCCS terminal includes access to Nuclear Weapons Accounting System • HQ, Third Army: Army component of Central Command activated in December 1982 to plan for deployment of airborne forces and Army special operations forces to Southwest Asia
Fort Stewart, Hinesville	HQ, 24th Infantry Division: nuclear units include 3 155mm and 8" artillery battalions • Naval Space Surveillance System receiver
Hawkinsville	Naval Space Surveillance System receiver
***King's Bay**	Naval Submarine Support Base: Submarine Squadron 16: homeport for 12 Poseidon submarines with Trident I missiles, base opened in 1980, includes nuclear weapons storage for some 406 warheads in Strategic Weapons Facility or aboard submarines in port, designated future homeport for the first Trident II missile submarines, full Trident training and refit facilities under construction • British Trident submarines will receive their missiles and be logistically supported from King's Bay
Moody AFB, Valdosta	347th Tactical Fighter Wing, TAC: nuclear-capable F-4E
Robins AFB	HQ, Air Force Reserve: adminstrative control of all Air Force reserve units • 19th Aerial Refueling Wing: KC-135 tankers, 19th Bombardment Wing deactivated in 1983 with 13 B-52Gs dispersed to other bases • Warner-Robins Air Logistics Center: logistic support of Air Force air-to-air and air-to-surface missiles
Savannah	Navy operated gunnery range used by SAC bombers for training[30]
Savannah AFS	702d Radar Squadron: JSS radar (base located within Hunter Army Airfield)
Statesboro	Statesboro RBS Site: 8th AF SAC nuclear bomb delivery practice site, part of the Strategic Training Range

Thomasville	FEMA Region IV "Federal Regional Center:" underground civil defense command center

HAWAII

Hawaii ranks 6th in facilities in the nuclear infrastructure and 14th with 345 nuclear warheads and has one of the largest concentrations of combat units in the U.S. Like Alaska, however, it is treated as a semi-overseas base where military operations will originate from in wartime. It is the military center for planning and command in the Pacific theater, for anti-submarine warfare (ASW), and naval and Marine Corps operations. Nuclear weapons command and control locations include the TACAMO base at Barbers Point, strategic communications facilities at Bellows AFS, Hickam AFB, Punamano AFS, and Wahiawa, and the underground Pacific Fleet operations center at Kunia.

***NAS Barbers Point, Oahu**	Patrol Wing 2/Barbers Point Air Patrol and Reconnaissance Group: 5 nuclear-capable P-3 squadrons, aircraft deploy to forward bases throughout the Pacific, 100 nuclear depth bombs are stored on the base, guarded by Marines • homebase for Carrier Air Wings when aircraft carriers are ported in Hawaii • Fleet Air Reconnaissance Squadron 3 (VQ-3): Pacific TACAMO radio relay squadron with EC-130 aircraft, moved from Guam in 1981–1982 • Naval Facility: processing station for SOSUS
Barking Sands, Kauai	Pacific Missile Range Facility: operates Barking Sands Tactical Underwater Range (BARSTUR), 700 sqare miles of highly instrumented underwater systems including bottom-mounted hydrophones and three dimensional tracking, range support for carrier battle group operations, ASW, submarine weapons tests, submarine vs. submarine operations, more than 900 missile launches per year for naval maneuvers and R&D tests • Naval Undersea Warfare Engineering Station Keyport, WA Det: RDT&E of nuclear-capable ASW weapons including ASROC/SUBROC testing • air defense fighter-interceptor dispersal base
Bellows AFS, Oahu	HF transmitter: part of the Pacific Giant Talk/Scope Signal III net, Mystic Star, Commando Escort, and the Global Command and Control system (receiver is located at Hickam AFB)
Camp H.M. Smith, Halawa Heights, Oahu	HQ, U.S. Pacific Command (PACOM): joint commander for all Pacific forces, coordinator of Pacific nuclear operations, WWMCCS terminal includes access to Nuclear Weapons Accounting System, Nuclear Capabilities Plan and Single Integrated Damage Analysis Capabilities System, alternate command post (ALCOP) is at Hickam AFB • HQ, Fleet Marine Force Pacific: commander of all Marine Corps forces in the Pacific
Ewa Beach, Oahu	transmitter supporting missile launches from WSMC
Fort Shafter, Honolulu, Oahu	HQ, Army Western Command: Army component of Pacific Command and commander of Army support forces in the Pacific • "Nuclear Weapons Support Branch, Maintenance Division"[31]
Haiku, Maui	OMEGA station operated by Coast Guard transmitting navigational signals on VLF to Pacific area
Hickam AFB, Honolulu IAP, Oahu	HQ, Pacific Air Forces (PACAF): command of all AF tactical fighter units in the Pacific, also Commander Joint Task Force 119: responsible for the defense of Hawaii, nuclear command and control facilities include PACAF "emergency action console" and WWMCCS terminal allowing access to the Nuclear Capabilities Plan and Nuclear Contingency Planning System • 548th Reconnaissance Technical Group: Pacific Command and PACAF nuclear targeting intelligence and assessment center • 834th Airlift Division: Pacific theater nuclear airlift coordinator • Pacific Command alternate command post (ALCOP) • 9th Airborne Command and Control Squadron: 4 EC-135J "Blue Eagle" Pacific Command airborne command centers • 6594th Test Group: specially configured C-130 aircraft which recover satellite reconnaissance film capsules in midair • 154th Tactical Fighter Group (HIANG): F-4C on 24-hour alert for the air defense of Hawaii • HF receiver: part of the Mystic Star net, Global Command and Control system, Giant Talk/Scope Signal III, and Commando Escort (transmitter at Bellows AFS) • Commando Escort Net control station • NEACP/ABNCP ground entry point • AN/MSC-54 mobile airborne command post ground entry point van • Hickam Automatic Digital Weather Switch: control of weather intercept

	units in the Philippines and Japan and liaison with the Japanese Meteorological Agency[32]
Kaena Point, Oahu	Hawaii Tracking Station, AF Satellite Control Facility: command and control of military satellites • DMSP tracking and command readout station • Kaena Point Station: high precision FPQ-14 tracking radar supporting midcourse analysis of missile launches from WSMC
Kahoolawe Island	entire island is restricted area used for bombardment including "simulated special [nuclear] weapons"[33]
MCAS Kaneohe, Oahu	1st Marine Brigade/Marine Aircraft Group 24: nuclear units include 1 artillery battalion • Hawaii Laboratory, Naval Ocean Systems Center: ocean surveillance R&D, specializing in optical detection and acoustics
Kokee AFS, Kauai	150th Aircraft Control and Warning Squadron (HIANG): Hawaii air defense direction center and radar station manned 24-hours
Kunia, Oahu	Pacific Fleet underground command facilities including Fleet Operations Control Center Pacific, command center for the Pacific area, WWMCCS terminal • Army command center for Hawaii • NSA/Joint intelligence indications and warning center[34]
Kure Island	Coast Guard LORAN-C Station: serving central Pacific chain
Lualualei, Oahu	Naval Magazine: conventional weapons storage and nuclear weapons logistics support • Naval Radio Transmitter Facility: HF and LF transmitter operating to the Pacific area, also used for navigation purposes
Makaha Ridge, Kauai	electronic warfare "threat emitter" simulating Soviet signals, supports naval training at Barking Sands
Makalapa, Pearl Harbor, Oahu	HQ, Pacific Fleet: command of naval forces in the Pacific, includes WWMCCS terminal • HQ, Naval Forces, Central Command (USNAVCENT): formerly Rapid Deployment Naval Forces, name changed June 1981, provides naval support for Southwest Asian contingencies
Mt. Heleakala, Maui	Maui Observation Station, DARPA: long-range, highly sensitive optics supporting missile launches from WSMC, tests of electro-optical sensors and advanced optics • Det 3, 1st Space Wing: Maui Optical Tracking and Identification Facility (MOTIF): visible light and long-wave infrared detection of space objects • GEODDS station for deep space detection
Mt. Kaala AFS, Oahu	169th Aircraft Control and Warning Squadron (HIANG): Hawaii air defense direction center located on Wheeler AFB complex and radar station manned 24 hours • Pacific Command airborne command post ground communications terminal[35]
Niihau Island	new AN/APS-134 radar to extend range and surveillance coverage of training and missile testing from Barking Sands
Palehua, Oahu	AF Solar Observing Optical Network (SOON) observatory
Pearl Harbor, Oahu	Naval Base: homeport for ships and submarines • Naval Shipyard: Naval Reactors Representitive Office • Naval Submarine Base: HQ, Submarine Force Pacific/Submarine Force Third Fleet (CTF 34): command and control of Pacific Fleet submarines, cruise missile targeting, submarine operating authority for the Hawaiian area, coordinates strategic submarine operations and targeting for Pacific-based Trident submarines • Submarine squadrons 1 and 17 • Polaris Materiel Office Pacific Det: strategic submarine logistics support unit, activated in November 1982 • Ford Island: HQ, Third Fleet: coordinates naval operations in the eastern Pacific and Bering Sea • Oceanographic Systems Pacific: control and central processing of SOSUS data in the Pacific • homeport of USNS Observation Island with Cobra Judy missile tracking radar used to monitor Soviet and Chinese missile testing
Punamano AFS	Commando Escort station[36]
Schofield Barracks, Oahu	HQ, 25th Infantry Division: nuclear units include 3 155mm M-198 artillery battalions
Upoli Point, Hawaii	Coast Guard LORAN-C Station: serving central Pacific chain

Wahiawa, Oahu	Naval Communications Area Master Station Eastern Pacific: central AUTODIN/AUTOVON switching center, main Defense Communications System station, satellite communications terminal to Calif., Korea, Okinawa, Japan, Guam, Kwajalein, Philippines, and Ft. Detrick, Md., and ground station for the Pacific Command airborne command post • Naval Radio Receiver Facility: HF receiver for fleet communications • Det C, Navy Astronautics Group: Transit satellite tracking and injection station • NAVSTAR monitoring station
Waikele, Oahu	munitions storage site of Naval Magazine Lualualei: possible nuclear weapons storage site
***West Loch, Pearl Harbor, Oahu**	main nuclear weapons storage site of Naval Magazine Lualualei: serves ships and submarines at Pearl Harbor and provides storage for other services, weapons stored include 100 Navy and Marine Corps bombs, 50 ASROC and 50 SUBROC warheads
Wheeler AFB, Oahu	1156th TOS, AFTAC: control of Pacific nuclear test detection network • Hawaiian ROCC: activated in 1984, control of 2 radars and interceptor aircraft in Hawaii • Wheeler Range Network Control Center, WSMC: switching center and data transfer site supporting missile launches and down-range sites from WSMC

IDAHO

Most of the nuclear-related facilities in Idaho support missile testing to White Sands, NM and SAC bomber training. No nuclear warheads are stored in the state.

Ashton	SAC operated mobile radar bomb scoring site, part of Strategic Training Range
Bayview	Acoustic Research Det, DTNSRDC: underwater acoustic trials at Lake Pend Oreille, a 1,150 foot quiet body of water used for submarine silencing research
Blue Butte	telemetry and radar site supporting tests from Shoofly to White Sands, NM
Edgemead	radar tracking site supporting tests from Shoofly to White Sands, NM
Grassmere	radar tracking site supporting tests from Shoofly to White Sands, NM
Hagerman	radar tracking site supporting tests from Shoofly to White Sands, NM
Idaho Falls	Idaho National Engineering Laboratory, DOE: GOCO facility operated by EG&G Idaho, Inc., Exxon Nuclear Idaho Co., and Westinghouse Electric, R&D of naval nuclear reactors, processing of spent fuel from naval reactors, nuclear research, storage of military nuclear waste, reservation covers 571,000 acres • Naval Nuclear Power Training Unit
Mountain Home AFB	366th Tactical Fighter Wing, TAC: 91 nuclear-capable F-111A, conducts F-111 crew training for the AF • dispersal base for B-52s from Castle AFB, CA • bombing range used by SAC bombers • future operations center and software support facility for west coast OTH-B radar • Idaho launch site support center, White Sands Missile Range, NM: including tracking radar[37]
Shoofly	Idaho Launch Site, White Sands Missile Range, NM: 800-mile extended range launch site supporting Pershing flights to White Sands, 4 radars at Shoofly support launches
Wilder	15th AF SAC radar bomb scoring nuclear bomb delivery practice site, part of the Strategic Training Range

ILLINOIS

Illinois houses the headquarters of the Army Armament Munitions and Chemical Command at Rock Island, responsible for Army nuclear weapons development, as well as the Military Airlift Command and Air Force Communications Command at Scott AFB.

Argonne	Argonne National Laboratory, DOE: GOCO operated by the University of Chicago, a small portion of the lab's work deals with nuclear weapons and waste management

Capital MAP, Springfield	183d Tactical Fighter Group (ILANG): nuclear-capable F-4D
Chanute AFB, Rantoul	AF Chanute Technical Training Center: training of crews and technicians in Minuteman and ICBM missile operations and maintenance
Chicago	HQ, FEMA Region V
NAS Glenview	Patrol Squadron 60 (VP-60): reserve nuclear-capable P-3 • Patrol Squadron 90 (VP-90): reserve nuclear-capable P-3
O'Hare IAP, Park Ridge	126th Aerial Refueling Wing (ILANG): KC-135 tankers
Rock Island	Rock Island Arsenal: HQ, Army Armament Munitions and Chemical Command: management and R&D of Army nuclear weapons, including artillery, missiles, and ADMs, new command activated in July 1983
Scott AFB	HQ, Military Airlift Command: nuclear weapons transportation worldwide • HQ, 23d Air Force: newly established MAC unit commanding AF special operations forces and SAC missile security police • HQ, Air Force Communications Command: manages AF non-tactical communications with field units at 429 locations worldwide • Global Command and Control Station[38]

INDIANA

The most significant nuclear facility in Indiana is the new National Emergency Airborne Command Post forward base at Grissom AFB. Airborne command post operations were relocated from Andrews AFB, MD to Grissom in 1983.

Crane	Naval Weapons Support Center: material, technical and logistic support to Navy programs, including ASW and submarine ballistic missile systems, more than 3,000 civilian employees
Dana	Coast Guard LORAN-C Station: serving northeast U.S. and Great Lakes chains
Ft. Wayne MAP	122d Tactical Fighter Wing (INANG): nuclear-capable F-4C
Grissom AFB, Peru/Bunker Hill	305th Aerial Refueling Wing, SAC: operates KC-135 tankers and 2 E-4 NEACP, forward operating base for the airborne command posts was relocated from Andrews AFB, MD in 1983 (the main base is Offutt AFB, NE) • 931st Aerial Refueling Group, AFRES: KC-135 tankers
Hulman Field, Terre Haute	181st Tactical Fighter Group (INANG): nuclear-capable F-4C

IOWA

Ames	Ames Laboratory, Iowa State University: a small portion of the laboratory is funded by DOE for nuclear materials safeguards and security research
Burlington	Iowa Army Ammunition Plant: former nuclear weapons final assembly plant, closed when final warhead assembly was consolidated at Pantex Plant, Amarillo, TX
Des Moines MAP	132d Tactical Fighter Wing (IAANG): nuclear-capable A-7D
Sioux City MAP	185th Tactical Fighter Group (IAANG): nuclear-capable A-7D

KANSAS

McConnell AFB is the center of the nuclear infrastructure in Kansas. Though the Titan II missile silos dispersed around it have begun to be dismantled, missiles will be replaced with B-1B bombers in early 1988. Four strategic communications sites, as well as Forbes Field and Salinas also support the SAC bomber force.

Andale	SACDIN terminal supporting McConnell AFB
Colby	GWEN relay node using commercial radio tower
Forbes Field, Topeka	190th Aerial Refueling Group (KSANG): KC-135 tankers
Fort Riley, Junction City	HQ, 1st Infantry Division: nuclear-capable units include 1 8" and 2 155mm artillery battalions, forward brigade is stationed in Goeppingen, West Germany

Manhattan — GWEN relay node using commercial radio tower

***McConnell AFB, Wichita** — 381st Strategic Missile Wing: 17 Titan II missiles in silos around Wichita, began deactivation in late 1984 • 384th Aerial Refueling Wing: 2 KC-135 squadrons, will receive 16 B-1Bs in early 1988 and convert to Bombardment Wing • 184th Tactical Fighter Group (KSANG): nuclear-capable F-4D training unit

Oxford — SACDIN terminal supporting McConnell AFB

Salinas — dispersal base for B-52s from Dyess AFB, TX at former SAC Schilling AFB

KENTUCKY

Fort Campbell — HQ, 101st Airborne Division (Air Assault): nuclear units include 1 155mm M-198 battalion

Louisville — Field Office, DMAHTC: supports preparation of mapping products, including support for nuclear weapon systems

Paducah — Gaseous Diffusion Plant, DOE: separates uranium for further processing

Richmond — 8th AF SAC radar bomb scoring nuclear bomb delivery practice site

LOUISIANA

Lousiana ranks 9th with 530 nuclear warheads deployed at Barksdale AFB. The base houses SAC's alternate command post, the headquarters of SAC's 8th Air Force, a bomber wing, and a major Air Force central nuclear warhead storage depot.

***Barksdale AFB, Bossier City** — HQ, 8th Air Force, SAC: includes operations of the SAC alternate underground command post • 2d Bombardment Wing: B-52G, KC-135 and KC-10, to receive ALCMs starting in December 1986, nuclear weapons supporting the Wing include 150 bombs and 60 SRAM missiles • 78th Aerial Refueling Squadron (Associate), AFRES: provides crews for KC-10 tankers • GWEN receive only station • Giant Talk/Scope Signal III master/area network control station for CONUS network • HQ, 1st Combat Evaluation Group, SAC: operates the SAC radar bomb scoring sites for nuclear bombing practice • 3097th Aviation Depot Squadron (SA-ALC): central AF nuclear weapons storage depot, including 225 bombs, 35 ALCMs, and 60 SRAMs

Camp Robinson, North Little Rock — training site for testing the security and safety of mobile nuclear weapons, including the ground-launched missile (GLCM)

Fort Polk, Leesville — HQ, 5th Infantry Division (Mechanized): nuclear units include 2 155mm and 1 8" artillery battalions

Grangeville — Coast Guard LORAN-C Station: serving southeast U.S. chain

Lake Charles — JSS radar

NAS New Orleans Belle Chase — Det 1, 87th Fighter Interceptor Squadron: nuclear-capable F-106 on alert • 139th Tactical Fighter Group (LAANG): nuclear-capable F-4C, to convert to F-15 in late 1985 • Patrol Squadron 94 (VP-94): reserve nuclear-capable P-3 • HQ, 4th Marine Air Wing: Marine Corps reserve command for aviation units

New Orleans — HQ, 4th Marine Division: Marine Corps reserve command for ground units • Coast Guard LORAN-C Monitor Station: serving southeast U.S. and Great Lakes chains

Slidell — JSS radar

MAINE

Maine is the forward north Atlantic base for a number of important nuclear-related installations: bomber and tanker bases at Bangor IAP and Loring AFB, a main P-3 ASW deployment base at Brunswick, and the VLF submarine communications station at Cutler. The state ranks 13th with 320 nuclear warheads deployed. The only operating over-the-horizon radar in the U.S. has elements at Bangor, Columbia Falls and Moscow.

Ashland — 8th AF SAC radar bomb scoring nuclear bomb practice site, part of the Strategic Training Range

Bangor IAP	101st Aerial Refueling Wing (MEANG): KC-135 tankers • operations and control center of OTH-B radar
***NAS Brunswick**	HQ, Patrol Wings Atlantic: controls P-3 operations in the Atlantic, command facilities include an ASW Operations Center • Patrol Wing 5: 12 nuclear-capable P-3C squadrons, the planes rotate to bases in Iceland, Bermuda, Sicily, Spain and the Azores • Advanced Underwater Weapons Det includes storage of at least 100 nuclear depth bombs[39]
Bucks Harbor AFS, Machias	JSS radar
Cape Elizabeth	Coast Guard LORAN-C Monitor Station: serving northeast U.S. and Canadian east coast chains
Caribou	Coast Guard LORAN-C Station: serving northeast U.S. and Canadian east coast chains, also serves as a synchronizer between the OTH-B receiver and transmitter sites in Maine • Global Command and Control Station
Caswell AFS	766th Radar Squadron: JSS radar
Charleston AFS, Dover-Foxcroft	Det 6, 14th Missile Warning Squadron: inactive FSS-7 SLBM early warning radar, can be brought back into service • 765th Radar Squadron: JSS radar
Columbia Falls	OTH-B receiver site
Cutler, East Machias	Naval Communications Unit: VLF transmitter, one of two main U.S. submarine communications sites with worldwide coverage, operates with 2 MegaWatts of power, the highest power level of any communications station in the world, also used for radionavigation purposes
Kittery	Portsmouth Naval Shipyard: overhaul of strategic missile submarines, 9,000 civilian employees
***Loring AFB, Limestone**	42d Bombardment Wing: B-52G and KC-135, secondary anti-ship missions with Harpoon, nuclear weapons stored on the base include 150 bombs and 60 SRAM missiles • Det 1, 49th Fighter Interceptor Squadron: F-106 with nuclear Genie missiles • Green Pine station • Global Command and Control System (site at Caribou)
Machias	SAC controlled 8th AF gunnery range used by B-52 bombers[40]
Moscow-Caratunk	OTH-B transmitter site, 3,000 foot long antenna array transmitting signals in 6 bands, full 180 degree coverage in 1986
Prospect Harbor	Det A, Navy Astronautics Group: Transit satellite tracking and injection station
Rosemount	Det 2, 1000th Satellite Operations Group: DMSP tracking and injection station

MARYLAND

Although no nuclear warheads are stored in Maryland, its ranks 3d in the U.S. with 35 facilities in the nuclear infrastructure. These facilities include the largest number of key U.S. nuclear-related communications sites anywhere in the world—at Annapolis, Brandywine, Camp David, Cheltenham, Davidsonville, Ft. Detrick, Ft. Ritchie, Olney, and Patuxent River—as well as numerous nuclear weapons research and technology laboratories.

Aberdeen	Aberdeen Proving Ground: Army Test and Evaluation Command material testing, including work on nuclear artillery and mobility testing of ground-launched cruise missiles • Army Pulse Radiation Facility: "provides a radiative environment simulating a portion of the nuclear weapons ground environment to determine the nuclear vulnerability of Army equipment and systems" • Army Ballistics Research Laboratory: R&D on propulsion dynamics, launch and flight dynamics, characteristics of targets and munitions, warhead dynamics, terminal and nuclear weapons effects, primary laboratory for design of nuclear artillery • Army Radiation Control Team[41]
Adelphi	Army Electronics R&D Command (ERADCOM): R&D on fire control, fuzing, weapons electronics and nuclear weapons effects, nuclear artillery • Harry

	Diamond Laboratories: R&D on fuzing (Pershing II, nuclear artillery), ordnance, nuclear weapons effects, and radar
Andrews AFB, Camp Springs	HQ, Air Force Systems Command (AFSC): manages AF RDT&E, including laboratories and nuclear weapons programs • 113th Tactical Fighter Wing (DCANG): nuclear-capable F-4D • Mystic Star Master Net Control Station for presidential and VIP communications • Global Command and Control System and Giant Talk/Scope Signal III station, radio sites at Brandywine and Davidsonville • Det 1, 4950th Test Wing: Project "Speckled Trout" • 1st Helicopter Squadron: operates "Crown Helo" for Presidential emergency evacuation and "Constant Blue" continuity of operations evacuation, as well as the DOD Joint Emergency Evacuation Plan • Nuclear Emergency Search Team (NEST): DOE nuclear recovery and anti-terrorism unit
Annapolis	Naval Radio Transmitter Facility: VLF/LF transmissions to Atlantic and Caribbean, also used for radio navigation purposes, primary means for communications with missile submarines
Bethesda	Armed Forces Radiobiology Research Institute: Defense Nuclear Agency laboratory conducting research on nuclear weapons effects and radiation
Bloodsworth Island, Crocheron	future site of EMP Radiation Environmental Simulator for Ships (EMPRESS II), to be activated in the late 1980s to test ships of the Atlantic Fleet against 7 million volt electrical charges
Blossom Point	Naval Research Laboratory ocean surveillance satellite tracking and command facility
Brandywine	Brandywine Communications Station: AFSATCOM UHF ground terminal • DSCS "special user terminal" (for contingency deployments worldwide) • NEACP ground entry point • Giant Talk/Scope Signal III and Global Command and Control system transmitter • Naval Research Laboratory radio antenna range[42]
Brighton Dam	Naval Surface Weapons Center Hydroacoustic Facility: test and assessment of underwater acoustic systems for naval weapons
Brookmont	Defense Mapping Agency Hydrographic/Topographic Center: mapping services including Digital Terrain Elevation Data for cruise missile programs, geodetic survey, satellite geophysics, 2,800 civilian employees
Camp David, Thurmont	White House Communications Agency alternate switchboard and emergency operations center
Carderock	David W. Taylor Naval Ships R&D Center (DTNSRDC): R&D on naval vehicles, acoustic silencing of submarines, design of Trident, nuclear survivability of ships and submarines, 1,600 civilian employees
Cheltenham	Naval Communications Unit Washington: primary Naval communications station for Washington, with HF transmissions worldwide, links to civilian MARISAT satellites
Chesapeake Beach	Naval Research Laboratory research facility
Davidsonville	Governors Bridge Communications Station: Global Command and Control System and Giant Talk/Scope Signal III receiver • Mystic Star and NEACP ground entry points
Derwood	National Civil Defense Computer Facility, FEMA
Emmitsburg	FEMA Emergency Management Institute: civil defense training
Fort Detrick	Army East Coast Telecommunications Center (ECTC): one of the nation's largest communications facilities, primary hub for satellite communications support to Washington, three SATCOM terminals, HF radio facilities, network control station for Atlantic DSCS satellite, AUTODIN switching center, and Moscow-Washington Direct Communications Link (DCL) (the "hotline")
Fort Meade	National Security Agency: signals intelligence collection, but also responsible for all nuclear weapons release and control codes and procedures • 770th Radar Squadron: JSS radar
Fort Ritchie, Cascade	HQ, 7th Signal Command: major Army command for fixed and strategic communications in the U.S. • administrative and computer support center (4203d Operational Data Processing Squadron of SAC) for the Alternate

	National Military Command Center located at Raven Rock, PA • Army Communications Support Activity: unit created in 1984 to restore military communications after a nuclear war
Germantown	Department of Energy staff offices including Division of Military Applications and Division of Naval Reactors • DOE satellite communications station
Indian Head	Naval Ordnance Station/Naval Explosive Ordnance Disposal Technology Center: nuclear weapons ordnance disposal training and technology for DOD, "maintain a rapid response technology support group for countering improvised nuclear devices as required by the joint memorandum of understanding between the DOD, DOE and FBI", 1,800 civilian employees[43]
Laytonsville	"Federal Regional Center": underground bunker for unidentified government agency
Maryland Point	Maryland Point Observatory, Naval Research Laboratory: high precision radio telscope used for Very Long Baseline Interferometry
North Beach	Naval Research Laboratory research station
Olney	Alternate National Warning Center: secondary civil defense bunker operated by FEMA • HQ, FEMA Region III and "Federal Regional Center": underground civil defense command center
Patuxent River	Naval Air Test Center: T&E of aircraft, ASW and attack weapons systems, 2,000 civilian employees • ASW Operational Test and Evaluation Squadron One (VX-1): aircraft include P-3C, EP-3A, S-3A, SH-3H, SH-2F • Oceanographic Development Squadron Eight (VXN-8): operates specially configured P-3 aircraft in Project Outpost Birdseye which conducts Arctic studies and SSBN operational area assessments, and Project Outpost Seascan, which conducts acoustic and oceanographic surveys • Fleet Air Reconnaissance Squadron Four (VQ-4): EC-130 TACAMO VLF radio relay aircraft for communications to missile submarines • Patrol Squadron 68 (VP-68): reserve nuclear-capable P-3 • EMP Radiation Environment Simulator for Ships (EMPRESS) and the EMP Simulator for Aircraft (EMPSAC) Facility, operated by the Naval Surface Weapons Center, Dahlgren, VA
Pomonkey	Naval Research Laboratory Free Space Antenna Range
Randle Cliff	Chesapeake Bay Det, Naval Research Laboratory: 167 acre R&D facility involved in radar, fire control, optics, communications, hypervelocity gun research, also balloon launch and tracking facility, experimental over-the-horizon radar, radar cross section measurements facility
Silver Hill	Air Force operated radio relay site serving Washington
Suitland	Naval Operational Intelligence Center (formerly Naval Ocean Surveillance Information Center): ocean surveillance center for the Navy • Naval Intelligence Support Center
St. Inigoes	Naval Electronics Systems Engineering Activity
Tilghman Island	Tilghman Island Test Facility, Naval Research Laboratory: test site supporting optical, radar and space systems R&D
Waldorf	Waldorf Radio Site, Naval Research Laboratory: 221 acre site involved in monitoring environmental phenomena, sensors include X-band and S-band antennas
White Oak	Naval Surface Weapons Center, White Oak Laboratory: "principle Navy RDT&E center for surface-ship weapon systems, ordnance, mines, and strategic systems support," including nuclear warhead fuzing and SUBROC development, 1,900 civilian employees[44]

MASSACHUSETTS

Massachusetts hosts nine technical facilities, radars, observatories, and elctronic research sites involved in a wide variety of work on nuclear weapons command and control systems and weapons electronics. Most are part of the Electronic Systems Division and Air Force Geophysics Laboratories at Hanscom AFB. No nuclear warheads are deployed in the state.

Boston	HQ, FEMA Region I: command center operated at Maynard

Cape Cod AFS, Buzzards Bay	6th Missile Warning Squadron: AN/FPS-115 Pave Paws, provides "tactical warning and supports attack assessment of an SLBM attack against the continental U.S. and southern Canada. Another mission is to provide warning support attack assessment of an ICBM attack against these areas," radar site abuts Otis ANGB[45]
Hamilton	Sagamore Hill Solar Observatory, AF Geophysics Laboratory • Sagamore Hill Radio Observatory, Air Weather Service
Hanscom AFB, Lexington	HQ, Electronic Systems Division: AF management of all electronic related and command and control R&D programs • Air Force Geophysics Laboratory: research on the effects of the geophysical environment on military systems, including extensive work in the fields of geodesy and seismology, contributes directly to the accuracy programs for ICBMs, monitors solar activity, 600 personnel
Ipswich	Electronic Systems Division research facility
Maynard	FEMA Region I "Federal Regional Center": underground civil defense command center
Nantucket	Coast Guard LORAN-C Station: serving northeast U.S. and Canadian east coast chains
North Truro AFS	762d Radar Squadron: JSS radar
Otis ANGB	102d Fighter Interceptor Wing (MAANG): nuclear-capable F-106 • AF Geophysics Laboratory Weather Test Facility
Plymouth	Electronic Systems Division "4th Cliff" research facility
Prospect Hill	Prospect Hill Research Station: joint Rome Air Development Center, NY/Electronics Systems Division research facility
NAS South Weymouth	Patrol Squadron 92 (VP-92): reserve nuclear-capable P-3
Sudbury	Sudbury Research Site: Ground-based Remote Sensing Facility, AF Geophysics Laboratory: weather research station stressing interpretation of storms that affect military operations
Waltham	Electronic Systems Division research facility
Watertown	Army Materiel & Mechanics Research Center
Westford	Millstone Hill Facility: MIT Lincoln Laboratory field research facility, including L-band radar, "Firepond" infrared tracking radar for precise tracking, "Haystack" X-band radar for geosynchronous orbit observations, and a very-long baseline interferometry observatory
Westover AFB, Holyoke	Giant Talk transmitter and receiver, part of the continental U.S. network, located on former SAC base, now a bomber dispersal site[46]

MICHIGAN

Michigan ranks 6th (tied with Texas) with 630 nuclear warheads deployed at two bomber bases: K.I. Sawyer AFB and Wurtsmith AFB. The extremely-low-frequency (ELF) antenna at Republic has been the center of controversy for years because of its role in communicating with nuclear submarines.

Battle Creek	FEMA Region V "Federal Regional Center": underground civil defense command center • Federal Emergency Management Agency Staff College
Bayshore	Bayshore RBS Site: 8th AF SAC nuclear bomb delivery practice site, part of the Strategic Training Range
Calumet AFS	665th Radar Squadron: JSS radar
Dunbar Forest	Coast Guard LORAN-C Monitor Station: serving northeast U.S. and Great Lakes chains
Empire AFS	JSS radar
Port Austin	JSS radar
Kincheloe AFB	former SAC base, remains a bomber dispersal base
***K.I. Sawyer AFB, Gwinn**	410th Bombardment Wing: B-52H and KC-135, nuclear weapons include 150 bombs and 60 SRAM missiles, to receive ALCMs in 1987 • 87th Fighter

	Interceptor Squadron: F-106 with nuclear Genie missiles, to convert to F-15 starting in late 1984
Lake Superior	SAC controlled 8th AF gunnery range used by bombers[47]
Port Austin AFS	754th Radar Squadron: JSS radar
Republic	partially completed ELF transmitter facility, three cables suspended from telephone poles in an "F" pattern, consisting of 56 miles of cable, construction to be completed in 1985–86
Sault Saint Marie AFS	753d Radar Squadron: JSS radar
Selfridge ANGB, Mount Clemens	191st Fighter Interceptor Group (MIANG): F-4C/D • 127th Tactical Fighter Wing (MIANG): nuclear-capable A-7D • Naval Air Facility Detroit: Patrol Squadron 93 (VP-93): reserve nuclear-capable P-3
***Wurtsmith AFB, Oscoda**	HQ, 40th Air Division, SAC: intermediate command controlling 3 SAC bases • 379th Bombardment Wing: B-52G and KC-135, nuclear weapons include 150 bombs, 60 SRAM missiles, and 200 ALCMs, 242 total ALCMs after full deployment

MINNESOTA

Baudette AFS	Coast Guard LORAN-C Station: serving the Great Lakes chain
Duluth IAP	148th Fighter Interceptor Group (MNANG): F-4C/D unit activated in 1984 • former SAGE command center of the 23d NORAD Region, moved to McChord AFB, WA
Finland AFS, Nashwauk	FAA owned and operated JSS radar
Rosemount	Det B, Navy Astronautics Group: Transit satellite tracking and injection station

MISSISSIPPI

Bay St. Louis	Naval Oceanography Command/Naval Ocean R&D Activity: naval and ocean systems R&D, tenant of the National Space Technology Laboratories (NASA), conducts oceanography research supporting nuclear weapons such as developing models for acoustic and ocean surveillance, provides direct support to DMA, research on marine seismic systems used to determine if nuclear explosions can be distinguished from earthquakes, work includes installation by the Glomar Challenger of seismic instruments in the northwest Pacific Ocean during 1983
Columbus AFB	former SAC bomber base, remains a dispersal base • GWEN relay site to be activated in 1985
Keesler AFB, Biloxi	920th Weather Reconnaissance Group: aerial weather collection and forecasting including nuclear test detection by air sampling, supports operations "Volant Met" and "Volant Cross" to collect weather reconnaissance in "data sparse areas" and in overwater aerial refueling areas • Keesler Technical Training Center: AF training in strategic missile command, control and communications • Giant Talk/Scope Signal III station opened in 1981[48]
Meridian	JSS radar
Silver Lake	Naval Space Surveillance System receiver

MISSOURI

The 150 Minuteman II missile silos around Whiteman AFB are the main element of the nuclear infrastructure in Missouri, as well as the DOE Kansas City plant which manufactures components for nuclear warheads.

El Dorado Springs	SACDIN terminal supporting Whiteman AFB
Kansas City	HQ, FEMA Region VII • Kansas City Plant, DOE: GOCO operated by Bendix, production of non-nuclear components of nuclear warheads,

	electrical systems, mechanical devices, plastics, foams, adhesives, 6,815 employees
Lambert Field, St. Louis	131st Tactical Fighter Wing (MOANG): nuclear-capable F-4C
St. Louis	DMA Aerospace Center: production of aeronautical charts, air target materials (large-scale air target/radar charts and urban area mosaics), digital data, point position data bases, space mission charts, geodetic and aerospace environmental data used in navigation and weapons guidance, 3,400 civilian employees
Tipton	SACDIN terminal supporting Whiteman AFB
Warrensburg	SACDIN terminal supporting Whiteman AFB
***Whiteman AFB, Knob Noster**	351st Strategic Missile Wing: 150 Minuteman II missiles in silos around Whiteman, missiles being upgraded with a remote retargeting capability under the NS-17 upgrade to be active in January 1986, 10 missiles are equipped with the Emergency Rocket Communications System (ERCS) instead of nuclear warheads for emergency communications, the "Oscar" Launch Control Facility is the only SAC control facility located on a main base[49]

MONTANA

The 200 Minuteman missile silos surrounding Malmstrom AFB are the main elements of the nuclear infrastructure in Montana, supported by six strategic communications facities.

Arlington	SACDIN terminal supporting Malmstrom AFB
Billings	GWEN relay site to be activated in 1985
Conrad AFS	SAC radar bomb scoring site for nuclear delivery practice, to become part of the Strategic Training Range in 1986
Forsyth	SAC radar bomb scoring site for nuclear delivery practice, part of the Strategic Training Range
Glasgow AFB	SAC bomber and tanker dispersal base
Great Falls IAP	120th Fighter Interceptor Group (MTANG): nuclear-capable F-106 • former command center of 24th NORAD Region • GWEN relay site to be activated in 1985 • SACDIN terminal supporting Malmstrom AFB
Harlowton	SACDIN terminal supporting Malmstrom AFB
Havre AFS	778th Radar Squadron: JSS radar • SAC radar bomb scoring site for nuclear bomb delivery practice, part of the Strategic Training Range
Kalispell AFS	FAA owned and operated JSS radar
***Malmstrom AFB, Great Falls**	341st Strategic Missile Wing: 150 Minuteman II and 50 Minuteman III missiles in silos around Malmstrom • former SAGE command center moved to McChord AFB, WA • former alternate command post (ALCOP) for NORAD, replaced by back-up facility (BUF) at Peterson AFB, CO • FAA owned/joint operated JSS radar
Opheim AFS	779th Radar Squadron: JSS radar
Ronan	GWEN relay site to be activated in 1985
Valier	SACDIN terminal supporting Malmstrom AFB

NEBRASKA

Strategic Air Command headquarters and the 7 facilities supporting survivable communications to Offutt AFB dominate the state. Offutt AFB is the location of the Joint Strategic Target Planning Staff, where the strategic nuclear war plan of the U.S. is prepared, and homebase of the SAC and National airborne command posts. In the southwest corner of the state, 85 Minuteman III missile silos are dispersed from F.E. Warren AFB in Wyoming.

Ainsworth	GWEN relay site
Bellevue	GWEN relay site supporting SAC headquarters at Offutt AFB

Elkhorn	Offutt Communications Annex 2: Giant Talk/Scope Signal III transmitter, part of the continental U.S. network • Green Pine net control station
Grand Island	Cornhusker Army Ammunition Plant: houses key SAC communications and command facilities, including serving as the probable HQ for the SAC headquarters emergency relocation team (HERT), a mobile SAC command center[50]
Hastings	Hastings RBS Site: 8th AF SAC nuclear bombing practice site, part of the Strategic Training Range, to be deactivated in late 1985
Hooper	Offutt Communications Annex 3: communications support for SAC headquarters
Offutt AFB, Omaha	HQ, Strategic Air Command: JCS "specified command" responsible for all bomber and land-based missile forces, SAC commander is also Director of the Joint Strategic Target Planning Staff, which prepares the Single Integrated Operational Plan (SIOP), the central nuclear war plan of U.S. nuclear forces, SAC headquarters includes an elaborate underground command center • 544th Strategic Intelligence Wing: processes and analyzes intelligence information to support selection of nuclear targets and preparation of the SIOP, operates the Strategic Targeting Intelligence Center • 1000th Satellite Operations Group: support for DMSP strategic weather satellites • Strategic Communications Division, AF Communications Command: operates the specialized communications and command systems supporting SAC forces • AF Global Weather Central: weather processing and forecasting, strategic support to ballistic missile warning, SAC forces and operations such as low-level bomber and cruise missile operations • AFSATCOM Master Control Center and Consolidated Ground Terminal • GWEN input/output station • 1st Airborne Command and Control Squadron: operation of the National Emergency Airborne Command Post fleet of 4 E-4 converted 747 planes, aircraft maintain alert at Offutt and at Grissom AFB, IN • 2d Airborne Command and Control Squadron: operates the SAC "Looking Glass" airborne command post fleet of 3 EC-135 planes, one plane is on airborne alert at all times, another is on ground alert as the Eastern Auxiliary Command Post • Giant Talk/Scope Signal III station (sites at Elkhorn and Scribner State)[51]
Scribner State Airfield	Giant Talk/Scope Signal III receiver, part of the continental U.S. net
Silver Creek	Survivable Low-frequency Communications System (SLFCS) LF transmitter and receiver: "to provide essential command control communications in support of SAC EWO [Emergency War Order] operations before, during and after a nuclear attack" • SAC airborne command post ground entry point, "UHF and HF radio ground entry functions supporting SAC PACCS [Post-attack Command and Control System]" • GWEN receive-only site[52]
Sunol	SACDIN terminal supporting F.E. Warren AFB, WY

NEVADA

Huge land areas of Nevada are controlled by the military to run the Nellis AFB, Nevada Test Site, Tonopah testing complex. Underground nuclear tests of the U.S. and Britian are conducted at the Nevada Test Site. Some 260 nuclear warheads are stored at the Air Force depot at Lake Meade Base.

Camp Mercury	HQ, Nevada Test Site, DOE: located adjacent to the Nellis AFB complex, this 1,350 square mile facility is the location of DOE and DOD underground nuclear weapons testing, as well as nuclear warhead testing for the British • Defense Nuclear Agency Test Division conducts DOD tests • Regional Seismic Test Network station • DOE Nuclear Emergency Search Team
Cherry Creek	microwave relay station supporting the AFFTC and cruise missile testing from PMTC to Utah
Egan	microwave relay station supporting the AFFTC and cruise missile testing from PMTC to Utah
Ely	telemetry station supporting the AFFTC and cruise missile testing from PMTC to Utah

Fallon AFS	JSS radar • Coast Guard LORAN-C Station: serving the U.S. west coast chain
Goshute	telemetry station supporting the AFFTC and cruise missile testing from PMTC to Utah
Hawthorne	Hawthorne RBS Site: 8th AF SAC nuclear bombing practice site, part of the Strategic Training Range, to be deactivated in 1985 (located on Hawthorne Army Ammunition Plant)
Indian Springs	Indian Springs AF Auxiliary Field: support to nuclear warhead testing at the Nevada Test Site • management of the Nellis AFB training range • Det 1, 57th FIghter Weapons Wing: helicopter support to DOE nuclear warhead testing, including providing airborne closed circuit television coverage of tests, provides post-test air sampling, security and airlift
***Lake Meade**	Lake Meade Base (Nellis Area 2): 3096th Aviation Depot Squadron (SA-ALC): nuclear storage depot of Nellis AFB, one of three AF central nuclear storage sites in the U.S., stores 225 nuclear bombs and 35 ALCMs
Nellis AFB	474th Tactical Fighter Wing: nuclear-capable F-16 • 57th Fighter Weapons Wing: operates F-4, F-5, F-15, F-16, and F-111 aircraft to support training on the Nellis Range • AF Tactical Fighter Weapons Center: conducts air combat training operations and exercises ("Red Flag") and operates the Nellis Range, which covers 6,000 square milies, training targets include nuclear bombing circles, simulated surface-to-air missile sites, a truck convoy, an airfield, an industrial area, and an ICBM launch site, used for tactical aircraft, bomber, GLCM training, and drop testing nuclear bomb shapes • British nuclear-capable Jaguars and Buccaneer aircraft train at Nellis regularly (see also Camp Mercury and Lake Meade Base)
Searchlight	Coast Guard LORAN-C Station: serving U.S. west coast chain
Shoshone	telemetry station supporting the AFFTC and cruise missile testing from PMTC to Utah
Tempiute	microwave relay station supporting the AFFTC and cruise missile testing from PMTC to Utah
Tonopah	Tonopah Test Range: located on the Nellis AFB complex and operted by Sandia Laboratories, NM, non-explosive aspects of nuclear weapons testing such as rocket launches and parachute tests
Worthington	microwave relay station supporting the AFFTC and cruise missile testing from PMTC to Utah

NEW HAMPSHIRE

Manchester AFS, New Boston	New Hampshire Satellite Tracking Station, AF Satellite Control Facility: tracking and control of reconnaissance satellites, communications facilities include an AN/FSC-78 DSCS satellite communications terminal
***Pease AFB, Portsmouth**	HQ, 45th Air Division, SAC: intermediate headquarters controlling 4 SAC bases in the northeast • 509th Bombardment Wing: FB-111A and KC-135, nuclear weapons on base include 125 bombs and 65 SRAM missiles • 157th Aerial Refueling Group (NHANG): KC-135 tankers
Portsmouth	(see Kittery, ME for Portsmouth Naval Shipyard)

NEW JERSEY

New Jersey is home to the primary nuclear transportation unit for the U.S. military. From McGuire AFB, specially trained crews fly regular missions throughout the world delivering warheads and components. Development of Army nuclear weapons largely centers at Picatinny Arsenal in Dover while Army communications are centered at Fort Monmouth.

Atlantic City AP	177th Fighter Interceptor Group (NJANG): nuclear-capable F-106
***Earle/Colts Neck**	Naval Weapons Station Earle: naval weapons storage depot providing homeport services for Atlantic Fleet ammunition ships assigned, base contains "classified ordnance facility" storing 100 nuclear warheads, more than 700 civilian employees, 235 man Marine Barracks provides security[53]

Ft. Monmouth, Red Bank	HQ, Army Communications and Electronics Command: development and acquisition of Army command, control and communications equipment • Army Satellite Communications Agency: management of the ground portions of the DSCS satellite and tactical satellite operations
Gibbsboro AFS	772d Radar Squadron: JSS radar
NAS Lakehurst	contingency nuclear storage site supported by Earle, used as transhipment point for nuclear weapons • Army operated satellite communications ground terminal, the major station on the east coast for communications with forces in Europe
McGuire AFB	HQ, 21st Air Force, MAC: coordinates nuclear weapons transportation in the Atlantic and European areas • 6th Military Airlift Squadron: the U.S. military "Prime Nuclear Airlift Force" for intercontinental missions, only long-range C-141 nuclear airlift unit, 20 specially trained crews • 170th Aerial Refueling Group (NJANG): KC-135 tankers • 108th Tactical Fighter Wing (NJANG): nuclear-capable F-4D[54]
Palermo	Palermo Communications Facility: unidentified strategic communications facility
Picatinny Arsenal, Dover	Army Armament Research and Development Center: nuclear weapons R&D, life cycle procurement and production support for Army nuclear weapons, development of future nuclear artillery guns, includes the Nuclear Munitions Project Office • "Surety Field Activity," Army Materiel Command • Army Large Caliber Weapon Systems Laboratory: R&D of nuclear warhead sections, artillery, safing, arming and fuzing components for Army nuclear Weapons, lead Army development laboratory for 155mm nuclear artillery and insertable nuclear components[55]
Sandy Hook	Coast Guard LORAN-C Monitor Station: serving the northeast U.S. chain
Trenton	Naval Air Propulsion Center: technical and engineering support for engines, including those of cruise missiles
Wildwood	Coast Guard LORAN-C Station (Experimental): serving northeast U.S. and Great Lakes chains

NEW MEXICO

New Mexico contains the most extensive nuclear weapons research, management, training and testing facilities and organizations in the U.S. Nuclear warheads are designed and fabricated in Los Alamos and White Sands Missile Range has a wide variety of testing facilities for delivery systems. The huge nuclear complexes at Holloman AFB and Kirtland AFB are intimately involved in every aspect of the development and management of the nuclear weapons stockpile. The nuclear weapons depot at Kirtland (formerly the Manzano base) is the Air Force's largest central storage site, ranking New Mexico 11th with 410 warheads.

Alamo Peak	telemetry site supporting missile launches at WSMR
Cannon AFB	27th Tactical Fighter Wing, TAC: 82 nuclear-capable F-111D with possible nuclear weapons storage
Carlsbad	Waste Isolation Pilot Plant Site, DOE: military nuclear waste storage
Contreas	GWEN relay site to be activated in 1985
El Huerfano	telemetry site supporting missile launches at WSMR
Elephant Butte	Naval Space Surveillance System receiver
Farmington	NEACP ground entry point[56]
Holloman AFB, Alamogordo	Armament Division, 6585th Test Group, AF Systems Command: T&E of navigational and guidance systems and reentry vehicles, facilities include Radar Target Backscatter Facility (RATSCAT) for radar cross section measurements of rockets, missiles, and reentry vehicles, tests take place on the White Sands Missile Range, weapons currently under test include MX, Trident, B-1B and B-52 avionics, and ALCM "Have Rust" program, Central Inertial Guidance Test Facility: missile and space guidance system T&E, inertial and stellar gyroscope and accelerometers R&D, supports Pershing, Trident, and MX AIRS guidance • Det 1, AF Geophysics Laboratory (Balloon

R&D Test Branch): high altitude balloon launches carrying gravimeters and other instruments to measure variations in the gravity field and the atmosphere • AF Solar Optical Observing Network (SOON) observatory • 49th Tactical Fighter Wing, TAC: provides F-15s on NORAD alert • 1025th Satellite Communications Squadron (Mobile): probable operator of the DSP satellite early warning system Mobile Ground Terminals

***Kirtland AFB, Albuquerque** — Albuquerque Operations Office, DOE: intermediate field office responsible for DOE nuclear weapons and materials transportation, operates more than 10 "safe secure trailers" (SSTs) used in shipments of nuclear materials and components in the U.S., coordinates the research, development, production and testing programs of the DOE, including stockpile management • Interservice Nuclear Weapons School: joint DOD and DOE training in nuclear weapons design, employment. management and safety • Defense Nuclear Agency Field Command management of the DOD nuclear weapons stockpile, also control the DNA Test Directorate located at the Nevada Test Site • Joint Nuclear Accident Coordinating Center: joint DOD and DOE nuclear accident emergency response center • AF Space Technology Center, AF Systems Command: supervision of AF laboratories dealing with strategic weapons and nuclear technology • AF Weapons Laboratory: principal AF exploratory and engineering development laboratory dealing with nuclear weapons, effects, vulnerability, survivability and safety, largest computational capability in DOD, operates the EMP "trestle test facility," the largest glue-laminated wood structure in the world used to test full sized aircraft against nuclear weapons effects, 1,025 personnel • Naval Weapons Evaluation Facility: principal Navy organization responsible for test, evaluation and technical support for naval nuclear weapons and components, conducts feasibility studies on new concepts and weapons, including Marine Corps nuclear weapons • 3098th Aviation Depot Squadron (SA-ALC): one of 3 central Air Force nuclear weapons storage sites in the U.S. (formerly Manzano Base), weapons in storage include 10 Genie warheads, 10 Titan II warheads, 225 bombs, 35 ALCMs, 50 GLCMs, 15 Minuteman II warheads, and 65 Minuteman III warheads • AF Inspection and Safety Center Directorate of Nuclear Surety • Nuclear Field Office, Army Materiel Command • Nuclear Support Office, AF Logistics Command • RSTN System Control and Receiving Station (SCARS), DOE: seismic data reception from 5 RSTN stations via INTELSAT satellite • Primary Nuclear Airlift Support Base • 150th Tactical Fighter Group (NMANG): nuclear-capable A-7D • Sandia National Laboratories, DOE: GOCO operated by Sandia Corporation, a subsidiary of Western Electric Company, RDT&E of all non-nuclear components of nuclear weapons, including control devices, parachutes, timing and fuzing mechanisms, the laboratory occupies 39,500 acres on Kirtland AFB[57]

Los Alamos — Los Alamos National Laboratory, DOE: GOCO operated by the University of California Board of Regents, R&D of nuclear weapons, design and testing of new warheads, only laboratory with capability of constructing entire prototype nuclear devices for tests, "weapons like devices in certain areas, and . . . large quantities of special nuclear materials" are present at the laboratory • RSTN station[58]

McGregor Range — supports Pershing 1 missile firings to WSMR

Mt. Taylor — telemetry site supporting missile tests to WSMR

Roswell AFB — former SAC bomber base, remains a bomber and tanker dispersal base

Silver City (Cliff) — FAA owned JSS radar

Socorro — Det 1, 1st Space Wing: GEODSS satellite tracking station (lcoated on Stallion Range of WSMR)

Sunspot — Solar Reserach Branch, AF Geophysics Laboratory: AF use of the Sacramento Peak Solar Observatory (located on WSMR)

White Sands/Las Cruces — White Sands Missile Range (WSMR): T&E of Army missiles, rockets, and reentry vehicles, range covers 40 by 100 mile area, includes nuclear effects testing facilities, largest overland missile test center in North America, location of first atomic explosion on what is now part of the range, site of over 33,000 missile firings since 1945, involved in the development of every Army nuclear missile, currently supports Pershing, ABRES, low-altitude anti-ballistic missiles, Assault Breaker, anti-tactical missiles, SRAM, over 3,000 precisely surveyed instrumentation sites support the range, 11 microwave relay stations, 3 telemetry sites, 14 tracking telescope sites, 20 video camera sites, and 18 radars are on the range • White Sands Solar Furnace: one of the largest furnaces in the world, capable of generating up to 5,000 degrees farenheit on a four-inch spot, used to simulate the extreme heat of a nuclear explosion • Nuclear Effects Facility: radiation chamber contains a fast burst reactor used to simulate nuclear weapons radiation

NEW YORK

With the largest U.S. Army nuclear weapons storage depot in the world at Seneca, New York ranks 2d with 1,900 nuclear warheads deployed. Seneca has become the center for storage of neutron bombs for the U.S. arsenal as a result of an August 1981 decision to build the weapons even though they would not be deployed overseas. Over 500 enhanced radiation warheads have since been stored at the base. Two SAC bomber bases, Griffiss AFB and Plattsburgh AFB also contribute to the high number of nuclear warheads. New York also ranks 7th in number of facilities in the nuclear infrastructure with 27, many of which are field research facilities of the Rome Air Development Center at Griffiss AFB.

Ava	Ava Test Annex: Rome Air Development Center (Griffiss AFB) research facility
Ballston Spa	Naval Nuclear Power Training Unit: naval nuclear reactor training
Dansville	JSS radar
Dresden	Lake Seneca Test Site, Naval Underwater Systems Center, Newport, RI
Forest Park	Forest Park Test Annex: Rome Air Development Center (Griffiss AFB) research facility
Fort Drum	Army training range used by SAC bombers • to be future location of Army division
Great Bend	Great Bend RBS Site: 8th AF SAC nuclear bombing practice site
***Griffiss AFB, Rome**	416th Bombardment Wing: B-52G and KC-135, first bomber unit to receive ALCM (September 1981), nuclear weapons include 150 bombs, 60 SRAM missiles, and 200 ALCMs (230 ALCMs at full deployment) • Rome Air Development Center, AF Systems Command: RDT and acquisition in the command, control, communications, information sciences and intelligence fields, supports systems such as Cobra Dane, satellite tracking radars and optics, ballistic missile defenses, lead laboratory in develoment of nuclear hardened electronics • Northeast ROCC: HQ, 24th NORAD Region/24th Air Division: control of air defense forces in the northeast U.S. • 49th Fighter Interceptor Squadron: nuclear-capable F-106 with Genie missiles
Hancock Field, Syracuse	former SAGE command center and HQ, 21st NORAD Region, closed with activation of the Griffiss AFB ROCC in 1983 • AUTODIN switching center
Lake Placid	DOE RSTN station located 25 miles west of Lake Placid
Lockport AFS	763d Radar Squadron: JSS radar
New York City	HQ, FEMA Region II
Newport	Rome Air Development Center (Griffiss AFB) research facility
Niagara Falls IAP	107th Fighter Interceptor Group (NYANG): F-4C/D
Ontario	Rome Air Development Center (Griffiss AFB) research facility: contains a tropospheric scatter range
***Plattsburgh AFB**	380th Bombardment Wing: FB-111A and KC-135, nuclear weapons include 125 bombs and 60 SRAM missiles
Quaker Hill	Quaker Hill Test Annex: Rome Air Development Center (Griffiss AFB) research facility
Riverhead, Long Island	FAA owned and operated JSS radar
Saratoga Springs AFS	656th Radar Squadron: JSS radar

***Seneca/Romulus**	Seneca Army Depot: major Army nuclear weapons storage site, supports east coast nuclear units and European deployments, 833d Ordnance Company (Special Ammunition General Support) provides nuclear warhead maintenance and storage support, nuclear warheads stored total some 1,300, including 60 ADMs, 575 8" artillery projectiles, both enhanced radiation (neutron bombs) and non-enhanced radiation versions, 90 Nike Hercules warheads, 50 155mm artillery projectiles, and 490 Lance missile warheads, both enhanced radiation and non-enhanced radiation versions • Coast Guard LORAN-C Station: serving the northeast U.S. and Great Lakes chains
Stockbridge	Stockbridge Test Annex: Rome Air Development Center (Griffiss AFB) research facility
Upton	Brookhaven National Laboratory, DOE: GOCO operated by Associated Universities, Inc., R&D on nuclear materials and waste, inertial confinement fusion
Utica (Remson)	JSS radar
Verona	Verona Test Annex: Rome Air Development Center (Griffiss AFB) research facility, including a tropospheric scatter range
Vienna	Rome Air Development Center (Griffiss AFB) research facility
Watertown AFS	655th Radar Squadron: JSS radar
West Milton, Schenectady	Naval Reactors Field Office: training
Youngstown	Youngstown Test Site: Rome Air Development Center (Griffiss AFB) research facility, including a tropospheric scatter range

NORTH CAROLINA

North Carolina is the east coast center for the Marines and Army airborne forces, and thus plays a key role in providing the forces for military operations in the Third World. No nuclear weapons are stored in the state.

Asheville	central U.S. government depository for all weather and meteorological data going back 100 years, contains the Geologic Survey depository for seismic data from the WWSSN and GDSN networks, military liaison offices include the AF Environmental Technical Applications Center that performs long-range prediction and analysis, and the AFTAC Data Processing Division and Data Reduction Center that processes and distributes nuclear test detection data
MCB Camp Lejeune	HQ, II Marine Amphibious Force/2d Marine Division: east coast Marine Corps HQ, including one division and support troops • 10th Marine Regt (Artillery) of the 2d Marine Division, comprised of 5 155mm nuclear-capable battalions • 2d Field Artillery Group provides long-range nuclear artillery support to Marine Corps operations, with 2 8" and 3 155mm batteries • Nuclear Ordnance Platoon, 2d Force Service Support Group: nuclear weapons technical support to Marine ground forces • 6th Marine Amphibious Brigade: HQ activated in 1983 for units earmarked to receive equipment from preposisitioned ships in the Middle East
Cape Hatteras, Buxton	Naval Facility: processing station for SOSUS, also provides data to ESMC for "broad ocean area sound fixing and ranging" in support of missile tests
Carolina Beach	Coast Guard LORAN-C Station: serving southeast U.S. and northeast U.S. chains
Cherry Point	Marine Corps gunnery range used by SAC bombers
MCAS Cherry Point	HQ, 2d Marine Aircraft Wing: nuclear-capable units include 2 A-4 squadrons, 2 AV-8B squadrons and 2 A-6 squadrons • Marine Wing Weapons Unit 2 (MWWU-2): nuclear weapons technical support for Marine air units
Fort Bragg, Fayetteville	HQ, XVIII Airborne Corps: command of Army airborne and rapid deployment forces, nuclear weapons support is provided by the 18th Field Artillery Brigade, with 155mm nuclear-capable artillery and the 1st Corps Support Command, responsible for maintenance and supply • HQ, 1st Special Operations Command: Army control of Special Forces units, some of which have ADM missions

Fort Fisher AFS, Kure Beach	Det 5, 14th Missile Warning Squadron: inactive FSS-7 SLBM detection early warning radar, could be brought back into service quickly • 701st Radar Squadron: JSS radar
MCAS New River	3 CH-53E heavy helicopter squadrons used in nuclear weapons transportation
Roanoke Rapids AFS	632d Radar Squadron: JSS radar
Seymour Johnson AFB	4th Tactical Fighter Wing: nuclear-capable F-4E, "dual-based" squadrons are committed to deployment in Europe • 68th Aerial Refueling Group, SAC: KC-135 tankers, formerly the 68th Bombardment Wing, the B-52Gs were redistributed to other bases in early 1982, Wing to receive KC-10 tankers in mid-1985

NORTH DAKOTA

North Dakota ranks 3d with 1510 nuclear warheads deployed and 10th with 19 facilities in the nuclear infrastructure. It houses two main SAC bases, Grand Forks AFB and Minot AFB, both housing a B-52 bomber wing as well as a Minuteman missile wing, two of only three such bases in the world. The early warning radar at Cavalier AFS is a key facility for determining the characteristics of a missile attack upon the U.S.

Benedict	SACDIN terminal supporting Minot AFB
Bismarck	Bismarck RBS Site: 15th AF SAC nuclear bombing practice site, part of the Strategic Training Range, to be deactivated in late 1985
Cavalier AFS	Concrete Missile Early Warning Station: Det 5, 1st Space Wing: operation of the Perimeter Acquisition Radar Characterization System (PARCS), the former anti-ballistic missile radar system, today it is used for attack assessments and characterization of missile attacks on the U.S., 1,800 mile range
Dickinson AFS	future Strategic Training Range site, to be activated in 1986
Edinburg	SACDIN terminal supporting Grand Forks AFB
Finley AFS	FAA owned and operated JSS radar
Fortuna AFS	780th Radar Squadron: JSS radar
***Grand Forks AFB, Emerado**	319th Bombardment Wing: B-52G and KC-135, received ALCMs in October 1983, will convert to 19 B-1Bs starting in September 1987, nuclear weapons include 150 bombs, 60 SRAM missiles, and 200 ALCMs (245 ALCMs at full deployment) • 321st Strategic Missile Wing: 150 Minuteman III missiles deployed in silos around the base, with some 480 Mk-12A warheads • GWEN receive only terminal
Hector Field, Fargo	119th Fighter Interceptor Group (NDANG): F-4C/D
Hope	SACDIN terminal supporting Grand Forks AFB
La Moure	Omega radionavigation station operated by the Coast Guard
Langdon	GWEN relay site to be activated in 1985
May	786th Radar Squadron: JSS radar
***Minot AFB**	HQ, 57th Air Division, SAC: intermediate command controlling SAC units in North Dakota • 5th Bombardment Wing: B-52H and KC-135, nuclear weapons include 150 bombs and 60 SRAM missiles • 91st Strategic Missile Wing: 150 Minuteman III, deployed in silos around the base, with 480 Mk-12A warheads • 5th Fighter Interceptor Squadron: nuclear-capable F-106 with Genie missiles, to convert to F-15 in 1985 • EC-135 airborne command posts from Ellsworth AFB, SD deploy to Minot for alert • GWEN receive only terminal
Norman	SACDIN terminal supporting Minot AFB
Pekin	SACDIN terminal supporting Grand Forks AFB
Stanley	SACDIN terminal supporting Minot AFB
Watford City (Alexander)	JSS radar

OHIO

Four main plants in the nuclear warhead production complex, Ashtabula, Fernald, Miamisburg and Piketon are located in Ohio. In addition, Wright-Patterson AFB in Dayton is the center of Air Force nuclear weapons logistics and bomber development. No nuclear warheads are stored in the state.

Ashtabula	Ashtabula Plant: plant owned by Reactive Metals, Inc. and under contract to DOE, fabrication of uranium received from Fernald Plant, OH for further processing at Hanford, WA and Savannah River, SC reactors
Fernald	Fernald Plant, Feed Materials Production Center, DOE: GOCO operated by NLO, Inc., conversion of uranium into finished target and fuel elements for nuclear materials production reactors
Gentile AFS, Dayton	AUTODIN switching center
Miamisburg	Mound Laboratory, DOE: GOCO operated by Monsanto Research Corporation, production of detonators, explosive timers, firing sets, and pyrotechnic devices for nuclear warheads, 1,900 employees
Newark AFS	Aerospace Guidance & Metrology Center, AF Logistics Command: repair of missile inertial guidance and navigation systems, assists in R&D of new missile guidance systems
Piketon	Portsmouth Gaseous Diffusion Plant, DOE: GOCO operated by Goodyear Atomic
Plumbrook	Coast Guard LORAN-C Monitor Station: serving northeast U.S. and Great Lakes chains
Rickenbacker ANGB, Columbus	160th Aerial Refueling Group (OHANG): KC-135 tankers • 121st Tactical Fighter Wing (OHANG): nuclear-capable A-7D • former SAC bomber base, remains a bomber dispersal base
Springfield MAP	178th Tactical Fighter Group (OHANG): nuclear-capable A-7D
Toledo-Express AP	180th Tactical Fighter Group (OHANG): nuclear-capable A-7D
Wright-Patterson AFB, Dayton	HQ, AF Aeronautical Systems Division. AF Systems Command: manages the development of air breathing systems including bombers and cruise missiles • 4950th Test Wing: operates the Advanced Range Instrumentation Aircraft (ARIA) in support of missile testing worldwide, stages out of 25 overseas bases, missions include collection of U.S. and Soviet missile and space telemetry, fleet consists of 7 EC-135N modified to serve as airborne telemetry terminals, supports missile launches from both ESMC and WSMC, ARIA fleet to convert to 6 C-18 and 2 C-135 by 1988, supports cruise missile testing as mobile relays of telemetry • HQ, AF Logistics Command: management, procurement, supply, transportation and maintenance in support of AF and reserve nuclear warheads and delivery systems • 906th Tactical Fighter Group, AFRES: nuclear-capable F-4D

OKLAHOMA

Oklahoma is home of the Army Field Artillery Center at Fort Sill, where artillery, Lance and Pershing II missile training is conducted and nuclear operational doctrine is developed. A Pershing II battalion and two Lance battalions at Fort Sill could be deployed overseas during crisis or as part of a military operation in the Third World. No nuclear warheads are stored in the state.

Altus AFB	340th Aerial Refueling Group, SAC: KC-135 tankers • dispersal site for B-52s from Dyess AFB, TX • SAC stand-by alternate command post[59]
Canton	GWEN relay node using commercial radio tower
Clinton-Sherman AFB, Clinton	former SAC base, remains a bomber and tanker dispersal base
Fort Sill, Lawton	Army Field Artillery Center and School: artillery and missile training and doctrinal development • HQ, III Corps Artillery: includes the 75th Field Artillery Bde, 212th Field Artillery Bde, and 214th Field Artillery Bde, containing 1st Battalion, 12th Field Artillery: Lance, committed to Central Command, and 6th Battalion, 33d Field Artillery: Lance, and 3d Battalion, 9th Field Artillery: Pershing II, first Pershing II unit, numerous

	nuclear-capable 155mm and 8" artillery battalions are also stationed at the base (60)
Tinker AFB, Midwest City	Oklahoma City Air Logistics Center: support of B-52 and B-1 bombers, including integration of Offensive Avionics Systems and cruise missiles. other systems supported include GLCM, A-7D, E-3A AWACs, airborne command posts, over 15,000 civilian employees • 552d Airborne Warning and Control Wing: homebase for the E-3 AWACS fleet, forward operations at Keflavik, Iceland, Kadena AB, Japan, and Saudi Arabia, includes the 3d Airborne Command and Control Squadron, providing NORAD support • AUTODIN switching center • 507th Tactical Fighter Group, AFRES: nuclear-capable F-4D
Tulsa MAP	138th Tactical Fighter Group (OKANG): nuclear-capable A-7D

OREGON

No nuclear warheads are stored in Oregon.

Boardman	Naval Weapons Systems Training facility: Navy operated bombing range used by SAC B-52 bombers
Buffalo Flats, Christmas Valley	future transmitter site for west coast OTH-B radar, to be fully operational in 1988
Coos Head, Charleston	Naval Facility: processing station for SOSUS
Kingsley Field, Klamath Falls	Det 1, 318th Fighter Interceptor Squadron: F-4C • JSS radar (Keno AFS) • GWEN relay site to be activated in 1985 • future systems support site for west coast OTH-B radar
Mt. Hebo AFS, Hebo	Det 2, 14th Missile Warning Squadron: inactive FSS-7 SLBM detection/early warning radar, could be returned to use quickly • 689th Radar Squadron: JSS radar
North Bend AFS	761st Radar Squadron: JSS radar • Coast Guard LORAN-C Monitor Station: serving west coast U.S. chain
Portland IAP	142d Fighter Interceptor Squadron (ORANG): F-4C/D
Salem (Dallas)	JSS radar

PENNSYLVANIA

The underground alternate military command center located in Raven Rock Mountain, near the Maryland border is the most critical instatllation in Pennsylvania. It is the primary Joint Chiefs of Staff operating center in wartime backing up the Pentagon. No nuclear warheads are stored in the state.

Benton AFS, Red Rock	648th Radar Squadron: JSS radar
Greater Pittsburgh IAP	171st Aerial Refueling Wing (PAANG): KC-135 tankers • 112th Tactical Fighter Wing (PAANG): nuclear-capable A-7D
Johnstown	GWEN relay site to be activated in 1985
Mechanicsburg	Naval Ships Parts Control Center/Fleet Material Support Office/Trident Refit Facility Quality Assurance Det: spare parts, components supply, maintenance support for naval ships and strategic missiles, Ships Parts Control Center monitors Navy nuclear Weapons for Pacific contingencies but located at non-Pacific storage sites[61]
Oakdale	JSS radar
Philadelphia	HQ, FEMA Region III
Raven Rock	Alternate National Military Command Center (ANMCC): "Site R," location of the underground hardened JCS command center, containing the Alternate Joint Communications Center (AJCC) and the AF Emergency Operations Center, internal redundant power generating capability, food and water supplies, full WWMCCS computer facilities includes access to the Single Integrated Damage Analysis Capabilities System, Nuclear Ordnance Monitoring System, and Nuclear Weapons Accounting System, the aboveground administrative support center is at Fort Ritchie, MD

Shippingport	Naval Reactors Office, DOE
Warminster	Naval Air Development Center: RDT&E for air warfare systems, including weapons, surveillance equipment, command, control and communications, and navigation, current projects include follow-on to TACAMO (E6-A), NAVSTAR, and balloon-borne VLF antennas
NAS Willow Grove, Horsham	Patrol Squadron 64 (VP-64): reserve nuclear-capable P-3 • Patrol Squadron 66 (VP-66): reserve nuclear-capable P-3

RHODE ISLAND

Newport	Naval Base: Naval Underwater System Center: "principal Navy RDT&E center for submarine warfare and submarine weapons systems," 1,600 civilian employees • Trident Command and Control Systems Maintenance Agency • Surface Group 4: homeport for 7 nuclear-capable ships[62]
Providence	DMA Field Office: prepares mapping products supporting nuclear weapons programs
Quonset Point	instrumentation site supporting missile tests from ESMC

SOUTH CAROLINA

South Carolina ranks 1st with the most nuclear warheads deployed. The Naval Weapons Station at Charleston stores 1,482 warheads, mostly ballistic missile warheads, as spares and for submarines undergoing overhaul. The normal compliment of three submarines in port at Charleston adds another 480 warheads. In addition, plutonium and tritium are produced at the Savannah River Plant, in Aiken.

Aiken	Savannah River Plant, DOE: GOCO operated by Dupont, production reactors manufacturing tritium and plutonium for nuclear warheads
Charleston AFB	Det 1, 48th Fighter Interceptor Squadron: nuclear-capable F-106 on alert
***Charleston**	Naval Base: main submarine and surface ship base • HQ, Submarine Forces Westlant: NATO SACLANT command • Cruiser-destroyer Group 2: homeport for nuclear-capable surface ships • Submarine Group 6: HQ for 31 ballistic missile submarines assigned in the Atlantic • Submarine Squadron 4: homeport for attack submarines • Naval Shipyard Charleston • Naval Supply Center Charleston: support for ballistic missile submarines • Fleet Ballistic Missile Training Center: initial and refresher training of submarine crews • Naval Weapons Station Charleston: located on the west bank of the Cooper River, 25 miles from Charleston, the weapons storage and support depot is the largest nuclear weapons storage site in the U.S., services and issues a wide variety of weapons, nuclear weapons stored include 20 SUBROC, 40 ASROC, 870 Poseidon warheads (for submarines in overhaul and storage), and 552 Trident I warheads (for submarines in overhaul and storage), more than 900 civilian employees, Marine Barracks with 463 men for security • Polaris Material Office Atlantic (located at the Naval Weapons Station): Poseidon submarine Refit Site IV, assembly, checkout, storage and loading of submarine missiles • Submarine Squadron 18: homeport for Poseidon submarines, about 3 are in port at any time, with some 480 warheads
Folly Beach	Coast Guard LORAN-C Station, also provides remote ranging support for missile launches from ESMC
Jedburg	FAA owned and operated JSS radar
McEntire ANGB	169th Tactical Fighter Group (SCANG): nuclear-capable F-16, first reserve F-16 unit
North Charleston AFS	792d Radar Squadron: JSS radar
Shaw AFB	HQ, 9th Air Force, TAC: also HQ, Air Forces, Central Command, command of 7 tactical fighter wings in the U.S. • 363d Tactical Fighter Wing: nuclear-capable F-16

SOUTH DAKOTA

South Dakota ranks 13th with 365 nuclear warheads deployed at and around Ellsworth AFB, which serves as both a B-52 bomber base and Minuteman II missile base.

Clark	GWEN relay node
***Ellsworth AFB Rapid City**	28th Bombardment Wing: B-52H and KC-135, to receive 32 B-1Bs in early 1987 along with ALCMs and additional KC-135s, nuclear weapons stored include 150 bombs and 60 SRAM missiles • 44th Strategic Missile Wing: 150 Minuteman II missiles in silos around the base • 4th Airborne Command Control Squadron: 4 EC-135s, including the SAC western auxiliary command post, and Airborne Launch Control Centers 1, 2, 3 • GWEN receive only site
Kodaka	SACDIN terminal supporting Ellsworth AFB
Opal	SACDIN terminal supporting Ellsworth AFB
Rapid City	DOE Regional Seismic Test Network station
Sioux Falls	114th Tactical Fighter Group (SDANG): nuclear-capable A-7D
Spearfish	SACDIN terminal supporting Ellsworth AFB

TENNESSEE

No nuclear warheads are stored in the state.

Arnold AFS, Manchester	Arnold Engineering Development Center: unique rocket engine, propulsion, space chambers and wind tunnel testing facilities supporting aerospace RDT&E in such areas as acceleration, turbojet/turbofan technology, B-1, ALCM, MX, reentry systems, Pershing, Trident, hardened mobile launchers, and Small ICBM
McGhee Tyson AP, Knoxville	134th Aerial Refueling Group (TNANG): KC-135 tankers
McMinnsville	DOE Regional Seismic Test Network (RSTN) station
NAS Millington, Memphis	Patrol Squadron 67 (VP-67): reserve nuclear-capable P-3s
Oak Ridge	Y-12 Plant, DOE: GOCO operated by Union Carbide Corporation, production of warhead and test device parts, lithium processing, uranium assembly, 5,878 employees • Oak Ridge National Laboratory, DOE: nuclear materials safeguards and security

TEXAS

Texas ranks 6th (tied with Michigan) with 630 nuclear warheads deployed and 9th with 22 facilities in the nuclear infrastructure. It houses two SAC bomber bases, Carswell AFB and Dyess AFB, as well as the final assembly and disassembly plant for all U.S. nuclear warheads. The San Antonio Air Logistics Center at Kelly AFB is responsible for managing the AF nuclear weapons stockpile.

Amarillo	PANTEX Plant, DOE: GOCO operated by Mason and Hanger-Silas Mason, final assembly and disassembly of nuclear warheads, including maintenance and modification, manufacture of high explosive components of warheads, conducts nuclear stockpile maintenance program, 2,280 employees • Amarillo IAP: used for transport of nuclear warheads and components in support of PANTEX Plant, also designated as dispersal site for B-52s from Dyess AFB, TX (former SAC bomber base)
Bergstrom AFB, Austin	HQ, 12th Air Force, TAC: control of AF tactical fighter units in the U.S. • HQ, 10th Air Force, AFRES: operational supervision of all tactical fighter units in Air Force Reserve • 924th Tactical Fighter Group: nuclear-capable F-4D • SAC bomber dispersal base
Brooks AFB, San Antonio	AF Aerospace Medical Division, AF System Command: nuclear radiation measurements and dosimetry research
***Carswell AFB, Fort Worth**	HQ, 19th Air Division, SAC: intermediate command of 6 SAC bases • 7th Bombardment Wing: B-52H and KC-135, nuclear weapons include 300 bombs and 120 SRAM missiles, to receive ALCMs in early 1985 and have 502 at full

	deployment • 301st Tactical Fighter Wing, AFRES: nuclear-capable F-4D • HQ, Automated Weather Network: main weather switch for AF, center for compiling intercepted weather data from foreign countries[63]
Denton	HQ, FEMA Region VI and "Federal Regional Center:" underground civil defense command center serving as National Warning Center No. 2, facilities for 500 people
***Dyess AFB, Abilene**	HQ, 12th Air Division, SAC: intermediate command of 4 SAC bases • 96th Bombardment Wing: B-52H and KC-135, designated as first B-1B base, to receive 26 bombers starting in late 1985, also to be site of B-1B crew training, B-52H aircraft to be relocated to Carswell AFB, nuclear weapons currently deployed include 150 bombs and 60 SRAM missiles
El Paso	FAA owned JSS radar
Ellington AFB	147th Fighter Interceptor Group (TXANG): F-4C/D • JSS radar
Fort Bliss, El Paso	Army Air Defense Center and School: Nike Hercules training and doctrine, includes the NATO Nike Hercules Main School • 3d Armored Cavalry Regiment: nuclear units include 3 155mm artillery batteries, committed for early deployment to Europe
Fort Hood, Killian	HQ, III Corps: designated for reinforcement of northern West Germany with forward HQ already established in the Netherlands, 13th Corps Support Command is main nuclear support unit • HQ, 2d Armored Division: nuclear units include 2 155mm and 1 8" artillery battalions, forward Brigade is located in Garlstedt, West Germany • 1st Cavalry Division: nuclear units include 2 155mm and 1 8" artillery battalions
Goodfellow AFB, San Antonio	imagery analysis and targeting training to be consolidated here in 1984–1985 • Pave Paws radar station to be activated 38 miles southwest of the base in March 1987
Houston	630th Radar Squadron: JSS radar
Kelly AFB, San Antonio	San Antonio Air Logistics Center (SA-ALC): Directorate of Special Weapons manages all nuclear bombs and warheads and reentry vehicles in AF custody, manages the AF nuclear stockpile, and provides logistics support for AF nuclear weapons, supplies specialized test and handling equipment, 15,000 civilian employees • 149th Tactical Fighter Wing (TXANG): nuclear-capable F-4C, to convert to F-16 in late 1986
Lackland AFB	FAA owned JSS radar
Lake Kickapoo	Naval Space Surveillance System main transmitter
Odessa	Odessa Radar Site: FAA owned JSS radar
Oilton	FAA owned JSS radar
Raymondville	Coast Guard LORAN-C Station: serving southeast U.S. chain
San Antonio	DMA Field Office: prepares mapping products in support of nuclear weapon systems
Sheppard AFB	Sheppard Technical Training Center: Titan II missile launch and maintenance training • SAC bomber and tanker dispersal base
Sonora	JSS radar

UTAH

Utah houses the Ogden Air Logistics Center, which is responsible for maintaining the land-based missile force, and the Utah Test and Training Range, which is involved in testing a wide variety of nuclear delivery systems. No nuclear warheads are stored in the state.

Cold Springs	telemetry site supporting tests from Green River to WSMR
Dugway	Dugway Proving Ground: 1,315 square mile training and testing range, part of the Utah Test and Training Range (see Hill AFB), used for operational testing of GLCM in field operations during 1982
Granite Peak	telemetry collection site supporting the AFFTC and cruise missile testing from PMTC to Utah

Green River — Green River Launch Site/Utah Test Complex (WSMR): mid-range launch site supporting Pershing tests to WSMR, includes tracking radar

Hill AFB, Ogden — Ogden Air Logistics Center: support for Minutemann, Titan and MX missiles, ERCS, F-4 and F-16 aircraft, 13,000 civilian employees (Utah's largest employer), operates the Hardness Test Center, including Minuteman II silo, Minuteman III silo, and launch control center mock-ups • Utah Test and Training Range: combined Hill/Wendover/Dugway Proving Ground range complex totaling 2,136 square miles, used for aircraft testing and training, cruise missile impact point for flights from Edwards AFB, CA or submarine launches from the Pacific Ocean, contains simulated targets for nuclear weapons training, the bombing range is used by SAC B-52 bombers • 388th Tactical Fighter Wing: nuclear-capable F-16, also conducts pilot training for Belgium • 6514th Test Squadron, AFFTC: DT&E of unmanned vehicles, cruise missiles and RPVs, helicopter recovery of cruise missile tests to the Utah range • 419th Tactical Fighter Wing, AFRES: nuclear-capable F-16 • 1954th Radar Evaluation Squadron, AF Communications Command: technical support for radar operations worldwide • Army Continental Communications Support Center: new command activated in 1984 with responsibility for restoring communications after a nuclear war

Moab — telemetry site supporting tests from Green River to WSMR

Salt Lake City IAP — 151st Aerial Refueling Group (UTANG): KC-135 tankers

Wendover — telemetry relay station supporting the AFFTC and cruise missile testing from PMTC to Utah

---

VERMONT

Burlington — 158th Tactical Fighter Group (VTANG): nuclear-capable F-4D

Windsor — GWEN relay site to be activated in 1985

VIRGINIA

Virginia ranks 5th in the U.S. with 31 facilities in the nuclear infrastructure and 8th with 542 nuclear warheads deployed. The military is mostly concentrated in the northern Virginia suburbs of Washington and in the Norfolk area. Obviously most important is the Pentagon, located in Arlington, supported by the key agencies responsible for nuclear weapons management which are dispersed in buildings and military facilities near Washington. The Atlantic Command and Atlantic Fleet HQ in Norfolk directs the operations of military forces in the Atlantic area. A number of key command centers and communications facilities supporting the Pentagon and Atlantic Command are also in the state, including the homebase for the "Scope Light" airborne command centers at Langley AFB and the infamous "Mount Weather" underground bunker in Bluemont.

Alexandria — HQ, Defense Nuclear Agency: responsible for management of the U.S. nuclear stockpile and development of new nuclear weapons concepts • VELA Seismological Center/Seismic Data Analysis Center: processing of nuclear detection data from satellites and ground monitoring stations, linked to numerous foreign seismic monitoring systems, including the Norwegian Seismic Array • Naval Research Laboratory research site at Coast Guard Radio Station • HQ, Army Materiel Command: responsible for Army weapons R&D, logistics and support

Arlington — Pentagon: National Military Command Center: WWMCCS main site, including Nuclear Ordnance Monitoring System, Single Integrated Damage Analysis System, Air Field Facility File, Nuclear Weapons Accounting System, Nuclear Capabilities Plan, Nuclear Contingency Planning System • Army Operations Center: WWMCCS facility, including access to Nuclear Weapons Accounting System • Navy Command Center: WWMCCS facility • HQ, Defense Communications Agency • Navy Strategic System Program Office: Trident submarine and missile development • Joint Cruise Missile Program Office

Bay Capes — future site of EMP Radiation Environmental Simulator for Ships (EMPRESS II), to be activated in the late 1980s, to test ships of the Atlantic Fleet against 7 million volt electric charges

Bedford	JSS radar
Bluemont	FEMA Special Facility and "Federal Regional Center:" "Mount Weather," civilian government relocation center, main facility built in the 1950s for evacuation of the top officials of the government
Cape Charles AFS	771st Radar Squadron: JSS radar
Chesapeake	Naval Satellite Communications Facility: main satellite terminal supporting Atlantic Command and Atlantic Fleet units in the Norfolk area
Culpepper	"Federal Regional Center:" underground bunker emergency relocation center for the Department of the Treasury
Dahlgren	Naval Surface Weapons Center: primary Navy R&D center for surface weapon systems and strategic systems support, including ballistic missile targeting, digital fire control, geoballistics, reentry body nosetips, heatshields, sensor windows, rocket nozzles and exit cones, main laboratory in support of Trident II accuracy program, "develops all test flight and operational fire control formulations for U.S. and U.K. SLBMs," lead laboratory for SM-2(N), also works on VLS, ASWSOW, Tomahawk, strategic fire control, and magnetic silencing, facilities include the DNA Casino Facility with the capability of simulating the electrical and mechanical effects in materials and electronic components which are produced by the X-ray output from nuclear weapons, 2,800 civilian employees • Naval Space Command: formed in 1983, responsible for Naval satellite systems, particularly ocean surveillance, TRANSIT, Naval Space Surveillance System and Navy portion of MILSTAR[64]
Dam Neck	Naval Ocean Processing Facility: integrated ocean surveillance information center for Atlantic Fleet
Driver	Naval Radio Transmitter Facility: high frequency radio station supporting Atlantic Command and Atlantic Fleet
Fort Belvoir, Alexandria	Army Engineer Topographic Laboratories: Army support to the Defense Mapping Agency • Army Nuclear and Chemical Agency: Army nuclear weapons development and management • Belvoir R&D Center/Mobility Equipment R&D Command: development of nuclear weapons physical security equipment • Davison Army Airfield: provides Army helicopters in support of government continuity of operations evacuation plans and the DOD Joint Emergency Evacuation Plan
Fort Lee AFS	former command center for 20th NORAD Region, closed with activation of new ROCC at Tyndall AFB, FL
Fort Monroe, Hampton	HQ, Army Training and Doctrine Command (TRADOC): development of Army doctrine and training plans
Fort Story	Explosive Ordnance Disposal Group Two: Navy nuclear EOD support to Atlantic Fleet
Langley AFB, Hampton	HQ, Tactical Air Command also, Air Forces Atlantic Command and Air Forces Readiness Command, mobile tactical strike force of nuclear-capable fighter aircraft • 48th Fighter Interceptor Squadron: F-15 strategic interceptor aircraft, converted from F-106 in 1981 • 6th Airborne Command and Control Squadron: operation of the Atlantic Command airborne command posts, 4 EC-135P "Scope Light" command centers, five full battle crews • 1st Tactical Fighter Wing: F-15, wing has dual air defense and ground attack mission and is committed to Central Command • HQ, Air Defense Tactical Air Command (ADTAC): operation of the radars and interceptors under the command of NORAD[65]
Little Creek	Naval Amphibious Base: Naval Special Warfare Group Two: special operations unit with ADM missions • Naval Satellite Communications Det
Newport News	shipyard responsible for missile submarine overhauls
NAS Norfolk	HQ, Naval Air Forces, Atlantic/Commander, Fleet Air: management of all naval aviation in the Atlantic • Tactical Support Wing One: responsible for airlift of nuclear weapons, both "vertical onboard delivery" to ships with helicopters and "carrier onboard delivery" to aircraft carriers with aircraft • a contingency nuclear storage site is operated at NAS Norfolk by Yorktown

	and is used for nuclear weapons transportation supporting the Naval Station and bases and ships in the Norfolk area
Naval Base, Norfolk	HQ, Supreme Allied Commander, Atlantic (SACLANT): NATO command responsible for the Atlantic area • Submarines Atlantic (SACLANT): operation of missile carrying submarines in support of NATO • HQ, Atlantic Command (CINCLANT): U.S. command, WWMCCS terminal including access to Nuclear Ordnance Monitoring System (NOMS), Coordinator of Atomic Operations, Single Integrated Damage Analysis Capabilities system, Nuclear Contingency Planning System • HQ, Western Atlantic Area (SACLANT), including Ocean Subarea and Submarine Forces, WESTLANT area • HQ, Atlantic Fleet, including Submarine Forces and Surface Forces • HQ, Second Fleet: headquarters aboard the USS Mount Whitney • HQ, Fleet Marine Force Atlantic • HQ, 4th Marine Amphibious Brigade: mission of deploying to Norway • Amphibious Group Two: Atlantic Fleet ships carrying Marines and Marine equipment • Nuclear Weapons Training Group, Atlantic • Carrier Groups 4/8 and Cruiser-destroyer Group 8: homeport for aircraft carriers and ships stationed in Norfolk • Naval Supply Center, Norfolk: "Nuclear Weapons Supply Department," supply of nuclear weapons components, including neutron generators and limited life components • Naval Communications Area Master Station, Atlantic • Fleet Ocean Surveillance Information Center: Atlantic Fleet ocean surveillance center[66]
NAS Oceana, Virginia Beach	Carrier Air Wings 1, 6, 7, and 8: home of HQ for aircraft carrier aviation components in the Norfolk area • Medium Attack Wing One: adminstrative control of nuclear capable A-6 squadrons in the Atlantic Fleet • Det 2, 23d Air Defense Squadron: JSS radar reporting to ROCC at Tyndall AFB, FL
Portsmouth	Norfolk Naval Shipyard: Underwater Explosions Research Division, DTNSRDC: supports the Defense Nuclear Agency in shock qualification of submarines
Quantico	Marine Air Facility: Marine Executive Squadron 1 (HMX-1): helicopter transportation support for the president, maintains a forward Det at Anacostia, DC, part of the evacuation force to relocate government officials from Washington in a nuclear war
Reston	Command and Control Technical Center, DCA: central control and operations of WWMCCS system, Joint Operations Planning System, Nuclear Weapons Accounting System
Richmond	Byrd IAP: 192d Tactical FIghter Group (VAANG): nuclear-capable A-7D
The Plains	JSS radar
***Yorktown**	Naval Weapons Station, Yorktown: Special Weapons Department operates nuclear weapons storage for naval units in the Norfolk area, estimated 542 warheads stored, including 300 Navy and Marine Corps bombs, 40 ASROCs, 25 SUBROCs, 32 Terriers, 25 Tomahawks, and 75 Marine Corps artillery warheads and ADMs, 45 nuclear depth bombs, weapons are guarded by 285 man Marine Barracks, 1,600 civilian employees
Wallops Island	NASA radars supporting missile launches from Wallops, ESMC in Florida, and Naval Air Test Center, Patuxent River, MD • Combat Systems Laboratory, Naval Surface Weapons Center: experimental operation of the AEGIS naval air defense system
Warrenton	Warrenton Training Center: reportedly contains Federal Relocation Center, underground bunker for unidentified government agency
Winchester	Army Interagency Communications Agency: communications unit supporting Mount Weather in Bluemont and other federal relocation centers in the Washington area
Woodbridge	Harry Diamond Laboratories Research Facility: nuclear weapons effects and EMP testing and R&D

WASHINGTON

Washington ranks 5th with 1,172 nuclear warheads deployed and 8th with 24 facilities in the nuclear infrastructure. The Trident submarine force is stationed at Bangor with nuclear storage at Silverdale. A B-52 bomber wing is stationed at Fairchild AFB. Plutonium for nuclear warheads is produced at the Hanford Reservation in Richland. A major station for communications with submarines is located at Jim Creek.

***Bangor**	Naval Submarine Base Bangor: Trident homeport in the Pacific, includes Trident Training Facility and Trident Refit Facility • Submarine Group 9 and Submarine Squadron 17: homeport for Trident missile submarines, average of 2 submarines and 384 warheads are estimated to be in dock at any time • Naval Communications Station Puget Sound: HF network control station for fleet communications • Naval Ammunition Annex (main nuclear weapons storage site at Silverdale)
Blaine AFS	757th Radar Squadron: JSS radar
Boeing Field, Seattle	dispersal base for B-52 bombers from Castle AFB, CA[67]
Bothell	HQ, FEMA Region X and "Federal Regional Center:" underground civil defense command center
Bremerton	Puget Sound Naval Shipyard
Carr Inlet, Puget Sound	Carr Inlet Range: principal west coast acoustic research and noise trials area for analysis of radiated and self noise of submarines, measures the acoustic signatures of Trident submarines[68]
Dabob	Dabob Range, NUWES Keyport: ASW weapons RDT&E, three dimensional underwater tracking
Everett	to be the homeport of the Nimitz carrier battle group starting in 1987
***Fairchild AFB, Airway Heights**	HQ, 47th Air Division, SAC: intermediate command of 4 SAC bases • 92d Bombardment Wing: B-52G and KC-135, nuclear weapons include 150 bombs, 60 SRAM missiles and 200 ALCMs (245 ALCMs at full deployment) • 141st Aerial Refueling Wing (WAANG): KC-135 tankers • Det 1, 1000th Satellite Operations Group: DMSP tracking and command readout station
Fort Lewis	HQ, I Corps: new HQ activated in 1983 to command 7th Infantry Division, 9th Infantry Division, and 172d Infantry Bde in Alaska • HQ, 9th Infantry Division: nuclear units include 3 155mm and 1 8" artillery battalions • base was used for GLCM field testing in 1982–1983
George	Coast Guard LORAN-C Station: serving Canadian west coast and U.S. west coast chains
Grant County AP	dispersal base for B-52s from Castle AFB, CA[69]
Hood Canal	Hood Canal Range, NUWES Keyport: ASW weapons RDT&E
Jim Creek, Oso	Naval Radio Station (Transmitting): main VLF transmitter to the Pacific, also used for radionavigation purposes
Keyport	Naval Undersea Warfare Engineering Station (NUWES): command and control system support for Trident submarines, depot maintenance and complete life cycle testing of all Navy ASW weapons, proof, testing and evaluation of underwater weapons, operates acoustic and tracking ranges, and numerous test ranges in the area, responsible for support of ASROC and SUBROC missiles
Makah AFS	758th Radar Squadron: JSS radar
McChord AFB	318th Fighter Interceptor Squadron: F-15 • Northwest ROCC/25th NORAD Region/25th Air Division: ROCC activated in June 1983 with deactivation of SAGE RCC, connected to radar sites via meteor burst communications • 36th Military Airlift Squadron: C-130 Prime Nuclear Airlift Force for inter-U.S. nuclear weapons transportation, 4 specially certified crews[70]
Mica Peak AFS	JSS radar
Pacific Beach	Naval Facility: processing station for SOSUS
Richland	Hanford Reservation, DOE: GOCO operated by Atlantic Richfield Hanford Company, United Nuclear Industries, production of weapon-grade plutonium

	in N-reactor, reprocessing of fuel in PUREX plant, reservation covers 365,000 acres
Seattle Tacoma AP	dispersal base for B-52 bombers from Castle AFB, CA
***Silverdale**	Strategic Weapons Facility Pacific: nuclear warhead and missile storage in support of Trident submarines at Bangor, weapons stored include 378 Trident I warheads • Polaris Material Office Pacific: Trident missile supply and maintenance • weapons guarded by 342 man Marine Barracks
Wenatchee	GWEN relay site to be activated in 1985
NAS Whidbey Island, Oak Harbor	Medium Attack Tactical Electronic Warfare Wing Pacific: 7 nuclear-capable A-6 squadrons, Marine Barracks provides probable storage of nuclear warheads • Patrol Squadron 69 (VP-69): reserve nuclear-capable P-3 • Coast Guard LORAN-C Monitor Station: serving Canadian west coast chain

WEST VIRGINIA

There are no facilities in the nuclear infrastructure and no nuclear weapons in the state. There is a very-long baseline interferometry observatory in Green Bank which is used for military research.

WISCONSIN

Antigo AFS	676th Radar Squadron: JSS radar
Clam Lake	ELF Test Facility: Navy experimental extremely-low frequency submarine communication system, 28 miles of antenna suspended from telephone poles in a perpendicular array, used in ELF test program with strategic and attack submarines, will operate in conjunction with ELF system in Republic, MI to provide worldwide coverage
Gen. Billy Mitchell Field, Milwaulkee	128th Aerial Refueling Group (WSANG): KC-135 tankers

WYOMING

F.E. Warren AFB houses 200 Minuteman III missiles in silos covering three states. The MX missile will be deployed in 100 silos starting in late 1986.

Douglas	SAC mobile radar bomb scoring site, part of the Strategic Training Range
***F.E. Warren AFB, Cheyenne**	HQ, 4th Air Division, SAC: intermediate command of 2 SAC bases • 90th Strategic Missile Wing: 200 Minuteman III missiles in silos spread out over 12,000 square miles of WY, CO, and NE, to be location of MX missile deployment in silos • Geodetic Survey Squadron, DMA • GWEN receive only station
Gillette	SAC mobile radar bomb scoring site, part of the Strategic Training Range
Little America	15th AF SAC mobile radar bomb scoring site, part of the Strategic Training Range
Meriden	SACDIN terminal supporting F.E. Warren AFB
Pinedale	Det 459, 1156th TOS: AFTAC nuclear test detection station
Powell	SAC mobile radar bomb scoring site, part of the Strategic Training Range
Wheatland	SACDIN terminal supporting F.E. Warren AFB

OUTSIDE THE UNITED STATES

Location	*Organization and Activity*

ANTIGUA

Located within the Latin American Nuclear-Free Zone, Antigua plays a key role in strategic submarine missile testing programs.

Naval Facility: former processing station for SOSUS closed in 1982-1984, base to be retained for other purposes • AN/FPQ-14 tracking radar doubles as satellite tracking system, telemetry collection station, command and control, timing and weather systems supporting missile testing from ESMC • Missile Impact Location System (MILS) underwater hydrophone target array 150 miles northeast of the island also supports missile tests from ESMC • satellite communications link to Cape Canaveral, FL[71]

ASCENSION ISLAND

Global Command and Control Station • NAVSTAR tracking, telemetry and control ground antenna and passive monitoring station • AN/FPQ-15 tracking radar doubles as satellite tracking system, optical station, telemetry collection station, timing, and weather systems supporting missile testing from ESMC • Missile Impact Location System (MILS) underwater hydrophone target array 36 miles southwest of the island supports missile tests from ESMC • Broad Ocean Area Sound Fixing and Ranging system supports missile tests from ESMC • AF Solar Observing Optical Network (SOON) observatory • Ascension Island Intercept: weather intercept facility • periodic nuclear-capable P-3 staging base[72]

AUSTRALIA

Two major strategic facilities are located in Australia, one of two main DSP satellite early warning ground stations at Nurrungar, and a Naval communications facility at North West Cape. Most of the other facilties are related to intelligence collection, space tracking and technology and nuclear test detection. There are also a number of additional minor technical facilities (Adelaide, Amberley, Hobart, Mundaring) involved in seismic research.

Alice Springs	Det 421, AFTAC: nuclear test detection station
Charters Towers	seismograph detection station operated by the University of Queensland for DARPA
Cocos Islands	periodic deployment base for nuclear-capable P-3s[73]
Darwin	port and airfield used by U.S. forces • B-52 bombers on "Busy Boomerang" and "Glad Customer" operations conduct ocean surveillance from the Darwin airfield • nuclear-capable ships call at the port
Exmouth, North West Cape	Naval Communications Station Harold E. Holt: one of two primary VLF communications stations broadcasting to submarines, operates on 2 million watts power, also used for radio navigation purposes • HF receiver and transmitter for communications with naval forces • FLTSATCOM and DSCS AN/MSC-61 satellite communications station[74]
Learmouth	AF Solar Observing Optical Network (SOON) observatory • periodic staging base for nuclear-capable P-3s
Narrogin	seismic detection station operated by Australian Bureau of Mineral Resources and funded by DARPA
Nurrungar	Woomera Air Station: "Joint Defence Space Communications Station," DSP satellite early warning "mission readout station," one of two main stations worldwide (the other is at Buckley ANGB, CO) linked to NORAD via satellite and submarine cable
Pine Gap (Alice Springs)	"Joint Defence Space Research Facility:" main ground station receiving data from reconnaissance and signals intelligence collection satellites
Woodside, Gippsland	OMEGA radionavigation station, operated by the Australian Department of Transportation

ARGENTINA

An OMEGA radionavigation station, operated by the Argentine Navy, is located at Trelew.

BAHAMAS

Located with the Latin American Nuclear-Free Zone, the Bahamas plays a key role in submarine training, testing and certification, as well as supporting strategic missile testing from ESMC.

Andros Island	Atlantic Underseas Test and Evaluation Center (AUTEC): deep water range for submarine systems undersea R&D, only permanent underwater noise measuring facility on the east coast of the U.S., used for Trident submarine certification trials, also key station in the missile submarine security and silencing programs and sonar testing, ASROC and SUBROC testing, instrumentation includes a hydrophone acoustic array fixed to a single cable which is buoyed 50 feet below the surface and anchored to the ocean floor, Weapons Range is a 5 by 15 mile tracking range used for ASW training and certification against mobile targets
Bassett Cove, GBI	timing transponder supporting missile testing from ESMC
Carter Cay, GBI	timing transponder supporting missile testing from ESMC
Deep Creek, Andros Island	down-range Site 6 of AUTEC
Eleuthera	Naval Facility: processing station for SOSUS, also serves as timing transponder supporting missile testing from ESMC
Fresh Creek, Andros Island	down-range Site 1 of AUTEC, command and control station
Gibson Cay, Andros Island	down-range Site 3 of AUTEC with converted Nike Hercules tracking radar
Golding Cay, Andros Island	down-range Site 4 of AUTEC
Grand Bahama Island (GBI)	tracking radar, telemetry collection station, command and control station, timing and weather systems supporting missile testing from ESMC • Missile Tracking Instrumentation System supporting missile tests from ESMC
Great Stirrup Cay	timing transponder supporting missile testing from ESMC
High Point Cay, Andros Island	down-range Site 7 of AUTEC
Marsh Harbour, Great Abaco Island	timing transponder supporting missile testing from ESMC
Salvador Point, Andros Island	down-range Site 2 of AUTEC with converted Nike Hercules tracking radar
Treasure Cay, Great Abaco Island	timing transponder supporting missile testing from ESMC
West End, GBI	timing transponder supporting missile testing from ESMC

BARBADOS

The Naval Facility, a former processing station for SOSUS, was closed in 1979.[75]

BELGIUM

Belgium is a member of NATO and site of its headquarters. One nuclear warhead storage site is located in the country, at Kleine Brogel AB, soon to be joined by a ground-launced cruise missile base at Florennes AB.

Brussels	North Atlantic Council: the governing body of NATO with a permanent International Staff, committees include the Nuclear Defense Affairs Committee and the Nuclear Planning Group, military planning and policy is the responsibility of the Defense Planning Committee • NATO Military Committee: highest military authority of NATO, supported by an International Military Staff and comprised of three joint allied commands: Allied Command Europe at Casteau-Mons, Belgium, Allied Command Atlantic at Norfolk, VA, and Allied Command Channel at Northwood, UK
Casteau-Mons	HQ, Allied Command Europe, also known as the Supreme Headquarters Allied Powers Europe: most important NATO military command responsible for continental European defense and preparation of the Nuclear Operations Plan of NATO, senior officer is known as the Supreme Allied Commander

	Europe (SACEUR) and is also the senior U.S. military commander in Europe, the commander of the U.S. European Command, with headquarters at Stuttgart, West Germany • Theater Mission Planning Center: one of three ground-launched cruise missile targeting centers in Europe
Florennes AB	485th Tactical Missile Wing: designated as ground-launched cruise missile main operating base, will receive 48 missiles on 12 launchers between 1986–1988
Helchteren	air-to-ground training range used for nuclear-related fighter training
Kester	NATO Satellite Earth Station: master control station for NATO communications satellites and NATO control terminal for DSCS
***Kleine Brogel AB**	7361st Munitions Support Squadron: nuclear warhead custodian for Belgian 10th Fighter Bomber Wing with 2 squadrons of 36 nuclear-capable F-16s (replaced F-104Cs in late 1981), some 25 nuclear bombs are stored at the base, nuclear warhead support has been provided to the Belgian Air Force at this base since 1962
Maisieres	NATO Airborne Early Warning Command (NAEW): control of NATO AWACs and British Nimrod early warning aircraft

BERMUDA

Bermuda's location in the Atlantic makes it an important ASW surveillance and operations base. Although no nuclear weapons are stored in Bermuda in peacetime, authorization has been given for deployment of 32 nuclear depth bombs there "for advanced readiness of ASW operations."

Hamilton	Island Commander Bermuda, SACLANT: NATO command
St. George	Kindley AFB: Naval Air Station: under command of Patrol Wings Atlantic, regular deployment airfield for nuclear-capable P-3 operations, command facilities include ASW Operations Center, designated deployment base for nuclear depth bombs in Advanced Underwater Weapons Det in wartime • LF transmitter/receiver • forward operating deployment base of TACAMO radio relay aircraft from Patuxent River, MD • NASA tracking radar and command and control station supporting missile testing from ESMC • Marine Barracks has nuclear weapons security role
South Hampton	NAS Annex: Naval Facility: processing station for SOSUS, also Broad Ocean Area Sound Fixing and Ranging System supporting missile testing from ESMC • HF radio facility for naval communications[76]
Tudor Hill	Tudor Hill Laboratory, Naval Underwater System Center, Newport, RI: anti-submarine warfare R&D

CANADA

As a member of NATO and partner in NORAD, Canada is closely linked with early warning and anti-submarine operations. Canada gave up its sole nuclear weapons role for its own forces in 1984 when it withdrew CF-101 interceptors and replaced them with CF–18s in air defense roles. It still ranks 2d in number of facilities in the overseas nuclear infrastructure with numerous radars and navigation stations. The ASW link with the U.S. includes close cooperation in maritime surveillance as well as authorization for the deployment of nuclear depth bombs in Canada "for wartime ASW operations."

Alert, Ellesmere Island, NWT	extremely-high frequency radio research site, used for experiments in high latitude propagation supporting the LES-8/9 experimental communications satellites and the future MILSTAR system, Alert is the northenmost active military facility in the world
Alsask	CADIN Pinetree radar
Argentia, Nfld	Naval Facility: processing station for SOSUS, "operates acoustic hydrophones planted off-shore in the Atlantic," also serves as Missile Tracking Instrumentation System (MTIS) and remote ranging station supporting missile tests from ESMC • Green Pine station[77]
Armstrong	CADIN Pinetree radar

CFB Bagotville, Alouette, Quebec	former nuclear warhead storage site for Genie missiles carried by CF-101, deactivated in 1984, nuclear weapons withdrawn in July 1984 with conversion from CF-101 to CF-18 aircraft, still a NORAD alert site with 2 aircraft on 5-minute alert[78]
Baldy Hughes	CADIN Pinetree radar
Barrington	CADIN Pinetree radar
Beausejour	CADIN Pinetree radar
Beaver Lodge	CADIN Pinetree radar
Broughton Island, NWT	DEW Line radar site (FOX 5) reporting to FOX Main site at Hall Beach
Byron Bay, NWT	DEW Line radar site (PIN 4) reporting to PIN Main site at Cape Parry
Cambridge Bay, NWT	DEW Line radar and CAM Main site • Green Pine station
Cape Dyer, NWT	DEW Line radar and DYE Main site • Green Pine station
Cape Hooper, NWT	DEW Line radar site (FOX 4) reporting to FOX Main site at Hall Beach
Cape Perry, NWT	DEW Line radar and PIN Main site • Green Pine station
Cape Race, Nfld	LORAN-C Station: operated by Canada, serving the Canadian east coast chain
Cape Young, NWT	DEW Line radar site (PIN 2) reporting to PIN Main site at Cape Perry
CFS Carp, Ont	Alternate HQ for Canadian government operations during nuclear war including link to NORAD
CFS Chatham, NB	former nuclear warhead storage site for Genie missiles carried by CF-101, deactivated in 1984, nuclear warheads withdrawn in July 1984 with conversion from CF-101 to CF-18 aircraft, still a NORAD alert site with 2 aircraft on 5-minute alert[79]
Chibougamau	CADIN Pinetree radar
Clinton Point, NWT	DEW Line radar site (PIN 1) reporting to PIN Main site at Cape Perry
CFB Cold Lake, Alta	dispersal base for B-52 bombers from Castle AFB, CA • training range used for cruise missile and fighter aircraft testing[80]
CFB Comox, Lazo, BC	former nuclear warhead storage site for Genie missiles carried by CF-101 interceptors, deactivated in 1984, nuclear warheads withdrawn in July 1984 with conversion from CF-101 to CF-18 aircraft, still a NORAD alert site with 2 aircraft on 5-minute alert • Canadian 407th Maritime Patrol squadron: 4 CP-140 Aurora aircraft closely linked to U.S. ocean surveillance and ASW operations, probable wartime deployment base for nuclear depth bombs supporting P-3 operations[81]
Dana	CADIN Pinetree radar
Dewar Lakes, NWT	DEW Line radar site (FOX 3) reporting to FOX Main site at Hall Beach
Ernest Harmon AB, Nfld	strategic interceptor dispersal base[82]
Falconbridge	CADIN Pinetree radar
Fort Churchill	AF Geophysics Laboratory rocket range
Fox Harbor, Lab	LORAN-C Station: operated by Canada, serving the Canadian east caost and Labrador Sea chains
CFS Gander, Nfld	strategic interceptor dispersal base • CADIN Pinetree radar
Gladman Point, NWT	DEW Line radar site (CAM 2) reporting to CAM Main at Cambridge Bay
Goose Bay AB, Lab	dispersal site for aerial refueling aircraft • strategic interceptor dispersal base • NATO flight training and bombing range • CADIN Pinetree radar • Goose Bay Ionospheric Observatory, AF Geophysics Laboratory: research on sub-arctic events including the aurora and polar cap absorbtion of radio waves, support of OTH-B radar research and operations • former SAC forward bomber base[83]
CFB Greenwood, NS	Canadian Maritime Air Group: 404th, 405th, and 415th Maritime Patrol squadrons: main CP-140 Aurora operating base, closely linked to U.S.

	surveillance and ASW operations, probable wartime deployment base for nuclear depth bombs supporting P-3 operations
Gypsumville	CADIN Pinetree radar
Halifax, NS	HQ, Canadian Atlantic Subarea, WESTLANT area, SACLANT: NATO command
Hall Beach, NWT	DEW Line radar and FOX Main site • Green Pine station
Holberg	CADIN Pinetree radar
Jenny Lind Island, NWT	DEW Line radar site (CAM 1) reporting to CAM Main at Cambridge Bay
Jervis Inlet, BC	Canadian Advanced Underwater Acoustic Measurement System: Jervis Inlet range used by NUWES, Keyport, WA for R&D and testing of U.S. ASW weapons
Kamloops	CADIN Pinetree radar
Komakuk, Yukon	DEW Line radar site (BAR 1) located on Herschel Island
Lac St. Denis	CADIN Pinetree radar
Lady Franklin Point, NWT	DEW Line radar site (PIN 3) reporting to PIN Main at Cape Parry
Longstaff Bluff, NWT	DEW Line radar site (FOX 2) reporting to FOX Main at Hall Beach
Mackar Inlet, NWT	DEW Line radar site (CAM 5) reporting to CAM Main at Cambridge Bay
Melville AS, Nfld	Green Pine station[84]
Moisie	CADIN Pinetree Radar
Montague, PEI	LORAN-C Monitor Station: operated by Canada, serving the Canadian east coast chain
Montapica	CADIN Pinetree radar
Moosonee	CADIN Pinetree radar
CFB Namao, Alta	aerial tanker and RC-135 intelligence collection aircraft alternate airfield[85]
Nanoose Bay, BC	Canadian Forces Maritime Experimental and Test Range/Nanoose Underwater Tracking Range: joint Canada-U.S. testing center includes a 15 mile range in the Strait of Georgia which varies from 2–5 miles wide and about 1,400 feet deep used for testing underwater detection systems and ASW weapons including air-dropped sonobuoys, NUWES Keyport, WA uses Nanoose for RDT&E of ASW weapons including ASROC and SUBROC missiles
Nicholson Peninsula, NWT	DEW Line radar site (BAR 4)
CFB North Bay, Hornell Heights, Ontario	HQ, Canadian Forces Air Defense Command: only hardened underground command center (other than NORAD) for air defense • Canadian ROCC: 2 ROCCs are located in North Bay • HQ, 22d NORAD Region[86]
Ottawa	HQ, Canadian Forces and Canadian National Defense Operations Center: operations center for Canadian Prime Minister participation in NORAD and receipt of early warning • Canadian Federal Warning Center: Canadian civil defense command center, connected to the U.S. National Warning Center at Cheyenne Mountain, CO
Pelly Bay, NWT	DEW Line radar site (CAM 4) reporting to CAM Main at Cambridge Bay
Port Hardy, BC	LORAN-C Station: operated by Canada, serving the Canadian west coast chain
Primrose Lake, Alta	Primrose Lake Air Weapons Evaluation Range: target point of U.S. ALCM test flights flown from northern Canada, 10,000 square kilometer area, test range also used for artillery and aircraft testing
Ramore	CADIN Pinetree radar
Red Lake, Ontario	DOE Regional Seismic Test Network (RSTN) station
St. Anthony, NB	LORAN-C Monitor Station and Control Site: operated by Canada, serving the Canadian east coast and Labrador Sea chains, also used as ground transponder to assist operations and testing of OTH-B radar in Maine[87]
St. Margarets, NB	22d NORAD Region alternate command post (ALCOP)[88]

Sandspit, BC	LORAN-C Monitor Station: operated by Canada, serving the Canadian west coast chain
Senneterre	CADIN Pinetree radar
Shepherd Bay, NWT	DEW Line radar site (CAM 3) reporting to CAM Main at Cambridge Bay
Shingle Point, Yukon	DEW Line radar site (BAR 2)
Sioux Lookout	CADIN Pinetree radar
Tuktoyaktuk, NWT	DEW Line radar site (BAR 3)
Vancouver, BC	COMPAC cable head used to relay early warning data from Nurrungar, Australia to NORAD HQ
Whitehorse, Yukon	aerial tanker and RC-135 intelligence collection aircraft alternate airfield
Williams Lake, BC	LORAN-C Station and Control Site: operated by Canada, serving the Canadian west coast chain
Winchelsea Island	computer site controlling ASW tests and operations on the Nanoose Bay Range
CFB Winnipeg, Westwin, Manitoba	HQ, Canadian Air Command: Canadian component of NORAD
Yellowknife, NWT	DOE Regional Seismic Test Network (RSTN) station
Yorkton, Sask	CADIN Pinetree radar

CAPE VERDE ISLANDS

An instrumentation site in the Cape Verde Islands supports missile testing from the ESMC.

DENMARK

Denmark is a NATO member and has a policy of not allowing nuclear weapons or foreign bases on its soil. Its ground forces assigned to Allied Land Forces Schleswig-Holstein and Jutland in Rendsburg, West Germany take part closely in nuclear weapons training and planning (see also Greenland).

Ejde, Faeroe Islands	LORAN-C Station: operated by Denmark, serving the Icelandic and Norwegian Sea chains
Karup	HQ, Allied Forces Baltic Approaches, AFNORTH: NATO command, including Allied Air Forces and Allied Naval Forces, Baltic Approaches
Thorshavn, Faeroe Islands	Island Commander Faeroes, EASTLANT, SACLANT: NATO command (see also Appendix C)

DIEGO GARCIA, BRITISH INDIAN OCEAN TERRITORY

Diego Garcia is the center of U.S. naval operations in the Indian Ocean. Authorization has been given for wartime deployment of nuclear depth bombs to the island to support P-3 aircraft operations.

Naval Air Facility: used as regular staging base for nuclear-capable P-3 aircraft on operations in the Indian Ocean • KC-135 aerial tanker forward operating base • Naval Support Facility: homeport for Maritime Prepositioning Ships of the 7th Marine Amphibious Brigade • "supports the presence of a carrier battle group in the Indian Ocean and operations of the RDF [Rapid Deployment Force]" • GEODDS satellite tracking site • DSCS satellite communications station • HF transmitter and receiver • NAVSTAR tracking and control ground anntenna and passive monitoring station[89]

GREECE

More than half of the facilities in the nuclear infrastructure in Greece support Greek military units that have nuclear weapons roles. 164 nuclear warheads are stored in the country, all for delivery by Greek military units. The Greek government has pledged that these weapons and bases will be removed by 1989. In addition, there are two communications stations, Kato Souli and Nea Makri, which serve as a link to U.S. strategic submarines.

***Araxos AB**	7061st Munitions Support Squadron: nuclear bomb custodian for Greek Air Force 116th Fighter Wing with F-104G, some 25 nuclear bombs are stored at the base

***Argyroupolis**	18th Field Artillery Det: nuclear warhead custodian for Greek Army Honest John missile unit
Athens	HQ, Eastern Mediterranean, AFSOUTH: NATO command
Canea, Souda Bay, Crete	NATO Allied Missile Firing Installation (NAMFI): NATO training range used by the U.S., Netherlands, Belgium, West Germany, and Greece for Lance and Honest John missile firing
***Drama**	88th Field Artillery Det: nuclear warhead custodian for Greek Army Honest John missile unit
***Elefsis**	HQ, 558th U.S. Army Artillery Group: central U.S. nuclear HQ and storage site for support of Greek forces, 10 sites around the country • 138th Ordnance Company: nuclear weapons storage and maintenance support for Army nuclear warheads stored in Greece, including 66 Honest John warheads, 43 8" artillery projectiles and 30 Nike Hercules missile warheads
***Erithea**	79th Air Defense Artillery Det: nuclear warhead custodian for Greek Air Force Nike Hercules unit
Hellenikon AB/Athens IAP	822d Strategic Squadron/Det 3, 306th Strategic Wing: ground support for rotational RC-135 strategic reconnaissance and KC-135 tankers • "Rivet Switch" supporting SAC intelligence communications • INFORM net HF radio station for air-ground communications[90]
Iraklion AB, Gourna, Crete	ground support for rotational KC-135 operations • INFORM net HF radio station • Det 315, AFTAC: nuclear test detection station[91]
***Karatea**	37th Air Defense Artillery Det: nuclear warhead custodian for Greek Air Force Nike Hercules unit
Kato Souli	Navy Radio Transmitter Facility: HF and LF naval transmitter, "provide Verdin LF submarine broadcasts" to the Mediterranean Sea and Indian Ocean supporting strategic missile submarines[92]
***Katsimidhi**	78th Air Defense Artillery Det: nuclear warhead custodian for Greek Air Force Nike Hercules unit
***Koropi**	76th Air Defense Artillery Det: nuclear warhead custodian for Greek Air Force Nike Hercules units
Mt. Hortiatis	communications site supporting nuclear weapons in Greece[93]
Mt. Parnis	European Command Control Console System (ECCCS) AN/MSQ-74 remote terminal supporting nuclear weapons in Greece[94]
Nea Makri	Naval Communications Station Greece: HF and LF receivers (transmitters at Kato Souli) supporting naval communications, strategic missile submarine communications, serves as a MEECN strategic communications receiver • Nea Makri Intercept Facility: weather intercepts[95]
***Perivolaki**	19th Field Artillery Det: nuclear warhead custodian for Greek Army Honest John unit
Preveza AB	forward operating base for NATO AWACs aircraft
Souda Bay, Crete	airfield supporting part time rotations of nuclear-capable P-3s
***Yiannitsa**	70th Field Artillery Det: nuclear warhead custodian for Greek Army 8" artillery unit

GREENLAND

Denmark has control of the defense and foreign affairs of Greenland and restricts nuclear weapons deployments although it allows foreign military bases. Four DEW line radars and one of three main ballistic missile early warning stations are on the island.

Angissoq	LORAN-C Station: operated by Denmark, serving the Labrador Sea and Icelandic chains
Easterly	DEW line radar
Gronnedal	Island Commander Greenland, SACLANT: NATO command
Kulusuk Island	DEW line radar (DYE-4)

Narsarssuak	ground transponder assisting testing and operations of the OTH-B radar in Maine[96]
Qiquatoqaq (Holsteinsberg)	DEW line radar (DYE-1) connected to Cape Dyer, Canada
Sondrestrom AB	4684th Air Base Group: operation of the former SAC base and maintenance of a bomber and tanker dispersal base, support to DEW line radar sites in Greenland and Canada
Thule AB	12th Missile Warning Squadron: BMEWS Site I, one of three Ballistic Missile Early Warning System stations, providing early warning and initial confirmation of missile launches after detection by DSP satellites, radars include 4 FPS-50 detection radars (400 feet wide by 165 feet high) and 1 FPS-49 tracking radar • Global Command and Control Station, Giant Talk/Scope Signal III transmitter and receiver • AF Satellite Control Facility satellite tracking and communications station[97]
Westerly	DEW line radar

GUAM

Guam is a commonwealth of the U.S. and treated as sovereign territory. It is the central nuclear weapons base in the western Pacific and support Navy, Marine Corps and Air Force weapons. The B-52 bombers at Andersen are the only such bombers stationed outside the U.S. Thirty percent of the land in Guam is controlled by the military.

NAS Agana/Brewer Field/Guam IAP	Patrol Wing 1 Det Agana/Patrol Squadron Agana/Marianas Patrol Group: supports a rotational nuclear-capable P-3 unit from Hawaii, Advanced Underwater Weapons Division maintains a nuclear depth bomb storage site and assembly operation, with the nuclear warheads stored at Santa Rita • Guam-based TACAMO radio relay squadron moved to Barbers Point, HI with deactivation of the Polaris submarine base in Guam, although Agana remains a priority alternate operating airfield[98]
***Andersen AB**	HQ, 3d Air Division: coordinates SAC operations in the Pacific • 43d Stategic Wing: B-52G and KC-135, nuclear weapons include 150 bombs, SRAM-capable bombers replaced B-52Ds without SRAMs in 1983, 60 SRAM missiles to be deployed by 1986 • Global Command and Control Station, Giant Talk/Scope Signal III system, part of the Pacific network (transmitter and receiver at Barrigada and Nimitz Hill) • SAC radar bomb scoring nuclear bombing practice site • AF Satellite Control Facility satellite tracking and communications station • NAVSTAR Monitor station • Coast Guard LORAN-C Monitor Station: serving the northwest Pacific chain, also a "Clarinet Pilgrim" submarine communications monitor station[99]
Apra Harbor	Naval Station: Submarine Group 7 Representitive Guam, operation of the former Polaris submarine base now supporting attack submarine operations in the western Pacific, homeport of the submarine tender Proteus and a nuclear-capable ammunition ship • ship repair facility[100]
Barrigada	Naval Communications Area Master Station Western Pacific: the hub of military communications in the central and western Pacific • Naval Radio Transmitter Facility: HF transmitters supporting the Pacific Fleet HICOM net and Giant Talk/Scope Signal III (Andersen Annex)
Finnegayan	Naval Communications Annex: submarine cable head terminal, DSCS satellite communications station linked to Hawaii, the Philippines, and Japan, AUTODIN switching center • Naval Radio Receiving Facility: HF recivers supporting the Pacific Fleet and SAC • Det 428, 1156th TOS, AFTAC: nuclear test detection station
Ritidian Point	Naval Facility: processing station for SOSUS
***Santa Rita**	Naval Magazine: main nuclear weapons storage site in the western Pacific supporting Navy and Marine Corps, weapons stored include 45 artillery projectiles, 75 bombs and 98 nuclear depth bombs • Marine Wing Weapon Unit 1 (MWWU-1): Marine Corps nuclear weapons unit in the western Pacific, moved from Iwakuni, Japan in 1982–83

Nimitz Hill	HQ, Naval Forces Marianas: senior military officer responsible for Guam and the Trust Territory of the Pacific Islands • unidentified strategic communications facility

ICELAND

Iceland is a NATO member that maintains no armed forces and does not allow nuclear weapons on its soil. The U.S., nonetheless, has its central ASW and air defense base in the north Atlantic in Iceland, and authorization has been given for deployment of 48 nuclear depth bombs at Keflavik "for wartime ASW operations."

Grindavik	Naval Radio Transmitter Facility: HF and LF communications • Green Pine station[101]
Hofn	667th Aircraft Control and Warning Squadron: NORAD controlled radar, not officially counted as part of the DEW line
Keflavik	HQ, Iceland Defense Force: sub-unified command of U.S. Atlantic Command, responsible for joint contingency plans • Naval Forces, Iceland: senior Navy command • Island Commander Iceland, EASTLANT, SACLANT: NATO command • Air Forces Iceland: senior AF command responsible for the air defense of Iceland • 57th Fighter Interceptor Squadron: F-4E, intercepted 170 Soviet aircraft in 1983, to upgrade to F-15 in 1986 • Naval Facility: processing station for SOSUS • Patrol Squadron Keflavik: rotational nuclear-capable P-3 operations from Brunswick, ME, command facilities include ASW Operations Center, designated to receive nuclear depth bombs in wartime • forward E-3A AWACs operations from Tinker AFB, OK • periodic deployment base for British Nimrod MR.2 ASW aircraft • Coast Guard LORAN-C Monitor Station and Control Site: serving the Icelandic and Norwegian Sea chains
Rockville (Sandgerdhi)	932d Aircraft Warning and Control Squadron: NORAD controlled radar, not officially counted as part of the DEW line • Naval Radio Receiver Facility: HF naval communications
Sandur	LORAN-C Station: operated by Iceland, serving the Icelandic and Norwegian Sea chains

ITALY

Italy is a NATO member and ranks 3d in nuclear warheads deployed in overseas countries with 549 warheads. Nuclear weapons support both U.S. and Italian Army, Air Force, and Navy units. The main U.S. bases are at Vicenza (for the Army), Aviano and Comiso (for the Air Force), and Naples, Gaeta and Sigonella (for the Navy). NATO operations in southern Europe and the Mediterranean are directed from Italian bases.

Affi	NATO Air Operations Center: underground command center of the 5th ATAF
Agnano (Naples)	HQ, Maritime Air Forces Mediterranean, AFSOUTH: NATO command
***Aviano AB, Pordenone**	40th Tactical Group: supports rotational nuclear-capable F-16s from Spain with nuclear strike mission, some 200 nuclear bombs are estimated to be stored on the base • INFORM net communications station
***Bovolone**	41st Air Defense Artillery Det: nuclear warhead custodian for Italian Air Force Nike Hercules unit[102]
Catania AB	adjacent to NAS Sigonella, home of nuclear-certified Italian Navy Atlantique ASW planes
***Catron (Montichiari)**	87th Air Defense Artillery Det: nuclear warhead custodian for Italian Air Force Nike Hercules unit
***Ceggia**	Team 3, 34th Air Defense Artillery Det: nuclear warhead custodian for Italian Air Force Nike Hercules unit
***Chioggia**	40th Air Defense Artillery Det: nuclear warhead custodian for Italian Air Force Nike Hercules unit
***Codogne**	29th Field Artillery Det: nuclear warhead custodian support for Italian Army Lance, not currently certified

Coltano	main Army communications station in Italy, including AUTODIN switching center • AN/GNC-39 satellite communications terminal
***Comiso AS, Sicily**	487th Tactical Missile Wing: main operating base for ground-launched cruise missiles, first operational in March 1984, will receive 112 missiles on 28 launchers
***Conselve**	34th Air Defense Artillery Det: nuclear warhead custodian for Italian Air Force Nike Hercules unit
***Cordovado**	Team 2, 34th Air Defense Artillery Det: nuclear warhead custodian for Italian Air Force Nike Hercules unit
Crotone	LORAN-C Monitor Station: serving the Meditteranean Sea chain
Decimomannu, Sardinia	air-to-ground training range used for nuclear bombing practice[103]
***Gaeta**	HQ, Sixth Fleet: headquarters for naval operations in the Meditteranean aboard the destroyer tender Puget Sound • HQ, Naval Striking and Support Forces Southern Europe, AFSOUTH: NATO designation of Sixth Fleet in wartime • HQ, Battle Forces Sixth Fleet (TF 60)/Carrier Group 2: homeport of Sixth Fleet aircraft carriers when in Italy, to become NATO TF 502 in wartime
***Ghedi-Torre AB**	7402d Munitions Support Squadron: nuclear bomb custodian for Italian Air Force 154th Gruppo with Tornado (replaced F-104G in late 1983), some 25 nuclear bombs are stored at the base
***La Maddalena, Sardinia**	Submarine Refit and Training Group: center of attack submarine operations and support in the Mediterranean, homeport of submarine tender Orion that can handle up to 3 attack submarines, nuclear weapons stored include 15 SUBROC missiles
Lampedusa	Coast Guard LORAN-C Station: serving the Meditteranean Sea chain
Latina	NATO Communications School
Licola	Naval Radio Transmitter Facility: HF communications in support of NATO and naval commands in Naples and Gaeta
***Longare**	"Site Pluto:" main nuclear weapons storage site for Army units in Italy and Vicenza-based units, 69th Ordnance Company: storage, maintenance and support of Army nuclear weapons in Italy, weapons stored include 24 ADMs and 50 155mm artillery projectiles for U.S. use, weapons supported for Italian military use include 60 Nike Hercules, 42 Lance warheads, and 29 8-inch artillery projectiles
Maniago	air-to-ground training range used by the Air Force for nuclear weapons training[104]
***Monte Calvarina**	47th Air Defense Artillery Det: nuclear warhead custodian for Italian Air Force Nike Hercules unit
Monte Nardello	"Creek Cruiser" AF ground-air communications station
Naples	HQ, Allied Forces South Europe (AFSOUTH) and Commander, U.S. Naval Forces Europe (headquarters in London): senior NATO command in Southern Europe and senior Navy officer in Europe, subordinate elements of AFSOUTH HQ includes Naval Forces Southern Europe, Commander, Western Mediterranean, Commander, Southern Mediterranean, and Commander, Submarine Forces Mediterranean • Deputy Commander, U.S. Air Forces Europe for Southern Area and Commander, Allied Air Forces Southern Europe, AFSOUTH: peacetime command of southern European air defenses • Submarine Group 8 (TF 64): operates attack submarines • Fleet Ballistic Missile Forces Sixth Fleet: strategic submarine operations in the Mediterranean, becomes NATO TF 442 in wartime, commands missile submarines in the Mediterranean • HQ, Maritime Surveillance and Reconnaissance Forces Sixth Fleet (TF-67): commands nuclear-capable P-3 and S-3 operations • HQ, Area ASW Forces Sixth Fleet • Naval Communications Area Master Station Mediterranean
***Oderzo**	12th Field Artillery Det: nuclear warhead custodian for Italian Army Lance unit

Portogruaro	HQ for Italian Army Lance missile brigade
***Rimini AB**	7401st Munitions Support Squadron: nuclear bomb custodian for Italian Air Force 5th Wing with F-104G/S, some 25 nuclear bombs are stored on the base
San Vito dei Normanni	"Creek Cruiser" AF ground-air communications station • AF Solar Optical Observing Network (SOON) observatory relocated from Iran in 1980
Santa Rosa (Rome)	HQ, Central Mediterranean, AFSOUTH: NATO command colocated with Italian Navy underground command center
***Sciaves**	11th Field Artillery Det: nuclear warhead custodian for Italian Army 8-inch artillery unit
Sellia Marina	Coast Guard LORAN-C Monitor Station and Control Station: serving Mediterranean Sea chain
***NAS Sigonella, Sicily**	Patrol Squadron Sigonella: rotational nuclear-capable P-3 operations, command facilities include ASW Operations, 63 nuclear depth bombs stored at Sigonella for use by P-3s, Italian Atlantiques at Catania and British Nimrods • Tactical Support Squadron 24 (VR-24): nuclear weapons transportation support for Sixth Fleet ships
Tavolara, Sardinia	NATO VLF communications station[105]
Trapani-Birgi AB	NATO AWACs forward operating base starting in 1985
Verona	HQ, Allied Land Forces Southern Europe, AFSOUTH: control of NATO Army units for land defense of northern Italy
Vicenza	HQ, Southern European Task Force (SETAF): senior Army command in the Mediterranean • 559th U.S. Army Artillery Group: control of nuclear weapons in support of Italian military units • 62d Engineer Company (ADM): nuclear storage at Longare • HQ, 5th Allied Tactical Air Force (5th ATAF): commands air units in Italy
***Zelo (Rovigo)**	44th Air Defense Artillery Det: nuclear warhead custodian for Italian Air Force Nike Hercules unit

JAPAN

The U.S. maintains the most extensive forward nuclear infrastructure in the Pacific region in Japan, even though the country maintains strict non-nuclear policies. It is the forward operating base for Naval and Marine forces as well as the central command for military operations in east Asia. Kadena AB on Okinawa is one of the most important U.S. overseas bases, housing strategic tankers, reconnaissance aircraft and communications. Nuclear weapons communications also take place from Owada, Tokorozawa and Yosami, as well as the five stations in Japan of the "Clarinet Pilgrim" network. Although no nuclear weapons are stationed in Japan, nuclear-capable forces include Marine Corps artillery and aviation units, P-3 aircraft, and the aircraft carrier Midway. A facility at Misawa Air Base also appears to be prepared to receive nuclear depth bombs in wartime.

Atsugi, Honshu	Naval Air Facility: HQ, Fleet Air Western Pacific: Seventh Fleet aviation command and land base of 2 nuclear-capable A-7 squadrons from the aircraft carrier Midway when it is in port
Camp S.D. Butler/Camp Courtney, Okinawa	HQ, III Marine Amphibious Force/HQ, 3d Marine Division/Landing Force Seventh Fleet (CTF 79): western Pacific Marine Corps HQ, including command of one division and support troops dispersed on Okinawa • III MAF command center • HQ, 9th Marine Amphibious Brigade
Camp Drake, Honshu	AUTODIN switching center (to move to Yokota AB in 1985–1986)
Camp Zama, Sagamihara, Honshu	HQ, U.S. Army Japan/IX U.S. Corps: Army HQ in Japan, skeleton organization for a Corps size formation without combat forces, maintains ammunition and fuel storage infrastructure in Japan, also has "Emergency Action Console" for receipt of nuclear orders • AN/MSC-46 satellite communications link to Philippines, South Korea, Guam, Hawaii, and California[106]
Camp Zukeran, Okinawa	HQ, 1st Marine Aircraft Wing: aviation component of III MAF • 12th Marine Regt (Artillery) of the 3d Marine Division, 3 M-198 155mm and 1 8-inch nuclear-capable artillery battalions

Fort Buckner, Okinawa	Army-operated AN/MSC-46 satellite communications link to South Korea, Guam, Hawaii, Philippines, and Diego Garcia • ground mobile force mobile satellite terminal • AUTODIN switching center
Fuchu AS, Honshu	AUTODIN switching center
Futenma, Okinawa	Marine Corps Air Station: CH-53D/E heavy helicopters used in nuclear weapons transportation
Gesashi, Okinawa	Coast Guard LORAN-C Station: serving the northwest Pacific chain, also "Clarinet Pilgrim" submarine communications station • AF LORAN-C/D Station: part of the "Commando Lion" network used for tactical long-range navigation and target location
Henoko, Okinawa	Nuclear Ordnance Platoon, 3d Marine Division located at former nuclear weapons storage site, technical support for nuclear artillery and ADMs, warheads are stored in Guam or aboard amphibious ships
Ie-Shima Island	Ie-Shima firing range used for simulated nuclear bombing training[107]
Iruma, Honshu	Pacific Command HF radio command and control station
Iwakuni, Honshu	Marine Corps Air Station: Marine Aircraft Groups 12 and 15 • Patrol Wing 1 Det Iwakuni: nuclear-capable P-3 deployment base • Marine Wing Weapon Unit 1 (MWWU-1) moved to Santa Rita, Guam in 1982–1983
Iwo Jima Island	Coast Guard LORAN-C Station: serving the northwest Pacific chain, also "Clarinet Pilgrim" submarine communications station
Kadena AB, Okinawa	HQ, 313th Air Division: Pacific Air Forces forward command for the western Pacific, has "Emergency Action Console" for receipt of nuclear orders • 376th Strategic Wing: SAC unit supporting forward deployed KC-135s in Okinawa (909th Aerial Refueling Squadron) and SR-71 and RC-135 strategic reconnaissance aircraft, 4 tankers on alert to meet nuclear missions • Patrol Wing 1 Det Kadena/Okinawa Air Patrol Group: nuclear- capable P-3s on rotation • Det 474, AFTAC: nuclear test detection station • NEACP/Pacific Command airborne command post ground command facility, including mobile MSC-54 ground entry point • Giant Talk/Scope Signal III master/area network control station • AFSATCOM ground terminal • Commando Escort station • 400th Munitions Maintenance Squadron (Theater): conventional ammunition storage in Japan, supervision of forward nuclear weapons storage in the Pacific, maintains "status documents for the Personnel Reliability Program"[108]
Kamiseya, Honshu	HQ, Patrol and Reconnaissance Force Seventh Fleet/HQ, Patrol Wing 1/Japan Air Patrol Group: coordinates tactical ocean surveillance and nuclear-capable P-3 operations in the western Pacific and Indian Ocean • Fleet Ocean Surveillance Information Facility (FOSIF) Western Pacific: ASW and ocean surveillance command center for the Seventh Fleet • Naval Radio Receiver Facility: HF and LF communications
Makiminato, Okinawa	3d Force Service Support Group: logistics and maintenance support of Marine Corps forces
Marcus Island (Minami Tori Shima)	Coast Guard LORAN-C Station: serving the northwest Pacific chain, also "Clarinet Pilgrim" submarine communications station
Misawa AB, Honshu	Northern Japan Air Patrol Group: directs rotational nuclear-capable P-3 operations, Advanced Underwater Weapons Shop on base may be contingency storage site for nuclear depth bombs • Det 422, AFTAC: nuclear test detection center • 432d Tactical Fighter Wing: new wing to receive 2 squadrons of 48 nuclear-capable F-16s beginning in 1985[109]
Owada, Honshu	Giant Talk/Scope Signal III, Global Command and Control System and Commando Escort receivers (from Yokota AB) • Owada Intercept Site: weather intercept facility[110]
Tokachibuto, Hokkaido	Coast Guard LORAN-C Station: serving the northwest Pacific chain, also "Clarient Pilgrim" submarine communications station • AF LORAN-C/D Station: part of the "Commando Lion" chain used for tactical long-range navigation and target location

Tokorozawa, Honshu	Giant Talk/Scope Signal III, Global Command and Control System and Commando Escort transmitters (from Yokota AB)
Totsuka, Honshu	Naval Radio Transmitter Facility: HF and LF station supporting Yokosuka and the Seventh Fleet
Tsushima Island	Omega station operated by the Japanese Maritime Safety Agency
White Beach, Okinawa	Amphibious Group 1/Amphibious Force Seventh Fleet (CTF 76)
Yokosuka, Honshu	HQ, Seventh Fleet: aboard the Blue Ridge, control of naval operations in the western Pacific and Indian Ocean • HQ, Naval Forces Japan: senior Navy command in Japan • Destroyer Squadron 15: homeport for surface ships in Japan • HQ, Submarine Force Seventh Fleet (CTF 74)/Submarine Group 7: submarine operating authority for the western Pacific and Indian Ocean areas • Carrier Group 3/Carrier Air Wing 5/Battle Force Seventh Fleet (CTF 70): homeport for the aircraft carrier Midway (land based air operations at Atsugi)
Yokota AB, Honshu	HQ, U.S. Forces Japan: sub-unified command, highest U.S. military HQ in Japan, includes WWMCCS terminal and "Emergency Action Console" to receive nuclear orders • HQ, 5th Air Force/U.S. Air Forces Japan: senior AF command in the western Pacific and east Asia • Global Command and Control station, Giant Talk/Scope Signal III and Commando Escort stations (sites at Owada and Tokorozawa) • Pacific airborne command post ground operations center and terminal including MSC-54 mobile ground entry point • TACAMO radio relay aircraft forward deployment base • Coast Guard LORAN-C Monitoring Station and Control Site: serving the northwest Pacific chain, also "Clarinet Pilgrim" submarine communications monitor station • AF LORAN-C/D Control Site: part of the "Commando Lion" tactical long-range navigation and target location system • Det 407, AFTAC: nuclear test detection station[111]
Yosami, Honshu	VLF/LF transmitter for attack and missile submarine communications worldwide, 8 250-meter towers, also used for radionavigation purposes[112]

JOHNSTON ATOLL

Johnston Atoll is an uninhabited U.S. territory southwest of Hawaii which is used for chemical weapons storage and serves as a Defense Nuclear Agency "Nuclear Readiness-to-Test Facility" maintaining a stand-by "overseas atmospheric nuclear test capability." A Coast Guard LORAN-C Master Station is also operated serving the central Pacific chain.[113]

KWAJALEIN ATOLL, MARSHALL ISLANDS

The Kwajalein Missile Range (KMR) is a national range operated by the Army Ballistic Missile Defense Systems Command. It serves as the target for ICBM and SLBM testing with land-based instrumentation for collecting data on the terminal portion of missile flights. Anti-ballistic missile research is conducted using missile tests to Kwajalein as targets. Technical facilities include the Kiernan Reentry Measurements Site "for space object identification through radar-imaging techniques," the DARPA Lincoln C-band Observable Radar (ALCOR), and the DARPA Long-rang Tracking and Instrumentation Y-Band Radar (ALTAIR). ALTAIR is also part of the of the Pacific Barrier anti-satellite program and used for satellite tracking. Missile testing to the ocean area near Kwajalein is monitored by transponders implanted and surveyed in the ocean floor and Caribou aircraft flying from Kwajalein. A NAVSTAR tracking, telemetry and control ground antenna and passive monitoring station is maintained at Kwajalein, as well as an LF communications transmitter.

LIBERIA

An Omega station is operated by the Liberian Ministry of Commerce Industry and Transportation at Paynesword

MIDWAY ISLAND

Midway Island is an uninhabited U.S. territory which serves as a stand-by naval base. A Pacific Missile Range Facility Det from Barking Sands, HI maintains an instrumentation station providing support for PMTC sound fixing and ranging. The Naval Facility Midway serves as a processing station for SOSUS.

The Naval Air Facility Midway supports rotational nuclear-capable P-3 aircraft deployments and would become the HQ of the Midway Air Patrol and Reconnaissance Group in wartime.

NETHERLANDS

The Netherlands is a NATO member and full participant in nuclear weapons plans and operations. Three nuclear storage sites and 81 warheads are stored in the country at Havelteberg, 't Harde, and Volkel. NATO headquarters for central Europe is also located at Brunssum.

Brunssum	HQ, Allied Forces Central Europe (AFCENT): subordinate NATO command of ACE responsible for central Europe, part of command center located within the deactivated Hendrik coal mine
***Havelteberg**	Johannes Post Kaserne: 8th Field Artillery Det, nuclear warhead custodian for Dutch Army Lance missile unit, some 42 warheads stored
Hoensbroek	AFCENT command center located in deactivated Emma mine
Maastricht	NATO 2d ATAF Joint Operations Center, Sector Operations Center/Allied Tactical Operations Center (SOC/ATOC) located in underground command center in Cannerberg • Tapjin Kaserne: HQ, III Corps (Forward): forward element of III Corps from Ft. Hood, TX forming nucleus of AFCENT reserve Corps of U.S. reinforcements for northern West Germany
Soesterberg	Camp New Amsterdam: INFORM network command and control station in stand-by status
Steenwijk	communications tributary supporting nuclear weapons
***'t Harde**	LTC Tonnet Kaserne: 23d Field Artillery Det, nuclear warhead custodian for Dutch Army 8" artillery unit, some 14 warheads stored
Valkenburg AB	Dutch Navy Number 320 Squadron: nuclear-certified P-3C unit with nuclear warheads stored in Britain
Vlieland Island	air-to-ground training range used for nuclear training
***Volkel AB**	7362d Munition Support Squadron: nuclear bomb custodial support for Dutch Air Force 311 and 312 Squadrons with F-16s, converted from F-104Gs in 1982–1984, some 25 bombs stored on the base
Woensdrecht AB	designated main operating base for 48 ground-launched cruise missiles, deployment scheduled to begin in 1986

NEW ZEALAND

Black Birch Astronomic Observatory (Blenheim) is a southern hemisphere observatory operated by the U.S. Naval Observatory.

NORWAY

Norway is a NATO member that does not allow nuclear weapons or foreign military bases on its soil. It houses, nonetheless, an important NATO command at Kolsaas and a number of intelligence collection and nuclear test detection stations operating for the the U.S. Secret Norwegian bases at Viksjofjell, Vardo, and Vadso also contribute to intelligence collection on Soviet strategic forces and missile testing.

Andoeya AB	airfield supporting part time rotational nuclear-capable P-3 operations[114]
Bodoe AB	HQ, Allied Forces North Norway, AFNORTH: NATO command • airfield supports part time rotational nuclear- capable P-3 operations[115]
Bratland	Omega station operated by the Norwegian Telecommunications Administration
Hamar	Norwegian Seismic Array (NORSAR): nuclear test monitoring conducted for U.S. Air Force, dispersed seismic array centered on Hamar, data processing center at Norwegian Defense Research Establishment, Kjeller
Helgeland (Novika)	VLF communications station operated by Norwegian government used for worldwide radionavigation
Karasjok	Norwegian operated seismic monitoring station reporting data to AFTAC

Kolsaas	HQ, Allied Forces Northern Europe (AFNORTH): NATO command responsible for Norway, Denmark, the Baltic and Schleswig-Holstein in West Germany
Oerland AB	forward operating location for NATO AWACs
Oslo	HQ, Allied Forces South Norway, AFNORTH: NATO command

OMAN

Masirah Island is used as a periodic staging base for nuclear-capable P-3 operations.

PANAMA

Located within the Latin American Nuclear-Free Zone, Panama houses a number of strategic communications and electronics facilities including a Mystic Star and airborne command post receiver at Howard AFB.

Albrook AFS	Global Command and Control System transmitter (receiver at Howard AFB)
Fort Kobbe	AN/GSC-39 satellite terminal providing presidential communications support to and from Panama[116]
Fort Randolph	Operating Location BN (OL-BN), AFTAC: nuclear test detection station[117]
Howard AFB	NEACP ground entry point serving the Mystic Star network • Global Command and Control System receiver • 1035th TOS, AFTAC: nuclear test detection station[118]
Semaphore Hill	long-range radar reporting to the JSS
Summit	Naval Radio Transmitter Facility: HF communications to naval forces

PHILIPPINES

Nuclear weapons are no longer permanently stored in the Philippines although stand-by storage is available for nuclear weapons at Cubi Point, Clark AB and Subic Bay. Subic Bay is the largest U.S. overseas naval installation and Clark AB is one of the largest overseas air bases.

Camp O'Donnell, Luzon	Global Command and Control System, Giant Talk/Scope Signal III, and Commando Escort transmitter (receiver at Dau)
Capas Tarlac, Luzon	Naval Radio Transmitter Facility: LF and HF transmitter (receiver at San Miguel)
Clark AB, Luzon	HQ, 13th Air Force: senior AF command in the Philippines, responsible for the south Pacific and southeast Asia • 3d Tactical Fighter Wing: nuclear-capable aircraft, includes "Emergency Action Facility" for receiving nuclear orders • Det 401, AFTAC: nuclear test detection station • Global Command and Control Station, Giant Talk/Scope Signal III, and Commando Escort station (sites at Dau and Camp O'Donnell) • DSCS Satellite Operations Center: links to Hawaii, Diego Garcia, Japan and South Korea • PACAF Emergency Response Explosive Ordnance Disposal (EOD) Team: mobile nuclear EOD for the Pacific[119]
Crow Valley, Luzon	Crow Valley Range: bombing range 13 miles northwest of Clark AB, RTA-2A (Realistic Target Area Two) "contains unscored simulated special weapons and tactical weapons targets," "the simulated special weapons target has 50 foot, 250 foot, 750 foot, 1,000 foot, and 2,000 foot radius concentric circles," targets include mock railyard complex[120]
NAS Cubi Point, Luzon	HQ, Carrier Striking Force Seventh Fleet/Carrier Group 5: homeport for aircraft carriers when forward deployed • Advanced Underwater Weapons Branch: "classified ordnance transshipment and contingencies activities," stand-by nuclear weapons storage site for ASW weapons including nuclear depth bombs and ASROC missiles • Patrol Wing 1 Det Cubi/Patrol Squadron Cubi/Philippine Air Patrol Group: supports regular nuclear-capable P-3 deployments[121]
Dau	Global Command and Control System, Giant Talk/Scope Signal III, Commando Escort receiver (transmitter at Camp O'Donnell) • NEACP, Pacific Command, and Mystic Star airborne command post ground entry

	point, including MSC-54 mobile ground entry point • Weather Intercept Control Unit and Intercept Facility
Del Monte, Bukidnon, Mindanao	Det 423, AFTAC: nuclear test detection station
Gozar	Operating Location AB (OL-AB), 848th ACWS: Philippine air defense radar
Los Frailes	Los Frailes target used in "simulated special weapons delivery training"[122]
Manila	Det 5, 1st Weather Wing: AF Solar Optical Observing Network (SOON) observatory at the Manila Observatory
Mt. Santa Rita	Naval Radio Link Station: relay station for Philippine bases
Nichols AB	Philippine Air Defense Control Center: air defense command center for the Philippines, including 13th Air Force Air Defense Unit
Parades	Operating Location AA (OL-AA), 848th ACWS: Philippine air defense radar
Paranal	Operating Location AC (OL-AC), 848th ACWS: Philippine air defense radar
San Miguel, Luzon	17th Surveillance Squadron: AN/GPS-10 radar part of the Pacific Barrier Radar (PACBAR) anti-satellite program, also used for satellite tracking • Naval Communications Station Philippines: HF and LF receiver (transmitter at Capas Tarlac) • San Miguel Weather Intercept Unit[123]
Scarborough Shoal	bombing range used for "simulated special weapons delivery training," located 148 miles from Cubi Point[124]
Subic Bay, Luzon	Naval Base: HQ, Naval Forces Philippines: senior Navy command in the Philippines, supports 10–12 ships and submarines in port at any time, facilities include Supply Center, Ship Repair Facility and Naval Magazine • Submarine Group 7 Representitive Subic • Marine Barracks provides base security and nuclear weapons support upon deployment of nuclear weapons to the Philippines
Tarbones, Nazasa Bay	Tarbones target used in "simulated special weapons delivery training"[125]
Villamor AB	Det 1, 13th Air Force: Air Force command center and combat operating staff for the Philippines
Wallace AS, Poro Point	848th Aircraft Control and Warning Squadron: joint U.S-Philippine Air Defense Direction Center with search and height finder radars

PORTUGAL

Portugal is a NATO member which does not allow the deployment of nuclear weapons on its home soil, but allows them in the Azores. Although no nuclear weapons are stored in the Azores in peacetime, authorization has been given for deployment of 32 nuclear depth bombs at Lajes "for wartime ASW operations." The Azores are a center for ASW operations and ocean surveillance.

Cinco Pincos, Terceira, Azores	Global Command and Control Station and naval HF transmitter (receiver at Villa Nova)[126]
Funchal, Madeira Island	Island Commander Madeira, IBERLANT: NATO command
Lajes, Terceira Island, Azores	HQ, U.S. Forces Azores/Naval Forces Azores: sub-unified command of Atlantic Command and senior naval command • Naval Air Facility: Patrol Squadron Lajes: supports full time rotational nuclear capable P-3 operations, command facilities include ASW Operations Center, will become deployment site for 32 nuclear depth bombs in wartime • Missile Tracking Instrumentation System and remote ranging station supporting missile launches from ESMC • Global Command and Control Station (sites at Cinco Pincos and Villa Nova)
Montijo	part time rotational nuclear-capable P-3 operations[127]
Oeiras	HQ, Iberian Atlantic Command, SACLANT: senior NATO command responsible for Spain, Portugal and the mid-Atlantic
San Miguel, Azores	Island Commander Azores, IBERLANT: NATO command
Santa Maria, Azores	Azores Fixed Acoustic Range: NATO ASW hydrophone array used for submarine training and ocean surveillance[128]

Villa Nova, Terceira Island, Azores	Global Command and Control Station and naval HF receiver (transmitter at Cinco Pincos)

PUERTO RICO

Puerto Rico is a territory of the U.S. located within the Latin American Nuclear-Free Zone. Authorization has been given, nonetheless, for deployment of 32 nuclear depth bombs to Roosevelt Roads "for wartime ASW operations." In addition, 13 nuclear-related facilities are maintained on the island, including two Mystic Star communications stations. Roosevelt Roads has also been designated as an alternate command center for missile submarines in the Atlantic if continental U.S. bases are destroyed.

Aguada	Naval Radio Facility: LF transmitter kept in non-operating caretaker status since 1974, to be activated to replace closed communications transmitter at Balboa, Panama[129]
Fort Allen, Juana Diaz	Mystic Star transmitter: part of the Presidential and VIP communications network[130]
Cape San Juan	future Coast Guard differential Omega radionavigation remote monitoring facility
Isabela	Naval Radio Transmitting Facility: HF and LF transmitters operated under contract, primary links from Puerto Rico to naval forces, Brandywine, MD, and Macdill AFB, FL
Muniz ANGB, San Jaun IAP	156th Tactical Fighter Group (PRANG): nuclear-capable A-7D
Pico del Este	radar and communications site supporting AFWTF, Roosevelt Roads, also serves as JSS radar
Point Borinquen	AF Solar Optical Observing Network (SOON) observatory located at the former SAC Ramey AFB
Punta Salinas	140th Aircraft Control and Warning Squadron (PRANG): air defense radar manned 24-hours
Punta Tuna	future Coast Guard differential Omega radionavigation facility, coverage in Eastern Caribbean only
Roosevelt Roads	Naval Station: HQ, U.S. Naval Forces Caribbean: command of naval forces in the Caribbean, including nuclear command and control function, contingency headquarters for ballistic missile submarine operations • HQ, Fleet Air Caribbean: command of aircraft, aircraft carrier and ASW operations in the Caribbean • former HQ for Antilles Defense Command, a sub-unified command of Atlantic Command, now replaced by U.S. Forces Caribbean, Key West, FL • Atlantic Fleet Weapons Training Facility (AFWTF): training range consisting of 200,000 square miles of sea areas supporting ship and submarine acceptance trials, ASW operations and test firings and large scale naval maneuvers • Advanced Underwater Weapons Branch: stand-by nuclear warhead storage site for 32 nuclear depth bombs to be deployed in wartime • periodic nuclear-capable P-3 staging base
Salinas	Mystic Star Control Console and Receiver Facility: part of the Presidential and VIP communications network[131]
Sebana Seca	Naval Radio Receiving Facility: primary receiver for fleet communications entering Puerto Rico and link from Davidsonville, MD and MacDill AFB, FL
Vieques Island	"inner range" of AFWTF, air-to-ground training range used for aircraft training, "Bullseye Target Two" is designated for practice nuclear bombing

SAIPAN, NORTHERN MARIANAS ISLANDS

The U.S. is planning to build a Pacific Barrier radar on Saipan, relocating a C-band radar from the ship USNS Arnold.

SEYCHELLES

The AF maintains a Satellite Control Facility satellite tracking and communicaions station on Mahe Island in the Seychelles.

SOUTH AFRICA

An inactive tracking radar and telemetry receiver supporting missile launches from ESMC is maintained in stand-by status in Pretoria.[132]

SOUTH KOREA

South Korea is the only forward U.S. base for storage of nuclear weapons in Asia, housing 151 warheads. The nuclear weapons are stored at one site and support the U.S Army and Air Force. The U.S. and South Korean militaries are fully integrated in terms of planning and operations.

Camp Ames, Taejon	HQ, Korean Ammunition Management System: main Army nuclear weapons support unit, with 78th Ordnance Company providing maintenance and assembly and U.S. Army Security Company providing security, nuclear warheads are stored at Kunsan AB, where the Army maintains a "maximum security area"
Camp Casey, Tongduchon	HQ, 2d Infantry Division: main U.S. combat unit in Korea, with both nuclear artillery and ADM missions
Camp Castle, Tongduchon	2d Engineer Bn, 2d Infantry Division: possible ADM mission
Camp Essayons, Uijongbu	6th Bn, 37th Field Artillery: 8-inch artillery of 2d Infantry Division, nuclear facilities include "Emergency Action Facility" to receive nuclear release orders
Camp Page, Chunchon	former HQ of 4th Missile Command which controlled Army Honest John missiles
Camp Red Cloud, Uijongbu	HQ, ROK/U.S. Combined Field Army: formerly HQ, I Corps (ROK/U.S. Group), joint command of a nine division force including the 2d Infantry Division
Camp Stanley, Uijongbu	HQ, 2d Infantry Division Artillery • 2 M-198 and 1 M-109 nuclear-capable artillery battalions, nuclear facilities include "Emergency Action Facility" and Special Weapons Training Facility[133]
Changsan	AF LORAN-C/D Monitor Station: part of the "Commando Lion" chain used for tactical long-range navigation and target location • Coast Guard LORAN-C Monitor Station: serving the northwest Pacific chain
Choejong San	Det 2, 1st Space Wing: GEODSS satellite tracking station
Hwedok	former HQ for 833d Ordnance Company and nuclear weapons storage site prior to relocation to Seneca Army Depot, NY in 1979
Koon-Ni	Nightmare Range: nuclear air-to-surface aircraft training range[134]
***Kunsan AB**	8th Tactical Fighter Wing: nuclear-capable F-16, replaced F-4D in 1981 • nuclear weapons storage site for Army and Air Force in South Korea, weapons stored include 60 bombs, 40 8-inch and 30 155mm artillery projectiles and 21 ADMs • Commando Escort station
Kwang Ju AB	AF LORAN-C/D Station: part of the "Commando Lion" network used for tactical long-range navigation and targeting • AF Korea alternate command center
Osan AB	314th Air Division/Air Forces Korea: top AF command in Korea, semi-hardened underground command center, the "Tree House" includes the joint ROK/U.S. Central Control Facility, an early warning and air defense center for South Korea and an "Emergency Action Facility" for receiving nuclear release orders • 51st Tactical Fighter Wing: nuclear-capable F-4E • SAC radar bomb scoring nuclear bombing practice site • Commando Escort station • AF LORAN-C/D Station: part of the "Commando Lion" network used for tactical long-range navigation and target location[135]
Pohang	AF LORAN-C/D Station: part of the "Commando Lion" network used for tactical long-range navigation and target location
Seoul	HQ, U.S. Forces Korea: sub-unified command of the Pacific Command, WWMCCS facilities include Nuclear Capabilities Plan, command facilities include "Emergency Action Console" for receiving nuclear release orders • ROK/U.S. Combined Forces Command: highest U.S./ROK operational HQ in South Korea, military command of forces in wartime, integrated planning

	and staff in peacetime • HQ, Eighth U.S. Army: top Army command in Korea
Songnam	"Tango" Combined Communications Operations Center: underground command center for U.S. Forces Korea, including WWMCCS facilities and "Emergency Action Console" for receiving nuclear release orders
Songso	AN/GSC-39 satellite terminal, main communications link to Japan and Hawaii
Taegu AB	497th Tactical Fighter Squadron: nuclear-capable F-4E • Alternate Tactical Air Control Center for South Korea
Tobongsan	Tobongsan Ammunition Center (near Uijongbu): stand-by forward nuclear weapons storage site for 2d Infantry Division
Wongju, Kangwondo	Det 452, AFTAC: nuclear test detection station

SPAIN

Spain is the newest member of NATO and already has an extensive nuclear infrastructure. Since 1979, the Spanish government has not allowed the stationing of strategic nuclear weapons in Spain, although the fate of nuclear depth bombs at Rota is unknown. Most likely the weapons have been withdrawn and Rota now serves as a stand-by base for wartime deployment. Two B-52 forward operating contingency bases are also maintained in Spain.

Bardenas Reales	nuclear bombing practice range, 70 percent of U.S. air-to-ground training in Europe takes place at this range, with the planes operating from Zaragoza AB[136]
Estaca de Vares	European airborne command center ground station[137]
Estartit (Gerona)	Coast Guard LORAN-C Station: serving the Mediterranean Sea chain
Guardamar del Segura	Naval Radio Station (Transmitter): inactive LF transmitter in partial maintenance status
Humosa	Humosa Radio Relay Station: AN/GSC-39 satellite communications terminal[138]
Inogues	"Creek Cruiser" AF command and control station and ground-to-air transmitter[139]
Moron AB	B-52 bomber standby dispersal base at former SAC base • Naval Radio Transmitter Facility: HF communications to the fleet[140]
Rota, Cadiz	Naval Station: former strategic submarine base (closed July 1979) • Fleet Ocean Surveillance Information Facility • Patrol Squadron Rota: supports nuclear-capable P-3 operations, command facilities include ASW operations center, wartime location for 32 nuclear depth bombs • Naval Radio Receiver Facility: HF communications and Rota weather intercept facility[141]
Soller	"Creek Cruiser" AF command and control station and ground-to-air transmitter[142]
Torrejon AB	HQ, 16th Air Force: senior AF command in southern Europe • 401st Tactical Fighter Wing: nuclear-capable F-16, makes regular deployments to Italy and Turkey • Giant Talk/Scope Signal III station • Det 313, AFTAC: nuclear detection station and support for "Olive Harvest" U-2 air sampling operations • Torrejon weather intercept facility[143]
Zaragoza AB	406th Tactical Fighter Training Wing: supports rotational aircraft deployments to train on the Bardenas Reales range • 34th Strategic Squadron: supports KC-135 forward operations • B-52 bomber stand-by forward operating base at former SAC base • Inform Net station in stand-by status[144]

TURKEY

Turkey is a member of NATO and ranks 4th overseas with 489 nuclear weapons deployed. Five nuclear-armed air bases in Turkey are within range of the Soviet Union. The main U.S. combat base at Incirlik in south central Turkey is also a key communications and staging base for the Middle East. Soviet missile tests are tracked from Pirinclik.

Alemdag	nuclear weapons communications relay between Cakmakli and Sahin Tepesi
Ankara	HQ, Northeastern Mediterranean, AFSOUTH: NATO command • HQ, The U.S. Logistics Group (TUSLOG): senior U.S. military command in Turkey
***Balikesir AB**	TUSLOG Det 184: nuclear bomb custodian for Turkish Air Force 191st and 192d Squadrons (Filos) with F-104G/S, some 25 nuclear bombs stored on the base
Belbasi	Det 301, AFTAC (TUSLOG Det 18): nuclear test detection station
***Cakmakli**	HQ, 528th U.S. Army Artillery Group (TUSLOG Det 67): central HQ and storage site for Army nuclear weapons in Turkey • 70th Ordnance Company (TUSLOG Det 168): storage, assembly and maintenance of Army nuclear weapons in Turkey, including 57 8-inch artillery projectiles and 132 Honest John warheads[145]
Cigli AB, Izmir	Air Force stand-by dispersal base for nuclear-capable aircraft[146]
***Corlu**	21st Field Artillery Det: nuclear warhead custodian for Turkish Army Honest John unit
Diyarbakir	support base for Pirinclik radars, includes DSCS satellite communications terminal linked to Lakehurst, NJ
***Erhac/Malatya AB**	TUSLOG Det 93: nuclear bomb custodian supporting Turkish Air Force 171st and 172d Squadrons (Filos) with F-4Es, some 25 bombs stored on the base
Erzincan	former nuclear weapons custodial site
***Erzurum**	27th Field Artillery Det: nuclear warhead custodian for Turkish Army Honest John unit, closest nuclear weapons storage site to the Soviet Union[147]
***Eskisehir AB**	7392d Munitions Support Squadron (TUSLOG Det 100): nuclear bomb custodian supporting Turkish Air Force 111th Squadron (Filo) with F-4E (formerly with F-100C/D/F aircraft), some 25 bombs stored on base[148]
***Incirlik AB**	39th Tactical Group (TUSLOG Det 10): supports up to 36 nuclear-capable F-4 and F-16 on rotation from Spain and the United States, some planes nuclear-loaded on quick reaction alert, one hour by air from the Soviet border • Global Command and Control Station, Giant Talk/Scope Signal III, INFORM Net, Cemetery Net transmitter/receiver • 1 of 3 HF radio stations for communications to Southwest Asia • Incirlik weather intercept facility • nuclear weapons storage site on base contains some 200 nuclear bombs[149]
Izmir	HQ, 6th Allied Tactical Air Force, AIRSOUTH/Allied Land Forces Southeastern Europe, AFSOUTH: senior NATO commands in Turkey
***Izmit**	14th Field Artillery Det: nuclear warhead custodian for Turkish Army Honest John unit
Kargaburun	Coast Guard LORAN-C Station: serving the Mediterranean Sea chain
Konya AB	forward operating base for NATO AWACs • air-to-ground training range used by U.S. aircraft from Incirlik for low-level nuclear bombing training[150]
***Murted AB**	TUSLOG Det 183: nuclear bomb custodian for Turkish Air Force 141st and 142d Squadrons (Filos) with F-104G/S, some 25 bombs stored on the base
***Ortakoy**	10th Field Artillery Det: nuclear warhead custodian for Turkish Army Honest John unit
Pirinclik	19th Surveillance Squadron: 2 AN/FPS-17 detection and 1 AN/FPS-79 tracking radar supporting long-range surveillance and intelligence collection on Soviet missile testing, also conducts satellite surveillance
Sahin Tepesi	European Command and Control Console System (ECCCS) mobile communications and control van supporting nuclear weapons in Turkey
Sirinyer	Joint Combat Operations Center/Air Defense Operations Center, 6th ATAF: NATO command center

TURKS AND CAICOS ISLAND

The U.S. maintains a Naval Facility on Grand Turk Island as a processing station for SOSUS. The tracking facility supporting missile launches from ESMC was closed in 1983.

UNITED KINGDOM

The U.K. is a member of NATO and closest nuclear ally of the U.S. The country is 2d behind West Germany with some 1,268 nuclear warheads deployed, twice as many as in the British national arsenal. Britain is the center of long-range Euro-strategic forces with 170 F-111 fighters at Lakenheath and Upper Heyford, Poseidon submarines at Holy Loch, and ground-launched cruise missiles. In addition, Britain houses important nuclear and naval commands which would be the center of northern Atlantic ASW operations and European land warfare in wartime.

RAF Alconbury	17th Reconnaissance Wing, SAC: organized in 1983 with deployment of first TR-1 reconnaissance aircraft overseas • designated as airfield and logistics support base for future ground-launched cruise missiles at Molesworth • INFORM Net station • stand-by nuclear storage capability is maintained on the base[151]
Barford St. John	Global Command and Control Station, Giant Talk/Scope Signal III transmitter (receiver at Croughton)
RAF Bentwaters	INFORM Net station
Brawdy, Wales	Naval Facility: processing station for SOSUS
RAF Brize Norton	B-52 bomber forward operating base at former SAC bomber base
Cowden	air-to-ground training range used regularly by F-111s for nuclear bombing practice
RAF Croughton	Global Command and Control Station, Giant Talk/Scope Signal III receiver (transmitter at Barford St. John) • 1 of 3 HF radio stations for communications to Southwest Asia • Croughton Automatic Digital Weather Switch, Weather Intercept Control Unit, Croughton Intercept Facility • European airborne command post satellite communications ground station • AUTODIN switching center[152]
Edzell	HF receiver for naval communications
RAF Fairford	11th Strategic Group, SAC: European Tanker Task Force of KC-135s, aircraft permanently deployed since late 1979, B-52 bomber forward operating base at former SAC bomber base • INFORM net station in stand-by status
Fylingdales Moor	Det 1, 12th Missile Warning Squadron: BMEWS Site III, one of three main early warning radars of the U.S. operated by Royal Air Force (see Appendix C)
***RAF Greenham Common**	501st Tactical Missile Wing: first ground-launched cruise missile main operating base activated in December 1983, eventual deployment of 6 missile flights with 96 missiles • INFORM Net station
High Wycombe AS (Daws Hill Lane)	Static War Headquarters, U.S. European Command: wartime command center containing Theater Mission Planning Center, one of three cruise missile targeting centers in Europe
RAF High Wycombe	HQ, U.K. Air Forces Command (UKAIR), ACE: NATO command equivalent of RAF Strike Command (see Appendix C)
Holbeach	air-to-ground training range used for nuclear bombing training
***Holy Loch, Firth of Clyde**	Fleet Ballistic Missile Refit Site 1/Submarine Squadron 14: forward base and support facilities for Poseidon submarines homeported at Groton, CT (where crews fly from), 3 submarines are in port at any time with some 510 warheads
Jurby	air-to-ground training range used for nuclear bombing training
***RAF Lakenheath**	48th Tactical Fighter Wing: 84 nuclear-capable F-111Fs, nuclear weapons stored on base include some 300 bombs • Det 348, AFTAC: nuclear test detection station • INFORM Net station in stand-by status
London	HQ, U.S. Naval Forces Europe/U.S. Commander Eastern Atlantic (USCOMEASTLANT), Atlantic Command: senior naval administrative and operational commands in Europe, WWMCCS terminal facilities include access to Nuclear Weapons Capabilities Plan and Nuclear Weapons Accounting System • HQ, Fleet Marine Force Europe (Designate): skeletal forward command activated in 1980 for Marine Corps operations in Europe

***Machrihanish**	Naval Aviation Weapons Facility Det, USCOMEASTLANT: nuclear depth bomb storage supporting U.S. and Dutch P-3 and British Nimrod operations, some 63 warheads stored on base
RAF Marham	B-52 bomber forward operating base (see also Appendix C)
RAF Mildenhall	HQ, 3d Air Force: senior AF command in U.K. • 10th Airborne Command and Control Squadron: 4 EC-135 "Silk Purse" European Command airborne command centers • 306th Strategic Wing, SAC: supports rotational RC-135 strategic reconnaissance aircraft and KC-135 aerial refueling operations in Europe • Giant Talk/Scope Signal III Area Network Control Station for European net • INFORM Net station • staging base for TACAMO radio relay aircraft
RAF Molesworth	designated main operating base for ground-launched cruise missiles, to house 4 missile flights totaling 64 missiles by 1988, nuclear weapons support and airfield at Alconbury
Mormond Hill	European airborne command post ground communications station
Northwood	HQ, Eastern Atlantic Command (EASTLANT), SACLANT: NATO command including Submarine Forces, Bay of Biscay Subarea, and Maritime Air Forces • HQ, Allied Command Channel (CINCHAN): NATO and U.K. national command, as national command (CINCFLT), it controls the U.K. Polaris submarine force, NATO command is one of three main commands of NATO and includes Maritime Air Forces Channel Command (COMMAICHAN) • U.S. Atlantic Fleet Submarine Forces Representitive (see also Appendix C)
Oakhanger	satellite control facility (see Appendix C)
Pitreavic, Rosyth	HQ, Northern Subarea, EASTLANT: NATO command, including Maritime Air Forces • HQ, Northern Channel Command (COMNORECHAN): NATO command, including Maritime Air Forces North Channel Command (COMMAIRNORECHAN) (see also Appendix C)
Plymouth	HQ, Central Subarea, EASTLANT: including Maritime Air Central Subarea • HQ, Plymouth Subarea, Channel Command
***St. Mawgan**	Naval Aviation Weapons Facility, USCOMEASTLANT: nuclear depth bomb storage for U.S. and Dutch P-3s, and British Nimrods, some 63 warheads are stored on the base
RAF Sculthorpe	former SAC bomber base in stand-by status • INFORM Net station in standby status
Shetland Islands	Coast Guard LORAN-C Monitoring Station: serving the Norwegian Sea chain
Thurso	LF transmitter operating to the North Atlantic and North Sea, Navy operated and jointly used by the British • AN/GSC-39 DSCS satellite communications station
***RAF Upper Heyford**	20th Tactical Fighter Wing: 72 nuclear-capable F-111Es, some 300 nuclear bombs stored on base • 42d Electronic Combat Squadron: EF-111 "Raven" electronic warfare aircraft • INFORM Net station in stand-by status
Wainfleet	air-to-ground training range used for nuclear weapons training
RAF Weathersfield	INFORM Net station in stand-by status

U.S. VIRGIN ISLANDS

This U.S. territory located within the Latin American Nuclear-Free Zone houses three testing installations which support strategic submarine and missile research and training.

Crown Mountain, St. Thomas	Crown Mountain Radar Site: tracking radar supporting AFWTF, Roosevelt Roads, Puerto Rico
Sprat Hall, St. Croix	control center of AFWTF underwater tracking range, 82 square mile acoustic range used for ASW exercises, submarine certification, Trident advanced magnetic silencing ("Linear Chair") • Sonobuoy Quality Assurance Facility, Naval Weapons Support Center, Crane, IN[153]

St. George, St. Croix	St. George Hill Radar Site: tracking radar supporting AFWTF, Roosevelt Roads, Puerto Rico

WEST GERMANY

The most extensive nuclear infrastructure in the world is located in West Germany, which ranks 1st with about 3,400 nuclear warheads and 241 nuclear-related facilities. U.S. Nuclear weapons in the country are earmarked for U.S., West German, Dutch, Belgian, and British use. Warheads include about 500 bombs, 340 Pershing 1as and IIs, 600 short-range Lance missile warheads, 320 Nike Hercules air defense missiles, about 1,200 155mm and 8-inch nuclear artillery projectiles, and 350 atomic demolition munitions (ADMs). The most extensive weapons deployments are in widely dispersed artillery units which have about 1,500 nuclear-certified guns. U.S. European Command headquarters in Stuttgart-Vaihingen is the highest level command in West Germany. Other important NATO and U.S. commands with nuclear functions are located at Frankfurt, Heidelberg, Pirmasens, Ramstein, Rheindahlen, Seckenheim, and Stuttgart-Moehringen. Wartime command centers are located at Birkenfeld, Boerfink, Feudenheim, Kalkar, Kindsbach, Massweiler, and Sembach. Kapaun Air Station in Vogelweh became a ground station for early warning satellites in 1983—one of three in the world—and is the most important strategic facility in Germany.

Adelheide/Delmenhorst, SchH	Lilienthal Kaserne: former nuclear warhead custodial site for West German Air Force Nike Hercules unit, now a communications tributary supporting nuclear weapons
Aachen, Nordr	Lutzon Kaserne: West German Army Lance missile ground support equipment training
Albersdorf, SchH	West German Army nuclear-certified 8-inch artillery unit
Altenbusek, Hessen	communications tributory supporting nuclear weapons
Altenrath, Nordr	Belgian Army nuclear-certified 155mm artillery unit
Amberg, Bayern	Pond Barracks: nuclear-certified 155mm artillery battery, 3d Squadron, 2d Armored Cavalry Regt
Ansbach, Bayern	Hindenberg Kaserne: HQ, 1st Armored Division: nuclear units include artillery and ADMs • Bleidorn Kaserne: nuclear-certified 155mm artillery units of VII Corps Artillery
Arolson, Hessen	West German Army nuclear-certified 155mm artillery unit
***Arsbeck, Nordr**	West German Air Force Pershing 1a Combat Alert Status site supporting Tevren Wing
Aschaffenburg, Bayern	Fiori Barracks: 1st Bn, 80th Field Artillery, VII Corps Artillery: 6 nuclear-certified Lance launchers
Augsburg, Bayern	Reese Barracks: HQ, VII Corps Artillery, 17th Field Artillery Bde: includes nuclear-certified 155mm and 8-inch artillery battalions in Augsburg
Augustdorf, Nordr	West German Army nuclear-certified 155mm artillery unit
Babenhausen, Hessen	HQ, 41st Field Artillery Bde, V Corps Artillery: includes 1 nuclear-certified 8-inch artillery battalion in Babenhausen
Bad Hersfeld, Hessen	McPheeter Barracks: nuclear-certified 155mm battery, 3d Squadron, 11th Armored Cavalry Regt
Bad Kissingen, Bayern	Daley Barracks: nuclear-certified 155mm battalion, 3d Infantry Division • nuclear-certified 155mm battery, 2d Squadron, 11th Armored Cavalry Regt
Bad Kreuznach, RP	Rose Barracks: HQ, 8th Infantry Division: nuclear units include artillery and ADMs
Bad Reichenhall, Bayern	West Germany Army nuclear-certified 155mm artillery unit
Bad Toelz, Bayern	Army Special Forces Det (Airborne) Europe: battalion-sized Green Beret unit with "behind-the-enemy-lines" Special ADM (SADM) mission
Bamberg, Bayern	Warner Barracks: nuclear-certified 155mm and 8-inch artillery battalions of VII Corps Artillery • 1 nuclear-certified 155mm artillery battalion, 1st Armored Divsion • nuclear-certified 155mm artillery battery, 2d Squadron, 2d Armored Cavalry Regt

Bann, RP	Bann Strategic Training Range: SAC radar bomb scoring and nuclear delivery practice • DMSP weather satellite tracking and receiving facility
Barme/Doerverden, Nieders	communications tributary supporting nuclear weapons
***Barnstorf/Diepholz, Nieders**	Eydelstadt Kaserne: 41st Air Defense Artillery Det: nuclear warhead custodian for West German Air Force Nike Hercules unit • communications tributary supporting nuclear weapons
***Baumholder, RP**	Smith Barracks: HQ, 8th Infantry Division Artillery, including 2 nuclear-certified 155mm and 1 8-inch artillery • Btry C, 5th Bn, 6th ADA: nuclear-certified Nike Hercules tactical firing site to be closed down by mid-1985
Bayreuth, Bayern	nuclear-certified 155mm artillery battery, 2d Armored Cavalry Regt
Bedburg	(see Putz)
***Bergen, Nieders**	Barker Barracks: 15th Field Artillery Det: nuclear artillery warhead custodian for British Army units
Bindlach, Bayern	Christensen Barracks: nuclear-certified 155mm artillery battery, 1st Squadron, 2d Armored Cavalry Regt
Birkenfeld, RP	NATO AFCENT War Headquarters collocated with West German Air Force 2d Air Division command post
Bitburg AB, RP	36th Tactical Figther Wing: 72 F-15C/D responsible for air defense of central Europe, 4 aircraft on "Zulu" alert • INFORM Net station
Bocksberg, Nieders	communications site supporting nuclear weapons
***Bodelsberg-Gorisried, Bayern**	West German Air Force Pershing 1a Combat Alert Status site supporting Landsberg Wing
Boerfink, RP	hardened underground command center for NATO AFCENT and AAFCE ground and air commands, commands operations in Central Europe • Tactical Fusion Center: indications and warning center for central Europe[154]
Borgholzhausen, Nordr	former Dutch Air Force Nike Hercules unit with nuclear warheads provided by Team C, 509th Air Defense Artillery Det, unit deactivated in 1983–84
Boettingen, BadenW	possible Army Pershing missile Combat Alert Status site
Boostedt, SchH	nuclear-certified West German Army 155mm artillery unit
Bramsche, Nordr	HQ, Dutch Air Force 12th Guided Missile Group: controls nuclear-certified Nike Hercules
Braunschweig, Nieders	nuclear-certified West German Army 155mm artillery unit
RAF Bruggen, Nordr	communications tributary supporting nuclear weapons (see also Appendix C)
***Buechel AB, RP**	7501st Munitions Support Squadron: nuclear bomb custodian for West German Air Force 33d Wing with nuclear-certified F-104Gs. some 25 bombs stored on base
***Bueren, Nordr**	Stockerbusch Kaserne: HQ, 5th U.S. Army Air Defense Artillery Group/27th Ordnance Company: nuclear warhead custodial HQ and storage site for all Nike Hercules missile units in West Germany, provides warhead site support at 31 locations, Dutch Army provides security guards for nuclear storage site
***Burbach/Lipper Hohe, Nordr**	Siegerland Kaserne: 52d Air Defense Artillery Det: nuclear warhead custodian for West German Air Force Nike Hercules unit
Butzbach, Hessen	Schloss Kaserne: nuclear-certified 155mm artillery battalion, 3d Armored Division • possible nuclear warhead storage site supporting 3d Armored Division units
***Crailsheim, BadenW**	McKee Barracks: 2d Battalion, 42d Field Artillery, VII Corps Artillery: 6 nuclear-certified Lance launchers
Dahn/Pirmasens, RP	Dahn Ammunition Depot: probable central nuclear storage site supporting U.S. Army, may have been closed

Dallau Eltzal, BadenW	former nuclear site of Battery A, 3d Battalion, 71st ADA: Nike Hercules unit withdrawn since 1983
Darmstadt, RP	Cambrai-Fritsch Kaserne: HQ, 32d Army Air Defense Command: responsible for Army air defense of Europe, including Nike Hercules operations
Darmstadt-Finthen, RP	Kelly Barracks: ADM unit assigned to V Corps
Datteln-Ahsen, Nordr	West German Air Force nuclear-certified Nike Hercules unit
Dedelstorf, Nieders	nuclear-certified West German Army 155mm artillery unit
Deilinghofen-Menden, Nordr	Peninsular Barracks: 69th Field Artillery Det: nuclear warhead custodian support for British Army, nuclear warheads stored at Hemer
Dellbruck-Koln, Nordr	Moorslede Kaserne: communications tributary and nuclear custodial unit supporting Belgian Army units
Delmenhorst, SchH	communications tributary supporting nuclear weapons (see also Adelheide)
Dexheim, RP	Anderson Barracks: former nuclear site of Battery B, 2d Battalion, 1st ADA: Nike Hercules unit closed since 1983 • ADM Platoon of 8th Infantry Division
Dichtelbach, RP	former nuclear site of Battery D, 2d Battalion, 1st ADA: Nike Hercules unit closed since 1983
Dieberg	(see Munster-Dieberg)
Dobraburg, RP	"Rivet Switch" ground communications terminal supporting SAC reconnaissance operations
Donauworth, Bayern	nuclear-certified West German Army 155mm artillery unit
***Dornum, Nieders**	Team D, 35th Air Defense Artillery Det: nuclear warhead custodian for West German Air Force Nike Hercules unit
***Doerverden, Nieders**	Niedersachsen Kaserne: 25th Field Artillery Det: nuclear warhead custodian for West German Army I Corps
***Duelmen, Nordr**	St. Barbara Kaserne: 81st Field Artillery Det: nuclear warhead custodian for West German Army I Corps
***Dunsen Bassum, Nieders**	Schill Kaserne: 5th Field Artillery Det: nuclear warhead custodian for West German Army I Corps
***Dueren Drove, Nordr**	43d Air Defense Artillery Det: nuclear warhead custodian for Belgian Air Force Nike Hercules unit, scheduled for retirement
Edewecht	(see Westerscheps)
Edingen, BadenW	HF radio site, hub for Cemetery Network in north Germany and the Netherlands
Erle-Schermbeck, Nordr	nuclear-certified Belgian Air Force Nike Hercules unit
Eschweiler, Nordr	Donnerberg Kaserne: West German Army Lance electronic components maintenance training
***Euskirchen-Billig, Nordr**	Team C, 43d Air Defense Artillery Det: nuclear warhead custodian for Belgian Air Force Nike Hercules unit, scheduled for retirement
Feudenheim, BadenW	NATO Central Army Group (CENTAG) underground command post
***Fischbach b. Dahn, RP**	Fischbach Ordnance Depot: HQ, 197th Ordnance Bn/64th Ordnance Co: major nuclear weapons storage site in support of U.S. VII Corps, over 1,600 acres
***Flensburg-Meyn, SchH**	nuclear weapons storage site of 294th Artillery Group supporting West German Army Lance and artillery units
Flensburg-Weiche, SchH	Von Briesen Ksn: HQ, 294th U.S. Army Artillery Group/99th Ordnance Det: nuclear warhead custodian for West German Army Lance and 8-inch artillery units in the NATO LANDJUT Corps (see Rendsburg)
Frankfurt, Hessen	Abrams Building: HQ, V Corps: command of U.S. Army units in West Germany in the northern sector, command facilities include "Emergency Action Console" for receiving nuclear firing orders • Drake Kaserne: HQ, 3d Armored Division: nuclear-certified units include artillery and ADMs • HQ, V Corps Artillery: nuclear-certified units include Lance and Artillery

Frankfurt-Hausen, Hessen	Pershing Modification and Exchange Facility: rework of Pershing 1a launchers and equipment to Pershing II standards
Friedberg, Hessen	Ray Barracks: nuclear-certified 155mm artillery battalion, 3d Armored Division
Fulda, Hessen	Down Barracks: nuclear-certified 155mm artillery battery, 1st Squadron, 11th Armored Cavalry Regt • ADM Platoon, 11th Armored Cavalry Regt
Furth	(see Nurnburg)
Fussen, Bayern	nuclear-certified West German Army 155mm artillery unit
Garlstedt, Nieders	nuclear-certified 155mm artillery battalion, 2d Armored Division (Forward)
Geilenkirchen AB, Nordr	main operating base of NATO Airborne Early Warning Force of E-3 AWACs, 18 aircraft to be deployed by 1985 • West German Air Force Pershing 1a unit moved to Tevren with deployment of AWACs
Geinsheim/Hassloch (Fronmuhle), RP	former nuclear site of Battery A, 2d Battalion, 56th ADA: Nike Hercules withdrawn since 1983
Gelnhausen, Hessen	Coleman Barracks: nuclear-certified 155mm artillery battalion, 3d Armored Division
***Giessen, Hessen**	Giessen Army Depot/River Barracks: HQ, 42d Field Artillery Bde, V Corps Artillery: 1 nuclear-certified 155mm and 1 8-inch artillery battalion • 3d Battalion, 79th Field Artillery: 6 nuclear-certified Lance launchers • nuclear storage site supporting V Corps Artillery • Stueben Kaserne: 30th Field Artillery Det: nuclear warhead custodian for West German Army Lance and artillery units of III Corps
Goeppingen, BadenW	Cooke Barracks: HQ, 1st Infantry Division (Forward): nuclear units include artillery and ADMs
Goettingen, Nieders	nuclear-certified West German Army 155mm artillery unit
***Grefrath Hinsbeck, Nordr**	Grefrath Kaserne: 507th Air Defense Artillery Det: nuclear warhead custodian for Belgian Air Force Nike Hercules unit, scheduled for retirement
Gross Sachsenheim, BadenW	former nuclear site of Battery B, 3d Battalion, 71st ADA: Nike Hercules withdrawn since 1983
Grossauheim, Hessen	Grossauheim Kaserne: possible nuclear weapons storage supporting U.S. Army
***Grossengstingen, BadenW**	Eberhard Finckh Kaserne: 84th Field Artillery Det: nuclear warhead custodian for West German Army Lance battalion of II Corps
Guenzburg, Bayern	Neue Kaserne: HQ, 512th U.S. Army Artillery Group: nuclear warhead HQ and storage site supporting West German Army II Corps and West German Air Force Pershing missile unit • Prinz Eugen Kaserne: 510th Ordnance Company: nuclear weapons storage and maintenance supporting West German military
***Hahn AB, RP**	50th Tactical Fighter Wing: 72 nuclear-certified F-16 (replaced F-4 in 1982), some 150 bombs are stored on the base • INFORM Net station
Hamburg-Fischbek	nuclear-certified West German Army 155mm artillery unit
Hamburg-Rahlstedt	nuclear-certified West German Army 155mm artillery unit
Hamminkeln, Nordr	communications tributory supporting nuclear weapons
***Hanau, Hessen**	Hutier Kaserne: HQ, 3d Armored Division Artillery: includes 1 nuclear-certified 155mm and 1 8-inch artillery battalion in Hanau • Fliegerhorst Kaserne: 1st Battalion, 32d Field Artillery, V Corps: 6 nuclear-certified Lance launchers, 1 nuclear-certified 8-inch artillery battalion, V Corps Artillery • Hessen Homburg Barracks: ADM Platoon, 3d Armored Division • nuclear weapons storage supporting V Corps and 3d Armored Division
Handorf	(see Muenster-Handorf)
Hardheim, BadenW	former nuclear site of Battery C, 3d Battalion, 71st ADA: Nike Hercules withdrawn after 1983

Hasselbach	(see Wuescheim)
Heidelberg, BadenW	Campbell Barracks: HQ, U.S. Army Europe (USAREUR): WWMCCS facilities include access to Nuclear Capabilities Plan • HQ, Central Army Group (CENTAG), AFCENT: NATO command over U.S., West German, and Canadian forces, 59th Ordnance Bde staff element signal team provides CENTAG with support to issue nuclear control orders to combat units • HQ, 4th Allied Tactical Air Force (4th ATAF): NATO air command for southern portion of West Germany
***Heilbronn, BadenW**	Badenerhof Kaserne: 23d Ordnance Company: nuclear weapons storage for Pershing missile unit • Battery A-B, 3d Battalion, 84th Field Artillery: 18 Pershing launchers
***Hemau, Bayern**	36th Field Artillery Det: nuclear warhead custodian for West German 4th Infantry Division
***Hemer Menden, Nord**	nuclear warhead storage site supporting British Army (see Deilinghofen)
***Herbornseelbach, Hessen**	Aartal Kaserne: HQ, 557th U.S. Army Artillery Group/96th Ordnance Company: nuclear warhead custodian and storage in support of West German Army III Corps, 2 Engineer platoons support ADM units of the West German Army III Corps
Herzogenaurach, Bayern	Herzo Artillery Base: HQ, 210th Field Artillery Bde, VII Corps Artillery: 1 nuclear-certified 8" artillery battalion and 2d Battalion, 377th Field Artillery: 6 nuclear-certified Lance launchers
Hinsbeck/Grefrath, Nordr	communications tributary supporting nuclear weapons
Hohenfels, Bayern	Security Site Training Facility: nuclear weapons security training site opened in 1981
***Hohenkirchen, Nieders**	Wangerland Kaserne: 35th Air Defense Artillery Det: nuclear warhead custodian for West German Air Force Nike Hercules unit
Homberg, Hessen	nuclear-certified West German Army 155mm artillery unit
Hontheim, RP	former nuclear site of Battery D, 5th Battalion, 6th ADA: Nike Hercules withdrawn since 1983
Idar Obserstein, RP	Strassburg Kaserne: nuclear-certified 155mm battalion, 8th Infantry Division
Immendingen, Bayern	nuclear-certified West German Army 155mm artillery unit
Inneringen, BadenW	former Pershing 1a Combat Alert Status site supporting Neu Ulm, closed in 1983
Ippweger Moor	(see Oldenburg)
Itzehoe, SchH	communications tributary supporting nuclear weapons
Jever AB, SchH	NATO Tornado weapons training unit
Jever Hohenkirchen, SchH	communications tributary supporting nuclear weapons
Kaiserslautern, RP	Polaski Barracks: 41st Ordnance Company: operates nuclear storage sites at Fischbach and Weilerbach
Kalkar, Nordr	NATO Operations Support Cell (NOSC): collocated with West German Air Force 3d Air Division command post, underground command center supporting air operations in the northern German area
Kapaun	(see Vogelweh)
Kapellen-Erft, Nordr	nuclear-certified Belgian Air Force Nike Hercules unit, scheduled for retirement
***Kaster, Nordr**	Team B, 43d Air Defense Artillery Det: nuclear warhead custodian for Belgian Air Force Nike Hercules unit, scheduled for retirement
***Kellinghusen, SchH**	Lilliencron Kaserne: 13th Field Artillery Det: nuclear warhead custodian for West German units of LANDJUT Corps (see Rendsburg)
Kemel, Hessen	nuclear-certified West German Air Force Nike Hercules unit
Kempten, Bayern	nuclear-certified West German Army 155mm artillery unit
Keil-Holtenau, SchH	HQ, Naval Forces Baltic Approaches, AFNORTH: NATO command

***Killianstadten, Hessen**	Nidda Kaserne: 501st Air Defense Artillery Det: nuclear warhead custodian for West German Air Force Nike Hercules unit
Kindsbach, RP	U.S. Air Forces Europe and 4th ATAF underground command center and static war HQ
Kirchgoens, Hessen	Ayers Kaserne: 1 nuclear-certified 155mm artillery battalion, 3d Armored Division
Kitzingen, Bayern	Larson Barracks: HQ, 3d Infantry Division Artillery, includes 1 nuclear-certified 8-inch artillery battalion in Kitzingen
Kleingartach, BadenW	Pershing 1a missile Combat Alert Status site
Korbecke, Nordr	66th Air Defense Artillery Det: nuclear warhead custodian for West German Air Force Nike Hercules unit, storage site at Soest
***Kornwestheim, BadenW**	Ludendorf Kaserne: ADM company, VII Corps
***Kriegsfeld-Gerbach, RP**	Kriegsfeld Ordnance Depot ("Northpoint"): 619th Ordnance Company: major nuclear weapons storage site
***Lahn Ems/Soegel, Nieders**	Muhlenberg Kaserne: HQ, 552d U.S. Army Artillery Group/162d Ordnance Company: nuclear warhead custodian and support for West German Army I Corps and I Netherlands Corps
Lahnstein, RP	nuclear-certified West German Army 155mm artillery unit
Landau, RP	former nuclear site of Battery B, 2d Battalion, 56th ADA: Nike Hercules withdrawn in 1983
***Landsberg am Lech, Bayern**	Ritter von Leeb Kaserne: 24th Field Artillery Det: nuclear warhead custodian for West German Air Force Pershing 1a unit with 36 launchers
Landshut, Bayern	nuclear-certified West German Army 155mm artillery unit
Landstuhl, RP	AN/FSC-78 satellite communications terminal, main station for U.S. forces in West Germany, linked to Berlin, Britain and the U.S. • satellite control facility for DSCS communications satellites
***Lechfeld AB, Bayern**	West German 32d Wing with nuclear-certified Tornado (converted from F-104G in 1984), some 25 nuclear bombs are believed to be stored on the base
***Lehmgrube, BadenW**	Von Steuben Kaserne: U.S. Pershing II missile Combat Alert Status site
***Leipheim, BadenW**	Riedheim Lager: 510th Ordnance Company: nuclear weapons storage site supporting Guenzburg
Lich, Hessen	nuclear-certified West German Air Force Nike Hercules unit
Liebenau, Nieders	nuclear-certified West German Air Force Nike Hercules unit
Linderhofe, Nordr	communications station supporting nuclear weapons
Lindsey Air Station	(see Wiesbaden)
Lipper Hohe	(see Burbach)
Lippstadt, Nordr	nuclear-certified British Army 155mm and 8-inch artillery units
Lohne-Vechta, Nieders	nuclear-certified West German Air Force Nike Hercules unit
Ludwigsburg	(see Kornwestheim)
Luttmersen, Nieders	nuclear-certified West German Army 155mm artillery unit
Marienheide, Nordr	nuclear-certified West German Air Force Nike Hercules unit
Massweiler, RP	U.S. Army Europe underground command center
***Memmingen AB, Bayern**	7261st Munitions Support Squadron: nuclear bomb custodian for West German Air Force 34th Wing with nuclear-certified F-104Gs, some 25 bombs are stored on the base
Menden	(see Hemer Menden)
***Miesau, RP**	Miesau Army Depot: 4th Ordnance Company: Nike Hercules support • HQ, 72d Ordnance Bn: Pershing and V Corps nuclear weapons support • largest U.S. ammunition depot outside U.S., 2,500 acres
Minden, Nordr	Herzug von Braunschweig Kaserne: West German Army III Corps ADM unit
Moenchengladbach	(see Rheindahlen)

Moehringen	(see Stuttgart-Moehringen)
***Montabaur, RP**	Westerwald Kaserne: 83d Field Artillery Det: nuclear warhead custodian for West German Army Lance unit
Muenchweiler, RP	HQ, 197th Ordnance Bn: provides nuclear warhead support to VII Corps and 32d AADCOM
***Muenster-Dieberg, Hessen**	Muenster Ammunition Depot/Pine Bks: 545th Ordnance Company: nuclear warhead support to 3d Armored Division and V Corps units
***Muenster-Handorf, Nordr**	Handorf Kaserne: HQ, 570th U.S. Army Artillery Group/583d Ordnance Company: nuclear warhead custodian for British, Belgian, and West German Army units
***Mulheim/Blankenheim, Nordr**	Team D, 43d Air Defense Artillery Det: nuclear warhead custodian for Belgian Air Force Nike Hercules unit, scheduled for retirement
Munsingen, BadenW	nuclear-certified West German Army 155mm artillery unit
***Mutlangen, BadenW**	Mutlangen Training Area: Pershing II missile training area and Combat Alert Status site supporting Schwaebisch Gmuend, initial deployment site of Pershing II in December 1983
Naumburg, Hessen	nuclear-certified West German Army 155mm artillery unit
***Neckars Ulm, BadenW**	Artillery Kaserne: Battery C-D, 3d Battalion, 84th Field Artillery: 18 Pershing launchers • Ammunition Storage Area: Pershing missile and warhead storage
***Neu Ulm, BadenW**	Nelson Barracks: 579th Ordnance Company: Pershing missile and warhead storage • Wiley Barracks: 1st Battalion, 81st Field Artillery: 36 Pershing launchers • 1 nuclear-certified 155mm artillery battalion, 1st Infantry Division (Forward)
Neuenburg vorm Wald, Bayern	nuclear-certified West German Army 155mm artillery unit
***Nienburg/Landendamm, Nieders**	Clauswitz Kaserne: 32d Field Artillery Det: nuclear warhead custodian for West German Army I Corps
Nordhorn, Nordr	Air Force air-to-ground training range used for nuclear training
***Norvenich AB, Nordr**	7502d Munitions Support Squadron: nuclear bomb custodian for West German Air Force 31st Wing with nuclear-certified Tornado (first Tornado unit formed in August 1983 replacing F-104Gs), some 25 bombs are stored on the base
Nuernberg, Bayern	Merrell Barracks: HQ, 2d Armored Cavalry Regt: includes ADM platoon in Nuernberg
Nuernberg-Fuerth, Bayern	Darby Kaserne: 1 nuclear-certified 8-inch artillery battalion, 1st Armored Division
Oberammergau, Bayern	Hotzendorf Kaserne: NATO School (SHAPE): numerous nuclear weapons training courses for Allied Command Europe officers including weapons employment and planning, ADM procedures, air delivered weapons, targeting and release
Oberauerbach, RP	former nuclear site of Battery D, 2d Battalion, 56th ADA: Nike Hercules withdrawn in 1983
Obersayn, RP	nuclear-certified West German Air Force Nike Hercules unit
***Oberoth b. Illertissen/Kettershausen, Bayern**	Pershing missile Combat Alert Status site
Oedingen-Elspe, Nordr	nuclear-certified West German Air Force Nike Hercules unit
Oldenburg, Nieders	nuclear-certified West German Army 8-inch artillery unit
***Paderborn, Nordr**	26th Field Artillery Det: nuclear warhead custodian for British Army units
Pforzheim, BadenW	former nuclear site of Battery D, 3d Battalion, 71st ADA: Nike Hercules withdrawn since 1983

***Pfullendorf, Bayern**	Generaloberst von Fritsch Kaserne: 2d Field Artillery Det: nuclear warhead custodian for West German Army 10th Armored Division, southernmost nuclear weapons unit in West Germany
***Phillipsburg, BadenW**	Salm Kaserne: 3d Field Artillery Det, nuclear warhead custodian for West German Army 12th Artillery Regt
***Pirmasens, RP**	Husterhoeh Kaserne: HQ, 59th Ordnance Brigade: responsible for all Army and NATO nuclear weapons in Europe, including stockpile management, maintenance, and nuclear weapons release procedures and training, operates Permissve Action Link Det for control of nuclear warheads • AUTODIN switching center • 22d Aviation Det: responsible for transport of nuclear weapons and components in West Germany and the Netherlands
Pruem, RP	Air force operated communications and control center including European Command and Control Console System (ECCCS) switch and European airborne command post ground entry point mobile van
Putz/Bedburg, Nordr	nuclear-certified Belgian Air Force Nike Hercules unit, scheduled for retirement
Quirnheim/Gruenstadt RP	former nuclear site of Battery C, 2d Battalion, 1st ADA: Nike Hercules withdrawn in 1983
***Ramstein AB, RP**	HQ, U.S. Air Forces Europe (USAFE): senior Air Force command in Europe • HQ, Allied Air Forces Central Europe (AAFCE): central direction and control of Air Forces in the central region • Combat Operations Intelligence Center (COIC): operates the WWMCCS system including access to the Nuclear Weapons Accounting System and Nuclear Capabilities Plan • 86th Tactical Fighter Wing: 48 nuclear-certified F-4E, to receive 72 F-16 in 1986, 2 aircraft on quick reaction alert • HQ, 7th Air Division: coordinates SAC contingency operations and KC-135 support in Europe • Operating Location, AF Weapons Laboratory, Kirtland AFB, New Mexico: Tornado and NATO F-16 certification, manages nuclear-compatibility, certification and safety program for non-U.S. NATO aircraft • 7450th Tactical Intelligence Squadron: nulcear targeting support to NATO and USAFE • 322d Airlift Division: coordinates nuclear weapons transportation within Europe • INFORM Net Alternate Net Control Station[155]
Regensburg, Bayern	nuclear-certified West German Army 8-inch artillery
Rendsburg, SchH	HQ, Allied Land Forces Schleswig-Holstein and Jutland (LANDJUT), AFNORTH: integrated Corps unit of West German and Danish Army units
Rhein Main AB, Hessen	37th Tactical Airlift Squadron: Primary Nuclear Airlift Force for Europe with 4 specially trained crews flying C-130 planes • INFORM Net Control Station
Rheine-Elte, Nordr	Dutch Air Force Nike Hercules unit, slated for deactivation in 1984–85
Rheindahlen, Moenchengladbach, Nordr	HQ, 2d Allied Tactical Air Force: NATO air command for northern West Germany • HQ, Northern Army Group (NORTHAG), AFCENT: NATO command responsible for ground units in northern West Germany • 59th Ordnance Bde staff element/signal team: provides nuclear control order services for NORTHAG and 2d ATAF (see also Appendix C for British units)
Rockenhausen	(see Schoenborn)
***Rodenkirchen, Nieders**	Team B, 35th Air Defense Artillery Det: nuclear warhead support to West German Air Force Nike Hercules unit
Salzwoog-Lemburg, RP	former nuclear site of Battery C, 2d Battalion, 56th ADA: Nike Hercules withdrawn after 1983
***Schoeppingen, Nordr**	Team B, 509th Air Defense Artillery Det: nuclear warhead custodian for Dutch Air Force Nike Hercules unit
Schoenborn, RP	former nuclear site of Battery A, 5th Battalion, 6th ADA: Nike Hercules withdrawn after 1983
Schwabach, BadenW	nuclear-certified 155mm artillery battalion, 1st Armored Divison

***Schwaebisch-Gmuend, BadenW**	Bismarck Kaserne: HQ, 56th Field Artillery Bde: Pershing II • Hardt Kaserne: 1st Battalion, 41st Field Artillery: 36 Pershing II launchers, first Pershing II unit in Europe
***Schwabstadl, Bayern**	Schwabstadl Kaserne: 74th Field Artillery Det: nuclear warhead custodian to 1st West German Army Mountain Division
Schwanewede, Nieders	nuclear-certified West German Army 155mm artillery unit
Schweinfurt, Bayern	Ledward Barracks: 2 nuclear-certified 155mm artillery battalions, 3d Infantry Division
Schweinsburg, BadenW	Schweinsburg Range: Pershing missile training area
Seckenheim b. Mannheim, BadenW	Hammond Barracks: HQ, Central Army Group (CENTAG): NATO ground command for southern West Germany • HQ, ACE Allied Mobile Force (AMF): NATO multinational rapid deployment force
Sembach AB, RP	HQ, 17 Air Force: U.S. Air Force command for central Europe • hardened underground command center controlling offensive operations in the 4th ATAF sector • INFORM Net Station in stand-by status
***Sennelager, Nordr**	Dempsey Barracks: 22d Field Artillery Det: nuclear warhead custodian for British Army Lance missile unit
***Siegelsbach Heilbronn, BadenW**	Siegelsbach Ordnance Depot: 525th Ordnance Company: nuclear weapons support to V Corps
Siegenburg, Bayern	Air Force air-to-ground training range used for nuclear weapons training
Soegel	(see Lahn Ems/Soegel)
***Soest Hohnesee (Buecke), Nordr**	66th Air Defense Artillery Det: nuclear warhead storage site
***Spangdahlem AB, RP**	52d Tactical Fighter Wing: 72 nuclear-certified F-4E, some 150 bombs are stored on base • INFORM Net Station in stand-by status
Stadtallendorf, Hessen	nuclear-certified West German Army 155mm artillery unit
Stuttgart-Moehringen, BadenW	Kelly Barracks: HQ, VII Corps: command of U.S. Army units in southern West Germany
Stuttgart-Nellingen, BadenW	Nellingen Kaserne: 2d Corps Support Command: nuclear weapons logistic support to VII Corps
Stuttgart-Vaihingen, BadenW	Patch Barracks: HQ, European Command: senior U.S. military command in Europe, WWMCCS facilities include full access terminal supporting European Coordinator of Atomic Operations, Nuclear Ordnance Monitoring System reporting terminal, European airborne command center secondary ground terminal, Nuclear Capabilities Plan, Nuclear Contingency Planning System, and Nuclear Weapons Accounting System • Theater Mission Planning Center: one of three cruise missile targeting and planning centers in Europe
***Syke-Sorhausen, Nieders**	Team D, 51st Air Defense Artillery Det: nuclear warhead custodian for West German Air Force Nike Hercules unit
Sylt	Coast Guard LORAN-C Station: serving Norwegian Sea chain
Tauberbischofsheim, BadenW	nuclear-certified West German Army 8-inch artillery unit
***Tevren, Nordr**	Fliegerhorst Kaserne: 85th Field Artillery Det: nuclear warhead custodian for West German Air Force Pershing 1a missile unit
Thumberg, Nieders	nuclear-certified Belgian Air Force Nike Hercules unit, scheduled for retirement
Treebeck-Schinnen	communications tributary supporting nuclear weapons
***Treysa/Schwalmstadt, Hessen**	Hardtberg Kaserne: 7th Field Artillery Det: nuclear warhead custodian for West German Army artillery units
Vogelweh, RP	Kapaun Air Station: Det 6, 1st Space Wing: DSP satellite early warning system Simplified Processing System station[156]
***Voerden, Nieders**	NATO Kaserne: 509th Air Defense Artillery Det: nuclear warhead custodian for Dutch Air Force Nike Hercules units

***Wackernheim, RP**	McCulley Barracks: former nuclear site of Battery A, 2d Battalion, 1st ADA: Nike Hercules withdrawn since 1983 • 28th Ordnance Comapny: major nuclear weapons storage site
Wagenfeld-Forlingen, Nieders	nuclear-certified West German Air Force Nike Hercules unit
Waldbrol, Nordr	nuclear-certified West German Air Force Nike Hercules unit
***Waldheide/Heilbronn, BadenW**	Pershing missile training area
Walldurn, BadenW	nuclear-certified West German Army 155mm artillery unit
Warendorf-Westkirchen, Nordr	nuclear-certified West German Air Force Nike Hercules unit
Weiden, Bayern	nuclear-certified West German Army 155mm artillery unit
***Weilerbach, RP**	Weilerbach Storage Point: nuclear weapons storage facility of 41st Ordnance Company providing Pershing missile and warhead support
Wentorf, SchH	nuclear-certified West German Army 155mm artillery unit
***Werl, Nordr**	4th Field Artillery Det: nuclear warhead custodian for I Belgian Corps including 4 battalions of Lance, 155mm, and 8-inch artillery
Wertheim	Peden Barracks: HQ, 72d Field Artillery Bde, VII Corps Artillery: includes 1 nuclear-certified 8-inch artillery battalion in Wertheim
***Wesel, Nordr**	Schill Kaserne: 1st Field Artillery Det: nuclear warhead support custodian for West German Army Lance unit
***Westerscheps/Edewecht, Nieders**	Team C, 51st Air Defense Artillery Det: nuclear warhead support for West German Air Force Nike Hercules unit
Wetzlar, Hessen	nuclear-certified West German Army 155mm artillery unit
Wiesbaden, Hessen	Wiesbaden AB: 1st Battalion, 333d Field Artillery: 6 nuclear-capable Lance launchers • Lindsey Air Station: 1157th TOS, AFTAC: European HQ for coordinating nuclear test detection
***Wiesmoor-Hinrichsfehn, Nieders**	Team C, 35th Air Defense Artillery Det: nuclear warhead custodian for West German Air Force Nike Hercules unit
Wildeshausen, Nieders	nuclear-certified West German Army 155mm artillery unit
Wildflecken, Bayern	Camp Wildflecken: ADM unit
Worms, RP	Taukkunen Barracks: HQ, 3d Ordnance Bn: supervises all maintenance of Army nuclear missiles in Europe, including maintaining an "operational readiness float" of spare missiles and warheads at storage depots
Wuerzburg, Bayern	Leighton Barracks: HQ, 3d Infantry Division: nuclear units include artillery and ADMs
Wuescheim/Hasselbach, RP	designated as future ground-launched cruise missile main operating base, former nuclear site of Battery B, 5th Battalion, 6th ADA: Nike Hercules withdrawn in 1983
Wurmburg	(see Pforzheim)
Xanten, Nordr	nuclear-certified Belgian Air Force Nike Hercules unit, scheduled for retirement
Zirndorf/Nuernburg, Bayern	Pinder Barracks: HQ, 1st Armored Division Artillery: includes 2 nuclear-certified 155mm artillery battalions in Zirndorf
Zweibrucken AB, RP	INFORM Net Station

YAP ISLANDS, FEDERATED STATES OF MICRONESIA

A LORAN-C Station serving the northwest Pacific chain and operating as part of the "Clarinet Pilgrim" submarine communications system is operated on Gagil-Tomil Island.

NOTES TO APPENDIX A

1. U.S. Navy, "Naval Station Adak Organization Manual," Naval Station Adak Instruction 5450.6F (June 15, 1981), p. 41.
2. U.S. Air Force, "Operations: Alert Planning Factors and Procedures," Castle AFB (93d Bombardment Wing) Regulation 55–4, (July 15, 1981); HASC, FY 1982 Military Construction, p. 209.
3. U.S. Air Force, "Organization and Mission-Field: 16th Surveillance Squadron," Space Command Regulation 23–33 (June 6, 1983).
4. SAC, FY 1984 DOD, pt. 2, p. 840.
5. U.S. Air Force, "Nuclear Airlift Operations," vol. 2, Military Airlift Command (MAC) Regulation 55–18 (Jan. 29, 1981).
6. HASC, FY 1981 Military Construction, p. 168.
7. Air Force Systems Command, Western Space and Missile Center, Western Test Range, "Landbased Instrumentation Handbook," (July 1, 1981), p. 2–35.
8. U.S. Air Force, "Organization and Mission—Field: 7th Missile Warning Squadron," Space Command Regulation 23–37 (May 16, 1983); U.S. Air Force, "Operations: Alert Planning Factors and Procedures," 320th Bombardment Wing Regulation 55–1 (Jan. 3, 1983).
9. U.S. Navy, *RDT&E Management Guide*, NAVSO P-2457, (Dec. 15, 1979) (Washington, DC: USGPO, 1979), p. F-4.
10. U.S. Navy, "Naval Weapons Station Concord, Mission and Functions of," Naval Sea Systems Command (NAVSEA) Instruction 5450.10A (Nov. 16, 1978), p. 3.
11. HAC, FY 1981 Military Construction, pt. 1, p. 1673.
12. U.S. Army, "Organization and Functions Manual, 7th Infantry Division," Fort Ord Regulation 10–2 (March 13, 1979), p. 16–2.
13. HASC, FY 1981 DOE, p. 608.
14. SAC, FY 1984 DOD, pt. 2, p. 840.
15. U.S. Navy, "Naval Weapons Station Concord, Missions and Functions," NAVSEA Instruction 5450.10A, p. 3.
16. HASC, FY 1981 Military Construction, p. 168.
17. HAC, FY 1982 Military Construction, pt. 1, p. 1172.
18. U.S. Air Force, "Flying Training: Bombing and Gunnery Ranges," Strategic Air Command (SAC) Regulation 55–1 (Jan. 15, 1981).
19. U.S. Navy, "NWS Seal Beach; Mission and Functions of," NAVSEA Instruction 5450.9A (May 13, 1981).
20. HASC, FY 1975 Military Construction, p. 304.
21. U.S. Air Force, "Nuclear Airlift Operations," MAC Regulation 55–18.
22. U.S. Marine Corps, "Aircraft Configuration and Equipment Requirements for Weapons Training Unit Three (AWTU-3), Conventional and Nuclear Weapons Training Courses," 3d Marine Air Wing Order 1543.3 (Oct. 20, 1982).
23. U.S. Air Force, "Units, Organizations, and Functions of Strategic Air Command Units," SAC Regulation 23–9 (July 31, 1981), p. 6–2; Air Force Systems Command, "Landbased Instrumentation Handbook," p. 2–3; see also *Air Force Magazine* (May 1984), p. 189.
24. HASC, FY 1981 Military Construction, p. 112; Joint SAC/SASC, FY 1981 Military Construction, p. 510.
25. SAC, FY 1984 DOD, pt. 2, p. 840.
26. Tom Bartlett, "MB: Yellow Water, Florida," *Leatherneck* (June 1983), pp. 35–45.
27. HAC, FY 1981 Military Construction, pt. 1, p. 1677.
28. U.S. Navy, Office of the Comptroller, "Distribution of Manpower in the United States by State," NAVSO P-1385 (Sept. 30, 1983).
29. Ibid; U.S. Navy, "U.S. Forces Caribbean, Key West, Florida: Staff Organization and Regulations Manual," COMUSFORCARIB Instruction 5400.1A (Oct. 26, 1982).
30. U.S. Air Force, "Flying Training: Bombing and Gunnery Ranges," SAC Regulation 55–1.
31. U.S. Department of Defense (DOD), OASD/M-RAL, "MILSTRIP Routing Identifier and Distribution Codes," DOD Directive 4140.17-M, supp. no. 1 (June 1982).
32. Air Force Communications Command, (AFCC), "Organization and Mission-Field: 1957 Communications Group," Pacific Communications Division Regulation 23–20 (Jan. 29, 1982); U.S. Air Force, "Automated Weather Network Management," Air Weather Service (AWS) Regulation 105–23 (Aug. 1, 1983).
33. U.S. Navy, Commander Third Fleet, "COMTHIRDFLT Manual of Fleet Operating Areas, Including Target, Test and Special Use Areas," COMTHIRDFLT Instruction 3120.1L, Change 1 (Sept. 13, 1982), p. VII-27.
34. U.S. Navy, Office of the Comptroller, "Navy Comptroller Manual," NAVSO P-1000–25, vol. 2, ch. 5, rev. 47, (Aug. 22, 1983), p. 5–49.
35. Air Force Communications Command, "Organization and Mission- Field: 1957th Communications Group," Pacific Communications Division Regulation 23–20 (Jan. 29, 1982).
36. Ibid.
37. U.S. Air Force, "Operations: Alert Planning Factors and Procedures," Castle AFB Reg. 55–4.
38. *Air Force Magazine* (May 1983), p. 76.
39. HAC, FY 1985 Military Construction, pt. 5, p. 424; U.S. Navy Comptroller, "Distribution of Manpower in the United States by State," NAVSO P-1385 (Sept. 30, 1983).
40. U.S. Air Force, "Flying Training: Bombing and Gunnery Ranges," SAC Reg. 55–1.
41. Department of Defense (DOD), Under Secretary of Defense for Research and Engineering, "Major Range and Test Facility Base Summary of Capabilities," DOD Directive 3200.11D (June 1983).
42. HASC, FY 1979 DOD, pt. 3, Book 1, pp. 162–163.
43. U.S. Navy, "U.S. Naval Explosive Ordnance Disposal Technology Center Organization Manual; Promulgation of," NAVEODTECHCEN Instruction 5450.2C (Jan. 9, 1984), p. I-3.

44. U.S. Navy, *RDT&E Management Guide* (Washington, D.C.: USGPO, 1979), p. F-4.
45. U.S. Air Force, "Organization and Mission-Field: 6th Missile Warning Squadron," SPACECOM Regulation 23–36 (May 16, 1983).
46. Air Force Communications Command (AFCC), "Organization and Mission—Field: 1st Aerospace Communications Group," Strategic Communications Division (SCD) Regulation 23–2 (July 31, 1981).
47. U.S. Air Force, "Flying Training: Bombing and Gunnery Ranges," SAC Reg. 55–1.
48. HAC, FY 1984 DOD, pt. 3, p. 350; HASC, FY 1982 Military Construction, p. 209.
49. SAC, FY 1984 DOD, pt. 1, p. 305.
50. Air Force Communications Command, "Organization and Mission—Field: 1st Aerospace Communications Group," SCD Reg. 23–2; U.S. Air Force, "Units, Organizations, and Functions of Strategic Air Command Units," SAC Reg. 23–9, p. 13–1.
51. Air Force Communications Command, "Organization and Mission—Field: 1st Aerospace Communications Group," SCD Reg. 23–2.
52. Ibid.
53. U.S. Navy, "Naval Weapons Station, Earle; Mission and Functions of," NAVSEA Instruction 5450.8B (Nov. 16, 1978).
54. U.S. Air Force, "Nuclear Airlift Operations," MAC Reg. 55–18.
55. U.S. Army, "Communications-Electronics: Authorized Addresses for Electrically Transmitted Messages," Army Regulation 105–32 (June 1, 1979).
56. SAC, FY 1984 DOD, pt. 2, p. 840.
57. U.S. Air Force, "Nuclear Airlift Operations," MAC Reg. 55–18.
58. HASC, FY 1980 DOE, p. 120.
59. Air Force Communications Command, "Organization and Mission—Field: 2002d Communications Squadron," Airlift Communications Division Regulation 23–13 (April 28, 1982).
60. SASC, FY 1984 DOD, pt. 2, p. 611.
61. U.S. Navy, "Navy Comptroller Manual," NAVSO P-1000–25, p. 5–61.
62. Ibid., p. 5–60
63. U.S. Air Force, "Automated Weather Network Management," Air Weather Service (AWS) Reg. 105–23.
64. U.S. Navy, "Organization Manual," Naval Surface Weapons Center Instruction 5450.1A (Aug. 1978), reprinted September 6, 1983 to include changes, p. 42; HAC, FY 1982 Military Construction, pt. 1, p. 1139.
65. HASC, FY 1981 Military Construction, p. 436, 444.
66. U.S. Department of Defense (DOD) "MILSTRIP Routing Identifier and Distribution Codes," DOD Directive 4140.17-M.
67. U.S. Air Force, "Operations: Alert Planning Factors and Procedures," Castle AFB Reg. 55–4.
68. U.S. Navy, "COMTHIRDFLT Manual of Fleet Operating Areas, Including Target, Test, and Special Use Areas; Promulgation of," Commander Third Fleet Instruction 3120.1L (June 14, 1982), p.II-37.
69. U.S. Air Force, "Operations: Alert Planning Factors and Procedures," Castle AFB Reg. 55–4.
70. Joint SAC/SASC, FY 1981 Military Construction, p. 676.; U.S. Air Force, "Nuclear Airlift Operations," MAC Reg. 55–18.
71. HAC, FY 1985 DOD, pt. 3, p. 315.
72. U.S. Air Force, "Automated Weather Network Management," Air Weather Service (AWS) Reg. 105–23.
73. Senate Foreign Relations Committee, "East-West Relations: Focus on the Pacific, Hearing," 97th Cong., 2d Sess. (June 16, 1982), p. 58.
74. U.S. Navy, "U.S. Naval Communication Station Harold E. Holt; Mission and Function of," NAVTELCOM Instruction 5450.25C (Feb. 2, 1983).
75. *New York Times* (Dec. 13, 1978), p. 6.
76. HAC, FY 1981 DOD, pt. 2, p. 671.
77. Congressional Research Service (CRS), "United States Foreign Policy Objectives and Overseas Military Installations," Report prepared for the Senate Foreign Relations Committee, 96th Cong., 1st Sess. (April 1979).
78. U.S. Department of Defense (DOD), "MILSTRIP Routing Identifier and Distribution Codes," DOD Directive 4140.17-M; *NATO's 15 Nations*, (Special no. 2, 1979), p. 44; "Canada Sends Nuclear Arms Back to U.S.," *Chicago Tribune* (Nov. 17, 1984), p. 5.
79. Ibid.
80. U.S. Air Force, "Operations: Alert Planning Factors and Procedures," Change 1, Castle AFB Reg. 55–4 (Jan. 1982).
81. U.S. Department of Defense (DOD), "MILSTRIP Routing Identifier and Distribution Codes," DOD Directive 4140–17-M; *NATO's 15 Nations*, (Special no. 2, 1979), p. 44; HASC, "Continental Air Defense," Hearing no. 97–54, 97th Cong., 2d Sess. (July 22, 1981); "Canada Sends Nuclear Arms Back to U.S.," *Chicago Tribune* (Nov. 17, 1984), p. 5.
82. U.S. Air Force, "Air Force Directory of Unclassified Addresses," Air Force Manual 10–4 (June 1982).
83. Congressional Research Service, "U.S. Foreign Policy Objectives, Report."
84. Ibid.
85. U.S. Air Force, "Operations—Aircrew and Staff Procedures," 6th Strategic Wing Regulation 55–2 (Sept. 30, 1983).
86. SASC, FY 1983 DOD, pt. 7, p. 4710.
87. *Aviation Week & Space Technology* (Aug. 16, 1982), p. 77.
88. Defense Communications Agency, "DCA" (Dec. 1982).
89. HAC, FY 1984 Military Construction, pt. 1, p. 1390.
90. SAC, FY 1980 Military Construction, p. 105; Air Force Communications Command, "Organization and Mission—Field: 2140th Communications Group," European Communications Division (ECD) Regulation 23–32 (May 27, 1982).
91. Congressional Research Service, "U.S. Foreign

Policy Objectives", Report; Air Force Communications Command, "2140th Communications Group," ECD Regulation 23-32.
92. U.S. Navy, "U.S. Naval Communications Station Greece; Mission and Functions of," Naval Telecommunications Command (NAVTELCOM) Instruction 5450.10D (Sept. 2, 1982).
93. Air Force Communications Command "2140th Communications Group," ECD Regulation 23-32.
94. Ibid.
95. U.S. Navy, "Naval Communications Station Greece," NAVTELCOM Instruction 5450.10D; U.S. Air Force, "Automated Weather Network Management," Air Weather Service Reg. 105-23.
96. *Aviation Week & Space Technology* (Aug. 16, 1982), p. 77.
97. HASC, FY 1982 Military Construction, p. 209.
98. U.S. Navy, "NAS Agana, Guam, Organization Manual," Naval Air Station Agana Instruction 5451.44 (Aug. 17, 1982), p. xi-4; HASC, FY 1984 DOD, pt. 5, p. 525.
99. SAC, FY 1980 Military Construction, p. 177.
100. HAC, FY 1984 Military Construction, pt. 4, pp. 150-151.
101. Joint SASC/SAC, FY 1981 Military Construction, p. 106.
102. *Army Times* (June 9, 1980), p. 41; U.S. Army, "Southern European Task Force Telephone Directory" (Jan. 1, 1969); U.S. Army Europe (USAREUR), "USAREUR Activity Address File and Directory, USAREUR Regulation 55-5 (Feb. 1, 1977).
103. SAC, FY 1980 Military Construction, p. 105.
104. HASC, FY 1982 DOD, pt. 5, p. 178.
105. *Signal Magazine* (Dec. 1980).
106. U.S. Army, "Communications Command Japan, Organization and Functions Manual," Communications Command Japan Regulation 10-1 (June 10, 1981).
107. HASC, FY 1982 DOD, pt. 5, p. 178.
108. Air Force Communications Command, "Organization and Mission— Field: 1962d Communications Group," Pacific Communications Division Regulation 23-47 (June 25, 1982); U.S. Air Force, "Organization and Functions, HQ 313th AD and Assigned Units," Pacific Air Forces (PACAF), HQ, 313th Air Division Regulation 23-4 (Feb. 28, 1983); U.S. Air Force, "Alert Planning Factors and Procedures," 376th Strategic Wing Regulation 55-1 (May 13, 1983).
109. HAC, FY 1981 Military Construction, pt. 4, p. 579.
110. U.S. Air Force, "Automated Weather Network Management," Air Weather Service Reg. 105-23.
111. HASC, FY 1982 Military Construction, p. 209.
112. U.S. Navy, "Mission and Functions of Naval Communications Station Japan," NAVTELCOM Instruction 5450.14C (Jan. 26, 1981).
113. HASC, FY 1984 Military Construction, p. 379; HAC, FY 1985 Military Construction, pt. 3, p. 575.
114. SAC, FY 1980 Military Construction, p. 94.
115. Ibid.
116. HASC, FY 1981 Military Construction, p. 138.
117. Air Force Technical Applications Center (AFTAC), "Manpower: Headquarters Detachments and Operating Location Organization/-Support Policy and Guidance," AFTAC Regulation 26-2 (Oct. 30, 1981).
118. SASC, FY 1980 Military Construction, p. 292.
119. HASC, FY 1982 Military Construction, p. 209; U.S. Air Force, "Automated Weather Network Management," Air Weather Service Reg. 105-23; Air Force Communications Command, "Organization and Mission—Field: 1961st Communications Group," Pacific Communications Division Regulation 23-12 (Oct. 23, 1981).
120. U.S. Air Force, "Airspace/Range Management in the Philippines," 13th Air Force Regulation 55-2 (March 1, 1982).
121. U.S. Navy, "Designation of Restricted Areas," COMNAVBASE SUBIC Instruction 5510.3A (Oct. 19, 1976); U.S. Navy, "Organization Manual, U.S. NAS Cubi Point," Cubi Point Instruction 5451.1H (May 19, 1983).
122. U.S. Air Force, "Airspace/Range Management in the Philippines," 13th AF Reg. 55-2.
123. *Air Force Magazine* (May 1983), p. 97; HAC, FY 1983 Military Construction, pt. 4, p. 528; U.S. Air Force, "Automated Weather Network Management," Air Weather Service Reg. 105-23.
124. U.S. Navy, "Commander, U.S. Facility Subic Bay Oparea Manual," COMUSFACSUBIC Instruction 3500.1 (May 28, 1982).
125. Air Force, "Airspace/Range Management in the Philippines," 13th AF Reg. 55-2.
126. Air Force Communications Command, "Organization and Mission— Field: 1936th Communications Squadron," Airlift Communications Division (ACD) Regulation 23-6 (April 28, 1982).
127. SAC, FY 1980 Military Construction, p. 94.
128. Congressional Research Service, "U.S. Foreign Policy Objectives," Report, p. 52.
129. Naval Telecommunications Communications Command, "Mission and Functions of U.S. Naval Communcations Station Puerto Rico," NAVTELCOM Instruction 5450.26D (Aug. 24, 1982).
130. Ibid.
131. Ibid.
132. U.S. Department of Defense (DOD), "Major Range and Test Facility Base," DOD Directive 3200.11D.
133. HASC, FY 1983 Military Construction, p. 161.
134. HAC, FY 1982 DOD, pt. 5, p. 178.
135. Air Force Communications Command, "Organization and Mission— Field: 2146th Communications Group," Pacific Communications Division Regulation 23-45 (Jan. 1, 1982).
136. SAC, FY 1980 Military Construction, p. 105; HASC, FY 1982 DOD, pt. 5, p. 178.
137. Air Force Communications Command, "Organization and Mission— Field: 1989th Communications Group," European Communications Division (ECD) Regulation 23-35 (May 3, 1982).
138. HAC, FY 1981 Military Construction, pt. 1, p. 1610.
139. Air Force Communications Command, "1989th Communications Group," ECD Reg. 23-35.

140. SAC, FY 1980 Military Construction, p. 105.
141. U.S. Air Force, "Automated Weather Network Management," Air Weather Service Reg. 105–23.
142. Air Force Communications Command, "1989th Communications Group," ECD Reg. 23–35.
143. U.S. Air Force, "Automated Weather Network Management," Air Weather Service Reg. 105–23.
144. SAC, FY 1980 Military Construction, p. 105; Air Force Communications Command, "Organization and Mission—Field: HQ SCD Organization and Functions," Strategic Communications Division (SCD) Pamphlet 23–1 (Sept. 30, 1981).
145. U.S. Army Europe (USAREUR), "USAREUR Activity Address File and Directory," USAREUR Reg. 55–5; HAC, FY 1981 Military Construction, pt. 1, p. 991ff; Defense Nuclear Agency (DNA), "Nuclear Accident Response Capability Listing," (Aug. 1, 1979) (Kirtland AFB, N.M.: DNA Field Command, 1979); "528th U.S. Army Arty Gp," *Field Artillery Journal* (March/April 1983), p. 48.
146. SAC, FY 1980 Military Construction, p. 105.
147. HAC, FY 1981 Military Construction, pt. 1, p. 991ff; U.S. Army Europe (USAREUR), "USAREUR Activity Address File and Directory," USAREUR Reg. 55–5.
148. *Air Force Times* (Oct. 20, 1980).
149. HASC, FY 1982 Military Construction, p. 209; U.S. Air Force, "Automated Weather Network Management," Air Weather Service Reg. 105–23.
150. HASC, FY 1982 DOD, pt. 5, p. 179.
151. U.S. Air Force Europe, "HQ, USAFE Munitions Bulletin," (April 1983).
152. HASC, FY 1982 Military Construction, p. 209; U.S. Air Force, "Automated Weather Network Management," Air Weather Service Reg. 105–23.
153. U.S. Department of Defense (DOD), "Major Range and Test Facility Base," DOD Directive 3200.11D.
154. "Streamlining Airpower for Theater Warfare," *Air Force Magazine* (Feb. 1978), p. 29; Defense Communications Agency, "DCA" (December 1982).
155. Air Force Weapons Laboratory, "Organization and Functions Chart Book, AFWL" (Oct. 24, 1983) (Kirtland AFB, N.M.: AFWL, 1983), p. 16.
156. Space Command, "Organization and Mission—Field: Detachment 6, 1st Space Wing," SPACECOM Regulation 23–47 (June 6, 1983).

Appendix B

Soviet Nuclear Weapons Infrastructure

INSIDE THE SOVIET UNION

Location	*Organization and Activity*
Abakan, Siberian MD	FROG Bn, unidentified Motorized Rifle Division: 4 FROG launchers
Abalakovo, Siberian MD	Hen Roost phased-array early warning radar under construction near Krasnoyarsk, faces northeast Pacific, also performs attack characterization and spacetrack
Akhalkalaki, Trans-Caucaucasus MD	FROG Bn, unidentified Motorized Rifle Division: 4 FROG launchers • FROG Bn, 10th Motorized Rifle Division: 4 FROG launchers
Aktubinsk, Central Asian MD	HQ, 1st Army: unlocated SCUD Bde assigned
Alabino, Moscow MD	FROG Bn, 2d Motorized Rifle Divsion: 4 FROG launchers
Aleksandrovsk, Far East MD	LORAN-C type "Pulsed Phase Radio Navigation System" (PPRNS), part of the eastern USSR chain • Air Base: Soviet Naval Aviation, reportedly used for bomber deployments
***Alekseyevka AB, Far East MD**	Soviet Naval Aviation Backfire B Regt: one of four SNA regiments, planes delivered in 1980, supports Pacific Fleet
***Aleysk, Siberian MD**	SS-18 ICBM main operating base
Alma-Ata, Central Asian MD	HQ, Central Asian Military District: includes unidentified Air Army • FROG Bn, unidentified Motorized Rifle Division: 4 FROG launchers (possibly located in Otar)
Amderma, Leningrad MD	LF transmitter operating to the Kara Sea
Anadyr AB, Far East MD	one of five Arctic Control Group airbases for forward staging operations of long-range bombers
Andreapol AB, Moscow MD	PVO SU-15 Flagon air defense interceptor Regt of the Moscow Air Defense District
Angarsk, Transbaikal MD	Hen House ICBM/SLBM early warning phased-array radar
Aral Sea	nuclear weapons testing site
Arkhangel'sk, Leningrad MD	HQ, 6th Army: unlocated SCUD Bde assigned • FROG Bn, 77th Motorized Rifle Division: 4 FROG launchers (possibly at Iskagorka) • HQ, Arkhangel'sk Air Defense District, PVO: Kola Peninsula and Northern Fleet air defense • Air Base: possible staging base for long-range bombers (may be located at Olenegorsk) • VLF transmitter used for submarine communications to White and Barents Seas
Artemovsk, Kiev MD	FROG Bn, unidentified Tank Division: 4 FROG launchers
Arzamas, Moscow MD	possible nuclear weapons research and development laboratory
Ashkabad, Turkestan MD	FROG Bn, unidentified Motorized Rifle Division: 4 FROG launchers • unidentified Artillery Division: possible nuclear-capable artillery (may be at Bikrava)
Ayaguz, Central Asian MD	FROG Bn, 15th Tank Division: 4 FROG launchers
Azgir, Central Asian MD	nuclear weapons testing area
Babstovo/Khabarovsk, Far East MD	FROG Bn, 194th Motorized Rifle Division: 4 FROG launchers
Baikonur	(see Tyuratam)
Baklashi, Transbaikal MD	FROG Bn, unidentified Motorized Rifle Division: 4 FROG launchers
Baku, Transcaucasus MD	HQ, 4th Army: unlocated SCUD Bde assigned • FROG Bn, 216th Motorized Rifle Division: 4 FROG launchers • former Air Defense District HQ, one of two former principal air defense HQ, disbanded in 1980–81
Baltiysk, Baltic MD	HQ, Baltic Fleet: homeport for cruisers, destroyers, cruise and ballistic missile submarines
Barabash/Kraskino, Far East MD	FROG Bn, 17th Motorized Rifle Division: 4 FROG launchers

Barnaul, Siberian MD	possible SS-20 IRBM base
Batumi, Transcaucasus MD	FROG Bn, unidentified Motorized Rifle Division: 4 FROG launchers • VLF transmitter for submarine communications to Black and Mediterranean Seas
Belaya Tserkov, Kiev MD	FROG Bn, 72d Motorized Rifle Division: 4 FROG launchers
***Belaya AB, Transbaikal MD**	Backfire Regt, Long Range Aviation: first introduced in 1978, Far East missions, near Usol'ye Sibirskoye
Belograd-Dnestrovskiy, Odessa MD	FROG Bn, unidentified Motorized Rifle Division: 4 FROG launchers
Belogorsk, Far East MD	HQ, unidentified Army: unlocated SCUD Bde assigned • possible Motorized Rifle Division (possibly in Svobodnyy)
Beloyarsk, Siberian MD	possible plutonium production facility
Beltsy, Odessa MD	FROG Bn, 33d Motorized Rifle Division: 4 FROG launchers
Berdichev, Carpathian MD	FROG Bn, 117th Tank Division: 4 FROG launchers
Bezhetsk AB, Moscow MD	PVO SU-15 Flagon air defense interceptor Regt of the Moscow Air Defense District
Bezrechnaya, Transbaikal MD	FROG Bn, unidentified Motorized Rifle Division: 4 FROG launchers
Bikrava	(see Ashkabad)
Birobidzhan, Far East MD	FROG Bn, unidentified Motorized Rifle Division: 4 FROG launchers • unidentified Artillery Division: possible nuclear-capable artillery
Biysk, Siberian MD	missile production factory, possibly affiliated with Nadiradize Design Bureau • solid motor and explosive production, largest producer of solid propellant for missiles • FROG Bn, 23d Motorized Rifle Division: 4 FROG launchers
Blagoveshchensk, Far East MD	FROG Bn, unidentified Motorized Rifle Division: 4 FROG launchers
***Bobruysk, Belorussian MD**	HQ, 5th Tank Army: unlocated SCUD Bde assigned • FROG Bn, 22d Tank Division: 4 FROG launchers • Bobruysk AB: Badger Regt of Smolensk Air Army, equipped with nuclear air-to-suface missiles
Bolgrad, Odessa MD	FROG Bn, 98th Motorized Rifle Division: 4 FROG launchers
Borisov, Belorussian MD	HQ, 7th Tank Army: unlocated SCUD Bde assigned • FROG Bn, 2d Motorized Rifle Division: 4 FROG launchers • FROG Bn, 34th Tank Division: 4 FROG launchers • FROG Bn, 47th Tank Division: 4 FROG launchers
Borisovskiy AB, Moscow MD	PVO Mig-25 Foxbat air defense interceptor Regt of the Moscow Air Defense District
Borzya, Transbaikal MD	FROG Bn, unidentified Motorized Rifle Division: 4 FROG launchers
Brest, Belorussian MD	FROG Bn, 50th Motorized Rifle Division: 4 FROG launchers • unidentified Artillery Division: possible nuclear-capable artillery
Bryansk, Moscow MD	Bryansk Zone (South), Moscow Air Defense District, PVO • LORAN-C type "Pulsed Phase Radio Navigation System" (PPRNS), part of the western USSR chain
Buyanksk, North Caucasus MD	4th Artillery Division: possible nuclear-capable artillery
***Byhkov AB, Belorussian MD**	Soviet Naval Aviation: 2 Backfire Regts supporting Northern Fleet, two of four Backfire regiments supporting the Navy
Charbarsovil, Far East MD	HQ, unidentified Air Army
Chebarkul, Ural MD	FROG Bn, unidentified Motorized Rifle Division: 4 FROG launchers
Chekhov, Moscow MD	unknown type ABM support radar, often referred to as "Chekhov" radar
***Chelyabinsk, Ural MD**	"Chelyabinsk 40:" reportedly main production and final assembly and disassembly facility for nuclear warheads, equivalent of U.S. PANTEX Plant in Amarillo, Texas
Cherkassy, Kiev MD	FROG Bn, 18th Tank Division: 4 FROG launchers

Chernigov, Kiev MD	HQ, 1st Tank Army: unlocated SCUD Bde assigned • FROG Bn, unidentified Motorized Rifle Division: 4 FROG launchers
Chernovtsy, Carpathian MD	FROG Bn, 66th Motorized Rifle Division: 4 FROG launchers
Chernyakhovsk AB, Baltic MD	nuclear-capable SU-24 Fencer Regt • also reportedly Soviet Naval Aviation TU-22 Blinder Regt, near Kaliningrad
***Chita, Transbaikal MD**	HQ, Far East Theater of Military Operations (TVD): responsible for Soviet forces in Far East, Transbaikal, Siberian and Central Asian MDs, as well as forces in Mongolia • HQ, Theater Air Defense District: newly established in 1982–1983 • HQ, Transbaikal Military District • HQ, unidentified Air Army • FROG Bn, 49th Tank Division: 4 FROG launchers • SRF Army intermediate HQ: 40–120 missiles assigned, controlling SS-20s • possible SS-20 IRBM main operating base
Chuguyev, Kiev MD	FROG Bn, 75th Tank Division: 4 FROG launchers
Dauriya, Transbaikal MD	FROG Bn, unidentified Motorized Rifle Division: 4 FROG launchers
***Derazhnya, Carpathian MD**	SS-19 ICBM main operating base at former SS-11 ICBM base • possible SS-20 IRBM main base
Dikson Ostrov, Siberian MD	VLF/LF transmitter used for long-range submarine communications to Arctic Ocean and Kara Sea
Dnepropetrovsk, Kiev MD	HQ, unidentified Tank Army: unlocated SCUD Bde assigned • SS-17 ICBM and SS-18 ICBM missile production facilities, possibly affiliated with the Yangel Design Bureau
Dobele, Baltic MD	FROG Bn, 24th Tank Division: 4 FROG launchers
Dodonovo, Siberian MD	reportedly one of three primary plutonium production facilities supporting nuclear weapons
Dolinsk-Sokol AB, Far East MD	SU-15 Flagon air defense interceptor Regt of the Far East Theater Air Defense District: home of the aircraft that shot down Korean Air Lines Flight 007 in 1983
***Dombarovskiy, Volga MD**	SS-18 ICBM main operating base
***Drovyanaya, Transbaikal MD**	SS-20 IRBM main operating base • SS-11 ICBM main operating base
Dushanbe, Central Asian MD	FROG Bn, 201st Motorized Rifle Division: 4 FROG launchers (possibly located in Frunze)
Dvina Gulf, Severodvinsk, Leningrad MD	shipyard building nuclear powered submarines, including November, Oscar, Yankee, Delta, and Typhoon classes
Dzambul, Central Asian MD	SRF Army intermediate HQ: formerly controlling SS-4 missiles (since retired), now controlling SS-20s
Dzemgi, Far East MD	FROG Bn, unidentified Motorized Rifle Division: 4 FROG launchers (possibly located in Kharborovsk)
Dzhusaly, Central Asian MD	satellite tracking station operated by SRF
Dzul'fa, Transcaucasus MD	FROG Bn, 75th Motorized Rifle Division: 4 FROG launchers
Evpatoria	(see Yevpatoria)
Fastov, Kiev MD	unidentified Artillery Division: possible nuclear-capable artillery
Feodosiya, Odessa MD	FROG Bn, 128th Motorized Rifle Division: 4 FROG launchers • submarine base, Black Sea fleet
***Gladkaya, Siberian MD**	SS-11 ICBM main operating base
Gor'kiy, Moscow MD	Gor'kiy Zone (East), Moscow Air Defense District, PVO • VLF transmitter used for worldwide submarine communications • shipyard building submarines, including Juliett, Charlie, and Papa cruise missile classes • FROG Bn, 15th Tank Division: 4 FROG launchers (possibly in Kovrov)
Gorodok AB, Carpathian MD	nuclear-capable SU-24 Fencer Regt

Grodno, Belorussian MD	HQ, 28th Army: unlocated SCUD Bde assigned
Groznyy, North Caucasus MD	FROG Bn, 24th Motorized Rifle Division: 4 FROG launchers
Guardeskoye	(see Oktyabirskoye AB)
Gusev (Gumbinnen), Baltic MD	FROG Bn, 26th Motorized Rifle Division: 4 FROG launchers
Gusmooresk, Transbaikal MD	FROG Bn, unidentified Motorized Rifle Division: 4 FROG launchers
Iliysk AB, Central Asian MD	nuclear-capable SU-24 Fencer Regt
***Imeni Gastello, Central Asian MD**	SS-18 ICBM main operating base
***Iokanga, Leningrad MD**	submarine base, Northern Fleet: reportedly homeport for new Typhoon missile submarines, located on the Kola Peninsula
***Irkutsk, Transbaikal MD**	HQ, Irkutsk Air Army: controls Backfire, Badger, Bear, and Bison long-range aviation bombers • Backfire Regt • FROG Bn, unidentified Motorized Rifle Division: 4 FROG launchers • missile impact area for testing from Kapustin Yar • Hen House ICBM/SLBM early warning phased-array radar (at Angarsk) • satellite tracking station operated by SRF
Itatka, Siberian MD	former SS-11 ICBM main operating base • FROG Bn, unidentified Motorized Rifle Division: 4 FROG launchers (possibly located in Tumen)
Ivano-Frankovsk, Carpathian MD	HQ, 38th Army: unlocated SCUD Bde assigned • FROG Bn, 70th Motorized Rifle Division: 4 FROG launchers
Izyaslav, Carpathian MD	FROG Bn, unidentified Motorized Rifle Division: 4 FROG launchers (possibly located in Uzhgorod)
Jonava, Baltic MD	FROG Bn, unidentified Motorized Rifle Division: 4 FROG launchers
Jurja	(see Yurya)
***Kaliningrad, Baltic MD**	Baltic Fleet submarine base: homeport of Golf II class with SS-N-5 missiles • HQ, Soviet Naval Aviation Baltic • VLF/LF transmitter operating worldwide and to Baltic and North Seas • HQ, 11th Army: unlocated SCUD Bde assigned • FROG Bn, 1st Tank Division: 4 FROG launchers • FROG Bn, 1st Motorized Rifle Division: 4 FROG launchers • unidentified Artillery Division: possible nuclear-capable artillery • HQ, 30th Air Army: status unknown • possible SS-4 IRBM and SS-20 IRBM main operating bases
Kalinkovichi, Belorussian MD	possible SS-20 IRBM main operating base
Kalinin, Moscow MD	unidentified Artillery Division: possible nuclear-capable artillery • satellite and space operations ground control center: one of two principal centers
Kamen-Rybolov, Far East MD	FROG Bn, 29th Motorized Rifle Division: 4 FROG launchers
Kamenskaya-Bugskaya, Carpathian MD	26th Artillery Division: possible nuclear-capable artillery
Kamyshlov, Ural MD	FROG Bn, unidentified Tank Division: 4 FROG launchers
Kandalaksha, Leningrad MD	FROG Bn, unidentified Motorized Rifle Division: 4 FROG launchers
Kapustin Yar, North Caucasus MD	ICBM missile testing range: used for short- and medium-range ballistic and cruise missiles, impact at Irkutsk and Sary Shagan • ABM research and test site supporting Sary Shagan
Karaganda, Central Asian MD	FROG Bn, unidentified Motorized Rifle Division: 4 FROG launchers (possibly located in Os')
***Kartaly, Ural MD**	SS-18 ICBM main operating base
Kazan, Volga MD	FROG Bn, 96th Motorized Rifle Division: 4 FROG launchers • Kazan North military airfield: used for technical support, near the Tupolov plant which produces Backfire bombers

Khabarovsk, Far East MD	HQ, Far East Military District • HQ, unidentified Air Army, status unknown • SRF intermediate Army HQ: controlls ICBMs and IRBMs (see Babstovo)
Khmel'nitskiy, Carpathian MD	FROG Bn, 17th Motorized Rifle Division: 4 FROG launchers
Kholmsk, Far East MD	LF transmitter, operating to Seas of Japan and Okhotsk
Khyshtym, Ural MD	plutonium fabrication and reprocessing plant, part of the nuclear weapons production complex, near site of 1958 accident
Kiev, Kiev MD	HQ, Theater Air Defense District: newly established in 1982–1983 • HQ, Kiev Military District • HQ, 17th Air Army • SLBM early warning phased-array radar built in the late 1970s • long-range OTH radar system nearby, facing southeast toward Chinese ICBM fields
***Kirov, Ural MD**	SRF intermediate Army HQ: controls 40–120 ICBMs and IRBMs • SS-20 IRBM main operating base
Kirovabad, Transcaucasus MD	FROG Bn, 31st Motorized Rifle Division: 4 FROG launchers
Kirovakan, Transcaucasus MD	FROG Bn, 26th Motorized Rifle Division: 4 FROG launchers
Kishinev, Odessa MD	HQ, 19th Army: unlocated SCUD Bde assigned
Kizyl-Arvat, Turkestan MD	FROG Bn, unidentified MRD: 4 FROG launchers
Klaipeda, Baltic MD	FROG Bn, unidentified Motorized Rifle Division: 4 FROG launchers
***Klin, Moscow MD**	Galosh ABM-1B missile complex: 2 launcher sites with 8 missiles each
Klyuchi, Far East MD	impact site on Kamchatka Peninsula for missile tests from Plesetsk, Tyuratam, the Barents Sea, and the White Sea (Nenoksa)
Kolpashevo, Siberian MD	satellite tracking station operated by SRF
***Komsomolsk-Na-Amure, Far East MD**	VLF transmitter used for communications and navigation, one of three stations in Omega-type network * FROG Bn, 73d Motorized Rifle Division: 4 FROG launchers • possible SS-20 IRBM main operating base • shipyard building ballistic missile submarines including Delta I, Golf, Yankee classes • OTH radar system (opposite Sakhalin Island) pointing northeast toward U.S. ICBM fields • SLBM early warning radar, possibly Hen Roost type, built in the late 1970s, facing southeast
Konotop, Kiev MD	FROG Bn, 7th Motorized Rifle Division: 4 FROG launchers
Kopu, Baltic MD	possible SS-20 IRBM main operating base
Korsakov, Far East MD	Korsakov AB: Soviet Naval Aviation nuclear-capable IL-38 May and Mail ASW aircraft • minor Pacific Fleet naval base located on Sakhalin Island
***Kostroma, Moscow MD**	SS-11 ICBM main operating base • SS-17 ICBM main operating base
Kotlas South AB, Leningrad MD	PVO Mig-25 Foxbat interceptor Regt of the Moscow Air Defense District
Kovel, Carpathian MD	unidentified Artillery Division: possible nuclear-capable artillery
Kovrov, Moscow MD	FROG Bn, unidentified Motorized Rifle Division: 4 FROG launchers (possibly located in Kursk) (see Gorkiy)
***Kozelsk, Moscow MD**	SS-11 ICBM main operating base • SS-19 ICBM main operating base
Kraskino	(see Barabash)
Krasnodar, North Caucasus MD	VLF transmitter: used for worldwide communications, also one of three stations in Omega-type radio navigation network
Krichev AB, Moscow MD	PVO Mig-25 Foxbat interceptor Regt of the Moscow Air Defense District
Krivoy Rog, Kiev MD	FROG Bn, 20th Tank Division: 4 FROG launchers
Kuybyshev, Volga MD	HQ, Volga Military District • FROG BN, 43d Motorized Rifle Division: 4 FROG launchers
Kuntsevo, Moscow MD	reported command post (underground) and airfield serving national level and SRF airborne command centers

Kursk East AB, Moscow MD	PVO Mig-23 Flogger interceptor Regt of Moscow Air Defense District (see also Kovrov)
Kushka, Turkestan MD	FROG Bn, unidentified Motorized Rifle Division: 4 FROG launchers
Kutaisi, Transcaucasus MD	HQ, 45th Army: unlocated SCUD Bde assigned • unidentified Artillery Division: possible nuclear-capable artillery
Kyakhta, Transbaikal MD	FROG Bn, 6th Tank Division: 4 FROG launchers
Kyzyl-kum Desert	reported launch site for ICBM tests
Leninakan, Transcaucasus MD	unidentified Artillery Division: possible nuclear-capable artillery • FROG Bn, 261st Motorized Rifle Division: 4 FROG launchers
Leningrad, Leningrad MD	HQ, Baltic Fleet: major shipyards and naval research and development activities, primarily for building destroyers and cruisers, some submarines • FROG Bn, 2d Tank Division: 4 FROG launchers • (Leningrad Military District and 13th Air Army HQ are located in Petrozavodsk)
Lenkoran, Transcaucasus MD	FROG Bn, 6th Motorized Rifle Division: 4 FROG launchers
Leonidovo, Far East MD	FROG Bn, 79th Motorized Rifle Division: 4 FROG launchers (located on Sakhalin Island)
Lepel, Belorussian MD	FROG Bn, 3d Tank Division: 4 FROG launchers
Lermontovka, Far East MD	FROG Bn, unidentified Motorized Rifle Division: 4 FROG launchers
Lesozavodsk, Far East MD	FROG Bn, unidentified Motorized Rifle Division: 4 FROG launchers
Liepaja, Baltic MD	Naval base: homeport for Golf II missile submarines assigned to the Baltic Fleet
Lipetsk, Moscow MD	reportedly alternate military command center for strategic forces
Litsa, Leningrad MD	submarine base, Northern Fleet
Lubny, Kiev MD	FROG Bn, unidentified Motorized Rifle Division: 4 FROG launchers
Lugansk, Kiev MD	FROG Bn, 4th Motorized Rifle Division: 4 FROG launchers (possibly located in Vorishilovgrad)
Lvov, Carpathian MD	HQ, Carpathian Military District • HQ, 57th Air Army • FROG Bn, 24th Motorized Rifle Division: 4 FROG launchers • ground satellite link for Washington-Moscow Direct Communciations Link ("Hot Line")
Lyaki, Transcaucasus MD	Hen Roost ICBM/SLBM early warning phased-array radar built in the late 1970s
Magadan, Far East MD	minor submarine base, Pacific Fleet
Magdagachi, Far East MD	former SS-4 IRBM base
Mariina-Gorka, Belorussian MD	FROG Bn, 8th Tank Division: 4 FROG launchers
Matotchkin Shar, Far East MD	VLF transmitter used for long-range submarine communications to Barents and Norwegian Seas (located on Novaya Zemlya Island)
Maykop, North Caucasus MD	FROG Bn, 9th Motorized Rifle Division: 4 FROG launchers
Mikhalevka, Kiev MD	Hen Roost ICBM/SLBM early warning phased-array radar built in the late 1970s
Mikhachkala, North Caucasus MD	4th Artillery Division: possible nuclear-capable artillery
Minsk, Belorussian MD	HQ, Belorussian Military District • HQ, 1st Air Army • FROG Bn, 120th Motorized Rifle Division: 4 FROG launchers • Hen House ICBM/SLBM early warning radar
Mirnaya, Transbaikal MD	FROG Bn, unidentified Motorized Rifle Division: 4 FROG launchers
Morshansk AB, Moscow MD	PVO SU-15 Flagon interceptor Regt of the Moscow Air Defense District

Moscow, Moscow MD	national military command center (alternate at Lipetsk), probably housing the Moscow link in the Moscow-Washington DCL ("Hot Line") • HQ, Strategic Rocket Forces • HQ, Air Force • HQ, Navy: operational command center for ballistic missile submarines • HQ, PVO, the PVO underground national command center is reported to be 50 kilometers from Moscow • HQ, Moscow Air Defense District, one of five principal Theater Air Defense HQs • HQ, Moscow Okrug Military District • HQ, 36th Air Army (Long Range Aviation)/"Moscow Air Army": controls 4 Bear and Bison bomber bases (3 in Ukraine, 1 in Far East) and 5 Arctic Control Group bases • 4 complexes of Galosh ABM-1B missiles (8 missiles per launch site) are located in a ring around Moscow, about 45 miles from its center • three radar types support the ABM complex: Dog House, Cat House and Try Add • Kurchatov Institute: nuclear weapons research and development center • Lebedev Physics Institute: performs X-ray laser research development
***Mozyr, Belorussian MD**	possiblc SS-20 IRBM main operating base
Mukachevo, Carpathian MD	FROG Bn, 128th Motorized Rifle Divisoin: 4 FROG launchers
Murmansk, Leningrad MD	FROG Bn, 45th Motorized Rifle Division: 4 FROG launchers (possibly located in Pechenga) • main naval bases often referred to as Murmansk are actually at Iokanga, Severomorsk, and Polyarnyy
Mys-Schmidta AB, Far East MD	one of five Arctic Control Group staging bases for long-range bombers
Mys Zhelaniya, Far East MD	LF transmitter operating to Arctic Ocean (located on Novaya Zemlya Island)
Nakhichevan, Transcaucasus MD	FROG Bn, 75th Motorized Rifle Division: 4 FROG launchers
Nakhodka, Far East MD	minor submarine and frigate base of the Pacific Fleet
Naro-Fominsk, Moscow MD	FROG Bn, 4th Tank Division: 4 FROG launchers • unidentified PARCS type radar for tracking and attack characterization
Naushki, Transbaikal MD	unidentified Artillery Division: possible nuclear-capable artillery
Nenoksa, Leningrad MD	SLBM launch test site 20 miles west of Severodvinsk, impact areas at Klyuchi and on Taymyr peninsula, used for SS-NX-20 SLBM development
Nikolayev, Odessa MD	FROG Bn, 92d Motorized Rifle Division: 4 FROG launchers • reportedly long-range OTH early warning radar • shipbuilding center building Kiev-class carriers, cruisers, destroyers, and smaller ships
Nizhneudinsk, Transbaikal MD	FROG Bn, unidentified Motorized Rifle Division: 4 FROG launchers
Novaya Zemlya Island Leningrad MD	active nuclear weapons testing area: underground explosions are set off in two locations
Novgorod, Leningrad MD	Hen House ICBM/SLBM early warning radar
Novocherkassk, North Caucasus MD	FROG Bn, unidentified Tank Division: 4 FROG launchers (possibly located in Uryupinsk)
Novograd-Volynskiy, Carpathian MD	FROG Bn, 13th Tank Division: 4 FROG launchers
Novo-Kazalinsk, Central Asian MD	satellite tracking or ground station operated by SRF
Novomoskovsk, Kiev MD	unidentified Artillery Division: possible nuclear-capable artillery
***Novopetrovskoye, Moscow MD**	Galosh ABM-1B missile complex with two launcher sites, each with 8 missiles
Novorossiysk, North Caucasus MD	FROG Bn, 73d Motorized Rifle Division: 4 FROG launchers
***Novosibirsk, Siberian MD**	HQ, Siberian Military District • HQ, unidentified Air Army • nuclear weapons production facility: components production and research • FROG Bn, unidentified Motorized Rifle Division: 4 FROG launchers • VLF transmitter: used for communications worldwide, also one of three stations

	in Omega-type radionavigation network • SS-20 IRBM main operating base • unidentified satellite tracking or ground station
Odessa, Odessa MD	HQ, Odessa Military District • HQ, 5th Air Army • FROG Bn, unidentified Motorized Rifle Division: 4 FROG launchers • VLF/LF transmitter operating worldwide and to the Black Sea area
***Oktyabirskoye AB, Odessa MD**	Soviet Naval Aviation Backfire Regt: one of four active Navy regiments, supports the Black Sea Fleet
***Olenegorsk, Leningrad MD**	Hen House ICBM/SLBM early warning radar • new phased-array radar under construction • Olenegorsk AB: Soviet Naval Aviation Bear-D ASW Regt supporting Northern Fleet • Arctic Control Group forward staging base, frequently visited by Backfire bombers
Olenek, Transbaikal MD	probable bomber base or bomber dispersal base
Olenya, Leningrad MD	submarine base, Northern Fleet
Olga, Far East MD	minor naval base of Pacific Fleet
***Olovyannaya, Transbaikal MD**	SS-11 ICBM main operating base • SS-20 IRBM main operating base
***Omsk, Siberian MD**	SRF Army intermediate HQ • SS-20 IRBM main operating base • FROG Bn, unidentified Tank Division: 4 FROG launchers
Orenburg, Volga MD	SRF Army intermediate HQ
Ordzhonikidze, North Caucasus MD	FROG Bn, unidentified Motorized Rifle Division: 4 FROG launchers
Osipovici, Belorussian MD	3d Artillery Division: possible nuclear-capable artillery
Otar	(see Alma-Ata)
Ovruch, Carpathian MD	FROG Bn, 23d Tank Division: 4 FROG launchers
Paldiski, Baltic MD	reportedly base for Golf II missile submarines of the Baltic Fleet
Pargolova, Leningrad MD	FROG Bn, 37th Motorized Rifle Division: 4 FROG launchers
Pavlograd, Kiev MD	rocket test facility used in SS-X-26 ICBM testing program
Pechenga	(see Murmansk)
Pechora, Ural MD	Hen Roost ICBM/SLBM early warning phased-array radar, facing the Arctic Ocean
Pereval Kurday, Central Asia MD	FROG Bn, 8th Motorized Rifle Division: 4 FROG launchers
***Perm, Ural MD**	SS-11 ICBM main operating base
***Pervomaysk, Odessa MD**	SS-19 ICBM main operating base at former SS-11 main operating base
***Petropavlovsk, Far East MD**	7th Squadron: main submarine base located in Taliniskaia Bay, homeport for 75% of the submarines in the Pacific Fleet, including Delta I/III, Yankee I classes • VLF transmitter used for long-range submarine communications worldwide, LF to Sea of Okhotsk and Bering Sea • LORAN-C type "Pulsed Phase Radio Navigation System" (PPRNS), part of the eastern USSR chain • satellite ground tracking station operated by SRF • FROG Bn, 22d Motorized Rifle Division: 4 FROG launchers (possibly located in Svobodnyy) • AB: PVO SU-15 Flagon Regt of the Far East Theater Air Defense District • (see also Sebuchar)
Petrozavodsk, Leningrad MD	HQ, Leningrad Military District • HQ, 13th Air Army • HQ, 6th Army: unlocated SCUD Bde assigned • LORAN-C type "Pulsed Phase Radio Navigation System" (PPRNS), part of the western USSR chain
Plesetsk, Leningrad MD	major missile test center, including launch complexes for satellites • ICBM test launch site with impact areas at Klyuchi and in the Sea of Okhotsk, used for crew training and operational testing, reportedly contains five new silos for 5th generation SS-X-24 and SS-X-26 ICBMs, and SS-X-25 mobile ICBM, launchers probably have an operational capability • missile production facility, possibly a part of the Chelomei design bureau

Pogranichnyy, Far East MD	FROG Bn, unidentified Tank Division: 4 FROG launchers (location uncertain, possibly Pogranichnaya) • FROG Bn, unidentified Motorized Rifle Division: 4 FROG launchers (possibly located in Sergeyevka)
Pokrovka, Far East MD	unidentified Artillery Division: possible nuclear-capable artillery
***Polotsk, Belorussian MD**	SS-20 IRBM main operating base • FROG Bn, unidentified Motorized Rifle Division: 4 FROG launchers
***Polyarnyy, Leningrad MD**	major submarine base of Northern Fleet: homeport for Yankee I, Delta I/II/III, Hotel III, and Golf III missile submarines
Poronaysk, Sakhalin Island, Far East MD	FROG Bn, 79th Motorized Rifle Division: 4 FROG launchers • Artillery Division: possible nuclear-capable artillery
***Postavy, Belorussian MD**	SS-20 IRBM main operating base
Pravdinsk AB, Moscow MD	PVO Mig-25 Foxhound-A interceptor Regt of the Moscow Air Defense District
Priozersk, Leningrad MD	FROG Bn, 64th Motorized Rifle Division: 4 FROG launchers (possibly located in Sapernaya)
Provideniya, Far East MD	LF transmitter operating to the Bering Sea • AB: possible Badger Regt and dispersal base
Pushkin, Leningrad MD	unidentified Artillery Division: possible nuclear-capable artillery
Pushkino, Moscow MD	"Pushkino" four face, 360-degree phased-array radar, part of the Moscow ABM system
Ramenskoye AB, Moscow MD	strategic aircraft test center, site of first observation of the Blackjack bomber
Raychikinsk, Far East MD	FROG Bn, unidentified Motorized Rifle Division: 4 FROG launchers
Riga, Baltic MD	HQ, 30th Air Army (status unknown)
Rostov, North Caucasus Md	HQ, North Caucasus Military District • VLF transmitter used for worldwide naval communications
Rovno, Carpathian MD	HQ, 13th Army: unlocated SCUD Bde assigned
Rzhev, Moscow MD	Rzhev Zone (West), Moscow Air Defense District, PVO
Saki AB, Odessa MD	Soviet Naval Aviation TU-22 Blinder Regt: supports Black Sea Fleet
Samarkand, Turkestan MD	FROG Bn, unidentified Motorized Rifle Division: 4 FROG launchers
Samtredia, South Caucasus MD	Samtredia East AB: nuclear-capable SU-24 Fencer Regt, located near Turkey
Sapernaya	(see Priozersk)
Sary Ozek, Central Asia MD	FROG Bn, unidentified Motorized Rifle Division: 4 FROG launchers
Sary Shagan, Central Asian MD	ABM and space research, development, and test facility • phased-array tracking and early warning radars
Sayda, Leningrad MD	submarine base, Northern Fleet
Sebuchar, Far East MD	FROG Bn, unidentified Motorized Rifle Division: 4 FROG launchers • FROG Bn, unidentified Tank Division: 4 FROG launchers
***Semipalatinsk, Central Asia MD**	nuclear weapons research, development, and test facility, including silos for ICBM testing • SS-20 IRBM main operating base • HQ, 1st Army: unlocated SCUD Bde assigned • unidentified Artillery Division: possible nuclear-capable artillery • FROG Bn, 165th Motorized Rifle Division: 4 FROG launchers (possibly located in Ust-Kamenogorsk)
Sergeyevka	(see Pogranichnyy)
Sevastopol, Odessa MD	HQ, Black Sea Fleet: main naval and submarine base
Severodvinsk, Leningrad MD	large shipyard for construction of ballistic missile submarines, including Delta and Typhoon classes
Severo Kuril'sk, Far East MD	LF transmitter operating to the Seas of Japan and Okhotsk

***Severomorsk, Leningrad MD**	HQ, Northern Fleet: major naval base, one of possibly three ballistic missile submarine bases supporting Northern Fleet (see also Polyarnyy and Iokanga) • naval armaments storage • VLF/LF transmitter operating worldwide and to the Arctic Ocean
Shadrinsk, Ural MD	former SS-11 ICBM main operating base
Simferopol, Odessa MD	FROG Bn, 126th Motorized Rifle Division: 4 FROG launchers • satellite tracking station operated by SRF • LORAN-C type "Pulse Phase Radio Navigation System" (PPRNS), part of the western USSR chain
Skopin, Moscow MD	unidentified Artillery Division: possible nuclear-capable artillery
Skrunda, Baltic MD	unidentified ICBM early warning radar
Slavuta, Carpathian MD	FROG Bn, unidentified Motorized Rifle Division: 4 FROG launchers
Slavyanka, Far East MD	unidentified Artillery Division: possible nuclear-capable artillery
Slonim, Belorussian MD	FROG Bn, unidentified Tank Division: 4 FROG launchers • LORAN-C type "Pulse Phase Radio Navigation System" (PPRNS), part of the western USSR chain
Slutsk, Belorussian MD	FROG Bn, 29th Tank Division: 4 FROG launchers
***Smolensk, Moscow MD**	HQ, 46th Air Army/"Smolensk Air Army": controls about 12 bomber bases in the western Soviet Union, with Backfire, Badger, and Blinder assigned, controls 390 bombers but no fighters • PVO Mig-23 Flogger interceptor Regt of the Moscow Air Defense District • SRF Army intermediate HQ • SS-4 IRBM main operating base
Smolyaninovo, Far East MD	FROG Bn, unidentified Motorized Rifle Division: 4 FROG launchers
***Smorgon, Belorussian MD**	SS-20 IRBM main operating base
Sol'tsy AB, Leningrad MD	Backfire bomber base of the Smolensk Air Army
Sortavala, Leningrad MD	FROG Bn, unidentified Motorized Rifle Division: 4 FROG launchers
Sovetsk, Baltic MD	FROG Bn, unidentified Motorized Rifle Division: 4 FROG launchers
Sovetskaya Gavan, Far East MD	one of three main Pacific Fleet naval bases, homeport for surface ships up to destroyer size and numerous support ships • possible Badger Regt and ASW aircraft deployment base
Sretensk, Transbaikal MD	FROG Bn, 34th Motorized Rifle Division: 4 FROG launchers
Staro Konstantinov AB, Carpathian MD	nuclear-capable SU-24 Fencer Regt
Sverdlovsk, Ural MD	HQ, Ural Military District • nuclear weapons/components production facility • FROG Bn, 77th Motorized Rifle Divison: 4 FROG launchers
***Svobodnyy, Far East MD**	FROG Bn, unidentified Motorized Rifle Division: 4 FROG launchers (possibly located in Petropavlovsk) • SS-11 ICBM main operating base • (see also Belogorsk)
Syzran, Volga MD	LORAN-C type "Pulse Phase Radio Navigation System" (PPRNS), part of the western USSR chain
Tallin, Baltic MD	naval base of the Baltic Fleet, homeport to surface ships up to cruiser size and submarines • FROG Bn, unidentified Motorized Rifle Division: 4 FROG launchers
Tambov, Moscow MD	FROG Bn, unidentified Motorized Rifle Division: 4 FROG launchers
Tapa, Baltic MD	possible SS-20 IRBM main operating base
Tartu AB, Baltic MD	possible long-range bomber base
***Tashkent, Turkestan MD**	HQ, Turkestan Military District • HQ, 6th Air Army • HQ, Southern Theater of Military Operations (TVD): includes forces in Turkestan, North Caucasus and Transcaucus MDs as well as Afghanistan • Theater Air Defense HQ • nuclear weapons testing site
***Tatischevo, Volga MD**	SS-19 ICBM main operating base

Taymyr Peninsula, Siberian MD	impact areas for SLBM tests from Nenoksa in the White Sea
Tazovskiy Peninsula, Siberian MD	nuclear weapons testing site
Tbilisi, Transcaucasus MD	HQ, Transcaucasus Military District • HQ, 34th Air Army • FROG Bn, 1st Tank Division: 4 FROG launchers • satellite tracking station operated by SRF
Termez, Turkestan MD	FROG Bn, 360th Motorized Rifle Division: 4 FROG launchers
***Teykovo, Moscow MD**	SS-11 and SS-19 ICBM main operating base
Tiksi AB, Transbaikal MD	one of five Arctic Control Group airbases for forward staging of long-range bombers
Tiraspol, Odessa MD	FROG Bn, 59th Motorized Rifle Division: 4 FROG launchers
Tolnichi, Far East MD	unidentified Artillery Division: possible nuclear-capable artillery
Tomsk, Siberian MD	satellite tracking station operated by SRF
Totskoye, Volga MD	FROG Bn, 21st Motorized Rifle Division: 4 FROG launchers • unidentified Artillery Division: possible nuclear-capable artillery
Troitsk, Ural MD	uranium enrichment plant producing nuclear weapons materials
Tsugol, Transbaikal MD	unidentified Artillery Division: possible nuclear-capable artillery
Tukums AB, Baltic MD	nuclear-capable SU-24 Fencer Regt
Tumen	(see Itatka)
Turka, Carpathian MD	unidentified Artillery Division: possible nuclear-capable artillery
Tyumen, Siberian MD	former SS-11 ICBM main operating base
Tyuratam, Central Asian MD	"Baikonur Cosmodrome:" main space launch and missile test center, principal test site for ICBMs/IRBMs/MRBMs, with impact areas at Kamchatka, and in the Pacific Ocean, 600 miles northeast of Midway and 600 miles southeast of Wake Islands • missile crew training and operational testing • new ICBM research, development, and testing facility, particularly for liquid fuel missiles • at least 18 SS-18 launchers are thought to have a contingency launch capability • although called the "Baikonur Cosmodrome," it is located 310 kilometers southwest of Baikonur
Ukraina AB, Far East MD	possible long-range bomber base
Ulan Ude, Transbaikal MD	satellite tracking and receiving station operated by SRF • FROG Bn, unidentified Motorized Rifle Division: 4 FROG launchers
Ungeny, Odessa MD	unidentified Artillery Division: possible nuclear-capable artillery
Ura Guba, Leningrad MD	submarine base, Northern Fleet
Uryupinsk	(see Novocherkassk)
Usol'y Sibirskoye	(see Belaya)
Ussuriysk, Far East MD	HQ, 5th Army: unlocated SCUD Bde assigned • FROG Bn, unidentified Motorized Rifle Division: 4 FROG launchers • unidentified Artillery Division: possible nuclear-capable artillery • satellite tracking station operated by SRF • LORAN-C type "Pulsed Phase Radio Navigation System" (PPRNS), part of the eastern USSR chain
Ust-Chaun, Transbaikal MD	possible bomber dispersal base
Ust-Kamenogorsk, Central Asian MD	possible long-range bomber base
Uzhgorod	(see Izyaslav)
***Uzhur, Siberian MD**	SS-18 ICBM main operating base: 64 silos with Mod 4 missiles, 10% of ICBM force
Vanino	(see Alexsandrovsk AB)
Verhkhnyaya Salda, Ural MD	SS-20 IRBM main operating base

Vilnius, Baltic MD	FROG Bn, unidentified Motorized Rifle Division: 4 FROG launchers
Vinnitsa, Carpathian MD	SRF intermediate Army HQ: controls IRBMs and ICBMs • HQ, unidentified Air Army: new formation with reorganization of the Air Force in early 1980s
Vinogradov, Carpathian MD	81st Artillery Division: possible nuclear-capable artillery
Vladimir, Far East MD	minor naval base of Pacific Fleet
Vladimir, Moscow MD	ground station for Washington-Moscow DCL ("Hot Line"): Soviet Molniya portion • SRF intermediate Army HQ: controls 40–120 unidentified missiles
Vladimir-Volynskiy, Carpathian MD	FROG Bn, 15th Motorized Rifle Division: 4 FROG launchers
Vladimirovka, North Caucasus MD	cruise missile and bomber testing center
***Vladivostok, Far East MD**	HQ, Pacific Fleet: one of three major naval bases in the Pacific • 5th Squadron: homeport for a wide variety of surface ships and submarines (60–70% of the ships in the Pacific Fleet), including ballistic missile submarines and two VTOL aircraft carriers • Backfire base in the vicinity (probably Alekseyevka) • VLF/LF transmitter providing submarine communications to the Sea of Japan and Pacific
Volnoye	(see Dnepropetrovsk)
Volgograd, North Caucasus MD	nuclear weapons testing area
Vorishilovgrad	(see Lugansk)
Vorkuta AB, Ural MD	one of five Arctic Control Group airbases for forward staging of long-range bombers
Voronezh AB, Moscow MD	possible long-range bomber base
Vozzhayevka, Far East MD	FROG Bn, unidentified Motorized Rifle Division: 4 FROG launchers
Vyborg, Leningrad MD	FROG Bn, 45th Motorized Rifle Division: 4 FROG launchers
Vypolzov, Kiev MD	FROG Bn, unidentified Tank Division: 4 FROG launchers
Yaroslav, Moscow MD	Yaroslav Zone (North), Moscow Air Defense District, PVO
Yaroslav-Tunoshnoye AB, Moscow MD	PVO Mig-23 Flogger G interceptor Regt of the Moscow Air Defense District
Yary, Leningrad MD	possible ABM early warning radar
***Yedrovo, Moscow MD**	SS-4 IRBM main operating base • SS-20 IRBM main operating base • SS-17 ICBM main operating base
Yefremov AB, Moscow MD	PVO Mig-23 Flogger G interceptor Regt of the Moscow Air Defense District • possible Backfire bomber base
Yerevan, Transcaucasus MD	HQ, 76th Army: unlocated SCUD Bde assigned • FROG Bn, unidentified Motorized Rifle Division: 4 FROG launchers
Yevpatoriya, Odessa MD	one of two principal space program ground control centers • satellite tracking station operated by SRF MD
***Yoshkar Ola, Ural MD**	SS-13 ICBM main operating base: 60 silos (entire SS-13 force)
***Yurya, Ural MD**	SS-20 IRBM main operating base
Yuzhno-Sakhalinsk, Far East MD	HQ, 15th Army: unlocated SCUD Bde assigned • FROG Bn, 342d Motorized Rifle Division: 4 FROG launchers • unidentified Artillery Division: possible nuclear-capable artillery
Zaprozh'ye, Odessa MD	2d Artillery Division: possible nuclear-capable artillery
Zavitinsk	(see Raychikinsk)
***Zhangiz Tobe, Central Asian MD**	SS-18 ICBM main operating base
Zhitomir, Carpathian MD	HQ, 8th Tank Army: unlocated SCUD Bde assigned

OUTSIDE THE SOVIET UNION

Location	*Organization and Activity*

ANGOLA

The Soviet Union has a major communications facility in Angola and maintains a near continous naval presence in port.

BULGARIA

Some 27 SCUD and 39 FROG Soviet missile launchers are deployed in Bulgaria, reportedly but unconfirmed at missile sites near Plotchik, Markovo, south of Plovdiv, Shabla, Petritch (near Karnobat), Kavarna/Kyutstendil, Haskovo, Harmanli, and Vidin. The Bulgarian Air Defense Forces, headquarters at Sliven, are committed to support Soviet PVO and 15th Air Army of the Odessa Military District. No nuclear warheads are believed to be stationed in Bulgaria.

CUBA

No Soviet nuclear warheads are deployed in Cuba, although the Soviets have developed a number of facilities which are part of the nuclear infrastructure. Two airfields, San Antonio de Los Banos and Jose Marti airport, support regular Bear-D reconnaissance and nuclear-capable Bear-F ASW visits to Cuba. The Bear-F planes began to operate from Cuba for the first time in 1983. Cienfuegos and Havana are used by Soviet naval forces. Havana and Lourdes house major satellite ground stations and Soviet intelligence gathering facilities. The Lourdes facility probably monitors U.S. missile testing from Cape Canaveral, Florida.

CZECHOSLOVAKIA

Nuclear weapons are deployed in Czechoslovakia for aircraft and Army missiles. The new SS-21 missiles have been forward stationed to replace the FROGs, and SS-22 long-range missiles have also been reportedly deployed.

Bruntal	FROG Bn, unidentified Tank Division: 4 FROG-7/SS-21 launchers
Ceske Budejovice	unidentified FROG/SS-21 Bn (general location)
Havlickuv Brod	possible FROG/SS-21 Bn (general location)
Kfomeriz	unidentified FROG/SS-21 Bn (general location)
Milovice, Prague	HQ, Central Group of Forces: senior Army command in Czechoslovakia • FROG Bn, unidentified Tank Division: 4 FROG-7/SS-21 launchers • HQ, 7th Air Army, CZAF: Air Defense HQ, probably integrated with Soviet PVO
Mlada-Boleslav	HQ, Army Boleslav: includes SCUD Bde with 9 SCUD-b launchers (general location) • FROG Bn, 18th Motorized Rifle Division: 4 FROG-7/SS-21 launchers
Olomouc	HQ, Army Olomouc: includes SCUD Bde with 9 SCUD-b launchers (general location)
Pilsen	unidentifed FROG/SS-21 Bn (general location)
Prague	satellite ground station operated by SRF
Pribram	possible SCUD Bde (general location)
Slany	possible SCUD Bde (general location)
Susice	unidentified FROG/SS-21 Bn (general location)
Tabor	possible FROG/SCUD/SS-21 Bde (general location)
Topolcany	unidentified FROG/SS-21 Bn (general location)
Vysoke Myto	FROG Bn, unidentified Motorized Rifle Division: 4 FROG-7/SS-21 launchers
Zvolen	FROG Bn, unidentified Motorized Rifle Division; 4 FROG-7/SS-21 launchers

EAST GERMANY

Nuclear weapons are deployed in East Germany for aircraft, Army missiles and possibly artillery. By mid-1985, all Soviet divisions in East Germany will be converted from the FROG missile to the SS-21. SS-22 long-range missiles have also been reportedly deployed. Each Motorized Rifle and Tank Division in East Germany has also received a battalion of 152mm nuclear-capable artillery in its Artillery Regiment.

Altes Lager	(see Juterbog)
Belgern	bomb range used for simulated nuclear bombing missions
Bernau	FROG Bn, 6th Motorized Rifle Division: 4 SS-21 launchers
Bernsdorf	SS-22 Bde, first deployment site outside Soviet Union
***Brand-Briesen AB**	nuclear-capable SU-24 Fencer Regt, converted from SU-7 in early 1982 • nuclear bomb storage site
Bruck	SCUD Bde, Military District I, East German Army: SCUD-b, not believed to be nuclear-certified (possibly in Stallberg)
Cottbus	HQ, 1st Air Defense Division, East German AF
Dallgow-Doberitz	FROG Bn, 35th Motorized Rifle Division: 4 SS-21 launchers
Dessau-Rosslau	FROG Bn, 7th Tank Division: 4 SS-21 launchers
Dresden	HQ, 1st Tank Army: includes SCUD Bde with 9 SCUD-b launchers (general location only) • FROG-7 Bn, East German Army: 4 FROG-7 launchers
Dresden-Klotzsche	FROG Bn, 11th Tank Division: 4 SS-21 launchers
Eberswalde	HQ, 20th Army: includes SCUD Bde with 9 SCUD-b launchers (general location only)
Eggersdorf	HQ, East German AF Air Defense Command
Eggesin	FROG-7 Bn, East German Army: 4 FROG-7 launchers
Erfurt	FROG-7 Bn, East German Army: 4 FROG-7 launchers
***Finsterwalde AB**	nuclear-capable Mig-27 Flogger D/J Regt • nuclear bomb storage
Frankfurt-Furstenberg	HQ, 2d Tank Army: includes SCUD Bde with 9 SCUD-b launchers (general location only)
Furstenwalde	satellite ground station for Molniya II communications satellites
Grimma	FROG Bn, 20th Motorized Rifle Division: 4 SS-21 launchers
Gross Dolln	(see Templin)
***Grossenhain AB**	nuclear-capable SU-17 Fitter D Regt • possible nuclear bomb storage
Halle	FROG Bn, 27th Motorized Rifle Division: 4 SS-21 launchers • FROG Bn, East German Army: 4 FROG-7 launchers
Hillersleben	FROG Bn, 47th Tank Division: 4 SS-21 launchers
Jena	FROG Bn, 20th (79?) Motorized Rifle Division: 4 SS-21 launchers
Juterbog	FROG Bn, 14th Motorized Rifle Division: 4 SS-21 launchers • Juterbog AB: possible nuclear bomb storage for aircraft
Klotzsche	(see Dresden)
Krampnitz	FROG Bn, 10th Tank Division: 4 SS-21 launchers
Letzlinger Heide, Magdeburg	training area used for surface-to-surface missile training, equipped with ground-launched cruise missile and Pershing missile mock-ups
Lutherstadt	(see Wittenberg)
Magdeburg	HQ, 3d "Shock" (Tank) Army: includes SCUD Bde with 9 SCUD-b launchers (general location only)
***Mirow-Rechlin Larz AB**	nuclear-capable Mig-27 Flogger D/J Regt • nuclear bomb storage
Naumburg-Saale	FROG Bn, 57th MRD: 4 SS-21 launchers
Neubrandenburg	SCUD Bde, East German Army: 9 SCUD-b launchers, not nuclear certified (general location only) • HQ, 2d Air Defense Division, East German AF
Neuruppin	FROG Bn, 12th Tank Division: 4 SS-21 launchers

***Neuruppin AB**	nuclear-capable Su-17 Fitter C Regt • possible nuclear bomb storage
Neustrelitz	FROG Bn, 9th Tank Division: 4 SS-21 launchers
Ohrdruf	FROG Bn, 39th Motorized Rifle Division: 4 SS-21 launchers
Parchim AB	possible nuclear bomb storage site
Perleberg-Prignitz	FROG Bn, 32d/212th Motorized Rifle Division: 4 SS-21 launchers
Potsdam	34th Artillery Division: nuclear-capable artillery, only Soviet Artillery Division stationed outside the Soviet Union
Rechlin-Larz	(see Mirow)
Retzow	bomb range used for simulated nuclear bombing missions
Riesa, Sachsen Zeithain	FROG Bn, 9th Tank Division: 4 SS-21 launchers
Rosslau	(see Dessau)
Rossow	bomb range used for simulated nuclear bombing missions
Sachsen Zeithain	(see Riesa)
Schwerin	FROG Bn, 94th Motorized Rifle Division: 4 SS-21 launchers • FROG Bn, East German Army: 4 FROG-7 launchers
Sperenberg	bomb range used for simulated nuclear bombing missions
Stendal-Altmark	FROG Bn, 207th Motorized Rifle Division: 4 SS-21 launchers
***Templin-Gross Dolln AB**	nuclear-capable Su-17 Fitter H Regt • probable nuclear bomb storage on base
Vogelsang-Templin	FROG Bn, 25th Tank Division: 4 SS-21 launchers
Weimar-Nohra	HQ, 8th Army: includes SCUD Bde with 9 SCUD-b launchers (general location only)
Wittenberg-Lutherstadt	FROG Bn withdrawn as part of withdrawal of 6th Tank Division in 1979
Zossen-Wunsdorf	HQ, Group of Soviet Forces, Germany (GSFG) • HQ, 16th Air Army: disbanded with tactical aircraft units assigned directly to Group of Soviet Forces

ETHIOPIA

The primary Soviet Navy logistical support base for in the Indian Ocean is at Dahlak Island. Johannes IV Airfield, Asmara also supports nuclear-capable IL-38 May ASW operations.

HUNGARY

Nuclear weapons are stored in Hungary for aircraft and Army missiles. In addition, unlocated nuclear-capable 152mm artillery units are assigned to Soviet forces in Hungary.

Binitza	HQ, 24th Air Army: HQ for forward deployed aircraft in Hungary and the southwestern Soviet Union
Budapest-Matyasfold	HQ, Southern Group of Forces: senior Soviet military command in Hungary
***Debrecen AB**	nuclear-capable SU-24 Fencer Regt, first Soviet deployment in Eastern Europe in August 1981
Esztergom	FROG Bn, 2d Tank Division: 4 FROG-7 launchers
Kecskemet	FROG Bn, unidentified Motorized Rifle Division: 4 FROG-7 launchers
Szekesfehervar	FROG Bn, 102d Motorized Rifle Division: 4 FROG-7 launchers (15 miles southeast of the city)
Szombathely	unidentified FROG unit (general location)
Tatabanya	unidentified FROG unit (general location)
Veszprem	FROG Bn, 5th Tank Division: 4 FROG-7 launchers (15 miles west of the city)

MONGOLIA

Barun Urt	FROG Bn, unidentified Motorized Rifle Division: 4 FROG launchers (possibly located in Buigan)
Choybalsan (Urf Durfal)	FROG Bn, unidentified Tank Division: 4 FROG launchers
Sayn-Shand	FROG Bn, unidentified Motorized Rifle Division: 4 FROG launchers (possibly located in Sumber Soma)

POLAND

Nuclear weapons are deployed in Poland for aircraft and Army missiles.

Borne	FROG Bn, 20th Tank Division: 4 FROG-7 launchers
Kielce	reportedly satellite ground station for Molniya II communications satellites
Legnica	HQ, Northern Group of Forces: senior Soviet military command in Poland • HQ, 4th Air Army "Legnica Air Army": new formation controlling forward deployed aircraft in Poland and north western Soviet Union, 180 bombers and 135 fighters assigned (formerly 37th Air Army)
Lodz	reportedly central communications station for Soviet forces in Poland
Swiebodzin	FROG Bn, 38th Tank Division: 4 FROG-7 launchers (possibly in Swietoszow)
***Szprotawa AB**	nuclear-capable SU-24 Fencer Regt • probable nuclear bomb storage site
***Zagan AB**	nuclear-capable SU-24 Fencer Regt • probable nuclear bomb storage site

SOUTH YEMEN

The Soviet Navy maintains port facilities in Aden and uses Socotra Island for anchorage and resupply of ships operating in the Indian Ocean. Nuclear-capable IL-38 May ASW planes operate from Aden International and Al Anad Air Base.

VIETNAM

The Soviet Navy has established a major submarine and ship base at Cam Ranh Bay, which also serves as a deployment base for Bear-D reconnaissance aircraft and Tu-16 Badger bombers (deployed since November 1983). Da Nang also supports Soviet naval forces and Bear-D reconnaissance landings. A satellite ground station operated by the SRF is located in Hanoi.

Appendix C

British Nuclear Weapons Infrastructure

INSIDE THE UNITED KINGDOM

Location	*Organization and Activity*
Aberporth, Dyfed	Upper Atmosphere Centre, Meteorological Office, MOD: radiosonde facilities for upper atmosphere measurements and forcasting at the Royal Aircraft Establishment range, aiding the military in ballistic missile targeting and fallout prediction
Aldermaston, Berkshire	Atomic Weapons Research Establishment: nuclear warhead design, research, model fabrication, and production, some 5,000 employees
Anstruther, Fife	HQ, Northern Scotland civil defence zone 11 (formerly SRHQ): responsible for initial post-nuclear war government functions in Fife, Tayside, Grampian, and Highland
Anthorn, Cumbria	NATO VLF transmitter used for communications with naval forces and submarines, also used for radionavigation
Armagh, County Armagh	HQ, Northern Ireland civil defence zone (formerly SRHQ): responsible for initial post-nuclear war government functions in Northern Ireland
Balado Bridge, Tayside	NATO SATCOM III satellite communications terminal
Barrow-in-Furness, Cumbria	nuclear submarine construction and refit yard, planned Trident submarine construction site • Submarine Installation and Test Establishment, MOD: test and evaluation of Royal Navy submarine propulsion equipment, including the PWR 2 nuclear reactor for the Trident-class submarine
Basingstoke, Hampshire	HQ, civil defence zone 62 (formerly SRHQ): responsible for initial post-nuclear war government functions in Hampshire, Berkshire, Oxfordshire, and Buckinghamshire
Bath-Foxhill, Avon	Director General (Submarines) Department, MOD: Trident submarine design, engineering development, and construction support, also "In-Service Submarine Group" for Polaris research, and Chief Naval Architect, responsible for submarine design standards, including signature reduction • Director General (Strategic Weapons Systems) Department, MOD: responsible for strategic missile system R&D, works with U.S. Liaison Officer to the British submarine program • Director General (Supplies and Transport, Armament Services), MOD: responsible for Trident armament engineering
Bath-Lansdown, Avon	Sector Control Centre, UKWMO: distributes attack warning information to regional branches, serves as emergency meteorological office to predict regional fallout
Bawburgh, Norfolk	HQ, civil defence zone 41 (formerly SRHQ): responsible for initial post-nuclear war government functions in Norfolk, Suffolk, and Cambridgeshire
Benbecula, Western Isles	RAF/UKADGE aircraft early warning radar station, also storage site of a "mobile strategic reserve" long-range radar • Administrative HQ, Royal Artillery Guided Weapons Range, Hebrides: supporting Lance missile tests from South Uist
RAF Benson, Oxfordshire	The Queen's Flight: 3 Andover CC.2 aircraft for VIP transport
Bentley Priory, Stanmore, Middlesex	HQ, Number 11 Group (Air Defence), RAF Strike Command: missile and aircraft early warning for Britain • HQ, UK Air Defence Region
Bishop's Court, County Down	RAF/UKADGE aircraft early warning radar station
Blacknest, Hampshire	Blacknest Research Station: nuclear test detection site operated by AWRE, Aldermaston
Bolt Head, Devon	HQ, civil defence zone 72 (formerly SRHQ): responsible for initial post-nuclear war government functions in Devon and Cornwall
RAF Boscombe Down, Salisbury, Wiltshire	RAF Tornado Operational Evaluation Unit: 4 Tornado GR.1 aircraft for weapons delivery and operational tactics trials, in liaison with the RAF Central Tactics and Trials Organization • Aeroplane and Armament

	Experimental Establishment: RD&T center for aircraft, including nuclear-capable Jaguars
Boulmer, Northumberland	RAF/UKADGE aircraft early warning radar station • Sector Operations Centre of UK Air Defense Region: control and reporting center linked to BMEWS radar at Fylingdales, receives information from 12 UKADGE radars
Bracknell, Berkshire	Meterological Office, MOD: provides weather support to all military branches, UKWMO, and to all nuclear weapon RDT&E establishments, conducts research on weather phenomena and communications
Brampton, Cambridgeshire	HQ, RAF Support Command: responsible for flight training and logistics support
Bridgend, Mid Glamorgan	HQ, civil defense zone 82 (formerly SRHQ): responsible for initial post-nuclear war government functions in Mid Glamorgan, Glamorgan, Dyfed, Powys, and Gwent
RAF Brize Norton, Oxfordshire	RAF transport and dispersal base • Squadron 101: 9 VC-10K.2/3 aerial refuelers, activated in 1984, 6 Lockheed L-1011 Tristars being converted to refueling planes, to enter service in 1984–1985
Buchan, Grampian	RAF/UKADGE aircraft early warning radar station • Sector Operations Centre of UK Air Defence Region: control and reporting center linked to BMEWS radar at Fylingdales, receives information from 12 UKADGE radars, also storage site for a "mobile strategic reserve" long-range radar
***Burghfield, Berkshire**	Royal Ordnance Factory: production center for final assembly of separate components into complete nuclear warheads • maintenance and overhaul of Polaris warheads from storage in Coulport, and probably other RN and RAF warheads • conducts nuclear weapons research • 600 employees
Butt of Lewis, Western Isles	LF transmitter used for communications to submarines and fleet
Calder Hall, Cumbria	British Nuclear Fuels Ltd nuclear power station: former military reactor producing plutonium for British nuclear warheads (ceased operation in 1964), current plutonium production presumed for U.K. military, materials may be transferred to U.S. plutonium reserve stockpile
Cape Wrath (Garvie Island), Highland	RAF bombing range: used by Jaguar aircraft assigned to West Germany, Tornados, and U.S. F-111s, F-4, and NATO F-104 nuclear-capable aircraft
Cardiff (Llanishen), South Glamorgan	Royal Ordnance Factory: manufacturing of tampers and other components for nuclear warheads
Chapelcross, Dumfries & Galloway	British Nuclear Fuels Ltd nuclear power station: former military reactor producing plutonium for British nuclear weapons (ceased operation in 1964), current plutonium production presumed for U.K. military, materials may be transferred to U.S. plutonium reserve stockpile • Tritium production for U.K. military
Chatham, Kent	Royal Navy base closed in 1984 • LF transmitter used for naval communications
Cheltenham, Gloucestershire	Government Communication Headquarters (GCHQ): British signals intelligence agency, equivalent of NSA, presumably produces codes and other control devices for British nuclear weapons
Chenies, North London	RAF Strike Command radio station
RAF Chilmark, Wiltshire	Number 11 Maintenance Unit (Ordnance): possible nuclear weapon system support, logistics, and storage center
Cleethorpes, Humberside	LF transmitter used for communications to submarines and fleet
RAF Coltishall, Norfolk	Squadrons 6, 41, and 54: Jaguar GR.1 aircraft in offensive support role, nuclear capability unknown
Copenacre, Hawthorn, Wiltshire	RN Store Depot, Copenacre: Polaris/Trident logistics support
RAF Cottesmore, Leicestershire	Tri-national Tornado Training Establishment: 22 British Tornado GR.1, 22 West German, and 7 Italian nuclear-capable aircraft

***Coulport, Loch Long, Strathclyde**	RN Armament Depot: Polaris warhead and missile storage, facilities to be expanded as part of the Trident program
Criggion, Powys	VLF transmitter operated by the Post Office, used for communications to the Navy and submarines
Crimond, Grampian	LF transmitter used for naval communications to the North Atlantic and North Sea
RNAS Culdrose, Helston, Cornwall	RN Air Station: Squadrons 814, 820, and 826: nuclear-capable Sea King HAS.5 ASW helicpoters • Squadrons 706 and 810: Sea King HAS.2/5 ASW aircrew training • Squadron 849: Sea King HAS.2 airborne early warning
Dean Hill, Salisbury, Wiltshire	RN Armament Depot: probable storage of nuclear depth bombs
Defford, Hereford and Worcester	NATO satellite communications station (reserve to Oakhanger)
Devonport	(see Plymouth)
Dounreay, Highland	RN Nuclear Propulsion Test Establishment: R&D of Trident PWR2 nuclear reactor
Dover, Kent	HQ, civil defence zone 61 (formerly SRHQ): responsible for initial post-nuclear war government functions in Kent, Surrey, and Sussex
Dundee, Tayside	Sector Control Centre, UKWMO: distributes attack warning information to regional branches, serves as emergency meteorological office to predict regional fallout
Easingwold, North Yorkshire	Home Defence College: civil defence training
East Kilbride, Strathclyde	HQ, Western Scotland civil defence zone (formerly SRHQ): responsible for initial post-nuclear war government functions in Strathclyde, Central, Dumfries & Galloway
Eskdalemuir, Dumfries & Galloway	Eskdalemuir Observatory, Natural Environment Research Council: geomagnetic and seismological research station
Eskmeals, Cumbria	Upper Atmosphere Centre, Meteorological Office, MOD: radiosonde facilities for upper atmosphere measurements and forcasting at the Proof and Experimental Establishment, aiding the military in ballistic missile targeting and fallout prediction
Farnborough, Hampshire	Royal Aircraft Establishment: aerospace R&D, "special weapons department" designs and tests nuclear bombs, conducts evaluation program for experimental NAVSTAR receivers • Meterological Research Flight: Hercules W.2 weather research aircraft
Faslane, Gareloch, Strathclyde	10th Squadron, Submarine Command: homeport for 4 Polaris submarines • Polaris Training School/Trident Training School • facilities to be expanded under the Trident program • HMS Neptune is location of Captain, 10th Submarine Squadron and Captain, Submarine Sea Training
Fiskerton, Lincolnshire	Sector Control Centre, UKWMO: distributes attack warning to regional branches, serves as emergency meteorological office to predict regional fallout
Forest Moor, North Yorkshire	RN radio receiver station
Foulness, Essex	facility of Atomic Weapons Research Establishment: possible nuclear test detection site (exact function unknown)
Fylingdales, North Yorkshire	Ballistic Missile Early Warning System (BMEWS) radars: operated by RAF, fully integrated into U.S. early warning system, detection of both strategic and theater (European) missile attacks, 3 AN/FPS-49 tracking radars
Goosnargh, Lancashire	Wartime National HQ, UK Warning and Monitoring Organization: responsible for assimilating and analyzing attack and fallout damage to help relocate military forces to surviving bases • Sector Control Centre, UKWMO: distributes attack warning information to branch offices, also serves as an emergency meterological office to predict regional fallout

Greatworth, Northamptonshire	RAF HF communications center, role uncertain
Hack Green, Cheshire	HQ, civil defence zone 102 (under construction): responsible for initial post-nuclear war government functions in Cheshire, Merseyside, and Manchester
Hartland Point, Devon	RAF/UKADGE aircraft early warning radar station
Hawthorn, Wiltshire	probable national government wartime HQ • probable underground wartime HQ for UK Land Forces, including the U.K. Commander-in-Chief Committee
Hertford, Hertfordshire	HQ, civil defence zone 42 (formerly SRHQ): resposible for initial post-nuclear war government functions in Hertfordshire, Bedfordshire, and Essex
Hexham, Northumberland	HQ, civil defense zone 21 (under construction): responsible for initial post-nuclear war government functions in Northumberland, Tyne and Wear, Durham, and Cleveland
RAF High Wycombe, Buckinghamshire	UK Regional Air Operations Centre: NATO/RAF HQ • HQ, RAF Strike Command: British equivalent of SAC, located at Naphill • HQ, UK Warning and Monitoring Organization • RAF Central Tactics and Trials Organisation (see also Appendix A)
***RAF Honington, Suffolk**	Tornado Weapons Conversion Unit: RAF weapons training with 22 nuclear-capable Tornado GR.1 aircraft, will become Squadron 45 in the event of mobilization • Squadron 9: 16 nuclear-capable Tornado GR.1, first operational squadron in 1982 • nuclear weapons storage site
Horsham, West Sussex	Sector Control Centre, UKWMO: distributes attack warning information to regional branches, serves as emergency meteorological office to predict regional fallout
Inskip, Lancashire	LF/HF transmitter used for communications to submarines and fleet
Kelvedon Hatch, Essex	HQ, civil defence zone 51 (formerly SRHQ): responsible for initial post-nuclear war government functions in Greater London
RAF Kinloss, Grampian	Number 18 Group Squadrons 120, 201, and 206: 18–20 nuclear-capable Nimrod MR.2 ASW aircraft, Nimrod AEW forward operating location • probable nuclear weapons storage site in wartime
Kinver, Hereford and Worcester	HQ, civil defense zone 92 (formerly SRHQ): responsible for initial post-nuclear war government functions in Hereford and Worcester, and Salop
Kirknewton, Lothian	HQ, Eastern Scotland civil defense zone 12 (formerly SRHQ): responsible for initial post-nuclear war government functions in Lothian and Borders
Larkhill, Wiltshire	HQ, The Royal School of Artillery: probable location of nuclear artillery training at Royal Aircraft Establishment range • Upper Atmosphere Centre, Meteorological Office, MOD: radiosonde facilities for upper atmosphere measurements and forcasting at the Royal School of Artillery, aiding the military in ballistic missile targeting, nuclear explosion characteristics, and fallout prediction
Kineton, Warwickshire	Army School of Ammunition, Central Ammuntion Depot: Lance ammunition and supply technical training, also offered to NATO personnel
Lerwick, Shetland Islands	Upper Atmosphere Centre, Meteorological Office, MOD: radiosonde facilities for upper atmosphere measurements and forecasting, aiding the military in ballistic missile targeting and fallout prediction
London	Ministry of Defence • Defence Situation Centre • Defence Communications Centre • Scientific Research and Development Branch, Home Office • Controller Research and Development Establishments, Research and Nuclear Programmes (CERN): top MOD official in charge of nuclear weapons procurement • Chief of Strategic Systems Executive • Director General Strategic Weapons Systems • Assistant Director Naval Warfare (Strategic Systems) • Assistant Chief Scientific Advisor (Nuclear): top scientific advisor to MOD on nuclear weapons policy • Deputy Controller (Aircraft Weapons and Electronics) Department: program manager for RAF strategic

	communications and electronics • Chief Scientist, RN, Strategic Systems Performance Analysis Group
RAF Lossiemouth, Grampian	Number 18 Group Squadrons 12 and 208: each with 15–16 nuclear-capable Buccaneer S.2B aircraft, used for "maritime strike," possible nuclear weapons storage • 237 Operational Conversion Unit: 10 nuclear-capable Buccaneer S.2B, secondary support role for RAF Germany in event of mobilization • 226 Operational Conversion Unit: 15 nuclear-capable Jaguar GR.1 aircraft, training • Squadron 8: 6 Shackleton AEW.2 aircraft, to be deactivated and replaced by Nimrod AEW.3 based at RAF Waddington
Loughborough, Leicestershire	HQ, civil defense zone 32 (formerly SRHQ): responsible for initial post-nuclear war government functions in Leicestershire and Northamptonshire
Machrihanish, Strathclyde	forward operating base for RAF Nimrods and other NATO ASW aircraft • U.S. nuclear weapons storage (see Appendix A)
Malvern, Hereford and Worcester	Royal Signals and Radar Establishment: R&D in early warning, radars, communications and electronics, facilities include long-range tracking radar • Meteorological Office Radar Research Laboratory: forecasting research and "special investigations"
RAF Marham, Norfolk	Squadrons 27 and 617: nuclear-capable Tornado GR.1 aircraft, possible nuclear weapons storage • Squadrons 55 and 57: 22 Victor K.2 aerial refueling aircraft • 232 Operational Conversion Unit: Victor K.2 training (see also Appendix A)
Neatishead, Norfolk	RAF/UKADGE aircraft early warning radar station • Sector Operations Centre of UK Air Defence Region: control and reporting facility linked to BMEWS at Fylingdales, receives information from 12 UKADGE radars
RAF Northolt, Middlesex	Squadron 32: 4 Andover and 6 HS.125 aircraft used for VIP transport and government communications
Northwood, Middlesex	aboveground and hardened underground NATO and UK command center: RN Command HQ, Polaris executive, (CTF 345), Commander-in-Chief, Fleet (CINCFLT), also UK Polaris operational commander • HQ, Number 18 Group, RAF Strike Command: provides forces to NATO EASTLANT and Channel Commands (see also Appendix A)
Oakhanger, Hampshire	NATO satellite communications terminal • Skynet ground station, largest EMP hardened structure in Europe • Hampshire British control station for DSCS "special user" network • joint U.S./British satellite control facility
Pitreavie Castle, Dunfermline, Fife	subordinate Naval command center to Northwood including alternate wartime HQ • HQ, Northern Maritime Air Region • LF transmitter operated by the British government (see also Appendix A)
Plymouth, Devon	RN command center (Mount Wise) • RN Armament Depots Bull Point and Ernesettle: probable storage of nuclear depth bombs supporting Devonport • LF transmitter operating to the local sea area • RAF Mount Batten: HQ, Southern Maritime Air Region
Plymouth-Devonport, Decon	RN dockyard: shipyard supporting attack submarine and surface warship refits and repairs • RN Base: houses location of Chief Staff Officer Nuclear • RN Hydrographic School
Portland, Dorset	RN Base • Portland Sea Training Area: facilities for joint ASW/ASUW exercises and trials with NATO navies • RNAS Portland: Squadron 815: 35 nuclear-capable Lynx HAS.2 ASW helicopters, Squadron 702: Lynx HAS.2/3 aircrew training, Squadron 829: 27 nuclear-capable Wasp HAS.1 ASW helicopters
Portland-Southwell, Dorset	Admiralty Underwater Weapons Establishment: R&D in anti-submarine warfare, operations of ranges and test facilities for submarine certification and testing • Director General (Underwater Weapons) Department, MOD: projects on ASW weapons
Portreath, Cornwall	air defense center and radar

Portsdown, Cosham, Hampshire — Admiralty Surface Weapons Establishment: R&D in naval communications, radar, weapons, missile targeting • Flag Officer Third Flotilla (Fort Southwick): commands helicopter/VSTOL carriers with nuclear-capable Sea King helicopters and Sea Harrier aircraft

Portsmouth, Hampshire — RN command center, Commander-in-Chief Naval Home Command • Number 2 Group (ASW) command center • Staff Officer Nuclear Training • LF transmitter operated to the English Channel • RN dockyards

Prestwick (HMS Gannet), Strathclyde — Squadron 819: 8 nuclear-capable Sea King HAS.2 ASW helicopters, responsible for anti-submarine protection of Faslane and Holy Loch submarine bases

Rona, Highland — Admiralty Marine Technology Establishment: post-refit underwater noise analysis of Polaris submarines

Rosehearty, Grampian — RAF bombing range: land-attack and maritime strike practice by nuclear-capable RAF Jaguar, Buccaneer, and U.S. F-111 aircraft

Rosyth, Firth of Forth, Fife — RN Dockyard: shipyard supporting Polaris, attack submarine and surface warship refits and repairs • LF transmitter operating to the North Sea

Rhydymwyn, Wales — possible government reserve wartime HQ

RAF Rudloe Manor, Box, Wiltshire — HQ, Defence Communications Network

Rugby, Warwickshire — primary VLF transmitter operating worldwide, one of three primary stations for submarine communications, also used for radionavigation • LF transmitter operating to the Atlantic and Mediterranean regions

St. Kilda, Western Isles — radar and telemetry site supporting Lance missile testing from South Uist

St. Mawgan, Cornwall — Squadron 42, Number 18 Group: about 5 nuclear-capable Nimrod MR.2 ASW aircraft • 236 Operational Conversion Unit: 3 nuclear-capable Nimrod MR.2 to become Squadron 37 during mobilization • Nimrod AEW forward operating location • U.S. nuclear weapons storage (see Appendix A) • forward operating base for RAF Buccaneer maritime strike aircraft

Saxa Vord, Shetland Islands — RAF/UKADGE aircraft early warning radar station

Shanwell, Tayport, Fife — Upper Atmosphere Centre, Meteorological Office, MOD: radiosonde facilities for upper atmosphere measurements and forecasting, aiding the military in ballistic missile targeting and fallout prediction

Shipton, North Yorkshire — HQ, civil defence zone 22 (formerly SRHQ): responsible for initial post-nuclear war government functions in Yorkshire and Humberside

Shoeburyness, Essex — Upper Atmosphere Centre, Meteorological Office, MOD: radiosonde facilities for upper atmosphere measurements and forcasting at the Proof and Experimental Establishment, aiding the military in ballistic missile targeting and fallout prediction, supports the AWRE at Foulness

Skendleby, Lincolnshire — HQ, civil defence zone 31 (formerly SRHQ): responsible for initial post-nuclear war government functions in Lincolnshire, Nottinghamshire, and Derbyshire

Slough, Berkshire — Admiralty Compass Observatory

South Clettraval, Western Isles — tracking radar supporting Lance missile testing from South Uist

Southport, Merseyside — HQ, civil defense zone 101 (formerly SRHQ): responsible for initial post-nuclear war government functions in Lancashire and Cumbria

South Uist, Western Isles — Royal Artillery Guided Weapons Range, Hebrides: operational training for the British Army on the Rhine's 50th Missile Regiment with Lance missiles, about 15 Lance firings per year since 1977, two launch areas at West Geirinish, target area in international waters south of St Kilda, range control located at Reuval • research projects of the Meteorological Office (Rockets Divsion) and AWRE Aldermaston including the firing of upper atmosphere rockets for work on nuclear missile targeting and nuclear explosion characteristics

Southwick, Hampshire	School of Maritime Operations and Maritime Tactical School, RN: ASW and surface warfare training for U.K. and other NATO naval personnel
Staxton Wold, North Yorkshire	RAF/UKADGE aircraft early warning radar station
Stevenage, Hertfordshire	technical support center for Polaris system, operated by British Aerospace Dynamics
Stornoway, Western Isles	future Nimrod and NATO ASW deployment base • possible future Buccaneer aircraft forward operating base • Upper Atmosphere Centre, Meteorological Office, MOD: radiosonde facilities for upper atmosphere measurements and forcasting, aiding the military in ballistic missile targeting techniques and fallout prediction
Surbiton, Surrey	Mapping and Charting Establishment, MOD: central military mapping agency, similar to the U.S. DMA
Swynnerton, Staffordshire	HQ, civil defense zone 91 (formerly SRHQ): responsible for initial post-nuclear war government functions in Staffordshire, West Midlands, and Warwickshire
Tain, Highland	RAF bombing range: training area covering some 2,500 acres, used by Jaguars from Lossiemouth, also used by RAF Buccaneers and Tornados, U.S. F-111s and F-4s, and NATO F-104s
Taunton, Somerset	Hydrographic Plans and Surveys Department, MOD: responsible for conducting hydrographic and oceanographic surveys with the RN Surveying Flotilla, supporting the British strategic submarine force
Teddington, Middlesex	Admiralty Marine Technology Establishment: R&D in the ocean environment, submarine noise reduction
Thurso, Highland	LF transmitter on U.S. base used by Britain for communications to the North Atlantic and North Sea (see also Appendix A)
Ullenwood, Gloucestershire	HQ, civil defense zone 71 (formerly SRHQ): responsible for initial post-nuclear war government functions in Gloucestershire, Avon, Somerset, Wiltshire, and Dorset
Upavon, Wiltshire	HQ, Number 1 Group, RAF Strike Command: intermediate command controlling 3 Tornado squadrons, 1 strategic reconnaissance unit, and refueling squadrons
RAF Waddington, Lincolnshire	3 squadrons of Nimrod AEW aircraft to replace Shackletons • Squadron 50: 6 Vulcan K.2 aerial refuelers, to be replaced by VC-10s at Brize Norton
West Byfleet, Surrey	Defence Operational Analysis Establishment: conducts war games and computer simulations to recommend force allocation options, including ASW forces in the eastern Atlantic Ocean
West Drayton, Middlesex	RAF Air Defence Data Centre
Westcott, Buckinghamshire	Propellants, Explosives and Rocket Motor Establishment: R&D on missiles, warheads, and explosives
West Freugh, Stranraer, Dumfries & Galloway	Instrumentation and Trials Department, Royal Aircraft Establishment: weapons range covering some 2,750 acres on land and 250 square miles off the coast, used for training in high-speed low-level air attack by Buccaneer and other RAF and NATO strike/attack aircraft
Wick, Highland	LF transmitter, probably deactivated
Wilton, Salisbury, Wiltshire	HQ, UK Land Forces: peacetime HQ • Joint Emergency Planning Staff • UK Commanders-in-Chief Committee • Joint Warfare Staff
Windscale (Sellafield), Cumbria	nuclear materials reprocessing plant, used for plutonium core fabrication and rework
Winterbourne Gunner, Wiltshire	Defence Nuclear, Biological, and Chemical Centre: Army training
RAF Wittering, Cambridgeshire	233 Operational Conversion Unit: Harrier GR.3 aircaft, to receive GR.5s in 1986/87, also conducts nuclear-capable Sea Harrier FRS.1 training

RAF Wyton, Huntington, Cambridgeshire	Squadron 51: 3 Nimrod R.1 strategic reconnaissance aircraft • Number 1 Photographic Reconnaissance Unit: 4 Canberra PR.9 aircraft • Electronic Warfare Avionics Unit: 1 Andover C.1 aircraft, trials and test platform
RNAS Yeovilton, Ilchester, Somerset	HQ, Fleet Air Arm • RN Squadrons 800, 801, and 809: nuclear-capable Sea Harrier FRS.1 aircraft, Squadron 899: Sea Harrier training

OUTSIDE THE UNITED KINGDOM

ASCENSION ISLAND

The Wideawake Airfield is a periodic deployment base for nuclear-capable Nimrod MR.2 ASW aircraft (see also Appendix A).

BERMUDA

Britain uses Kindley Naval Air Station as a periodic deployment base for nuclear-capable Nimrod MR.2 ASW aircraft and operates an LF transmitter to the Western Atlantic from Bermuda (see also Appendix A).

CANADA

Britain conducts air training exercises with U.S. and Canadian air forces at Cold Lake, Alberta and Goose Bay, Labrador with nuclear-capable Buccaneer, Harrier, and Tornado aircraft (see also Appendix A).

CYPRUS

The Akrotiri base on Cyprus is a periodic deployment base for nuclear-capable Nimrod MR.2 ASW aircraft and Buccaneer strike aircraft.

DENMARK

An RAF/UKADGE aircraft early warning radar station is located at Sornfelli in the Faeroe Islands

FALKLAND ISLANDS

Britain operates an LF transmitter to the Southern Atlantic area from Port Stanley. About 5 nuclear-capable Sea King HAS.5 ASW helicopters have also been stationed at Stanley Airfield since the Falklands War. Nuclear-capable Nimrod MR.2 ASW and Buccaneer aircraft have also deployed to Stanley Airfield since November 1983.

GIBRALTAR

Britain maintains a naval base and dockyard on Gibraltar which serves as a temporary homeport for rotational ships which carry nuclear-capable ASW helicopters and a periodic deployment base for nuclear-capable Nimrod MR.2 ASW, Buccaneer, and Jaguar aircraft. An LF transmitter also operates to the Eastern Atlantic, Mediterranean and north Indian Ocean. HQ, Gibralter Mediterranean Command, NATO, is also located there.

ICELAND

Keflavik is a periodic deployment base for nuclear-capable Nimrod MR.2 ASW aircraft (see also Appendix A).

NETHERLANDS

Britain uses the bombing range at Vlieland for its nuclear-capable Buccaneer and Tornado aircraft stationed in West Germany (see also Appendix A).

TURKEY

Konya Air Base is a proposed forward deployment base for Nimrod AEW aircraft assigned to NATO (see also Appendix A).

UNITED STATES of AMERICA

Britain maintains a number of activities in the U.S.: at Cape Canaveral AFS, Florida; King's Bay, Georgia; Nellis AFB and Nevada Test Site, Nevada; and Dahlgren, Virginia (see also Appendix A).

Location	*Organization and Activity*
	WEST GERMANY
***RAF Brueggen**	Squadrons 14, 17, 20, and 31: nuclear-capable Jaguar GR.1 aircraft, will convert to Tornado GR.1s in 1984–1985 • Number 431 Maintenance Unit: supports all RAF aircraft in Germany, probable nuclear weapon system support, logistics, and storage
RAF Gutersloh	Squadrons 3 and 4: currently assigned non-nuclear Harrier fighters, squadrons will transition to nuclear-capable Harrier GR.5 aircraft in 1987–1988
***RAF Laarbruch**	Squadrons 15 and 16: nuclear-capable Tornado GR.1 aircraft, completed conversion from Buccaneer S.2 in March 1984, a third Tornado GR.1 squadron will be transferred from RAF Honington in 1986, in addition to another Tornado reconaissance squadron
Muenchen-Gladbach	HQ, Royal Air Forces, Germany (RAFG): all 14 squadrons are assigned to the 2d Allied Tactical Air Force, 6 squadrons are presently nuclear-capable, increasing to 9 by 1989
Rheindahlen	HQ, British Army on the Rhine (BAOR): nuclear units include the 50th Missile Regiment with 12 Lance launchers, 3 regiments of dual capable 8" and 155mm artillery guns, warheads for both systems held in U.S. custodial units in West Germany (see Appendix A)

Appendix D

French Nuclear Weapons Infrastructure

INSIDE FRANCE

Location	*Organization and Activity*
Aix-en-Provence, Bouches-du-Rhone	HQ, 4th Air Defense Region: regional air defense control center • Détachement Militaire de Control (DMC) 80/940, CAFDA
***Apt-St. Christol (air Base 200), Vaucluse**	HQ, Brigade de Missiles Stratégiques 04/200: central support base for land-based S-3 IRBMs on Plateau d'Albion, 18 missiles in two flights located in outlying underground silos • probable training site for personnel assigned to S-3 launch control centers
***Avord (Air Base 702), Cher**	HQ, 94th Escadre de Bombardement (EB): Bomber Squadron EB 1/94 with Mirage IVA, to be disbanded in 1986–87 • nuclear bombs stored in a Dépôt-Atelier Munitions Spéciales (DAMS) • Squadron 3/93, 93d Escadre de Ravitaillement en Vol (ERV): operates C-135F aerial refueling aircraft
***Belfort, Terr de Belfort**	plutonium enrichment facilities, with possible military use • 74th Army Artillery Regiment: 6 Pluton launchers, 1,000 military personnel
Bordeaux (area), Gironde	Centre d'Études Scientifiques et Techniques d'Aquitaine, under the Military Applications Branch of the Commissariat à l'Énergie Atomique: nuclear weapons effects research, including simulated blasts on nuclear power stations, EMP simulation tests (exact location unknown)
Bordeaux-Gironde AB, Gironde	HQ, 3d Air Defense Region, CAFDA: regional air defense control center
Bordeaux-Mérignac (Air Base 106), Gironde	Centre D'Instruction des Forces Aériennes Stratégiques (CIFAS 328): major strategic training base with 4 Mirage IV used for crew training, 13 Mirage IIIB used for operational conversion and aerial refueling training, 5 Noratlas N-2501/SNB (Système Navigation Bombardement) fitted with Mirage IV radar and avionics and used for navigation and bombardment training
Brest, Finistere	LF radio transmitter used for submarine and fleet communications to the NE Atlantic • Centre de Détection et de Control (CDC) 08/927: primary military control and reporting center • shipyard: construction and overhaul of Foch & Clemenceau aircraft carriers • HQ, Naval Commander-in-Chief Atlantic Region (CECLANT) • Préfet Maritime de la Deuxième Region • (see also Île Longue, Roches Douvres, and Soument) • Etablissement Principal du Service Hydrographique et Oceanographique de la Marine (EPSHOM): responsible for conducting hydrographic and oceanographic surveys in support of the French strategic submarine force, FOST
Bruyères-le-Chatel, Essone	Centre d'Études de Bruyères-le-Chatel: under the Military Applications Branch of CEA, possible nuclear warhead research
Cadarache, Bouches-de-Rhone	Service Technique des Construction et Armes Navales: subsidiary of CEA, designs and constructs nuclear submarine reactors, designs prototype reactors for future SSBNs, including the Inflexible-class
***Cambrai (Air Base 103), Nord**	Mirage IVA bomber dispersal base, with intermittant deployments of 4 bombers • nuclear bomb storage in Dépôt-Atelier Munitions Spéciales (DAMS) • an underground wartime command post is reportedly planned here
Cannes, Alpes-Maritimes	Division Systèmes Balistique et Spatiaux, Aerospatiale: supervises strategic missile series production, conducts R&D on future SX mobile and M5 SLBM missiles, operates EMP simulators for individual missile components, operates missile guidance and control loop simulators
***Cazaux (Air Base 120), Gironde**	Bomber Squadron EB 2/91: Mirage IVA, converting to Mirage IVP with ASMP nuclear air-to-surface missiles in 1986–87 • nuclear bomb storage in a Dépôt-Atelier Munitions Spéciales (DAMS) • Centre de Tir et de Bombardement: bombing range
Chalais-Meudon, Paris	HQ, Office National d'Études et de Recherches Aérospatiales (ONERA): French national aerospace R&D organization, includes research on early warning radars, stealth aircraft technology, electronic warfare, and cruise missiles

Chateaudun, Eure-et-Loir	601st Entrepôt d'Armée de l'Air: maintenance unit for French military aircraft, combining storage, repair and disposal facilities, possible nuclear weapons or components storage
Chateaulin, Finistère	41st Infantry Regiment: tasked with protection of strategic submarine installations, 1,400 personnel
Chatillon, Hauts-de-Seine	Division Engins Tactiques, Aerospatiale: design and R&D of Pluton missiles and future ASMP nuclear air-to-surface missiles, includes prototype production
Cherbourg, Manche	La Direction Technique des Constructions Navales (DTCN): naval shipyard involved in construction of missile submarines • Préfet Maritime de la Première Region • Naval Base: homeport of testbed submarine Gymnote supporting Force Océanique Sratégique (FOST) SLBM missile development • LF radio transmitter used for submarine communications to the northeast Atlantic
Chinon, Indre-et-Loire	Électricité de France (EdF) graphite-moderated reactors: former military plutonium source, may be reactivated upon decommissioning of Marcoule military production reactor
Cinq-Mars-La-Pile, Indre-et-Loire	Centre de Détection et de Control (CDC) 07/927: hardened military control and reporting center, including early warning search and height finder radars • 609 Entrepôt d'Armée de L'Air: nuclear weapon system logistic support and possible storage
Colmar (Air Base 132), Haut-Rhin	HQ, 13th Escadre de Chasse (EC): one Mirage IIIE aircraft squadron, nuclear capability unknown
Contrexeville, Vosges	Centre de Détection et de Control (CDC) 05/902: primary military control and reporting center collocated with early warning radar
Cotar, Landes	Station de Flanquement: telemetry and tracking station supporting missile launches from Landes
***Creil (Air Base 110), Oise**	contingency bomber dispersal base for Mirage IVA, former active base • probable nuclear bomb storage in a Dépôt-Atelier Munitions Spéciales (DAMS)
Creys-Malville, Isere	Superphénix 1200 megawatt breeder reactor, could be used for weapons plutonium production in the future
Croix d'Hins, Gironde	VLF/LF radio transmitter, could be used for submarine communications worldwide
Dijon (Air Base 102), Cote-d'Or	HQ, 2d Escadre de Chasse (EC): 2 Mirage IIIE squadrons, nuclear capability unknown
Doullens, Somme	Centre de Détection et de Control (CDC) 05/925: primary military control and reporting center collocated with early warning radar
Drachenbronn, Bas-Rhin	Centre de Détection et de Control (CDC) 05/901: hardened primary military control and reporting center collocated with early warning radar
Evreux (Air Base 105), Eure	51 Escadrille Électronique (Aubrac), Commandemant des Transmissions de l'Armee de l'Air: formed in 1977 with one specially modified DC-8 (Sarig) • 64 Escadre de Transport, Commandemant Du Transport Aérien Militaire: 10 Transall C-160 modified for aerial refueling in support of strategic bombers • 4 Transall C-160 modified for VLF airborne relay (similar to U.S. TACAMO) for emergency communications to submarines, operational by 1987.
Fontenay-aux-Roses, Hauts-de-Seine	Centre d'Études Nucléaire de Fontenay-aux-Roses, CEA: conducts fundamental nuclear physics research, possible military applications
Gramat, Lot	Centre d'Études de Gramat, Établissement Technique Central de l'Armement: nuclear weapons effects research including fixed and mobile EMP simulators
Grenoble, Isere	Centre d'Études Nucléaires de Grenoble, CEA: nuclear weapons research
Hagenau	(see Oberhoffen)
Houilles, Yvelines,	HQ, Force Océanique Stratégique (FOST): strategic submarine force underground command center

Hourtin, Gironde	Station de Flanquement: telemetry and tracking station supporting missile launches from Landes
Hyeres NAS, Var	Naval aviation Squadron 17F: home of 12 carrier-based nuclear-capable Super Étendard aircraft
***Île Longue, Brest, Finistere**	submarine base: homeport and support installations supporting the strategic submarine force, storage for missiles and TN61 warheads, 250 personnel working with strategic missiles
***Istres (Air Base 125), Bouches-du-Rhone**	contingency bomber dispersal base for Mirage IVA, former active bomber base • probable nuclear bomb storage in Dépôt-Atelier Munitions Spéciales (DAMS) • Aerial Refuelling Squadron 1/93 (ERV 1/93): C-135F aerial refueling aircraft • Fighter Squadron 4/7 (EC 4/7): nuclear-capable Jaguar A aircraft, to be replaced by Mirage 2000N in 1989–90 • test site for Mirage 2000N aircraft • Centre Militaire de Control CMC) 85/940
Kerlouan, Finistère	VLF radio transmitter, could be used for submarine communications worldwide
La Hague, Manche	Établissement de La Hague: operated by Compagnie General de Matières Nucléaires (COGEMA), subsidiary of CEA, plutonium reprocessing site for military and commercial use
La Vallée du Rhône, Vaucluse	Centre d'Études Nucléaires de la Vallée du Rhône, CEA: nuclear research
Landes	Centre d'Essais des Landes (CEL): missile launch and test center extending from Biscarosse (north) to Mimizan (south) with some 130 km of French coastline (from Point d'Arcachon to Bayonne near the Spanish border) becoming a restricted area during launches, over 6,000 firings since 1966, 110 tests of SLBMs and IRBMs, and 40 of Pluton SRBMs, missile firings are toward the southwest, to the ocean area beyond the Azores, where tracking and telemetry sites are maintained, three silos at Landes for tests • 3 Douglas DC-7C AMOR aircraft are used for midflight tracking • Naval Test and Measurement Group: responsible for tracking missile re-entry to impact phase from ships • nuclear weapons effects research also takes place at CEL, including EMP simulation on completed missiles
Landivisiau NAS, Finistère	Naval aviation Squadrons 11F and 14F: home of 24 carrier-based nuclear-capable Super Étendard aircraft
Lann-Bihoué NAS, Morbihan	Squadron 23: maritime patrol support services to Pacific Test Center with Atlantique aircraft
Lanvéoc-Poulmic NAS, Finistere	Squadron 32: provides protection for submarine base at Île Longue with Super Frelon ASW helicopters • early warning radar supporting military center at Brest
***Laon-Couvron, Aisne**	60th Army Artillery Regiment: 6 Pluton launchers, 1,000 military personnel
La Regine, Aude	LF radio transmitter used for submarine and fleet communications to the Mediterranean Sea
Le Bourget (Air Base 104), Seine St. Denis	Escadre de Transport 3/60: VIP transport for French government
Les Mureaux, Yvelines	HQ, Division Systèmes Balistique et Spatiaux, Aerospatiale: RD&T laboratory and production site of ballistic missiles, including M4 development and EMP testing, along with its facilities at Cannes and Saint-Médard this division is responsible for RD&T and production of current (M20, M4, and S3) and future (Hadès SSM, and SX mobile IRBM) missile systems, 150 personnel working on nuclear effects projects, developed mobile EMP simulators for use on S3 IRBMs in their silos
Lessay, Manche	LORAN-C Station: experimental transmissions by the Service Technique des Constructions et Armes Navales
Limeil-Valenton, Val-de-Marne	Centre d'Études de Limeil-Valenton: under the Military Applications Branch of CEA, function unknown
Limoges, Haute-Vienne	603d Entrepôt d'Armée de l'Air: nuclear weapon system support and logistics including service to Jaguar aircraft

***Luxeuil (Air Base 116), Haute-Saone**	contingency bomber dispersal base for Mirage IVA, former active bomber base • probable nuclear bomb storage in Dépôt-Atelier Munitions Spéciales (DAMS) • HQ, 4th Escadre de Chasse (EC): 2 nuclear-capable Mirage IIIE squadrons, to convert to Mirage 2000N in 1988 • 339th Centre Prediction et Instruction Radar (CEAA): 2 Mystere 20 SNA radar training aircraft used for intercept training for radars and fighter pilots
***Mailly, Aube**	3d Army Artillery Regiment: 6 Pluton launchers, 1,000 military personnel
Malakoff, Hauts-de-Seine	nuclear warhead fuze production plant • EMP simulators (fixed and mobile) operated by Thomson-CSF and Aerosptiale
Marcoule, Gard	Centre Atomique de Marcoule: nuclear materials production plant, including G3 unit, military plutonium production reactor, to be decommissioned by 1985 • SAP pilot plant for plutonium reprocessing, new TOR plutonium reprocessing unit to be operational by 1985 • Phenix 250 megawatt prototype breeder reactor, operating since 1973, thought to provide plutonium to the military branch of the CEA • Celestin I & II heavy water moderated reactors producing tritium
Metz, Moselle	HQ, État-major de Corps d'Armée (1st Corps): command of four Army divisions, with operational control and support of the Pluton force • HQ, 1st Air Region
Metz-Frescaty (Air Base 128), Moselle	HQ, 1st Commandement Aérien Tactique (1 CATAC): commands 19 fighter squadrons, 5 of nuclear-capable Mirage IIIE's and Jaguar A's • 54th Escadrille Électronique, Commandement des Transmissions de L'Armée de L'Air: 8 Noratlas equipped with offensive electronic warfare equipment
Miramas, Bouches-du-Rhône	Établissement de Miramas, COGEMA, CEA: materials production site (lithium 6 & 7) for nuclear weapons related purposes
Modane, Savoie	Office National d'Études et de Recherches Aérospatiales (ONERA): wind tunnel used for trajectory studies for nuclear weapons (ASMP and M4 RVs)
***Mont-de-Marsan (Air Base 118), Landes**	HQ, 91st Escadre de Bombardement (EB): includes Bomber Squadron EB 1/91 with Mirage IVA, to convert to Mirage IVP with ASMP nuclear air-to-surface missiles in 1986–87 • nuclear bomb storage in Dépôt-Atelier Munitions Spéciales (DAMS) • Aerial Refueling Squadron 2/93 (ERV 2/93): C-135F aerial refuelers • Centre de Détection et de Control (CDC) 04/930: primary military control and reporting center collocated with early warning radar • Centre d'Expérimentations Aériennes Militaires: aircraft flight testing, navigation and target practice, including the Mirage IVP with ASMP nuclear air-to-surface missiles
Mt. Angel (Nice), Alpes-Maritimes	Centre de Détection et de Control (CDC) 05/943: primary military control and reporting center collocated with early warning radar
Mt. Verdun (Lyons), Rhone	alternate national military command center and backup air defense HQ for CAFDA, underground hardened facility • Centre de Détection et de Control (CDC) 05/942: primary military control and reporting center collocated with early warning radar
Nancy (AB), Meurthe-et-Moselle	HQ, 3d Escadre de Chasse (EC): 2 Mirage IIIE and 1 Jaguar squadrons, nuclear capability unknown
Narbonne, Aude	Centre de Détection Satellite (CDS) 15/944 • secondary military control center, collocated with early warning radar
Oberhoffen, Bas-Rhin	32d Army Artillery Regiment: 6 Pluton launchers, 1,000 military personnel (also known as Hagenau)
Orange (Air Base 115), Vaucluse	contingency bomber dispersal base for Mirage IVA, former active bomber base (disbanded in late 1983) • probable nuclear bomb storage in Depot-Atelier Munitions Speciales (DAMS)
Orly, Val-de-Marne	Détachement Militaire de Control (DMC) 80/920, CAFDA
Paris	HQ, Ministry of Defense and military services • HQ, Armée de l'Air: including two nuclear commands, one strategic and one tactical
Pierrelatte, Drome	gaseous diffusion uranium enrichment plant for weapons purposes, operational since 1964

Point d'Arcachon, Gironde	Station de Flanquement: telemetry and tracking station supporting missile launches from Landes
Prunay, Loir-et-Cher	Centre de Détection Satellite (CDS) 15/914 • secondary military control center
Quimper, Finistere	new missile tracking facility supporting long-range missile tests on the Landes Range shot from submarines off the coast
***Reilhanette, Drôme**	2d Post Central de Tir: HQ and launch control center for flight of 9 S3 IRBMs located in underground silos
Ripault, Indre-et-Loire	Centre d'Études du Ripault: under the Military Applications Branch of CEA, function unknown (exact location unknown)
Rocamadour, Lot	607th Entrepôt d'Armée de l'Air: possible nuclear weapon system support and logistics
Rochefort, Charente-Maritime	Naval Aviation school: training of Super Étendard crews for carrier-based operations
Roches Douvres, Brest, Finistére	navigation, propulsion system, command and control and launch procedures training base for missile submarines
Romilly-sur-Seine (Air Base 914), Aube	secondary military control center collocated with early warning radar
Romorantin-Pruniers, Loir-et-Cher	602d Entrepôt d'Armée de l'Air: possible nuclear weapon system support and logistics
Rosnay, Le Blanc, Indre	main VLF radio transmitter used for submarine communications worldwide • ELF system also being developed for communications with submarines
Rustrel, Vaucluse	1st Post Central de Tir: HQ and launch control center for flight of 9 S3 IRBMs located in underground silos
Saclay, Essonne	Centre d'Études Nucléaires de Saclay, CEA: nuclear weapons research
S. Assise, Essonne	VLF radio transmitter operated by Administration des Postes et Telecommunications, could be used for submarine communications in emergency
St. Christol	(see Apt-St. Christol)
***St. Dizier (Air Base 113), Haute-Marne**	Bomber Squadron EB 2/94: Mirage IVA, to be disbanded in 1986–87 • nuclear bomb storage in Dépôt-Atelier Munitions Spéciales (DAMS) • HQ, 7th Escadre de Chasse (EC): 3 Jaguar A/E squadrons, two operational nuclear-capable squadrons and one conversion training, to be replaced by Mirage 2000N in 1989–90
Saint-Germain-en-Laye, Yvelines	HQ, État-major de Corps d'Armée (3d Army): Pluton support
Saint-Medard en Jalles, Gironde	Centre d'Achèvement et d'Essais des Propulseurs et Engins: one of two specialized centers run by the Direction Technique des Engins (D.T.En) which researches, constructs and tests the engines and propulsion systems for land and sea-based ballistic missiles, Aerospatiale is prime contractor • Établissement d'Aquitaine, Division Systèmes Balistique et Spatiaux, Aerospatiale: RD&T and production of missiles and components, conducts EMP and thermal testing for missile components using Europe's largest plasma torch to simulate atmospheric reentry temperatures for RVs
Savigny-en-Septaine, Cher	605th Entrepôt d'Armée de l'Air: possible nuclear weapons system support and logistics
Soument, Brest, Finistère	training base for strategic submarine force
Soustons, Landes	LORAN-C Station: experimental transmissions by the Service Technique des Constructions et Armes Navales
Strasbourg (Air Base 124), Bas-Rhine	HQ, État-major d'Armée (1st Army): Pluton command and control
***Suippes, Marne**	25th Army Artillery Regiment: 6 Pluton launchers, 1,000 military personnel • air-to-ground bombing and training range used by U.S. Air Force

Taverny (Air Base 921), Val-d'Oise	National Military Command Center: underground HQ of all three legs of French nuclear forces, Presidential command center for nuclear C3 (submarine HQ at Houilles) • État Major de la Defense Aérienne 900: HQ, Commandement Air des Forces de Defence Aérienne (CAFDA), French NORAD equivalent, receiving data from 8 primary and 2 secondary regional air defense centers, also linked to NATO NADGE network extending air defense early warning thousands of miles • HQ, Forces Aériennes Stratégiques (FAS): French equivalent of SAC, strategic arm of Armée de l'Air, controls missile and bomber force
Toul (Air Base 136), Meurthe-Mosselee	HQ, 11th Escadre de Chasse (EC): 3 Jaguar squadrons, one assigned to overseas rapid deployment role, nuclear capability unknown
***Toulon, Var**	Naval Base: homeport of two Clemenceau-class aircraft carriers equipped with nuclear-capable Super Étendard aircraft • Préfet Maritime de la Troisième Region • LF radio transmitter used by submarines in the Mediterranean Sea • differential Omega station
Toulouse, Haute-Garonne	608th Entrepôt de l'Armée de l'Air: nuclear weapon system support and logistics, possible storage
Tricastin, Ardeche	gaseous diffusion uranium enrichment facility with possible military functions
Valduc, Cote-d'Or	Centre d'Études de Valduc, under the Military Applications Branch of CEA: function unknown
Varennes	606th Entrepôt de l'Armée de l'Air: nuclear weapon system support and logistics, possible storage (exact location unknown)
Vaujours, Seine-St.Denis	Centre d'Etudes de Vaujours, under the Military Applications Branch of CEA: function unknown
Vernon, Eure	Laboratoire de Recherches Balistique et Aérodynamiques, one of two specialized centers run by the Direction Technique des Engins (D.T.En): RDT&E of engines and guidance for ballistic missiles, prime contractor is Aerospatiale
Villacoublay (Air Base 107), Yvelines	HQ, 2d Air Region (Paris) • Groupe des Liaison Aériennes Ministérielles 1/60: French president's plane (Caravelle)

OUTSIDE FRANCE

Location	*Organization and Activity*

DJIBOUTI

The Djibouti Naval Base is a regular deployment base for naval vessels and is occassionally visited by aircraft carriers. Air Base 188 also supports U.S. P-3 deployments and French naval aircraft.

FRENCH POLYNESIA

Location	*Organization and Activity*
Faaa NAS, Tahiti	Escadrille de Servitude 12: 8 Neptune and Gardian aircraft provide maritime patrol and surveillance services at the Pacific Test Center
Fangataufa	location of former atmospheric test site, being considered as a second site for possible underground nuclear testing, reported under construction due to sinking of Mururoa Atoll
Hao (Air Base 185)	Section Alouette du Pacifique: 4 Alouette helicopters providing support to the Pacific Test Center
Mururoa Atoll	Centre d'Experimentation du Pacifique (CEP): former atmospheric and current underground nuclear testing at the Pacific Test Center • Escadrille de Servitude 27: 5 Super Frelon helicopters providing airlift support
Papeete, Tahiti (Air Base 197)	LF radio transmitter operated by the Marine Nationale • Direction Technique des Construction Navales: dockyards for overhauling ships assigned to the Pacific Test Center • Escadron de Transport d'Outre-Mer 82 (ETOM 82): airlift supporting nuclear testing

MARTINIQUE

The Marine National operates an LF transmitter on Fort de France for communications to the central and south Atlantic.

NEW CALEDONIA

The Marine National operates an LF transmitter on Noumea-La Tontouta.

PORTUGAL

France operates a number of facilities in the Azores which support missile testing from Landes. A missile tracking station is operated at Florès and Santa Maria airfield supports AMOR aircraft used in tracking and telemetry collection in connection with missile testing.

LA REUNION

The Port des Galets Naval base is occasionally visited by French aircraft carriers when deployed to the Indian Ocean. France also operates the Omega Station at Mafate.

SENEGAL

The Forces Armées Françaises operates an LF radio transmitter at Dakar.

UNITED STATES OF AMERICA

Nuclear-capable Jaguar A aircraft of the Force Aerienne Tactique train in low-altitude bombing at Nellis AFB, Nevada (see also Appendix A).

WEST GERMANY

France's État-major de Corps d'Armée (II Corps) at Baden-Baden commands three French divisions in West Germany, at Freiburg, Landau and Trier. Pluton nuclear missile support comes from units across the border in France.

Appendix E

Chinese Nuclear Weapons Infrastructure

Location	*Organization and Activity*
Antu	satellite tracking station
Baotou (Paotow)	production plant for nuclear weapons material • missile production and flight test center
Beijing	HQ, Peoples Liberation Army: command and control of entire military and nuclear forces, commands include the 2d Artillery, responsible for nuclear weapons (the name of the 2d Artillery was changed in 1984) • Ballistic Missile Technology Institute • Aerodynamics Research Institute: operates wind tunnel facilities similar to NASA's Langley Research Center
Bohai Gulf	SLBM test launch site south of Huludao
Changchun	satellite tracking station • laser research and development center supporting defense/space programs
Changde	VLF transmitter with worldwide communications coverage
Changxing	missile test center and launch site for IRBM and SLBM test range
Chengdu	missile component factory • satellite tracking station
Chongqing	new space launch center, used for geosynchronous orbit satellite launches
Dalian	(see Luda)
Datong	VLF transmitter with regional communications coverage to naval forces
Fuzhou	VLF transmitter with regional communications coverage to naval forces • satellite tracking station
Guangzhou	naval base and submarine construction yard
Haikou, Hainan Island	HQ, 2d Submarine Flotilla, South Sea Fleet
Hainan Island	missile test center and launch site for IRBM test range
Haiyan (Koko Nor)	Haiyan Nuclear Plant: nuclear weapons development and assembly center
Harbin	bomber production plant • Heilongjiang Laser Infrared Experimental Center: supports defense/space programs
Hohhot	hardened underground central government shelter • airfield with underground control facilities • missile fuel factory
Hong Yuan	uranium enrichment plant for nuclear weapons material production
Huludao	North Sea Fleet naval base • Han-class attack submarine and Xia-class missile submarine construction yard • submarine-launched ballistic missile (SLBM) test-launch center
Jiangnan	shipyard constructing Romeo-class attack submarines
Jinxi	Jinxi Missile Test and Development Center: main military test, development, and launch center for SLBMs and ICBMs • 2d Artillery Corps command training center and college: missile and nuclear weapons training
Jingyu	missile test-launch center
Jiuquan	uranium mine and processing plant producing enriched uranium
Jiuzhan	uranium mine used for nuclear weapons material production
Kashi	satellite tracking station
Koko Nor	(see Haiyan)
Kunming	astrophysics research center supporting defense/space programs
Lanzhou (Lanchow)	Lanzhou Gaseous Difusion Plant: uranium enrichment, major nuclear weapon material production facility (15 mi north of Lanzhou) • ordnance factory: produces missile and warhead components
Lhasa	satellite tracking station
Lop Nur (Lop Nor)	only Chinese nuclear weapons test site • terminus of missile flight tests from Shuangchengzi

Luda (Dalian)	Honqui Shipyard: homeport and construction site of Golf-class missile test submarine (SSB) • North Sea Fleet naval base
Lushun	North Sea Fleet naval base and submarine school • VLF transmitter with regional communications coverage to naval forces
Mashan	uranium mine used for nuclear weapons material production
Nagqu	CSS-1 and CSS-2 missile base and test center (300 kilometers north of Lhasa)
Nanjing	satellite tracking station
Nanning	satellite tracking station
Nanyang	uranium mine used for nuclear weapons material production
Ningbo	VLF transmitter with regional communications coverage to naval forces
Quingdao	HQ, North Sea Fleet • 1st Submarine Flotilla: most likely future Xia-class strategic submarine base • submarine school
Shanghai	HQ, East Sea Fleet • naval base • ship and submarine construction yard for Romeo-class attack submarines • missile factory • fuel factory • Institute of Technical Physics: supports defense/space programs • laser research and development center • space tracking station
Shenyang	aircraft factory producing B-6 (Tu-16) bomber • missile assembly plant • fuel factory
Shuangchengzi (Shuang Ch'eng Tse)	Shuangchengzi Launch Complex: primary space/defense missile test launch and satellite launch center (satellite launch complex and 2d Artillery missile launch facility located on opposite sides of Ruo Shui river)
Taklimakan desert	MRBM/IRBM missile impact point from northwest Manchuria launch site
Taiyuan	missile component factory • missile fuel factory
Tianjin	satellite tracking station
Urumqui	uranium enrichment/fabrication plant for nuclear weapons material production • satellite tracking station
Weinan	Weinan Center for Space Tracking, Telemetry and Control: central space tracking facility, controls a seven-station network
Wuzhai	MRBM missile test center and range, also used for SLBM testing and development from 1975–78
Wuzhang	shipyard building Romeo-class diesel attack submarines
Xia Chuan	uranium mine used for nuclear weapons material production
Xian (Sian)	missile assembly plant • fuel factory • space tracking station
Xiangxiang	missile fuel factory
Xingyang	missile test tracking facility
Xisha, Paracel Islands	satellite tracking station
Yaxian	VLF transmitter with regional communications coverage to naval forces
Yulin, Hainan Island	HQ, 3d Submarine Flotilla: possible future SSBN base • submarine school
Yumen	nuclear materials production facility
Zhangiang	HQ, South Sea Fleet • VLF transmitter with regional communications coverage to naval forces
Zhaosu	satellite tracking station

(Note: names in parentheses indicate Wade-Giles spelling)

Sources for Appendices

Appendix A: U.S. Nuclear Weapons Infrastructure

Air Force Association, *Air Force Magazine* (annual "Air Force Almanac" edition published each May).

Robert J. Archer, *United States Military Aviation: The Air Force* (Leicester, U.K.: Midland Counties Publications, 1980).

Association of the U. S. Army, *Army Magazine* (annual "Green Book" edition published each October).

Canadian Department of National Defence, *Defence in the 70's* (Ottawa: Queen's Printer, 1971).

International Telecommunications Union, International Frequency Registration Board, *International Frequency List,* vol. 1 and 1982 supplement (Geneva: ITU, 1979).

U.S. Air Force, Air Force Manual 10–4, "Air Force Directory of Unclassified Addresses" (June 1982).

———, Air Force Communications Command (AFCC), PCN UE501H10B, "AFCC Active Units Listing" (Sept. 27, 1982).

———, AFCC, Pacific Communications Division (PCD) Regulation 23–12, "Organization and Mission—Field: 1961st Communications Group" (Oct. 23, 1981).

———, AFCC, PCD Regulation 23–20, "Organization and Mission—Field: 1957th Communications Group" (Jan. 29, 1982).

———, AFCC, PCD Regulation 23–44, "Organization and Mission—Field: 1956th Communications Group" (Nov. 16, 1981).

———, AFCC, PCD Regulation 23–45, "Organization and Mission—Field: 2146th Communications Group" (Jan. 1, 1982).

———, AFCC, PCD Regulation 23–47, "Organization and Mission—Field: 1962d Communications Group" (June 25, 1982).

———, AFCC, European Communications Division Regulation 23–36, " Organization and Mission—Field: TUSLOG Detachment 16" (Nov. 14, 1979) (includes all Air Force communications facilities in Turkey).

———, AFCC, Strategic Communications Division (SCD) Pamphlet 23–1, "Organization and Mission—Field: HQ SCD Organization and Functions" (Sept. 30, 1981).

———, AFCC, SCD Regulation 23–2, "Organization and Mission—Field: 1st Aerospace Communications Group" (July 31, 1981).

———, AFCC, SCD Regulation 23–15, "Organization and Mission—Field: 33rd Communications Group" (July 15, 1982).

———, AFCC, SCD Regulation 23–39, "Organization and Mission—Field: 2192d Communications Squadron" (Aug. 26, 1982).

———, Air Force Systems Command (AFSC), Eastern Space and Missile Center (ESMC), *Abbreviated Instrumentation Handbook,* SP 83–1, (Jan. 1983) (Patrick AFB, FL: ESMC, 1983).

———, AFSC, Air Force Flight Test Center, *AFFTC User's Handbook,* (April 1978) (Edwards AFB, CA: AFFTC, 1978).

———, Strategic Air Command Regulation 50–4, vol. 1, "Training: Bombing/Navigation-/AGM Operations (RCS: SAC-DOT (M&SA) 7105)" (June 28, 1982).

U.S. Army, U.S. Army Europe (USAREUR) Pamphlet 350–220, "Local Training Areas" (July 28, 1977).

———, USAREUR Pamphlet 450–45, "USAREUR Installations" (Sept. 23, 1977).

———, USAREUR Regulation 350–220, "Training Management Areas" (Dec. 21, 1982).

———, USAREUR Regulation 55–5, "USAREUR Activity Address File and Directory," (Feb. 1, 1977).

———, "U.S. Army Europe Telephone Directory," 1982.

———, Army Communications Command (USACC) Korea Regulation 10–1, "Organization and Functions Manual: 1st Signal Brigade" (March 1, 1981).

———, Army Pamphlet 210–1, "United States Army Installations and Major Activities" (April 1976).

———, Army Corps of Engineers, "Inventory of Army Military Real Property: The United States," (annual) (Sept. 30, 1982).

———, Army Corps of Engineers, "Inventory of Army Military Real Property: Outside the United States" (annual) (Sept. 30, 1982).

———, Training Circular 25–1, "Training Land: Unit Training Land Requirements" (Aug. 4, 1978).

———, Army Regulation 105–32, "Authorized Addresses for Electronically Transmitted Messages" (July 1979).

———, White Sands Missile Range, "Technical Capabilities Summary" (May 1983).

U.S. Congress, Congressional Budget Office, *Strategic Command, Control, and Communications: Alternative Approaches for Modernization* (Washington, D.C.: USGPO, 1981).

U.S. Department of Defense, "Base Structure Annex to Manpower Requirements Report" (annual) (Fiscal years 1979, 1980, 1981, 1982, 1983, and 1984).

———, "Global AUTOVON Defense Communications System Directory" (annual) (Dec. 1982).

———, DOD Directive 3200.11-D, "Major Range and Test Facility Base Summary of Capabilities" (June 1983).
———, Defense Communications Agency, "Defense Communcations System Northwest Pacific Region: Resource, Inventory and Allocation Pamphlet" (Sept. 1982).
———, Defense Nuclear Agency Field Command, Joint Nuclear Accident Coordinating Center, "1979 Nuclear Accident Response Capability Listing" (Aug. 1, 1979).
———, Military Communications- Electronics Board, "Joint Department of Defense Plain Language Address Directory" (Aug. 1982).
———, Office of the Assistant Secretary of Defense for Manpower, Reserve Affairs and Logistics (OASD/MRAL), DOD Directive 4140.17-M, "MILSTRIP Routing Identifier and Distribution Codes," supp. no. 1 (June 1982).
———, OASD/MRAL, DOD Directive 4525.6L, "Mail Distribution Scheme—Military Post Office Location List" (Nov. 1981).
U.S. Department of Transportation, Coast Guard Commandant Instruction MI6562.4, "Specification of the Transmitted LORAN-C Signal" (July 1981).
———, "Coast Guard Radionavigation Bulletin No. 13" (Dec. 13, 1983), p. 6.
———, *Coast Guard Radionavgation Systems Book, Part 2: LORAN-C* (Washington, D.C.: U.S. Coast Guard, 1983).
U.S. Navy, Office of the Chief of Naval Operations (OPNAV) P09B2-107, "Standard Navy Distribution List, Part 1" (Oct. 1982).
———, Chief of Naval Operations (OPNAV) P09B2-105, "Standard Navy Distribution List, Part 2 and Catalog of Naval Shore Activities" (Jan. 1978).
———, OPNAV Instruction 3111.14U, "Homeports and Permanent Duty Stations, Establishment, Disestablishment, and Modification of Activities of the Operating Forces of the Navy," Change 9 (Feb. 1, 1984).
———, OPNAV Report 5750-1, "Command History, David W. Taylor Naval Ship Research and Development Center for Calendar Year 1982" (1983).
———, Office of the Comptroller, (NAVSO) P-1385, "Distribution of Manpower in the United States by State" (Sept. 1983).
———, Office of the Comptroller, (NAVSO) P-1000-25, "Navy Comptroller Manual," vol. 2, ch. 5, rev. 47 (Sept. 1983).
———, Naval Explosive Ordnance Disposal Technology Center (NAVEODTECHCEN) Instruction 5450.2C, "Organization Manual" (Jan. 9, 1984).
———, Naval Telecommunications Command (NAVTELCOM), NTP 3 SUPP-1 (B), "U.S. Navy Plain Language Address Directory" (May 15, 1979).
———, NAVTELCOM Instruction C5450.12C, "Naval Communication Area Master Station EASTPAC Honolulu; Mission and Functions of" (partially declassified) (Oct. 7, 1980).
———, NAVTELCOM Instruction 5450.16A, "Tasks and Functions for Naval Communications Unit Key West" (Jan. 13, 1976).
———, NAVTELCOM Instruction 5450.24C, "Naval Communications Area Master Station LANT; Mission and Functions of" (Sept. 2, 1982).
———, NAVTELCOM Instruction C5450.31E, "Naval Communication Station San Diego; Mission and Functions of" (partially declassified) (April 18, 1983).
———, NAVTELCOM Instruction 5450.32C, "Naval Communication Station Stockton; Mission and Functions of" (Jan. 29, 1979).
———, Naval Underwater System Center, Technical Document 4980A, "Atlantic Undersea Test and Evaluation Center: Handbook and Visitor's Guide" (March 20, 1981).

Appendix B: Soviet Nuclear Weapons Infrastructure

Desmond Ball, *Targeting for Strategic Deterrence,* Adelphi Paper no. 185 (London: International Institute for Strategic Studies, 1983).
Robert Berman and John Baker, *Soviet Strategic Forces: Requirements and Responses* (Washington, D.C.: Brookings Institution, 1983).
John Beukers, *A Review and Applications of VLF and LF Transmissions for Navigation and Tracking* (Bohemia, N.Y.: Beukers Laboratories, n.d.), p. 12.
Kensuke Ebata, "Cam Ranh Bay: Forward Base of the Soviet Pacific Fleet," *Jane's Defence Weekly* (July 21, 1984), p. 66.
International Telecommunications Union, International Frequency Registration Board, *International Frequency List,* 10th ed. vol. 1, and 1982 supplement (Geneva: ITU, 1979).
David Isby, *Weapons and Tactics of the Soviet Army* (London: Jane's, 1981).
Geoffrey Kemp, *Nuclear Forces for Medium Powers: Part 1: Targets, Weapons Systems and Deterrence,* Adelphi Paper no.106 (London: International Institute for Strategic Studies, 1974).
Phillip J. Klass, "U.S. Scrutinzing New Soviet

Radar," *Aviation Week & Space Technology* (Aug. 22, 1983), p. 19.

Andreus Maislinger, "Landerbericht Österreich: Neue Österreichische Friedensbewegungen," *Mediatus* (April 1984), pp. 8–9.

"Omega Offers Immediate INS Backup," *Aviation Week & Space Technology* (Oct. 3, 1983), p. 153.

Norman Polmar, *Guide to the Soviet Navy* (Annapolis, Md.: U.S. Naval Institute Press, 1983).

Thomas Ries, "Defending the Far North," *International Defense Review* (July 1984), pp. 873–880.

Clarence Robinson, "Soviet SALT Violations Feared," *Aviation Week & Space Technology* (Sept. 22, 1980), p. 15.

Harriet Fast Scott and William F. Scott, *The Armed Forces of the USSR* (Boulder, Colo.: Westview Press, 1979).

"Soviet Far East Bases," *Jane's Defence Weekly* (April 14, 1984), pp. 560–562.

"Soviets Improve Moscow Air Defence," *Jane's Defence Weekly* (Feb. 18 1984), p. 231.

U.S. Department of Defense, *Soviet Military Power* (1st ed. Sept. 1981; 2d ed. March 1983; 3d ed. April 1984).

———, Defense Mapping Agency, "Operational Navigational Chart" Series of the Soviet Union (various years, 1978 to 1983).

———, Joint Chiefs of Staff, *United States Military Posture* (various years).

U.S. Department of Energy, "Summary of Foreign Nuclear Detonations Through December 31, 1983" (Las Vegas, Nev.: Nevada Operations Office, 1984).

U.S. Department of Transportaion, *Coast Guard Radionavigation Systems Book, Part 2: LORAN-C* (Washington, D.C.: U.S. Coast Guard, 1983), pp. 21–61.

Bruce W. Watson, *Red Navy at Sea: Soviet Naval Operations on the High Seas, 1956–1980* (Boulder, Colo.: Westview Press, 1983).

Derek Wood, "Soviets' Northern Fleet disabled . . .'Not Viable' for Six Months," *Jane's Defence Weekly* (July 14, 1984), p. 3.

Appendix C: British Nuclear Weapons Infrastructure

Paul Beaver, *The Encyclopedia of the Modern Royal Navy,* (Cambridge: Patrick Stevens, 1982).

British Defence Directory, vol. 1, no. 2 (June 1982), and vol. 3, no. 1 (March 1984) (Oxford: Brassey's Defence Publishers, quarterly)

Denis J. Calvert, "RAF Germany Re-equips," *Armed Forces* (Dec. 1983), pp. 451–455.

Duncan Campbell, *War Plan U.K.* (London: Burnet, 1982).

James W. Canan, "NATO on the Upbeat," *Air Force* (Sept. 1984), pp. 134–147.

Steve Conner, "Search Begins for Bomb Test Victims," *New Scientist* (Oct. 6, 1983), p. 3.

Margaret Gowing, *Independence and Deterrence: Britain and Atomic Energy, 1945–1952,* 2 vols. (New York: St. Martin's, 1974).

William Hill, "384 Warheads for UK Trident Force," *Jane's Defence Weekly* (June 9, 1984), pp. 913–917.

"International Air Forces and Military Aircraft Directory," AL-258/4/83, Aviation Advisory Services, Milavnews, (April 1983), pp. 75–84A.

International Telecommunications Union, International Frequency Registration Board, *International Frequency List,* vol. 1 (Geneva: ITU, 1979).

Stan Openshaw, Philip Steadman, and Owen Greene, *Doomsday: Britain After Nuclear Attack* (Oxford: Basil Blackwell, 1983).

Antony Preston, "Training Royal Navy Style—a Visit to HMS Dryad," *Jane's Defence Weekly* (Nov. 3, 1984), pp. 803–807.

Malcolm Spaven, *Fortress Scotland: A Guide to the Military Presence* (London: Pluto Press, 1983).

"Submarine Machinery Test Equipment," *Navy International* (Aug. 1984), p. 506.

" The West Wires Up for Armageddon," *New Scientist* (April 19, 1984), p. 25.

"Tornado Build-up Accelerates for RAF and Luftwaffe," *Aerospace Daily* (Nov. 8, 1983), p. 43.

U.K. House of Commons, *House of Commons Defence Committee Report, Summer 1984* (London: HMSO, 1984)

U.K. House of Commons, "The Future of the United Kingdom's Nuclear Weapons Policy," Sixth Report from the Expenditure Committee, Session 1978–79 (London: H.M. Stationery Office, 1979), p. 241.

U.K. Ministry of Defence, *Annual Report on the Meteorological Office,* 1976, 1980, 1981 and 1982 (London: H.M. Stationery Office, annual)

U.K. Ministry of Defence, *Selected Accessions List of the Map Library,* List no. 2/84 (Surbiton, U.K.: MOD Mapping and Charting Establishment, 1984).

U.K. Ministry of Defence, *Statement on the Defence Estimates, Parts I and II,* (1980, 1981, 1983, and 1984) (London: H.M. Stationery Office, annual)

"U.K. Radar Chain," *Jane's Defence Weekly* (Nov. 3, 1984), p. 763.

U.S. Army, Europe, "Training: Course Catalog of Institutional Training Courses—Non-USAREUR Courses," USAREUR Pamphlet 350–206 (Oct. 4, 1983), p.32.

U.S. Department of Transportation, *Coast Guard Radionavigation Systems Book, Part II: LORAN-C,* (Washington, D.C.: U.S. Coast Guard, 1983), pp.21–61.

U.S. Navy, Strategic Systems Project Office, "Initial and Replenishment Material Requirements for the United Kingdom Polaris Program," SSP Instruction 4614.2D (Feb. 23, 1979), p. 11.

Tom Wilkie, "Old Age Can Kill the Bomb," *New Scientist* (Feb. 16, 1984), pp. 27–32.

Appendix D: French Nuclear Weapons Infrastructure

"A la 7e Escadre de chasse 100 000 heures sur Jaguar," *Air et Cosmos* (April 30, 1983), p. 33.

Edward W. Bassett, "France to Modernize Nuclear Forces," *Aviation Week & Space Technology* (June 16, 1980), p. 268.

Daniel Blanc, *La Sûreté Nucléaire* (Paris: Presses Universitaires de France, 1982), p. 47.

Christian Brac de la Perrière, "The French Navy Atlantic Command," *Naval Forces* (No. 1/1983), p. 15.

Comité pour le Désarmement Nucleaire en Europe, "CODENE," *Disarmament Campaigns,* No. 18 (Jan. 1983), p. 8.

Comité pour le Désarmement Nucléaire en Europe, "La Dissuasion Française? Une Cible Pour Les Missiles," map prepared by CODENE (Paris: CODENE, 1983).

Commissariat à l'Énergie Atomique, *Rapport Annuel 1983* (Paris: Commissariat à l'Énergie Atomique, 1983).

Shirley Compard, "La Parade Existe," *Aerospatiale Revue* (March 1984), pp. 4–7.

"Final test of French M-4 SLBM," *Jane's Defence Weekly* (March 17, 1984), p. 392.

"France not ruling out using Superphénix plutonium for weapons," *Nucleonics Week* (April 28, 1983), pp. 2–3.

"France to Decommision Three Early Units," *Nuclear News* (May 1984), p. 81.

Hubert Haenel, La Défense Nationale (Paris: Presses Universitaires de France, 1982).

Jolyon Howarth, "Lethal Legacy of France," *Journal of European Nuclear Disarmament* (June/July 1983), p. 18.

International Telecommunications Union, International Frequency Registration Board, *International Frequency List,* vol. 1 and 1982 supp. (Geneva: ITU, 1979).

Paul A. Jackson, *French Military Aviation* (Leicester, U.K.: Midland Counties, 1979).

———, "More Mirages. . .Fewer Illusions," *Air International* (Nov. 1976), pp. 213–219.

"La force nucléaire tactique française en 1980," *Air et Cosmos* (July 12, 1980), p. 80.

Pierre Langereux, "Aerospatiale: l'Activité Balistique Décroît au Profit de l'Espace," *Air et Cosmos* (May 28, 1983), p. 10.

Jeffrey M. Lenorovitz, "France Updating Mirage 4P Bomber For Operations With ASMP Missile," *Aviation Week & Space Technology* (Nov. 26, 1984), pp. 63–64.

Jeffrey M. Lenorovitz, "Weak Economy Hinders Mitterrand Plan," *Aviation Week & Space Technology* (April 18, 1983), p. 74.

Roger May, *La France a la Bombe* (Paris: Gallimard, 1959).

Colonel Yvan Malaganne, "The French Air Force," *NATO's 15 Nations* (special issue no. 2, 1979), pp.52–55.

Jacques Ohanessian, "La Première Base Française De L'Espace," *Science et Vie* (Jan. 1967), pp. 110–114.

Alain Pigear, "The French Nuclear Triad," *Ground Defense International,* 74(4) (1981), pp. A1-A8.

"Revue aérienne à la base d'Orange le 14 juillet," *Air et Cosmos* (April 16, 1983), p. 12.

Alain Rudrauf, "Electromagnetic Pulse Simulators: EMP on tap," *Defense Electronics* (no. 1, 1984), pp. 83–86.

Jean-Claude Salvinien, "Mirage 2000's for the 'Cigognes' Squadron," *Aerospatiale Revue* (Sept. 1984), p. 25.

Robert Salvy, "The Air Defense of France: Plugging the Low-Level Gaps," *International Defense Review* (May 1983), pp. 571–577.

"Search for a new radar horizon," *New Scientist* (Aug. 11, 1983), p. 414.

Jacques Soppelsa, *Géographie des Armaments* (Paris: Masson, 1980).

"Space and Ballistic Systems Division: Military Programs," Aérospatiale Brochure DIC/R No. 86/83 S3 (Les Mureaux: Aérospatiale, 1983).

"Space and Ballistic Systems Division: The Division, Its Vocations and Facilities," Aérospatiale Brochure DIC/R No. 86/83 S1 (Les Mureaux: Aérospatiale, 1983).

"Tactical Missiles," Aérospatiale Brochure DRP/R No. 95/81 (Châtillon: Aérospatiale, 1981).

"Brandt-Armements participates in the annual

USAF Red Flag exercise," Thomson Newsletter (April 16, 1984)

U.S. Congress, Senate Foreign Relations Committee, U.S. Security Issues in Europe: Burden Sharing and Offset, MBFR and Nuclear Weapons" (comm. print, Dec. 2, 1973) (Washington, D.C.: USGPO, 1973).

U.S. Department of Transportation, Coast Guard, Radionavigation Bulletin 9 (June 1982), p. 1.

U.S. Naval Observatory, "Daily Time Differences and Relative Phase Values," 4(925) (Oct. 25, 1984) (Washington D.C.: NAVOBSY, 1984) pp. 6–7

Appendix E: Chinese Nuclear Weapons Infrastructure

S.K. Ghosh and Sreedhar, *China's Nuclear and Political Strategy,* (New Delhi: Young Asia, 1975).

Government Business Worldwide Report (March 24, 1980), p. 4202.

Bradley Hahn, "China in Space," *China Business Review* (July/Aug. 1984), pp. 12–24.

———, "China in the SLBM Club," *Pacific Defence Reporter* (Feb. 1984), pp. 17–20.

International Institute for Strategic Studies, *Military Balance 1983–84* (London: IISS, 1983).

International Telecommunications Union, International Frequency Registration Board, *International Frequency List,* 1982 supp. to 1979 ed. (Geneva: ITU, 1982).

Harlan Jencks, *From Muskets to Missiles: Politics and Professionalism in the Chinese Army 1945–1981* (Boulder, Colo.: Westview, 1982).

John Moore, ed., *Jane's Fighting Ships 1982–83,* and 1983–84, (London: Jane's, annual).

Antony Preston, "The PLA Navy's Underwater Deterrent," *Jane's Defence Weekly* (April 28, 1984), pp. 659–660.

John Scherer, ed. *China Facts & Figures Annual* (Gulf Breeze, Fla.: Academic International Press, annual) vol. 1, 1978, p. 77; and vol. 4, 1981, p. 115.

U.S. Defense Intelligence Agency, *Handbook on the Chinese Armed Forces* (Washington, D.C.: DIA DDI-2680–32-76, July 1976).

———, "Unclassified Communist Naval Orders of Battle," DDB-1200–124-83 (June 1983).

Selected Bibliography

This bibliography is limited to those general sources that could be useful in further understanding the nuclear battlefields and the nuclear infrastructure. Resources mentioned as specific sources for the appendices and chapter notes are, for the most part, not repeated. In addition, general sources that are critical to any understanding of military issues and the nuclear arms race are not included. Key documents are annual reports such as *Defense of Japan,* issued by the Japanese Defense Agency; *Statement on the Defence Estimates,* issued by the British Ministry of Defence; *Defense/Defence,* issued by the Canadian Department of National Defense; the U.S. Secretary of Defense's *Annual Report to Congress,* the U.S. Joint Chiefs of Staff *Military Posture Statement,* and *Soviet Military Power.* These and other other general publications are discussed in William M. Arkin, *Research Guide to Current Military and Strategic Affairs* (Washington, D.C.: Institute for Policy Studies, 1981).

Aberdeen Campaign for Nuclear Disarmament, *Living on the Frontline* (Aberdeen, U.K.: Aberdeen People's Press, 1981).

James V. Albertini, "Hawaii: Life under the Gun," *Bulletin of the Atomic Scientists* (March 1981): 50–57.

Jim Albertini, Nelson Foster, Wally Inglis, and Gil Roeder, *The Dark Side of Paradise: Hawaii in a Nuclear World* (Honolulu: Catholic Action of Hawaii, 1980).

Thomas B. Allen and Norman Polmar, "The Silent Chase: Tracking Soviet Submarines," *New York Times Magazine* (Jan. 1, 1984): 12–17 ff.

William M. Arkin, Andrew Burrows, Richard Fieldhouse, and Jeffrey I. Sands, "Nuclearization of the Oceans," background paper for the Symposium on the Denuclearization of the Oceans, Norrtalje, Sweden, May 11–14, 1984 (Stockholm: Myrdal Foundation, Jan. 1984).

William M. Arkin and Richard W. Fieldhouse, "Nuclear Weapon Command, Control and Communications," in *World Armaments and Disarmament: SIPRI Yearbook 1984* (London: Taylor & Francis, 1984).

Desmond Ball, *Can Nuclear War Be Controlled* ?, Adelphi Paper 169 (London: International Institute for Strategic Studies, 1981).

———, *A Suitable Piece of Real Estate: American Installations in Australia* (Sydney: Hale & Iremonger, 1980).

James Bamford, *The Puzzle Palace: A Report on NSA, America's Most Secret Agency* (Boston: Houghton Mifflin Company, 1982).

Bell Laboratories, "ABM Research and Development at Bell Laboratories: Project History" (written for Army Ballistic Missile Defense Systems Command under contract DAHC60–71-C-0005) (Whippany, N.J.: Bell Laboratories, 1975).

Bruce Bolt, *Nuclear Explosions and Earthquakes: The Parted Veil* (San Francisco: W.H. Freeman, 1976).

Iris Borg, "Nuclear Explosives: The Peaceful Side," *New Scientist* (March 8, 1984): 10–13.

Andrew Boyd, *An Atlas of World Affairs,* 7th ed. (London: Methuen, 1983).

Paul Bracken, *The Command and Control of Nuclear Forces* (New Haven, Conn.: Yale University Press, 1983).

George W. Bradley, *From "Missile Base" to "Gold Watch": An Illustrated History of The Aerospace Guidance and Metrology Center and Newark Air Force Station* (Newark AFS, Ohio: AGMC History Office, Air Force Logistics Command, 1983).

"Britain and the Bomb: The New Statesman Papers on Defence and Disarmament," *New Statesman Report No. 3* (London: New Statesman, 1981).

Burghfield Peace Camp, *ROF Burghfield: A Nuclear Weapons Factory* (Burghfield, U.K.: Burghfield Peace Camp, 1982).

Cambridge City Council, "Cambridge and Nuclear Weapons" (Cambridge, Mass.: Cambridge City Council, n.d. (1983)).

Duncan Campbell, *The Unsinkable Aircraft Carrier: American Military Power in Britain* (London: Michael Joseph, 1984).

———, *War Plan UK: The Truth about Civil Defence in Britain* (London: Burnett Books, 1982).

Canadian Department of External Affairs, "Agreement with the United States of America on Test and Evaluation of U.S. Defence Systems in Canada," Communique No. 15 (Feb. 10, 1983).

Center for Defense Information, "Preparing for Nuclear War: President Reagan's Program," *Defense Monitor* 10(8) (1982).

Thomas B. Cochran, William M. Arkin, and Milton M. Hoenig, *Nuclear Weapons Databook, vol. 1: U.S. Nuclear Forces and Capabilities* (Cambridge, Mass.: Ballinger, 1984).

John M. Collins, *U.S.-Soviet Military Balance: Concepts and Capabilities 1960–1980* (New York: McGraw Hill, 1980).

Alvin J. Cottrell and Thomas H. Moorer, *U.S. Overseas Bases: Problems of Projecting American Military Power Abroad* (Beverly Hills, Calif.: Sage Publications, 1977).

Danny J. Crawford and Ann A. Ferrante, "The Marine Corps in 1982," *Proceedings* (naval review issue, May 1983): 66 ff.

P.M. Dadant, "Shrinking International Airspace as a Problem of Future Air Movements: A Briefing," *Rand Report* R-2178-AF (Santa Monica, Calif.: RAND, 1978).

Savannah Davis, Naomi Harmon, and Craig Simpson, *New Mexico, The Military and the Bomb* (Albuquerque: New Mexico People and Energy, 1980).

Thijs de la Court, Deborah Pick, and Daniel Nordquist, *The Nuclear Fix: A Guide to Nu-*

clear Activities in the Third World (Amsterdam: World Information Service on Energy, 1982).

Daniel Deudney, *Space: The High Frontier in Perspective* (Washington: Worldwatch Institute Paper 50, Aug. 1982).

———, *Whole Earth Security: A Geopolitics of Peace* (Washington: Worldwatch Institute Paper 55, July 1983).

Keith A. Dunn, "Constraints on the USSR in Southwest Asia: A Military Analysis," Orbis 25(3) (Fall 1981): 607–29.

Benjamin M. Elson, "Magnetosphere Studied as VLF Transmission Aid," *Aviation Week & Space Technology* (Dec. 20, 1978): 64–65.

Energy and Technology Review, Special Issue: Treaty Verification (Livermore,Calif.: Lawrence Livermore National Laboratory, May 1983).

Lawrence Freedman, *Britain and Nuclear Weapons* (London: Macmillan, 1980).

Oswald H. Ganley and Gladys D. Ganley, *To Inform or To Control? The New Communications Networks* (New York: McGraw-Hill, 1982).

S.K. Ghosh and Sreedhar, eds., *China's Nuclear and Political Strategy* (New Delhi: Young Asia Publications, 1975).

Carole Giangrande, *The Nuclear North: The People, the Regions and the Arms Race* (Toronto: Anansi, 1983).

Paul H. B. Godwin, *The Chinese Tactical Air Forces and Strategic Weapons Program: Development, Doctrine and Strategy* (Maxwell AFB, Ala.: Air University, April 1978).

Colin Gray, *The Geopolitics of the Nuclear Era* (New York: Crane Russak, 1977).

Olafur Grimsson and Angus McCormack, *The Nuclear North Atlantic* (London: European Nuclear Disarmament, 1982).

Bradley Hahn, "PRC Submarine-launched Ballistic Missile Development," *Proceedings* (Oct. 1979): 132–35.

Richard Halloran, "Navy Trains to Battle Soviet Submarines in Arctic," *New York Times*, May 19, 1983, A-1.

———, "Report to Congress Provides Figures for Nuclear Arsenal," *New York Times*, Nov. 15, 1983, A-15.

Robert E. Harkavy, *Great Power Competition for Overseas Bases: The Geopolitics of Access Diplomacy* (New York: Pergamon Press, 1982).

Peter Herring, "Lights in the Night Sea," *New Scientist* (Feb. 23, 1984): 45–48.

Alan Hyman, "Long Range Navigation," *Aerospace International* (March/April 1981): 26–30.

Interchurch Peace Council (Netherlands), *Opslag en Transport van Kernwapens* (1982), also translated into German as *Lagerung und Transport von Atomwaffen* (Munchen: Informationsburo fur Friedenspolitik, 1982).

B. Jasani, ed., *Outer Space: A New Dimension of the Arms Race* (London: Taylor & Francis, 1982).

Harlan W. Jencks, *From Muskets to Missiles: Politics and Professionalism in the Chinese Army, 1945–1981* (Boulder, Colo.: Westview, 1982).

Mary Kaldor and Dan Smith, eds., *Disarming Europe* (London: Merlin Press, 1982).

David E. Kaplan, ed., *Nuclear California: An Investigative Report* (San Francisco: Greenpeace/Center for Investigative Reporting, 1982).

Thomas H. Karas, *Implications of Space Technology for Strategic Nuclear Competition*, Occasional Paper No. 25 (Muscatine, Iowa: Stanley Foundation, 1981).

Geoffrey Kemp, "The New Strategic Map," *Survival* (March/April 1977): 50–59.

Michael Kidron and Ronald Segal, *The State of the World Atlas* (New York: Simon & Schuster, 1981).

Michael Kidron and Dan Smith, *The War Atlas: Armed Conflict—Armed Peace* (New York: Simon & Schuster, 1983).

Philip Klass, *Secret Sentries in Space* (New York: Random House, 1971).

Lowell L. Klessig and Victor L. Strite, *The ELF Odyssey: National Security versus Environmental Protection* (Boulder, Colo.: Westview, 1980).

Albert Langer, Owen Wilkes, and N.P. Gleditsch, *The Military Functions of Omega and Loran-C* (Oslo: Peace Research Institute (PRIO), 1971).

Peter Laurie, *Beneath the City Streets: The Secret Plans to Defend the State* (London: Granada, 1983).

William H. Lewis, "How a Defense Planner Looks at Africa," in Helen Kitchen, ed., *Africa: From Mystery to Maze* (Lexington, Mass.: Lexington Books, 1976).

Ian Lind, *Neighborhood Nukes: Nuclear Weap-*

ons in Local Communities, An Organizer's Guide to Information and Action (Baltimore: Vacant Lots Press, March 1981).

Burkhard Luber, *Bedrohungsatlas Bundesrepublik Deutschland* (Wuppertal, FRG: Jugenddienst-Verlag, 1982).

MITRE Corporation, *The First Twenty Years: A History of the MITRE Corporation (1958–1978)* (Bedford, Mass.: MITRE, 1979).

Kari Mottola, *Nuclear Weapons and Northern Europe* (Helsinki: Finnish Institute of International Affairs, 1983).

Lieutenant Comander David G. Muller, "China's SSBN in Perspective," *Proceedings* (March 1983): 125–27.

Stephen M. Myer, *Soviet Theater Nuclear Forces: Part 1: Development of Doctrine and Objectives,* Adelphi Paper No. 187 (London: International Institute for Strategic Studies, 1984).

———, *Soviet Theater Nuclear Forces: Part 2: Capabilities and Implications,* Adelphi Paper No. 188 (London: International Institute for Strategic Studies, 1984).

Roland Paul, *American Military Commitments Abroad* (New Brunswick, N.J.: Rutgers University Press, 1973).

Robert Poole and Steve Wright, The Richardson Institute Study Group on Civil Defence, *Target North West: Civil Defense & Nuclear War in Cumbria, Lancashire, Manchester, Merseyside & Cheshire* (University of Lancaster: Richardson Institute, 1982).

Barbara B. Poppe, Debbi A. Naab, and John S. Derr, "Seismograph Station Codes and Characteristics," (Washington, D.C.: U.S. Geological Survey, Circular 791, 1978).

Antony Preston, "The PLA Navy's Underwater Deterrent," *Jane's Defence Weekly* (April 28, 1984): 659–60.

Peter Pringle and William Arkin, *S.I.O.P.: The Secret U.S. Plan for Nuclear War* (New York: W.W. Norton, 1983).

Project Ploughshares, "Make Canada a Nuclear Weapon Free Zone," *Ploughshares Monitor* 3(6) (n.d.).

Ernie Regehr and Simon Rosenblum, eds., *Canada and the Nuclear Arms Race* (Toronto: Lorimer, 1983).

Research Institute for Disarmament Development and Peace, *What the Russians Know Already and the Italians Must Not Know* (Rome: Research Institute for Disarmament Development and Peace, Aug. 1983 and March 1984).

Geoff Richards, "Transit: The First Navigational Satellite System," *Spaceflight* (Feb. 1979).

Jeffrey Richelson, "The Keyhole Satellite Program," *Journal of Strategic Studies* (June 1984): 248–78.

Paul Rogers, *Guide to Nuclear Weapons 1984–85* (Bradford, UK: University of Bradford School of Peace Studies, 1984).

Charles Shishkevish, "Soviet Seismographic Stations and Seismic Instruments, Part 1, A Report Prepared for Defense Advanced Research Projects Agency," *Rand Report* R-1204-ARPA (Santa Monica, Calif.: RAND, May 1974).

Ruth Leger Sivard, *World Military and Social Expenditures* (Leesburg, Virg.: World Priorities, annual).

Michael Skinner, *USAFE: A Primer of Modern Air Combat in Europe* (Novato, Calif.: Presidio Press, 1983).

Society for Human Exploration, *The Nuclear War Atlas* (Victoriaville, Quebec: Society for Human Exploration, 1982).

Jacques Soppelsa, *Géographie des Armements* (Paris: Masson, 1980).

Robert G. Sutter, *Chinese Nuclear Weapons and American Interests: Conflicting Policy Choices* (Washington, D.C.: Congressional Research Service, Sept. 27, 1983).

Lynn R. Sykes and Jack F. Evernden, "The Verification of a Comprehensive Nuclear Test Ban," *Scientific American* (Oct. 1982): 47–55.

"Technology in War and Peace," *IEEE Spectrum* 19(10) (special issue) (Oct. 1982).

U.S. Air Force, Air Command and Staff College, *The European Military Environment: NATO and the Warsaw Pact, Volume 1, The European Environment,* (Maxwell, Ala.: Air University, n.d.).

———, "Nuclear Safety: Safety Rules for the CF-101/AIR-2A/W25 Weapon System," Air Force Regulation 122–7 (July 31, 1978).

U.S. Air Force, Air Force Communications Command, "Air Force Communications Command: Chronology, Leaders, and Lineage 1938–1981" (Scott AFB, Ill.: AFCC, 1982).

———, "Air Force Communications Command: Providing the Reins of Command, 1938–1981,

An Illustrated History" (Scott AFB, Ill.: AFCC, 1981).

U.S. Air Force, Air Force Geophysics Laboratory, "AFGL Fiscal Year 1984 Air Force Technical Objectives Document," AFGL-TR-82–0293, Special Report No. 232, (Hanscom AFB, Mass.: Air Force Geophysics Laboratory, Nov. 1982).

———, "Report on Research For the Period January 1979-December 1980," AFGL-TR-82–0132 (Hanscom AFB, Mass.: Air Force Geophysics Laboratory, 1982).

U.S. Air Force, Air Force Global Weather Central, "History of Air Force Global Weather Central (AFGWC), Offutt Air Force Base, Nebraska, 1 January 1983–30 June 1983," Mary J. Carr, ed. (Sept. 30, 1983).

U.S. Air Force, Air Force Satellite Control Facility, "Historical Brief and Chronology, 1954–1981" (Sunnyvale AFS, Calif.: AFSCF, 1982).

U.S. Air Force, Air Force Systems Command, "History: Electronic Systems Division, Air Force Systems Command, 1 October 1981—30 September 1982," vol. 1 (declassified) (Hanscom AFB, Mass.: ESD, 1983).

———, "History of the 6585th Test Group, 1 October 82–30 September 83," (Holloman AFB, N.M.: 6585th Test Group, 1983).

———, "Space and Missile Systems Organization: A Chronology, 1954–1979," (Los Angeles: SAMSO, 1980).

U.S. Air Force, Eastern Space and Missile Center, "T&E Support Resource Plan FY 82–89, Part II: Eastern Space and Missile Center," (Patrick AFB, Fla.: ESMC, n.d.).

U.S. Air Force, Space Command, "Weather: Atmospheric Effects on Detecting/Tracking Radars," Regulation 105–3 (May 20, 1983).

U.S. Air Force, Strategic Air Command, "Intelligence: Mission Support Imagery," Regulation 200–9 (May 21, 1984).

———, "Intelligence: Functions and Responsibilities," Regulation 200–14 (Feb. 10, 1984).

U.S. Air Force, Tactical Air Command, "History of the Tactical Fighter Weapons Center —1982, vols. 1–4" (Secret, partially declassified) (Nellis AFB, Nev.: TFWC, 1983).

———,"TAC Quarterly Status Report, Vol. 2, December 31, 1983," (Nellis AFB, Nev.: Tactical Fighter Weapons Center, 1983).

U.S. Arms Control and Disarmament Agency, "An Analysis of Civil Defense in Nuclear War" (Washington, D.C.: ACDA, Dec. 1978).

U.S. Army, Army Armament Research and Development Command (ARRADCOM), "Organization and Functions: Mission and Major Functions of the United States Army Armament Research and Development Command," Regulation 10–1, Jan. 31, 1977, with changes through July 6, 1982 (Dover, N.J.: AARADCOM, 1979).

U.S. Army, Army Communications Command, "History of the United States Army Communications Command from Origin through 1976" (Ft. Huachuca, Ariz.: Army Communications Command, 1979).

U.S. Army, Army Missile Command, "Organization, Mission and Functions," Oct. 1, 1979, with changes through 1983, (Redstone Arsenal, Ala.: MICOM, 1979).

U.S. Central Intelligence Agency, *Polar Regions Atlas* (Washington, D.C.: GPO, 1978).

U.S. Congress, House International Relations Committee, "United States Military Installations and Objectives in the Mediterranean," report prepared by the Congressional Research Service (March 27, 1977).

U.S. Congress, Joint Economic Committee, "Allocation of Resources in the Soviet Union and China, Hearings," (annual, 1974-).

U.S. Congress, Senate Foreign Relations Committee, "United States Foreign Policy Objectives and Overseas Military Installations," report prepared by the Congressional Research Service (April 1979).

———, United States Security Agreements and Commitments Abroad, 9 vol., Hearings before the Subcommittee on United States Security Agreements and Commitments Abroad, 91st Cong., 2nd Sess. (Washington, D.C.: GPO, 1970).

U.S. Defense Intelligence Agency, "Defense Intelligence Report, Soviet Self Propelled Artillery," DDI-1130–6-76 (May 1976) (partially declassified).

———, "A Guide to Foreign Tactical Nuclear Weapon Systems Under the Control of Ground Force Commanders," DST-1040S-541–83 (Sept. 9, 1983) (partially declassified).

———, "Handbook on the Chinese Armed Forces," DDI-2680–32-76 (July 1976).

———, "Unclassified Communist Naval Orders of Battle," DDB-1200–124-83 (June 1983).

U.S. Department of Defense, "Major Range and

Test Facility Base Summary of Capabilities," Directive 3200–11D (1983).
U.S. Department of Energy, "Announced United States Nuclear Tests: July 1945 through December 1982," NVO-209, rev. 3, annual (Las Vegas: Nevada Operations Office, 1983).
U.S. Department of State, "Atlas of United States Foreign Relations," DOS Publication 9350 (June 1983).
U.S. Department of Transportation, Coast Guard Commandant Instruction P165662.2, "OMEGA Global Radionavigation: A Guide for Users" (Nov. 1983).
———, Coast Guard Radionavigation Bulletin, compiled ed. (Jan. 1978—Dec. 1982).
U.S. Navy, Pacific Fleet, "COMTHIRDFLT Manual of Fleet Operating Areas, Including Target, Test, and Special Use Areas; Promulgation of," Commander Third Fleet Instruction 3120.1L (June 14, 1982).
U.S. Navy, David Taylor Naval Ship R&D Center, "Organizational and Functional Manual," DTNSRDC Instruction 5400.1D (July 7, 1981, with changes through Jan. 13, 1984).
U.S. Navy, Naval Material Command, "CNM-Commanded Research and Development Centers; Missions and Functions of," NAVMAT Instruction 5450.27C (Aug. 1, 1983).
U.S. Navy, Naval Observatory, "Descriptive Summary of Research and Development Program Fiscal Year 1984: Astronomy and Astrophysics" (n.d. (1983)).
———, "The Naval Observatory: Its Unique Mission" (Washington, D.C.: NAVOBSY, June 1979).
———, "Organization and Regulations Book," NAVOBSY Instruction 5400.1C (June 3,1982).
U.S. Navy, Naval Ocean Systems Center, "A Guide to U.S. Navy Command, Control, and Communications," Technical Document 247 (San Diego: NOSC, 1979).
U.S. Navy, Naval Oceanographic Office, "Oceanographic Survey Support Plans: FY 84 —FY 89" (Bay St. Louis, Miss.: NOO, 1983).
U.S. Navy, Naval Research Laboratory, *1983 Fact Book* (Washington, D.C.: NRL, 1983).
———, *1982 Review,* (Washington, D.C.: NRL, 1982).
U.S. Navy, "Naval Surface Weapons Center Brief, Sept. 30, 1982" (Dahlgren, Virg.: SWC, 1982).
U.S. Navy, "Naval Undersea Warfare Engineering Station: Publication 5400(3)," 13ND-NUWES-P5400(3) (Newport, Wash.: NUWES, 1979).
U.S. Navy, "Naval Weapons Center Brief, Sept 30, 1983," (China Lake, Calif.: NWC, 1983).
U.S. Navy, Naval Weapons Support Center "Organization Manual, August 1, 1983, with changes through January 30, 1984" (Crane, Ind.: NWSC, 1983).
U.S. Navy, Office of Naval Research, "Contract Research & Technology Program," NAVSO P-3589 (April 1982).
U.S. Navy, Pacific Missile Test Center, "Annual Report: Fiscal Year 1982" (Point Mugu, Calif.: PMTC, 1983).
Mark Wade, "The Chinese Ballistic Missile Program," *International Defense Review* (Aug. 1980): 1190–92.
Captain Thomas D. Washburn, "The People's Republic of China and Nuclear Weapons: Effects of China's Evolving Arsenal" (University of South Carolina, M.A. Thesis, March 15, 1979) (Washington, D.C.: National Technical Information Service, ADA 067350, 1979).
Western Union Telegraph Company, Government Systems Division, "Information for AUTODIN II Subscribers" (McLean, Virg.: Western Union, 1981).
Owen Wilkes, *Spacetracking and Space Warfare* (Oslo: Peace Research Institute (PRIO), 1978).
Owen Wilkes and Nils Petter Gleditsch, *Intelligence Installations in Norway: Their Number, Location, Function and Legality* (Oslo: Peace Research Institute (PRIO), 1979).
Robert S. Winohur and Rene E. Gonzalez, Jr., "Ocean Science and Military Use of the Ocean," *Oceanus* (Winter 1983).
Edward Zuckerman, *The Day After World War III: The U.S. Government's Plans for Surviving a Nuclear War* (New York: Viking, 1984).

Glossary

AAC: Alaskan Air Command, headquarters at Elmendorf AFB, Alaska

AAFCE: Allied Air Forces Central Europe, NATO command, headquarters at Ramstein AB, West Germany

AAP: Army ammunition plant

AB: airbase

ABM: anti-ballistic missile

ABNCP: airborne command post

ACCHAN: Allied Command Channel, NATO command, headquarters at Northwood, United Kingdom

ACE: Allied Command Europe, NATO command, headquarters at Casteau-Mons, Belgium

ACR: armored cavalry regiment

ACLANT: Allied Command Atlantic, NATO command, headquarters at Norfolk, Virginia

ACMI: air combat maneuvering instrumentation, aircraft testing and training ranges used by United States and allies

ACWS: aircraft control and warning squadron

ADA: air defense artillery

ADGE: air defense ground environmant

ADM: atomic demolition munition

ADS: aerospace defense squadron, operate air defense radars in the United States

AF: Air Force

AFB: Air Force base

AFCC: Air Force Communications Command, headquarters at Scott AFB, Illinois

AFCENT: Allied Forces Central Europe, NATO command, headquarters at Brunssum, Netherlands

AFFTC: Air Force Flight Test Center, headquarters at Edwards AFB, California

AFGL: Air Force Geophysics Laboratory, headquarters at Hanscom AFB, Massachussets

AFGWC: Air Force Global Weather Central, located at Offutt AFB, Nebraska, provides SAC and military with weather support

AFLC: Air Force Logistics Command, headquarters at Wright-Patterson AFB, Ohio

AFNORTH: Allied Forces Northern Europe, NATO command, headquarters at Kolsaas, Norway

AFRES: Air Force Reserve

AFS: Air Force station

AFSATCOM: Air Force satellite communications system, a worldwide, survivable command and control network between the NCA and nuclear forces

AFSC: Air Force Systems Command, headquarters at Andrews AFB, Maryland

AFSCF: Air Force Satellite Control Facility, headquarters at Sunnyvale AFS, California

AFSOUTH: Allied Forces Southern Europe, NATO command, headquarters in Naples, Italy

AFTAC: Air Force Technical Applications Center, headquarters at Patrick AFB, Florida

ALANG: Alabama Air National Guard

ALC: air logistics center

ALCM: air-launched cruise missile

ALCOP: alternate command post

ANGB: Air National Guard base

ANMCC: Alternate National Military Command Center, located at Raven Rock, Pennsylvania

ARANG: Arkansas Air National Guard

ARG: aerial refueling group

Arty: artillery

ARW: aerial refueling wing

ASAT: anti-satellite

ASM: air-to-surface missile

ASROC: anti-submarine rocket

ASW: anti-submarine warfare

ASWOC: anti-submarine warfare operations center

ATAF: Allied Tactical Air Force (NATO)

ATOC: Allied Tactical Operations Center (NATO)

AUTEC: Atlantic Undersea Test and Evaluation Center, located at Andros Island, Bahamas; subordinate to NUSC

AUTODIN: automatic digital network

AUTOVON: automatic voice network

AUW: advanced underwater weapons, a U.S. pseudonym used for naval nuclear depth bombs

AWACS: airborne warning and control system

AWS: Air Weather Service, headquarters at Scott AFB, Illinois

AZANG: Arizona Air National Guard

BARSTUR: Barking Sands tactical underwater range, located at Barking Sands, Oahu, Hawaii

Bde: brigade

Bks: barracks

BMD: ballistic missile defense

BMEWS: ballistic missile early warning system

Bn: battalion

Btry: battery

BS: bombardment squadron

BUF: back-up facility

BW: bombardment wing, with either B-52 or FB-111 aircraft. The typical wing contains one bomber squadron with 14 to 16 B-52s or 15 FB-111, and one aerial refueling squadron with 15 KC-135 tanker aircraft

C³: command, control, and communications

C³CM: command, control, and communications countermeasures

CAANG: California Air National Guard

CADIN: continental air defense integration north. A 24-radar network named CADIN-Pinetree across southern Canada provides tactical warning, tracking, and attack assessment

CAFDA: Commandement Air des Forces de Défense Aérienne, French air defense command

CARGRU: aircraft-carrier group

CATAC: Commandement Aérien Tactique, French tactical air command

CDC: centre de detection et de control, French air defense command and control center

CEA: Commissariat à l'Énergie Atomique, French atomic energy commission

CEL: Centre d'Essais des Landes, French missile test launch center

CENTAG: Central Army Group, NATO command, headquarters at Seckenheim, West Germany

CENTCOM: Central Command, headquarters at MacDill AFB, Florida

CEVG: combat evaluation group, SAC unit that operates nuclear bomb practice sites

CFB: Canadian Forces Base

CFS: Canadian Forces Station

CINC: commander-in-chief

CINCHAN: Commander-in-Chief, Channel, NATO command, headquarters at Northwood, United Kingdom

CINCLANT: Commander-in-Chief, Atlantic, headquarters at Norfolk, Virgina

CINCPAC: Commander-in-Chief, Pacific, headquarters at Camp H.M. Smith, Hawaii

CNM: Chief of Naval Material

CNO: Chief of Naval Operations, Navy equivalent to Chief of Staff

CO: company

COANG: Colorado Air National Guard

COC: combat operations center

COG: continuity of government

Commando Escort: Pacific Air Forces HF radio command and control system, six stations provide the primary ground-to-air link to aircraft and the Pacific Command airborne command post

COOP: continuity of operations plan

CRUDESGRU: cruiser-destroyer group

CVW: aircraft-carrier air wing

CZAF: Czechoslovakian Air Force

DAMS: dépôt-atelier munitions spéciales, French nuclear weapon storage site, located at airbases

DARCOM: Army Material and Development Readiness Command, headquarters at Alexandria, Virginia

DARPA: Defense Advanced Research Projects Agency, headquarters at Arlington, Virginia

DCA: Defense Communications Agency, headquarters at Alexandria, Virginia

DCANG: District of Columbia Air National Guard

DCL: Direct Communications Link, Moscow-Washington "hot line"

DCS: defense communications system

DESRON: destroyer squadron

Det: detachment

DEW: distant early warning

DIA: Defense Intelligence Agency, headquarters in the Pentagon, offices located at Bolling AFB, Washington, D.C.

Div: division

DMA: Defense Mapping Agency, headquarters at the Naval Observatory in Washington, D.C.

DMAAC: DMA Aerospace Center, located in St. Louis, Missouri

DMAHTC: DMA Hydrographic and Topographic Center, located in Washington, D.C.

DMSP: Defense Meteorological Satellite Program

DNA: Defense Nuclear Agency, headquarters in Alexandria, Virginia

DOD: Department of Defense

DOE: Department of Energy

DSCS: Defense Communications Satellite System

DSP: Defense Support Program, U.S. early warning satellite system

DTNSRDC: David W. Taylor Naval Ship Research and Development Center, headquarters at Carderock, Maryland

EASTLANT: Eastern Atlantic command, NATO command, headquarters at Northwood, United Kingdom

EB: escadre de bombardement, French bomber wing, under FAS

EC: escadre de chasse, French aircraft attack wing, under FATAC

ECM: electronic countermeasures EGA: East German Army

EGAF: East German Air Force

EHF: extremely high frequency

ELF: extremely low frequency, wavelength used primarily to communicate with submarines

EMP: electromagnetic pulse

Eng: engineer

EOD: explosive ordnance disposal

EPG: Army Electronic Proving Grounds, headquarters at Ft. Huachuca, Arizona

ERADCOM: Army Electronics Research and Development Command, headquarters at Adelphi, Maryland

ERCS: emergency rocket communications system

ERV: escadre de ravitaillement en vol, French aerial refueling wing

Escadre: wing (French)

ESD: Air Force Electronics Systems Division, headquarters at Hanscom AFB, Massachussets, subordinate to Air Force Systems Command

ESMC: Eastern Space and Missile Center, headquarters at Patrick AFB, Florida

ETR: Eastern Test Range, missile test range operated by ESMC

EWO: emergency war order

FA: field artillery

FAA: Federal Aviation Administration

FAS: Forces Aériennes Stratégiques, French strategic air command

FATAC: Force Aérienne Tactique, French tactical air command

FBM: fleet ballistic missile

FCRC: federal contract research center

FEMA: Federal Emergency Management Agency

FIS: fighter interceptor squadron

FIW: fighter interceptor wing

FLANG: Florida Air National Guard

FLTSATCOM: fleet satellite communications system

FMF: Fleet Marine Force

FMFLANT: Fleet Marine Force Atlantic

FMFPAC: Fleet Marine Force Pacific

FOC: full operational capability

FORSCOM: Army Forces Command, headquarters at Ft McPherson, Georgia

FOSIC: Fleet Ocean Surveillance Information Center

FOSIF: Fleet Ocean Surveillance Information Facility

FOST: Force Océanique Stratégique, French strategic nuclear submarine force

FRC: Federal Regional Center

FROG: free-rocket-over-ground, division level short-range missile; latest version is FROG-7 (Soviet)

FSSG: Force Service Support Group, Marine Corps unit

FY: fiscal year

GCHQ: Government Communications Headquarters, British signals intelligence agency headquarters at Cheltenham, United Kingdom

GCI: ground control intercept

GEODSS: ground-based electro-optical deep space surveillance

Giant Talk: Strategic Air Command HF long-range radio communications network, 14 stations, operates continuously as the primary link to bombers, being upgraded to Scope Signal III

GLCM: ground-launched cruise missile

Global Command and Control System (formerly Air Force Aeronautical Stations): HF two-way communications network to aircraft, 16 stations, used for retransmission of Emergency Action Messages, control site and transmitter/receiver usually separated by 10 to 20 miles

GOCO: government-owned contractor-operated

Gp: group

Green Pine: Strategic Air Command Northern Area ultra high frequency line of sight radio communications network, 13 stations, supplementing the Giant Talk network in northern latitudes

GWEN: ground wave emergency network, an emergency communications network in the U.S. being built to survive a nuclear attack by having 300 to 500 communications stations

HF: high frequency

HF/SSB: high frequency single sideband

HIANG: Hawaii Air National Guard

HQ: headquarters

IAANG: Iowa Air National Guard

IAP: international airport

ICBM: intercontinental ballistic missile

ICF: inertial confinement fusion

ILANG: Illinois Air National Guard

INANG: Indiana Air National Guard

Inf: infantry

IRBM: intermediate-range ballistic missile

Inform Net: Air Forces Europe HF point-to-point radio command and control network, 13 active, 9 stand-by stations

I/O: input/output, refers to control stations in the CWEN network

IOC: initial operational capability

JCS: Joint Chiefs of Staff

JEEP: joint emergency evacuation program, "essential" government workers to be evacuated to shelters for continuation of U.S. government after a nuclear war

JSS: joint surveillance system

JTF: joint task force

JTFAK: Joint Task Force Alaska, wartime command responsible for Alaskan defense

km: kilometer

KSANG: Kansas Air National Guard

Ksn: kaserne (barracks)

LAANG: Louisiana Air National Guard

LANTCOM: Atlantic Command, U.S. Unified Command, headquarters at Norfolk, Virginia

LF: low frequency

LORAN-C: long-range aids to navigation, modification C, used for submarine navigation and communications (Clarinet Pilgrim network), also used for accurate alignment and synchronization of missile tests

MAB: Marine Amphibious Brigade

MAC: Military Airlift Command

MACG: Marine Air Control Group

MAF: Marine Amphibious Force

MAG: Marine Air Group

MAP: municipal airport

MAU: Marine amphibious unit

MAW: Marine Air Wing

MC: Marine Corps

MCAS: Marine Corps Air Station

MD: military district (Soviet)

MEANG: Maine Air National Guard

Mech: mechanized

MEECN: minimum essential emergency communications network

MIANG: Michigan Air National Guard

MICOM: Army Missile Command, headquarters at Redstone Arsenal, Alabama

MNANG: Minnesota Air National Guard

MOANG: Missouri Air National Guard

MOB: main operating base

MP: military police

MRD: motorized rifle division

MSBS: mer-sol balistique stratégique, submarine-launched ballistic missile (French)

MUNSS: munition support squadron, Air Force nuclear weapons custodial/maintenace unit supporting NATO nuclear units

MWS: missile warning squadron

MWWU: Marine Wing Weapons Unit

Mystic Star: Presidential HF radio communications network, 14 stations, many colocated with Global C2 stations

NADGE: NATO air defense ground environment, a system of air defense radars and control stations throughout Europe

NAS: Naval air station

NASA: National Aeronautics and Space Administration

NATO: North Atlantic Treaty Organization

NAVCAMS: Naval Communications Area Master Station

NAVSPASUR: Naval space surveillance system, subordinate to Naval Space Command, both have headquarters at Dahlgren, Virginia

NAVSTAR: navigation system using time and ranging, U.S. navigation satellite system

NCA: National Command Authority

NCMC: NORAD Cheyenne Mountain Center, NORAD's hardened command center

NDANG: North Dakota Air National Guard

NEACP: national emergency airborne command post

NHANG: New Hampshire Air National Guard

NJANG: New Jersey Air National Guard

NORAD: North American Aerospace Defense Command, headquarters at Peterson AFB, Colorado

NOSC: Naval Ocean Systems Center, headquarters at San Diego, California

NRF: Naval Reserve Force

NRL: Naval Research Laboratory, headquarters in Washington, D.C.

NSA: National Security Agency, headquarters at Ft. Meade, Maryland

NSWC: Naval Surface Weapons Center, Dahlgren, Virginia, and White Oak, Maryland

NUSC: Naval Underwater Systems Center, located at Newport, Rhode Island

NUWES: Naval Underwater Weapons Evaluation Station, headquarters at Port Hueneme, Calfornia

NWC: Naval Weapons Center, headquarters at China Lake, California

NWS: Naval Weapons Station

NWSC: Naval Weapons Support Center, headquarters at Crane, Indiana

NYANG: New York Air National Guard

OL: operating location

ORANG: Oregon Air National Guard
Ord: ordnance

OTH: over-the-horizon

OTH-B over-the-horizon backscatter

OUSDRE: Office of the Under Secretary of Defense for Research and Engineering

PAANG: Pennsylvania Air National Guard

PACCS: post-attack command and control system, SAC airborne command posts

PACFLT: Pacific Fleet

PACOM: Pacific Command, U.S. Unified Command, headquarters at Camp H.M. Smith, Hawaii

PAR: phased-array radar

PARCS: perimeter acquisition radar attack characterization system

PATWING: patrol wing

PAVE PAWS: precision acquisition of vehicle entry—phased array warning system, U.S. SLBM early warning radar system

PLA: People's Liberation Army, Chinese military

PMRF: Pacific Missile Range Facility, headquartered at NAS Barbers Point, Hawaii

PMTC: Pacific Missile Test Center, headquarters at Point Mugu, California

PNAF: primary nuclear airlift force

PPRNS: Pulse Phased Radio Navigation System (Soviet)

PRANG: Puerto Rico Air National Guard

PVO: Voiska protivovozdushnoi oborony or Voiska PVO, Soviet Air Defense Forces

QRA: quick reaction alert

RAF: Royal Air Force (British)

R&D: research and development

RADC: Rome Air Development Center, headquarters at Griffiss AFB, New York

RADS: radar squadron, operating air defense radars in the United States

RBS: radar bomb scoring

RCC: regional control center

RD&T: research, development, and testing

RDT&E: research, development, testing, and evaluation

REDCOM: Readiness Command, U.S. Unified Command, headquarters at MacDill AFB, Florida

Regt: regiment

RN: Royal Navy (British)

RNAS: Royal Navy Air Station (British)

ROCC: region operations control center, 8 command centers for the NORAD Joint Surveillance System of air defense radars

ROF: Royal Ordnance Factory (British)

ROK: Republic of Korea

RSTN: regional seismic test network

SAC: Strategic Air Command, headquarters at Offutt AFB, Nebraska

SACCS: SAC airborne command and control system

SACDIN: SAC digital network

SACEUR: Supreme Allied Commander Europe, NATO command, headquarters in Stuttgart-Vaihingen, West Germany

SACLANT: Supreme Allied Commander Atlantic, NATO command, headquarters in Norfolk, Virginia

SAGE: semi-automated ground environment

SAM: surface-to-air missile

SAMSO: Space and Missile Systems Organization, headquarters in Los Angeles, California

SCANG: South Carolina Air National Guard

Scope Signal III: follow-up radio system for Giant Talk

SCUD: SS-1 Army level mid-range battlefield missile; latest version is SCUD-b (Soviet)

SDANG: South Dakota Air National Guard

SEEK IGLOO: radar system replacing the Alaskan air defense radars

SHAPE: Supreme Headquarters Allied Powers Europe, NATO headquarters at Casteau-Mons, Belgium

SIOP: single integrated operational plan

SLBM: submarine-launched ballistic missile

SLCM: sea-launched cruise missile

SLFCS: survivable low-frequency communications system

SMW: strategic missile wing

SNA: Soviet Naval Aviation

SNLE: sous-marin nucléaire lanceur d'engins, nuclear-powered ballistic missile submarine (French)

SOC: sector operations center

SOON: solar observing optical network, operated by the Air Force

SOSUS: sound surveillance system

SPACECOM: Space Command, headquarters at Peterson AFB, Colorado

Sqn: sqadron

SRAM: short-range attack missile

SRBM: short-range ballistic missile

SRF: Strategic Rocket Forces (Soviet)

SRHQ: sub-regional headquarters, British command centers

SRW: strategic reconnaissance wing

SSB: strategic nonnuclear-powered ballistic missile submarine

SSBN: strategic nuclear-powered ballistic missile submarine

SSBS: sol-sol balistique stratégique, land-based strategic ballistic missile (French)

SSM: surface-to-surface missile

STR: strategic training range, SAC bombing and navigation training site

STRC: strategic training range complex, network of SAC STR sites

SUBDEVRON: submarine development squadron

SUBGRU: submarine group

SUBROC: submarine rocket

SUBRON: submarine squadron

SW: strategic wing

TAC: Tactical Air Command, headquarters at Langley AFB, Virginia

TD: tank division (Soviet)

T&E: test and evaluation

TF: task force

TFG: tactical fighter group, in the reserve forces, smaller than a TFW

TFTW: tactical fighter training wing

TFW: tactical fighter wing, many of which are nuclear-certified, with either F-4, F-16, F-111, or A-7 aircraft, normally comprising 72 aircraft in 3 squadrons

TFWC: Tactical Fighter Weapons Center, headquarters at Nellis AFB, Nevada

TNANG: Tennessee Air National Guard

TOG: technical operations group (AFTAC)

TOS: technical operations squadron (AFTAC)

TRADOC: Army Training and Doctrine Command, headquarters at Ft. Monroe, Virginia

TRANSIT: Navy navigation satellite system, being replaced by NAVSTAR

TTW: tactical training wing

TUSLOG: Turkish-U.S. Logistics Group

TVD: theater of military operations (Soviet)

TXANG: Texas Air National Guard

UHF: ultra high frequency

u/i: unidentified

UKADGE: U.K. air defense ground environment

UKWMO: U.K. Warning and Monitoring Organisation

USAREUR: U.S. Army Europe

USGPO: U.S. Government Printing Office

UTANG: Utah Air National Guard

UTTR: Utah Test and Training Range, headquarters at Hill AFB, Utah

VLBI: very long baseline interferometry

VLF: very low frequency

VP: patrol squadron, Navy unit flying maritime patrol aircraft

VSTOL: vertical/short take-off and landing

VTANG: Vermont Air National Guard

VTOL: vertical take-off and landing

WAANG: Washington Air National Guard

WESTLANT: Western Atlantic command, NATO command, headquarters in Norfolk, Virginia

WIANG: Wisconsin Air National Guard

WSMC: Western Space and Missile Center, headquarters at Vandenberg AFB, California

WSMR: White Sands Missile Range, located in New Mexico

WTR: Western Test Range, missile range of WSMC

WWMCCS: worldwide military command and control system

Subject Index

Geographic Index

About the Authors

William M. Arkin is Fellow and Director of Nuclear Weapons Research at the Institute for Policy Studies in Washington, D.C. He is author of *Research Guide to Current Military and Strategic Affairs* (1981) and *S.I.O.P.: The Secret U.S. Plan for Nuclear War* (1983, with Peter Pringle), and co-editor of the acclaimed *Nuclear Weapons Databook* series (with Thomas B. Cochran). Mr. Arkin is a Washington columnist for the Bulletin of the Atomic Scientists and writes on military affairs. He has lectured in West Germany, the Netherlands, Britain, Japan, Iceland, Sweden, and Puerto Rico.

Richard W. Fieldhouse is a Research Associate with the Arms Race and Nuclear Weapons Research Project of the Institute for Policy Studies. He received his B.A. in Political Science from Bates College in 1980. He has specialized in nuclear weapons research ever since and has contributed to a number of books and professional papers. He will be a visiting researcher at the Stockholm International Peace Research Institute (SIPRI) in Sweden during 1985-1986.